HANDBOOK OF MIDDLE AMERICAN INDIANS, VOLUME 5

Linguistics

HANDBOOK OF MIDDLE AMERICAN INDIANS

EDITED AT MIDDLE AMERICAN RESEARCH INSTITUTE, TULANE UNIVERSITY

ROBERT WAUCHOPE, *General Editor*

MARGARET A. L. HARRISON, *Associate Editor*

LORE M. COLBY, *Assistant Editor*

INIS PICKETT, *Administrative Assistant*

FRANK T. SCHNELL, JR., DAVID S. PHELPS,

THOMAS S. SCHORR, *Art Staff*

ASSEMBLED WITH THE AID OF GRANTS FROM THE NATIONAL SCIENCE FOUNDATION, AND THE SPONSORSHIP OF THE NATIONAL RESEARCH COUNCIL COMMITTEE ON LATIN AMERICAN ANTHROPOLOGY

HANDBOOK OF MIDDLE AMERICAN INDIANS

ROBERT WAUCHOPE, General Editor

VOLUME FIVE

Linguistics

NORMAN A. McQUOWN

Volume Editor

UNIVERSITY OF TEXAS PRESS AUSTIN

Published in Great Britain by the
University of Texas Press, Ltd., London

International Standard Book No. 0-292-73665-7
Library of Congress Catalog Card No. 64-10316
Copyright © 1967 by the University of Texas Press
Manufactured in the United States of America
All rights reserved
Second printing, 1972

The preparation and publication of the
Handbook of Middle American Indians
has been assisted by grants from
the National Science Foundation.

CONTENTS

1. History of Studies in Middle American Linguistics 3
   Norman A. McQuown

2. Inventory of Descriptive Materials 9
   William Bright

3. Inventory of Classificatory Materials 63
   María Teresa Fernández de Miranda

4. Lexicostatistic Classification 79
   Morris Swadesh

5. Systemic Comparison and Reconstruction 117
   Robert Longacre

6. Environmental Correlational Studies 161
   Sarah C. Gudschinsky

7. Type Linguistic Descriptions 177

   A. Classical Nahuatl. 179
      Stanley Newman

   B. Classical Yucatec (Maya) 201
      Norman A. McQuown

   C. Classical Quiche 249
      Munro S. Edmonson

   D. Sierra Popoluca 269
      Benjamin F. Elson

   E. Isthmus Zapotec 291
      Velma B. Pickett

   F. Huautla de Jiménez Mazatec. 311
      Eunice V. Pike

   G. Jiliapan Pame 331
      Leonardo Manrique C.

   H. Huamelultec Chontal 349
      Viola Waterhouse

8. Language-in-Culture Studies 369
   Miguel León-Portilla

References 385

HANDBOOK OF MIDDLE AMERICAN INDIANS, VOLUME 5

Linguistics

GENERAL EDITOR'S NOTE

The manuscripts for the following articles were submitted at various dates over a period of several years. Because of revisions and minor updatings made from time to time, it is difficult to assign a date to each article. In some cases, an indication of when an article was completed can be had by noting the latest dates in the list of references at the end of each contribution.

1. History of Studies in Middle American Linguistics

NORMAN A. McQUOWN

Shortly after the conquest of Middle America by the soldiers of the Spanish Crown, the priests of the Church began serious study of the indigenous languages spoken there, in order to be able to preach the gospel, to convert and educate the heathen, and to provide the civil authorities with a linguistic vehicle to facilitate local government. The first descriptive linguistic *grammars* were modeled on the Spanish grammar of Antonio de Nebrija (1492); this, in turn, was an attempt to explain the grammar of the Spanish of his times in Classical Latin terms. Typical of these, Andrés de Olmos (1547) published the first grammar of Nahuatl, the language of the Aztec overlords of Tenochtitlan and the official trade language of large stretches of Middle America. Olmos is reputed also to have prepared grammars of Huastec and of Totonac at about the same period. Similar grammars of the 16th century are those for *Mixtec* (Reyes, 1593), *Nahuatl* (Molina, 1571a; Rincón, 1595), and *Tarascan* (Gilberti, 1558; Lagunas, 1574). The 17th century saw those of Maldonado (16th C) for *Cakchiquel*, of Albornoz (1691) for *Chiapanec*, of Morán (1685–95) for *Cholti*, of Reynoso (1644) for *Mam*, of Basalenque (1640) for *Matlatzinca*, of Carochi (1645), Gáldo Guzmán (1642), Guerra (1692), and Vetancurt (1673) for *Nahuatl*, of Vico (1675?) for *Quiché*, of Coronel (1620) and San Buenaventura (1684) for *Yucatec Maya*, and of González (1672) for *Zoque*. For the 18th century, we have those of Angel (18th C?), Flores (1753), Torresano (1754), and Ximénez (1750?) for *Cakchiquel*, Tapia Zenteno (1767) for *Huastec*, Quintana (1729) for *Mixe*, Aldama y Guevara (1754), Cortés y Zedeño (1765), Vázquez Gaztelu (1726), and Tapia Zenteno (1753) for *Nahuatl*, Lombardo (1702) for *Opata*, Sánchez (1747) and Neve y Molina (1767) for *Otomi*, Moran (1720) for *Pocomchi*, Zúñiga (1720) for *Pocomam*, Anleo (1744) and Ximénez (1750?) for *Quiché*, Rinaldini (1743) for *Tepehuan*, Zambrano Bonilla (1752) for *Totonac*, and Ara (16th C) for *Tzeltal*. The Zambrano still professes to be "conforme a el Arte de Antonio Nebrija," and reminds us that the grammatical tradition begun by Nebrija in 1492 still held sway almost 300 years later.

During this early period *catechisms, breviaries, confessionaries*, and the like were composed for the use of the representatives of the church. Sahagún (1575–77), in addition, as the "first ethnographer," taught his Indian informants how to write down, in the Nahuatl of Tenochtitlan-Tlaltelolco, copious *texts* descriptive of the society and culture out of which came the rulers of the Aztec

3

empire. Genealogical and historical *chronicles* were also written down by Indian scribes in the Maya-speaking portions of Middle America, chiefly in Yucatan and in the Quiché-dominated highlands of Guatemala. Local *records* were also kept in Nahuatl as a governmental *lingua franca* (by Nahuatlatos trained by the priests) and, though much less frequently, in other languages as well. Such records were plentiful in the 16th and 17th centuries, and not wholly lacking at even later periods.

To serve the priests who were being trained to preach in the local languages, during this period, special *dictionaries* were compiled. Noteworthy are those of Angel (18th C), Coto (17th C), Santo Domingo (1693), and Varela (17th C?) as well as those of several anonymous authors (?) for *Cakchiquel*, of Ortega (1732) for *Cora*, of Basalenque (1642a, b) for *Matlatzinca*, of Alvarado (1593) for *Mixtec*, of Arenas (see editions under his n.d.), Molina (1555, 1571b), and of two anonymous authors (1590, 1598) for *Nahuatl*, of an anonymous author (1750) for *Otomí*, of Morán (n.d.) for *Pocomam*, of Barrera (1745), Basseta (1698?), Calvo (1726), and Vico (17th C?), and of several anonymous authors (17th and 18th C?) for *Quiché*, of Gilberti (1559) for *Tarascan*, of Ara (1571) and Guzmán (16th C) for *Tzeltal*, of an anonymous author (18th C) for *Yaqui*, of Ciudad Real (1600?) and of an anonymous author (17th C) for *Yucatec* Maya, of Córdova (1578) for *Zapotec*, and of an anonymous author (1733) for *Zoque*. Such grammars, religious texts, and dictionaries are heavily concentrated in the last half of the 16th century, thin out in the 17th, and build up again in the middle of the 18th century.

Not until the 19th century was there another resurgence of interest in indigenous languages, with reprints (Beltrán de Santa Rosa María, 1859) of earlier versions of some items, first printings (anon., 1862, 1884, 1887, 1890, 1893a, 1893b; Córdova, 1886; Valle, 1925) of some older manuscript

(Cárdenas, 17th C?; anon., 1800) items, and the beginnings of not completely Latinate linguistic descriptions (Sandoval, 1810; Tellechea, 1826; Chimalpopoca G., 1869; Nájera, 1870; Brasseur de Bourbourg, 1872; Sánchez, 1877; Caballero, 1880; Siméon, 1885; Basalenque, 1886; Palma, 1886; Stoll, 1887, 1888; Pineda, 1888; Alejandre, 1890; Los Reyes, 1891; Belmar, 1892, 1897, 1898, 1899, 1900, 1901a, 1901b, 1902a, 1902b; La Grasserie and Léon, 1896; La Grasserie, 1898; Zavala, 1898; Zavala and Medina, 1898; Patiño, 1907; Romero Fuentes, 1910; Diguet, 1911; Dolores, 1911–14, 1923; León, 1911; Boas, 1913; Mason, 1917, 1923; Pérez, 1866–77; Tozzer, 1921; LaFarge, 1927; LaFarge and Byers, 1931; Schuller, 1925a; Sapper, 1927; Preuss, 1932, 1935; Angulo, 1933; Schultze-Jena, 1933; Gómez, 1935; Radin, 1935a; Becerra, 1937; Fernández, 1937; Gates, 1938; Pacheco Cruz, 1938) which came in with the development of linguistics as a science in the late 19th and early 20th centuries. Among such later studies in the first category are an anonymous (1893b) for *Otomí*, Valle (1925) for *Pame*, Beltrán (1859) for *Yucatec* Maya, and Córdova (1886) for *Zapotec*; in the second, the anonymous (1884) for *Cakchiquel*, the (1890) for *Cahita*, and the (1862) for *Pima*, the anonymous (1887) and (1893a) for *Zapotec*; in the third an anonymous manuscript (1800) for *Zapotec*, and the Cardénas manuscript (17th C?) for *Kekchí* of Coban; and in the fourth, a wide variety of descriptive materials, a fair part of them based on previous descriptions, some small quantity of genuinely new descriptions, some of these still fairly Latinate, others beginning to shake loose from the earlier tradition of grammatical description. In this last category, then, we have Belmar (1901) for *Amusgo*, Boas (1913) for *Chatino*, Angulo (1933) for *Chichimec*, Belmar (1899), and León (1911) for *Chocho*, Becerra (1937) and LaFarge (1927) for *Chol*, Belmar (1900) for *Chontal de Oaxaca*, Gómez (1935) and Preuss (1932 and 1935) for *Cora*, Belmar

(1902b) for *Cuicatec*, Alejandre (1890) for *Huastec*, Belmar (1901) for *Huave*, Diguet (1911) for *Huichol*, Stoll (1887) for *Ixil*, LaFarge and Byers (1931) for *Jacaltec*, Belmar (1892) for *Mazatec*, Belmar (1902a) and La Grasserie (1898) for *Mixe*, Caballero (1880), Chimalpopoca (1869), Sandoval (1810) and Siméon (1885) for *Nahuatl*, Dolores (1911–14 and 1923) for *Papago*, Fernández (1937) and Stoll (1888) for *Pocomchí*, Schultze-Jena (1933) for *Quiché*, Sapper (1927) for *Tapachultec*, Tellechea (1826) for *Tarahumara*, Basalenque (1886), La Grasserie (1898) and León, and Nájera (1870) for *Tarascan*, Mason (1917) for *Tepecano*, Radin (1933) for *Tlappanec*, Belmar (1897) for *Trique*, Pineda (1888) for *Tzeltal*, Schuller (1925) for *Tzotzil*, Mason (1923) for *Yaqui*, Brasseur (1872), Gates (1938), Pacheco (1938), Pérez (1866–77 and 1898), Romero (1910), Tozzer (1921), and Zavala (1898) for *Yucatec* (Maya), Los Reyes (1891) for *Zapotec*, and La Grasserie (1898) and Sánchez (1877) for *Zoque*.

The modern period may be said to have begun with Boas, with Mason, and with others trained by Boas, Sapir, Bloomfield, and their students. In the mid-thirties of the present century William Cameron Townsend founded the Summer Institute of Linguistics (The Wycliffe Bible Translators) and began a program of linguistic studies whose primary intent was the eventual production of New Testament translations for all the indigenous languages of the Americas. During the 25 years between 1935 and 1960, all the languages of Mexico and Guatemala had received attention, and a sizable quantity (Summer Institute of Linguistics, 1960) of descriptive linguistic publications on these languages had appeared. It is no accident that of the eight linguistic sketches presented in this volume of the Handbook of Middle American Indians four are the work of members of the Summer Institute of Linguistics, as are two of the theoretical chapters of this volume. The total impact to date of SIL-workers on Middle American linguistics is substantial, and it will become more so as increasing quantities of SIL materials still in files are made available. Other linguistic workers with academic or governmental affiliations, with orientation toward scientific research or toward practical application, have collaborated on both counts with SIL members. Increasingly serious scientific research is being carried on in Middle American languages, both descriptive and historical, oriented toward both linguistic structure and linguistic content (McQuown, 1960b). The establishment, in the Universidad Nacional Autónoma de México, of the Seminario de Cultura Nahuatl and the Seminario de Cultura Maya, as well as the founding, in Quezaltenango, in Guatemala, of the Academia de la Lengua Quiché, augurs well for the future of philologically organized studies of the structure and content of materials in the three "classical" languages of Middle America, those with considerable quantities of immediate postconquest documentary materials. We have therefore included in this volume grammatical sketches of Classical *Nahuatl*, Classical (Yucatec) *Maya*, and Classical *Quiché* representing the Uto-Aztecan and the Mayan families of languages. Each of the other five sketches represents an additional family (or subfamily) of Middle American languages: *Sierra Popoluca*—Mixe-Zoque-Popolucan, *Zapotec*—Zapotecan (Otomanguean), *Mazatec*-Mazatecan (Otomanguean), *Pame*—Otopamean (Otomanguean), and *Chontal de Oaxaca*—Hokaltecan. These eight sketches are representative not only of a variety of linguistic structures, but also of a range of approaches descriptive of such structures. Contrastive inspection of the internal organization of the sketches (as evidenced in their Tables of Contents) will demonstrate that although there is almost universal agreement on the basic principles of linguistic analysis, there is almost none on the logistics of the presentation of descriptive results. Current linguistic journals (Aboriginal linguistics, Acta linguistica,

Anthropological linguistics, General linguistics, International journal of American linguistics, Investigaciones lingüísticas, Language, Lingua, México antiguo, Miscellanea phonetica, Monographs of the Institute of Languages and Linguistics of Georgetown University, Phonetica, Revista Mexicana de estudios antropológicos, Tlalocan, and Word) provide, in their indexes, an inventory of publications in the Middle American linguistic field, and an idea of the quantity and quality of recent publications. William Bright and María Teresa Fernández de Miranda provide in this volume annotated inventories of descriptive and of classificatory materials, respectively. Classificatory theory and results are treated by Swadesh (lexicostatistically) and by Longacre (comparatively and reconstructively). Extra-linguistic correlations are handled by Gudschinsky (anthropologically) and by León Portilla (philologically).

All these presentations make passing reference to general theoretical problems involving the problems of Middle American languages and in some instances even more general linguistic problems. The techniques of linguistic analysis in Middle America have shifted from description in terms of a single model language (Latin) to description of each language in its own terms. These latter descriptions, deprived of a single model for presentation of the resultant analytic data, have become ever more diverse in pattern. This diversity in presentation reflects in part increasing diversity in descriptive models, a result which, although it may be salutary in the development of a young science, must present a source of difficulty to the nonspecialist who attempts by comparison of two or more linguistic descriptions to gain some contrastive insight into the structures of the languages described. It behooves the linguists of the next decade to devote some time to the problem of interconvertibility of linguistic descriptive statements, if they hope to make their efforts more generally intelligible. The techniques

of historical linguistics in Middle America during the past decade have seen increasing application of the lexicostatistical tool for the purposes of preliminary classification where such classification is lacking on other grounds and for the posing of historical problems where the results of lexicostatistical classification and classification deriving from systemic comparison and reconstruction differ. Systemic comparison and reconstruction has likewise made considerable progress in Middle America during the past decade, and some initial attempts at inferring proto-cultures from proto-lexicon have been made public. It is to be expected that the detection of smaller genetic differences will become possible and that finer genetic distinctions will become feasible in direct proportion to the finer structural detail of improved descriptions. As ever-finer structural correspondence-matrices are set up, the fine-meshed sieve which they provide for screening out noninherited lexical and grammatical material will make possible the tracing of such linguistic material to its points of origin, and an ever-more reliable linguistic contribution to culture history. Reliable extra-linguistic correlations for linguistic features, in turn, may be expected to result from continued improvement in the techniques of archaeological reconstruction, ethnohistorical inference, and contemporary socio-cultural description. Machine processing of linguistic and of extra-linguistic cultural data, finally, will make possible the prompt testing of explanatory hypotheses, the equally quick rejection of untenable ones, and the formulation of new ones, in what we hope will be an ever more fruitful dialectic. Improvement in the products of this research-oriented dialectic will make available to all who would make practical application of them ever-more useful tools for human betterment. We hope that the present volume will serve not merely to outline past events and the current state of research in Middle American linguistics but also to show the way toward this last goal.

6

REFERENCES

Albornoz, 1691
Aldama y Guevara, 1754
Alejandre, 1890
Alvarado, 1593
Angel, 18th C, *a, b, c*
Angulo, 1933
Anleo, 1744
Anonymous, 1590, 1598, 17th C *a–f*, 18th C *a, b,*
   1733, 1750, 1800, 1862, 1884, 1887, 1890, 1893a, b
Ara, 16th C, 1571
Arenas, n.d.
Barrera, 1745
Basalenque, 1640, 1642a, 1642b, 1886
Basseta, 1698
Becerra, 1937
Belmar, 1892, 1897, 1899, 1900, 1901a, 1901b,
   1902a, 1902b
Beltrán de Santa Rosa María, 1859
Boas, 1913
Brasseur de Bourbourg, 1872
Caballero, 1880
Calvo, 1726
Cárdenas, 17th C
Carochi, 1645
Chimalpopoca Galicia, 1869
Ciudad Real, 1600
Col. de gramáticas, 1904
Córdova, 1578a, 1578b, 1886
Coronel, 1620
Cortés y Zedeño, 1765
Coto, 17th C
Diguet, 1911
Dolores, 1911–14, 1923
Fernández, 1937
Flores, I. J., 1753
Galdo Guzmán, 1642
Gates, 1938
Gilberti, 1558, 1559
Gómez, 1935
González, 1672
Guerra, 1692
Guzmán, 16th C
LaFarge, 1927
—— and Byers, 1931
La Grasserie, 1898
—— and León, 1896
Lagunas, 1574
León, N., 1911
Lombardo, 1702
Los Reyes, 1891

McQuown, 1960b
Maldonado, 16th C
Mason, 1917, 1923
Molina, 1555, 1571a, 1571b
Morán, F., 1685–95
Morán, P., n.d., 1720
Nájera, 1870
Nebrija, 1492
Neve y Molina, 1767
Olmos, 1547
Ortega, 1732
Pacheco Cruz, 1938
Palma, 1886
Patiño, 1907
Pérez, 1866–77, 1898
Pineda, 1888
Preuss, 1932, 1935
Quintana, 1729
Radin, 1933
Reyes, 1593
Reynoso, 1644
Rinaldini, 1743
Rincón, 1595
Romero Fuentes, 1910
Sahagún, 1575–77
San Buenaventura, 1684
Sánchez, 1877
Sánchez de la Baquera, 1747
Sandoval, 1810
Santo Domingo, 1693
Sapper, 1927
Schuller, 1925a
Schultze-Jena, 1933
Siméon, 1885
Stoll, 1887, 1888
Summer Inst. Linguistics, 1960
Tapia Zenteno, 1753, 1767
Tellechea, 1826
Torresano, 1754
Tozzer, 1921
Valle, 1925
Varela, 17th C
Vázquez Gaztelu, 1726
Vetancurt, 1673
Vico, 17th C, 1675
Ximénez, 1750
Zambrano Bonilla, 1752
Zavala, 1898
—— and Medina, 1898
Zúñiga, 1720

2. Inventory of Descriptive Materials

WILLIAM BRIGHT

This inventory is a selected and annotated bibliography of published materials on the phonologies, grammars and lexicons of the native Middle American languages, from Molina's *Vocabulario* of 1555 down to works published in 1966. Items are arranged alphabetically by author and numbered in that order; the indexing which follows—by language, historical period, and type of material—refers to these numbers.

There were eight bases for selection of these entries.

1. Middle American languages are taken to include those spoken from the northern border of Mexico to the southern extreme of the Mesoamerican culture area (as defined by Kirchhoff, 1943). In the north, I include those border languages which have substantial numbers of speakers in Mexico, such as Pima-Papago; I exclude Diegueño and Apache. In the south, the listing includes Lenca, Cacaopera, Chorotega, Subtiaba, and Mangue; but it stops short of Jicaque, Paya, Sumo, Miskito, Ulua, and the languages of Costa Rica. The Black Carib language, as a recent arrival in Mesoamerica, is excluded.

2. Materials existing only in manuscript are not listed. Microfilms have been included only when they are part of a regularly distributed series, notably the dissertations made available by University Microfilms, Ann Arbor, and the Microfilm Collection of Manuscript Materials on Middle American Cultural Anthropology, issued by the University of Chicago Library.

3. Studies which are primarily oriented toward linguistic comparison are excluded from this bibliography, even though they often contain lexical data not available elsewhere. To supplement this inventory, therefore, readers should also consult the Inventory of Classificatory Materials which follows.

4. Texts in Middle American languages are included only when they appear to have immediate usefulness for linguistic study. The large body of Christian devotional literature in aboriginal languages is thus excluded. But texts in the native tradition, when recorded or edited by linguistically sophisticated scholars, and accompanied by translation, are included.

5. Some of the primers and other literacy materials published recently by the Summer Institute of Linguistics include word lists of sufficient size to be of use to the linguist. Such materials, when I have been able to see them, are listed here. Other literacy publications, including the many that I have not seen, are omitted.

6. Other types of material which are excluded are those dealing with kinship termi-

9

nology, with onomastics, with ethnolinguistic relationships, with linguistic acculturation, and with aboriginal writing systems. Book reviews are not listed except when they contain new data or offer new analyses.

7. In the case of the two Middle American languages on which the most has been written, namely Aztec and Maya, I have been more selective than elsewhere. This means that nearly all publications from the 16th and 17th centuries are included, but that many later works are omitted. The reasons have been expressed by Gates (1924):

In every language and dialect, the Sixteenth century writers wrote down what they found, and by sheer necessity (helped often by great linguistic keenness) gave exquisitely accurate recordings. There was little attempt at theorizing; it was first-hand reporting. In the later Seventeenth they began to elaborate, wiping out "irregularities" they did not understand, or which were dying out under Spanish contact. And then in the Eighteenth they openly "corrected" and formalized the languages themselves, to what they thought they ought to be—to make "good language." In the Nineteenth, practically everything became worthless.

In the 20th century, of course, improved techniques of linguistic study have brought about great improvement, and a larger percentage of works on Aztec and Maya are found suitable for inclusion in this listing.

8. Aid in compiling this bibliography was derived from many previously published bibliographies, to which the reader may also turn for items excluded here. All but two of these are listed in Gibson, 1960; the additional ones are those of the Summer Institute of Linguistics, 1960, 1964.

ABBREVIATIONS

AA	American Anthropologist. Menasha, Wisc.
An. Mus. Nac.	Anales del Museo Nacional (de Arqueología, Historia y Etnología). México.
An. Soc. Geog. Hist.	Anales de la Sociedad de Geografía e Historia. Guatemala.
Anth. Ling.	Anthropological Linguistics. Bloomington, Ind.
APS-P	American Philosophical Society, Proceedings. Philadelphia.
BAE-R	Bureau of American Ethnology, Annual Report. Washington.
Bol. Soc. Mex. Geog. Estad.	Boletín de la Sociedad Mexicana de Geografía y Estadística. México.
Diss. Abs.	Dissertation Abstracts. Ann Arbor, Mich.
ICA-P	International Congress of Americanists, Proceedings.
IJAL	International Journal of American Linguistics. Baltimore.
Inv. Ling.	Investigaciones Lingüísticas. México.
JSAP	Journal de la Société des Américanistes. Paris.
Lg.	Language, the Journal of the Linguistic Society of America. Baltimore.
Méx. Ant.	El México Antiguo. México.
Mic. Coll.	Microfilm Collection of Manuscript Materials on Middle American Cultural Anthropology. Chicago, University of Chicago Library.
Rev. Etno.	Revista de Etnología, Arqueología y Lingüística. San Salvador.
Rev. Ling.	Revue de Linguistique et de Philologie Comparée. Paris.
Rev. Mex. Est. Antro.	Revista Mexicana de Estudios Antropológicos. México.
UCPAAE	University of California Publications in American Archaeology and Ethnology. Berkeley and Los Angeles.

INVENTORY

ADAM, LUCIEN

1   1877a   Du polysynthétisme, de l'incorporation, de la composition et de l'emboîtement dans la langue Nahuatl. *Rev. Ling.*, 9: 231–54.

2   1877b   Du polysynthétisme et de la formation des mots dans les langues Quiché et Maya. *Rev. Ling.*, 10: 34–74.

3   1877   La langue Chiapanèque: observations grammaticales, vocabulaire méthodique, textes inédits, textes rétablis. Vienne.

Based on Pinart, 1875, and on MSS of Joan Núñez, 1633. Includes Chiapanec-French vocabulary and devotional texts.

ADÁN, ELFEGO

4   1922   Los Cuicatecos actuales. *An. Mus. Nac.*, 4a época, 1: 137–54.

Includes Spanish-Cuicatec word and phrase lists and paradigms, pp. 141–47.

AGREDA, EL PADRE

5   1888   Arte de la lengua Otomí . . . escrita por el Dr. L. Darapski. Anales del Museo Michoacano, año 1, entregas 3–4. Morelia.

Cited in *Boletín Bibliográfico de Antropología Americana*, 18.2: 297, but not included in the bound volumes of the *Anales* which I have seen.

ALDAMA Y GUEVARA, JOSEPH AUGUSTÍN DE

6   1754   Arte de la lengua Mexicana. México.

Said to be only a compendium of previous writers' statements. Not seen.

ALEJANDRE, MARCELO

7   1870   Noticia de lengua Huasteca. *Bol. Soc. Mex. Geog. Estad.*, 2a época, 2: 733–90.

Sketch of phonetics and grammar, with Spanish-Huastec vocabulary.

8   1890   Cartilla Huasteca con su gramática, diccionario y varias reglas para aprender el idioma. . . . México.

Includes grammar, Spanish-Huastec and Huastec-Spanish vocabularies, conversational sentences, and devotional text with interlinear translation.

ALEMÁN, L.

9   1884   Grammaire élémentaire de la langue Quichée. Publiée par A. Blomme. Supplément au Compte-Rendu du Congrès International des Américanistes. Copenhague.

Grammatical sketch from MS of 1842.

ALLEMAN, VERA MAE

10   1952   Vocabulario Zapoteco del Rincón. Primera parte, Zapoteco-Español. Segunda parte, Español-Zapoteco. México.

ALVARADO, FRANCISCO

11   1593   Vocabulario en lengua Misteca. . . . México.

Not seen. Data from this source appear in Arana and Swadesh, 1965.

ALVAREZ, ALBERT

11a   1965   Some Papago puns. *IJAL*, 31: 106–07.

Punning texts with translation and explanation.

ANDERSON, ARABELLE

12   1957   Two Chol texts. *Tlalocan*, 3: 313–16. México.

ANDRADE, MANUEL J.

13   1946a   Materials on the Huastec language. *Mic. Coll.*, no. 9. Chicago.

Posthumous field notes, prepared for publication by A. M. Halpern and Mark H. Watkins. Consists of typed and handwritten MS, including transcriptions of texts recorded on phonograph discs. Phonological, grammatical, and lexical materials.

14   1946b   Materials on the Mam, Jacaltec, Aguacatec, Chuj, Bachahom, Palencano, and Lacandon languages. *Mic. Coll.*, no. 10. Chicago.

See 1946a. Includes Mam texts transcribed by Rev. and Mrs. H. D. Peck and Rev. E. F. Sywulka.

15   1946c   Materials on the Quiché, Cakchiquel, and Tzutuhil languages. *Mic. Coll.*, no. 11. Chicago.

See 1946a. Includes comparative word list of Quiché, Cakchiquel, Jacaltec, and Mam.

16   1946d   Materials on the Kekchi and Pokoman languages. *Mic. Coll.*, no. 12. Chicago.

See 1946a.

17   1955   A grammar of modern Yucatec. *Mic. Coll.*, no. 41. Chicago.

Posthumous MS edited by S. L. Bradshaw. Contains Maya phonology, summary of grammar, detailed morphology, long section on "usage" of certain constructions, and a long note on the pronunciation of Classical Maya.

See also Bowman, 1959.

ANDREWS, HENRIETTA

18   1949   Phonemes and morphophonemes of Temoayan Otomi. *IJAL*, 15: 213–22.

19   1950   Vocabulario Otomí de Tasquillo, Hidalgo. Primera parte, Otomí-Español. Segunda parte, Español-Otomí. México.

             Contains notes on the alphabet used.

ANDREWS, HENRIETTA, AND DORIS BARTHOLOMEW

20   1956   Aprendamos a leer en Otomí. Cartilla Otomí para los que saben leer en Castellano. Otomí—dialecto de San Felipe y Santiago, San Juan Jiquipilco, Estado de México. México.

             Contains word lists.

ANGULO, JAIME DE

21   1925   The Chontal language (dialect of Tequixistlán). *Anthropos*, 20: 1032–52. St. Gabriel-Mödling.

             Brief vocabulary, grammatical sketch, and short texts.

22   1926a   The development of affixes in a group of monosyllabic languages of Oaxaca. *Lg.*, 2: 46–61, 119–33.

             Discussion of pronominal elements in Zapotec, Mixtec, Chinantec, Mazatec, Cuicatec, Chatino, and Chocho.

23   1926b   Tone patterns and verb forms in a dialect of Zapotek. *Lg.*, 2: 238–50.

             Grammatical function of tone in dialect of Teotitlán del Valle, with short analyzed text.

24   1926c   L'emploi de la notion d' "être" dans la langue Mixe. *JSAP*, 18: 1–7.

             Includes analyzed text.

25   1933   The Chichimeco language (central Mexico). *IJAL*, 7: 152–94.

             Grammatical notes, paradigms, stem lists, and analyzed text.

ANLEO, BARTOLOMÉ DE

26   1865   Arte de la lengua Quiché o Utlateca, edited . . . by E. G. Squier. London.

             From MS of 1744. Not seen.

ANONYMOUS

27   1818   Gramática del Zotzil. n.p.

             Serves as basis for Schuller, 1925. Not seen.

28   1890   Vocabulario para aprender con perfección el Quecchí. Cobán, Guatemala.

             Not seen.

29   1938   Vocabulario Zutuhil, traducido al Castellano y usado por los indígenas de Santiago Atitlán, Departamento de Sololá. *Revista de Educación*, 6: 259–60, 7: 15. Guatemala.

             Paradigms, phrase list, and Tzutuhil-Spanish word list.

ARANA OSNAYA, EVANGELINA, AND MAURICIO SWADESH

29a   1965   Los elementos del Mixteco antiguo. México.

             Mixtec-Spanish stem list, based on Alvarado, 1593, and A. Reyes, 1593, plus material from modern dialects; notes on structure; Spanish-Mixtec index.

ARANA XAJILÁ, FRANCISCO HERNÁNDEZ
    See Villacorta C., 1934.

ARAUZ, PRÓSPERO

30   1926   Frases del Pipil. *Rev. Etno.*, 1: 209–12. San Salvador.

             Reprinted in *Anales del Museo Nacional "David J. Guzmán"*, 1.2: 70–73 (San Salvador, 1950).

31   1960   El Pipil de la region de los Itzalcos. San Salvador.

ARENAS, PEDRO DE

32   1611   Vocabulario manual de las lenguas Castellana y Mexicana, en que se contienen

las palabras, preguntas, y respuestas más comunes y ordinarias que se suelen ofrecer en el trato y communicación entre españoles e indios. México.

Many later editions; the latest in Puebla, 1887. A French version, translated by Charles Romey, is: Guide de la conversation en trois langues, Français, Espagnol et Mexicain (Paris, 1862).

ARREOLA, JOSÉ MARÍA

33   1934   Tres vocabularios dialectales del Mexicano. *Inv. Ling.*, 2: 428–43.

Word and phrase lists from two Aztec dialects of Jalisco and from one of Colima.

ARROYO, VÍCTOR MANUEL

34   1955   Elementos de gramática Otomí. [México.]

Sketch of phonetics and grammar; three texts with interlinear translation. The author was assisted by E. E. Wallis of the Summer Institute of Linguistics.

ASCHMANN, HERMAN P.

35   1956a   Totonaco phonemes. *IJAL*, 12: 34–43.

Includes text with literal and free translations.

36   1946b   Totonac categories of smell. *Tlalocan*, 2: 187–89. Azcapotzalco.

Lexical classification of odors.

37   1953   Los dos niveles de composición en el verbo Totonaco. *Rev. Mex. Est. Antro.*, 13: 119–22.

Derivational vs. inflectional levels.

38   1962   Vocabulario Totonaco de la Sierra. Serie de vocabularios indígenas Mariano Silva y Aceves, 7. México.

Totonac-Spanish and Spanish-Totonac, with appendices on phonology and grammar.

ASCHMANN, HERMAN P., AND WILLIAM L. WONDERLY

39   1952   Affixes and implicit categories in Totonac verb inflection. *IJAL*, 18: 130–45.

AULIE, EVELYN WOODWARD

40   1948   Chol dictionary. *In* Summer Institute of Linguistics, 1948. 30 pp.

Chol-English dictionary.

See also Yourison, 1948.

AULIE, WILBUR

41   1957   High-layered numerals in Chol (Mayan). *IJAL*, 23: 281–83.

Description of numeral system permitting count up to 8000.

ÁVILA, FRANCISCO DE

42   1717   Arte de la lengua Mexicana. . . . México.

BAEGERT, JOHANN JACOB

43   1773   Nachrichten von der amerikanischen Halbinsel Californien. . . . Mannheim.

Spanish translation by Pedro R. Hendrichs: Noticias de la península americana de California . . . (México, 1942). English translation by M. M. Brandenburg and C. L. Baumann: Observations in Lower California (Berkeley and Los Angeles, 1952). Chapter 10 consists of notes on the Waicuri language.

BAER, PHILLIP AND MARY

44   1948   The Lacandon song of the jaguar. *Tlalocan*, 2: 376. Azcapotzalco.

Song text of nine sentences.

45   1950   Materials on Lacandón culture of the Petáh (Pelhá) region. *Mic. Coll.*, no. 34. Chicago.

Contains "A tentative description of Lacandón phonemes," pp. 331–34.

BAEZO, PERFECTO

46   1832   Vocabulario de las lenguas Castellana y Maia. *Bulletin de la Société de Géographie de Paris*, 1st series, 18: 215–17.

Appended to Juan Galindo, Mémoire sur les ruines de Palenqué, pp. 198–214. The language is apparently Chol.

BARREDA, NICOLÁS DE LA
46a   1730   Doctrina christiana en lengua chinanteca. México.

> Facsimile edition, ed. by Howard F. Cline (Museo Nacional de Antropología, serie científica, 6), México, 1960; includes extensive linguistic commentary, including Spanish-Chinantec and Chinantec-Spanish vocabularies extracted from Barreda's text. Some of these materials had been earlier reprinted by Brinton, 1892a.

BARRERA VÁSQUEZ, ALFREDO
47   1946   La lengua Maya de Yucatán. *Enciclopedia Yucatanense*, 6: 205–92. México.
> Phonology and detailed grammar.

See also Colop D., 1927.

BARRIENTOS, LUIS
See Pinart, 1875.

BARRITT, WESTBROOK
48   1956   The phonemic interpretation of 'accent' in Father Rincón's "Arte Mexicana." *General Linguistics*, 2: 22–29. Louisville.
> Suggests that accent is distinctive within the Aztec word. *See* Bright, 1960.

BARTHOLOMEW, DORIS
See Andrews and Bartholomew, 1956.

BASALENQUE, DIEGO
49   1714   Arte de la lengua Tarasca. México.
> Reprinted by Antonio Peñafiel, México, 1886. The reprinting includes a grammatical restatement by Francisco Pimentel.

BASAURI, CARLOS
50   1929   Monografía de los Tarahumaras. México.
> Includes notes on pronunciation, word lists, and eight texts with interlinear and free translations.

51   1931   Tojolabales, Tzeltales y Mayas. Breves apuntes sobre antropología, etnografía y lingüística. México.
> Includes Tojolabal phonology, Spanish-Tojolabal vocabulary, paradigms, and text.

BASCOM, BURT
52   1954   Tepehuane (Northern): Dialect of Baborigame, Chihuahua. Tepehuane (Southern): Dialect of Xoconostle, Durango. *In* Key, 1954, pp. 312–33.

53   1959   Tonomechanics of Northern Tepehuan. *Phonetica* 4: 71–88. Basel.

See also Pike, K. L., and Bascom, 1959.

BEALS, RALPH L.
54   1945   Ethnology of the Western Mixe. *UCPAAE*, 42: 1–175.
> Short vocabulary, pp. 135–38.

BECERRA, MARCOS E.
55   1910   Estudio lexicológico. *Bol. Soc. Mex. Geog. Estad.*, 30: 97–112 (5a época, tomo 4).
> Reproduces data on Camotán dialect from Peccorini, 1909, and shows it to be a form of Chortí.

56   1934   Los Chontales de Tabasco: Estudio etnográfico y lingüístico. *Inv. Ling.*, 2: 29–36.
> Includes short word list, with some material for dialect comparison.

57   1937a   Los Chiapanecas. *Inv. Ling.*, 4: 214–53.
> Includes Chiapanec-Spanish and Spanish-Chiapanec vocabularies.

58   1937b   Vocabulario de la lengua Chol. *An. Mus. Nac.*, 5a época, 2: 249–78.
> Spanish-Chol vocabulary.

BEEKMAN, JOHN AND ELAINE
59   1953   Vocabulario Chol. Primera parte, Español-Chol. Segunda parte, Chol-Español. México.
> Contains notes on alphabet used.

BELMAR, FRANCISCO
60   1891   Disertación sobre las lenguas Zapoteca, Chinanteca, Mixe, y Trike y comparación con el Zoque y el Mixteco. México.

Not seen.

61   1892   Ligero estudio sobre la lengua Mazateca. Oaxaca.

Paradigm grammar, Mazatec-Spanish root list, and Biblical text with interlinear translation and grammatical notes. Lexical materials are republished by Lehmann, 1920, pp. 905–06.

62   1897   Ensayo sobre la lengua Trike. Oaxaca.

Grammatical notes, phrase lists, Spanish-Trique vocabulary, and Trique-Spanish word lists of plants, animals, and place names.

63   1899   El Chocho. Oaxaca.

Contains grammatical notes and Spanish-Chocho vocabulary. Not seen.

64   1900   Estudio de el Chontal. Oaxaca.

Notes on Tequistlatec grammar, phrase lists, Spanish-Tequistlatec vocabulary, and stories. Excerpts were reprinted in Manuel Martínez Gracida, Historia antigua de la Chontalpa Oaxaqueña (México, 1910).

65   1901a   Investigación sobre el idioma Amuzgo que se habla en algunos pueblos del Distrito de Jamiltepec. Oaxaca.

Includes Spanish-Amuzgo vocabulary. Not seen.

66   1901b   Estudio del Huave. Oaxaca.

Contains grammatical notes and Spanish-Huave vocabulary.

67   1901c   Breve noticia del idioma Papabuco, del pueblo de Elotepec. Oaxaca.

Grammatical notes and Spanish-Zapotec-Papabuco vocabulary.

68   1902a   Estudio del idioma Ayook. . . . Oaxaca.

Mixe grammary, Mixe-Spanish dictionary, list of phrases and sentences.

69   1902b   Investigaciones sobre la lengua Chatina. Oaxaca.

Dialect comparisons, grammatical notes, and Chatino-Spanish vocabulary.

70   1902c   El Cuicateco. Oaxaca.

Grammatical notes, Cuicatec-Spanish stem list, and Spanish-Cuicatec vocabulary.

71   1905   Lenguas indígenas de México. Familia Mixteco-Zapoteca y sus relaciones con el Otomí. Familia Zoque-Mixe. Chontal. Huave y Mexicano. México.

Contrastive notes on languages of Oaxaca. Grammatical sketches of Huave, Tequistlatec, Aztec, Mixe, and Zoque. Appendix contains texts (mostly Bible translations) in these languages, and phrase lists in Cuicatec, Mazatec, Chinantec, Otomí, and in the Aztec dialect of Teotitlán, Oaxaca.

See also Quintana, 1729, and Reyes, Gaspar, 1891.

BELTRÁN DE SANTA ROSA, PEDRO

72   1746   Arte de el idioma Maya, reducido a succintas reglas, y semilexicon Yucateco. . . . México.

Reprinted, Mérida, 1859. "By far the best of the early works"—Tozzer, 1921, p. 164. Includes Maya-Spanish word lists.

BERENDT, C. H.
See Means, 1917.

BERLIN, BRENT

72a   1962   Esbozo de la fonología del Tzeltal de Tenejapa, Chiapas. *Estudio de Cultura Maya,* 2: 17–36. México.

72b   1963a   A possible paradigmatic structure for Tzeltal pronominals. *Anth. Ling.,* 5.2: 1–5.

72c   1963b   Some semantic features of reduplication in Tzeltal. *IJAL,* 29: 211–18.

BERLIN, BRENT, AND A. KIMBALL ROMNEY

72d   1964   Descriptive semantics of Tzeltal numeral classifiers. *In* A. K. Romney and R. G. D'Andrade, eds., Transcultural studies in cognition. *AA,* vol. 66, no. 3, pt. 2, pp. 79–97.

BIONDELLI, BERNARDINO, ED.

73   1858   Evangeliarium epistolarium et lectionarium Aztecum sive Mexicanum ex antiguo codice Mexicano nuper reperto depromptum cum præfatione interpretatione adnotationibus glossario edidit Bernardinus Biondelli. Mediolani.

Biblical texts in Aztec translation by Bernardino de Sahagún, followed by an Aztec-Latin vocabulary.

74 1869 Glossarium Azteco-Latinum et Latino-Aztecum curâ et studio Bernardino Biondelli collectum ac digestum. Mediolani.

      Aztec-Latin and Latin-Aztec vocabularies, the former reproduced from Biondelli, 1858. Not seen.

BLAIR, ROBERT W.

74a 1964 Yucatec Maya noun and verb morpho-syntax. Indiana University dissertation. Ann Arbor, University Microfilms.

      Summary in *Diss. Abs.*, 25: 6606, 1965.

BLIGHT, RICHARD AND FAITH

75 1956–57 Cartilla Otomí (Otomí de Tenango de Doria, Hidalgo.) Parts 1–3. México.

      Contains Otomí-Spanish vocabulary at the end of each part.

BLOM, FRANS, AND OLIVER LAFARGE

76 1927 Tribes and temples, a record of the expedition to Middle America conducted by the Tulane University of Louisiana in 1915. 2 vols. New Orleans.

      Vol. 2 contains appendices by LaFarge: I. The Popoluca language of San Martín Pajapan, Ver. (pp. 455–64). II. Comparative word lists: "Yocotan," Chontal, Tzeltal, Chaneabal (Tojolabal), Jacalteca (pp. 465–85). III. "Yocotan" grammar (pp. 487–98). IV. "Yocotan" texts (pp. 499–502). V. Tzeltal texts (pp. 503–04). "Yocotan" is a variety of Chontal.

BLOMME, A.

    See Alemán, 1884.

BOAS, FRANZ

77 1913a Notes on the Chatino language of Mexico. *AA*, 15: 78–86.

      Grammatical notes, English-Chatino vocabulary, and short text.

78 1913b Phonetics of the Mexican language. *ICA-P*, 18: 107–08. London.

      Aztec dialects of the Valley of Mexico and of Pochutla, Oaxaca.

79 1917 El dialecto Mexicano de Pochutla, Oaxaca. *IJAL*, 1: 9–44.

      Notes on pronunciation and grammar; Pochutla-Spanish and Spanish-Pochutla vocabularies. The latter vocabulary was reprinted by Lehmann, 1920, pp. 1075–80.

80 1920 Cuentos mexicanos de Milpa Alta D. F. *Journal of American Folklore*, 33: 1–24. Lancaster, Pa.

BOWER, BETHEL

81 1948 Stems and affixes in Tepehua numerals. *IJAL*, 14: 20–21.

BOWER, BETHEL, AND DOROTHY HERZOG

82 1958 Lhīmak'alhkāma'. Cartilla en Tepehua. Parts 1–3. México.

      Contains Tepehua-Spanish vocabularies at the end of each part.

BOWMAN, ELIZABETH

83 1959 An attempt at an analysis of modern Yucatec from a small corpus of recorded speech. *Anth. Ling.*, 1.4: 43–86.

      Texts transcribed from discs made by M. Andrade in 1933; phonemic and grammatical sketch based on this and on Andrade's grammar, 1955.

BRADLEY, CHARLES H.

83a 1965 A linguistic sketch of Mixteco of Jicaltepec. Cornell University dissertation. Ann Arbor, University Microfilms.

      Summary in *Diss. Abs.*, 26: 4646, 1966.

BRADSHAW, S. L.

    See ANDRADE, 1955.

BRAMBILA, DAVID, AND JOSÉ VERGARA BIANCHI

84 1953 Gramática rarámuri. México.

      Very detailed (644 pp.) Tarahumara grammar, on traditional models. Transcription appears near-phonemic.

BRASSEUR DE BOURBOURG, CHARLES ÉTIENNE

85   1861   Coup d'oeil sur la nation et la langue des Wabi. . . . *Revue Orientale et Américaine*, 5: 261–71. Paris.

Republished, *Archives de la Société Américaine de France*, nouv. sér., 1: 131–42 (Paris, 1875). Contains short French-Huave word list and paradigm. This was republished in León, 1904b.

86   1862   Gramática de la lengua Quiché. Grammaire de la langue Quichée Espagnole-Française mise en parallèle avec les deux dialectes, Cakchiquel et Tzutuhil, tirée des manuscrits des meilleurs auteurs guatémaliens. Ouvrage accompagné de notes philologiques, avec un vocabulaire . . . servant d'introduction au Rabinal-Achi, drame indigène avec sa musique originale, texte Quiché et traduction Française en regard. (Collection de Documents dans les Langues Indigènes . . . , vol. 10.) Paris.

Grammar in Spanish, with added French glosses and French footnotes. Quiché-Spanish-French vocabulary of roots. Republished by Jorge Luis Arreola, Guatemala, 1961.

87   1870   Manuscrit Troano. Études sur le système graphique et la langue des Mayas. Vol. 2. Paris.

This volume consists of grammar, chrestomathy, and Maya-French-Spanish dictionary. Republished as: Dictionnaire, grammaire et chrestomathie de la langue Maya (Paris, 1872). The grammar is based on that of San Buenaventura, 1684. The entire work has been criticized, both by Brinton and by Tozzer, 1921, as being of little value.

BRETON, A. C.

88   1919   Notes on Pokomchi (Guatemala). *Man*, 19: 7–12. London.

Lexical notes extracted from a MS of the 17th century.

BREWER, FORREST AND JEAN

88a   1962   Vocabulario Mexicano de Tetelcingo, Morelos: Castellano-Mexicano, Mexicano-Castellano. Serie de vocabularios indígenas Mariano Silva y Aceves, 8. México.

BRIGGS, ELINOR

88b   1961   Mitla Zapotec grammar. México.

Emphasis on morphology.

BRIGHT, WILLIAM

89   1960   'Accent' in Classical Aztec. *IJAL*, 26: 66–68.

Identifies Aztec 'accent,' proposed by Barritt, 1956, as based on vowel length.

BRINTON, DANIEL G.

90   1884a   A grammar of the Cakchiquel language of Guatemala, translated from a MS in the Library of the American Philosophical Society, with an introduction and additions. *APS-P*, 21: 345–412.

Based on anonymous MS of 1692.

91   1884b   On the language and ethnologic position of the Xinca Indians of Guatemala. *APS-P*, 22: 89–97.

English-Xinca vocabulary, from an unpublished MS.

92   1885   The annals of the Cakchiquels. The original text, with a translation, notes and introduction. Brinton's Library of Aboriginal American Literature, no. 6. Philadelphia.

Includes Cakchiquel-English vocabulary.

93   1886   Notes on the Mangue, an extinct dialect formerly spoken in Nicaragua. *APS-P*, 23: 238–57.

Spanish version: Notas sobre el Mangue, traducidas y anotadas por Marcos E. Becerra, *An. Mus. Nac.*, 4a época, 3: 399–419 (México, 1925). Material reprinted in Lehmann, 1920, pp. 848–57. Consists of Mangue vocabulary and sentences, from unpublished MSS.

94   1887   On the so-called Alaguilac language of Guatemala. *APS-P*, 24: 366–77.

Contains vocabulary of an Aztec dialect of Guatemala.

95   1888   On the Chane-abal (four-language) tribe and dialect of Chiapas. *AA*, o.s., 1: 77–96.

Spanish version: El Chane-abal, traducido y anotado por Marcos E. Becerra, *An. Mus. Nac.*, 4a época, 4: 331–53 (1926). Contains grammatical notes and vocabulary from the Tojolabal language.

96   1892a   Observations on the Chinantec language of Mexico. *APS-P*, 30: 22–31.

Text extract and English-Chinantec vocabulary, based on Barreda, 1730.

97   1892b   On the Mazatec language of Mexico and its affinities. *APS-P*, 30: 31–39.

Contains English-Mazatec vocabulary, reproduced in Lehmann, 1920, pp. 903–05.

98   1892c   Chontales and Popolucas, a contribution to Mexican ethnography. *ICA-P*, 8: 556–64. Paris.

Contains short word lists of Tequistlatec, Chontal of Tabasco, Matagalpa, and Mixe.

99   1895   The Matagalpan linguistic stock of Central America. *APS-P*, 34: 403–15.

Grammatical notes and vocabulary of Cacaopera, based mainly on Mendoza, 1895.

BROCKWAY, EARL

99a   1963   The phonemes of North Puebla Náhuatl. *Anth. Ling.*, 5.2: 14–18.

See also Harding and Brockway, 1954.

BUELNA, EUSTAQUIO, ED.

100   1893   Luces del Otomí o gramática del idioma que hablan los indios Otomíes en la República Mexicana. Compuesto por un padre de la Compañía de Jesús. México.

Publication of anonymous MS from around 1770, in which various unpublished grammatical notes and vocabularies are brought together. Includes Otomí-Spanish and Spanish-Otomí dictionaries.

See also Velasco, 1737.

BURKITT, ROBERT

101   1902   Notes on the Kekchi language. *AA*, n.s., 4: 441–63.

Notes on pronunciation; texts; notes on numerals and on personal names.

BUSCHMANN, J. C. E.

102   1856   Die Pima-Sprache und die Sprache der Koloschen. *Abhandlungen der Königliche Akademie der Wissenschaften*, 1856: 321–432. Berlin.

Contains grammatical notes on Pima and an English-Pima vocabulary, based on the fragmentary published data of the time.

BYERS, DOUGLAS

See LaFarge and Byers, 1931.

CALDERÓN, EUSTORGIO

103   1908   Estudios lingüísticos. I. Las lenguas de Yupiltepeque y del Barrio Norte de Chiquimulilla en Guatemala. II. Las lenguas de Oluta, Sayula, Texistepec en el Istmo de Tehuantepec en México. Guatemala.

Said to be reprinted from *Repertorio Salvadoreño* for 1891–92, but I have not been able to see that publication. Part I deals with Xinca grammar and vocabulary; this is republished by Lehmann, 1920, pp. 739–67. The Xinca-Spanish vocabulary, through the letter M, is also published as: Ensayo lingüístico sobre el Pupuluca y otra lengua india del sudeste de Guatemala, congénere del Pupuluca, precedido de un corto vocabulario de ambos idiomas, *An. Soc. Geog. Hist.*, 16: 74–80, 156–63 (1939); this publication is stated to be from an uncompleted MS of 1890. Calderón's part II is a vocabulary of three languages which are sometimes lumped together as "Popoluca of Veracruz," but which are here misleadingly referred to as Mixe. This material is republished by Lehmann, 1920, pp. 771–79; and also, further mislabeled, as: Vocabulario Sinca [!], *An. Soc. Geog. Hist.*, 16: 231–48 (1940).

104   [*nil*]

105   [*nil*]

CÁRCERES, PEDRO DE

106   1907   Arte de la lengua Othomí (siglo XVI). Lo publica por vez primera el Dr. N. León. *Bolétin del Instituto Bibliográfico Mexicano*, 6: 39–155. México.

CARLSON, RUTH

See Eachus and Carlson, 1966.

CAROCHI, HORACIO

107   1645   Arte de la lengua Mexicana con la declaración de los adverbios della. México.

Reprinted in Colección de gramáticas de la lengua Mexicana 1: 395–538, supplement to *An. Mus. Nac.*, 1a época, tomo 5 (1892).

108   1759   Compendio del arte de la lengua Mexicana, dispuesto . . . por el P. Ignacio de Paredes. México.

Reprinted, *Bol. Soc. Mex. Geog. Estad.*, 4a época, 4: 147–216, 313–38, 422–32, 559–73, 623–733 (1897). Reprinted in México, 1902. Reprinted in Puebla, 1910, along with Molina's Vocabulario of 1571. This is perhaps the most useful source on Classical Aztec.

CARRANZA, JOSEPH DE

109   1900   Arte donde se contienen todos aquellos rudimentos y principios preceptivos que conducen a la lengua Mexicana. Primera edición. Colección de gramáticas de la lengua Mexicana, 2: 47–224, supplement to *An. Mus. Nac.*, 1a época, tomo 7.

Publication of MS from the late 18th century.

CARREÑO, ALBERTO MARÍA

     See Reynoso, 1644.

CASTELLS, F. DE P.

110   1902   Método Quiché: libro para enseñar á leer en lengua Quiché á los indígenas de Guatemala. Los Angeles, Calif.

Contains word and phrase lists, paradigms, and devotional texts with interlinear translation.

CASTRO G., CARLO ANTONIO

111   1955   La pluralización en Pame Meridional. *Rev. Mex. Est. Antro.*, 14: 213–18.

CHARENCEY, HYACINTHE DE

112   1876   Mélanges sur différents idiomes de la Nouvelle Espagne. Paris.

Republished as: Sur différents idiomes de la Nouvelle Espagne, in the author's Mélanges de Philologie et Paléographie Américaines (Paris, 1883), pp. 37–67. Contains the following materials copied from MSS in the library of Brasseur: Chiapanec-French vocabulary, notes on grammar of Tzotzil and Tzeltal (the latter from a MS by Juan de Rodaz), French-Kekchi vocabulary, and Kekchi grammatical notes.

113   1879   Vocabulaire Français-Nagranda. *Rev. Ling.*, 12: 334–37.

Subtiaba vocabulary.

114   1883   Vocabulaire Français-Maya. *Actes de la Société Philologique*, 13: 1–87. Alençon.

Also published separately, Alençon, 1884.

115   1884   De la formation des mots en langue Maya. *ICA-P*, 5: 379–426. Copenhague.

116   1885   Vocabulaire de la langue Tzotzil. *Mémoires de l'Académie Nationale des Sciences, Arts et Belles-Lettres de Caen*, 1885: 251–89. Caen.

Also published separately. Consists of Spanish-Tzotzil vocabulary from MS of Manuel Hidalgo, 1735.

117   1886   Abrégé de grammaire de la langue Tzotzil avec texts d'après le manuscrit du R. P. Don Manuel Hidalgo. *Rev. Ling.*, 19: 170–88.

Grammar notes and devotional texts from MS of the 18th century.

118   1889   Vocabulario Tzotzil-Español. Dialecto de los indios de la parte oriental del Estado de Chiapas. *Rev. Ling.*, 22: 247–73.

Also published separately, Orléans, 1890.

119   1890   Étude sur la langue Mam. *ICA-P*, 7: 389–403. Berlin.

Includes texts and Mam-French vocabulary.

120   1891   Des suffixes en langue Quichée. *Mémoires de l'Académie Nationale des Sciences, Arts et Belles-Lettres de Caen*, 1891: 205–78. Caen.

Also issued separately, 1892. Lists suffixes alphabetically, with discussion of each.

121   1896   Mélanges sur quelques dialectes de la famille Maya-Quichée. *JSAP*, o.s., 1: 43–60.

Also issued separately, Paris, 1897. The parts are: 1. De quelques particularités du verbe et de la conjugaison en langue Quichée. 2. Rectification d'un texte en langue Maya. 3. Des voix verbales en Maya.

122   1912   De la formation des voix verbales en Tzotzil. *ICA-P*, 17: 167–75. Buenos Aires.
             See also Quintana, 1733; Reyes, A., 1593; and Reynoso, 1644.

CHRISTIANSEN, L. D.
123   1937   Totonaco. *Inv. Ling.*, 4: 151–53.
             Notes on phonology and grammar.

CHURCH, CLARENCE AND KATHERINE
123a   1960   The Jacaltec noun phrase. *In* Elson, 1960, pp. 159–70.
123b   1966   Jacaltec grammar. *In* Mayers, 1966, pp. 206–18.

CIUDAD REAL, ANTONIO DE
             See Martínez Hernández, 1929.

CLARK, LAWRENCE E.
124   1959   Phoneme classes in Sayula Popoluca. *Studies in Linguistics*, 14: 25–33. Buffalo.
124a   1960   Vocabulario Popoluca-Castellano, Castellano-Popoluca: Dialecto de Sayula, Veracruz. (Serie de vocabularios Mariano Silva y Aceves, 4.) México.
             Includes notes on pronunciation and a morphological sketch.
124b   1962   Sayula Popoluca morpho-syntax. *IJAL*, 28: 183–98.

CLINE, HOWARD F.
             See Barreda, 1730.

COLLARD, HOWARD
125   1954   Mayo: Dialect of Tetanchopa, Sonora. *In* Key, 1954, pp. 347–65.

COLLARD, HOWARD AND ELIZABETH
125a   1962   Vocabulario Mayo: Castellano-Mayo, Mayo-Castellano. Serie de vocabularios indígenas Mariano Silva y Aceves, 6. México.

COLOP D., FERNANDO
126   1927   Vocabulario del idioma Kakchiquel traducido al Español. Quezaltenango, Guatemala.
             Republished with corrections and Quiché equivalences added by Remigio A. Marroquín, ed. by Alfredo Barrera Vásquez, *An. Mus. Nac.*, 5a época, 3: 239–54. Consists of Spanish-Cakchiquel word and phrase lists.

CÓRDOVA, JUAN DE
127   1578a   Arte en lengua Zapoteca. México.
             Republished as: Arte del idioma Zapoteco . . . , bajo la dirección y cuidado del Dr. Nicolás León (Morelia, 1886).
128   1578b   Vocabulario en lengua Zapoteca. México.
             Facsimile edition: Vocabulario Castellano-Zapoteco, introducción y notas de Wigberto Jiménez Moreno (México, 1942).
             See also Peñafiel, 1887.

CORONEL, JUAN
129   1620   Arte en lengua Maya recopilado y enmendado. México.
             Reprinted in Martínez Hernández, 1929.

CORTÉS Y ZEDEÑO, GERÓNIMO THOMÁS DE AQUINO
130   1765   Arte, vocabulario, y confesionario en el idioma Mexicano, como se usa en el Obispado de Guadalaxara. Puebla.
             Not seen.

CORUNA Y COLLUDO, ANTONIO DE
131   1880   Zoque—the language spoken at Santa María de Chimalapa, and at San Miguel and Tierra Blanca, in the State of Chiapas, Mexico. Translated by J. A. Dacus. *Transactions of the St. Louis Academy of Science*, 4.1: 36–42. St. Louis, Missouri.
             Contains vocabulary and Lord's Prayer.

CORZO, ÁNGEL M.
132   1929   Algunos vocablos pertenecientes a los dialectos hablados por diferentes tribus del Estado de Chiapas. *Quetzalcoatl*, 1.2: 15–18. México.
             Short word lists from several villages, in several Mayan dialects (including Tzotzil and Tojolabal) and in Zoque.

COVARRUBIAS, MIGUEL

133   1954   Mexico South, the Isthmus of Tehuantepec. New York.

Generalities on the Zapotec language, pp. 304–10; Zapotec texts with free translation, pp. 299–300, 312–13, 315–17, 346–47. An appendix contains word lists in Zapotec of Juchitán, Nahuat of Cosoleacaque, Tequistlatec, Huave, Sierra Popoluca, Mixe, and Zoque (the last three collected by George and Mary Foster).

COWAN, FLORENCE HANSEN

134   1937   Report on the Mazateco dialect—morphology and grammar. *Inv. Ling.* 4: 144–47.

Under name of "Florencia Hansen."

See also Cowan, George M. and Florence, 1947.

COWAN, GEORGE M.

135   1947   Una visita a los indígenas Amuzgos de México. *Anales del Instituto Nacional de Antropología e Historia*, 2: 293–301. México.

Includes section on language, with notes on phonemic system.

136   1948   Mazateco whistle speech. *Lg.*, 24: 280–86.

Account of how whistling of Mazatec tones is used as substitute for speech.

136a   1965   Some aspects of the lexical structure of a Mazatec historical text. Summer Institute of Linguistics of the University of Oklahoma, Publications in linguistics, 11. Norman, Okla.

A study of "the collocational habits of lexical items".

COWAN, GEORGE M. AND FLORENCE

137   1947   Mazateco: Locational and directional morphemes. *Aboriginal Linguistics*, 1: 3–9. Cuernavaca.

COWAN, MARION

138   1956   Gramática Castellana-Tzotzil. México.

Not seen.

CRAWFORD, JOHN CHAPMAN

138a   1963   Totontepec Mixe phonotagmemics. Summer Institute of Linguistics, Publications in linguistics, 8. Norman, Okla.

Phonemes and their arrangements.

CROFT, KENNETH

139   1951   Practical orthography for Matlapa Nahuatl. *IJAL*, 17: 32–36.

Suggests combined phonemic and morphophonemic basis.

140   1953   Matlapa Nahuatl II: Affix list and morphophonemics. *IJAL*, 19: 274–80.

141   1954   Matlapa Nahuatl III: Morpheme arrangements. *IJAL*, 20: 37–43.

142   1957   Nahuatl texts from Matlapa, S.L.P. *Tlalocan*, 3: 317–33. México.

CRUMRINE, LYNNE S.

142a   1961   The phonology of Arizona Yaqui, with texts. University of Arizona, Anthropological papers, 5. Tucson.

Yaqui as transplanted from Sonora to Arizona.

CURTIS, E. S.

143   1908   The North American Indian. Vol. 2. Cambridge, Mass.

Pima and Papago word lists, pp. 118–23.

DACUS, J. A.

See Coruna y Colludo, 1880.

DARAPSKI, L.

See Agreda, 1888.

DAVIS, MARJORIE

144   1954   Translating from FL Cuicateco to TL English. *IJAL*, 20: 302–12.

Five-stage translation of a text from the "From Language" Cuicatec to the "Target Language" English.

See also Needham and Davis, 1946.

DAVIS, MARJORIE, AND MARGARET WALKER

145   1955   Cuicateco: Morphemics and morphophonemics. *IJAL*, 21: 46–51.

DEDRICK, JOHN M.

146   1946   How Jobeʔeso Roʔi got his name. *Tlalocan*, 2: 163–66. Azcapotzalco.
Yaqui text with literal and free translations.

147   1954   Yaqui (Cáhita): Dialect of Vicam, Sonora. *In* Key, 1954, pp. 334–46.

DELGATY, ALFA

147a   1961   Notes on dependent versus independent nouns in Tsotsil. *In* A William Cameron Townsend en el vigésimoquinto aniversario del Instituto Lingüístico de Verano, pp. 413–19.

DELGATY, COLIN C.

147b   1960   Tzotzil verb phrase structure. *In* Elson, 1960, pp. 83–125.

147c   1964   Vocabulario Tzotzil de San Andrés, Chiapas. Serie de vocabularios indígenas Mariano Silva y Aceves, 10. México.
Tzotzil-Spanish and Spanish-Tzotzil.

DÍAZ BARRIOS, EDUARDO
See Herbruger and Díaz Barrios, 1956.

DÍAZ FLORES, RAYMUNDO

148   1945   Textos en idioma Cora. Escuela Nacional de Antropología, Pub. 3. México.
Seven texts with interlinear translation, written by a native speaker in a phonemic alphabet.

DIGUET, LÉON

149   1911   Idiome Huichol, contribution à l'étude des langues mexicaines. *JSAP*, n.s., 8: 23–54.
Grammatical notes, paradigms, word lists, and text, based on author's field work.

DIRECCIÓN GENERAL DE CARTOGRAFÍA, GUATEMALA

149a   1962   Alfabetos oficializados de trece principales idiomas indígenas de Guatemala. Diccionario Geográfico de Guatemala, vol. 2, pp. 415–50. Guatemala.
Explanations of phonemic orthographies for Achí, Aguacatec, Cakchiquel, Chuj, Ixil, Jacaltec, Kanjobal, Kekchí, Mam, Pocomam, Quiché, and Tzutuhil.

DOBLADO LARA, JORGE

150   1951   Vocabularios Lencas de Honduras. *Anales del Museo Nacional "David J. Guzmán"* 2.6: 73–79. San Salvador.
Word lists of five dialects, collected at the end of the 19th century.

DOLORES, JUAN

151   1913   Papago verb stems. Introduction by A. L. Kroeber. *UCPAAE*, 10: 241–63.

152   1923   Papago nominal stems. Edited by J. Alden Mason. *UCPAAE*, 20: 19–31.

DOMÍNGUEZ, FRANCISCO
See Zambrano Bonilla, 1752

DOUGLASS, CELIA M.
See Mendenhall, Celia Douglass.
See also Supple and Douglass, 1949.

DYK, ANNE

153   1951   Vocabulario de la lengua Mixteca de San Miguel el Grande, Oaxaca. México.
Spanish-Mixtec and Mixtec-Spanish, preceded by notes on phonetics and grammar.

154   1959   Mixteco texts. Summer Institute of Linguistics, University of Oklahoma, Linguistics series, no. 3. Norman, Okla.
Texts followed by Mixtec-Spanish vocabulary, with notes on phonemics and morphophonemics.

DYK, ANNE, AND BETTY STOUDT

154a   1965   Vocabulario Mixteco de San Miguel el Grande. Serie de vocabularios indígenas Mariano Silva y Aceves, 12. México.
Mixtec-Spanish and Spanish-Mixtec, with notes on transcription and on grammar.

EACHUS, FRANCIS, AND RUTH CARLSON

154b   1966   Kekchi. *In* Mayers, 1966, pp. 110–24.
Grammatical sketch with sample text.

ECKER, LAWRENCE

155   1937   Los dos metoros (un cuento Otomí). *Inv. Ling.*, 4: 254–61.

Short text with free translation and grammatical notes.

156   1947   La incorporación del objeto al verbo en Otomí y Mexicano. *ICA-P*, 27.2: 269–77. México.

157   1952   Compendio de gramática Otomí, introducción a un diccionario Otomí-Español. *Anales del Instituto Nacional de Antropología e Historia*, 4: 121–74. México.

Introduction to an unpublished dictionary, compiled from López Yepes 1826, Neve y Molina 1767, and Buelna 1893. Includes text, "Los dos metoros."

EDMONSON, MUNRO S.

157a   1965   Quiche-English dictionary. Publications of the Middle American Research Institute, Tulane University, 30. New Orleans.

Materials compiled from colonial and modern sources, including the MS Vocabulario of Domingo de Basseta (1698?) and the anonymous Franciscan Vocabulario of 1787, as well as material from Brasseur 1862, Fernández 1892, Friedrich 1955, Selis Lope 1953, Teletor 1959, Xec and Maynard 1954, and other published and unpublished sources.

EKSTROM, J.

158   1954   [Vocabularies as listed below.] *In* Key, 1954.

Nahuatl of Zongolica, Veracruz, pp. 60–72; Nahuatl of San Agustín Oapan, Guerrero, pp. 95–102; Nahuatl of Atzacualoya, Guerrero, pp. 103–09; Nahuatl of Topiltepec, Guerrero, pp. 110–17; Nahuatl of La Cimienta, San Luis Potosí, pp. 220–26 (see note under Key, 1954); Nahuatl of Xochihuehuetlan, Guerrero, pp. 227–38; Varohío, pp. 374–81.

ELLIOTT, RAYMOND

158a   1960   Ixil (Mayan) clause structure. *In* Elson, 1960, pp. 129–54.

ELLIOTT, RAYMOND AND HELEN

158b   1966   Ixil. *In* Mayers, 1966, pp. 125–39.

Grammatical sketch with sample text.

ELSON, BEN

159   1947a   Sierra Popoluca syllable structure. *IJAL*, 13: 13–17.

160   1947b   The Homshuk: a Sierra Popoluca text. *Tlalocan*, 2: 193–214. Azcapotzalco.

161   1960   Sierra Popoluca morphology. *IJAL*, 26: 206–23.

161a   1960b   Gramática del Popoluca de la Sierra. Universidad Veracruzana, Biblioteca de la Facultad de Filosofía y Letras, 6. Xalapa.

161b   1960c   Mayan studies, I. Edited by Ben Elson. Summer Institute of Linguistics of the University of Oklahoma, Linguistic series, 5. Norman, Okla.

Contents: Cakchiquel grammar, by W. Cameron Townsend, pp. 3–79; Tzotzil verb phrase structure, by Colin Delgaty, pp. 83–125; Ixil clause structure, by Ray Elliott, pp. 129–54; The Jacaltec noun phrase, by Clarence and Katherine Church, pp. 159–70.

161c   1961   Person markers and related morphemes in Sierra Popoluca. *In* A William Cameron Townsend en el vigésimoquinto aniversario del Instituto Lingüístico de Verano, pp. 421–30. México.

161d   1965   Sierra Popoluca intonation. *In* Homenaje a Juan Comas, vol. 1, pp. 177–89. México.

ENGEL, RALPH, AND ROBERT E. LONGACRE

161e   1963   Syntactic matrices in Ostuacan Zoque. *IJAL*, 29: 331–44.

ESCALANTE HERNÁNDEZ, ROBERTO

161f   1961   El Pima Bajo ('obnók). *Anales del Instituto Nacional de Antropología e Historia*, 14: 349–52 (published 1962). México.

Phonology of lower Pima.

161g   1962   El Cuitlateco. Instituto Nacional de Antropología e Historia, Depto. de Investigaciones Antropológicas, Publicaciones, 9. México.

Grammatical sketch and vocabulary, from field work with the last surviving speaker.

161h   1963   Material lingüístico del oriente de Sonora: Tonichi y Pónida. *Anales del Instituto Nacional de Antropología e Historia*, 16: 149–78 (published 1964). México.

Data on two contemporary Uto-Aztecan dialects of eastern Sonora, perhaps to be identified with Ópata.

ESCANDÓN, LUIS A.

162   1891   Arte del idioma Otomí. *In his* Ensayo histórico-geográfico estadístico del Distrito de Itzmiquilpan. México.

Grammatical sketch with paradigms.

FERNÁNDEZ, JESÚS

162   1937–38 Diccionario Poconchí. *An. Soc. Geog. Hist.*, 14: 47–70, 184–200.

Pocomchí-Spanish.

FERNÁNDEZ, LEÓN

164   1892   Lenguas indígenas de Centro América en el Siglo XVIII según copia del Archivo de Indias hecha por el Licenciado don León Fernández y publicada por Ricardo Fernández Guardia y Juan Fernández Ferraz. San José de Costa Rica.

Word lists prepared at the order of Charles III of Spain in 1788–89. Among languages included are Quiché, Kekchi, Pocomchi, Cakchiquel, Tzutuhil, Pocomam, "Pupuluca" (an unidentified Mayan dialect), Chol, Tzotzil, Tzeltal, "Chanabal" (Tojolabal), "Subinha" (Kanjobal), Mam, Zoque, and Chiapanec. Part of these were reprinted as: Lenguas indígenas de Guatemala en el Siglo XVIII, *An. Soc. Geog. Hist.*, 24: 107–58 (1949). The Chiapanec material was reproduced by Lehmann, 1920, pp. 888–94.

FERNÁNDEZ DE MIRANDA, MARÍA TERESA

165   1953   Las formas posesivas en Ixcateco. *Memoria del Congreso Científico Mexicano*, 12: 159–70. México.

Morphophonemic and morphological description, with Ixcatec-Spanish noun vocabulary.

166   1959   Fonémica del Ixcateco. Instituto Nacional de Antropología e Historia, Pub. 3 México.

166a   1961   Diccionario Ixcateco. Instituto Nacional de Antropología e Historia, Dirección de Investigaciones Antropológicas, Publicaciones, 7. México.

Ixcatec-Spanish and Spanish-Ixcatec, with morphological notes and texts.

FERNÁNDEZ FERRAZ, JUAN

See Fernández, León, 1892.

FERNÁNDEZ GUARDIA, RICARDO

See Fernández, León, 1892.

FERRERO, JOSÉ

167   1920   Pequeña gramática y diccionario de la lengua Tarahumara. México.

Includes Spanish-Tarahumara dictionary.

168   1924   Diccionario Tarahumar-Castellano. México.

Includes addenda and corrigenda to Ferrero, 1920.

FLORES, ILDEFONSO JOSEPH

169   1753   Arte de la lengua metropolitana del reyno Cakchiquel o Guatemalico, con un. parallelo de las lenguas metropolitánicas de los reynos Kiché, Cakchiquel, y Tzutuhil. . . . Guatemala.

Cakchiquel grammar, followed by comparisons with Quiché and Tzutuhil.

FOSTER, GEORGE M.

170   1940   Notes on the Popoluca of Veracruz. Instituto Panamericano de Geografía e Historia, Pub. 51. México.

Includes Sierra Popoluca vocabulary, pp. 31–41.

FOSTER, MARY L. AND GEORGE M.

171   1948   Sierra Popoluca speech. Smithsonian Institution, Institute of Social Anthropology, Pub. 8. Washington.

Phonology, brief grammar, analyzed text, and short vocabulary.

See also Covarrubias, 1954.

FOX, DAVID
171a   1966   Quiche grammatical sketch. *In* Mayers, 1966, pp. 60–86.
            Includes sample text.

FRAENKEL, GERD
172   1959   Yaqui phonemics. *Anthro. Ling.*, 1.5: 7–18.

FRIEDRICH, JOHANNES
173   1955   Kurze Grammatik der alten Quiché-Sprache im Popol Vuh. *Abhandlungen der Akademie der Wissenschaften und der Literatur in Mainz, Geistes- und sozialwissenschaftliche Klasse*, Jahrgang 1955, nr. 4 (pp. 310–449). Wiesbaden.

FUENTE, J. DE LA
174   1947   Los Zapotecos de Choapan, Oaxaca. *Anales del Instituto Nacional de Antropología e Historia*, 2: 143–205. México.

            Word list, pp. 196–204.

FUENTES, E. A.
175   1903   Palabras Huaves coleccionadas en 1870 para el Instituto Smithsoniano. México.
            Not seen.

GAGE, THOMAS
176   1648   The English-American his travail by sea and land; or, a new survey of the West-Indies ... with a grammar, or some few rudiments of the Indian tongue, called, Poconchi, or Pocoman. London.

            Various later editions, including London, 1928. Spanish version of linguistic section: Rudimentos gramaticales de la lengua Poconchí o Pocomán, traducción por José Antonio Villacorta C., *An. Soc. Geog. Hist.*, 14: 455–64 (1938).

GALDO GUZMÁN, DIEGO DE
177   1642   Arte Mexicano. México.

            Reprinted in Colección de gramáticas de la lengua Mexicana, 1: 281–394, supplement to *An. Mus. Nac.*, 1a época, tomo 4 (1890–92).

GALINDO, JUAN
       See BAEZO, 1832.

GARIBAY K., ÁNGEL MARÍA
178   1934   Morfemas nominales en Otomí, contribución a la morfología de esta lengua. *An. Mus. Nac.*, 5a época, 1: 291–323.
            Description of noun derivation.

179   1940   Llave del Náhuatl. Colección de trozos clásicos, con gramática y vocabularios, para utilidad de los principiantes. Otumba, Mexico.
            Revised edition, México, 1961.

GARVIN, PAUL L.
180   1947   Distinctive features in Zoque phonemic acculturation. *Studies in Linguistics*, 5: 13–20. Norman, Okla.
            Re-analysis, in terms of acoustic features, of Wonderly, 1946a.

GASSÓ, LEONARDO
181   1903   Gramática Rarámuri o Tarahumara. México.
            Grammar according to strict Latin model; devotional texts, some with interlinear translation.

GATES, WILLIAM EDMOND
182   1938   A grammar of Maya. Maya Society, Pub. 13. Baltimore.
            Consists mostly of grammatically classified word lists.

GATSCHET, ALBERT S.
183   1877   Der Yuma-Sprachstamm. *Zeitschrift für Ethnologie*, 9: 341–50, 366–418. Berlin.
            Includes word lists of Cochimí, Kiliwa, and "H'taäm" (perhaps the "Akwa'ala" of Gifford and Lowie, 1928).

184   1883   Der Yuma-Sprachstamm, 2. *Zeitschrift für Ethnologie*, 15: 123–47. Berlin.
            Includes Seri word list.

185   1886   Der Yuma-Sprachstamm, 3. *Zeitschrift für Ethnologie*, 18: 97–122. Berlin.

Includes word list from Yuman dialect of Santa Catalina, Lower California; and Seri-German vocabulary by Alphonse L. Pinart.

GEBUTA QUEJ, FRANCISCO DÍAZ
See Villacorta C., 1934.

GEOFFROY RIVAS, PEDRO

186   1956   Status morfológico de las conjunciones Nahuas. *Tlatoani*, 2a época, no. 10, pp. 39–40. México.

Description using the "valence" terminology of Richard Pittman.

GERDEL, FLORENCIA
See Slocum and Gerdel, 1965.

GIBSON, LORNA F.

187   1956   Pame (Otomi) phonemics and morphophonemics. *IJAL*, 22: 242–65.

GIFFORD, E. W., AND R. H. LOWIE

188   1928   Notes on the Akwa'ala Indians of Lower California. *UCPAAE*, 23: 339–52.

Brief vocabularies of Akwa'ala, "Yukaliwa," and Cocopa.

GILBERTI, MATURINO

189   1558   Arte de la lengua de Michoacán. [México.]

Reprinted as: Arte de la lengua Tarasca o de Michoacán, ed. Nicolás León (México, 1898).

190   1559   Vocabulario en lengua de Mechuacán. México.

Tarascan-Spanish, with a separate list of verb roots, and Spanish-Tarascan. Reprinted as: Diccionario de la lengua Tarasca o de Michoacán, ed. Antonio Peñafiel (México, 1901). The root list was reprinted as: Raíces de la lengua Tarasca, Colección Siglo XVI, 3 (México, 1959). The entire work was again republished (title: Diccionario . . .) in Guadalajara, 1962.

GIRARD, RAFAEL

191   1940–41   El Chortí. *Revista del Archivo y Biblioteca Nacionales*, 19: 111–13, 185, 244–45. 310–11, 365–66, 426–28, 498–99, 555–56, 625–26, 281–82, 746–47; 20: 43–44, 113–14, 175–76, 247–48, 369–72. Tegucigalpa, Honduras.

Word lists, paradigms, sentences.

192   1949   Los Chortís ante el problema Maya. 5 vols. México.

Vol. 1, pp. 91–138, contains word lists, with notes on pronunciation and grammar.

GÓMEZ, ANICETO M.

193   1935   Estudios gramaticales de la lengua Cora que se habla en el Territorio de Tepic. *Inv. Ling.*, 3: 79–142.

Discussion of phonology and grammar, with paradigms; two texts of the Pater Noster.

GONZÁLEZ, LUIS
See Grasserie, 1898.

GONZÁLEZ CASANOVA, PABLO

194   1920   Un cuento en Mexicano de Milpa Alta, D.F. *Journal of American Folklore*, 33: 25–27. Lancaster, Pa.
Aztec text with interlinear translation.

195   1922a   Un cuento en Mexicano. *Méx. Ant.*, 1: 291–309.
Aztec text from Tepoztlán, Morelos, in close phonetic transcription, with literal and free translations and grammatical notes.

196   1922b   El Mexicano de Teotihuacán. *In* Manuel Gamio, ed., La población del Valle de Teotihuacán. Vol. 2, pp. 595–648. México.
Notes on phonetics and morphology; text; Aztec-Spanish vocabulary.

197   1925   Nota sobre la lengua Chinanteca. *An. Mus. Nac.*, 4a época, 3: 103–08.
Contains Spanish-Chinantec vocabulary by Ángel Soliz.

198   1930   Un vocabulario Chichimeca. *ICA-P*, 23: 918–25. New York.

199   1946   Cuentos indígenas. Edición bilingüe Náhuatl y Española. Biblioteca de Filología y Lingüística Indígenas, I. México.
Fourteen Aztec folk tales in conventional (i.e., non-phonemic) orthography.

GOUBAUD CARRERA, ANTONIO
See Stoll, 1884.

GRASSERIE, RAOUL DE LA

200   1898   Langue Zoque et langue Mixe. Grammaire, dictionnaire, textes traduits et analysés. Bibliothèque Linguistique Américaine, 22. Paris.

Zoque grammar, Spanish-Zoque and Zoque-French dictionaries, based on MS of Luis González, Arte breve y vocabulario de la lengua Tzoque, 1672. Grammatical notes on modern Zoque, after Sánchez, 1877. Mixe grammatical notes, word lists, and texts, after Quintana, 1733.

GRASSERIE, RAOUL DE LA, AND NICOLÁS LEÓN

201   1896   Langue Tarasque. Grammaire, dictionnaire, textes traduits et analysés. Bibliothèque Linguistique Américaine, 19. Paris.

Based on materials from Basalenque 1714, Lagunas 1574, Gilberti 1558 and 1559.

GRIMES, JOSEPH E.

202   1953   *Review of* J. Alden Mason, The language of the Papago of Arizona. *IJAL*, 19: 313–15.

Attempts to establish Papago phonemes on the basis of Mason's phonetic data.

203   1954   Nahuatl of Ostotitla, Veracruz. *In* Key, 1954, pp. 52–59.

204   1955   Style in Huichol structure. *Lg.*, 31: 31–35.

Stylistic variation on the phonetic level, analyzed as reflecting two co-existent phonemic systems.

205   1959   Huichol tone and intonation. *IJAL*, 25: 221–32.

206   1960   Spanish-Nahuatl-Huichol monetary terms. *IJAL*, 26: 162–65.

Description of Huichol system for counting money, noting Spanish and Nahuatl influences.

206a   1964   Huichol syntax. Janua linguarum, series practica, 11. The Hague.

Includes text analysis and notes on verb morphology.

See also McIntosh and Grimes, 1954a, 1954b.

GRIMES, JOSEPH E., AND W. NYMAN, JR.

207   1954   Nahuatl of Pómara, Michoacán. *In* Key, 1954, pp. 73–94.

GUDSCHINSKY, SARAH C.

208   1958   Native reactions to tones and words in Mazatec. *Word*, 14: 338–45. Limoges.

209   1959   Mazatec kernel constructions and transformations. *IJAL*, 25: 81–89.

Grammatical sketch according to transformational analysis, as developed by Z. S. Harris.

210   1959b   Discourse analysis of a Mazatec text. *IJAL*, 25: 139–46.

Text with discourse analysis according to techniques of Z. S. Harris, using transformational analysis of Mazatec grammar.

See also Pike, E. V., and Gudschinsky, 1952.

GUERRA, JUAN

211   1692   Arte de la lengua Mexicana según la acostumbran hablar los indios en todo el Obispado de Guadalaxara, parte del de Guadiana, y del de Mechoacán. México.

Republished by Alberto Santoscoy, Guadalajara, 1900. Includes Aztec-Spanish word list of the Jalisco dialect.

GUEVARA, MIGUEL

212   1862   Arte doctrinal y modo general para aprender la lengua Matlaltzinga.... Año de 1638. *Bol. Soc. Mex. Geog. Estad.*, 1a época, 9: 197–260.

Grammatical notes, paradigms, word lists, sentences.

HAEDO, FRANCISCO

213   1731   Gramática de la lengua Otomí.... México.

Not seen.

HALE, KENNETH LOCKE

214   1959   A Papago grammar. Indiana University dissertation. Ann Arbor, University Microfilms.

27

Phonology and morphology-syntax of Pima-Papago. Summary in *Diss. Abs.*, 20: 1773, 1960.

214a   1965   Some preliminary observations on Papago morphophonemics. *IJAL*, 31: 295–305.

HALPERN, A. M.
See Andrade, 1946a.

HAMP, ERIC P.

215   1954   Componential restatement of syllable structure in Trique. *IJAL*, 20: 206–09.
Based on data from Longacre, 1952.

216   1957   Stylistically modified allophones in Huichol. *Lg.*, 33: 139–42.
Based on data from Grimes, 1955.

HANSEN, FLORENCIA
See Cowan, Florence Hansen.

HARDING, B., AND E. BROCKWAY

217   1954   Nahuatl of Tlaxpanaloya, Puebla. *In* Key, 1954, pp. 208–19.

HARRIS, MARGARET

218   1947   Nombres clasificadores Chontales. *Anales del Instituto Nacional de Antropología e Historia*, 2: 303–06. México.
Title mistranslates "noun classifiers," suffixes attached to numerals in Chontal of Tabasco.

See also Keller and Harris, 1946.

HARRISON, W. ROY

219   1953   The mason: a Zoque text. *Tlalocan*, 3: 193–204. México.

HARRISON, W. ROY AND MARGARET B.

220   1948   Diccionario Español-Zoque y Zoque-Español. Glendale, Calif.

HART, HELEN LONG

221   1957   Hierarchical structuring of Amuzgo grammar. *IJAL*, 23: 141–64.
Grammatical sketch based on K. L. Pike's "grammemic" (later "tagmemic") theory.

HASLER, JUAN

221a   1960   Los fonemas del náhuat de Los Tuztlas. *Estudios de Cultura Nahuatl*, 2: 129–34. México.

HENDRICHS PÉREZ, PEDRO R.

222   1939   Un estudio preliminar sobre la lengua Cuitlateca de San Miguel Totolapan, Gro. *Méx. Ant.*, 4: 329–62.
Contains grammatical notes, paradigms, and brief Spanish-Cuitlatec word list.

223   1946   Por tierras ignotas, viajes y observaciones en la región del Río de las Balsas. Vol. 2. Pan American Institute of Geography and History, Pub. 83. México.
Spanish-Aztec vocabularies in four dialects, pp. 78–124. Aztec texts, pp. 125–29. Cuitlatec grammatical notes and Spanish-Cuitlatec vocabulary, pp. 130–244. Cuitlatec texts, pp. 244–46.

224   1947   Breve informe del idioma Cuitlateco. *ICA-P*, 27, 1st session, 2: 289–95. México.
Contains grammatical notes.

See also Weitlaner, 1939b.

HERBRUGER, ALFREDO, JR., AND EDUARDO DÍAZ BARRIOS

225   1956   Método para aprender a hablar, leer y escribir la lengua Cakchiquel. Vol. 1. Guatemala.
Pedagogical grammar, including word lists, paradigms, sentences for memorization, exercises, and readings.

HERNÁNDEZ, EUSEBIO, AND A. L. PINART

226   1897   Pequeño vocabulario de la lengua Lenca. Petite Bibliothèque Américaine, vol. 8. Paris.
Not seen. Spanish-Lenca vocabulary republished by Lehmann, 1920, pp. 671–86.

HERNÁNDEZ, FORTUNATO

227   1902   Las razas indígenas de Sonora y la Guerra del Yaqui. México.

Grammatical notes on Cáhita, pp. 185–93, based on Velasco, 1737. Spanish-Cáhita and Cáhita-Spanish vocabularies, pp. 194–233. English-Seri and Spanish–Seri word lists, paradigms, and phrases, pp. 237–69, from MSS of W. J. McGee, A. L. Pinart, and others. A smaller part of McGee's data was also published in his The Seri Indians, *BAE-R*, 17: 299–344 (Washington, 1896).

HERZOG, DOROTHY
    See Bower and Herzog, 1958.

HESS, HARWOOD
227a   1962   The syntactic structure of Mezquital Otomí. University of Michigan dissertation. Ann Arbor, University Microfilms.
        See summary in *Diss. Abs.*, 23: 3365, 1963.

HESS, HARWOOD AND PATRICIA
228   1956   Dictionary of Otomi, Spanish, and English. México.

HESTERMANN, FERD.
    See Reyes, Gaspar, 1931.

HIDALGO, MANUEL
    See Charencey, 1885 and 1886.

HILTON, KENNETH S.
229   1947   Palabras y frases de las lenguas Tarahumara y Guarijío. *Anales del Instituto Nacional de Antropología e Historia*, 2: 307–13. México.
230   1954   Tarahumara: dialect of Samachique, Chihuahua. *In* Key, 1954, pp. 300–11.
231   1959   Vocabulario Tarahumara y Español. Serie de vocabularios indígenas Mariano Silva y Aceves, 1. México.
        Tarahumara-Spanish and Spanish-Tarahumara, preceded by grammatical notes.

HOCKETT, CHARLES F.
232   1947   Componential analysis of Sierra Popoluca. *IJAL*, 13: 258–67.
        Phonemic restatement of data from Elson, 1947.

HÖLTKER, GEORG
233   1930   Dvandvaähnliche Wortkuppelung im Aztekischen. *Wiener Beiträge zur Kulturgeschichte und Linguistik*, 1: 349–58. Wien.

HOOGSHAUGEN, SEARLE
233a   1959   Three contrastive vowels lengths in Mixe. *Zeitschrift für Phonetik*, 12: 111–15. Berlin.

HOOGSHAUGEN, SEARLE AND HILDA
234   1956   Ayuuc alfabeto, en el idioma Mixe de Coatlán. México.
        Includes word list.

HORCASITAS, FERNANDO
235   1958   Nahuatl for beginners. México.
        Mimeographed textbook, with English-Aztec and Aztec-English vocabularies.

HOYO, EUGENIO DEL
235a   1960   Vocablos de la lengua Quinigua de los indios Borrados del Noreste de México. *Humanitas*, Anuario del Centro de Estudios Humanísticos, Universidad de Nuevo León, 1.1: 489–515. México.
        Listing and attempted analysis of words in the Quinigua language, gleaned from MSS of the 16th–18th centuries. Some items suggest Coahuiltecan affiliation.
235b   1965   El cuadernillo de la lengua de los indios Pajalates (1732) por Fray Gabriel de Vergara, y El confesonario [sic] de indios en lengua Coahuilteca. Publicaciones del Instituto Tecnológico y de Estudios Superiores de Monterrey, Serie: Historia, 3. Monterrey.
        Fragmentary data on two extinct languages of northwestern Mexico.

INSTITUTO INDIGENISTA NACIONAL, GUATEMALA
236   1947   Trayectoria del Instituto. Lenguas indígenas. *Boletín del Instituto Indigenista Nacional*, 2: 115–21. Guatemala.
        Explanation of an alphabet for Cakchiquel, based on work by Mark Hanna Watkins.

237 1950 Alfabetos para los cuatro idiomas indígenas mayoritarios de Guatemala: Quiché, Cakchiquel, Mam y Kekchí. Publicaciones Especiales del Instituto Indigenista Nacional, no. 10. Guatemala.

Includes information on phonetics.

JACKSON, FRANCES
See Supple and Jackson, 1952.

JENKINS, JOYCE
238 1958 Morphological phoneme sequences in Eastern Otomi. *Phonetica*, 2: 1–11. Basel.

Phonemes and their distribution with reference to morpheme boundaries.

JIMÉNEZ, TOMÁS FIDIAS
239 1937 Idioma Pipil, o Nahuat de Cuzcatlán y Tunalán, hoy República de El Salvador en la América Central. San Salvador.

Includes grammar, Pipil-Spanish phrase and word lists, and Spanish-Pipil lexicon. Partly reprinted in *Tzunpame*, 1: 19–32 (1941), 5: 44–51 (1946), 7: 123–33 (1948). San Salvador.

JIMÉNEZ MORENO, WIGBERTO
See Córdova, 1578b.

JOHNSON, JEAN BASSETT
240 1939 Some notes on the Mazatec. *Rev. Mex. Est. Antro.*, 3: 142–56.

Includes phonetic and grammatical notes.

241 1954a Varohio. *In* Key, 1954, pp. 366–73.
242 1954b Pima Bajo: dialect of Onabas, Sonora. *In* Key, 1954, pp. 382–89.
242a 1962 El idioma Yaqui. Instituto Nacional de Antropología e Historia, Depto. de Investigaciones Antropológicas, Publicaciones, 10. México.

Structural sketch, texts, and Yaqui-Spanish vocabulary.

JOHNSON, JEAN BASSETT, AND IRMGARD WEITLANER DE JOHNSON
243 1947 Un vocabulario Varohío. *Rev. Mex. Est. Antro.*, 9: 27–45.

Includes notes on phonetics, plus some phrases and sentences.

244 1954 Opata: dialect of Tonichi, Sonora. *In* Key, 1954, pp. 390–97.

JONES, WILLIAM
245 1915 Kickapoo tales, collected by William Jones. Translated by Truman Michelson. Publications of the American Ethnological Society, vol. 9. Leyden.

Text and free translation on facing pages.

JUNTA COLOMBINA DE MÉXICO
246 1893 Vocabulario Castellano-Zapoteco. Publicado por la Junta Colombina de México con motivo de la celebración del Cuarto Centenario del Descubrimiento de América. México.

Publication of 18th-century MS.

KAUFMAN, TERRENCE S.
246a 1963 Tzeltal grammar. University of California (Berkeley) dissertation. Ann Arbor, University Microfilms.

See summary in *Diss. Abs.*, 24: 5400, 1964.

KELLER, KATHRYN C.
247 1955 The Chontal (Mayan) numeral system. *IJAL*, 21: 258–75.
248 1959 The phonemes of Chontal (Mayan). *IJAL*, 25: 44–53.
See also Yegerlehner and Voegelin, 1957.

KELLER, KATHRYN C., AND MARGARET HARRIS
249 1946 Masculine crab and mosquitoes: two Chontal texts. *Tlalocan*, 2: 138–40. Azcapotzalco.

Mayan Chontal, i.e. of Tabasco.

KELLER, KATHRYN C., AND LULU REBER
250 1958 Yoco t'an, La primera cartilla del idioma Chontal de Tabasco. México.

Chontal-Spanish word list at end.

KELLER, KATHRYN C., AND SOL SAPORTA

251   1957   The frequency of consonant clusters in Chontal. *IJAL*, 23: 28–35.

KEY, HAROLD

252   1954   Vocabularies of languages of the Uto-Aztecan family, collected by Harold Key. *Mic. Coll.*, no. 38. Chicago.

Some vocabularies are supplemented by sentences, some by grammatical notes. The contents are:

Aztec dialects:
Tetelcingo, Morelos, by R. S. Pittman and F. Brewer, pp. 1–9.
Mecayapan, Veracruz, by H. Law, pp. 10–22.
Atlaiaca, Guerrero, by A. McKinlay, pp. 23–38.
Xalacapan, Puebla, by H. Key, pp. 39–51.
Ostotitla, Veracruz, by J. Grimes, pp. 52–59.
Zongolica, Veracruz, by J. Ekstrom, pp. 60–72.
Pómaro, Michoacán, by J. Grimes and W. Nyman Jr., pp. 73–94.
San Agustín Oapan, Guerrero, by J. Ekstrom, pp. 95–102.
Atzacualoya, Guerrero, by J. Ekstrom, pp. 103–09.
Topiltepec, Guerrero, by J. Ekstrom, pp. 110–17.
San Pedro Tototepec, México, by H. Key, pp. 118–25.
Acatlan and Tulapa, Puebla, by G. Stairs, pp. 126–33.
Santo Domingo, Sonsonate, El Salvador, by E. F. Sywulka, pp. 134–43.
Nahuizalco, El Salvador, by J. G. Todd, pp. 144–51.
Tlaxcala, Tlaxcala, by H. Key, pp. 152–59.
Huejotzingo, Puebla, by A. Wares, pp. 160–68.
Tlanepantla, Puebla, by H. Key, pp. 168–75.
Chilac, Puebla, by H. Key, pp. 176–83.
Topilejo, D. F., by H. Key, pp. 184–91.
Xoxocotla, Morelos, by H. Key, pp. 192–99.
Metztla, Puebla, by H. Key, pp. 200–07.
Tlaxpanaloya, Puebla, by B. Harding and E. Brockway, pp. 208–19.
La Cimienta, San Luis Potosí, by J. Ekstrom, pp. 220–26. (Perhaps a mistake for La Pimienta, Hidalgo, on the San Luis Potosí border.)
Xochihuehuetlan, Guerrero, by J. Ekstrom, pp. 227–38.
Xochixtlahuaca, Guerrero, by C. Stewart, pp. 239–43.
Pochutla, Oaxaca (from Boas, 1917), pp. 247–54.
El Salvador (from Arauz, 1926), pp. 255–62.
"Classical" Nahuatl (from Sahagún, 1957), pp. 263–70.
Durango and Michoacán (from Guerra, 1692), pp. 271–78.
Huichol: La Piedra Gorda, Nayarit, by J. McIntosh and J. Grimes, pp. 279–91.
Cora: San Pedro Ixcatán, Nayarit, by A. McMahon, pp. 292–99.
Tarahumara: Samachique, Chihuahua, by K. Hilton, pp. 300–11.
Tepehuane (northern): Baborigame, Chihuahua, by B. Bascom, pp. 312–19.
Tepehuane (southern): Xoconostle, Durango, by B. Hart, pp. 320–33.
Yaqui (Cáhita): Vicam, Sonora, by J. Dedrick, pp. 334–46.
Mayo: Tetanchopa, Sonora, by H. Collard, pp. 347–65.
Varohio by Jean B. Johnson, pp. 366–73.
Varohio by J. Ekstrom, pp. 374–81.
Pima Bajo: Onabas, Sonora, by Jean B. Johnson, pp. 382–89.
Opata: Tonichi, Sonora, by Jean B. and Irmgard Johnson, pp. 390–97.
Tepecano (from Mason, 1917), pp. 398–405.
Papago: Sells, Arizona, by D. Saxton, pp. 429–41.
Papago (from Dolores, 1913), pp. 442–49.

253   1960   Stem construction and affixation of Sierra Nahuat verbs. *IJAL*, 26: 131–45.

KEY, HAROLD AND MARY

254   1953a   The phonemes of Sierra Nahuat. *IJAL*, 19: 53–56.

255   1953b   Vocabulario Mejicano de la Sierra de Zacapoaxtla, Puebla. México.

Spanish-Nahuat and Nahuat-Spanish, preceded by notes on pronunciation and grammar.

See also McKinlay and Key, 1949.

KINGDON, R.

256   1948   sapoʻteko. *Le Maître Phonétique*, no. 90, pp. 24–25. Hertford, England.

Phonetic transcription of text, "The North Wind and the Sun," with interlinear translation.

KROEBER, A. L.

257   1931   The Seri. Southwest Museum Papers, 6. Los Angeles.

Contains short vocabulary.

258   1934   Uto-Aztecan languages of Mexico. Ibero-Americana, 8. Berkeley.

Brief word lists of Sinaloa Aztec, Ópata, Cáhita (Yaqui and Mayo), and Varohío.

See also Dolores, 1913.

KURATH, WILLIAM

259   1945   A brief introduction to Papago, a native language of Arizona. University of Arizona Social Science Bulletin, no. 13. Tucson.

Notes on pronunciation and grammar, six texts with interlinear and free translation.

KURATH, WILLIAM, AND EDWARD H. SPICER

260   1947   A brief introduction to Yaqui, a native language of Sonora. University of Arizona Social Science Bulletin, no. 15. Tucson.

Notes on pronunciation and grammar, six texts with interlinear and free translations, Yaqui-English vocabulary.

KUTSCHER, G.

261   1958   Ein von Walter Lehmann gesammeltes Mexicano-Märchen und Vokabular (Mexicano von Chilapa, Staat Guerrero). *Miscellanea Paul Rivet*, 1: 533–72. México.

Includes Aztec-Spanish vocabulary from Chilapa and short word lists from two other localities.

LaFARGE, OLIVER, AND DOUGLAS BYERS

262   1931   The year-bearer's people. Middle American Research Series, 3. New Orleans.

Contains section on the Jacaltec language, including grammar, texts, and Jacaltec-English dictionary. Also included are vocabularies of Chuj, Chaneabal, Santa Eulalia, and Mam.

See also Blom and LaFarge, 1927.

LAGUNAS, JUAN BAPTISTA DE

263   1574   Arte y diccionario con otras obras en lengua Michuacana. México.

Tarascan grammar and Tarascan-Spanish dictionary. Reprinted by Nicolás León, Supplement to Anales del Museo Michoacano, años 1–3 (Morelia, 1890).

LANDERO, CARLOS F.

264   1890   Estudio sobre la lengua Huichola. *La República Literaria*, 5: 694–702. Guadalajara.

Contains short word list.

LARDÉ Y LARÍN, JORGE

265   1950   El idioma Lenca en Chilanga. *Anales del Museo Nacional "David J. Guzmán"*, 1.1: 53–56. San Salvador.

Lenca-Spanish word list, compiled from previous publications and from a list made by the Alcalde Municipal of Chilanga in 1909.

LARÍN DE LARDÉ, BENIGNA

266   1926   Diccionario Lenca-Español. *Rev. Etno.*, 1: 223–48, 291–304.

Compiled from previously published materials. Reprinted, as far as the letter P, in *Revista del Archivo y Biblioteca Nacionales*, 30: 239–47, 338–42, 444–45, 31: 75–79 (Tegucigalpa, 1951–52).

267   [*nil*]

LARIOS, HIERÓNIMO

268   1607   Arte de la lengua Mame. México.

Not seen.

LARSEN, RAYMOND S.

269   1953   Proclíticos pronominales del dialecto Huasteco que se habla en el Estado de San Luis Potosí. *Rev. Mex. Est. Antro.*, 13: 117–18.

270   1955   Vocabulario Huasteco del Estado de San Luis Potosí. México.

Huastec-Spanish and Spanish-Huastec, preceded by notes on pronunciation and grammar.

LARSEN, RAYMOND S., AND EUNICE VICTORIA PIKE

271   1949   Huasteco intonations and phonemes. *Lg.*, 25: 268–77.

LATHROP, MAXWELL D., JR.

272   1937   Report of a partial study of the Tarascan dialect. *Inv. Ling.*, 4: 111–29.

Notes on phonology and morphology.

273   1953   Trabajos realizados para condicionar el idioma Tarasco como vehículo de educación. *Memoria del Congreso Científico Mexicano*, 12: 175–80. México.

Contains data on the phonemic system. Author's name is given as "Máximo Léthrop."

LAW, HOWARD W.

274   1949   Gulf Aztec texts and dictionary. *In* Summer Institute of Linguistics, 1949, pp. 556–707.

English-Aztec dictionary in dialect of Mecayapan, Veracruz.

275   1954   Nahuatl of Mecayapan, Veracruz. *In* Key, 1954, pp. 10–22.

276   1955   The phonemes of Isthmus Nahuat. *Méx. Ant.*, 8: 267–78.

Phonemic description, with text, of the dialect earlier called "Gulf Aztec" by the author.

277   1957   Tamákasti: a Gulf Nahuatl text. *Tlalocan*, 3: 344–60. México.

278   1958   Morphological structure of Isthmus Nahuat. *IJAL*, 24: 108–29.

278a   1966   Obligatory constructions of Isthmus Nahuat grammar. Janua linguarum, series practica, 29. The Hague.

Tagmemic grammar with analyzed text.

LEAL, MARY

279   1950   Patterns of tone substitution in Zapotec morphology. *IJAL*, 16: 132–36.

LEAL, MARY AND OTIS

280   1954   Noun possession in Villa Alta Zapotec. *IJAL*, 20: 215–16.

281   1956   Aprendamos a leer en Zapoteco. Libro de transición para los que saben leer en Castellano. Zapoteco—dialecto de Yatzachi el Bajo, región de Villa Alta, Estado de Oaxaca. México.

Contains word lists.

LEGTERS, D. BRAINERD

282   1937   Story of a hunter. *Inv. Ling.*, 4: 302–07.

Maya text with literal and free translations, plus notes on phonetics.

LEHMANN, WALTER

283   1915   Über die Stellung und Verwandschaft der Subtiaba-Sprache der Pazifischen Küste Nicaraguas und über die Sprache von Tapachula in Südchiapas. *Zeitschrift für Ethnologie*, 47: 1–34. Berlin.

Includes word lists of Subtiaba and of Tapachultec II. See also Lehmann, 1920.

284   1920   Zentral-Amerika. Teil I, Die Sprachen Zentral-Amerikas in ihren Beziehungen zueinander sowie zu Süd-Amerika und Mexiko. 2 vols. Berlin.

Issued on microtext cards by H. A. Gleason Jr. (Hartford, Conn., 1956). The work is a compendium of grammatical information, vocabularies, and texts from most of the languages of Central America, excluding the Mayan family. Some Mexican languages are also covered. Lehmann reprints much material previously published, as well as material from unpublished MSS and from his own field notes. Of the languages included in this bibliography, Lehmann provides information on the following:

Cacaopera (Matagalpan), pp. 604–23, including data of Mendoza, 1895.

Lenca, pp. 668–722, including data of Squier, 1858; Hernández and Pinart, 1897; Membreño, 1897; and Peccorini, 1910.

Xinca, pp. 727–68, including data of Brinton, 1884, and Calderón, 1908.

Oluta, Sayula, and Texistepec, pp. 769–79, from Calderón, 1908.

Tapachultec II, pp. 780–81, from Sapper, 1912.

Mangue, pp. 842–64, including data of Squier, 1852, and Brinton, 1886.

Chiapanec, pp. 881–900, including data of Pinart, 1875, Charencey, 1876; and L. Fernández, 1892.

Mazatec, pp. 903–10, including data of Brinton, 1892, and Belmar, 1892.

Subtiaba, pp. 919–69, including data of Squier, 1853.

Tlapanec, pp. 969–78, including data of León, 1912.

Aztec, pp. 1027–83, including data of Scherzer, 1885; Stoll, 1884; Brinton, 1887; Boas, 1912; and Starr, 1902.

See also Kutscher, 1958.

LEON, FRANCES

284a 1962 Revisión de la fonología del Otomí. *Anales del Instituto Nacional de Antropología e Historia*, 15: 315–30 (published 1963). México.

LEON, FRANCES, AND MORRIS SWADESH

285 1949 Two views of Otomi prosody. *IJAL*, 15: 100–05.

Takes issue with the analysis of Sinclair and Pike, 1948.

LÉON, JUAN DE

286 1955 Diccionario Quiché-Español. Guatemala.

LÉON, NICOLÁS

286a 1886 Silabario del idioma Tarasco o de Michoacán. Morelia.

Word lists for pronunciation practice, with Spanish glosses. A revised version appeared in *Anales del Museo Michoacano*, 2: 139–54 (Morelia, 1889).

287 1903a Los Comanches y el dialecto Cahuillo de la Baja California. *An. Mus. Nac.*, 1a época, 7: 263–78.

Contains Spanish-"Cahuillo" vocabulary from Ensenada, Baja California; León mistakenly identifies it with Uto-Aztecan Cahuilla of Southern California. It appears, however, to be a Yuman dialect; see A. L. Kroeber, Supposed Shoshoneans in Lower California, *AA*, n.s., 7: 570–72 (1905).

288 1903b Vocabulario en lengua Tepehua que se habla en el Estado de Hidalgo. . . . *An. Mus. Nac.*, 1a época, 7: 298–301.

Spanish-Tepehua word list.

289 1903c Vocabulario del dialecto llamado Tepehua que se habla en Huayacocotla, . . . Estado de Veracruz. *An. Mus. Nac.*, 1a época, 7: 301–04.

Word list of what is evidently a dialect not of Tepehua but of Otomí.

290 1903d Vocabulario en lengua Cuitlateca de Totolapam, Estado de Guerrero. *An. Mus. Nac.*, 1a época, 7: 304–07.

Spanish-Cuitlatec word list.

291 1903e Vocabulario del dialecto Tepecano del Pueblo de Azquetlan, Estado de Jalisco. *An. Mus. Nac.*, 1a época, 7: 307–09.

Spanish-Tepecano word list.

292 1904a Noticia de un dialecto nuevo del Matlaltzinca. *Boletín del Museo Nacional*, 2a época, 1: 201–04. México.

Word list collected by F. Plancarte.

293 1904b Catálogo de la colección de antigüedades Huavis del Estado de Oaxaca existentes en el Museo Nacional de México. México.

Includes Huave-Spanish word lists copied from Brasseur, 1861, and Starr, 1900, and the longer vocabulary from Belmar, 1901b.

294 1912 Vocabulario de la lengua Popoloca, Chocha o Chuchona, con sus equivalentes en Castellano, colectado y arreglado bajo un solo alfabeto. *An. Mus. Nac.*, 3a época, 3: 1–58.

Combined Chocho-Spanish and Spanish-Chocho vocabulary; Chocho phrase list; miscellaneous word lists of Popoloca, Mixe and Tlapanec. The last-named is reprinted by Lehmann, 1920, pp. 971–72.

See also Cárceres, 1907; Córdova, 1578a; Gilberti, 1558; Grasserie and León, 1896; and Lagunas, 1574.

LÉTHROP, MÁXIMO

See Lathrop, Maxwell D., Jr.

LEVANTO, LEONARDO
See Peñafiel, 1887.

LEWY, ERNST

295   1937   Die Sprache der Quiché (Kiče) von Guatemala. *Anthropos*, 32: 929–58. St. Gabriel-Mödling.

Grammatical sketch based on Schultze-Jena, 1933.

LIND, JOHN O.

295a   1964   Clause and sentence level syntagmemes in Sierra Popoluca. *IJAL*, 30: 341–54.

LOMBARDO, NATAL

296   1702   Arte de la lengua Teguima vulgarmente llamada Ópata. México.

See also Pimentel, 1863.

LONGACRE, ROBERT E.

297   1952   Five phonemic pitch levels in Trique. *Acta Linguistica*, 7: 62–82. Copenhagen.

298   1955   Rejoinder to Hamp's "Componential restatement of syllable structure in Trique". *IJAL*, 21: 189–94.

See Hamp, 1954.

299   1959   Trique tone morphemics. *Anthro. Ling.*, 1.4: 5–42.

299a   1965   Transformational parameters in tagmemic field structures. *Georgetown Monograph Series on Languages and Linguistics*, 18: 43–58. Washington.

Contrasting grammatical structures of Zoque, Sierra Popoluca, and Mixe.

299b   1966   Trique clause and sentence: a study in contrast, variation, and distribution. *IJAL*, 32: 242–52.

See also Engel and Longacre, 1963.

LÓPEZ OTERO, DANIEL

300   1914   Gramática Maya. Mérida.

Called "a very good grammar" by Tozzer, 1921, p. 167. Includes word lists.

LÓPEZ YEPES, JOAQUÍN

301   1826   Catecismo y declaración de la doctrina cristiana en lengua Otomí, con un vocabulario del mismo idioma. México.

Includes notes on pronunciation and a Spanish-Otomí dictionary.

LORENZANA, SERAPIO D.

302   1896   Un intérprete Huasteco. México.

Spanish-Huastec phrase and word lists.

LOWIE, R. H.
See Gifford and Lowie, 1928.

LUNA CÁRDENAS, JUAN

303   1951   Gramática analítica del idioma Tarasco. México.

Notes on pronunciation and grammar.

LYMAN, LARRY

303a   1964   The verb syntagmemes of Choapan Zapotec. *Linguistics*, no. 7, pp. 16–41. The Hague.

MCARTHUR, HARRY

303b   1966   Xinca. *In* Mayers, 1966, pp. 309–12.

Short word lists collected from the few surviving speakers.

MCARTHUR, HARRY AND LUCILLE

304   1956   Aguacatec (Mayan) phonemes within the stress group. *IJAL*, 22: 72–76.

304a   1966   Aguacatec. *In* Mayers, 1966, pp. 140–65.

Grammatical sketch with sample text.

MCGEE, W. J.
See HERNÁNDEZ, F., 1902.

MCINTOSH, JOHN B.

305   1945   Huichol phonemes. *IJAL*, 11: 31–35.

306   1949a   Cosmogonía Huichol. *Tlalocan*, 3: 14–21. Azcapotzalco.
                 Text with free translation.

307   1949b   Huichol texts and dictionary. *In* Summer Institute of Linguistics, 1949, pp. 1–337.
                 Contains Huichol-Spanish dictionary and Spanish-Huichol verb list.

McINTOSH, JOHN B., AND JOSEPH R. GRIMES

308   1954a   Niuqui 'Íquisicayari. Vixárica niuquiyári, Teivári niuquiyári hepáïsita. Vocabulario Huichol-Castellano, Castellano-Huichol. México.
                 Appendices give notes on pronunciation and grammar.

309   1945b   Huichol: La Piedra Gorda, Nayarit. *In* Key, 1954, pp. 279–91.

McKAUGHAN, HOWARD P.

310   1954   Chatino formulas and phonemes. *IJAL*, 20: 23–27.
                 Formulae for phonemic distribution.

McKAUGHAN, HOWARD P. AND BARBARA

311   1951   Diccionario de la lengua Chatina. México.
                 Spanish-Chatino and Chatino-Spanish; notes on pronunciation; paradigms.

McKINLAY, ARCH

312   1954   Nahuatl of Atliaca, Guerrero. *In* Key, 1954, pp. 23–28.

McKINLAY, ARCH, AND HAROLD AND MARY KEY

313   1949   Puebla Sierra Aztec texts and dictionary. *In* Summer Institute of Linguistics, 1949, pp. 338–555.
                 Contains Spanish-Aztec dictionary.

McMAHON, A.

314   1954   Cora: San Pedro Ixcatán, Nayarit. *In* Key, 1954, pp. 292–99.

McMAHON, A. AND M.

315   1959   Vocabulario Cora y Español. Serie de vocabularios Mariano Silva y Aceves, 2. México.
                 Spanish-Cora and Cora-Spanish, with sections on pronunciation and grammar.

McQUOWN, NORMAN A.

316   1941a   La fonémica de un dialecto Náhuatl de Guerrero. *Méx. Ant.*, 5: 221–32.
                 Contains Nahuatl-Spanish word list.

317   1941b   La fonémica del Cuitlateco. *Méx. Ant.*, 5: 239–54.
                 Contains Cuitlatec-Spanish word list.

318   1942   La fonémica de un dialecto Olmeca-Mexicano de la Sierra Norte de Puebla. *Méx. Ant.*, 4: 61–72.
                 Includes Aztec-Spanish word list and three untranslated texts.

319   1947   La fonémica del Totonaco. *ICA-P*, 27, 1st session, 2: 306–12. México.

MAK, CORNELIA

320   1948   Vocabulario comparativo de cuatro dialectos del idioma Mixteco. México.
                 Not seen.

321   1950   A unique tone perturbation in Mixteco. *IJAL*, 16: 82–86.

322   1953   A comparison of two Mixtec tonemic systems. *IJAL*, 19: 85–100.

323   1958   The tonal system of a third Mixtec dialect. *IJAL*, 24: 61–70.

MALDONADO DE MATOS, MANUEL

324   1918a   Vocabulario de la lengua Szinca. Edición fotostática. Boston.
                 Not seen.

325   1918b   Arte de la lengua Szinca. Edición fotostática. Boston.
                 Not seen.

MALER, TEOBERT

326   1885   Sur quelques langues du Mexique. Lengua de los Totonacos de Xhopala en el Distrito de Papantla. *Actes de la Société Philologique*, 14: 205–08. Paris.
                 Short word lists of Totonac and Zoque.

MARROQUÍN, REMIGIO A.
See Colop D., 1927.

MARTÍNEZ GRACIDA, MANUEL
See Belmar, 1900.

MARTÍNEZ HERNÁNDEZ, JUAN, ED.

327   1969   Diccionario de Motul Maya-Español atribuído a Fray Antonio de Ciudad Real y Arte de lengua Maya por Fray Juan Coronel. Mérida.

Dictionary from MS of the 16th century; grammar from Coronel, 1620.

MARTÍNEZ RÍOS, JORGE

327a   1961   Los estudios lingüísticos en el Estada de Oaxaca, México. *Revista Mexicana de Sociología*, 23: 933–71. México.

Survey with detailed bibliography.

MASIN, INÉS

327b   1926   El Pipil de Izalco. *Rev. Etno.*, 1: 259–64.

List of words and phrases.

MASON, J. ALDEN

328   1917   Tepecano, a Piman language of Western Mexico. *Annals of the New York Academy of Sciences*, 25: 309–416. New York.

Phonology, morphology, and four texts with translation and analysis.

329   1918   Tepecano prayers. *IJAL*, 1: 91–153.

Thirty-seven texts with interlinear and free translations.

330   1923   A preliminary sketch of the Yaqui language. *UCPAAE*, 20: 195–212.

Notes on phonetics and grammar, based on Velasco, 1737; two short texts with analysis.

331   1950   The language of the Papago of Arizona. Philadelphia.

Phonology and grammar.

See also Dolores, 1923.

MAYERS, MARVIN

332   1957   Pocomchi verb structure. *IJAL*, 23: 165–70.

333   1958   Pocomchi texts with grammatical notes. Summer Institute of Linguistics, University of Oklahoma, Linguistic series, 2. Norman, Okla.

Includes Pocomchi-English lexicon.

333a   1960   The phonemes of Pocomchí. *Anth. Ling.*, 2.9: 1–39.

333b   1966   Languages of Guatemala. Janua linguarum, series practica, 23. The Hague.

Sketches of the Mayan languages of Guatemala: Achí, by M. Shaw and H. Neuenswander, pp. 27–48; Quiché, by D. Fox, pp. 60–86; Pocomchí, by M. and M. Mayers, pp. 102–09; Kekchí, by F. Eachus and R. Carlson, pp. 114–24; Ixil, by R. and H. Elliott, pp. 132–39; Aguacatec, by H. and L. McArthur, pp. 154–65; Mam, by E. Sywulka, pp. 178–95; Jacaltec, by C. and K. Church, pp. 206–18; Chuj, by K. and B. Williams, pp. 225–34; Chortí, by H. Oakley, pp. 243–50; Mopan Maya, by M. and R. Ulrich, pp. 261–71; plus a Xinca word list, by H. McArthur, pp. 309–12.

MAYERS, MARVIN AND MARILYN

334   1956   Vocabulario Pocomchí. México.

Not seen.

334a   1966   Pocomchi. *In* Mayers, 1966, pp. 87–109.

Grammatical sketch with sample text.

MAYNARD, GAIL
See Xec and Maynard, 1954.

MAZA, ANTONIO DE LA

335   1947   La nación Pame. *Bol. Soc. Mex. Geog. Estad.*, 63: 493–575.

Includes verb paradigms and Pame-Spanish vocabulary.

MEANS, PHILIP AINSWORTH

336   1917   History of the Spanish conquest of Yucatan and of the Itzas. Papers of the Peabody Museum, Harvard University, vol. 7. Cambridge, Mass.

        Appendix contains word list from the Itzá dialect of Maya, collected by C. H. Berendt in 1866–67.

MECHLING, WILLIAM H.

337   1912   The Indian linguistic stocks of Oaxaca, Mexico. *AA*, n.s., 14: 643–82.

        Includes Amuzgo word list, as well as shorter comparative lists from other languages.

MEDINA, A.

    See Zavala and Medina, 1898.

MEMBREÑO, ALBERTO

338   1897   Hondureñismos: Vocabulario de los provincialismos de Honduras. Segunda edición. Tegucigalpa.

        An appendix contains vocabularies of several Central American languages, including Lenca; this is reprinted in Lehmann, 1920, pp. 671–92. The first and third edition of Membreño do not contain these vocabularies.

MENDENHALL, CELIA DOUGLASS, AND JULIA SUPPLE

339   1948   Tojolabal texts and dictionary. *In* Summer Institute of Linguistics, 1948, texts pp. 60–156, dictionary unpaged.

        Contains Tojolabal-English dictionary.

    See also Douglass, Celia M.

MENDOZA, EUFEMIO

    See Nájera, 1870.

MENDOZA, JEREMÍAS

340   1895   El pueblo de Cacaopera. *La Universidad*, 5: 436–43. San Salvador.

        Not seen. Contains linguistic data on a dialect of Matagalpan; republished by Lehmann, 1920, pp. 604–23. See also Brinton, 1895.

MERRIFIELD, WILLIAM R.

340a   1963   Palantla Chinantec syllable types. *Anth. Ling.*, 5.5: 1–16.

340b   1965   Palantla Chinantec grammar. Cornell University dissertation. Ann Arbor, University Microfilms.

        Summary in *Diss. Abs.*, 26: 5426, 1966.

MICHELSON, TRUMAN

    See Jones, 1915.

MILLER, W. S.

341   1937   La lengua Mixe o Ayuc. *Inv. Ling.*, 4: 130–33.

        Description of phonetic system.

MOLINA, ALONSO DE

342   1555   Aqui comiença un vocabulario en la lengua Castellana y Mexicana. México.

        Not seen.

343   1571a   Vocabulario en lengua Castellana y Mexicana. México.

        Reprinted, Leipzig, 1880, and Puebla, 1910; facsimile edition, Madrid, 1944. Spanish-Aztec and Aztec-Spanish.

344   1571b   Arte de la lengua Mexicana y Castellana. México.

        Reprinted in Colección de gramáticas de la lengua Mexicana 1: 127–224, supplement to *An. Mus. Nac.*, 1a época, tomo 4 (México, 1886). Facsimile edition, Madrid, 1945.

345   1937   Molina redivivo o nuevo diccionario Náhuatl-Español y Español-Náhuatl. *Inv. Ling.*, 3: 357–403, 4: 175–82.

        Molina, 1571a, as revised and enlarged, principally by Miguel Trinidad Palma. Publication proceeded as far as the word *campaxoa* in the Nahuatl-Spanish section, and was then discontinued.

MOLINA, ARCADIO G.

346   1889   El jazmín del Istmo. Principios generales para aprender a leer, escribir y hablar la

lengua Zapoteca, acompañados de un vocabulario Español-Zapoteco y Zapoteco-Español. Oaxaca.

A later edition, 1892. Neither edition seen.

347   1894   La rosa del amor. Frases en Español y Zapoteco. San Blas, Tehuantepec.

Not seen.

MORÁN, FRANCISCO

348   1935   Arte y diccionario en lengua Choltí. Maya Society, Pub. 9. Baltimore.

Photostat reproduction of a MS condensation of a lost MS work of 1625. Author's name mistakenly given on title page as "Pedro." Contains Spanish-Choltí vocabulary.

MORRISON, MAY

See Waterhouse and Morrison, 1950.

MOSER, EDWARD AND MARY

349   1961   Vocabulario Seri: Seri-Castellano, Castellano-Seri. Serie de vocabularios indígenas Mariano Silva y Aceves, 5. México.

350   1965   Consonant-vowel balance in Seri (Hokan) syllables. *Linguistics*, no. 16, pp. 50–67. The Hague.

NÁGERA Y YANGUAS, DIEGO DE

351   1637   Doctrina y enseñanza de la lengua Mazahua.... México.

What appears to be a republication (but without this title) is in *Actes de la Société Philologique*, 27: 239–94, 28: 169–304 (Paris, 1898–99). There is a facsimile edition, México, 1952. The work contains grammatical notes, word lists, and both devotional and conversational texts with phrase-by-phrase translation.

NÁJERA, MANUEL DE SAN JUAN CRISÓSTOMO

352   1837   De linguâ Othomitorum dissertatio. *Transactions of the American Philosophical Society*, n.s., 5: 249–96. Philadelphia.

Contains lists of verb forms and a short Otomí-Latin vocabulary. Spanish version: Disertación sobre la lengua Otomí (México, 1845).

353   1870   Gramática del Tarasco. Morelia.

Reprinted as: Gramática de la lengua Tarasca..., ed. Eufemio Mendoza, *Bol. Soc. Mex. Geog. Estad.*, 2a época, 4: 664–84 (1872). Reprinted again, México, 1944.

NEBAH, PARISH PRIEST OF

354   1935   Arte y vocabulario de la lengua Ixil con doctrina y confesionario. Maya Society Pub. 14. Baltimore.

Photostat reproduction of MS of 1824, entitled: Doctrina y confesionaria en lengua Ixil precedidos de un corto modo para aprender la lengua y ritual de matrimonio, por cura párroco de Nebah. Contains paradigms and short word list, but no statements of grammar.

NEEDHAM, DORIS, AND MARJORIE DAVIS

355   1946   Cuicateco phonology. *IJAL*, 12:139-46.

Phonemics and morphophonemics.

NEUENSWANDER, HELEN

See Shaw and Neuenswander, 1966.

NEVE Y MOLINA, LUIS DE

356   1767   Reglas de orthographía, diccionario, y arte del idioma Othomí. México.

Reprinted, México, 1863. Includes Spanish-Otomí vocabulary. Italian version: Grammatica della lingua Otomí esposta in Italiano dal conte Enea Silvio Vincenzo Piccolomini (Roma, 1841). This work also served as basis for the work entitled Élements de la grammaire Othomi, *Revue Orientale et Américaine*, 8: 15–49 (Paris, 1862).

NIDA, EUGENE A.

357   1937   The Tarahumara language. *Inv. Ling.*, 4: 140–44.

Notes on phonology and morphology.

NIDA, EUGENE A., AND MOISÉS ROMERO C.

358   1950   The pronominal series in Maya (Yucatec). *IJAL*, 16: 193–97.

NOYES, ERNEST
359 1957 Grammar and lexicon of Black Carib and Lexicon of Cholti and Chorti. *Mic. Coll.*, no. 39. Chicago.

Contains Choltí-Spanish lexicon, based on Morán, 1935; and Chortí-English lexicon, based on Wisdom, 1950.

NÚÑEZ, JOAN
See Adam, 1887.

NYMAN, W., JR.
See Grimes and Nyman, 1954.

OAKLEY, HELEN
359a 1966 Chorti. *In* Mayers, 1966, pp. 235–50.

Grammatical sketch with sample text.

OLIVARES, JUAN
See Warkentin and Olivares, 1947.

OLMOS, ANDRÉS DE
360 1875 Grammaire de la langue Nahuatl ou Mexicaine. Composée en 1547, et publiée avec notes, éclaircissements, etc., par Rémi Siméon. Paris.

Also published as: Arte para aprender la lengua Mexicana, Colección de gramáticas de la lengua Mexicana, 1: 1–126, supplement to *An. Mus. Nac.*, 1a época, tomo 3 (México, 1885–86).

OLSON, DONALD AND ANNE
361 1956 Trescientos palabras en tres idiomas. México.

Contains vocabulary of Ocotlán Zapotec. Not seen.

ONORIO, JUAN MANUEL
362 1924 El dialecto Mexicano de Cantón de los Tuxtlas (Veracruz). *Méx. Ant.*, 2: 159–91.

Aztec-Spanish vocabulary; miscellaneous lists of words, phrases, and sentences; texts with free translation.

OROZCO, GILBERTO
363 1946 Tradiciones y leyendas del Istmo de Tehuantepec. México.

Zapotec-Spanish word lists, pp. 196–212.

ORTEGA, JOSÉ DE
364 1732 Vocabulario en lengua Castellana y Cora. México.

Reprinted in *Bol. Soc. Mex. Geog. Estad.*, 1a época, 8: 561–605 (1860). Also reprinted, Tepic, 1888.

OVERHOLT, EDWARD
364a 1961 The tonemic system of Guerrero Mixteco. *In* A William Cameron Townsend en el vigésimoquinto aniversario del Instituto Lingüístico de Verano, pp. 597–626. México.

PACHECO CRUZ, SANTIAGO
365 1912 Compendio del idioma Yucateco . . . . Mérida.

Later editions have title: Compendio del idioma Maya; most recent seen is the fifth (Mérida, 1955). A pedagogical textbook; includes conversation and Maya-Spanish vocabulary.

PALMA, MIGUEL TRINIDAD
See Molina, Alonso, 1937.

PAREDES, IGNACIO DE
See Carochi, 1759.

PARRY, C. C.
366 1853 Vocabulary of the language of the Pimo Indians. *In* vol. 3, pp. 460–62, of Henry Rowe Schoolcraft, Information respecting the history, condition and prospects of the Indian tribes of the United States. Philadelphia.

PATIÑO, CELESTINO
367 1907 Vocabulario Totonaco. Xalapa-Enríquez, Mexico.

Spanish-Totonac and Totonac-Spanish vocabularies for each of the parts of speech: paradigms; conversations.

PECCORINI, ATTILIO

368   1909   Ligeros apuntes sobre el dialecto Camotán. *Centro América Intelectual*, 2a época, nos. 7–9. San Salvador.

    Not seen. Deals with Chortí; data republished in Becerra, 1910.

369   1910   Dialecte Chilanga. *JSAP*, n.s., 7: 163–30.

    Lenca word lists and paradigms. Republished by Lehmann, 1920, pp. 693–99; and by Schuller, 1925b.

370   [*nil*]

PECK, H. D.

    See Andrade, 1946b.

PEÑAFIEL, ANTONIO, ED.

371   1887   Gramática de la lengua Zapoteca por un autor anónimo que agregó a su obra otro "Arte," por el P. Fray Andrés Valdespino, las reglas de las partículas por Fray Juan de Córdova, el confesionario en Zapoteco del Valle por el R.P.P. Gral. Fray Antonio Vellón...; la administración de los sacramentos en idioma Zapoteco, y otro confesionario en lengua Zapoteca de Tierra Caliente, o de Tehuantepec. Obra copiada o escrita en Oaxaca por el año de 1823. México.

    Also includes Spanish-Zapotec word list from San Bernardo Miztepeque, collected in 1856 by Leonardo Levanto.

372   ca. 1895   Lenguas mexicanas. [México?]

    This book, unbound and without title page, was bought in Mexico City in 1959. It bore the penciled notation, "Peñafiel, Lenguas Indígenas"; the title indicated in the printer's signatures, however, is "Leng. Mex." It contains word lists of about 200 items each for the dialects of some hundred localities in the states of Tlaxcala, Puebla, Morelos, and Hidalgo; the lists are signed by the local residents who prepared them, and are dated between 1880 and 1894. Two vocabularies (pp. 188–96) are of Otomí, one (pp. 316–20) is of Totonac, and two (pp. 320–29) are of Popoloca; all the rest are of Aztec dialects.

    I cannot find this book in any published bibliography or catalog. Its existence, however, and the authorship of Peñafiel are confirmed by three references.

    First is the work by Robelo, 1889, with title: Vocabulario comparativo Castellano y Nahuatl ... para contestar el cuestionario filológico formulado por la Dirección General de Estadística de la República Mexicana. The word list of Robelo is identical with that of the work under discussion, and Peñafiel was in charge of the Dirección General de Estadística at this period.

    Second is the statement of Mechling, 1912, p. 643: "In the year 1886 Dr. Antonio Peñafiel collected vocabularies of native languages from all parts of Mexico.... The volume of these vocabularies that has been printed deals entirely with the well-known Mexican of the Central Plateau region.... With the other four volumes into which Peñafiel divides his manuscripts nothing has been done, although it is hoped that they will soon be published by the Mexican Government."

    Third, excerpts from the Distrito Federal vocabularies were published by Urbano Lavín in 1922, who states (*An. Mus. Nac.*, 4a época, 1: 82) that his list was "formado por el Sr. Peñafiel."

    The material contained in this book should be especially valuable for the study of Aztec dialectology. For further information, see now Juan A. Hasler, Tetradialectología Nahua, *in* A William Cameron Townsend en el vigésimoquinto aniversario del I.L.V. (México, 1961), esp. p. 455, fn. 2.

    See also Basalenque, 1714, and Gilberti, 1559.

PÉREZ, JUAN PÍO

373   1866–77   Diccionario de la lengua Maya. Mérida.

    Maya-Spanish.

374   1898   Coordinación alfabética de las voces del idioma Maya que se hallan en el Arte y obras del Padre Fr. Pedro Beltrán de Santa Rosa con las equivalencias Castellanas que en las mismas se hallan. Mérida.

    Maya-Spanish and Spanish-Maya dictionary, the latter based on the MS Ticul Dictionary of 1690.

PÉREZ, MANUEL

375   1713   Arte de el idioma Mexicano. México.

PFEFFERKORN, IGNAZ

376   1794–95   Beschreibung der Landschaft Sonora.... 2 vols. Köln.

Vol. 2, chap. 11, contains notes on the Pima language. English version: Sonora, a description of the province, translated and annotated by Theodore E. Treutlein (Albuquerque, 1949).

PICCOLOMINI, ENEA SILVIO VINCENZO
See Neve y Molina, 1767.

PICKETT, VELMA B.

377   1951   Nonphonemic stress: a problem of stress placement in Isthmus Zapotec. *Word,* 7: 60–65.

378   1953   Las construcciones de los verbos del Zapoteco del Istmo, de Juchitán, Oaxaca. *Memoria del Congreso Cienfitico Mexicano*, 12: 191–98. México.

379   1953–55   Isthmus Zapotec verb analysis. *IJAL*, 19: 292–96, 21: 217–32.

380   1959   Vocabulario Zapoteco del Istmo. Serie de Vocabularios Indígenas Mariano Silva y Aceves, 3. México.

Spanish-Zapotec and Zapotec-Spanish dictionary, with appendices on pronunciation, dialect variation, and grammar.

381   1960   The grammatical hierarchy of Isthmus Zapotec. Language Dissertation no. 56. Baltimore.

"Analysis and description of the syntactic structure..., [using] a modification of the tagmemic model of Kenneth L. Pike."

PIERSON, ESTHER

382   1953   Phonemic statement of Popoloca. *Lingua*, 3: 426–29. Haarlem.

See also Williams and Pierson, 1950.

PIÉRZON, G. DE

383   1951   Palabras o frases del Nahuat o Pipil como se habla en Izalco. *Anales del Museo Nacional "David J. Guzmán"*, 2.5: 85. San Salvador.

PIKE, EUNICE VICTORIA

384   1937   Mazateco fonetics. *Inv. Ling.*, 4: 148–50.

385   1948   Problems in Zapotec tone analysis. *IJAL*, 14: 161–70.

Variations of tone in Zapotec of Villa Alta.

386   1949   Texts on Mazatec food witchcraft. *Méx. Ant.*, 7: 287–94.

With literal and free translations.

387   1951   Tonemic-intonemic correlation in Mazahua (Otomi). *IJAL*, 17: 37–71.

388   1954   Phonetic rank and subordination in consonant patterning and historical changes. Miscellanea Phonetica, 2: 25–41, supplement to *Le Maître Phonétique*. Hertford.

Includes description of Mazatec phonemes.

389   1956   Tonally differentiated allomorphs in Soyaltepec Mazatec. *IJAL*, 22: 57–71.

PIKE, EUNICE VICTORIA, AND SARAH C. GUDSCHINSKY

390   1952   Vocabulario Mazateco. México.

Mazatec-Spanish only. Revised and amplified edition, 1957.

See also Pike, K. L., and E. V. Pike, 1947; Larsen and E. V. Pike, 1949.

PIKE, KENNETH L.

391   1937   Una leyenda Mixteca. *Inv. Ling.*, 4:262–70.

Text with free translation, plus a description of Mixtec phonetics.

392   1944   Analysis of a Mixteco text. *IJAL*, 10: 113–38.

Includes interlinear and free translations, with a detailed analysis.

393   1945a   Tone puns in Mixteco. *IJAL*, 11: 129–39.

Text containing eight puns, with explanation.

394   1945b   Mock Spanish of a Mixteco Indian. *IJAL*, 11: 219–24.

Includes text with literal translation.

395   1946a   Another Mixteco tone pun. *IJAL*, 12: 22–24.
Includes text with literal and free translations.

396   1946b   Phonemic pitch in Maya. *IJAL*, 12: 82–88.

397   1947a   Grammatical prerequisites to phonemic analysis. *Word*, 3: 155–72. Baltimore.
Includes section on "Phonological characteristics of Mixteco morphemes".

398   1947b   A text involving inadequate Spanish of Mixteco Indians. *IJAL*, 13: 251–57.
Text with free translation and commentary.

399   1948   Tone languages, a technique for determining the number and type of pitch contrasts in a language, with studies in tonemic substitution and fusion. University of Michigan Publications, Linguistics, vol. 4. Ann Arbor.
Chap. 7, "Tonemic perturbations in Mixteco, with special emphasis on tonomechanical subclasses." Chap. 8, "Tonemic perturbations in Mazateco, with special emphasis on tonemic fusion."

400   1949   A problem in morphology-syntax division. *Acta Linguistica*, 5: 125–38. Copenhagen·
Discussion based mainly on Mixtec data.

401   1953   A note on allomorph classes and tonal technique. *IJAL*, 19: 101–05.
Discussion based on tonal system of Mixtec.

PIKE, KENNETH L., AND BURT BASCOM
402   1959   Instrumental collaboration on a Tepehuan (Uto-Aztecan) pitch problem (with Ralph P. Barrett.) *Phonetica*, 3: 1–22. Basel.

PIKE, KENNETH L., AND EUNICE VICTORIA PIKE
403   1947   Immediate constituents of Mazateco syllables. *IJAL*, 13: 78–91.
IC analysis on phonological level.

PIKE, KENNETH L., AND MILTON WARKENTIN
403a   1961   Huave: A study in syntactic tone with low lexical functional load. *In* A William Cameron Townsend en el vigésimoquinto aniversario del Instituto Lingüístico de Verano, pp. 627–42. México.

See also Sinclair and Pike, 1948.

PIMENTEL, FRANCISCO
404   1863   Vocabulario manual de la lengua Ópata. *Bol. Soc. Mex. Geog. Estad.*, 1a época, 10: 287–313.
Ópata-Spanish vocabulary extracted from works of Natal Lombardo.

405   1874   Cuadro descriptivo y comparativo de las lenguas indígenas de México. Segunda edición única completa. 3 vols. México.
Contains sketches and vocabularies derived from earlier publications, including Nahuatl of Jalisco (Guerra, 1692), Ópata (Lombardo, 1702), "Heve" (Ópata) (Smith, 1861d), Cáhita (Velasco, 1737), Pima (Smith, 1862b), Tepehuan (Rinaldini, 1743), Tarahumara (Tellechea, 1826), Cora (Ortega, 1732), Tarascan (Lagunas 1574, Gilberti 1559, Basalenque 1714), Mixtec (Reyes 1593, Alvarado 1593), Zapotec (Córdova, 1578), Maya (San Buenaventura, 1684), Quiché (Brasseur, 1862), Mam (Reynoso, 1644), Huastec (Tapia Zenteno, 1761), Totonac (Zambrano Bonilla, 1752), Otomí (Neve y Molina, 1767), and Mazahua (Nájera y Yanguas, 1637). Also contains material not previously published for Huichol, Seri, Matlaltzinca, and Pame.

See also Basalenque, 1714.

PINART, ALPHONSE L., ED.
406   1875   Arte de la lengua Chiapaneca compuesto por el M. R. Padre Fray Juan de Albornoz y Doctrina cristiana en la misma lengua escrita por el Padre Mtro. Fray Luis Barrientos. Bibliothèque de Linguistique et d'Ethnographie Américaines, vol. 1. Paris and San Francisco.
Grammar from MS of 1691, catechism from MS of 1690.

407   1897   Vocabulario castellano-k'ak'chi. Paris.
Not seen.

See also Gatschet, 1886; Hernández, E., and Pinart, 1897; Hernández, F., 1902.

PINEDA, VICENTE
408   1887   Gramática de la lengua Tzel-Tal . . . . Chiapas.

Republished, 1888, in: Historia de las sublevaciones indígenas habidas en el Estado de Chiapas; Gramática de la lengua Tzel-tal ... y diccionario de la misma (Chiapas.) Contains Tzeltal-Spanish dictionary.

PITTMAN, RICHARD S.

409 1945 La historia de Pedro Sa-kinemilea. *Tlalocan*, 2: 10–17. México.
      Aztec texts in dialect of Tetelcingo, Morelos.

410 1948 Nahuatl honorifics. *IJAL*, 14: 236–39.
      "Reverential" forms in the morphology of the Tetelcingo dialect.

411 1949 Tetelcingo Aztec texts and dictionary. *In* Summer Institute of Linguistics, 1949, pp. 708–824.
      Contains Spanish-Aztec and Aztec-Spanish dictionary.

412 1954 A grammar of Tetelcingo (Morelos) Nahuatl. Language Dissertation no. 50. Baltimore.
      Includes texts with literal and free translation and short Aztec-English verb list.

412a 1961 The phonemes of Tetelcingo (Morelos) Nahuatl. *In* A William Cameron Townsend en el vigésimoquinto aniversario del Instituto Lingüístico de Verano, pp. 643–51. México.

PITTMAN, RICHARD S., AND F. BREWER

413 1954 Nahuatl of Tetelcingo, Morelos. *In* Key, 1954, pp. 1–9.

PLANCARTE, F.
   See León, 1904a.

PREUSS, KONRAD THEODOR

414 1912 Die Nayarit-Expedition: Text-Aufnahmen und Beobachtungen unter Mexikanischen Indianern. Erster Band, Die Religion des Cora-Indianer in Texten nebst Wörterbuch. Leipzig.
      Extensive Cora texts with interlinear and free translations and grammatical notes; Cora-German dictionary.

415 1932 Grammatik der Cora-Sprache. *IJAL*, 7: 1–84.

416 1934 Wörterbuch Deutsch-Cora. *IJAL*, 8: 81–102.

PRIDE, KITTY

416a 1961 Numerals in Chatino. *Anth. Ling.*, 3.2: 1–10.

416b 1965 Chatino syntax. Summer Institute of Linguistics of the University of Oklahoma, Publications in linguistics, 12. Norman, Okla.
      Includes analyzed text.

QUINTANA, AGUSTÍN DE

417 1729 Arte de la lengua Mixe. Puebla.
      Republished by Francisco Belmar, Oaxaca, 1891. Not seen.

418 1733 Confessionario en lengua Mixe, con ... un compendio de voces Mixes, para enseñarse a prononciar la dicha lengua. Puebla.
      Republished by H. de Charencey, *Actes de la Société Philologique*, 18: 185–335 (Paris, 1890); also issued separately, Alençon, 1890. Contains word lists for pronunciation practice, numerical terms, and list of body parts.

RADIN, PAUL

419 1925 The distribution and phonetics of the Zapotec dialects: a preliminary sketch. *JSAP*, 17: 27–76.
      Contains comparative word list of Zapotec dialects. "Unfortunately full of typographical errors," according to Radin, 1946, p. 153.

420 1929 Huave texts. *IJAL*, 5: 1–56.
      Some with literal and free translations, some with free translation only.

421 1930 A preliminary sketch of the Zapotec language. *Lg.*, 6: 64–85.
      Partly corrected in Radin, 1943–44.

422 1933a Notes on the Tlappanecan language of Guerrero. *IJAL*, 8: 45–72.
      Notes on grammar; English-Tlapanec vocabulary.

423   1933b   Mixe texts. *JSAP*, 25: 41–64.

With interlinear and free translations.

424   1935   An historical legend of the Zapotecs. Ibero-Americana, no. 9. Berkeley.

Zapotec text with English translation.

425   1943–44   Cuentos y leyendas de los Zapotecos. *Tlalocan*, 1: 3–30, 134–54, 194–226. Sacramento, Calif.

Also issued separately as: Cuentos de Mitla (Sacramento, 1945). Consists of texts, preceded by a general discussion of the Zapotec language.

426   1946   Zapotec texts: dialect of Juchitan-Tehuano. *IJAL*, 12: 152–72.

Ten texts with free translations.

REBER, LULU
See Keller and Reber, 1958.

REKO, V. A.
See Reyes, Gaspar, 1931.

RENSCH, CALVIN R.
426a   1963   Some aspects of Chinantec grammar: A tagmemic view. *Georgetown Monograph Series on Languages and Linguistics*, 16: 81–88. Washington.

REYES, ANTONIO DE LOS
427   1593   Arte en lengua Mixteca. México.

Reprinted, Puebla, 1750. Republished by H. de Charencey, Alençon, 1889; also in *Actes de la Société Philologique* 18: 1–96 (Paris, 1890). Contains word lists: reverential vocabulary, body parts, kinship terms, and place names. Data from this source appear in Arana and Swadesh, 1965.

REYES, GASPAR DE LOS
428   1891   Gramática de las lenguas Zapoteca-Serrana y Zapoteca del Valle. Oaxaca.

Published by Francisco Belmar, from MS of 1700.

429   1931   Quellenschriften zur mexikanischen Linguistik. Das verschollene Manuskript des Gaspar de los Reyes: Gramática Zapoteca del Valle (1700). Nach der Handschrift kopiert von V. A. Reko in Oaxaca, Mexiko. Herausgegen von Ferd. Hestermann. *Mitteilungen der Anthropologischen Gesellschaft in Wien*, 61: 331–50. Wien.

REYNOSO, DIEGO DE
430   1644   Arte, y vocabulario en lengua Mame . . . . México.

Republished by H. de Charencey, Paris, n.d.; the "Vocabulario" also in *Actes de la Société Philologique*, 25: 267–351 (Paris, 1897). The "Vocabulario" was again republished by Alberto María Carreño, with grammatical notes, as: Vocabulario de la lengua Mame (México, 1916).

RINALDINI, BENITO
431   1743   Arte de la lengua Tepeguana, con vocabulario, confesionario, y catecismo . . . México.

Grammar, conversational text with free translation, and Spanish-Tepehuan vocabulary.

RINCÓN, ANTONIO DEL
432   1595   Arte Mexicana. México.

Reprinted in Colección de gramáticas de la lengua Mexicana, 1: 225–80, supplement to *An. Mus. Nac.*, 1a época, tomo 4 (1888–89). Contains short Aztec-Spanish vocabulary.

ROBBINS, FRANK E.
432a   1961a   Palabras nasales sin vocales fonéticas en el Chinanteco de Quiotepec. *In* A William Cameron Townsend en el vigésimoquinto aniversario del Instituto Lingüístico de Verano, pp. 653–56. México.

432b   1961b   Quiotepec Chinantec syllable patterning. *IJAL*, 27: 237–50.

432c   1965   Quiotepec Chinantec grammar. Cornell University dissertation. Ann Arbor, University Microfilms.

Summary in *Diss. Abs.*, 26: 3320, 1965.

ROBELO, CECILIO

433 1889 Vocabulario comparativo Castellano y Nahuatl ... para contestar el cuestionario filológico formulado por la Dirección General de Estadística de la República Mexicana. Segunda edición. Cuernavaca.

Spanish-Aztec word list with morphological analyses of terms. Cf. Peñafiel, 1895.

See also Siméon, 1902.

ROBLES URIBE, CARLOS

433a 1962 Manual del Tzeltal: ensayo de gramática del Tzeltal de Bachajón. Universidad Iberoamericana, Publicaciones de antropología, Lingüística, 1. México.

Phonology, morphology, and syntax, with index of words cited.

433b 1964 Investigación lingüística sobre los grupos indígenas del Estado de Baja California. *Anales del Instituto Nacional de Antropología e Historia*, 17: 275–301 (published 1965). México.

Vocabularies from Yuman dialects, identified as Paipai, Ku'ahl, Cochimí, Cocopa, and Kiliwa. The term "Cochimí" here seems to be inappropriately applied to a Diegueno dialect.

ROCHAC, ALFONSO

434 1951 Vocabulario Náhuat o Pipil de Izalco. *Anales del Museo Nacional "David J. Guzmán"*, 2.7: 46–48. San Salvador.

Spanish-Pipil vocabulary.

RODAZ, JUAN DE

See Charencey, 1876.

ROMERO CASTILLO, MOISÉS

434a 1958 Los fonemas del Chichimeco-Jonaz. *Anales del Instituto Nacional de Antropología e Historia*, 11: 289–99 (published 1960). México.

434b 1961a Morfemas clasificadores del Maya-Yucateco. *In* A William Cameron Townsend en el vigésimoquinto aniversario del Instituto Lingüístico de Verano, pp. 657–62. México.

434c 1961b Formas pronominales del Maya-Yucateco. *Anales del Instituto Nacional de Antropología e Historia*, 14: 345–48 (published 1962). México.

434d 1963 Los fonemas del Maya-Yucateco. *Anales del Instituto Nacional de Antropología e Historia*, 16: 179–92 (published 1964). México.

Includes sample text and lexicon of examples.

See also Nida and Romero, 1950.

ROMNEY, A. KIMBALL

See Berlin and Romney, 1964.

ROSALES, CARLOS J. (supposed author)

435 1919 Gramática del idioma Cachiquel escrita en 1748 .... Publícala por vez primera ... Daniel Sánchez García. Guatemala.

Contains short vocabulary, Kiché-Spanish-Cakchiquel-Tzutuhil.

RUEGSEGGER, MANIS AND JANE

436 1955 Vocabulario Zapoteco. México.

Dialect of Miahuatlan. Not seen.

RUSSELL, FRANK

437 1908 The Pima Indians. *Annual Report of the Bureau of American Ethnology*, 26: 3–389. Washington.

Contains extensive texts of songs and speeches, with interlinear and free translations.

RUVALCABA, J. MELQUIADES

438 1935 Vocabulario Mexicano de Tuxpan, Jalisco. *Inv. Ling.*, 3: 208–14.

Comments and corrections to Arreola, 1934.

S. D. O.

439 1923 Breve vocabulario del dialecto Kekchí con un apéndice de 25 conversaciones del uso más vulgar entre la clase indígena. Guatemala.

Kekchi-Spanish vocabulary and conversations.

SÁENZ DE SANTA MARÍA, CARMELO

439a 1940 Diccionario Cakchiquel-Español. Guatemala.

Based on MS of Francisco de Varea, Calepino en lengua Cakchiquel, plus published materials. Preceded by notes on grammar.

SAHAGÚN, BERNARDINO DE (supposed author)

439b 1947 Aztec manuscript dictionary (1590). *Mic. Coll.*, no. 37. Chicago.

Aztec-Spanish-Latin dictionary.

See also Biondelli, 1858; Schultze-Jena, 1950, 1952.

SAN BUENAVENTURA, FRANCISCO GABRIEL DE

439c 1684 Arte de la lengua Maya. México.

Reprinted, México, 1888, by Joaquín García Icazbalceta.

SÁNCHEZ, JOSÉ MARÍA

439d 1877 Gramática de la lengua Zoque. México.

Reprinted, Cuadernos de Chiapas no. 13 (Tuxtla Gutiérrez, 1948). Presents Zoque grammar in catechism form; morphology taught mainly through paradigms.

439e 1895 La lengua Tzotzil en Chiapas, explicaciones grammaticales, dogmáticas e instructivas. . . . San Cristóbal las Casas.

Grammar and Spanish-Tzotzil vocabulary from anonymous MS of 1804.

SÁNCHEZ GARCÍA, DANIEL

See Rosales, 1919.

SANTOSCOY, ALBERTO, ED.

439f 1889 Nayarit, colección de documentos inéditos. . . . . Guadalajara.

Contains Cora-Spanish word list, pp. 64–68.

See also Guerra, 1692.

SAPORTA, SOL

See Keller and Saporta, 1957.

SAPPER, KARL THEODOR

439g 1895 Die Gebräuche und religiösen Anschauungen der Kekchí-Indianer. *Archives Internationales d'Ethnographie*, 8: 195–215. Leyden.

Contains Kekchi prayer texts with free translations.

439h 1897 Das nördliche Mittel-Amerika nebst einem Ausflug nach dem Hochland von Anahuac. Braunschweig.

Contains vocabulary of about 200 words in Huastec, Chicomuceltec, Yucatec, Peten, Mopan, Chol, Chortí, Chontal, Tzeltal, Tzotzil, Tojolabal, Chuj, Motocintlec, Mam, Jacaltec, Ixil, Aguacatec, Quiché, Cakchiquel, Tzutuhil, Uspantec, Kekchi, Poconchi, and Pocomam. Taken in part from Stoll, 1884.

440 1907 Choles und Chorties. *ICA-P*, 15.2: 423–65. Québec.

Chortí, Chol, and Pocomam word lists; Chortí and Pocomam paradigms and sentences.

441 1912 Ueber einige Sprachen von Südchiapas. *ICA-P*, 17, 2d session, pp. 295–320. México.

Contains word list of Tapachultec II; vocabularies of Huastec, Chicomuceltec Motocintlec, Jacaltec, and Mam; and sentences in Motocintlec and Chicomuceltec. The Tapachultec II is reproduced in Lehmann, 1920, pp. 780–81.

442 1927 La lengua Tapachulteca. *Méx. Ant.*, 2: 259–68.

Contains word list, Spanish-Tapachultec I.

SARAVIA, RAMÓN G.

443 1895 Vocabulario gramatical del Español y Quechí. Coban, Guatemala.

Not seen.

SAXTON, DEAN

444 1954 Papago: dialect of Sells, Arizona. *In* Key, 1954, pp. 429–41.

444a 1963 Papago phonemes. *IJAL*, 29: 29–35.

SCHERZER, KARL

445 1855 Sprachen der Indianer Zentral-Amerika's. *Sitzungsberichte der Kaiserlichen Akademie der Wissenschaften*, Philosophisch-Historische Klasse, 15: 28–37. Wien.

Contains word lists of Tlascaltec (Pipil) of Izalco, Quiché of Ixtlahuacan, Pocomchí of Palin, and "Pupuluca-Katschikel" (i.e. Cakchiquel) of Santa María.

446 1857 Wanderungen durch die mittelamerikanischen Freistaaten Nicaragua, Honduras und San Salvador. Braunschweig.

Contains German-Pipil word list from Izalco.

SCHOEMBS, JAKOB

447 1905 Material zur Sprache von Comalapa in Guatemala. Dortmund.

Cakchiquel word lists, texts, and 3407 sentences (arranged mainly by verb stems), with German and Spanish equivalents.

448 1906 Beiträge zur Kenntnis der Mayasprachen. Dortmund.

Not seen.

449 1949 Aztekische Schriftsprache: Grammatik (mit Lautlehre), Text und Glossar. Heidelberg.

Includes long text passage from Sahagún's Historia general, with Aztec-German glossary.

SCHOENHALS, ALVIN AND LOUISE

449a 1965 Vocabulario Mixe de Totontepec: Mixe-Castellano, Castellano-Mixe. Serie de vocabularios indígenas Mariano Silva y Aceves, 14. México.

Includes appendices on phonology and grammar.

SCHULLER, RUDOLF

450 1925a El dialecto Maya-K'iché llamado Api, Apay, Apayac. *Rev. Etno.*, 1: 123–24.

Not seen.

451 1925b Primera contribución al estudio de las lenguas indígenas de El Salvador. Dialecto de Chilanga, Departamento de San Miguel, según los apuntes de Atilio Peccorini. *Rev. Etno.*, 1: 127–35, 305–14.

Lenca word lists, paradigms, and sentences; based on the same MS as Peccorini, 1910.

452 1925c La lengua Ts'ots'il. *IJAL*, 3: 193–218.

Sketch of phonology and grammar, with Spanish-Tzotzil-Maya word lists. Based on anonymous Gramática del Zotzil, 1818.

See also Valle, 1892.

SCHULTZE-JENA, LEONHARD

453 1933 Indiana, I: Leben, Glaube und Sprache der Quiché von Guatemala. Jena.

Extensive Quiché texts with German translation, grammar, and Quiché-German analytical vocabulary. Cf. Lewy, 1937.

454 1935 Indiana, II: Mythen in der Muttersprache der Pipil von Izalco in El Salvador. Jena.

Pipil texts with free translation, grammar, and analytic glossary.

455 1938 Indiana, III: Bei den Azteken, Mixteken und Tlapaneken der Sierra Madre del Sur von Mexiko. Jena.

Grammatical notes, texts, and vocabularies for Mixtec and for Tlapanec.

456 1957 Alt-Aztekische Gesänge, nach einer in der Biblioteca Nacional von Mexiko aufbewahrten Handschrift übersetzt und erläutert. Quellenwerke zur alten Geschichte Amerikas aufgezeichnet in den Sprachen der Eingeborenen, VI. Stuttgart.

Nahuatl texts and German translation on facing pages, followed by a full analytical lexicon.

456a 1950 Wahrsagerei, Himmelskunde und Kalender der alten Azteken, aus dem aztekischen Urtext Bernardino de Sahagún's übersetzt und erläutert... Quellenwerke zur alten Geschichte Amerikas, 4. Stuttgart.

Aztec text with German translation and detailed analytical vocabulary.

456b 1952 Gliederung des alt-aztekischen Volks in Familie, Stand und Beruf, aus dem aztekischen Urtext Bernardino de Sahagún's übersetzt und erläutert... Quellenwerke zur alten Geschichte Amerikas, 5. Stuttgart.

Aztec text with German translation and detailed analytical vocabulary.

SCOULER, JOHN

457   1841   Observations on the indigenous tribes of the Northwest coast of America. *Journal of the Royal Geographical Society*, 11: 215–51. London.

Contains Pima word list, pp. 246–50. This also appears on p. 129 of Albert Gallatin, Hale's Indians of Northwest America, *Transactions of the American Ethnological Society*, 2: xxiii-clxxxviii, 1–130 (New York, 1848).

SEDAT S., GUILLERMO

458   1955   Nuevo diccionario de las lenguas K'ek'chi' y Española. Chamelco, Alta Verapaz, Guatemala.

Kekchi-Spanish and Spanish-Kekchi, preceded by a note on pronunciation.

SEILER, HANSJAKOB, AND GÜNTER ZIMMERMANN

458a   1962   Studies in the phonology and morphology of classical Nahuatl, I: Orthographic variation *o/u*, its phonological and morphological implications. *IJAL*, 28: 243–50.

SELIS LOPE, MARIO

459   1937   Vocabulario Español-Quecchi. 3a ed., corregida y aumentada. Coban, Alta Verapaz, Guatemala.

Word lists, phrase lists, short devotional texts. Only this edition was available to me; but a 5th edition, 1953, is reported.

SHAW, MARY, AND HELEN NEUENSWANDER

459a   1966   Achi. *In* Mayers, 1966, pp. 15–48.

Grammatical sketch with sample text.

SIMÉON, RÉMI

460   1885   Dictionnaire de la langue Nahuatl ou Mexicaine. Paris.

Aztec-French dictionary, preceded by a brief grammar. Reprinted, Graz, 1963.

461   1902   Estudios gramaticales del idioma Náhuatl ... traducidos con notas y adiciones por el Lic. Cecilio A. Robelo. Appendix to Collección de Gramáticas de la Lengua Mexicana, vol. 2, supplement to *An. Mus. Nac.*, 1a época, tomo 3. Another Spanish version has been published by Enrique Torroella, *Estudios de Cultura Nahuatl*, 3: 137–201 (México, 1962).

See also Olmos, 1875.

SINCLAIR, DONALD E., AND KENNETH L. PIKE

462   1948   The tonemes of Mesquital Otomi. *IJAL*, 14: 91–98.

SKINNER, LEO E.

462a   1962   Usila Chinantec syllable structure. *IJAL*, 28: 251–55.

SLOCUM, MARIANNA C.

463   1948   Tzeltal (Mayan) noun and verb morphology. *IJAL*, 14: 77–86.

464   1950   Vocabulario Tzeltal. México.

Spanish-Tzeltal and Tzeltal-Spanish. Not seen.

SLOCUM, MARIANNA C., AND FLORENCIA L. GERDEL

464a   1965   Vocabulario Tzeltal de Bachajón: Castellano-Tzeltal, Tzeltal-Castellano. Serie de vocabularios indígenas Mariano Silva y Aceves, 13. México.

Includes appendix on numeral classifiers.

SMITH, T. BUCKINGHAM

464b   1861b   Mame vocabulary. *Historical Magazine*, 5: 117–18. New York.

465   1861b   Vocabulary of the Nevome, as spoken by the Pima of Moris, a town of Sonora. *Historical Magazine*, 5: 202–03. New York.

Grammatical notes, English-Pima vocabulary, and devotional texts.

466   1861c   The Opata language. *Historical Magazine*, 5: 236. New York.

English-Opata vocabulary.

467   1861d   A grammatical sketch of the Heve language, translated from an unpublished Spanish manuscript by Buckingham Smith. Shea's Library of American Linguistics, no. 3. New York.

From MS with title: Arte y vocabulario de la lingua Dohema, Heve ó Eudeva; this is identified with Opata. Includes English-Heve vocabulary.

468   1862a   Vocabulary of the Eudeve, a dialect of the Pima language, spoken in Sonora. *Historical Magazine*, 6: 18–19. New York.

English-Pima word list.

469   1862b   Grammar of the Pima or Névome, a language of Sonora, from a manuscript of the XVIII century. Shea's Library of American Linguistics, no. 5 New York.

SMITH, PAUL AND DOROTHY
470   1955   Vocabulario Chinanteco. México.

Dialect of Ojitlan. Not seen.

SOLÍS ALCALÁ, ERMILO
471   1949   Diccionario Español-Maya. [Mérida?]

SOLIZ, ÁNGEL
See González Casanova, 1925.

SOUSTELLE, JACQUES
472   1935   Deux contes Otomis. *JSAP*, 27: 1–12.

Interlinear and free translations, with some grammatical notes.

473   1937   La famille Otomi-Pame du Mexique Central. Travaux et Mémoires de l'Institut d'Ethnologie de l'Université de Paris, vol. 26. Paris.

Includes phonetics, morphology and syntax of the Otomí dialect of San José del Sitio, Méx.; notes on Otomí dialects and Otomí style; sketches of Mazahua, Matlaltzinca and Ocuiltec, Pame, and Chichimec (Jonaz).

474   1938   Un vocabulaire Cora. *JSAP*, 30: 141–45.

Publication of an anonymous MS, containing a miscellany of words and phrases.

475   1951   Documents sur les langages Pame et Jonaz du Mexique Central (Hidalgo, Querétaro et San Luis Potosí). *JSAP*, 40: 1–20.

Word lists and paradigms.

SOUSTELLE, JACQUES, AND R. J. WEITLANER
476   1935   Canciones Otomíes. *JSAP*, 27: 304–24.

Song texts with interlinear and free translations.

SPEAR, JOHN C.
477   1872   Report on the geology, mineralogy, natural history, inhabitants and agriculture of the Isthmus of Tehuantepec. *In* R. W. Shufeldt, Reports of explorations and surveys to ascertain the practicability of a ship-canal between the Atlantic and Pacific Oceans, by the way of the Isthmus of Tehuantepec, pp. 99–139 (Washington).

Contains vocabularies of "Logue" (Zoque) and Zapotec, pp. 128–32.

SPICER, EDWARD H.
See Kurath and Spicer, 1947.

SPOTTS, HAZEL
478   1953   Vowel harmony and consonant sequences in Mazahua (Otomi). *IJAL*, 19: 253–58.

479   1956   Some post-conquest changes in Mazahua. *IJAL*, 22: 208–11.

Comparison of the modern language with that recorded by Nágera y Yanguas, 1637.

480   1957   Yo mindyo. Cuentos de coyotes en el idioma Mazahua. México.

Contains Mazahua-Spanish vocabulary.

See also Stewart and Spotts, 1954, 1956.

SQUIER, EPHRAIM GEORGE
481   1852   Nicaragua, its people, scenery, monuments, and the proposed interoceanic canal. 2 vols. New York and London.

Grammatical notes on "Nagrandan," i.e. Subtiaba, and word lists of Subtiaba and Chorotegan, pp. 315–27. These were reprinted in the author's Observations on the archaeology and ethnology of Nicaragua, *Transactions of the American Ethnological Society*, 3: 83–158 (1853). The Chorotegan is also reprinted by Lehmann, 1920, pp. 844–48, and the Subtiaba on pp. 924–28.

482   1858   The states of Central America. New York and London.

Comparative word list of Lenca dialects, pp. 253–55; reproduced in Lehmann, 1920, pp. 668–70. Word lists of two Pipil dialects, pp. 339–40. Spanish version: Apuntamientos sobre Centro-América (Paris, 1856).

See also Anleo, 1865.

STAIRS, GLENN

483   1954   Nahuatl of Acatlan and Tulapa, Puebla. *In* Key, 1954, pp. 126–33.

STAIRS, GLENN AND EMILY

484   1956–57   Cartilla Huave. Parts 1–3. México.

    Short Huave-Spanish vocabularies at the end of each part.

STARK, DONALD S.

485   1947   Mixteco: complex phonemes. *Aboriginal Linguistics*, 1: 10–15. Cuernavaca.

STARR, FREDERICK

486   1900   Notes upon the ethnography of southern Mexico. Expedition of 1898. . ., 1899. . ., 1900. *Proceedings of the Davenport Academy of Sciences*, 8: 1–90. Davenport, Iowa.

    Comparative word list of Trique, Mixe, Huave, Tequistlatec, Chinantec, Mazatec, Chocho, Tepehua, and Totonac, facing p. 88.

487   1902   Notes upon the ethnography of southern Mexico. Expedition of 1901. *Proceedings of the Davenport Academy of Sciences*, 9: 1–109. Davenport, Iowa.

    Aztec word and phrase list from Citlaltepec, Veracruz, pp. 74–81; partly reproduced in Lehmann, 1920, pp. 1080–81. Spanish-Chol-English vocabulary by Henry Rau, pp. 82–89. Comparative word list of Huastec, Maya, Zoque, Chiapanec, Tzotzil, and Chol. The Chiapanec is reproduced by Lehmann, 1920, pp. 897–98.

STEFFEL, MATTHÄUS

488   1791   Tarahumarisches Wörterbuch. . . . Brünn.

    Reprinted in Christoph Gottlieb von Murr, ed., Nachrichten von verschiedenen Ländern des spanischen Amerika, Erster Theil (Halle, 1809), pp. 293–388. German-Tarahumara and Tarahumara-German vocabularies; short list of Latin sentences with Tarahumara translations.

STEWART, C.

489   1954   Nahuatl of Xochixtlahuaca, Guerrero. *In* Key, 1954, pp. 239–46.

STEWART, DONALD AND SHIRLEY

490   1958   Cartilla Mazahua. México.

    Mazahua-Spanish vocabulary, pp. 113–31.

STEWART, DONALD AND SHIRLEY, AND HAZEL SPOTTS

491   1954   Vocabulario Mazahua. México.

    Mazahua-Spanish and Spanish-Mazahua.

STOLL, OTTO

492   1884   Zur Ethnographie der Republik Guatemala. Zürich.

    Includes vocabularies of Pipil, Pupuluca de Conguaco, Chortí, Pocomam, Chol, Alagüilac, and Aguacatec; also a grammatical sketch of Cakchiquel. Vocabularies reprinted in Lehmann, 1920, are: Aguacatec, pp. 786–69; Pipil, pp. 1062–69. Spanish version: Etnografía de la República de Guatemala, traducida del alemán con prólogo y notas por Antonio Goubaud Carrera (Guatemala, 1938). Second edition: Etnografía de Guatemala (Guatemala, 1958).

493   1885   Supplementary remarks to the grammar of the Cakchiquel language of Guatemala. . . . *APS-P*, 22: 255–68.

    Comments on Brinton, 1884a.

494   1887   Die Sprache der Ixil-Indianer. . . . Leipzig.

    Contains Ixil-German vocabulary; comparative vocabulary of Aguacatec, Mam, Jacaltec, and Chuj; and a list of Aguacatec sentences.

495   1888   Die Maya-Sprachen der Pokom-Gruppe, 1. Teil. Die Sprache der Pokonchi-Indianer. Wien.

    Grammar of Pocomchi, followed by notes on Pocomam, three short texts, and a Pocomchi-German vocabulary.

496 1896 Die Maya-Sprachen der Pokom-Gruppe, 2. Teil. Die Sprache der K'ekchi-Indianer, nebst einem Anhang: die Uspanteca. Leipzig.

Kekchi grammar, brief textual materials, and Kekchi-German vocabulary. Notes on Uspantec grammar, with Uspantec-German vocabulary.

497 1928 Das Vokabular der Sprache von Aguacatán No. II (Guatemala). *Mitteilungen der Geographisch-Ethnographischen Gesellschaft*, Ergänzungsheft 1. Zürich.

Word list, Spanish and Aguacatec II, with some equivalents in Aguacatec I.

STOUDT, BETTY
See Dyk and Stoudt, 1965.

SUMMER INSTITUTE OF LINGUISTICS, field workers of
498 1948 Materials on Mayan languages of Mexico: Texts and dictionaries in Chol, Tojolabal, and Tzotzil by field workers of the Summer Institute of Linguistics, during the period 1939–1948. *Mic. Coll.*, no. 26. Chicago.

Chol texts and dictionary, by Ruth Hitchner Yourison and Evelyn Woodward Aulie. Tojolabal texts and dictionary, by Celia Douglass Mendenhall and Julia Supple. Tzotzil texts and dictionary, by Nadine Douglass Weathers. Text pages are numbered consecutively, 1–215; dictionaries are interspersed with different numbering or none. See individual authors for further information.

499 1949 Huichol and Aztec texts and dictionaries. *Mic. Coll.*, no. 27. Chicago.

Huichol texts and dictionary, by John B. McIntosh, pp. 1–337. Puebla Sierra Aztec texts and dictionary, by Arch McKinlay and Harold and Mary Key, pp. 338–555. Gulf Aztec texts and dictionary, by Howard W. Law, pp. 556–707. Tetelcingo Aztec texts and dictionary, by Richard S. Pittman, pp. 708–824. See individual authors for further information.

500 1958 *Maticleerocan Totajtol* I, Primera Cartilla Mejicana, Dialecto del Istmo. México.

Aztec-Spanish vocabulary at end.

501 1959a *Caña Jun*, Aprenda a leer. Primera cartilla en el idioma Chol de Tila. México.

Chol-Spanish vocabulary at end.

502 1959b *La' laj q'uel jun*, La primera cartilla en el idioma Chol de Tumbalá y Español. México.

Chol-Spanish vocabulary at end.

503 1960 *Ra Haho 'nɛ rá Xaha*. Primera cartilla en el idioma Otomí de la Sierra. —*Ra Yotoro 'nɛ rá x'ɑyo*. Segunda cartilla en el idioma Otomí de la Sierra. México.

Otomí-Spanish vocabulary at end of each part; dialect of Huehuetla, Hidalgo.

SUPPLE, JULIA, AND CELIA M. DOUGLASS
504 1949 Tojolabal (Mayan) phonemes and verb morphology. *IJAL*, 15: 168–74.

SUPPLE, JULIA, AND FRANCES JACKSON
505 1952 Vocabulario Tojolabal. México.

Not seen.

See also Mendenhall and Supple, 1948.

SWADESH, MORRIS
506 1949 El idioma de los Zapotecos. *In* L. Mendieta y Núñez, ed., Los Zapotecos, monografía histórica, etnográfica y económica, pp. 415–48 (México).

Sketch of phonemics and grammar, notes on syntax, comparative word list of three dialects.

506a 1963 El tamaulipeco. *Rev. Mex. Est. Antro.*, 19: 93–104.

Identification of an extinct language of Tamaulipas, with a short vocabulary gleaned from colonial records.

See also Arana and Swadesh, 1965; Leon and Swadesh, 1949.

SWANTON, JOHN R.
507 1940 Linguistic material from the tribes of Southern Texas and Northeastern Mexico. *BAE-B*, 127. Washington.

Includes vocabularies of Coahuiltec, Comecrudo, Cotoname and Maratino, with reverse indexes.

SYWULKA, E. F.

508   1954   Nahuatl of Santo Domingo Sonsonate, El Salvador. *In* Key, 1954, pp. 134–43.

508a   1966   Mam grammar. *In* Mayers, 1966, pp. 178–95.

               Includes sample text.

            See also Andrade, 1946b.

TAPIA ZENTENO, CARLOS DE

509   1747   Arte de la lengua Huasteca. México.

               Not seen.

510   1753   Arte novísima de la lengua Mexicana. México.

               Reprinted in Colección de gramáticas de la lengua Mexicana 3: 1–42, supplement to *An. Mus. Nac.*, 1a época, tomo 3 (1885).

511   1767   Noticia de la lengua Huasteca. . . . México.

               Grammar, Spanish-Huastec vocabulary, and catechism.

TELETOR, CELSO NARCISO

512   1942   Breve manual de conversación (Quiché-Castellano). Guatemala.

               Not seen.

513   1951   Epítome Quiché. Guatemala.

               Grammatical sketch, paradigms, and phrase list.

513a   1959   Diccionario Castellano-Quiché y voces Castellano-Pokomam. Guatemala.

               Spanish-Quiché and Spanish-Pocomam vocabularies.

TELLECHEA, MIGUEL

514   1825   Compendio gramatical para la inteligencia del idioma Tarahumar. México.

               Reprinted, *Bol. Soc. Mex. Geog. Estad.*, 1a época, 4: 145–66 (1854). Reprinted again, Puebla, 1900.

TERMER, FRANZ

515   1930   Über die Mayasprache von Chicomucelo. *ICA-P*, 23: 926–36. New York.

               Contains German-Chicomuceltec-Huastec word list.

TERNAUX-COMPANS, HENRI, ED.

516   1840–41   Vocabulaire des principales langues du Mexique. *Nouvelles Annales des Voyages*, 88: 5–37, 92: 257–87. Paris.

               Parallel vocabularies of Aztec (from Molina 1571), Cakchiquel (from an anonymous MS of the 16th century), Maya (from Beltrán 1746), Otomí (from an undated MS of Alonso Urbano), Huastec (from Tapia Zenteno 1747), Zapotec (from Córdova 1564, 1578), Mixtec (from Reyes 1593), Cáhita (from Velasco, 1737), Tarahumara (from Tellechea 1826), and Totonac (from Zambrano Bonilla, 1752).

THORD-GRAY, I.

517   1955   Tarahumara-English English-Tarahumara dictionary, and an introduction to Tarahumara grammar. Coral Gables, Florida.

TODD, J. G.

518   1954   Nahuatl of Nahuizalco, El Salvador. *In* Key, 1954, pp. 144–51.

TORRESANO, ESTÉBAN

519   1754   Arte de la lengua Kakchikel, incluyendo un paralelo de las lenguas Kiché, Cakchiquel y Zutuhil. Guatemala.

               Not seen.

TORROELLA, ENRIQUE

            See Siméon, 1902.

TOWNSEND, WILLIAM CAMERON

519a   1960   Cakchiquel grammar. *In* Elson, 1960, pp. 3–79.

               Pedagogical sketch of morphology, written in 1926.

TOZZER, ALFRED M.

520   1906   Notes on the Maya pronoun. Boas Anniversary Volume, pp. 85–87. New York.

521   1912   A classification of Maya verbs. *ICA-P*, 17, 2d session, pp. 233–37. México.

522   1921   A Maya grammar with bibliography and appraisement of the works cited. Papers of the Peabody Museum, Harvard University, vol. 9. Cambridge, Mass.

Description of phonetics and grammar, based on author's field work. Five texts with interlinear and free translations. Comparative vocabulary of Yucatec dialects.

Troike, Rudolph Charles

523   1959   A descriptive phonology and morphology of Coahuilteco. University of Texas dissertation. Ann Arbor, University Microfilms.

Analyzes data from Bartolomé García's Manual para administrar los Santos Sacramentos (México, 1760). Includes short sample of edited text. Summary in *Diss. Abs.*, 20: 2793, 1960.

523a   1963   A contribution to Coahuilteco lexicography. *IJAL*, 29: 295–98.

Ulrich, Matthew and Rosemary

523b   1966   Mopan Maya. *In* Mayers, 1966, pp. 251–71.

Grammatical sketch with sample text and short word list.

Upson, Jessamine

524   1956   Some Chatino riddles analyzed. *IJAL*, 22: 113–16.

Twenty riddles with linguistic analysis and glossary.

525   1960   A preliminary structure of Chatino. *Anthro. Ling.* 2.6: 22–29.

Morphological sketch.

Urbano, Alonso
See Ternaux-Compans, 1840–41.

Valdespino, Andrés
See Peñafiel, 1887.

Valle, Francisco

526   1892   Quaderno de algunas reglas y apuntes sobre el idioma Pame. *In* Conde de la Viñaza, Bibliografía Española de lenguas indígenas de América, pp. 287–314 (Madrid).

Publication of an 18th-century MS, containing material on pronunciation and grammar. Also published as: Única gramática conocida de la lengua Pame, ed. by Rudolf Schuller (México, 1925).

Varea, Francisco de
See Sáenz de Santa María, 1940.

Vázquez Gastelu, Antonio

527   1689   Arte de la lengua Mexicana. Puebla.

Several later editions exist. Reprinted in Colección de Gramáticas de la lengua Mexicana, 2: 1–44, supplement to *An. Mus. Nac.*, 1a época, tomo 3 (1885).

Velasco, Juan B. de (supposed author)

528   1737   Arte de la lengua Cáhita. México.

Reprinted, with introduction and notes by Eustaquio Buelna, México, 1890. The reprint edition contains Spanish-Cáhita and Cáhita-Spanish vocabularies.

Velázquez, G. G.

529   1934   Vocabulario Otomí del pueblo de Santa María Mazatla, Mex. *Inv. Ling.*, 2: 54–58.

Spanish-Otomí word list.

Velde, Paul van de

530   1933   Breve vocabulario comparado del idioma Zapoteco. *Inv. Ling.* 1: 251–57.

Comparative vocabulary of three Zapotec dialects.

Vergara, Gabriel de
See Hoyo, 1965.

Vergara Bianchi, José
See Brambila and Vergara Bianchi, 1953.

Vetancurt, Agustín

531   1673   Arte de lengua Mexicana. México.

Reprinted in Colección de gramáticas de la lengua Mexicana, 1: 539–620, supplement to Biblioteca Mexicana Histórica y Lingüística, Cuadernos 1–4 (1901–04).

Villacorta C., José Antonio

532   1933   Estudios sobre lingüística guatemalteca. *An. Soc. Geog. Hist.*, 10: 41–81, 170–205, 331–73, 431–77.

"Extructura [sic] de las lenguas indígenas guatemaltecas," pp. 87–132, containing notes on Quiché and Cakchiquel. All this is reprinted in Villacorta, 1934.

533 1934 Memorial de Tecpán-Atitlán (Anales de los Cakchiqueles) por Francisco Hernández Arana Xajilá y Francisco Díaz Gebuta Quej. Texto y traducción revisados con notas y estudios sobre lingüística guatemalteca por J. Antonio Villacorta C. Guatemala.

In addition to reprinting Villacorta, 1933, contains "Vocabulario de las principales voces usadas en el Memorial de Tecpán-Atitlan" (Cakchiquel-Spanish), pp. 361–78.

VILLALPANDO, LUIS DE
534 1571 Diccionario de la lengua Maya. México.

Not seen.

VOEGELIN, CARL F.
535 1956 Linear phonemes and additive components. *Word*, 12: 429–43. Limoges.

Includes phonemic inventories, for typological purposes, of Chatino, Totonac, and Aguacatec.

VOEGELIN, FLORENCE M.
See Yegerlehner and Voegelin, 1957.

WALLIS, ETHEL
536 1956 Simulfixation in aspect markers of Mezquital Otomi. *Lg.*, 32: 453–59.

536a 1964 Mezquital Otomi verb fusion. *Lg.*, 40: 75–82.

WALLIS, ETHEL, ET AL.
537 1956 Diccionario Castellano-Otomí, Otomí-Castellano. Cuadernos del Patrimonio Indígena del Valle del Mezquital, no. 1. Itzmiquilpan, Mexico.

See also Arroyo, 1955.

WARES, ALAN
538 1954 Nahuatl of Huejotzingo, Puebla. *In* Key, 1954, pp. 160–67.

See also Yegerlehner and Voegelin, 1957.

WARKENTIN, MILTON
See Pike and Warkentin, 1961.

WARKENTIN, MILTON AND CLARA
539 1947 Diccionario Huave. México.

Revised and expanded as Vocabulario Huave, México, 1952.

WARKENTIN, MILTON, AND JUAN OLIVARES
540 1947 "The holy bells" and other Huave legends. *Tlalocan*, 2: 223–34. Azcapotzalco.

Texts with literal and free translations.

WARKENTIN, VIOLA
See Whittaker and Warkentin, 1965.

WATERHOUSE, VIOLA
541 1949 Oaxaca Chontal: Sentence types and text analysis. *Méx. Ant.*, 7: 299–314.

This and the next two listings deal with the Tequistlatec language.

542 1962 The grammatical structure of Oaxaca Chontal. Indiana University Research Center in Anthropology, Folklore, and Linguistics, Publications, 19. Bloomington, Ind.

Grammar and phonology.

WATERHOUSE, VIOLA, AND MAY MORRISON
543 1950 Chontal phonemes. *IJAL*, 16: 35–39.

WATKINS, MARK HANNA
See Andrade, 1946a; Instituto Indigenista Nacional, 1947.

WEATHERS, KENNETH AND NADINE
544 1949 Diccionario Español-Tzotzil y Tzotzil-Español. México.

Not seen.

545 1956 Spanish-Tzotzil grammar. México.

Not seen.

WEATHERS, NADINE

546   1947   Tsotsil phonemes with special reference to allophones of *b. IJAL*, 13: 108–11.

547   1948   Tzotzil texts and dictionary. *In* Summer Institute of Linguistics, 1948.
               Texts, pp. 157–215. Tzotzil-English dictionary, not paginated.

548   1950   Morphological analysis of a Tzotzil (Mayan) text. *IJAL*, 16: 91–98.

WEITLANER, ROBERT J.

549   1933   El dialecto Otomí de Ixtenco, Tlaxcala. *An. Mus. Nac.*, 4a época, 8: 667–92.
               Contains comparative vocabulary of three Otomí dialects.

550   1939a   Beitrag zur Sprache der Ocuilteca von San Juan Acingo. *Méx. Ant.*, 4: 297–328.
               Phonetic sketch; comparative vocabulary of Ocuiltec, Matlaltzinca, and Otomí.

551   1939b   Notes on the Cuitlatec language. *Méx. Ant.*, 4: 363–73.
               Contains vocabulary collected by Pedro Hendrichs.

552   1939c   Los Chinantecos. *Rev. Mex. Est. Antro.*, 3: 195–216.
               Includes grammatical notes.

553   1947   The phonemic system of Chinantec, dialect of Chiltepec, Oaxaca. *ICA-P*, 27, 1st
               session, 2: 313–21. México.
               Includes text with interlinear translation.

554   1948   Un idioma desconocido del Norte de México. *ICA-P*, 28: 205–27. Paris.
               Unclassified language of Naolán, Tamaulipas.

WEITLANER, ROBERT J., AND IRMGARD WEITLANER DE JOHNSON

555   1943   Acatlán y Hueycantenango, Guerrero. *Méx. Ant.*, 6: 140–202.
               Contains vocabularies of three Aztec dialects, of Tlapanec, and of "Popoloca-
               Tlapaneco."
       See also Soustelle and Weitlaner, 1935.

WEITLANER DE JOHNSON, IRMGARD
       See Johnson and Weitlaner de Johnson, 1947 and 1954; Weitlaner and Weitlaner de John-
       son, 1943.

WHORF, BENJAMIN LEE

556   1946   The Milpa Alta dialect of Aztec. *In* Linguistic Structures of Native America, pp.
               367–97. Viking Fund Publications in Anthropology, no. 6. New York.
               Phonology and grammar, with notes on Classical Aztec and on the dialect of Tepoz-
               tlán.

WHIPPLE, A. W.

557   1856   Vocabularies of North American languages. U. S. War Department, Reports of
               explorations and surveys to ascertain the most practicable and economical route
               for a railroad from the Mississippi River to the Pacific Ocean, 3: 54–103 (Wash-
               ington).
               Contains short English-Pima word list, p. 94.

WHITTAKER, ARABELLE, AND VIOLA WARKENTIN

557a   1965   Chol texts on the supernatural. Summer Institute of Linguistics of the University
               of Oklahoma, Publications in linguistics, 13. Norman, Okla.
               Texts with word-for-word translation and a Chol-English glossary.

WILLENBRINK, ANTONINE

558   1935   Notes on the Pima Indian language. [Santa Barbara, Calif.]
               Mimeographed grammar with extensive Pima-English word lists.

WILLIAMS, ANN, AND ESTHER PIERSON

559   1950   Diccionario Español-Popoloca, Popoloca-Español. México.
               Contains section on pronunciation.

WILLIAMS, KENNETH AND BARBARA

559a   1966   Chuj. *In* Mayers, 1966, pp. 219–34.
               Grammatical sketch with sample text.

WISDOM, CHARLES

560   1950   Materials on the Chorti language. *Mic. Coll.*, no. 28. Chicago.

Grammatical notes, texts, and Chortí-English lexicon. Mostly handwritten materials, photographed from file cards and notebooks.

WONDERLY, WILLIAM L.

561   1946a   Phonemic acculturation in Zoque. *IJAL*, 12: 92–95.

Two alternate phonemic analyses; sample text with free translation. Reprinted in K. L. Pike, Phonemics, pp. 202–06 (Ann Arbor, 1947).

562   1946b   Textos en Zoque sobre el concepto del nagual. *Tlalocan*, 2: 97–105. Azcapotzalco.

Texts on witchcraft, with free translations.

563   1947   Textos folklóricos en Zoque: Tradiciones de los alrededores de Copainalá, Chiapas. *Rev. Mex. Est. Antro.*, 9: 135–63.

With free translations.

564   1951–52   Zoque I–VI. *IJAL*, 17: 1–9, 105–23, 137–62, 235–51; 18: 35–48, 189–202.

Phonology and morphology, followed by text with detailed analysis.

See also Aschmann and Wonderly, 1952.

XEC, PATRICIO, AND GAIL MAYNARD

564a   1954   Diccionario Quiché preliminar: Quiché-Espanol, Espanol-Quiché. Quezaltenango (mimeographed).

Not seen.

XIMÉNEZ, FRANCISCO

565   1952   Arte de las tres lenguas Cakchiquel, Quiché, y Tzutuhil. Tratado segundo de todo lo que debe saver un ministro para la buena administración de estos naturales. *Mic. Coll.*, no. 36. Chicago.

Microfilm of 16th-century MS.

YEGERLEHNER, JOHN, AND FLORENCE M. VOEGELIN

566   1957   Frequencies and inventories of phonemes from nine languages. *IJAL*, 23: 85–93.

Includes phonemic inventories, for typological use, of Chontal de Tabasco (by Kathryn Keller) and of Tarascan (by Alan Wares).

YOURISON, RUTH HITCHNER

557   1948   Chol texts. *In* Summer Institute of Linguistics, 1948, pp. 1–59.

Includes brief phonemic description. Edited by Evelyn Woodward Aulie.

ZAMBRANO BONILLA, JOSÉ

568   1752   Arte de la lengua Totonaca.... Lleva añadido una Doctrina de Naolingo, con algunas vozes de la lengua de aquella Sierra, y de esta de acá ... su autor el Lic. D. Francisco Domínguez. Puebla.

Grammar followed by lists of minimal pairs, kinship terms, and body parts. Appended is a comparative word list of the dialects of Papantla and of Naolingo.

ZAVALA, M., AND A. MEDINA

569   1898   Vocabulario Española-Maya. Mérida.

ZEPEDA, FRANCISCO DE

570   1560   Artes de los idiomas Chiapaneco, Zoque, Tzendal y Chinanteco. [México?]

Title is variously cited; apparently no copies of this work remain in existence. "Chinantec" here means Tzotzil.

ZIMMERMANN, GÜNTER

See Seiler and Zimmermann, 1962.

INDEX

The following index of languages refers to the item numbers assigned in the body of the bibliography. Under each language, references are classified into four historical periods: Early, 1500–1650; Middle, 1650–1850; Late, 1850–1930; and Recent, 1930–1960. This classification refers to date of composition, when known, rather than to date of publication; so that a 16th-century MS first published in 1880 is listed as "Early," not "Late."

Under each historical period, references are classified according to their content, under five headings: General, Phonology, Grammar, Lexicon, and Texts. This classification reflects the *principal* topics contained in each reference; thus a grammar with only a few texts appended would be listed under "Grammar" alone, and not under "Texts." Works which deal briefly with several categories, but extensively with none, are classified as "General."

ACHÍ
  Recent: Phonology, 149a
          Grammar, 459a
AGUACATEC I
  Late: General, 494
       Lexicon, 439h, 492
  Recent: General, 14
       Phonology, 149a, 304, 535
       Grammar, 304a
AGUACATEC II
  Late: Lexicon, 497
AKWA'ALA (*see also* YUMAN)
  Late: Lexicon, 188
ALAGÜILAC
  Late: Lexicon, 94, 492
AMUZGO
  Late: General, 65
       Lexicon, 337
  Recent: General, 135
       Grammar, 221
AZTEC (*see also* ALAGÜILAC, PIPIL)
  Early: Grammar, 107, 177, 344, 360, 432
       Lexicon, 32, 342, 343, 345, 439b
  Middle: Grammar, 6, 42, 108, 109, 130, 211, 375, 510, 527, 531
       Lexicon, 130, 211
  Late: General, 71, 79, 196, 284, 405
       Phonology, 78
       Grammar, 1, 461
       Lexicon, 73, 74, 362, 372, 433, 460, 487
       Texts, 80, 194, 195, 362
  Recent: Phonology, 48, 89, 99a, 139, 221a, 254, 276, 316, 318, 412a, 458a, 556
       Grammar, 140, 141, 156, 179, 186, 233, 235, 253, 278, 278a, 410, 412, 449, 556
       Lexicon, 33, 88a, 133, 158, 179, 203, 207, 217, 235, 252, 255, 258, 261, 274, 275, 312, 313, 316, 318, 411, 413, 438, 449, 456, 456a, 456b, 483, 489, 500, 538, 555
       Texts, 142, 179, 199, 261, 274, 277, 313, 409, 411, 412, 449, 456
BACHAHOM
  Recent: General, 14
CACAOPERA, *see* MATAGALPAN
CÁHITA
  Middle: Grammar, 528
  Late: General, 227, 330, 405
       Lexicon, 528
  Recent: General, 260
       Phonology, 142a, 172
       Grammar, 242a
       Lexicon, 125, 125a, 147, 242a, 258
       Texts, 146, 242a
CAKCHIQUEL
  Early: Grammar, 565
       Lexicon, 516

Middle: Grammar, 90, 169, 435, 519
       Lexicon, 164
Late: Grammar, 492, 493, 519a
       Lexicon, 92, 126, 439h, 445, 447
       Texts, 92, 447
Recent: General, 15, 225, 532
       Phonology, 149a, 236, 237
       Lexicon, 439a, 533
CHANEABAL, *see* TOJOLABAL
CHATINO
  Late: General, 69, 77
       Grammar, 22
  Recent: Phonology, 310, 535
       Grammar, 416a, 416b, 525
       Lexicon, 311
       Texts, 524
CHIAPANEC
  Early: Grammar, 570
  Middle: Grammar, 406
       Lexicon, 164
  Late: General, 284
       Grammar, 3
       Lexicon, 3, 112, 487
       Texts, 3
  Recent: Lexicon, 57
CHICHIMEC
  Recent: General, 25, 473, 475
       Phonology, 434a
       Lexicon, 198
CHICOMUCELTEC
  Late: General, 441
       Lexicon, 439h, 515
CHINANTEC
  Middle: Texts, 46a
  Late: General, 60, 71, 96
       Grammar, 22
       Lexicon, 197, 486
  Recent: Phonology, 340a, 432a, 432b, 462a, 553
       Grammar, 340b, 426a, 432c, 552
       Lexicon, 470
CHOCHO
  Late: General, 63
       Grammar, 22
       Lexicon, 294, 486
CHOL
  Middle: Lexicon, 164
  Late: Lexicon, 439h, 440, 487, 492
  Recent: Grammar, 41
       Lexicon, 40, 58, 59, 501, 502, 557a
       Texts, 12, 557a, 567
CHOLTÍ
  Early: Grammar, 348
       Lexicon, 348
  Recent: Lexicon, 359
CHONTAL (of Oaxaca), *see* TEQUISTLATEC
CHONTAL (of Tabasco)
  Late: General, 76
       Lexicon, 98, 439h
  Recent: Phonology, 248, 251, 566
       Grammar, 218, 247
       Lexicon, 56, 250
       Texts, 249
CHOROTEGAN
  Late: Lexicon, 481

CHORTÍ
  Late: General, 191, 192, 368, 440
            Lexicon, 55, 439h, 492
  Recent: Grammar, 359a, 560
            Lexicon, 359, 560
            Texts, 560
CHUJ
  Late: Lexicon, 439h
  Recent: General, 14
            Phonology, 149a
            Grammar, 559a
COAHUILTEC
  Middle: Texts, 235b
  Recent: Phonology, 523
            Grammar, 523
            Lexicon, 507, 523a
COCHIMÍ
  Late: Lexicon, 183
COCOPA
  Late: Lexicon, 188
  Recent: Lexicon, 433b
COMECRUDO
  Recent: Lexicon, 507
CORA
  Middle: Lexicon, 364
  Late: General, 405
            Lexicon, 414, 439f
            Texts, 414
  Recent: General, 193
            Grammar, 415
            Lexicon, 314, 315, 416
            Texts, 148, 476
COTONAME
  Recent: Lexicon, 507
CUICATEC
  Late: General, 4, 70, 71
            Grammar, 22
  Recent: Phonology, 355
            Grammar, 145
            Texts, 144
CUITLATEC
  Late: Lexicon, 290
  Recent: General, 222, 223, 224, 551
            Phonology, 317
            Grammar, 161g
            Lexicon, 161g, 317
GUAICURA, see WAICURI
GUARIJÍO, see VAROHÍO
HUASTEC
  Middle: General, 511
  Late: General, 7, 405
            Grammar, 8
            Lexicon, 8, 302, 439h, 441, 487, 515
            Texts, 8
  Recent: General, 13
            Phonology, 271
            Grammar, 269
            Lexicon, 270
HUAVE
  Late: General, 66, 71, 85
            Lexicon, 175, 293, 486
            Texts, 420
  Recent: Phonology, 403a

            Lexicon, 133, 484, 539
            Texts, 540
HUICHOL
  Late: General, 149, 405
            Lexicon, 264
  Recent: Phonology, 204, 205, 216, 305
            Grammar, 206a
            Lexicon, 206, 307, 308, 309
            Texts, 306, 307
IXCATEC
  Recent: Phonology, 166
            Grammar, 165
            Lexicon, 166a
IXIL
  Middle: General, 354
  Late: General, 494
            Lexicon, 439h, 441
  Recent: Phonology, 149a
            Grammar, 158a, 158b
JACALTEC
  Late: Lexicon, 76, 439h
  Recent: General, 14, 265
            Phonology, 149a
            Grammar, 123a, 123b
            Lexicon, 15
JONAZ, see CHICHIMEC
KANJOBAL
  Middle: Lexicon, 164
  Recent: Phonology, 149a
KEKCHÍ
  Middle: Lexicon, 164
  Late: General, 101, 439
            Grammar, 122, 496
            Lexicon, 28, 112, 407, 439h, 443, 496
            Texts, 439g
  Recent: General, 16
            Phonology, 149a, 237
            Grammar, 154b
            Lexicon, 458, 459
KICKAPOO
  Late: Texts, 245
KILIWA
  Late: Lexicon, 183, 188
  Recent: Lexicon, 433b
LACANDÓN
  Recent: General, 14
            Phonology, 45
            Texts, 44
LENCA
  Late: General, 284, 369, 451
            Lexicon, 150, 226, 265, 266, 338, 482
MAM
  Early: Grammar, 268, 430
            Lexicon, 430
  Middle: Lexicon, 164
  Late: General, 119, 405
            Lexicon, 439h, 441, 464b
  Recent: General, 14
            Phonology, 149a, 237
            Grammar, 508a
            Lexicon, 15
MANGUE
  Late: General, 284
            Lexicon, 93

MARATINO
  Recent: Lexicon, 507
MATAGALPAN
  Late: General, 99, 284, 340
           Lexicon, 98
MATLALTZINCA
  Early: General, 212
  Late: General, 405
           Lexicon, 292
  Recent: General, 473
           Lexicon, 550
MAYA (Yucatec) (*See also* Mopan)
  Early: Grammar, 129, 327
           Lexicon, 327, 534
  Middle: Grammar, 72, 439c
           Lexicon, 46, 72
  Late: General, 365, 405, 448
           Grammar, 2, 115, 121, 300, 520, 521, 522
           Lexicon, 114, 336, 373, 374, 439h, 487,
             569
  Recent: General, 83, 363
           Phonology, 396, 434d
           Grammar, 17, 47, 74a, 182, 358, 434b,
             434c
           Lexicon, 471
           Texts, 282
MAYAN, unidentified (*see also* "PUPULUCA")
  Late: Lexicon, 132, 450
MAYO, *see* CÁHITA
MAZAHUA
  Early: General, 351
  Late: General, 405
  Recent: General, 473, 479
           Phonology, 387, 478
           Lexicon, 480, 490, 491
MAZATEC
  Late: General, 61, 71, 284
           Grammar, 22
           Lexicon, 97, 486
  Recent: General, 240
           Phonology, 136, 208, 384, 388, 403
           Grammar, 134, 136a, 137, 209, 210, 389,
             399
           Lexicon, 390
           Texts, 386
MEXICANO, *see* AZTEC
MIXE
  Middle: Grammar, 417
           Lexicon, 418
  Late: General, 60, 68, 71, 200, 284
           Grammar, 24
           Lexicon, 98, 294, 486
  Recent: Phonology, 138a, 233a, 341
           Grammar, 299a
           Lexicon, 54, 133, 234, 449a
           Texts, 423
MIXTEC
  Early: Grammar, 427
           Lexicon, 11
  Late: General, 405
           Grammar, 22
  Recent: Phonology, 83a, 321, 322, 323, 364a, 397,
             485
           Grammar, 83a, 399, 400, 401, 455

Lexicon, 29a, 153, 154a 320, 455
           Texts, 154, 391, 392, 393, 394, 395, 398,
             455
MOPAN
  Recent: Grammar, 523b
MOTOTZINTLEC
  Late: General, 441
           Lexicon, 439h
NAGRANDA, *see* SUBTIABA
NAHUA, NAHUAT, NAHUATL, *see* AZTEC
NAOLAN
  Recent: General, 554
OCUILTEC
  Recent: General, 473, 550
OLUTA (Popoluca of Veracruz)
  Late: Lexicon, 103
ÓPATA
  Middle: Grammar, 296
  Late: General, 405
           Grammar, 467
           Lexicon, 404, 466, 467
  Recent: General, 161h
           Lexicon, 244, 258
OTOMÍ
  Early: Grammar, 106
  Middle: General, 352
           Grammar, 213, 301, 356
           Lexicon, 301, 356, 516
  Late: General, 71, 405
           Grammar, 5, 100, 162
           Lexicon, 100, 289, 372
  Recent: Phonology, 18, 238, 284a, 285, 462, 473
           Grammar, 34, 156, 157, 178, 227a, 473,
             536, 536a
           Lexicon, 19, 20, 75, 228, 503, 529, 537,
             549, 550
           Texts, 155, 472, 476
PAJALATE
  Middle: General, 235b
PALENCANO
  Recent: General, 14
PAME
  Middle: General, 526
  Late: General, 405
  Recent: General, 335, 473, 475
           Phonology, 187
           Grammar, 111
PAPABUCO
  Late: General, 67
PAPAGO, *see* PIMA-PAPAGO
PIMA-PAPAGO
  Middle: General, 376
           Lexicon, 457
  Late: General, 405, 465
           Grammar, 102, 469
           Lexicon, 143, 151, 152, 366, 468, 557
           Texts, 437
  Recent: General, 259
           Phonology, 161f, 202, 214, 214a, 331,
             444a
           Grammar, 214, 331, 558
           Lexicon, 242, 444, 558
           Texts, 11a
PIPIL (*see also* AZTEC)

Late: Lexicon, 30, 327a, 445, 446, 482, 492
Recent: General, 31
Grammar, 239, 454
Lexicon, 239, 383, 434, 454, 508, 518
Texts, 454

POCOMAM
Early: Grammar, 176
Middle: Lexicon, 164
Late: General, 440, 495
Lexicon, 439h, 492
Recent: General, 16
Phonology, 149a
Lexicon, 513a

POCOMCHI
Early: Grammar, 176
Middle: Lexicon, 164
Late: Grammar, 495
Lexicon, 88, 439h, 445, 495
Recent: Phonology, 333a
Grammar, 332, 333, 334a
Lexicon, 163, 333, 334
Texts, 333

POPOLOCA
Late: Lexicon, 294, 372
Recent: Phonology, 382
Lexicon, 555, 559

POPOLUCA of Veracruz, *see* OLUTA, SAYULA,
SIERRA POPOLUCA, TEXISTEPEC

"PUPULUCA" (Mayan)
Middle: Lexicon, 164

PUPULUCA of Conguaco
Late: Lexicon, 492

QUINIGUA
Recent: Lexicon, 235a

QUICHÉ
Early: Grammar, 565
Middle: Grammar, 26, 169, 519
Lexicon, 164
Late: General, 110, 405
Grammar, 2, 9, 86, 87, 120, 121
Lexicon, 86, 87, 439h, 445
Texts, 87
Recent: General, 15, 512, 513, 532
Phonology, 149a, 237
Grammar, 171a, 173, 295, 453
Lexicon, 157a, 286, 453, 513a, 564a

SAYULA (Popoluca of Veracruz)
Late: Lexicon, 103
Recent: Phonology, 124
Grammar, 124b
Lexicon, 124a

SERI
Late: General, 227, 405, 453
Lexicon, 184, 185
Recent: Phonology, 350
Lexicon, 257, 349

SIERRA POPOLUCA (Popoluca of Veracruz)
Late: General, 76
Recent: General, 171
Phonology, 159, 161d, 232
Grammar, 161, 161a, 161c, 295a, 299a
Lexicon, 133, 170
Texts, 160

SUBTIABA
Late: General, 284, 481
Lexicon, 113, 283

TAMAULIPEC
Recent: Lexicon, 506a

TAPACHULTEC I
Late: Lexicon, 442

TAPACHULTEC II
Late: Lexicon, 283, 284, 441

TARAHUMARA
Middle: Grammar, 514
Lexicon, 488
Late: General, 50, 405
Grammar, 167, 181
Lexicon, 167, 168
Recent: General, 357
Grammar, 84, 517
Lexicon, 229, 230, 231, 517

TARASCAN
Early: Grammar, 189, 263
Lexicon, 190, 263
Middle: Grammar, 49
Late: General, 405
Grammar, 201, 353
Lexicon, 201, 286a
Texts, 201
Recent: General, 272, 303
Phonology, 273, 566

TEPECANO
Late: General, 328
Lexicon, 291
Texts, 329

TEPEHUA
Late: Lexicon, 288, 486
Recent: Grammar, 81
Lexicon, 82

TEPEHUANE
Middle: General, 431
Late: General, 405
Recent: Phonology, 53, 402
Lexicon, 52

TEQUISTLATEC (Chontal of Oaxaca)
Late: General, 21, 64, 71
Lexicon, 98, 486
Recent: Phonology, 542, 543
Grammar, 541, 542
Lexicon, 133
Texts, 541

TEXISTEPEC (Popoluca of Veracruz)
Late: Lexicon, 103

TLAPANEC
Late: General, 294
Recent: General, 422
Grammar, 455
Lexicon, 455, 555
Texts, 455

TOJOLABAL
Middle: Lexicon, 164
Late: General, 95
Lexicon, 76, 132, 439h
Recent: General, 51
Phonology, 504
Grammar, 504

Lexicon, 339, 505
Texts, 339

TOTONAC
Middle: Grammar, 568
Lexicon, 568
Late: General, 326, 367, 405
Lexicon, 372, 486
Recent: General, 123
Phonology, 35, 319, 535
Grammar, 37, 39
Lexicon, 36, 38

TRIQUE
Late: General, 60, 62
Lexicon, 486
Recent: Phonology, 215, 297, 298
Grammar, 299, 299b

TZELTAL
Early: Grammar, 570
Middle: Lexicon, 164
Late: Grammar, 112, 408
Lexicon, 76, 408, 439h
Recent: Phonology, 72a, 433a
Grammar, 72b, 72c, 72d, 246a, 433a, 463
Lexicon, 464, 464a

TZOTZIL
Early: Grammar, 570
Middle: Grammar, 27, 117, 439e
Lexicon, 116, 164, 439e
Late: General, 452
Grammar, 112, 122
Lexicon, 118, 132, 439h, 487
Recent: Phonology, 546
Grammar, 138, 147a, 147b, 545, 548
Lexicon, 147c, 544, 547
Texts, 547

TZUTUHIL
Early: Grammar, 565
Middle: Grammar, 169, 519
Lexicon, 164
Late: Lexicon, 439h
Recent: General, 15
Phonology, 149a
Lexicon, 29

USPANTEC
Late: Lexicon, 439h, 496
VAROHÍO
Recent: Lexicon, 158, 229, 241, 243, 258
WAICURI
Middle: General, 43
XINCA
Late: General, 103, 284
Grammar, 325
Lexicon, 91, 103, 324
Recent: Lexicon, 303b
YAQUI, see CÁHITA
YUCATEC, see MAYA
YUMAN of Baja California (see also AKWA'ALA, COCOPA, KILIWA)
Late: Lexicon, 183, 185, 287
Recent: Lexicon, 433b
ZAPOTEC
Early: Grammar, 127
Lexicon, 128
Middle: Grammar, 428, 429
Lexicon, 246
Late: General, 60, 346, 347, 371, 405, 419
Grammar, 22, 23
Lexicon, 477
Recent: General, 133, 421, 425, 506
Phonology, 377, 385
Grammar, 88b, 279, 280, 303a, 378, 379, 381
Lexicon, 10, 174, 281, 361, 363, 380, 436, 530
Texts, 256, 424, 425, 426
ZOQUE
Early: Grammar, 570
Middle: Lexicon, 164
Late: General, 71, 131
Grammar, 200, 439d
Lexicon, 132, 200, 326, 477, 487
Texts, 200
Recent: Phonology, 180, 561, 564
Grammar, 161e, 299a, 564
Lexicon, 133, 220
Texts, 219, 562, 563

REFERENCES

Gates, 1924
Gibson, G. D., 1960

Kirchhoff, 1943
Summer Inst. Linguistics, 1960, 1964.

3. Inventory of Classificatory Materials

MARÍA TERESA FERNÁNDEZ DE MIRANDA

The following bibliographic selection comprises for the most part those works which have permitted the establishing of the present linguistic classification of Mesoamerican languages. In order to facilitate the treatment of the languages which are closely related to the linguistic families of Mesoamerica, the northern limit of the Mesoamerican cultural aggregate has been extended somewhat to the north until it coincides with the present frontier between Mexico and the United States. The southern limit has not been changed.

No work before the second half of the 19th century appears in the bibliography, since the norm followed for the selection of materials has been that of including only those that mark an advance in our knowledge of the linguistic relations of the area, or which indicate connections meriting more thorough investigations.

For each linguistic group, the pertinent works are arranged and annotated in chronological order. After each citation comes a partial commentary and, at the end of the article, a general evaluation. Cross references are frequent; they always refer to the place in which the complete bibliographic citation is found or to works which are closely related to it. To avoid the abuse of such references, it seemed preferable to put

into the bibliographic section the various linguistic classifications in addition to the bibliographic works to which we refer repeatedly in the commentaries, except in cases which provide only special information about particular languages.

The order followed in presenting the different groups, families, or isolated languages is as follows:

Hokan (Subtiaba, Serian-Tequistlatecan, Coahuiltecan, Yuman and Guaicurian Families)
Uto-Aztecan
Otomanguean (Otomian, Popolocan, Manguean, Mixtecan, Zapotecan, and Chinantecan Families)
Zoquean
Mayan
Mísquito-Sumo-Matagalpa
Totonacan
Tarascan
Cuitlatecan
Huavean
Xincan, Lencan, Jicaquean, and Payan

The criterion which governed the preparation of this article—and which has obliged me occasionally to be perhaps too categorical in judgments—is that of the rigorous application of the method of comparison and of reconstruction which alone seems to have supplied so far the greatest wealth of convincing proof of linguistic affinities.

HOKAN STOCK

Subtiaba Family

LEHMANN, WALTER
  1920 Zentral-Amerika. 2 vols. Berlin.
        By inspection of vocabularies forms
        a group consisting of Tlappaneca-Yopi,
        Maribichicoa-Guatajiaguala and Maribio
        (Subtiaba).

SAPIR, EDWARD
  1925 **The Hokan affinity of Subtiaba in**
        Nicaragua. *Amer. Anthr.*, 27: 402–35,
        491–527.
        Establishes the relationship between
        Subtiaba-Tlappaneco and Hokan by
        means of lexical proofs, phonology and
        especially morphology. Postulates in
        provisional form broader relations of a
        possible Hokan Siouan group.

RADIN, PAUL
  1933 Notes on the Tlappanecan language of
        Guerrero. *IJAL*, 8: 45–72.
        By means of the examination of Tlap-
        panec and Subtiaba materials, proves
        that both are subdialects of the same
        language. Includes a list of morpho-
        logical similarities between Subtiaba,
        Tlappanec and Hokan.

WEITLANER, ROBERTO J., AND IRMGARD WEIT-
LANER DE JOHNSON
  1942–47 Acatlan y Hueycantenango, Gro.
        El Mex. Antiguo, 6: 140–604.
        Shows by inspection of Tlappanecan,
        Popoloca-Tlappanecan and Subtiaba
        vocabularies that the two Tlappanec
        dialects, primarily the Popoloca, are
        more conservative than is Subtiaba.

Serian and Tequistlatecan (Chontal de Oaxaca)
Families

BRINTON, DANIEL G.
  1891 The American race: a linguistic classi-
        fication and ethnographic description
        of the native tribes of North and South
        America. New York. Ed. española:
        Buenos Aires, 1946.
        By inspection of vocabularies postu-
        lates a relation between Yuman, Seri,
        and Tequistlatec, and between Yuman,
        Seri and Guaicura.

  1892 Chontales and Populucas: a contribu-
        tion to Mexican ethnography. *8th*
        Int. Cong. Amer. (Paris), pp. 556–64.
        Shows by inspection of a lexical com-
        parison that Chontal of Oaxaca is re-
        lated to the Yuman family. Suggests
        that perhaps the Chontales of Guerrero
        may be related to the same family.

KROEBER, A. L.
  1915 Serian, Tequistlatecan and Hokan.
        Univ. California Pub. Amer. Archaeol.
        and Ethnol., 11: 279–90.
        Examines comparative vocabularies of
        Chontal, Seri, Mohave, and other Hokan
        languages. Points out some phonemic
        correspondences, in order to establish
        the unity of Tequistlatecan, Serian and
        Yuman.

Coahuiltecan Family

SWANTON, JOHN R.
  1915 Linguistic position of the tribes of
        southern Texas and northwestern Mex-
        ico. *Amer. Anthr.*, 17: 17–40.
        Examines lexical lists of Coahuiltecan
        languages in order to determine the pro-
        portions of mutual resemblances. Swan-
        ton feels that Karankawa, Coahuiltec,
        Comecrudo and Cotoname constituted a
        branch of Coahuiltecan, a group which
        appears to have had two main divisions:
        (1) Coahuiltec, Comecrudo and perhaps
        Karankawa, with which Atakapa was
        most closely related; (2) Cotoname and
        Tonkawa.

SAPIR, EDWARD
  1920 The Hokan and Coahuiltecan languages.
        IJAL, 1: 280–90.
        From inspection of comparative vo-
        cabularies, Sapir thinks that the Hokan
        and Coahuiltecan languages had a com-
        mon origin.

BRIGHT, WILLIAM
  1955 A bibliography of the Hokan-Coahuilte-
        can languages. *IJAL*, 21: 276–85.
        Supposes without demonstrating it
        that Naolan is related to the Hokan-
        Coahuiltecan languages and that per-
        haps it can be identified with Janambre
        or Tamaulipec.

Yuman and Guaicurian Families

BRINTON, DANIEL G.
  1891 *See* Serian and Tequistlatecan fam-
        ilies.

BELMAR, FRANCISCO
  1912 *See* Uto-Aztecan family.
        Includes Guaicura and Cochimi-Lai-
        mon in the Yuman or Nahuatlan family.

KROEBER, A. L.
  1943 Classification of the Yuman languages.
        Univ. California Pub. Ling., 1: 21–40.
        On the basis of a comparative vo-
        cabulary of Walapai, Mohave, Maricopa,
        Yuman, Kahwan, Cocopan, Diegueño,
        Akwa'ala, and Kiliwa, establishes the
        comparative phonetics of the Yuman

languages and an outlined reconstruction of the original form.

MASSEY, WILLIAM C.
1949 Tribes and languages of Baja California. *SW. Jour. Anthr.*, 5: 272–307.
Work with an historical emphasis. Includes classifications of the Yuman and Guaicurian language families.

Remote Relationships of Hokan

RIVET, PAUL
1926 Les Malayo-Polynésiens en Amérique. *Jour. Soc. Amer. Paris*, 18: 141–278.
By inspection of vocabulary and grammatical forms, establishes the relationship of the various Hokan languages (Coahuiltecan, Serian-Tequistlatecan, and Subtiaba Families) on the one hand, and numerous Malayo-Polynesian languages on the other. Hokan is shown to be related more to Melanesian than to Polynesian or Indonesian.

HARRINGTON, JOHN P.
1943 Hokan discovered in South America. *Jour. Washington Acad. Sci.*, 33: 334–44.
Quechua is compared with some Hokan languages: Yana, Chimariko, Choctaw, Salinan, Subtiaba, Pomo, Washo, Esselen, and sporadically, Shasta and Chontal. Presents some phonetic correspondences and a list of common morphological characteristics.

The affiliation of Hokan with the Yuman, Serian-Tequistlatecan, Subtiaban and Coahuiltecan families (Kroeber, 1915; Sapir, 1920, 1925; Radin, 1933) is generally accepted. Nevertheless, the strict application of the comparative method and of reconstruction has been scarce: Yuman (Kroeber, 1943) and the relation of this with Serian-Tequistlatecan (Kroeber, 1915) are exceptions.

The supposed relation of Hokan with Naolan (Bright, 1955) is not proved; neither is the relationship of Tamaulipec, Olive, Pison, Janambre and Maratino with the Coahuiltecan languages demonstrated. Their genetic identification offers great difficulties because they are extinct languages and because of the scarcity of data on many of the languages. The inclusion of Guaicura-Pericu in the Yuman family is doubtful (Brinton, 1891): according to prevalent opinion it does not resemble either Yuman or Hokan.

A possible tie of the Hokan languages with the Malayo-Polynesian on the one hand (Rivet, 1926), and of the Hokan languages and Quechua on the other (Harrington, 1943), has been proposed, but with no convincing proof.

UTO-AZTECAN FAMILY

BUSCHMANN, JOH. CARL, ed.
1859 Die Spuren der aztekischen Sprache im nördlichen Mexico und höheren amerikanischen Norden. *König. Akad. der Wissensch.*, 12: 819. Berlin.
By inspection of vocabularies and of some grammatical forms, tries to establish the relations of the Sonoran languages (Tarahumara, Tepehuan, Cahita, Cora) with Aztec, Tubar, Yaqui, Eudeve, Opata and Pima on one hand, and with Ute, Comanche, Shoshone, Hopi, Chemehuevi, Cahuilla, Gabrieleño, Juaneño and Kechi on the other.

1864 Grammatik der sonorischen Sprachen. 1a part, pp. 361–453; 2a part, 1869, pp. 67–266; 3a part, 1868, pp. 23–215. Berlin.
By means of an examination of phonetic systems and of some grammatical formations, tries to find Aztec characteristics in the Sonoran languages; furthermore, the study of the number system induces Buschmann to infer the resemblance of the four Sonoran languages with each of the languages included in the above work.

CHARENCEY, HYACINTHE DE
1883 Mélanges de philologie et paléographie Américaines. 195 pp. Paris.
Taking off from the relationship established by Buschmann (1859, 1964) by inspection of lexical comparisons and some grammatical formations, divides the Sonoran languages into two groups: 1) Oregonian, with Comanche, Gabrieleño, Shoshone, Ute, Hopi and 2) Mexican with Pima, Tarahumara, Tepehuan, Tubar, Yaqui, Eudeve, Opata, Cora and Aztec (pp. 3–36).

STOLL, OTTO
1884 *See* Mayan family.
Shows a relationship between Pipil and Aztec, by inspection of vocabularies.

BRINTON, DANIEL G.
1887 On the so-called Alagüilac language of Guatemala. *Proc. Amer. Phil. Soc.*, 24: 366–77.
Shows that Alagüilac is an almost pure form of Nahuatl, by inspection of the Alagüilac materials of San Agustin Acasaguastlan and the Nahuatl of Molina.

1891 *See* Serian and Tequistlatecan families.
Divides Uto-Aztecan into three branches: Shoshonean, Sonoran, and Nahuatlan. Includes a comparative vocabulary of Tarahumara, Pima, Nahuatl, Ute, Heve, Tepehuan, Opata, and Cora.

BELMAR, FRANCISCO
1912 Lenguas de la familia nahuatlana: su clasificación. *17th Int. Cong. Amer.*, segunda sesión, Mexico, pp. 238–50.

Examines pronoun forms of Mexican, Opata, Eudeve, Pima, Tepehuan, Tarahumara, Cora, and Cahita, in order to demonstrate the relationship between those languages.

SAPIR, EDWARD
1915 Southern Paiute and Nahuatl: a study in Uto-Aztecan. *Amer. Anthr.*, 17: 98–120, 306–28; *Jour. Soc. Amer. Paris*, n.s., 10: 379–425, 1919, 11: 433–88.

In order to demonstrate the unity of Uto-Aztecan, the following languages are compared morphologically and phonologically and systematic phonemic correspondences are established: Sonoran, Southern Paiute, Shoshonean, Cora, Pápago, Tübatulabal, Luiseño-Cahuilla, Mono, Pima, Huichol, Cahita, Tepecano, Hopi, Gabrieleño, Tarahumara, Fernandeño, Bankalachi, Gitanemuk, Tepehuan, Shikanyam and Serrano.

MASON, J. ALDEN
1917 Tepecano, A Piman Language of Western Mexico. *Ann. New York Acad. Sci.*, 25: 309–416.

Lexical and grammatical inspection of Tepehuan, in order to demonstrate that it has notable similarities with Tepecano and that it differs little from Upper and Lower Piman. It seems, Mason states, that the most distant members of the group, Tepecano of Mexico and Pima of Arizona, have a closer relationship to each other than Tepecano has with adjacent languages.

BOAS, FRANZ
1920 El dialecto mexicano de Pochutla, Oaxaca. *IJAL*, 1: 9–43.

A descriptive comparison which includes some lexical comparisons between the Mexican of the Valley and that of Pochutla.

SAUER, CARL
1934 The distribution of aboriginal tribes and languages in northwestern Mexico. *Ibero-Amer.*, no. 5, pp. 1–94.

Historically oriented study which treats of the identification and grouping of the tribes and languages of northwestern Mexico.

KROEBER, A. L.
1934 Uto-Aztecan languages of Mexico. *Ibero-Amer.*, no. 8, pp. 1–28.

Classifies the Uto-Aztecan languages on the basis of lexical comparisons and establishes some phonetic correspondences without postulating a reconstruction. It rejects the old Sonoran grouping of the Uto-Aztecan languages and divides the latter into the following groups: Shoshonean, Pima-Tepehuan, Cahita-Opata-Tarahumara, Nahuatl and a group of languages of uncertain affinities or unclassified for lack of proof. The linguistic position of Huichol is considered doubtful.

WHORF, B. L.
1935 The comparative linguistics of Uto-Aztecan. *Amer. Anthr.*, 37: 600–08.

Compares similar structures of roots in the Uto-Aztecan languages and reconstructs the proto-phonemes, demonstrating their reflexes in a few of the languages. Recognizes the existence of some small well-defined groups: Piman, Shoshone-Comanche, Ute-Chemehuevi, and Cora-Huichol. By finding great resemblances between Uto-Aztecan, Penutian, Totonac, Kiowa and Mayan, Whorf proposes grouping these into one large family, Macro-Penutian. However, he presents no proof to corroborate his hypothesis.

MASON, J. ALDEN
1936 The classification of the Sonoran languages. *In* Essays in Anthropology Presented to A. L. Kroeber, pp. 183–98.

Offers a classification of a geographical type of the Sonoran languages, followed by a "correction," in which Mason rectifies his opinions (this article was written in 1923) in accord with the more recent studies by Kroeber (1934), Sauer (1934), and Whorf (1935). Includes appendix by Whorf with the corrected classification of Mason and with some changes made by Whorf himself in the terminology and in the groupings. The following groups are included: Taracahitian, Coran, Nahuatlan and Piman.

WHORF, B. L.
1937 The origin of Aztec tl. *Amer. Anthr.*, 39: 265–74.

By means of a comparison of the various Uto-Aztecan languages, proves that the "tl" is a local development in Aztec or in central Nahuatl and not an original sound of Uto-Aztecan.

WHORF, B. L., AND TRAGER, G. L.
1937 The relationship of Uto-Aztecan and Tanoan. *Amer. Anthr.*, 39: 609–24.

On the basis of lexical and phonological proofs establish relationship between Uto-Aztecan and Tanoan. The authors point out, nevertheless, that in spite of the similarity of their structures, these languages are different in aggregate. This is also true for their phonetic systems. A comparison by systematic phonemic correspondences is presented for the various Uto-Aztecan languages, including the reconstruction of the preceding common stage.

WEITLANER, ROBERTO J., AND IRMGARD WEITLANER DE JOHNSON
1942–47 *See* Subtiaba family.
They offer a comparative list of Mexican dialects of Acatlan, Gro., Hueycantenango, Gro. (Pastor dialect), and Mexican.

WEITLANER, ROBERTO J.
1947 Un idoma desconocido del norte de México. *28th Int. Cong. Amer.*, pp. 205–27.
By inspection of vocabularies of Naolan, Pame, Hokan-Siouan languages, and Uto-Aztecan, finds some similarities between the first and the Cahita subgroup of the Uto-Aztecan family.

DAVILA GARIBI, J. IGNACIO
1951 ¿Es el coca un idioma taracahita? *In* Homenaje a Alfonso Caso, pp. 143–51.
On comparing scanty Coca case material with Tarahumara and Cahita, finds six substantives which are almost identical semantically and structurally; too few, it is judged, to affirm a relationship.

SHAW MATSON, DANIEL
1953 Comparación lingüística entre algunos idiomas de la familia yuto-azteca. *Mem. Cong. Cién. Mexicano*, 12: 181–90.
Finds lexical and morphological resemblances between Nahuatl, Papago, Tepecano, Tarahumara and Huichol, on examining the vocabularies of these languages.

The linguistic position of the Uto-Aztecan family as the southern branch of the Aztecan-Tanoan group is accepted in general by all of the specialists. More than a century ago, lexical similarities were found between some of its members (Buschmann, 1859) and, somewhat later, analogies in its grammatical structure (Buschmann, 1891) which permitted this author to create his "sonorische Gruppen" with the subsequent tripartite division into Shoshonean, Sonoran, and Nahuatlan branches (Brinton, 1891). The present linguistic distribution has been gradually attained thanks to various studies (Mason, 1917, 1936; Sauer, 1934; Whorf, 1936, 1937) and to a few works based on comparison and reconstruction (Sapir, 1915, 1919; Kroeber, 1934; Whorf, 1935; Whorf and Trager, 1937).

The Uto-Aztecan family is comprised of three divisions: Taracahitian, Aztecoid and Piman (McQuown, 1955), each with numerous members. It is difficult, however, to establish with absolute certainty the relations of many of the languages or dialects here grouped, for example Suma, Jumano, Lagunero, Cazcan, Coca, Tecuexe, Colotlan, Guachihil and Zacatec, because of the paucity of existing data for some, and for others there is doubt of the correct attribution of certain vocabularies to certain vanished tribes, and for all it is impossible to obtain more data because of their complete extinction. The analogies believed to have been discovered between Naolan and Cahita (Weitlaner, 1947) have not been demonstrated.

The attempt to create a large Macro-Penutian family (Whorf, 1935) is a very suggestive hypothesis that has not yet been proved.

OTOMANGUEAN GROUP

Otomian Family

CHARENCEY, HYACINTHE DE
1883 *See* Uto-Aztecan family.
By vocabulary inspection establishes the Pirinda-Otomi family, subdivided into Pirinda-Matlatzinca and Mazahua-Otomi (pp. 78–88). Affirms that Pirinda has some points of contact with the Mixtec, Totonac and Tarascan languages (pp. 3–36).

BRINTON, DANIEL G.
1897 On the affinities of the Otomi language with Athabascan dialects. *10th Int. Cong. Amer.* (1894), pp. 151–62.
By means of a vocabulary inspection, compares the Otomi, Meco, Mazahua, Pame, and Pirinda families with twelve Athabascan dialects. Discovers some mutual similarities and feels that a more intensive study may prove a possible relationship.

BELMAR, FRANCISCO
1905b *See* Mixtecan family.

CHARENCEY, HYACINTHE DE
1906 Sur les idiomes de la famille Chichimèque. *14th Int. Cong. Amer.* (1904), pp. 159–91.
Examines lexical and grammatical forms of Serrano (perhaps identical with Meco or Jonaz), Pame or Chichimeco, Otomi, Mazahua, Matlatzinca and Tepehua of Huaynacotla, Ver. It is established that Tepehua is an Otomi dialect, that Mazahua is somewhat removed from Otomi, and that Pirinda or Matlatzinca is apparently more different. The group is renamed Chichimec.

BELMAR, FRANCISCO
1910 See Tarascan family.

LEHMANN, WALTER
1920 See Subtiaba family.
By vocabulary inspection, forms a linguistic group of the Otomi, Chocho-Popoloca, Trique, Ixcatec, Mazatec, Chiapanec and Mangue languages.

SOUSTELLE, JACQUES
1937 La famille Otomi-Pame du Mexique central. *Univ. Paris, Travaux et Mémoires de l'Institut d'Ethnologie*, 26: 16–571.
By a lexical inspection and inspection of some grammatical formations establishes a close affinity between Ocuiltec-Matlatzinca, Pame-Chichimec and Otomi-Mazahua. Believes Matlatzinca-Ocuiltec is the closer to Otomi-Mazahua and that both constitute a central-southern group in contrast to the northern group formed by Pame-Chichimec.

ECKER, LAWRENCE
1936–39 Relationship of Mixtec to the Otomian languages. *El Mex. Antiguo*, 4: 209–40.
Examines some general and basic characteristics of the phonetics and structure of Mixtec and Otomi. Presents a list of phonemic correspondences to prove their relationship.

WEITLANER, ROBERTO J.
1936–39 Beitrag zur Sprache der Ocuilteca von San Juan Acingo. *El. Mex. Antiguo*, 4: 297–328.
In order to demonstrate the relationship between Matlatzinca and Otomi, studies vocabularies of the Matlatzinca dialects of San Francisco and of Mexicaltzingo, the language of San Juan Acingo and Otomi.

NEWMAN, STANLEY, AND ROBERTO J. WEITLANER
1950 Central Otomian I: Proto-Otomi reconstructions. Central Otomian II: Primitive central Otomian reconstructions. *IJAL*, 16: 1–19, 73–81.
A comparison by systematic phonemic correspondences of eleven Otomi and two Mazahua dialects with the objective of reconstructing Proto-Otomi and Proto-Mazahuan respectively. This is followed by another comparison of both proto-languages for the purpose of postulating a Proto-Otomi-Mazahua language (Primitive Central Otomian).

SOUSTELLE, JACQUES
1951 Documents sur les langages Pame et Jonaz du Mexique central (Hidalgo,

Queretaro, San Luis Potosí). *Jour. Soc. Amer. Paris*, 40: 1–20.
This article contains a vocabulary of the Pame dialects of Jiliapan and Alaquines compared with the Pame material of Soriano, and another of Jonaz of Soriano compared with present-day forms.

WEITLANER, ROBERTO J. (in collaboration with E. Arana Osnaya, J. Hasler, and O. Uribe)
1953 Proto-Otomi-Matlatzinca: Reconstrucciones de Proto-Otomi III. *Mem. Cong. Cién. Mex.*, 12: 199–206.
A comparison, by systematic phonemic correspondences, of Proto-Central Otomian with Matlatzinca-Ocuiltec and a reconstruction of the former common period. Reconstructions are not included.

BARTHOLOMEW, DORIS
1959 Proto-Otomian-Pame. M.A. thesis, Univ. Pennsylvania.
Comparison of systematic phonemic correspondences between Proto-Otomi and Pame. Preliminary reconstruction of Proto-Otomian-Pame.

1960 Some revisions of Proto-Otomi consonants. *IJAL*, 26: 317–29.
Revision of the phonemic system of Proto-Otomi (Newman and Weitlaner, 1950) with the addition of three other Otomian dialects. It is followed by a new comparison with systematic phonemic correspondences, and by a modified reconstruction of Proto-Otomian.

Popolocan Family

BRINTON, DANIEL G.
1893 On the Mazatec language of Mexico and its affinities. *Proc. Amer. Phil. Soc.*, 31: 31–39.
Brinton (1891) included Chocho and Mazatec within the Zapotec-Mixtec group. Here he rectifies this opinion and postulates, by inspection of vocabularies, the relation of Mazatec to two remote and independent groups: Chiapanec and "Costarricense" (Talamanca, Boruca, Bribri, Viceita).

LEÓN, NICOLÁS
1905 Los Popolocas. Conferencias del Museo Nacional de México, Sección de Etnología, no. 1, Mexico. Also in *An. Mus. Nac. México*, 2a ep., pp. 103–20.
As the result of grammatical and lexical comparisons (which are not presented) the existence of a relationship between Chocho, Popoloca and Mixtec is maintained.

1912 Vocabulario de la lengua popoloca, chocha o chuchona con sus equivalentes en castellano. *An. Mus. Nac. México*, Número extraordinaire dédié au 18 Cong. Inter. Amér., México, 58 pp.

Proves, by inspection of vocabularies, that there is no relationship between Popoloca of Puebla and the Popolucas of Veracruz and Sayula.

MECHLING, WILLIAM H.
1912 The Indian linguistic stocks of Oaxaca. *Amer. Anthr.* jn.s., 14: 643–82.

By inspection of vocabularies integrates the Mazatecan family with the Chocho-Popolocan, Mazatecan-Ixcatecan, and Trique languages.

LEHMANN, WALTER
1920 *See* Otomian.

GONZÁLEZ CASANOVA, PABLO
1926 Los idiomas popolocas y su clasificación. *An. Mus. Nac. Arqueol., Hist. y Etnol.*, 5a ep., 1: 497–536.

By means of the inspection of vocabularies and of some morphological formations, forms the Popolocan family with these: Popoloca, Chocho, Ixcatec, and Mazatec (?) languages.

WEITLANER, ROBERTO J.
1942 La rama olmeca del grupo Macro-Otomangue. *In* Mayas y Olmecas, pp. 33–35.

Examining the phonemic systems, consonant groups and lexicographical similarities (which are not included, because this is a summary), concludes that Popoloca, Ixcatec, and Chocho have intimate mutual relationships and that Mazatec shows a close affinity with them.

FERNÁNDEZ DE MIRANDA, MARÍA TERESA
1951 Reconstrucción del protopopoloca. *Rev. Mex. Estud. Antr.*, 12: 61–93.

A comparison, by systematic phonemic correspondences, of Ixcatec, Chocho, and Popoloca, with reconstruction of the former common stage. Mazatec was not included since it shows a more distant relationship.

GUDSCHINSKY, SARAH C.
1953 Proto-Mazateco. *Mem. Cong. Cién. Mex.*, 12: 171–74.

A comparison by systematic phonemic correspondences of four Mazatecan dialects and a reconstruction of Proto-Mazatecan.

1959 Proto-Popotecan: A comparative study of Popolocan and Mixtecan. *IJAL*, Memoir 15, pp. 1–118.

Comparison by systematic phonemic

correspondences of Proto-Mazatec with Ixcatec, Popoloca and Chocho, in order to reconstruct Proto-Popolocan, and of Proto-Mazatec with Proto-Mixtecan, in order to postulate the previous common stage, Proto-Popotecan. It contains, besides, the reconstruction of some grammatical features of this last proto-language.

HAMP, ERIC P.
1958 Protopopoloca internal relationships. *IJAL.*, 64: 150–53.

Places Chocho-Popoloca last in the series of splits in the Popolocan family, Ixcatec off from these at an earlier stage, and Mazatec off from these at a still earlier period—these splits being determined by inspection and structural weighting of shared structural innovations, innovations by addition or replacement, rather than by loss. Hamp characterizes such innovations as the "only criterion for genetic proximity."

1960 Chocho-Popoloca innovations. *IJAL.*, 26: 62

Emends and adds to list of common Chocho-Popoloca innovations presented in *IJAL*, 24: 150–53, and emphasizes the futility of classifications of languages based on "mere appearances." Structural weighting of all criterial items is essential.

FERNÁNDEZ DE MIRANDA, MARÍA TERESA, AND ROBERTO J. WEITLANER
1961 *See* Manguean family.

Manguean Family

BELMAR, FRANCISCO
1905b *See* Mixtecan family.

Examines the Chiapanec and Nagrandan vocabularies with the object of showing some relations and differences between these languages, on the one hand, and Huave on the other.

LEHMANN, WALTER
1920 *See* Otomian family.

WEITLANER, ROBERTO J., AND IRMGARD WEITLANER DE JOHNSON
1942–47 *See* Subtiaba family.

By the examining of semantic differences and similarities, as well as of some mutations, postulates that the separation of Tlappaneco-Subtiaba was after that of Chiapaneco-Mangue but before the Nahuatl emigration.

FERNÁNDEZ DE MIRANDA, MARÍA TERESA, AND ROBERTO J. WEITLANER
1961 Sobre algunas relaciones de la familia mangue. *Anthr. Ling.*, 3 (7): 1–99.

A comparison of old (in the majority) Chiapanec and Manguean materials, by means of systematic phonemic correspondences, in order to reconstruct Proto-Chiapanec-Mangue, and from this a comparison of the Proto-Chiapanec-Mangue with Proto-Popoloca (Gudschinsky, 1959) and with Proto-Mixtecan (Longacre, 1957) in order to postulate the Proto-Popolocan-Manguean stage.

Mixtecan Family

CHARENCEY, HYACINTHE DE
1883 *See* Otomian family.

BELMAR, FRANCISCO
1905a Indian tribes of the state of Oaxaca and their languages. *13 Int. Cong. Amer.* (1902), pp. 193–202.
Groups the languages of Oaxaca within one family, Mixtec-Zapotec, which is divided into two branches: (a) Zapotec, with Zapotec and dialects, Papabuco, Chatino and dialects, and Chinantec; (b) Mixtecan with Amuzgo, Mazatec, Ixcatec (a dialect of Mazatec), Cuicatec, Popoloca (Chocho), Trique, and Mixtec with various dialects.

1905b Lenguas indígenas de México. Familia Mixteco-Zapoteca y sus relaciones con el otomí. Familia Zoque-Mixe. Chontal. Huave y Mexicano. 374 pp. Mexico.
By means of an examination of phonetics, of the formation of words, of the grammatical and lexical categories, reaffirms the preceding grouping, adding the Otomi language to the Mixtecan division because of the notable analogies which it presents.

LEÓN, NICOLÁS
1905 *See* Popolocan family.

MECHLING, WILLIAM H.
1912 *See* Popolocan family.
By inspection of vocabularies, groups the Mixtec, Cuicatec, and Amuzgo (?) languages in a Mixtec family.

LEHMANN, WALTER
1920 *See* Otomian family.

GONZÁLEZ CASANOVA, PABLO
1933 *See* Zoquean family.

WEITLANER, ROBERTO J.
1942 *See* Popolocan family.
By study of phonemic systems, consonant groups, and lexicographical similarities (without including them, for this is a summary) it is determined that Trique, Mixtec, Cuicatec are related to

one another. Provisionally, Amuzgo is considered connected to the languages cited.

LONGACRE, ROBERT E.
1957 Proto-Mixtecan. *Indiana Univ. Research Center in Anthr., Folklore, and Ling.* Pub. 5; *IJAL*, 8 + 195 pp.
Comparison, by systematic phonemic correspondences, of Mixtec, Cuicatec and Trique (Amuzgo was not regularly included) and a reconstruction of Proto-Mixtecan. This is the first successful reconstruction of a tonal system and various grammatical traits of a Proto-Mesoamerican language.

MAK, CORNELIA, AND ROBERT E. LONGACRE
1960 Proto-Mixtec phonology. *IJAL*, 26: 23–40.
Comparison of 28 Mixtecan dialects, by systematic phonemic correspondences, and reconstruction of Proto-Mixtec from the previous Proto-Mixtecan stage on.

ARANA OSNAYA, EVANGELINA
1960 Relaciones internas del Mixteco-Trique. *An. Inst. Nac. Antr. Hist.*, 12: 219–73.
Comparison by systematic phonemic correspondences of Mixtec, Cuicatec, Trique, and Amuzgo, and a reconstruction of the common ancestor, in order to fortify conclusions based upon lexicostatistics.

LONGACRE, ROBERT E., AND RENÉ MILLON
1961 Proto-Mixtecan and Proto-Amuzgo vocabularies: a preliminary cultural analysis. *Anthr. Ling.*, 3: 1–44.
Preliminary analysis of a selection of the reconstructed vocabularies of Proto-Mixtecan and Proto-Amuzgo-Mixtecan, for the purpose of a protocultural reconstruction.

FERNÁNDEZ DE MIRANDA, MARÍA TERESA, AND ROBERTO J. WEITLANER
1961 *See* Manguean family.

Zapotecan Family

BELMAR, FRANCISCO
1905a *See* Mixtecan family.
1905b *See* Mixtecan family.
1910 *See* Tarascan.

MECHLING, WILLIAM H.
1912 *See* Popolocan family.
By inspection of vocabularies, forms the Zapotecan family with Zapotec, Soltec, and Chatino.

ANGULO, JAIME DE
1925 The linguistic tangle of Oaxaca. *Lang.*, 1: 96–102.

On the basis of a superficial lexical examination and of certain traits of monosyllabism, proposes a possible linguistic affinity between Zapotec, Chatino, Mixtec, Cuicatec, Mazatec, Chocho, and Chinantec.

RADIN, PAUL
1925 The distribution and phonetics of the Zapotec dialects: a preliminary sketch. *Jour. Soc. Amer. Paris*, 17: 27–76.

By inspection of vocabularies and enumeration of phonetic changes, groups the Zapotec dialects into six divisions: (1) Valle, (2) Tehuano, (3) Serrano, (4) Nexitzo, (5) Vijana, (6) Miahuatlán. Divisions 1 and 2 form a unit as opposed to 3; division 4 contrasts also with 1 and 2; divisions 4 and 5 show more points of contact with 3 than with 1.

ANGULO, JAIME DE
1926 The development of affixes in a group of monosyllabic languages of Oaxaca. *Lang.*, 2: 46–61, 119–33.

Studies some grammatical traits of Chatino, Mazatec, Chinantec, Chocho, Cuicatec, Mixtec and Zapotec. His opinion is that a brief examination is sufficient to prove that these languages are not semantically allied, perhaps not even related; nevertheless, they remain joined as a group or family by their morphological similarities. Inspects various comparative lists with the object of demonstrating the semantic relation between Mixtec-Cuicatec, Mazatec-Chocho, and perhaps Zapotec-Chatino.

VAN DER VELDE, PAUL
1933–34 Breve vocabulario comparado del idioma zapoteco. *Inves. Ling.*, 1 251–57.

It comprises three vocabularies: one apparently modern and two old ones.

ANGULO, JAIME DE, AND L. S. FREELAND
1935 The Zapotecan linguistic group: a comparative study of Chinantec, Chocho, Mazatec, Cuicatec, Mixtec, Chatino and especially of Zapotec proper and its dialects. *IJAL*, 8: 1–38.

They consider the languages cited in the title to be independent, although an examination of their similar morphological structures would permit grouping them. These structural and to a certain point semantic similarities, they think, are the result of linguistic borrowing and of mutual influences. Because of this they tend not to accept the hypothesis that these constitute a "linguistic family" in the usual sense, which implies genetic relationship. They prove (including a list of 100 semantic items with

equivalents in all the languages in question) that, semasiologically, they are too different.

SWADESH, MORRIS
1947 The phonemic structure of Proto-Zapotec. *IJAL*, 13: 220–30.

A comparison by systematic phonemic correspondences of three Zapotec dialects (with sporadic examples of another) which represent the principal divisions of Zapotec. Preliminary reconstruction of the common ancestral language.

1949 El idioma de los Zapotecos. *In* Los Zapotecos: monografía histórica, etnográfica, y económica. Univ. Nac. Autónoma Mex., México, pp. 415–48.

In the historical linguistics section, reproduces part of the previous work modifying slightly the reconstructions. Points out that the so-called Zapotec dialects—forms actually mutually unintelligible—ought to be considered as languages.

Chinantecan Family

MECHLING, WILLIAM H.
1912 *See* Popolocan family.
Chinantec, with its different dialects, constitutes the Chinantec family.

WEITLANER, ROBERTO J., AND PABLO SMITH
1957 Notas sobre la fonología del idioma proto-chinanteco: un informe preliminar. Summer Inst. Linguistics, Mexico. Unpublished.

Comparison by provisional systematic phonemic correspondences based on nine Chinantec dialects and a reconstruction of the Proto-Chinantec stage.

Although the unity of the Otomanguean group has not yet been wholly established, there are now various comparative and reconstructive studies on its 6 families in addition to others on interfamilial relationships.

In the Otomian branch the Otomi-Mazahua-Pame relation has been proven (Newman and Weitlaner, 1950; Bartholomew, 1959) and that of the first two with Matlatzinca-Ocuilteco (Weitlaner and others, 1953). The Popolocan and Manguean familes are already established, as are their relationship with the Mixtecan family (Fernández de Miranda, 1951; Gudschinsky, 1953, 1959; Fernández de Miranda and Weitlaner, 1961). The Mixtecan branch is also reconstructed (Longacre, 1957; Mak and Longacre, 1960; Arana Osnaya, 1960; Longacre and Millon, 1961), lacking only the determination of the exact position of Amuzgo. Some relationships between the Zapotecan languages have been proposed (Swadesh, 1957) and a revision and enlargement, including Chatino, is in preparation (Fernández de Miranda). Likewise there is an outline of Proto-Chinantecan (Smith and Weitlaner, 1957).

It remains, then, to finish the integration of this group, to round out internally the Otomian, Chinantecan and Zapotecan families and then to test the genetic relation between them and the unified sector Popolocan-Mixtecan-Manguean.

ZOQUEAN FAMILY

CHARENCEY, HYACINTHE DE
1883 *See* Uto-Aztecan family.
> By inspection of vocabularies subdivides the Zoque-Mixe family into two groups: Tapijulapan with two or three dialects, and Zoque-Mixe (pp. 69–78).

STOLL, OTTO
1884 *See* Mayan family.
> Through the examination of a short vocabulary of Pupuluca of Guatemala, Mixe, Tzeltal, and Tzotzil, he points out the possible relation of the first with Zoque and Popoluca.

BELMAR, FRANCISCO
1902 Lenguas indígenas del estado de Oaxaca: estudio del idioma Ayook. xxxiv + 205–26 pp. Oaxaca.
> Examines the phonetic systems and some grammatical formations of the languages that he includes in the Zoquean family; divides it into Zoque (various dialects) and Ayook (Mixe and dialects).

CALDERÓN, EUSTORGIO
1908 Estudios lingüísticos. I. Las lenguas (Sinca) de Yupiltepeque y del barrio norte de Chiquimulilla en Guatemala. II. Las lenguas de Oluta, Sayula y Texistepec en el Istmo de Tehuantepec, en México. Guatemala.
> Studies the vocabularies of the Oluta, Sayula, and Texistepec languages to show the differences between them.

BELMAR, FRANCISCO
1912 *See* Uto-Aztecan family.
> Includes Zoque-Mixe in the Yuman or Nahuatlan family.

MECHLING, WILLIAM H.
1912 *See* Popolocan family.
> Groups Zoque and Mixe in the Zoquean family.

RADIN, PAUL
1916 On the relationship of Huave and Mixe. *Amer. Anthr.*, 18: 411–21.

Also *Jour. Soc. Amer. Paris* (1914–1919), 11: 489–99.
> By inspection of vocabularies, of some grammatical formations and of phonetic systems, postulates the relationship between the Mixe-Zoque and Huave languages.

LEHMANN, WALTER
1920 *See* Subtiaba family.
> Based on an examination of vocabularies, establishes a linguistic group with Mixe-Zoque, Tapachultec I, Aguacateca II (?), Xinca, and Lenca.

RADIN, PAUL
1924 *See* Mayan family.

FREELAND, L. S.
1931 The relationship of Mixe to the Penutian family. *IJAL*, 6: 28–33.
> Semasiological study and study of some grammatical formations of Mixe and of various Penutian languages, to propose a connection of the first with Penutian.

GONZÁLEZ CASANOVA, PABLO
1933 Un idioma austronesio en México. *An. Mus. Nac. Arqueol., Hist. Etnol.*, 4a ep., 8: 203–10.
> By inspection of lexical comparisons between the Zoquean, Trique, and Cuicatec languages and those of Australia, Polynesia, and Melanesia, shows some similarities between both groups, insufficient, he says, to establish genetic affinity. Suggests, as an explanation of these similarities, the possible existence of a small Austronesian nucleus mixed with the indigenous population.

McQUOWN, NORMAN A.
1942 Una posible síntesis lingüística Macro-Mayance. *In* Mayas y Olmecas, pp. 37–38.
> By lexical comparisons and by comparison of the phonetic and morphological structure (which is not presented), assumes a probable relationship between Totonac-Tepehua and Mixe-Zoque, thus creating the Totonac-Zoquean family, which together with the Mayan, would make up the larger Macro-Mayan family.

FOSTER, GEORGE M.
1942 The geographical, linguistic and cultural position of the Popoluca of Veracruz. *Amer. Anthr.*, 45: 531–45.
> Reviews the various relations proposed for the Popoluca of Veracruz with respect to the rest of the languages of the Mixe-Zoque family. Considers as separate Popolucan languages those of the Sierra, of Texistepec, of Oluta and of Sayula, because of their mutual unin-

telligibility. The first two, he points out, come closer to Zoque and the last to Mixe.

WONDERLY, WILLIAM L.

1949 Some Zoquean phonemic and morphophonemic correspondences. *IJAL*, 15: 1–11.

Comparison by systematic phonemic correspondences of 10 Zoque dialects, Tapachultec, Popoluca of the Sierra and a Mixe dialect, in order to reconstruct the common previous stage. Also presents a graphic representation of the isoglosses of some morphophonemic changes.

1953 Sobre la propuesta filiación lingüística de la familia totonaca con las familias zoqueana y mayense. *In* Huastecos Totonacos y sus Vecinos, pp. 105–13.

Considers that a relation between the Totonac, Zoquean and Mayan families (McQuown, 1942) is not evident. Although they share some cognates, without the establishment of systematic correspondences it is impossible to affirm any relationship. Believes that there is, nevertheless, a somewhat greater similarity between the Zoquean and Mayan families.

The grouping of the Mixe, Zoque, Popolucas of the Sierra, of Texistepec, of Oluta and of Sayula, Tapachulteca I and Aguacateca II languages within the Zoquean family is recognized without discussion. Nevertheless, with the exception of a partial study based on the method of comparison and reconstruction (Wonderly, 1949) there is no work of a similar kind which treats of the family in its entirety and permits proof of the supposed affinity without room for doubt.

The relations of the Zoquean family with Huave (Radin, 1916), Xinca, Lenca and other languages situated to the south (Lehmann, 1920), although accepted by some linguists, has not been proven satisfactorily. The relationship with the Totonac and Mayan families (Radin, 1924; McQuown, 1942), besides the tie with Penutian (Sapir, 1929; Freeland, 1931), well enough received in general, are not solidly established.

MAYAN FAMILY

BRASSEUR DE BOURBOURG, CHARLES ÉTIENNE

1862 Grammaire de la langue Quichée Espagnole-Française mise en parallèle avec ses deux dialectes, cakchiquel et tzutuhil.... xvii + 246 pp. Paris.

Through inspection of Quiche, Cak-chiquel and Tzutuhil materials, points out the differences among them.

ADAM, LUCIEN

1878 Examen grammatical comparé de seize langues américaines. *2d Int. Cong. Amer.* (1877), 2: 161–244.

Includes the examination of some grammatical traits of the Maya and Quiche languages, in order to test their relationship.

CHARENCEY, HYACINTHE DE

1883 *See* Uto-Aztecan family.

Mentions some phonetic changes among the Mayan languages as well as other modifications which distinguish the Western group (Quiché, Cakchiquel, Pokomchí) from the Eastern (Mam, Tzeltal, Chortí). Offers a classification of the family and designates it as Mam-Huastec (pp. 89–121). In another chapter (p. 122 *et passim*) he also calls it the Tapichulane-Huastec family divided into Tapachulan and Quiche-Huastec. Finally, studies some grammatical formations of Quiche, Pokomchí, Maya, Tzotzil and Huastec.

STOLL, OTTO

1884 Zur Ethnographie der Republik Guatemala. ix + 176 pp. Zürich. Ed. españolas: Guatemala, 1938 and 1958.

By inspection of a comparative vocabulary of 16 Mayan languages establishes the sequence of the different divisions of the common trunk (Maya of Yucatan) into branches—Huastec, branches from Guatemala (with many subsequent subdivisions), Tzeltal (also subdivided afterwards) and lastly, Mopán.

1885 Supplementary remarks to the grammar of the Cakchiquel language of Guatemala. *Proc. Amer. Phil. Soc.*, 22: 255–68.

Shows certain phonological changes or retentions between Cakchiquel and Maya foreshadowing the possibility of postulating rules of change. Assumes that the Quiche group was one of the earliest branches to separate from the common Mayan ancestor.

CHARENCEY, HYACINTHE DE

1890 Étude sur la langue Mam. *7th Int. Cong. Amer.* (1888), pp. 389–403.

Through the examination of grammatical traits and of lexical forms of Mam, Quiche and Maya, tries to establish the position of the first within the Maya-Quiche family. Establishes that Mam comes closer to the western group, the most archaic and, more specifically, to Quiche.

73

BRINTON, DANIEL G.

1892 *See* Serian and Tequistlatecan families.

Indicates that the Chontal languages of Tabasco and those of Honduras belong to the Maya group.

SAPPER, KARL

1897 Das Nördliche Mittelamerika nebst einem Ausflug nach dem Hochland von Anahuac. xi + 436 pp. Braunschweig.

Includes a comparative vocabulary of 25 Mayan languages and dialects (many originating in Stoll) and one map of linguistic distribution that covers an area from part of Oaxaca and Veracruz to El Salvador.

BELMAR, FRANCISCO

1905a *See* Huavean family.

SAPPER, KARL

1912 Ueber einige Sprachen von Südchiapas. *17th Int. Cong. Amer.*, pp. 295–320.

Assumes that the Chiapas Guatemala highlands were the cradle of the Mayan peoples and from that area part of them emigrated to the lowland zone of the Gulf of Mexico, forming the present-day Huastecs. Includes a comparative vocabulary of Huastec, Chicomuceltec, Motocintlec, Jacaltec, and Mam.

GATES, W. E.

1920 Distribution of the several branches of the Mayance linguistic stock. *In* S. G. Morley, The Inscriptions at Copan, pp. 605–15. *Carnegie Inst. Wash.*, Pub. 219.

Presents a classification of the Mayance family and several observations, for example: Cholti and Chorti constitute in general one language only; Chol is more closely related to the Tzeltal branch (Stoll's opinion, 1884); Yucatecan Maya is at times distinct from the dialects of the south and frequently is similar to the mountain dialects of Guatemala, though rarely to Tzeltal-Chol, etc.

SCHULLER, RUDOLF

1920 Zur sprachlichen Verwandtschaft der Maya-Qu'itsé mit den Carib-Aruác. *Anthropos*, 14/15: 465–91.

By inspection of grammatical similarities and lexical comparison, tries to establish the relation between the Carib-Arawak and Mayan languages.

TOZZER, ALFRED M.

1921 A Maya grammar with bibliography and appraisement of the works noted. *Papers Peabody Mus., Harvard Univ.*, no. 9, ix + 301 pp.

Includes a classification of the Mayan languages and a critical bibliography.

RADIN, PAUL

1924 The relationship of Maya to Zoque-Huave. *Jour. Soc. Amer. Paris*, n.s., 16: 317–24.

By examination of some morphologic traits and of a short vocabulary, tries to establish the genetic relationships between Huave-Zoque-Mixe and Maya.

SCHULLER, RUDOLF

1925 La lengua Ts'ots'il. *IJAL*, 3: 193–218.

Compares by phonological, morphological, and lexical inspection, Maya, Quiche, Tzeltal, Tzotzil, Huastec, and Mam, in order to prove that Tzotzil belongs to the Maya-Quiche family.

LaFARGE, OLIVER

1927 A record of the expedition to Middle America, conducted by the Tulane University of Louisiana in 1925. *Middle Amer. Research Ser.*, Pub. 2, pp. 453–504.

Examination of the vocabularies of Tzeltal, Yocotán, and Chontal, on the one hand, and of Chañabal and Jacaltec, on the other. He thinks that Yocotán is only a dialectical variant of Chontal and that although it can be included in the same division as Tzeltal, its relationship is not as close as the existent one between Tzeltal-Tzotzil or Tzeltal-Chañabal.

SCHULLER, RUDOLF

1938 *See* Xincan.

BECERRA, MARCOS E.

1934 Los Chontales de Tabasco: estudio etnográfico y lingüístico. *Invest. Ling.*, 2: 29–36.

By inspection, compares the languages of Chontalpa, Tabasco with Maya, to prove that it is Mayan. Presents then a comparative description of Chontal, Chol and Maya and a classification of the Mayan languages.

KROEBER, A. L.

1939a Cultural and natural areas of native North America. *Univ. California Pub. Amer. Archaeol. and Ethnol.*, 38: 1–242.

Includes a classification of the Mayan family (pp. 112–114).

1939b The historical position of Chicomuceltec in Mayan. *IJAL*, 10: 159–60.

Comparison of the Mayan languages in order to establish that there is a closer relationship between Chicomuceltec and Huastec than between Chicomuceltec and the rest of the languages of the family. Assumes that Chicomuceltec may have been a remnant left by the Huastecs upon emigrating or a part of the emigrated group that returned.

HALPERN, A. M.
1942 A theory of Maya tš-sounds. *Carnegie Inst. Wash., Notes on Middle Amer. Archaeol. ana Ethnol.*, no. 13.

Classification of the Mayan family, based on a partial comparison of the systematic phonemic correspondences of most of the languages which it embraces; puts special emphasis on the reflexes of the palatals.

MCQUOWN, NORMAN A.
1942 *See* Zoquean family.

GOUBAUD CARRERA, ANTONIO
1946 Distribución de las lenguas indígenas actuales de Guatemala. *Bol. Inst. Indig. Nac., Guatemala*, 1: 63–76.

Classification of Guatemala languages indicating their geographic distribution.

MCQUOWN, NORMAN A.
1955 The indigenous languages of Latin America. *Amer. Anthr.*, 57: 501–69.

Comparison by systematic phonemic correspondences with reconstruction, of various Mayan languages: Cakchiquel, Chuh, Huastec, Mam and Yucatec.

1956 The classification of the Mayan languages. *IJAL*, 22: 191–95.

Classification based on the lexical comparison of Huastec, Mam and Yucatec, languages for which there are adequate descriptive materials. For the majority of the other Mayan languages the author used vocabularies he had collected which permitted the formation of preliminary phonemic outlines.

MAYERS, MARVIN K.
1960 The linguistic unity of Pocomam-Pocomchi. *IJAL*, 26: 290–300.

Comparison by systematic phonemic correspondences of four dialects of Pocomam and two of Pocomchí, with reconstruction. (Cf. Article 4 for conclusions based on this method.)

There are relatively few studies of the Mayan languages to which have been applied the methods of comparison and reconstruction: Mam, Huastec and Proto-Mayan, with the occasional inclusion of Cakchiquel, Chuh and Yucatecan (McQuown, 1955), the first two languages named and Yucatecan (McQuown, 1956), Pocomam and Pocomchi (Mayers, 1960) and representatives of various Mayan divisions (Halpern, 1942); this last is the most extensive although limited to reflexes of the palatals.

On the other hand, works abound which refer to simple lexical or grammatical comparisons which have been used for the concoction of numerous classifications (Bourbourg, 1862; Stoll, 1884; Charencey, 1883, 1890; Sapper, 1897, 1912; LaFarge, 1927; Kroeber, 1939). Among the principal classifications, cited in chronological order, are those of Stoll, 1884; Gates, 1920; Tozzer, 1921; Mendizábal and Jiménez Moreno, 1936; Kroeber, 1939; Mason, 1940; Halpern, 1942; Rivet, 1952; McQuown, 1956. All these exhibit major or minor differences among them, owing, evidently, to insufficient knowledge concerning various members of the family.

An attempt has been made to relate the Mayan languages with Huave (Belmar, 1905a), with this tied to the Zoquean family (Radin, 1942), with the Totonac-Zoquean family (McQuown, 1942) and with the Carib-Arawak languages (Schuller, 1920), without achieving a satisfactory demonstration of any of these relationships.

The supposition that the cradle of the Mayan peoples was the region of the Chiapas-Guatemala highlands (Sapper, 1912), is suggested again in a study on migration theory (A. Richard Diebold, Jr., "Determining the Centers of Language Groups, *IJAL*, 26: 1–10); although enjoying considerable acceptance, it needs the reinforcement of the linguistic test.|

MÍSQUITO-SUMO-MATAGALPA FAMILY

BRINTON, DANIEL G.
1895 On the Matagalpan linguistic stock of Central America. *Proc. Amer. Phil. Soc.*, 34: 403–15.

Considers the proposition that Matagalpa has no genetic relationships with its neighbors—Nahua, Lenca, Ulua and Mísquito—but that it is profoundly influenced by them in its lexicon.

LEHMANN, WALTER
1910 Ergebnisse einer Forschungsreise in Mittel-Amerika und Mexico, 1907–1909. *Zeitsch. für Ethn.*, 46: 687–749.

Establishes, by inspection of materials, the relationships among the Mísquito, Ulua, Sumo-Tawahka, and Matagalpa languages.

1920 *See* Subtiaba family.

Reaffirms the previous relationship by means of an examination of vocabularies, and presents a subdivision of the family that has been widely accepted.

CONZEMIUS, EDUARD
1929 Notes on the Mísquito and Sumo languages of eastern Nicaragua and Honduras. *IJAL*, 5: 57–115.

Studies a comparative vocabulary of

five Mísquito and five Sumo dialects to show the relationship between both languages.

1932 Ethnographical survey of the Mísquito and Sumo Indians of Honduras and Nicaragua. *Smith. Inst., Bur. Amer. Ethnol.*, Bull. 106, vi + 191 pp.

Treats of the different subtribes of the Mísquito and Sumo. Assumes that the former were originally a Sumo subtribe.

The Mísquito, Sumo, and Matagalpa languages with their corresponding subdivisions, appear to be grouped by various authorities into only one independent family (Lehmann, 1910, 1920; Sapir, 1929a; Rivet, 1952) or included as members of more extensive groups such as Mísquito-Xinca (P. W. Schmidt, 1926), Chibcha-Mísquito (Mendizábal and Jiménez Moreno, 1936).

In spite of the almost general acceptance of such relationships, some doubt should be raised concerning the mutual internal relationships or the relationship with the Chibchan group (Mason, 1940). It is certain that until now there has been no application of the comparative method which has allowed the certain affirmation of the partial or total affinity of the languages in question, nor of their relationship with geographically nearby groups.

TOTONACAN FAMILY

CHARENCEY, HYACINTHE DE
1883 *See* Uto-Aztecan family.

Without presenting evidence, asserts that the Totonac family shows surprising analogies with the Mam-Huastec family and, to a lesser extent, with the Chichimec languages (pp. 3–36).

BELMAR, FRANCISCO
1912 *See* Uto-Aztecan family.

Includes Totonac in the great Yuman or Nahuatlan family.

WHORF, B. L.
1935 *See* Uto-Aztecan family.

McQUOWN, NORMAN A.
1942 *See* Zoquean family.

ARANA OSNAYA, EVANGELINA
1953 Reconstrucción del proto-totonaco. *In* Huastecos, Totonacos y sus vecinos, pp. 123–30.

Comparison by systematic phonemic correspondences of three Totonac dialects and one of Tepehua; reconstruction of the common antecedent stage.

There have been various attempts to determine precisely the linguistic position of Totonac. Similarities have been found with the Otomian,

76

Zoquean, Mayan, Uto-Aztecan and Penutian families (Charencey, 1883; Belmar, 1912; Whorf, 1935; McQuown, 1942) without offering, in any case, definite proofs.

Up to now the only verified relationship is that between Totonac and Tepehua (Arana Osnaya, 1953).

TARASCAN

CHARENCEY, HYACINTHE DE
1883 *See* Otomian family.

BELMAR, FRANCISCO
1910 El Tarasco y sus relaciones con las lenguas de la familia Mixteco-Zapoteca-Otomí. *16th Int. Cong. Amer.* (1908), pp. 611–25.

The linguistic relationships of Tarascan are still unknown. It has been surmised, without demonstrating it, that there is a possible relationship with the Otomian, Mixtecan and Zapotecan families (Charencey, 1883; Belmar 1910).

CUITLATECAN

WEITLANER, ROBERTO J.
1939 Notes on the Cuitlatec language. *El Mex. Antiguo*, 4: 363–73.

The inspection of Ocuiltec and Cuitlatec materials (with the occasional inclusion of Otomi, Matlatzinca, Pame, Mazahua and Chinantec forms) permits the observation of some phonetic similarities and similarities in the syllabic structure of words. Morphologically, it is observed, both are quite distant; Cuitlatec appears to approximate the Hokan group although lexically it has little similarity to Tlappaneco or Subtiaba.

HENDRICHS PÉREZ, PEDRO R.
1946 Por tierras ignotas. *México*, 1: 260, 2: 253.

By inspection of materials, finds some similarities between Cuitlatec and Tlappanec, Xinca and, particularly, Quiche.

Cuitlatec is, to date, an unclassified language. It has been believed that some analogies were discovered between this language and Ocuiltec (Weitlaner, 1939), Tlappanec, Xinca and Quiche (Hendrichs, 1946).

HUAVEAN

BELMAR, FRANCISCO
1905a *See* Mixtecan family.

Through inspection of vocabularies and of some grammatical formations, finds relationships between Huave and the Maya-Quiche group, pointed out previously (Orozco y Berra, 1864).

RADIN, PAUL

1916   *See* Zoquean family.

1924   *See* Mayan family.

One objective has been to establish a direct relationship of Huave to the Mayan family (Orozco y Berra, 1864; Belmar, 1905a), or an indirect relationship through the Zoquean family (Radin, 1916, 1924), but none of these attempts has had a firm basis of comparison and reconstruction. Because of this, in spite of the almost general acceptance of the existence of this tie, the linguistic position of Huave is still uncertain.

XINCAN, LENCAN, JICAQUEAN AND PAYAN

CHARENCEY, HYACINTHE DE

1883   *See* Uto-Aztecan family.

Without presenting proofs, places Xinca and Populuca (Conguaco) in the Mam-Huastec family (pp. 89–121).

BRINTON, DANIEL G.

1885   On the Xinca Indians of Guatemala. *Proc. Amer. Phil. Soc.*, 22: 89–97.

Compares old vocabularies of the Xinca dialects (Sinancatan, Jupiltepeque and Jutiapa). Is of the opinion that Xinca belongs to a different linguistic group from Maya or Nahuatl.

LEHMANN, WALTER

1920   *See* Zoquean family.

Asserts that Xinca is related to Lenca, Mixe-Zoque, Chontal of Oaxaca and the Chumash-Salinan languages of California.

SCHULLER, RUDOLF

1928   Las lenguas indígenas de Centro América, con especial referencia a los idiomas de Costa Rica. xiii + 132 pp.

By lexical inspection, finds close relationships between Xinca and the Maya-Quiche languages on the one hand, and Carib-Arawak on the other. Also finds Maya-Quiche-Carib-Arawak elements in the Lenca, Cacaopera, Paya, Jicaque, Tlappaneco-Yopi languages, the languages of Costa Rica, of Western Panama and, in general, concludes, that the majority of the Central American languages are related to both groups.

The Xincan, Lencan, Jicaquean and Payan languages are most suitably treated together, not because their affinity has been proven but because of the assumed relationships that are thought to have been found between all or some of them. They have been included, for example, in a Maya-Quiche-Carib-Arawak group (Schuller, 1928), a Mísquito-Xinca group (Schmidt, 1926), the Penutian group (Sapir, 1929a) and a Paya-Lenca group, which includes Jicaque but not Xinca, considered as "a tie between Zoque-Maya and Chibcha-Mísquito?" (Mendizábal and Jiménez Moreno, 1936).

The relationship of Xinca with the Zoquean family (included at times in the Mayan-Zoquean) has been supported by various linguists (Lehmann, 1920; Rivet, 1952). The former suggests, besides, a linguistic link between Xinca-Lenca and Hokan languages. They have also found analogies between Xinca-Populuca of Conguaco and the Mayan family (Charencey, 1883). For none of these relationships have conclusive proofs been furnished.

For some, the fact that these languages are found in a zone of contact with other languages has favored a theory of numerous mutual influences (Lehmann, 1920); for some others they are treated as true mixed languages with double or multiple roots (Mason, 1940).

To summarize, one can say that the linguistic position of these languages has not yet been elucidated and that they ought to be considered, for the moment, as independent languages.

A total accounting of the linguistic situation of Mesoamerica lets us appreciate the relative scantiness of the advances achieved through the scientific use of the methods of comparison and reconstruction. The general classification of the different linguistic groups and families of Mesoamerica has remained almost static for about a quarter of a century, though one must recognize the total or partial strengthening of the postulated relationships between members of some families, and, occasionally, within the families.

The principal interest of scholars has been directed toward the consolidation of Otomanguean, a goal which it is hoped will be reached in the fairly near future.

The state of the rest of the linguistic families is not as gratifying. In Mayan, we are relying on some recent production which soon will be enlarged by the results of investigations now in process. There are also isolated modern works on the Yuman, Zoquean and Totonacan families; for the rest, on the other hand, from Uto-Aztecan to Mísquito-Sumo-Matagalpa, there have been no new contributions in twenty-odd years.

The linguistic position of the languages considered here as independent—Tarascan, Cuitlatec, Huave, Xinca, Lenca, Paya and Jicaque, among others—is as yet not elucidated.

Larger groups such as Zoquean, Mayan and Totonacan, or even more ambitious ones such as Macro-Penutian, which claims to encompass the Penutian, Uto-Aztecan, Mayan and Totonacan families, or such as the proposed relationships between Mesoamerican, and Malayo-Polynesian or South American languages, although accepted by some, do not have the necessary scientific backing. It remains to consider them as mere hypothetical areas which it would be advantageous to explore.

REFERENCES

Hervás y Panduro, 1800
Ibarra Grasso, 1958
Johnson, F., 1940
León, N., 1901, 1902, 1922
McQuown, 1960b
Mason, 1939, 1940
Meillet and Cohen, 1924
Mendizábal and Jiménez Moreno, 1936, 1937, 1939
Müller, 1888
Muñoz y Manzano, 1892

Orozco y Berra, 1864
Parra and Jiménez Moreno, 1954
Pimentel, 1874–75
Radin, 1919, 1944
Sapir, 1929a
Schmidt, P. W., 1926
Thomas, 1902
—— and Swanton, 1911
Vivó, 1941

4. Lexicostatistic Classification

MORRIS SWADESH

0. Introduction
1. Antecedents and history
2. Over-all classification
3. Tarasco
4. Otopamean
5. Oaxacan
6. Chinanteco
7. Huave
8. Subtiaba-Tlappaneco
9. Manguean
10. Cuitlateco
11. Misuluan
12. Chibchan
13. Yutonahuan
14. Lencan and Xincan
15. Mayan
16. Mixean
17. Totonacan
18. Coahuiltecan
19. Procedure
20. Lists for classifying the Coahuilan languages

0. INTRODUCTION. Prehistory, which has to be inferred from available evidence, can make good use of genetic classifications of language. Their special value results from the fact that human communities normally continue in the use of traditional tongues, and only rarely adopt those of their neighbors. In any event, linguistic change is slow and follows more or less traceable norms. Four main principles can be used: (1) Where different languages have certain kinds of similarities which must stem from a single earlier speech form, the peoples speaking them must have once formed a single community or at least have had very intimate and extended contact with descendants of that community. (2) Since degrees of similarity among related languages imply degrees of recency of separation or of continued contact after separation, inferences can be drawn bearing on the time and place of prehistoric unity and contacts. (3) Cognate words, discovered in the process of demonstrating the common origin of two or more languages, give evidence of old culture traits or features of the physical environment in their common period. (4) Some words, not having cognates among the languages of a related set and identifiable as loans from specific sources, give evidence of prehistoric culture contacts with other groups. The application of these principles to prehistory depends on the linguistic determination and evaluation of genetic affinities.

One form of linguistic classification may be described as purely compartmental. The languages of a given area are divided into groups considered to be unrelated among themselves and each containing only cognate tongues. The cognate sets may then be divided and subdivided into mutually exclusive subsets, each of which contains members considered equally divergent from all the members of the other parallel groupings. This conception, in extreme form, is based on a rigid model of language differentiation. It assumes that a language is homogeneous until the speech community splits, and that on splitting each fraction begins a period of separate development unconnected with the remaining segments. An alternate type of classification, the interlocking, recognizes degrees of affinity depending not only on the recency of separation but also on the amount of contact during the period of differentiation. This way of viewing linguistic diversification is in keeping with the known fact that linguistic communities develop regional variants, with relatively greater similarity among neighboring dialects and least similarity where there is the greatest geographic and social distance. Abrupt differences usually result from the disappearance of intermediate types, for example, because of the expansion of some at the cost of others.

Those who use the first form of classification do not necessarily deny the subtleties of language differentiation, although they may possibly minimize them to some extent. Their main reason for compartmentalizing may be operational, because it seems easier to make reconstructions based on the concept of coordinate lines of evidence pointing toward a monolithic prototype traced from equidistant sister languages; or because they lack confidence in existing techniques for subtler forms of reconstruction. Nevertheless, it is important for the nonlinguist prehistorian to know that there has been experimentation in procedures for evaluating degrees of affinity and of interconnecting languages according to presumed contacts through time. Lexicostatistics is one of several such procedures, important at this moment in the development of Middle American comparative linguistics because it has been considerably used in the last eight years, either as a principal or as an auxiliary technique of classification. Another method which has been much used, sometimes independently of and sometimes in correlation with lexicostatistics, is that of isoglosses.

If linguistic classification is to aid in the reconstruction of culture prehistory, it is desirable, insofar as possible, that it include clues to the time depth of the divergences. There cannot actually be any simple measure of time, because divergence reflects the combined effect of duration and degree of separation; a given amount of difference may come from, say, five centuries of complete lack of contact between two originally identical speech forms, or from a thousand years of partial separation. However, the problem can at least be narrowed by determining a minimum time depth. For example, in the hypothetic case just mentioned, it might be possible, from the comparison of the two languages, to deduce that the separation could not have been less than five centuries. In a set of related languages, among which one can establish minimum divergence time between each two of them, one knows that the group as whole has a time depth equal to or exceeding that of the largest minimum separation found anywhere in the complex. To obtain an upper limit of divergence time, one may compare the languages of the immediate group with other more distantly related tongues. Having obtained, through such procedures, maximum and minimum time estimates, one has some chance of relating the segmentation of the linguistic group to archaeologically known culture sequences.

Lexicostatistic glottochronology is the only technique so far which gives any sort of a direct measure of minimum time depth. Though based on long established linguistic principles, it is still a new procedure, needing further research and experimentation. Some scholars have held that linguistic change is not sufficiently predictable to permit any measure of time depth, and this is essentially the case with the great bulk of linguistic material. However, "basic" vocabulary has considerable stability and is relatively little affected by cultural changes. Lexicostatistic divergence measures, based on this portion of language, have by now been attempted in thousands of individual cases and have produced results that relate more or less well with other evidence. In consequence, it seems justified to hold that lexicostatistic time depths can be of value in studies of prehistory. It is of course necessary to use them with reasonable caution and to understand how they are obtained, to what degree the evidence favors or leaves in doubt their reliability, and what are the possibilities of future improvement. These matters are considered in the present article along with a report on linguistic classifications obtained with the help of lexicostatistics in Middle America.

The present status and outlook of glottochronology has been well stated by Hymes (1960, p. 3):

In the last decade glottochronology has excited international interest and acquired a literature of its own. To the anthropologist it promises a measure of time depth for language families without documented history, and yet another linguistic example of regularity in cultural phenomena.

It is tempting to think of reasons why glottochronology should not work, and some find it hard to accept the fact that it can. It is tempting for an anthropologist to use even provisional findings of linguistic relationship and time depth, and some find it hard to not to accept them uncritically. Either may be unfortunate. Extreme skepticism delays the maturity of glottochronology, and of lexicostatistics, the field of which it is so far a part. Rash use of provisional results may give way to rash disillusionment.

1. ANTECEDENTS AND HISTORY. From the very beginnings of comparative linguistics, it has been recognized that amount of change must be related to time, a principle which has been well stated, for example, in Sapir's words (1916, p. 76): "The greater the degree of linguistic differentiation within a stock the greater is the period of time that must be assumed for the development of such differentiation." This formulation lacks only a specific mention of degree of separation as an independent variable. Although this second factor has been recognized theoretically for almost a century (J. Schmidt, 1872; Schuchardt, 1900) and is on occasion used in the interpretation of otherwise conflicting comparative evidence, it has tended to be disregarded in general practice.

The use of quantity of divergence, either as a measure of time plus degree of separation or as an aid in the genetic classification of languages, was at first a matter of global judgment on the part of each scholar. In the early years of the present century we begin to encounter the application of statistical devices. For example, Kroeber, Barrett, and Dixon counted and obtained percentages of cognates between each pair of languages in a family to help determine subgroupings; that is, dialects showing a relative high per cent of cognates were considered to be closer together genetically than those with lower percentages. The same procedure applied to supposedly unrelated languages, in the hopes of clarifying prehistoric contacts, resulted in the discovery of three new genetic groups, Penutian, Hokan and Ritwan (Dixon and Kroeber, 1919). This type of lexicostatistics was employed from time to time in comparative works. Around 1930 it began to be used in studies of Middle American languages (for example by Weitlaner, cited in Longacre, 1957).

Sapir, beginning around 1915 (see particularly 1916), applied quantitative concepts in a very different manner. It consisted in drawing an analogy between the over-all divergences in a set of languages being studied with that found in historically known cases, for example, comparing the amount of phonetic, structural and phonological differentiation in some Amerindian group with that of Germanic, Romance or Indo-European, and inferring that the time of separation must have been equal to, greater or less than these instances. Although he did not actually count and calculate percentages of agreements, his approach was similar to that of present-day glottochronology in the fact that it used historical control cases, and permitted a judgment of the time-depth.

In the thirties, Czekanowski and others (see Kroeber and Chretien, 1937) took up the problem of the statistical measurement of affinities, using indexes of sameness and difference, based on sets of selected phonological, structural and lexical traits. And Loukotka developed a lexicostatistical technique for the classification of South American languages, which employed a standard list of 36 meanings and grouped languages according to the percentage of apparent cognates.

The impulse that led to the development of lexicostatistic glottochronology came from outside the linguistic field. In 1948, noting the success and importance of archeological dating by radioactive carbon, I sought a comparable technique based on a predetermined measure of the resistance to change in linguistic material. The most suitable part of language for this purpose seemed to be vocabulary, since it provides a large number of individual items, but these had to be non-cultural elements, "basic" words, long recognized by linguistic-science to be the least affected by the ups and downs of culture history. It was not expected that the index of time depth would prove even remotely accurate, but only that it would provide some kind of objective orientation for time estimates. The author supposed that there was some lower limit to the rate of retention, conditioned by the fact that language is the principal means of communication in every society and has to serve continuously through the generations, but he believed that changes sometimes occurred much more slowly. When he formed a diagnostic word list and applied it to some historically known control cases, that is languages in which material was available for an earlier and a later period, he was surprised to find some approximate agreement in the retention rates (Swadesh, 1951). Lees (1953) extended the test to several historic instances, using special caution to guarantee

the date of the samples compared and applying significance tests to the results; his results tended to confirm the existence of an approximately constant level of retention in basic-vocabulary lists.

The purpose of establishing an index of retention was to obtain a minimum measure of prehistoric separation time derivable from a count of similarities and differences in cognate historic languages. It was necessary on the one hand to determine an average or normal rate in basic vocabulary, and on the other hand to provide a technique for relating the languages under study to such a rate. The measuring instrument is the diagnostic word-list, consisting of a standardized set of semantic items, defined in a convenient operational language, whether English, Spanish, French, Russian (to mention some used so far) or any other. One obtains the most-used every-day expression for each item in each of the linguistic complexes being compared. Comparing two lists, one scores for agreements, that is, whether they do or do not use the same original element to express a given semantic item, sameness being judged apart from variations in phonetic or morphologic detail that may reflect normal alternations in a given stage of a language or historic changes, as long as they do not involve the replacement of one essential form with another. To obtain the rate of retention between two stages of a language, one earlier and the other later, one divides the logarithm of the per cent of retained items by the number of time units which separate the two samples. The average of retention rates in all the test cases is taken as the index for determining minimum time of separation in the unknown cases. The typical application to prehistory consists of comparing the diagnostic lists of two languages, known or supposed to have once been identical. Assuming independence of development, or, in other words, that the substitutions in one line of development agree only by accident with those in the other, a minimum separation time is obtained by dividing the logarithm of common retention by twice that of the unit retention. In practice, to avoid laborious arithmetic and mechanical errors, one uses precalculated equivalence tables (see Swadesh, 1960e, p. 103).

As might be expected, the use of lexicostatistic glottochronology has raised many questions of theory and practice, some of minor detail, others of broad principle. Particularly interesting has been the application of the method to many different language groups in all parts of the world, with important improvements in theory and technique coming out of this experience. Developments have been summarized and analyzed by Hymes (1960). From this work and from the nature of other subsequent studies, it seems evident that the scientific examination of the rate and nature of vocabulary change has come to be recognized as an essential problem of linguistics and the science of culture, and it is to be expected that the future will bring better and more accurate applications of glottochronology to the problems of prehistory. At the current moment, comparative linguists differ considerably in the place they grant to lexicostatistics in their work. Some regard it with considerable suspicion or reserve judgment for a distant future when it has been thoroughly tested from every angle or when it has undergone improvements. Others, like myself, while recognizing the need for continued study, consider it a valuable tool even in its present state. Needless to say, as is true of other evidence used by prehistorians, its indications need to be treated, not as immutably certain prehistoric events, but only as clues to be tested against other lines of evidence.

The application of glottochronologic lexicostatistics to Middle American languages began soon after its first discovery, and has continued to be used by a number of different scholars. In consequence this field is thus far one of the best studied lexicostatistically. It is also an area in which the technique has been subjected to serious critical evaluation by scholars who question either the validity of the method or specific results obtained with it in given cases.

The first study of Middle American languages in the light of glottochronologic lexicostatistics was a brief treatment of the Uto-Nahuan group, submitted by the present author to the Round Table Conference of the Sociedad Mexicana de Antropología in 1951. However, it was not published in its original form, but later expanded into somewhat more complete analysis of the group mentioned with a special focus on Nahua (1954c). In the meantime there appeared a paper relating Jicaque to Hokan (Greenberg and Swadesh, 1953) and another on the relationship of Huastec to Yucatec in the Mayan family (Swadesh, 1953). The method was applied to the Popolocan group by María Teresa Fernández de Miranda (1956). An interesting study of Mazatec dialect gradation as measured by lexicostatistics was made by Sarah Gudschinsky (1958a). Bright (1956) returned to the question of Hokan-Coahuiltecan interrelation ships in the light of glottochronology, including a consideration of the effect of insufficient material and inadequate knowledge of phonology.

Most significant for the development of lexicostatistics in the Middle American field was its inclusion in a project of the Consejo de Lenguas Indígenas, relative to the linguistic complex known as "Oto-Manguean," begun in 1956 in anticipation of the Oaxaca Round Table Conference of the Sociedad Mexicana de Antropología. The aim was to gather materials in the field and to make the necessary comparative study of them, in order to confirm or correct the theory of relationship among these languages. To this end, several students of the Escuela Nacional de Antropología did survey work in various parts of Oaxaca in the vacation period, December 1956 to February 1957, collecting vocabulary and grammatical notes along with data on place names, kinship and selected points of ethnography, in towns speaking Zapoteco, Mixteco, Chocho-Popoloca and Chinanteco. Comparable data from other areas were supplied by workers of the Instituto Nacional Indigenista and of the Summer Institute of Linguistics, stationed in various Oaxacan towns. These materials and published data were submitted to comparative study in a research seminar conducted by Robert J. Weitlaner, María Teresa Fernández de Miranda, and myself, in the academic year of 1957.

In July 1957, the Consejo de Lenguas Indígenas held a conference, called the Semana Lingüística (Linguistic Week), on the subject of Glottochronology and the Oto-Manguean Languages. Its aims were: (1) to examine certain criticisms which had been made as to the validity of glottochronology, as a basis of deciding to what extent this procedure could and should be used in the Oto-Manguean project; (2) to provide an opportunity for linguists to present studies on various languages; and (3) to help bring together the conclusions to be presented in the main linguistic report for the Oaxaca conference. Although it was intended to publish the papers and discussions in a single volume soon after the conference, this part of the plan has not yet materialized. A number of the papers were circulated in mimeographed form or have been subsequently published elsewhere. As a basis for the methodological consideration, Hymes prepared a paper on "The Strategy of Lexicostatics" and Longacre one on "Some Recent Criticisms of Glottochronology." Two sessions of the conference were devoted to the discussion of this subject, ending with statements by Pedro Bosch-Gimpera, speaking as an archaeologist, by Paul Kirchhoff, as an ethnologist, and by William L. Wonderly, as a linguist. A final resolution was then adopted, recognizing that glottochronology was evidently a valuable tool for prehistory, even though it had to be used with caution; the main reservations were (1) that the time

depths found are not absolute, but minimum, measures, and (2) that the method still needs considerable further research and experimentation. In other sessions of the week-long conference, members of the Oto-Manguean seminar presented papers on the glottochronology of Chinantecan, "Macro Mixtecan" (Mixtecan, Cuicatecan, Amuzgo and Trique), and Chatino-Zapotecan. These and additional lexicostatistic time depths were incorporated into the paper prepared for the Oaxaca Round Table Conference (Weitlaner, Fernández de Miranda, and Swadesh, 1960). In general, the previous Oto-Manguean hypothesis was confirmed, but it was suggested that Tlappanecan and possibly Huave should be included; Chinantecan appeared to be somewhat removed from the others, in terms of the lexicostatistic tests made.

The year 1957 also saw the publication of *Proto-Mixtecan* by Longacre, mentioning lexicostatistic counts made by Weitlaner, Fernández de Miranda, and Gudschinsky; and the presentation of Arana's thesis—(published in 1959), giving the lexicostatistic position of a number of dialects of Mixtecan in relation to each other and to Cuicatec, Amuzgo and Trique.

In 1958 there appeared Hale's study, *Internal Diversity in Uto-Aztecan*. Although it was apparently made without knowledge of the present author's previous work, the results agree to a remarkable extent (commented in Hymes, 1960, p. 23). In the Americanist Congress of that year, several papers involving lexicostatistics were presented. In one, by Arana Osnaya (published 1959b), the isolated Cuitlatec language was shown to be related to Uto-Nahuan and to Chibchan, and more distantly to other language groups. In another, read by title and not published, Yolanda Lastra attempted the placement of the Chibchan languages by lexicostatistics. In a third, Manrique (1958) gave an internal classification of the Oto-Pamean languages. As part of my paper on

84

the linguistics of the region between the high culture areas, I (1959a) attempted to give an over-all classification of American languages, using lexicostatistics as the criterion. This classification was radically revised before the publication of the paper, and was later further modified in three subsequent publications (Swadesh, 1959b, 1959c, 1960b); an additional modification, recognizing the continuity of "Macro-Mayan" and "Macro-Hokan," appears for the first time in the present article.

In 1959 two conferences gave occasion for the presentation of further lexicostatistic work. In the Chiapas Round Table Conference, held in San Cristobal de las Casas in May, McQuown presented the linguistic results of the Chiapas project of the University of Chicago; in it, lexicostatistics had been employed, along with other techniques: (a) to determine whether Tzeltal and Tzotzil should be considered as two languages or as a single dialect continuum; (b) to place Tzeltal and Tzotzil with respect to other languages of the Maya family; and (c) to discover phenomena of internal linguistic variation within each town. Weitlaner, Fernández de Miranda, and Swadesh (1959) employed lexicostatistics to confirm the relationship of Mangue to the Popolocan family and to Mixtecan using the cognate percentages not for dating but for determining degrees of relationship among the reconstructed proto languages of Manguean, Popolocan and Mixtecan. In another paper (1960c) I attempted to give the glottochronologic relations of all the Chiapas languages to each other. One of the new relations pointed out in this paper, that of Xinca and Lenca to Mayan and to Uto-Nahuan, was taken up in greater detail in a study by Roberto Escalante and Lorraine Faier (1959) presented before the Annual Meeting of the American Anthropological Association, held in Mexico, in December of the same year. On the occasion of this meeting, the Escuela Nacional de Antropología e Historia distributed a specially prepared pamphlet on the Indian languages of Mexico (Swadesh, 1959c), with a revised lexicostatistic classification.

In a monograph on the relations of the Popolocan family to Mixtecan, Cuicatec, and Trique, Gudschinsky (1959c) implied that these relations were far closer than any involving Zapotecan. This stimulated the present author to prepare a revised synthesis and evaluation of the evidence for internal grouping of the languages of the Oto-Manguean complex. Besides giving lexicostatistic figures and documentation, it examines structural and phonetic isoglosses, holding them to be in consonance with the lexicostatistics. Evidence, both lexicostatistic and isoglottic, was offered for the inclusion of Huave in a single continuum with Zapotecan-Mixtecan-Trique-Popolocan and Otopamean. However, by the time the paper appeared in print, continuing studies suggested the further inclusion of Chinantecan, Manguean-Tlappanecan, Lencan, Xincan, Mayan, Yuto-Nahuan and still other stocks. In a paper prepared for the Americanist Congress of Vienna and in a popular monograph (Swadesh, 1960b) a complex was proposed with the name of "Macro-Mayan" and which included the bulk of the languages of Middle America. In these same papers, a new synthesis was offered for all American languages, grouped into six major nets, related among each other and with farther relationship extending to all the languages of the world.

Toward the end of 1960 a thorough lexicostatistic study of the Mayan group was attempted (Swadesh, 1960d), characterized by full or nearly full diagnostic lists for all but two languages of the stock and a concise technique for indicating items counted cognate. The data was arranged in a form adapted to use in an electronic computer, and the calculations were made electronically. This made it possible and easy to include all possible correlations, since all of the 253 pairs among 23 languages could be computed in about an hour. Since the time factor has on occasion led to a limitation of the number of counts made, this procedure promises to improve lexicostatistic work in the future.

After the submission of this article and before its publication, glottochronological studies have produced some realignments of the relationships presented here. The most notable in connection with Middle American languages is the determination of a relationship of intermediate time-depth between Tarasco and the previously recognized Maya-Mixezoquean-Totonacan complex (Swadesh, 1966). As calculated by Arana Osnaya (1966), Mixezoquean, Totonacan, and Tarasco form a continuum in this order, for which she suggests the name Porhezoquean. Confirming previous notions, Mixezoquean is the closest to Mayan, and Tarasco to Quechua. Mayan, Porhezoquean, and Quechuan are thus adjoining divisions in the Macro-Mayan phylum. Zuñi is found to flank Maya as well as Tarasco, on the basis of the 41–50 mc. criterion, discussed farther on. The regrouping is indirectly supported by recent demonstration that Zuñi aligns with California Penutian (Newman, 1964) and Chipaya of Bolivia with Mayan (Olson, 1964, 1965).

Longacre (1966) has proposed a realignment of Amuzgo, separating it from Mixtecan and making it just another division of Otomanguean. His evidence seems to me to be based on a one-sided concept of common innovation, involving a reliance on a very few points of phonology without regard for the phenomena of isoglottic areal extension of similar features, which so often shape the total picture. This leaves his case inconclusive.

2. OVER-ALL CLASSIFICATION. Before the use of lexicostatistic techniques of classification, the languages of Middle America were divided among a series of broad groups, including Macro-Penutian, Hokan-Coahuiltecan, Uto-Nahuan (Uto-Aztecan), Mayan or Macro-Mayan, Misulpayan, Macro-Chibchan, along with certain isolated unclassified languages, like Tarasco, Cuitlateco, Jicaque, Guaicura. Some of the groups were well established, with a more or less developed theory of phonological correspondence among the member languages, a known characteristic structure

and numerous identified cognates; others were more or less tentative, based upon the observation of some structural feature, supported perhaps by a scattering of lexical similarities. Moreover, quite aside from the amount of scientific knowledge that had been accumulated, there were evidently great differences in the closeness of relationship. For example, even though both Hokan-Coahuiltecan and Uto-Nahuan could be supported by scientific evidence, it was obvious that the former was far more diversified and, by inference, represented a great deal more time depth. In some cases there were conflicting theories as to the affinities of the groups, and much skepticism as to the reality of certain relationships. In sum, the theories of several generations of comparative linguists had posed many problems which demanded solution. Ideas as to the precise mode of solving them varied. Some placed their main faith in attempts at reconstruction: if one tried to reconstruct a proto language and if the effort succeeded, this would obviously indicate genetic unity. Others thought that the best key was provided by isoglosses or perhaps the discovery of a set of common structural features, or a sufficiently good list of lexical agreements. Obviously, a combination of these criteria was worth more than any of them taken alone. At certain points quantitative problems would have to be considered, in order to determine whether greater or lesser degrees of affinity were involved.

The use of glottochronologic lexicostatistics gave a new aspect to the problem of language classification. The technique permitted a quick preliminary judgment as to the possibilties of relationship between two languages, obtainable by the simple comparison of a fairly short list of words from each of them; or between two families by taking lists representing at least one language from each of them. In this way it was possible to confirm McQuown's theory that Totonacan, Zoquean and Mayan were probably related to each other, and that Huave, considered by some to belong with Zoquean, stood at a distance from any of the other three (Swadesh, 1954b); further, that Chibchan was related to Yuto-Nahuan (*op. cit.*). However, such preliminary comparisons left open doubts due to uncertain cognate identification. This called for careful study of phonologic agreements covering not only the words contained in the 100-item diagnostic list but also a sufficient amount of additional material to establish or to at least make probable the historical reality of the assumed phonemic developments. It was also necessary to develop a structural theory for each linguistic group, to support the lexical agreements and to eliminate the possibility that the vocabulary similarities might be due to lexical borrowings alone.

Still other problems arose from the fact that not all the languages of each set are equally related to those of another grouping. Thus, Chinanteco appeared to be a long way from Zapotecan as long as it was compared with the Isthmus dialect, but proved to be not nearly so remote from that of Ixtlan. Again much depends on the discovery of the correct intermediate groups Thus, the comparison of Manguean with Mayan and Uto-Nahuan did not suggest itself as at all promising until each of them was compared with Lencan.

These facts account for the uneven progress of lexicostatistic classification of Middle American languages. The first efforts, aimed mainly at testing previous theories, shed new light on certain points of affinity while leaving others unchanged. Gradually something like a total picture was brought into focus, with some details still unclear or distorted. Even today (1961) we do not have the last word. New studies in comparative phonology and improved etymological knowledge of individual words will modify some of the present-day lexicostatistic counts. Furthermore, the application of the technique in thorough fashion

to areas in which we now have only a sampling, will doubtless cause some regrouping of the families. Nevertheless, we are closer to a definitive over-all classification than at any time so far.

If, as the evidence I have studied seems to show, the languages of Middle America are genetically related to each other and to those of the rest of America and possibly of the whole world, there can no longer be any question as to whether languages are related but only as to how closely. With reference to those of Middle America, with the exception of some for which we have so far been unable to find the necessary lexical data, we are able to offer a provisional classification placing them all within a single continous network. Supporting evidence has been published for much of the complex (see Swadesh, 1954b, 1960a, 1960c; Arana, 1959b), and some additional proof is given for the first time in the present article.

The affirmation of kinship is based on the existence of common elements far greater than could be produced by chance and in number and type not attributable to borrowing. If a critic (Longacre, 1961a) has described our evidence for Zapotecan-Huave kinship as "tantalizing and suggestive" but holds that "it may well be questioned whether or not such data . . . constitute a demonstration of the alleged relationship," it is evidently because he does not relate the problem to the statistical measure of the chance factor; nor does he propose any alternate technique. For similarities involving two or more phonemes pure chance would give approximately one or two instances in a list of 100 elements, but the case in point shows over 20, about 10 times more than the chance factor. Much remains to be done in the line of determining exact phonetic correspondences, structural divergence and semantic change, in order to make full use of the evidence for historical reconstruction, but the proof of relationship as such is already strong. The

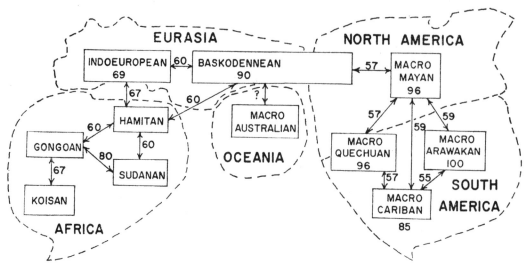

FIG. 1—THE WORLD LINGUISTIC NET. Divergences in minimum centuries.

critic mentioned also takes exception to the idea of "multilateral and gradient" relations as "a novel view of linguistic kinship—a view which all but jettisons any useful concept of linguistic relationship" (*op. cit.*, pp. 10, 9). Actually there is nothing novel about this principle, since it was formulated over 80 years ago and has been re-emphasized many times since then. Longacre himself recognizes the concept, for he says (1961a, p. 408): "Within a bona fide dialect net ... the situation is indeed somewhat as Swadesh posits, in that dialect borrowing at a relatively early stage of differentiation often leaves its traces in a bewildering web of isoglosses." Evidently the problem is not whether "multilateral and gradient" relations exist, but only whether those proposed are genuine. This question we leave to future scientific study, urging only that the strength of each case be considered on the basis of the actual evidence and not merely in the light of the enthusiasm of its proponent or the vehemence of its critic.

Tentative time depths lexicostatistically calculated among Middle American languages go as high as 95 minimum centuries. In certain difficult extreme points, where no serious attempt has yet been made to determine time depth, one supposes that the figure will prove higher.

The relationship among the languages takes the form of a more or less continuous network. The division of the net is possible only if one takes, more or less arbitrarily, definite criteria of divergence. For the purpose of fixing a limited number of major groups, which may be called phyla, we have taken 50 minimum centuries as the breakpoint, uniting languages in one set if they have 50 mc. or less divergence with respect to some other included language and making a separation where all the members of one group show more than 50 mc. of divergence with respect to all those in the other. This gives evidently 11 phyla in the world linguistic net, five in America. We break down the units of this net into major divisions using a criterion of 40 mc. The classification of Middle American languages is thus shown in figure 2. The further breakdown of each division is discussed in subsequent sections of the present chapter.

The diagrams show minimum divergence time as presently calculated. The figures within each box represent the largest amount as between extreme languages within the unit. The figures appearing on the dividing lines between divisions and on the double-headed arrows connecting phyla represent the minimum divergence between adjoining groups. Inter-phylum

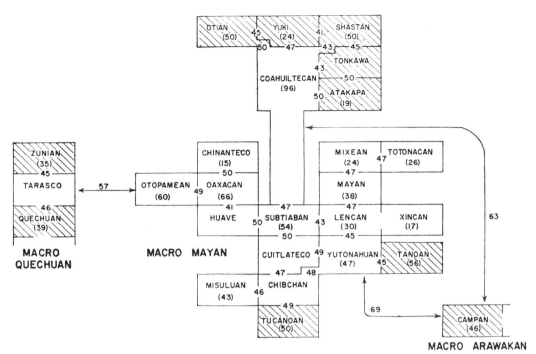

FIG. 2—INTERRELATIONSHIPS OF MIDDLE AMERICAN LANGUAGES

divergences have been calculated only in a few cases, hence are not necessarily the only contact points among them. In all instances, the unit of divergence is the minimum century (mc.), that is, we represent the least amount of centuries in which the divergence might have developed, as calculated lexicostatistically.

It will be seen that the divisions of phyla in our scheme agree in large part with the old long-recognized families and stocks. The broader groups of earlier theories in many cases are found to constitute continuous parts of one of our phyla. However, there are also points of contact among these continua which were not suspected previous to the use of the lexicostatistic method.

It has been found in the past that a re-examination of diagnostic lists after a period of detailed study frequently gives a different measure of lexicostatistic divergence, sometimes a little greater, often a little less than that previously found. Sometimes, too, new interrelations among the groups are found by bringing new lan-

guages into the study, since one of them may prove to be intermediate in the chain of relationship. Some day there will be enough study of the comparative phonology and morphological detail of the cognate languages to eliminate or at least to minimize uncertainties in the lexicostatistic counts. For the moment our results continue to be provisional.

In the discussion of the make-up of linguistic groups we often have to decide whether we are dealing with mere variants of one language or separate tongues. We have here adopted the criterion of 5 mc.; that is, if one can pass from one speech type to the next without exceeding this criterion, we speak of the dialects of a single language. If the measure is more than 5 mc. but not more than 10 mc., we speak of a "close complex." From 11 mc. to 25 mc. we use as criterion of a "family." In giving names to the complexes we use the -an ending (e.g., Popolocan, Mixtecan) for families and more disparate groups, but not for "close complexes."

It should not be forgotten that the sepa-

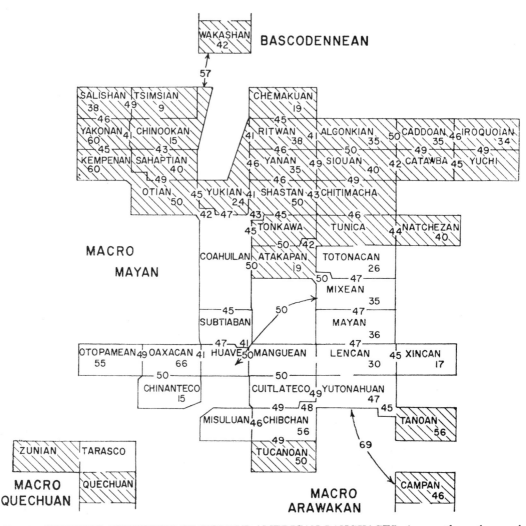

Fig. 3—INTERRELATIONSHIPS OF MIDDLE AMERICAN LANGUAGES. Among themselves and with other New World languages. Divergences in minimum centuries.

ration of the languages into phyla is relative. For example, we find that Tarasco-Matlatzinca is measured at only 7 mc. more divergent than the limit of 50 mc., which would have led to setting up a continuous phylum in the place of the present Macro-Mayan and Macro-Quechuan. Similarly Yutonahuan and Coahuiltecan approach Campan of the Macro-Arawakan net. Since the counts are tentative, it is not impossible that corrections in the future may modify the present picture.

As things stand, we find that the bulk of Middle American languages belong to a single continuum, called, purely for con-

venience, Macro-Mayan. This entity consists of 15 divisions which are located, in their entirety or in a substantial part, within Middle America; it also includes Tucanoan in South America and a number of divisions in North America, including Sapir's Hokan-Siouan; his Penutian; and his Algonkian-Mosan, except for Wakashan. In addition, we have in Middle America, a single language, Tarasco, belonging to Macro-Quechuan, a phylum located in South America except for Tarasco and Zunian (Zuni-Keres) in Mexico and North America.

The comparison of the relationship dia-

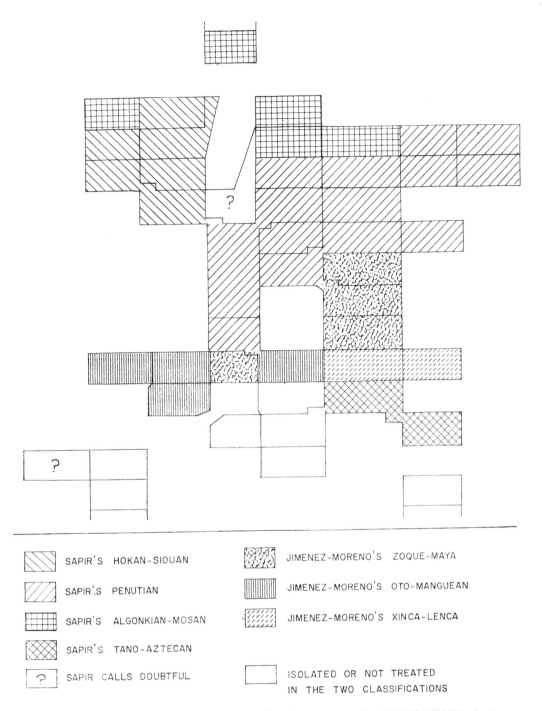

FIG. 4—A COMPARISON OF LEXICOSTATISTIC WITH OTHER CLASSIFICATIONS. Lexicostatistic classification shown by the collocation of the boxes, as in the larger diagram.

Legend:

- SAPIR'S HOKAN-SIOUAN
- SAPIR'S PENUTIAN
- SAPIR'S ALGONKIAN-MOSAN
- SAPIR'S TANO-AZTECAN
- ? SAPIR CALLS DOUBTFUL
- JIMENEZ-MORENO'S ZOQUE-MAYA
- JIMENEZ-MORENO'S OTO-MANGUEAN
- JIMENEZ-MORENO'S XINCA-LENCA
- ISOLATED OR NOT TREATED IN THE TWO CLASSIFICATIONS

gram, showing the order of linguistic affinities, with the geographic distribution of the peoples in historic times, leads to some inferences of prehistoric movements. One does not assume that all the linguistic differentiation took place in the present locations. The general scheme of affinities as seen here must have begun in the breadth

91

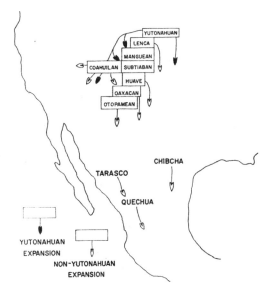

Fig. 5—PREHISTORIC MOVEMENTS OF LANGUAGES

of the northern continent above Mexico, rather than in the narrow funnel-shaped area of middle America. In the general movement southward, languages of the Macro-Quechuan complex must have anteceded those of Macro-Mayan, but Zunian and Tarasco moved less rapidly and continued in contact with Macro-Mayan groups. It is evident that Yutonahuan did not change location bodily but stretched out territorially, its vanguard maintaining contact with Cuitlatec and Chibchan while it still occupied large territories to the north. Various groups which had been to the north must have by-passed a number of Yutonahuan tribes to get to their present locations. The vanguard of Coahuiltecan languages intercrossed and in part went ahead of those belonging to Mixean and Mayan.

In all such attempts at inferring prehistoric movements from lexicostatistic data, it should be remembered that the more distant affinities are the hardest to calculate and that, in consequence, only a small part of the points of minimum divergence are as yet known. Without doubt, future studies will make possible improved arrangements of the data in better keeping

with the actual prehistory. In very tentative fashion, one might suggest a reorientation of part of the diagram, with Mixean, Mayan, Lencan and Yutonahuan more to the north and with languages like Oaxacan and Otopamean in the south alongside Chibchan.

3. TARASCO. Lexicostatistics confirms the isolated status of Tarasco, for counts attempted with various other languages have shown no affinity at less than about 45 mc. of divergence, the figure found with relation to Zuni to the north and with Quechua to the south. These more distant relationships place Tarasco in the phylum we have called Macro-Quechuan, the bulk of whose members are located in South America, with only Tarasco and Zuni-Keresan in the north. The affinity of Tarasco with Quechua and Aymara is reflected also in structure, since all of them show pronounced development of suffixing and some agreement in the kinds of suffixes used. In the field of phonetics, it is interesting to note that Zuni has glottalized stops alongside the simple, Tarasco has aspirates, whereas Keresan, Quechua and Aymara use all three. Presumably the triple contrast is archaic, whereas Tarasco and Zuni have each eliminated one of the types. Structural differences of Zuni and of Keresan with respect to Tarasco and Quechua may be due in part to long separation and in part to differences in trend even when they formed part of a single speech community; in technical terms, they were separated by a structural isogloss.

The closest affinity so far observed between Tarasco and Macro-Mayan languages is that of Tarasco-Matlatzinca, with a count of 57 mc. If this is at least approximately correct, the inference is that Tarasco anciently was in less intimate contact with Otopamean languages than with Zuni and Quechua. Presumably some dialects now lost were located in between early forms of the languages mentioned but with a stronger separation on the Macro-Mayan side.

We list below the words of Quechua and Tarasco which were counted cognate in obtaining the index of divergence. Zuni forms (marked Z.) are given where they appear to be also cognate. It is interesting to note the proportion of three-way agreements, which come to 7 per cent. With about a fourth cognates for Quechua-Tarasco and the same amount of Tarasco-Zuni, one would expect one-sixteenth to agree in all three, and the actual amount practically coincides with the expectable.

'what'	*ima*	*emáŋka*
'no'	*mana*	*ámpi*
'many'	*as-kha*	*kani-*
'woman'	*war-mi*	*wali*
'root'	*saphi*	*siráŋka* (Z. *lakʷimo-*)
'small'	*hu-cʔu*	*sapí* (Z. *¢ʔa-*)
'skin'	*qara*	*si-kʷiri* (Z. *¢ʔikkʷa*)
'blood'	*yawar*	*yuli-ri*
'grease'	*tika*	*tepári*
'horn'	*waqra*	*si-waŋkʷa*
'tail'	*cupa*	*chéti*
'feather'	*pura*	*phuŋkʷári*
'mouth'	*simi*	*pen-cúmi-*
'tongue'	*qalu*	*katámpa* (Z. *honni*)
'teat'	*kʔin-cu*	*i¢u-*
'die'	*wañu-*	*wáli-*
'kill'	*wañu-ci-*	*wán-ti-ku-*
'come'	*hamu-*	*hula-* (Z. *ʔi-*)
'say'	*ni-*	*ali-*
'moon'	*kila*	*kukála*
'star'	*quylur*	*hós-kʷa*
'hot'	*qʔuñi*	*holé-* (Z. *kʔali*)
'burn'	*kana-*	*kuli-* (cf. T. *khali-*, Z. *kʔusa* 'dry')
'road'	*ñañ* (*šnan)	*šaŋá-ru-* (Z. *ʔona-*)
'white'	*yura*	*urá-*
'night'	*tuta*	*cúri-* (Z. *tehli-*)
'cold'	*ciri*	*¢ira-* (Z. *te¢ʔe*)

4. OTOPAMEAN. The unity of Otomian, Matlatzinca-Ocuilteco, Chichimeco Jonaz, and Pemean has long been recognized. The lexicostatistical analysis of Manrique (1958) confirms the grouping, defines the relative position of its members in terms of degrees of divergence, and gives estimates of minimum time depth. Other studies (e.g., Swadesh, 1960a) place the group with respect to other linguistic entities. The lexicostatistic figures which follow are based on Manrique, as revised in the present volume.

Pamean consists of Northpame and Southpame, which are fairly divergent and have to be plotted separately because they show noticeably different relationship with reference to other subdivisions of Otopamean. Southpame comes within 30 mc. of Matlatzinca, thus permitting Pame and Matlatzinca-Ocuilteco to be joined in a single subdivision of Otopamean, which may be called Matlatzincan.

The greatest internal divergence is 55 mc., found between Chichimeca Jonaz and either Matlatzinca or Otomian. Pamean is intermediate, showing 34–36 mc. of divergence from Jonaz, 30–45 mc. in relation to the others. Southpame has evidently developed in closer contact to Otomian and Matlatzinca, since it shows divergences of 36 mc. and 30 mc. with these as against 45 mc. and 40 mc. for Northpame. The internal divergence of Pamean has been found to be 17 mc. That of Otomian 16; within Otomi, dialects show up to 8 mc. of divergence. Only a preliminary figure for Matlatzinca-Ocuilteco divergence has been determined; it is approximately 10 mc. The remaining division of Otopamean, namely Chichimeca Jonaz, is a single language without notable dialect divergences.

Of external divergences, the closest that has been observed is between Mazahua (Otomian) and Ixcateco of the Popolocan subdivision of Oaxacan. The measure is 49 mc., falling below our break-point, which places Otopamean in the Macro-Mayan network. Another outward point of contact is the measure of 57 mc. of divergence between Matlatzinca and Tarasco, providing the link between Macro-Mayan and Macro-Quechuan, as already mentioned.

5. OAXACAN. We propose the name Oaxacan for a group of languages almost entirely

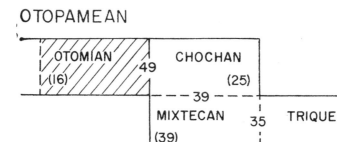

OTOPAMEAN

FIG. 6—INTERNAL AND EXTERNAL RELATIONSHIPS OF OAXACAN. Divergences in minimum centuries.

within the state of Oaxaca and occupying the bulk of its territory in colonial times. It includes eight languages or close complexes: Mazateco, Chocho-Ixcateco-Popoloco, Amuzgo, Mixteco, Cuicateco, Trique, Zapoteco, Chatino. The unity of various sets and combinations among these languages was recognized beginning long ago, but there were uncertainties as to which and how many languages belonged together. With the use of the lexicostatistic diagnostic technique, it was possible to marshall evidence for kinship and to define the sequence of the members within a single network.

Gudschinsky (1959c) gives the lexicostatistic internal divergence of Mazateco at 10 mc. Fernández de Miranda (1956) finds 12 mc. of divergence in Chocho-Popoloco-Ixcateco, in a triangle showing C-P 8 mc., P-I 12 mc., I-C 9 mc.; Mazateco of Huautla shows 23–24 mc. of divergence with reference to the former three languages. These findings confirm the relatively close unity of a family of languages, including the four languages mentioned, which may be called Chochan.

Mixteco is a large network of local dialects, with up to 15 mc. of divergence (Arana, 1959a). From one town to the next, the divergence is often no more than 2–4 mc., but at certain points the separation is

more marked. In this respect, Chigmecatitlan-Tlaltempan and Cuyamecalco-San-Juanico stand apart from each other and from the large remaining complex. Thus it might be correct to recognize three Mixtec languages, but common usage applies a single name to all of them. A relatively close farther relationship between Cuicateco and Mixteco is recognized by all scholars; Arana (1959a) finds the divergence to be 25 mc. at the closest, with respect to the Mixteco dialect of Mechoacan, and at the farthest 31 mc., with respect to Tlaltempan. Based on the smaller figure, Cuicateco-Mixtecan may be called a linguistic family. Amuzgo has been found to have 29–35 mc. of divergence from Mixteco, showing minimum disparity with reference to such dialects as Cuyamecalco and Huitepec, and maximum with regard to Mechoacan; Amuzgo-Cuicateco divergence was found to be 39 mc. Since no other language showed a divergence of 30 mc. or less with respect to any of the three and since they at their closest points fall within this figure, Mixteco, Cuicateco and Amuzgo may be regarded as a subdivision of Oaxacan; we call the group Mixtecan.

Slightly further removed stands Trique, with 34–39 mc. of divergence from Mixteco; 39 mc. with reference to Cuicateco and 45

94

with respect to Amuzgo. Its closest contact in Mixteco was found with relation to the Santo Tomas dialect, the farthest with respect to Cuyumecalco (Arana, 1959a). Longacre (1961a) strongly objects to the "separation" of Trique from Mixteco-Cuicatecan, even though the amount of added divergence is only 6 mc. In support of his position, he adduces counts of common phonetic features and of shared meanings among Mixteco, Cuicateco and Trique, showing that some patterns of greater and less agreements do not coincide with those of lexicostatistics. His use of this supposed evidence is merely negative, in that while it does not necessarily support the lexicostatistic findings, neither does it demonstrate his own theory. Moreover, Longacre has himself said (1961a, p. 401): "...the grain of truth in glottochronology is... that languages in their most intimate and and basic stocks of vocabulary TEND to change at about the same rate." But no one has ever found, and there is indeed evidence to the contrary, that phonetic changes take place at anything like a constant rate. Hence the number of phonetic isoglosses cannot be used as a measure of time nor as an index of degree of relationship, except in an extremely approximate sense. The relevance of Longacre's data on "shared meanings" as an index of divergence lacks a definition as to the extent to which it mixes basic vocabulary and culture terms, and the degree in which it may be influenced by the uneven amounts of material, in terms of number of dictionary items and of dialect variations, used in the study. In another portion of this critique (1961a, p. 12), Longacre in effect endorses the lexicostatistic findings. Thus, while admitting that "Glottochronologic counts have indeed established that Mixteco-Cuicateco share slightly more basic vocabulary than do any other two of the three languages," he holds that "...this is somewhat to be expected in that Mixtec and Cuicatec have apparently been in unbroken contact since the common Proto-Mixtec period." Now, in the normal interpretation of lexicostatistical evidence, divergence is precisely the product of time of separation as tempered by degree of continued contact. Hence the supposed objection amounts only to a suggestion as to the specific manner in which the divergences came about.

With reference to Zapotecan, there are insufficient figures on the dialects to give an adequate picture of their cohesions. The few available scores seem to confirm the existence of three or four separate languages in a close complex. The maximum divergence among them is about 20 mc. Chatino is separate, with from 18 to 24 mc. of divergence from various Zapoteco dialects, the closest being Miahuatlan, linguistically as well as geographically. Chatino and Zapoteco together thus form a family of languages constituting a subdivision of Oaxacan.

In the totality of Oaxacan, Mixtecan is central. It is removed from Chochan by 39 mc., as scored between Ixcateco and San Miguel Mixteco. With respect to Zapotecan, 36 mc. of divergence have been found between San Miguel Mixteco and Ixtlán Zapoteco. The closest Mixteco-Trique figure is 34 mc., as already mentioned. The largest internal divergence of Oaxacan as a whole seems to be 66 mc., found between Mazateco and Isthmus Zapoteco. Another extreme dimension is that of Mazateco and Trique, tentatively placed at 64 mc.

The closest external ties of Oaxacan are with Otopamean, Huave and Chinanteco, as represented by: Mazahua-Ixcateco, 49 mc.; Huave-Zapoteco (Isthmus dialect), 41 mc.; Chinanteco-Zapoteco (Ixtlán dialect) 50 mc. or Chinanteco-Trique 49 mc.

6. CHINANTECO. Divergences up to 15 mc. have been found among local forms of Chinanteco, which is apparently a close complex of several languages. Just how many is not clear as yet. The group is relatively isolated. Outside affinities of 49 mc.

and 50 mc. have been found for Ojitlán-Chinanteco with relation to Trique and to Ixtlán-Zapoteco, but the comparison is phonologically difficult. It is possible that future studies will show the glottochronologic relationship to be somewhat closer, or that it be set a little further off. In the latter case, Chinanteco would stand apart from the present Macro-Mayan network, but it seems improbable that it could turn out to be far removed.

We give below the possible agreements on which the lexicostatistic counts were made.

	OJITLÁN	TRIQUE	IXTLÁN
'I'	hna	yuɴh	inteʔ
'thou'	ʔni	reʔ/roʔ	luʔ
			(*liʔwi)
'we'	hnyaʔa	yuɴh/neʔ	—
'this'	la	nah	nui
'all'	lahi	niʔ	—
'one'	haɴ	ʔngo	—
'two'	ʔoɴ	wwih	—
'man'	¢a-ñiʔ	naʔu	—
'bark'	kʷoʔ	ki	—
'skin'	naloʔi-	nnih	—
'grease'	no	nami	—
'tail'	ci-koɴ	dune	ṣu-pana
		(*cukne)	
'ear'	rikʷa-	rakih	naka (?)
'nose'	ciʔyi-	dakiɴ	ṣinaʔ
'mouth'	ʔo	duʔwa	ruʔa
'knee'	ci-hni	cuh	ṣifi
'heart'	mi-ciy	nimaɴ	—
'hear'	ni	g-uni	iyenini
'know'	ñi	g-iniʔi	—
'rain'	hmi	gumaɴ	—
'fire'	yi	yaʔaɴ	yiʔ
'burn'	kaka	ko	—
'white'	ga¢i	te	¢i¢¢i
'night'	ci	zaʔ	—
'that'	haa	—	nua
'small'	piʔmiʔ	—	ṣ-kʷicutoʔ
'seed'	mi-¢i	—	fe¢iʔ
'root'	lu	—	lu
'flesh'	ci-hwi	—	¢itta
'teat'	citiʔ	—	ṣi¢iʔ

	OJITLÁN	TRIQUE	IXTLÁN
'drink'	ʔiɴ	—	iʔya
'stand'	siɴʔ	—	θu
'sand'	si	—	yuṣi
'hot'	ci	—	¢aʔa
'full'	cikaɴʔ	—	¢aʔ
'name'	la	—	laʔisiɴ

7. HUAVE. Our information is that there are only minor local dialect differences within Huave itself. External relations suggested previous to the application of lexicostatistics were with Mixean (Radin, 1916) and with Mayan and Totonacan (Jiménez Moreno and Mendizabal, 1930). The new technique confirms these relations, showing a divergence of 50 mc. with respect to Zoque and somewhat greater with languages of the other two groups. However, a much closer relation was discovered with Zapotecan of the Oaxacan division, 41 mc. having been found with Isthmus Zapoteco (Swadesh, 1960a). Other divergences within the 41–50 mc. range are 47 with Subtiaba and 50 mc. with Chiapaneco. Since the division to which the last mentioned language belongs occupies an intermediate position between Subtiaban and Lencan and the latter stands between Mayan and Yutonahuan, Huave has ties at two different points in the relationship continuum. This phenomenon, by no means isolated and paralleled for example by the place of Tocharian in Indo-European, is presumably due to a shift in the contacts among the languages of a network and the establishment of new contacts sufficiently early and of enough duration to affect the proportion of common conservation of a notable portion of basic vocabulary.

In order to test the correctness of the lexicostatistic conclusion, an examination was made of (a) general structural features, (b) specific structural elements, and (d) various points of phonology (in part published in Swadesh, 1960a, and in part not yet ready for publication). These several criteria confirm the intermediate position of

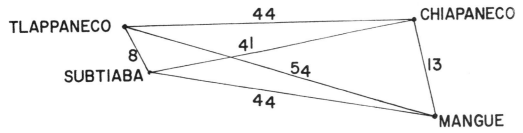

FIG. 7—INTERRELATIONS OF THE SUBTIABAN LANGUAGES

Huave, revealing important points of contact in both of the implied directions. The highest percentage of common structural features turned out to be with Otomian, on one side, and with Tzeltal Mayan, on the other. Of specific structural items, the greatest number of agreements was with Zapotecan, and, next in order, several other Oaxacan languages.

8. SUBTIABA-TLAPPANECO. We have here a close complex with an internal divergence of 8 mc., consisting of Subtiaba in Nicaragua and Tlappaneco on the Oaxacan border of the state of Guerrero in Mexico. The close relationship of the two languages was noted long before the use of glottochronology. As to farther connections, Sapir (1925) showed a kinship with his Hokan-Coahuiltecan. By the glottochronologic criterion, Subtiaba was found to show 49 mc. of divergence with respect to Jicaque, 47 mc. to Seri or Washo, and 45 mc. to Salinan. The dispersed location of these points of linguistic contact may in part be due to difficulties in obtaining an accurate count of cognates, but are certainly also connected with the very evident ancient dislocation of Coahuiltecan languages, as will be seen farther on.

In addition, the application of lexicostatistics has revealed a previously unsuspected relationship, even closer than that just mentioned, with another group not examined by Sapir, namely Manguean, made up of Chiapaneco and Mangue. A divergence of 41 mc. was found between Subtiaba and Chiapaneco at the point of closest agreement, 54 mc. between Tlappaneco and Mangue at the farthest, and

intermediate measures in the other two combinations (Swadesh, 1960a). Structural similarities support the relationship.

9. MANGUEAN. The two languages which make up this group, Chiapaneco and Mangue located respectively in the state of Chiapas (Mexico) and in Costa Rica, show 13 mc. of divergence. This represents simply a concrete measure of a close relationship previously noted. External affinities, in addition to those with Huave and Subtiaba as already mentioned, include 50 mc. between Chiapaneco and Cuitlateco.

10. CUITLATECO. An isolated language, Cuitlateco was first placed genetically by Arana (1959b) by means of the lexicostatistic procedure, applied with respect to a large number of different languages geographically related in all directions from the entity in question. The closest affinities were found with Paya of the Chibchan group and Nahua of Yutonahuan. A reexamination of the test vocabularies in the light of more recent new phonologic insights confirm these relationships, but reduce the divergence figures somewhat, and also indicate a connection on a similar level with Manguean. The divergence figures as now calculated are 47 mc. with Paya, 49 mc. with Nahua, and 50 mc. with Chiapaneco.

11. MISULUAN. This group consists of the Mísquito language, the close complex Matagalpa-Cacaopera, and another close complex Sumo-Ulua-Taguasca. The order of relationship of the three subdivisions is that indicated, with Matagalpa-Cacaopera forming the middle link of a chain relationship. The inner divergence of the middle complex is 10 mc., that of Sumo-Ulua-

Taguasca 11 mc. The largest divergence of the chain, between Mísquito and Ulua, is 43 mc.

Of external connections, the closest is between Ulua and Paya of the Chibchan division, divergent at 46 mc.

12. CHIBCHAN. Only preliminary lexicostatistic studies have been made of Chibchan. The maximum of internal divergence found so far is 56 mc., as between Guatuso and Cuna, but it is possible that somewhat greater divergences may be found. There seem to be three major divisions, two consisting of a single language each, Paya and Guatuso, while the third one embraces a fairly numerous complex of languages extending into South America. We tentatively suggest Raman as a possible name for the large main subdivision, based on the first language counting from the north. It shows internal divergences at least up to 50 mc., for Rama-Terraba.

The closest external ties of Chibchan include that between Paya and Cuitlateco estimated at 47 mc.; 48 mc. between Rama and Nahua; 46 mc. between Paya and Ulua of the Misuluan division; 49 mc. between Muisca and Coto of the Tucanan division.

13. YUTONAHUAN. Uto-Aztecan, Yutaztecan or Yutonahuan is a linguistic stock widespread in North America, as well as in Mexico and Central America. It has been studied for some time, and, in consequence, lexicostatistic counts can be made with considerable confidence. Doubtlessly because of this, two independently made studies produced almost identical figures (Swadesh, 1954c; Hale, 1958, 1959).

The largest divergence we have found is 47 mc. as between Monachi (Northern Payute) and Nahua. On the criteria of 30 mc. and 20 mc., the stock falls into four main branches, two of them with subdivisions, as follows:

1. Yutan. Max. divergence 38 mc. between Luiseño and Monachi.
   a. Nemmean: Monachi, Shoshoni-Co-

manche, Ute-Chemehuevi. 19 mc. between Payute and Monachi. The name is based on the word for "man."
   b. Tubatulabal.
   c. Cahuilla. Apparently a close-complex of several languages.
2. Hopi.
3. Tamaulipeco. This entity, represented by a short word-list of San Maratino, was formerly supposed to be related to Coahuiltean, but the few items of diagnostic vocabulary place it rather in Yutonahuan.
4. Nahuan. Maximum divergence, 45 mc. between Papago and Pochuteco Nahua.
   a. Papago-Tepecano. A close complex with 8 mc. of divergence.
   b. Sonoran: Cahita (Yaqui-Mayo), Opata, Guarojío, Tarahumara. Maximum divergence 24 mc. between Cahita and Tarahumara.
   c. Coran: Cora, Huichol. Divergence 15 mc.
   d. Nahua-Teco. A close complex, consisting of: a main grouping of Nahua dialects; Classical Nahua or Mexihca, which seems to be relatively separate from the foregoing; Pochuteco; Caxcán, Teco-Tecoxquin and other forms now lost, and not accurately placed. Divergence is 15 mc. for the first three components.

The closest external relations include: Hopi with Tano 45 mc.; Nahua with Lenca 45 mc.; Nahua with Paya of the Chibchan division, 48 mc.; Nahua with Cuitlateco 49 mc.

14. LENCAN AND XINCAN. Lencan (Swadesh, 1960c; Escalante and Faier, 1959) consists of two languages, Lenca and Chilanga, with a divergence provisionally estimated at 20 mc. External contacts include a divergence of 45 mc. between Lenca and Nahua; the same figure between Chilanga and Xinca; 47 mc. between Lenca and Quiche of the Mayan stock.

Xincan has been studied in two samples, which are evidently distinct languages, divergent about 17 mc., even though they are known by a single name. These speech forms belong to the villages of Chiquimulilla and Guazacapan. The only relatively close contact so far found is with Lencan, as already noted.

Observations of phonologic correspondences of Lencan and Xincan with Mayan, Mixean, and Totonacan, serving as a guide in the comparisons, have been published (Swadesh, 1960c).

15. MAYAN. Although there has never been any doubt of the unity of the Mayan stock, scholars have differed in their theories of its internal classification. McQuown's study (1956) based upon ample knowledge of phonology and using the criteria of isoglosses, offers two possible arrangements, one "cautious" and the other "less cautious." It is evident both in the alternate solutions and in the detail of isoglosses that this is not an easy group to subdivide. By lexicostatistic criteria (Swadesh, 1960d), one finds an integration in every direction. The largest internal divergence, between Huasteco and Mame, is 36 mc. Our usual criterion of 30 mc. as a lesser break-point gives no subdivision; that is, there is no language and no grouping of languages which exceeds 30 mc. of divergence from all others. The criterion of 20 mc. divides Mayan into two parts, a small one consisting of Huasteco and Cotoque, with 10 mc. of mutual divergence, and a large one embracing all the remaining languages, with divergences up to 30 mc. If we then pass to 10 mc. as a norm, the result is to tie together a few sets of languages in close complexes, namely Yucateco-Lacandon (6 mc.), Tzeltal-Tzotzil (7 mc.), Chol-Chontal (7 mc.), Rabinal-Quiche-Uspanteco-Cakchiquel (8 mc.), Pokomam-Pokomchí (about 10 mc., but the count is uncertain), but there remain a large number of discrete entities.

To obtain a useful subdivision of the Mayan stock, it is convenient to take 14 mc. as the break-point for the subdivision

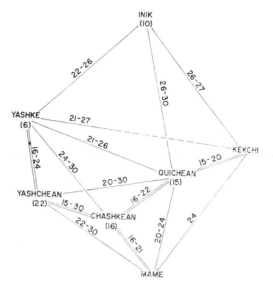

FIG. 8—INTERRELATIONSHIPS OF THE MAYAN LANGUAGES. Divergences in minimum centuries.

of the main division. The scheme is as follows:

I. Inik (10 mc.), that is Huasteco-Cotoque.
II. Winikan. Maximum divergence 30 mc.
   1. Yucateco-Lacandón or Yashke. Divergence 6 mc.
   2. Yaxchean. Maximum divergence 22 mc. between Chuh and Tzotzil. Composed of: Chuh, Tojolabal, Chorti, Chontal-Chol, Tzeltal-Tzotzil.
   3. Chaxkean. Max. div. 16 mc. between Jacalteco and Aguacatec. Consists of: Jacalteco, Ixil, Aguacateco, and Motocintleco.
   4. Mame.
   5. Quiché complex. Max. div. 15 mc. between Quiché and Pocomchí. Consists of: Quiché-Uspanteco-Cakchiquel-Rabinal and Pocomam-Pokomchí.
   6. Kekchi.

Minimum centuries of divergence of each language from each of the others are given in Swadesh, 1960d. The external relationships have not yet been worked out with care. As mentioned, the divergence between Lenca and Quiché has been estimated at 47 mc. and a similar figure has been found between Tzeltal and Zoque of the Mixean stock (see also Swadesh, 1954b).

16. MIXEAN. This group includes a complex of speech forms, known as Popoluca, Mixe, and Zoque in different areas. It is not clear to what extent these names correspond to notable linguistic boundaries. They may be merely names given in each region to languages of one more or less continuous family. The maximum divergence so far found is 24 mc. Besides these forms of Mixean, an evidently related vocabulary was once obtained from an old woman in the otherwise Mayan town of Aguacatán (Lehmann), which perhaps preserve the last remnants of another parallel linguistic branch. A lexicostatistic count of 35 mc. was obtained with reference to Zoque of Copainalá; since the measure was based on a very small sample, this figure should be corrected to 42 mc. However, it is possible that the vocabulary was merely a garbled recollection of Zoque. For this reason, we disregard the Aguacateco vocabulary in giving the internal divergence of Mixean The closest external contacts are with Mayan, as already mentioned, and with Totonacan. In both cases a divergence of 47 mc. was found.

17. TOTONACAN. This group, with an internal divergence estimated at 26 mc., consists of two languages, Totonaco and Tepehua. It is reported that each has its local variants, but there are no lexicostatistic data as to the amount of dialectal divergence.

18. COAHUILTECAN. As here defined on the basis of lexicostatistics (see §20), Coahuiltecan (or, more briefly, Coahuilan), consists of certain languages belonging to Sapir's Hokan-Coahuiltecan, plus Jicaque and Guaicura, not considered by him. Apart from a few counts made with altogether inadequate data, the maximal internal divergence is 88 mc. between Washo and Salina. The internal make-up is difficult to determine because of the frag-

100

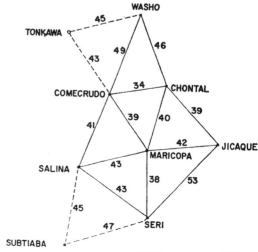

FIG. 9—INTERRELATIONS OF COAHUIL-TECAN LANGUAGES. Divergences in minimum centuries.

mentary data on several of the component languages. On the basis of available evidence as thus far studied, the following subdivisions are suggested:

a. Chumashan, with perhaps 46 mc. of divergence.

b. Salina-Antonino, with 6 mc. of divergence.

c. Serian, with 49 mc. divergence (Esselen-Seri), consisting of: Seri, Yuma, Esselen.

d. Quiriguan, with 36 mc. of divergence: Quirigua, Alazapa, Cotoname.

e. Comecrudo.

f. Clamcochean, with 28 mc. of divergence: Clamcoche, Coahuilteco.

g. Karankawa.

h. Chontal of Oaxaca.

j. Jicaque.

External contacts of Coahuiltecan are with other languages belonging to Sapir's Hokan-Coahuiltecan, with "Otian" (Miwok-Costanoan) and with Yukian. Thus we have: 42 mc. between Chumash and Mariposa Miwok; 47 mc. between Washo and Wappo Yukian; 43 mc. between Washo and Pomo (our Shastan); 45 mc. between Comecrudo and Tonkawa; 50 mc. between Comecrudo and Atakapa; 45 mc. between Salina and Subtiaba.

19. PROCEDURE. The lexicostatistic procedure can be used as an auxiliary device at various stages of comparative linguistic study, beginning with that in which data is scarce and theory elemental, and advancing to the point where all possible evidence is in and thoroughly analyzed, with a highly developed notion of phonological and structural correspondences and a full compilation of etymological evidence. It should be emphasized that in dealing with the native languages of Middle America, a good part of the terrain is still in early exploration and nowhere has a truly advanced stage of development been reached. Before the advent of lexicostatistics, serious scholars recognized the value of an over-all view and attempted to sketch out, as well as they could, the interrelations of the languages. The new technique both facilitates the enterprise and offers additional foundation for preliminary judgments, but the counts in such cases are less secure than in fields, like Yutonahuan and Mayan, where relatively advanced knowledge exists. In consequence, the results obtained in first estimates have often had to be modified after closer study. We take this to be an inevitable danger in all first explorations, which does not destroy but only limits their value. The counts we have cited in the present article are usually second or third efforts, representing improvements over initial explorations. Some perhaps approach finality, others still fall far short of it. In order to provide a basis for estimating the value of each count, it is proposed to describe in some detail the procedure used, indicating what conditions make for or impede the obtention of a firm score. We give, as an illustration of one of the more difficult problems of comparison, the data, procedure, and results connected with the lexicostatistic placement of Coahuiltecan languages. The discussion is not aimed at proving or determining the limits of the tendency toward a common retention rate in basic vocabulary but to give some idea to what extent our present estimates anticipate those which may appear after more complete study.

The first step in taking a glottochronologic count is to collect the diagnostic word-lists for two or more languages. Wherever possible, we have tried to obtain these from persons who know each language or from field linguists in a position to make the necessary tests of the correctness of each word. The norm requested was that for each item on the test list the common every-day equivalent in the language should be given. Where two words are in use, the more common one should be given; two or more equivalents are to be taken only when it is impossible to make a choice. A technically accurate translation was not called for, but rather the way in which the given concept would normally be referred to (for example, if a language uses the same word for "skin" and "bark," this element should be given in both cases and not a descriptive phrase specifying each item separately). When the words could not be obtained from a qualified expert, they were taken from published or manuscript material. Misunderstandings and difficulties in finding the proper equivalent of the items sometimes have led to errors, discovered only later or still unknown, but this is evidently a very minor factor. More serious is the problem of defective lists, due to the lack of data. In various instances short lists were used in first calculations, but could be replaced later by relatively complete ones. Experience in such cases shows that the short lists tend to include relatively more persistent words, and scores obtained from them generally give smaller divergences than those from full lists. In consequence, the practice was adopted of adding 20 per cent to divergences obtained from 50 or less word-pairs, and 10 per cent to those scored with 51–75 items. This has given better concordance between earlier and later scores, where it was possible to improve the word-lists, but it is not a mathematically derived or accurate correction.

The second step in lexicostatistics is to compare the corresponding words in each pair of lists and judge whether or not they are cognate in each case. This step is full of problems. The rest may be laborious but involves no uncertainties: one divides the number of presumed cognates by the total number of word-pairs to obtain a percent of correspondence; consulting the table of equivalences, one converts the percentage into the number of minimum centuries. If there are 75 or less word-pairs, one adds 10 per cent or 20 per cent to the mc. for the reasons already stated. As the number of languages in a group increases, there is a geometric increase in the number of pairs: thus, there are 45 pairs among 10 languages, but 190 in 20, and 435 among 30. The large amount of counting, calculating, and consulting of tables can be accomplished quickly with the aid of electronic computers.

The agreements which one attempts to score for lexicostatistics are words of common origin. In some cases they are easily recognized because of overwhelming correspondence of the entire sequence of sounds. Sometimes they are obscured by marked phonetic changes in one of both languages of the comparison, by reductions and transpositions, by the presence of formative affixes, the coalescence of the original common element with some other with which it once formed a compound but which may have become subsequently reduced to the size and appearance of a simple root. Two approaches have to be used to recognize cognates accurately. One is phonologic: to work out the rules of correspondence between the sounds of the two languages. The other is etymological: to build up a body of information on the development of each word in each language, using the data of related languages to provide clues as to what happened step by step insofar as it may be possible. Both approaches have been used in the lexicostatistic studies of

Middle American languages, but it is only to a limited extent that the necessary data is available as yet.

Not all languages present the same difficulties of cognate identification, since this is dependent upon the amount of reduction, transposition, and fusion that has taken place. The more distant connections are sometimes the more difficult to handle, but not necessarily. For example, Amuzgo is harder to compare with Mixteco than Maya with Wintun (of California), but the former gives a considerably higher percentage of cognates once one has recognized them.

There has been some tendency to reject unclear cognates in making preliminary cognate counts. This inevitably leads to increasing the divergence. When the same counts are later made with better knowledge, a higher count results. On the other hand, a very loose criterion leads to errors of overestimation.

There is a technique which is convenient in all cases and which helps avoid errors in difficult counts, giving some of the advantages of adequate phonologic and etymologic knowledge. It consists in making the count for a large number of languages together. The words for the same item in all the languages are examined together and one attempts to set up common forms for those elements which appear to be cognate. If there is more than one set of cognates for a given meaning, they are all set down and each assigned a convenient arbitrary symbol, say the first consonant in the reconstruction or some other letter if the first procedure would confuse two protoforms. The words in the lists are marked with the appropriate symbol. When the cognate count is made, or when the data are being prepared for processing in an electronic computer, one only needs to note the letter symbols, cognates being scored where the letters coincide for a given word. In this scheme, the same letter may be used for quite different elements in different word sets. There may be instances of the same original element turning up in different points in the list; for example, what is *sun* in one set may also appear as the expression for *moon, star,* or *hot.* Such cases reflect the development of the words and help fix etymologies, but do not affect the cognate count as such, since agreements are counted only when two languages use the same element for the same meaning.

The use of this procedure of identifying cognates is shown in connection with the problem of the Coahuilan languages, probably the most difficult in Middle America, not only because of phonological complications but also because of the great number of languages for which only very fragmentary materials are available. We included in the study languages which we presumed, from earlier study, would belong together in a single division of the relational network and others which might prove to be next nearest relatives. In addition, Campa and Nahua were taken in in the expectation that they would illustrate next farther relatives; and English was added to show how a very divergent language contrasts with those less remote. The results of the count changed some of the expected alinements in a greater or lesser degree.

Word-lists were obtained from fieldworkers in the case of Seri from Edward Moser; Jicaque from Doris Stone; Chontal from Viola Waterhouse. In other instances they were taken from published sources. The time of all the lists is modern, except that of Nahua, which is classical Mexihca of four centuries back. In the divergence scores, we have added 2 mc. to all those involving Nahua, that is, half the time difference, to equalize the temporal implication.

It will be seen that the phonology of the languages in our illustration is fairly complicated. We have also supposed strong reductions and fusions in some cases.

In addition to the material in the diagnostic word-lists, we were able to guide ourselves also by Sapir's comparisons (1917, 1920, 1925) and by other data in our files. However, it should be distinctly emphasized that we are uncertain about many of the cognate identifications. The aim is not to set down proven etymologies but to obtain a preliminary measure of degrees of relationship among a number of languages. By the same token the common forms shown for each set of words need not be accurately reconstructed; they are merely a mode of showing the possibility of common origin in the words. In a future revision, it is planned to include a number of additional languages, particularly Hokan and Otian; to correct the phonological rules; and to operate with fuller etymological data.

The lexicostatistic measures obtained among the languages are shown in the lower left half of Table 1. The upper right portion shows the number of word-pairs available for comparison in each combination, a figure needed to indicate where added caution is called for. We have also put a question mark after each score obtained with 20 word-pairs or less and an asterisk after those made with more than 20 but not more than 40.

An individual lexicostatistic measure based on very few items is not to be relied on, but where there are relatively consistent results for an entire set of languages, this can be given some weight. Thus Guaicura shows notable similarities with most of the Coahuiltecan languages. Except for the comparison with Cotoname, where no agreements were found in 8 word-pairs (the infinite lexicostatistic score shown in the table by 999), and except for three other instances in which the score goes above 100 mc. the measures cluster around 50 mc. and are in keeping with the general pattern of Coahuiltecan languages. Guaicura would thus seem to be rather definitely a language of this grouping. Klamkosh and Coahuilteco, which are a bit better provided with words for comparison, give notably more consistent evidence of belonging in the group.

TABLE 1—INTERRELATIONS OF COAHUILTECAN LANGUAGES AND SOME OTHERS

AVAILABLE WORD-PAIRS

	ENGL	ATAK	TONK	WASH	KARA	KLAM	COAH	COTO	COME	CHON	SERI	MARI	ESSE	CHUM	SALI	GUAI	JICA	SUBT	NAHU	CAMP
ENGL	ENGL	100	94	88	43	28	29	39	99	100	92	84	35	71	87	16	99	98	100	100
ATAK	76	ATAK	94	88	43	28	29	39	99	100	92	84	35	71	87	16	99	98	100	100
TONK	67	50	TONK	84	43	27	28	38	93	94	87	80	34	68	85	16	93	92	94	94
WASH	76	60	45	WASH	40	26	29	37	88	88	82	77	34	66	79	16	88	87	88	88
KARA	151	59	96	55*	KARA	11	17	22	43	43	41	39	20	36	41	9	42	42	43	43
KLAM	55*	96*	44*	91*	32?	KLAM	5	16	28	28	25	25	11	23	24	2	28	28	28	28
COAH	80*	80*	115*	38*	58?	36?	COAH	16	29	29	27	26	13	24	26	11	28	29	29	29
COTO	140*	124*	76*	60*	52*	47?	72?	COTO	36	36	37	35	18	32	37	8	39	39	39	39
COME	126	50	43	49	40	64*	50*	36	COME	99	92	84	35	71	87	16	99	98	99	99
CHON	90	76	67	46	54	55*	47*	44	34	CHON	92	84	35	71	87	16	99	98	100	100
SERI	71	71	71	67	60	46*	54*	96	45	50	SERI	79	33	65	86	14	87	91	92	92
MARI	96	90	60	50	64*	56*	47*	54	39	40	38	MARI	33	65	75	14	83	82	84	84
ESSE	115*	115*	49*	36*	68	41?	55*	60?	36?	49*	43*	32*	ESSE	35	35	10	35	35	35	35
CHUM	128	54	66	63	80*	60*	52*	72	69	69	69	88	36*	CHUM	65	14	71	71	71	71
SALI	76	71	60	96	56	64*	76?	56	41	47	42	43	36*	35	SALI	16	87	86	87	87
GUAI	72?	102?	47?	163?	44?	28?	47*	999?	55?	47?	102?	64?	124?	49?	16	GUAI	16	16	16	16
JICA	67	71	80	47*	80	54*	47*	76?	49	39	53	42	47*	54	42	28?	JICA	98	99	99
SUBT	109	60	67	49	96	64*	43*	140*	71	76	47	50*	59*	74	45	999?	49	SUBT	98	98
NAHU	69	87	69	69	61	78*	82*	93*	62	82	52	59*	82*	66	47	74?	51	65	NAHU	100
CAMP	76	67	60	80	64	115*	38*	218*	63	96	71	80	54*	84	71	72?	63	76	69	CAMP

DIVERGENCE IN MINIMUM CENTURIES

104

Our distant control case, English, shows scores of from 67 mc. to 151 mc. with respect to the other languages. The large variation, we presume to be due partly to the difficulty of identifying cognates accurately in languages which have been diverging so long and partly to the roughness of the measure at large time depths (a single presumed cognate may make a difference of 10 mc. in upper parts of the scale).

The divergences of Atakapa with respect to Coahuiltecan, from 50 mc. to 90 mc. not counting the shortest lists, of Tonkawa, 43–96 mc., of Nahua, 47–82 mc., and of Campa, 63–96 mc., are in keeping with what one might be expected in next farther relatives. In general, the variation between lower and higher limits is found to be in keeping with geographic position. For instance, Atakapa is closest to Comecrudo and farthest from Maricopa and Jicaque.

And Tonkawa is closest to Comecrudo and Washo, farthest from Jicaque. Only Subtiaba shows disparity with geography, having less divergence from Washo and Salina than from Chontal. This of course could be due to errors in the lexicostatistics, but might also reflect a prehistoric migration, separating it from old neighbors. Verification or correction should be sought in comparative linguistics by continued study and improved phonological, structural and lexical theory; and in other, independent lines of evidence for prehistory.

The general pattern of affinities in proportion to geographic location is found in large measure among the languages of the Coahuiltecan set. At points where the relation departs from this form, one should think of the possibility of population shifts at rates or in directions that broke the older conformation.

20. Lists for classifying the Coahuilan languages

English	- 'I/me'	- 'you (thou)'	- 'we'	T 'this'	T 'that'
Washo	N *le*	M *mi*	N *lem*	T *witi*	TH *hati*
Tonkawa	- *saaya*	N *naaya*	K *kewsaaka*	T *tee*	HW *wee, heʔe-*
Atakapa	- *wi*	N *na*	Y *yukit*	H *a*	Y *ya*
Karankawa	N *nay*	W *awa*	—	T *tal*	—
Klamkosh	—	—	—	—	—
Coahuiltec	—	M *hamin*	—	—	T *tu*
Cotoname	—	—	—	—	—
Comecrudo	Y *yen*	N *nana*	Y *yeynan*	T *tokom*	T *tom*
Seri	Y *ʔe*	M *me*	Y *ʔe*	— *ʔip-kix*	N *ʔin-kix*
Maricopa	N *ña*	M *maaña*	—	T *vada-*	N *ñaa-*
Esselen	N *ene*	NM *nemi*	N *leʔe*	—	NH *haynihi*
Chumash	N *noʔo*	P *piʔi*	K *kiku*	H *kay, he*	H *ho*
Salina	- *keʔ*	N *noʔ*	K *kaʔ*	N *na*	HW *wa, he*
Guaicura	- *be*	WT *tey, ew*	K *ke-*	T *ha-tupe*	Y *eyri*
Chontal	Y *iyáʔ*	M *imáʔ*	NY *iyank̆*	T *tyáʔa*	T *tiil'a*
Jicaque	N *naum*	P *hip*	K *kup*	H *huk*	H *hup*
Campa	N *na-*	W *awi-*	N *na-*	H *óka*	H *óra*
Nahua	N *ne-*	T *te-*	T *te..-n*	N *iniin*	N *inoon*
Subtiaba	N *ik-u, -lu*	- *ik-a*	N *hece-lu*	N *ka-la*	W *ka-wi*
Common	N **ʔe-ne*	M **ʔe-me-na*	N **ʔe-ne*	T **to/te*	T **to/te*
	Y **ʔe-ya*	T **te*	K **ke*	N **ne*	W **we*
		P **hi-pi*	Y **ʔe-ya*	H **he-ka*	H **ho*
		N **na*			N **ni*
		W **a-we*			Y **ye*

English	Q 'who'	Q 'what'	- 'not'	Q 'all'	M 'many'
Washo	Q khutina	Q khuŋathe	S es	M mile	- t?ekyu
Tonkawa	S sik	C hecuu	K kapay	- lum?at	- haa?as
Atakapa	S sa	- sok	K ha	M mon	W hew
Karankawa	—	—	MK kom	—	W wal
Klamkosh	—	—		—	
Coahuiltec	—	Q pin	M -aham	T tawahayo	WP apaw, ohaw
Cotoname	—	T tca	S sa	—	
Comecrudo	T tan, wawtek	T tete	MK kam	YM mawel, yawet	- yawet
Seri	Q ki?ya	C ?ašaré?eya	M m-	Q k-ooχo	K katχo
Maricopa	Q makye-	- av-	- walya		
Esselen	—			—	—
Chumash	- ayi			Y yula	W uhu
Salina	T ta	T tas-	K ko	S k-isili?p	K kaya, kaxʷen
Guaicura	—		R -ra	P pu	
Chontal	N nee	T tes	M mas	P pił-ki	W atáhu
Jicaque	Q pak	C cum	RM amasere	P pona	P peluk
Campa	N hánika	Q páita	RK ka, éro, te	M mároni	- oseki
Nahua	- aak	T λe	MK ka?amo	S iškic	M miek
Subtiaba	S sulu-lu	- mana	K a-	T tuwa	P ba-ñu
Common	T *ta S *so/se Q *qʷe N *ha-neke	T *tes Q *qʷe P *-pa C *he-cu	K *qhaw M *ma R *-ro S *?e-sa	P *pol/pel M *mor S *ese T *towa Y *yew Q *qhʷol	P *pel W *he-wel M *mel/mol K *ka

English	- 'one'	- 'two'	P 'big'	- 'long'	- 'small'
Washo	N laḱa	Q hesken	Y t-?iyeli	W t-?eme	C peheɕiŋ
Tonkawa	- wee?is	Q ketay	Q kʷaalow	W haway	W wixʷan
Atakapa	N ta-nuk	- cik	K hec	- mank	C hicon
Karankawa	SN naɕa	- haykya	Y yaan	—	Q kʷan, niktam
Klamkosh	—	—	—	—	
Coahuiltec	P pil	Q ahte	—	—	C šan
Cotoname	—	—	K katam	—	Q kʷosam
Comecrudo	P pe-	- ale-	K -kmat	W woskam	QK kisox
Seri	ST tašo	Q kokx	K kákox	K kaoksχax	K kisil, ?eke
Maricopa	S ?ašent	Q xavik	W vatay	Q aqol	—
Esselen	P pek	Q hulah	Y yakiske	—	Q ukus
Chumash	P paka	Q iškomo	K χax	—	
Salina	T t?oyu	Q xakis	K k-eɕaa?	Q kʷaka	Q skunthuy?
Guaicura	—	—	Q apanne		
Chontal	- ñúlyi	Q ukwé?	W ?awé	- ítuki	W awá
Jicaque	P pani	Q mat (*nqʷet)	Q penne	K kamn	CW cik-way
Campa	P aparo	Q apite	- ántiáro	- ántiáro	- -rihani
Nahua	S see	- ome	W weei	W weya-k	- tepi-ton
Subtiaba	N imba	Q apu	- -mba, -dagu	—	C risi, cici
Common	N *nokʷa P *paki S *se T *te	Q *qʷet	Q *qʷen W *way Y *yan K *qhec	W *wey Q *qhʷal	Q *qʷens W *wey C *cin K *kis

English	- 'woman'	- 'man'	- 'person'	- 'fish'	- 'bird'
Washo	K *t-hamomo*	WK *t-heliwhu*	N *t-ʔanu*	T *atʔapi*	T *sisu*
Tonkawa	- *kʷaan*	K *haaʔakoon*	T *tickan*	W *nes-walʔa-n*	KQ *koolʔa*
Atakapa	K *kis*	Y *sak-yol*	S *isak*	- *nti*	T *soksos*
Karankawa	—	- *usi*	—	- *am*	Q *kutn*
Klamkosh	—	K *ahaks*	—	K *kiles*	Q *kʷe*
Coahuiltec	T *tayaw, taw*	W *haw*	P *pil*	—	—
Cotoname	K *katam*	W *wawnahe*	- *hayma*	—	KQ *komyom*
Comecrudo	K *kem*	K *knax*	TS *estok*	T *atwis, pak*	K *xam*
Seri	N *nwam*	K *ktam*	N *nwike*	S *šixkám*	- *šik*
Maricopa	T *θeñaʔaka*	- *ʔiipáa*	P *paʔiipáa*	T *ʔaċi*	T *ciša*
Esselen	T *tanuc*	K *henoc*	—	S *šalul*	—
Chumash	N *eneq*	- *ohoy*	- *ku*	- *alilimu*	T *swiw*
Salina	N *leneʔ*	N *luway*	T *tam*	N *swaʔn*	T *saaxe*
Guaicura	N *anay*	—	T *ti*	—	—
Chontal	K *akáňoʔ*	- *akwéʔ*	S *asáns*	T *atyú*	K *akáʔ*
Jicaque	K *kep*	Y *yom*	- *mahaieesii*	K *kul*	T *cepay*
Campa	- *cináme*	- *širámpari*	S *ašáninka*	S *šima*	- *wánkitácari*
Nahua	- *siwaa-*	K *okic-*	T *ʎaaka-*	- *micin*	T *tootoo-*
Subtiaba	- *rab-agu*	N *rabu*	N *rabu*	K *eki*	T *diwi, ñuʔu*
Common	K **qhem*	W **hawen*	T **tami*	K **qel*	T **tow/ȼow*
	N **ʔeneqh*	K **qhen*	S **ʔese*	W **wan*	K **qam*
	T **ten*	Y **yol*	P **pen*	T **ʔatew*	Q **kʷe*
		N **new*	N **new*	S **šey*	

English	- 'dog'	- 'louse'	T 'tree'	S 'seed'	N 'leaf'
Washo	C *suku*	—	T *twetiš*	Y *yaka*	—
Tonkawa	Q *ʔekʷan*	- *hankapowełp*	Y *heeylapan*	K *xeel*	S *xaa-sey*
Atakapa	C *sul*	N *nin*	- *nes*	S *so*	W *te-was*
Karankawa	K *kis*	—	Q *akʷini*	—	—
Klamkosh	—	—	—	—	—
Coahuiltec	—	—	—	—	—
Cotoname	Q *kʷaw*	—	T *dopah*	—	—
Comecrudo	K *klam*	Y *ak*	Y *hay*	K *hekel*	S *sel*
Seri	K *ʔaχš*	- *ʔask, ʔai*	Y *ʔeʔe*	C *šiχiʔik*	S *istx*
Maricopa	K *ahara*	N *heʔel*(D)	Y *ʔaʔii*	—	WS *wal*(D), *saq*(D)
Esselen	C *šoʔošo*	—	Y *ii*	—	—
Chumash	C *ȼun, stin*	—	- *pon*	—	- *kap*
Salina	CK *xuȼay*	Y *ike*	Q *kelpa*	- *tanat*	S *sta*
Guaicura	—	—	—	—	—
Chontal	- *milya*	Y *aykʷíx*	Y *ʔeeh*	- *emés*	P *ípela*
Jicaque	C *cio*	T *tut*	Y *yo*	S *-setel*	N *lohan*
Campa	C *ocíti*	N *íne*	- *incáto*	S *-iȼoki*	S *-ši*
Nahua	C *cici*	T *atemi-*	Q *kʷáwi-*	- *ac-*	PS *-iswa-*, *ʎapal-*
Subtiaba	- *ruwa*	Y *yaha*	- *isi*	Y *yaha*	N *ina*
Common	C **cuqu*	Y **yakha*	Y **ʔe-yaqh*	S **sew*	S **selta*
	Q **eqʷew*	N **yine*	T **tew*	Y **yakha*	W **wałi*
	K **eqeł*	T **tem*	Q **qwe*	K **qhel*	P **pela*
					N **new*

107

English	N 'root'	P 'bark'	- 'skin'	P 'flesh'	- 'blood'
Washo	W *itewia*	—	Q *-ayike*	P *apši*	K *t-ašaŋ*
Tonkawa	—	—	Q *ʔek*	W *ʔawas*	- *ʔoon*
Atakapa	W *wil*	T *tal*	T *til*	- *al*	- *posk*
Karankawa	—	—	—	—	—
Klamkosh	—	—	—	—	—
Coahuiltec	—	—	—	W *ahaw*	K *ha¢*
Cotoname	—	—	—	M *kemas*	S *seh*
Comecrudo	Y *yemo*	T *paketle*	S *emol*	W *ewem*	K *kyal*
Seri	- *ʔeʔe-χái*	- *-naił*	- *ʔa-naił*	P *ʔapχási*	K *ʔait*
Maricopa	S *šamaa*	—	Q *ʔakʷely*	M *himat*	K *-iixʷet*
Esselen	—	—	—	—	K *mahʔana*
Chumash	N *alu*	—	—	- *saman*	K *axulis*
Salina	- *tepaso*	—	TP *spnat, ɾal*	M *maʔt*	K *aakat*
Guaicura	—	—	—	—	—
Chontal	Y *imé*	- *esmí*	S *esmí*	P *išik̓*	K *ahwa¢'*
Jicaque	S *-sil*	P *polohansi*	P *polok*	P *biš*	S *as*
Campa	- *pari¢a*	- *taki*	- *-mešina*	W *-wá¢i*	- *-iráha*
Nahua	N *-nelwa-*	P *-šipewal-*	P *ewa-*	N *naka-*	S *es-*
Subtiaba	- *ahmo*	- *osto*	S *sanhay*	N *nay*	KS *eʔedi, ecu*
Common	Y **yem*	T **tel*	P **pewal*	M **qhemat*	K **ʔaqʷhat*
	W **wił*	P **pewal*	T **tel*	P **pekhi*	S **ʔese*
	N **new*		S **ʔeseme*	N **nak*	
	S **šel*		Q **ʔeqʷel*	W **ʔawa¢*	

English	P 'bone'	K 'grease'	Q 'egg'	- 'horn'	T 'tail'
Washo	P *t-ipikeŋ*	- *t-itum*	Y *yakul*	Y *t-emesu*	—
Tonkawa	—	K *xaa*	N *haalol*	—	T *tan*
Atakapa	T *ci*	- *enk*	Q *ku*	- *noh*	T *tew*
Karankawa	—	—	T *dahome*	—	—
Klamkosh	—	—	—	- *teke-dolan*	—
Coahuiltec	—	—	—	—	—
Cotoname	—	—	—	Y *yomo*	S *asehuka*
Comecrudo	K *klemi, xi*	C *caw*	Y *yaw*	Y *yemo*	P *ep*
Seri	KT *šiχ-ítak*	SK *šixi-ʔáχ*	P *ipχ*	—	P *ip*
Maricopa	K *isaka*	SC *say*(D)	- *skawa*(D)	Q *iikʷé*	P *he*
Esselen	- *iya*	—	—	—	—
Chumash	- *se*	—	T *stum*	—	—
Salina	K *-axak*	- *upent*	T *teeteknel*	—	P *i¢heʔp*
Guaicura	—	—	—	—	—
Chontal	K *ekał*	- *manteka*	P *apiʔé*	- *kaacu*	P *ífpo*
Jicaque	P *posus*	C *icel*	PN *naypuk*	- *pac*	- *nan*
Campa	- *-tónki*	K *kehíci*	- *-i¢óki*	- *-¢éiki*	- *-ríši*
Nahua	- *omi-*	C *ciyawisso-*	T *-te-*	Q *kʷakʷawi-*	P *kʷiƛa-pil-*
Subtiaba	K *isu*	- *dasu*	N *raga*	- *šihi*(D)	S *siyu*
Common	K **ʔikheli*	C **cel*	Q **qʷew*	Y **yem*	P **hep̓aw*
	P **po*	K **khe*	T **ten*	Q **qʷew*	T **te*
	T **ton*		Y **ya*		S **ʔasey*
			N **nak*		
			P **pek*		

English	P 'feather'	K 'hair'	K 'head'	K 'ear'	Q 'eye'
Washo	—	- t-ayuš	K t-ihep	P -phisew	- wiki
Tonkawa	- ʔeʔeyon	K xʔaak	KT taakey	N henicxayʔan	L -yoxlʔoolok
Atakapa	- naw	T tes	- isat	N ani	L wol
Karankawa	—	—	—	—	—
Klamkosh	M am-dolkok	K ekya-aykuy	K okea	—	Q ikus
Coahuiltec	—	—	—	—	—
Cotoname	- kʷay	Q makʷat	Q makʷat	—	- arokʷan
Comecrudo	M ham	N elah	N elah	N ali	- huy
Seri	S šikína	K -kopχʷ	N ʔalit	M ʔásla	T ʔáto
Maricopa	—	K hiʔíš	- iiʔé	M ismályka	T iidó
Esselen	—	K khataseh	K khataseh	T tuksusu	—
Chumash	—	Q oqʷon	N nokš	T tu	T tuku, hutaš
Salina	S asax, syet	K s-poket, -kiht	- oophak	K iskoʔol(D)	- sokenet
Guaicura	—	—	—	—	—
Chontal	M imi	Q awáh	Q awáh	M asmás	- áʔu
Jicaque	M mik	N lala	Q bis	P beram	P pep
Campa	- -wánki	C -iši	T -ito	- -yempíta	Q -ki
Nahua	P iʔwi-	C ¢on-	Q kʷaai-	N nakas-	P iiš
Subtiaba	- gidusi	TC suhu, tasu	T ecu	M ñaw	T situ
Common	M *hemik P *pet/pel S *ʔasey	Q *axʷat C *con N *laqh T *tes K *qha	Q *axʷat N *noqh K *qhep T *ʔetu	M *asmalk T *tuk N *hane P *pel K *qor	P *pos T *to Q *qʷe L *wel

English	N 'nose'	- 'mouth'	T 'tooth'	T 'tongue'	- 'claw'
Washo	S šuyep	K haŋa	Y t-iyek	- matut	—
Tonkawa	Y yamʔacxan	K kala	YT hentaycan	N netxal	C sʔaac
Atakapa	W uc	K kat	T oc	N nel	C coh
Karankawa	—	—	Y e	—	—
Klamkosh	N -alwak	- -akʷoy	T dolonakin	N lean	—
Coahuiltec	—	—	—	—	—
Cotoname	Y yah	—	—	—	—
Comecrudo	Y yah	K hal	Y iy, heywuy	P ehpen	C esok, xayepo
Seri	- ʔaf	T ʔatén	T ʔatást	P ʔapl	—
Maricopa	Y iihú	- iiyáa	TY iidoo	P iipaly	—
Esselen	S hošis	—	—	—	—
Chumash	SN noxoš	K ík	S sa	N elew	- exway
Salina	N enenat	L elik	S suluknay	P ipal	—
Guaicura	N -namu	—	—	—	—
Chontal	N layñ'al	K akó	Y aʔáẏ	P apal	- añelúx
Jicaque	N mik	L lala	- bis	P beram	- pep
Campa	W -wón¢o	- -wánte	Y -áhi	N -néne	S -setáki
Nahua	Y yaka-	K kama-	T ƛan-	NP nene-pil-	S iste-
Subtiaba	- dako	T danwa	S siñu	T duha	C šñaño
Common	Y *yaqh N *nem-yaqh S *hešu W *wonc	K *qham L *le T *ten	T *ten Y *heyaki S *sen	P *nel-pel N *nel T *tonqʷ	C *coqh S *set

109

English	- 'foot'	K 'knee'	K 'hand'	P 'belly'	N 'neck'
Washo	- *mayop*	M *mokho*	T *t-atu*	K *¢ikukuš*	P *t-ipu*
Tonkawa	N *naatan*	K *yacicxeeloon*	T *hityan*	S *ʔasoy*	- *yaklʔaxan*
Atakapa	K *hikat*	M *te-mak*	- *wos*	K *kom*	N *nte*
Karankawa	K *kekeya*	—	M *e¢ma*	—	—
Klamkosh	E *-eham*	K *-klas*	M *sumahaha*	- *-luk*	P *-sebek*
Coahuiltec	—	—	M *maw*	—	—
Cotoname	E *ayesem*	—	—	K *koh*	—
Comecrudo	E *emi*	P *yapo*	M *mapi*	- *wah*	M *amo*
Seri	K *ʔatoaχátx*	—	- *ʔanopx*	- *ʔayáχ*	P *ʔayap*
Maricopa	E *iimé*	P *meme-puka*	- *isolya*	T *iitó*	MP *mipuk*
Esselen	—	—	—	—	N *luluseh*
Chumash	K *tem, ɨkeniš*	T *stuko*	- *pu*	SK *akšewe*	N *ni*
Salina	KE *isxeep*	—	M *menen*	PK *ika, epen*	N *e¢ʼay, lakay*
Guaioura	—	—	—	—	—
Chontal	E *amɨš*	K *ankónné*	M *amáane*	K *akúʔu*	N *anukma*
Jicaque	E *sam*	- *dile*	M *mas*	K *gol*	M *men*
Campa	K *-iti*	- *-yérito*	K *-áko*	- *-mótiha*	- *-¢áno*
Nahua	K *ikši-*	T *ƛankʷai-*	M *maai-*	T *iʔte-*	- *kec-*
Subtiaba	N *nahku*	T *tugomiw*	M *ñaw, ñanu*	S *sšambo*	P *hapu*
Common	E **sem*	M **moqho*	M **men*	K **qho*	N **neqʷ*
	K **qeti*	K **ken*	K **qem*	S **ʔaša*	P **ya-puk*
	N **na*	T **tuko*	T **hitali*	P **pen*	M **mo*
		P **ya-puka*		T **iʔte*	

English	T 'teat'	K 'heart'	L 'liver'	- 'drink'	- 'eat'
Washo	T *šu*	M *t-emli*	L *t-ilek*	M *ime*	M *emlu, iw*
Tonkawa	N *nayʔoman*	- *yacanan*	- *teyey*	M *xane-*	Y *yaxa-*
Atakap	N *nik*	S *so*	K *keck*	M *am*	Y *yah*
Karankawa	K *kanin*	- *lahama*	—	Q *akʷeten*	K *aknamas*
Klamkosh	—	—	—	Q *kʷay*	—
Coahuiltec	T *tam*	KS *hasal*	—	—	M *ham*
Cotoname	K *knam*	—	—	- *wahe*	M *hahame*
Comecrudo	K *knem*	KS *kayasel*	- *am*	M *kam*	K *kay*
Seri	—	M *ʔámoš*	Y *ʔiyas*	S *k-ɨsi*	Q *kóʔit*
Maricopa	KN *ñamayʔa(D)*	- *iiwáa*	- *tipsi(D)*	S *asi-*	M *amá-*
Esselen	—	—	—	S *ešeʔwne*	M *ama*
Chumash	K *kutet*	K *ayapis*	S *sal*	M *aqmil*	S *alšun*
Salina	—	K *eexiway*	S *asx*	S *-isim*	QS *isx, lam, khutex*
Guaicura	—	—	—	—	—
Chontal	- *páalʔe*	- *ʔáañima*	- *énteda*	S *snak-*	S *saago-*
Jicaque	T *so¢*	- *fos*	S *sem*	S *senibii*	- *laa*
Campa	T *-¢ómi*	S *-asánkani*	Y *-yácire*	- *ire*	- *-a*
Nahua	T *ciciwal-*	- *yoolloʔ-*	L *el-*	- *aaƛi*	Q *kʷa*
Subtiaba	T *dudu-, cici*	K *giga*	K *giko*	S *-ña*	S *-su*
Common	K **kan*	K **qhaysel*	S **sel*	Q **xʷan*	M **qhama*
	T **tutu/cucu*	S **sel*	K **qe*	S **sen*	Q **qʷe*
	N **nay*	M **ʔemali*	L **ʔelek*	M **qhama*	Y **yaqha*
			Y **yac*		K **qha*
					S **seq*

English	- 'bite'	S 'see'	K 'hear'	K 'know'	- 'sleep'
Washo	K *kithi*	K *ikhi*	T *tamal*	S *ašašesi*	M *elsumi*
Tonkawa	- *nace-*	Y *yaace-*	K *soskoona*	S *hatxese-*	- *coxana-*
Atakapa	C *caw*	K *hu*	K *naks*	K *uhc*	W *oy*
Karankawa	—	- *ca*	—	- *kʷas*	M *im*
Klamkosh	—	—	—	—	M *neyanama*
Coahuiltec	—	—	- *cey*	—	—
Cotoname	—	—	—	—	M *mackuka*
Comecrudo	Q *kʷam*	- *mah*	- *ye*	Y *yanam*	M *emet*
Seri	K *kašni*	Y *?á?o*	K *χii*	Y *ɨya*	K *kim*
Maricopa	C *cakyew*	Y *ayúu*	- *?a?avk-*	Y *uyaxʷ*(D), *ṣpo*	M *ašmá*
Esselen	—	—	—	—	- *acinisi*
Chumash	—	K *qoti*	—	—	W *we*
Salina	T *-itpetmak*	Y *yam-*	- *pesnoxo*	Y *yum*	K *kaw*
Guaicura	—	—	—	—	—
Chontal	T *tex-*	S *siñy-*	T *taýk-*	S *išiñak*	M *sma-*
Jicaque	Q *kʷakusi*	K *kuñuka*	- *mapokas*	- *wiskoskreye*	K *-kakoha*
Campa	C *-ácikakéro*	- *-néri*	K *-kamákero*	- *-iotéro*	M *-máhi*
Nahua	K *-keɖoma*	- *itta*	K *-kaki*	M *mati*	K *koci*
Subtiaba	- *-uyu*	Y *-yanga*	T *-daco*	M *-mañu*	K *-gapu, -gu*
Common	K **ket*	Y **yam*	K **na-qaq*	M **men-t*	M **ese-nma*
	Q **qʷe*	K **qo*	T **ta*	Y **yenm*	W **wey*
	C **cak*	S **se*		S **?ese*	K **ko*
	T **te*			K **qen*	

English	- 'die'	K 'kill'	S 'swim'	P 'fly'	W 'walk'
Washo	- *yuli*	Y *yatki*	S *yesuka*	Y *yešuwa*	KY *iye*
Tonkawa	W *hewawa-*	Y *yaaloona-*	S *sooya-*	Y *yoxa-*	K *ha-*
Atakapa	K *kaw*	- *nima*	N *lul*	K *kaw*	W *wank*
Karankawa	M *mal*	- *ahuk*	N *natawa*	—	Y *ye*
Klamkosh	—	—	—	—	- *sotah*
Coahuiltec	K *hum*	- *cap*	—	—	—
Cotoname	W *watho*	W *wathu-ka*	—	—	—
Comecrudo	P *plaw*	K *kamaw*	K *akikete*	K *kolmas*	KY *kiye*
Seri	K *?akχkmi?*	- *aokʷ*	K *kákat*	K *kap*	K *ki?tim*
Maricopa	P *?apooy-*	P *tapuy*	—	Y *ayer*	W *av?áak*
Esselen	P *tepoške*	—	—	—	N *neni*
Chumash	K *kšan*	- *siniwe*	- *pakiwiwin*	P *ahulpet, skoyoyu*	—
Salina	K *axaptep, sitip*	K *okoṙo, wile*	N *-lapatene*	- *mal*	- *isa*
Guaicura	P *pibi*	—	—	—	—
Chontal	M *máṁa*	P *pilk-*	S *soyy-*	- *ñufk-*	W *wa-*
Jicaque	P *nipi*	- *tinan*	K *kopoydeska*	- *vianarteme*	W *wiška*
Campa	K *-kamáki*	K *-ákiri*	M *-amáti*	- *-aranáki*	N *-anite*
Nahua	M *miki*	- *mik-tia*	M *-maneh*	P *paλaani*	Y *yaw*
Subtiaba	K *-gañu*	- *-d-eria*	- *-wengu*	K *-hka*	K *-hka, -cu*
Common	P **pol*	P **pol*	S **swey*	Y **yex*	Y **ye*
	M **mor*	K **qe*	M **man*	P **pet/pel*	W **wan*
	W **wey*	Y **yal*	K **ka*	K **kaw*	N **nen*
	K **qa*		N **nel*		K **kha*

111

English	Q 'come'	N 'lie'	C 'sit'	T 'stand'	K 'give'
Washo	P ipi	- maš-am	YK kekel	Y yal	S -ešl
Tonkawa	- haa-ta-	- hecne-	Y yela-	PY yalapa	K ʔeke-
Atakapa	Q m-ok	- ti	K ke	T tat	M mis
Karankawa	Q gas	—	K hakes	Y yeȼo	P bawus
Klamkosh	—	—	—	—	—
Coahuiltec	—	—	—	—	- a
Cotoname	—	—	P pawe	P pawya	—
Comecrudo	Y kye, nak	—	YP el-paw	YP nelpok	Y -yema
Seri	Q kafp	—	T ʔantkix	K kfit	SM ʔas, móši
Maricopa	- adii	—	—	W hivʔawm	K kʷii-
Esselen	Y eyoʔene	—	—	—	Y yuk, tuhwesa
Chumash	—	—	N leken	- nowo	K xiks
Salina	Y yax	—	C aselʔ	T etakox	- anikhoʔ
Guaicura	—	—	—	—	K ken, utewri-
Chontal	P páʔpa	N nóy-	P pang-	K kask-	K kuuy
Jicaque	Q kʷasii	P pewš	C haȼe	K kiibuhus	K gaȼ
Campa	Q koake	P -ponáke	C -ȼointa	K -kátia	P -pémpiro
Nahua	W waallaw, wiiȼ	K koliwki	T -λalia	K iʔkak	M -maaka
Subtiaba	Q -ca, -kuy, -ʔa	K gapo	T -taw, kamo	W -wihi	SM -šno, -mada
Common	Y *ye	P *pol	P *pa	Y *yel	M *men
	W *wan	K *qa	C *ce	T *ten	K *qen
	Q *qwem	N *ne	Y *yel	K *qat	S *šel
	P *pe		T *tel	P *pa	P *pe
			K *qel	W *hewe	Y *yew

English	- 'say'	S 'sun'	M 'moon'	T 'star'	- 'water'
Washo	T it	P t-ipe	- t-ipe	M malosaŋ	- t-ime
Tonkawa	- new-, hepi	T taaxas	N naʔasʔooʔoot	T tawsew	K ʔaax
Atakapa	- wan	K kakaw	- iti-yils	K kakaw hicon	K kawkaw
Karankawa	K kawpn	—	—	—	K kley
Klamkosh	—	K klos	W awil	—	K kley
Coahuiltec	K ka	—	N anwa	—	N ni
Cotoname	—	N o	—	—	K ah
Comecrudo	K kiwa, ekna	N al	K kan	K ketekʷi	PK ah, papak
Seri	K káiton	S šaʔ	—	S ʔašoxkanox	K ʔax
Maricopa	- ʔaʔi	N ʔanyáa	K xalyá	M hamuse	K axá
Esselen	—	N asi	—	TM amutatay	K asanah
Chumash	—	N ališap	W awaya	K aqewo	K o
Salina	K hekaʔ	N naʔ	—	T raȼwan	K ȼxaʔ
Guaicura	K hake	—	—	—	—
Chontal	K ko-	N elʔóra	M múulʔa	S sanná	K ahá
Jicaque	K kubereka	T doʔȼak	M mumi	- pul	K isu
Campa	K -kántero	TP pátoa	K kaširi, pisar	- impókiro	N niha
Nahua	T iʔtoa	T toonatiw	M meeȼ-	T siiλalin	P aa-
Subtiaba	T -data	K -ahka-	K ukuu	T caagwaN(D)	K iya
Common	K *he-qa	N *ʔanise	M *mol-t	T *ȼeter	K *ʔakha
	T *eto	K *qa	N *ʔani	K *qaw	P *pel
		T *ten	K *qaqan	M *hamo	N *ne
		P *pe	W *ʔaw		
		S *so			

English	- 'rain'	T 'stone'	S 'sand'	- 'earth'	- 'cloud'
Washo	—	T *tek*	- —	M *ŋawa*	T *tawmahun*
Tonkawa	- *yoomʔa*	T *yatexan*	K *xees*	- *haac*	- *yoomʔam-eykewʔan*
Atakapa	K *kawkawk*	W *way*	- *yew*	- *ne*	T *itans*
Karankawa	- *wiasn*	—	—	—	—
Klamkosh	—	—	K *kohon*	—	—
Coahuiltec	—	—	—	T *tap*	—
Cotoname	—	—	—	- *pen*	—
Comecrudo	- *mapel*	W *woyekʷel*	W *wawen*	M *kamla*	PM *mapel*
Seri	K *ipka*	K *ʔast*	K *ikx*	M *ʔamt*	- *ʔókax*
Maricopa	K *ikʷe*	W *ʔavii*	S *salyʔay*	M *amar*	- *ʔakʷé*
Esselen	—	K *šefe*	—	M *maȼa*	M *mec*
Chumash	- *tuhuy*	K *χⁱp*	K *has*	S *šuxp*	- *sⁱksi*
Salina	N *lesxayʔ*	K *sxap*	S *ȼinȼi*	S *sxoʔ*	P *payʔ*
Guaicura	—	—	—	T *atem-ba*	—
Chontal	K *akʷⁱ*	P *apíh*	- *antomáȼ*	M *amáȼ*	T *iȼimhma*
Jicaque	K *hive*	P *pe*	S *sus*	M *amara*	M *mol*
Campa	N *inkáni*	P *mápi*	- *impanéki*	- *kipáci*	M *menkóri*
Nahua	K *kiyawi-*	T *te-*	S *šal-*	T *ʎaal-*	M *miš-*
Subtiaba	N *d-undii-lu*	K *siinu*	W *hwilu*	M *umba*	T *duN(D)*
Common	K **khewke* N **ʔene*	T **te-qhep* K **qhaphi* W **way* P **pe*	S **sal* K **qhes* W **hewen*	M **ʔa-mat* T **ta* S **šoxo*	M **mel-c* P **pel* T **tam*

English	M 'smoke'	- 'fire'	- 'ash'	- 'burn'	P 'path'
Washo	—	- *t-ʔiyu*	P *ȼaphul*	T *tʔothika*	N *mahaletia*
Tonkawa	K *hakocan*	N *naxcan*	- *keewan*	N *nawa-*	N *naax*
Atakapa	P *puh*	Q *kicons*	T *temon*	N *law*	N *wank-ne*
Karankawa	N *anawa*	Q *humhe, kʷaci*	—	—	—
Klamkosh	—	—	- *ahoma*	Q *kʷoylsem*	—
Coahuiltec	—	—	—	—	—
Cotoname	K *kom*	M *man*	S *-semel*	- *-met*	N *al*
Comecrudo		NQ *klwen, len*			
Seri	N *ʔankáχat*	M *ʔamák*	- *ʔantimak*	Q *kitax*	W *ʔáʔo*
Maricopa	K *axway*	W *ʔaʔaw*	- *kʷaxʔóo*	—	W *uñi, yim, way*
Esselen	- *huma*	N *anah*	—	—	—
Chumash	T *tow*	N *ni*	P *alspawa*	—	—
Salina	T *ratet*	W *rʔaw*	—	T *ronʔ*	- *takeʔ*
Guaicura	—	—	—	—	—
Chontal	K *ikušiš*	WQ *unkʷa*	P *apiʔ*	N *ñáaloo-*	N *áne*
Jicaque	M *mus*	W *ava*	P *pew*	T *topes*	W *ahumuk*
Campa	K *káca*	T *cíci*	S *samámpo*	- *amórekáke*	W *awóci*
Nahua	P *pok-*	T *ʎe-*	- *neš*	T *-ʎa-tia*	P *oʔ-(*poʔ)*
Subtiaba	K *guni*	W *agu*	T *idi*	Q *-gamo*	- *gamba*
Common	P **pok* N **ʔane* K **qo* M **me* T **to*	W **ʔawa* N **ʔane* M **ʔama* Q **kʷa*	P **pew* T **ʔete* S **sem*	N **law* T **to* Q **qʷa*	P **pet* N **ʔana* W **ha-wanki*

English	- 'mountain'	- 'red'	K 'green'	K 'yellow'	Q 'white'
Washo	- haŋa	S -šošoŋi	C -ȼaȼami	- -ȼaȼami	P -phophoy
Tonkawa	T naatoon	S samox	TK xʔaton	M makik	M maslik
Atakapa	- ne-mak	- kuc	T tat	- tat	Q kop
Karankawa	—	- tamoyika	—	—	P peka
Klamkosh	—	—	—	—	—
Coahuiltec	—	—	—	—	—
Cotoname	—	M msay	—	—	M mesoy
Comecrudo	W way	M pamsol	Y yaluy	L yaluy	P pepuk
Seri	- ʔast	- kiʔw, kʔeł	Y yaiłkʷoił, χpanáms	- nwásoł	Q koχp
Maricopa	W avi	N ñihwitk	K xašami	K khwesam	- ñiily-
Esselen	—	—	—	—	—
Chumash	T tuptup, ošlomol	- tasin	—	—	- owow
Salina	T loyam, ṙophoyo	- ȼkaten?	—	K xawat	M maṙal
Guaicura	—	—	—	—	—
Chontal	W iwáalay	M mul'	- verde	- amariyo	P fuh
Jicaque	N neven	N nikip	C ȼu	L lu	P pe
Campa	T toŋkári, otiši	- kirá, kitiónka	K kenáfi-	K kitéri-	- kitamaro-
Nahua	T tepee-	- cicil-tik	T ten-ki	K kos-tik	S istaa-k
Subtiaba	N anwa	N -anga	C -aša	M -ohmo	S -iša, ticu
Common	W *way T *to N *new	M *mes S *semo N *nek	C *ca K *qen T *ten	L *yalu K *qhewe M maqhma	P *phek M *mes K *qʷoqʷp/qʷy S *ʔise

English	P 'black'	- 'night'	K 'hot'	K 'cold'	P 'full'
Washo	Y -yawi	T ta-phawit	- yasaŋka	M methu	P -iphula
Tonkawa	K kaxaw, capxew	- ʔooʔa	K xalal	K koowa-	P ha-pce-na
Atakapa	M mel	T iti	N ilu	K akcaw	P puk
Karankawa	MP ma, pal	—	—	—	—
Klamkosh	—	—	—	- delin	—
Coahuiltec	—	T cum	—	—	—
Cotoname	P pay	P pay	—	- hewes	—
Comecrudo	MP pal, -mol, yataw	- klul	- -sowetyaw	S -sekyaw	- kam
Seri	P k-opoł	- iʔámok	K kméke	P ʔaapł	—
Maricopa	T tiñam	T tiñam	- ʔapily	—	—
Esselen	—	—	—	—	—
Chumash	K akimi	- sulkunu	—	—	—
Salina	- sawwat	- smakhay?	—	PS epṙa, ȼnetel	P apewn
Guaicura	—	—	—	—	—
Chontal	- úmi	P ipugi?	N iñú?	S sítʸa	- lamáa
Jicaque	T te	TP pušte	- ehawa, eyampe	S cose	P pit
Campa	K kisá-	- osáite	K kácininká-	- -kácinká-	- -háka
Nahua	YP ya-pal-	- yowal	- toton-ki	S sekʷis-	- ten-tok
Subtiaba	T -dagina	T -duʔu	K -hka	M ma	- -ahni
Common	P *pal T *tem Y *yaw M *mel	T *tem P *phel	N *new K *kar	S *sati K *ḱel M *me P *peλ	P *pol

English	N 'new'	Q 'good'	- 'round'	- 'dry'	N 'name'
Washo	—	M t-aŋaw	—	—	T -tiye-
Tonkawa	S hosas	- henos	PT talmay, kopul	—	—
Atakapa	N il	T tol	T koctols	- cak	N enk
Karankawa	—	- pla	- laakum	—	—
Klamkosh	—	Q kʷist-baha	—	—	—
Coahuiltec	—	MQ kapan, manam	—	—	W aw
Cotoname	—	Q knah	—	—	—
Comecrudo	N -lex	- -lex, -sex	P -wapel	PW -ptaw, -wel	N lekaw
Seri	N nwaki?	Q kipe	—	Q kʷótix	T ?atási
Maricopa	—	Q aχotk	Y yeryer(D)	—	- amulʸ
Esselen	—	—	—	—	—
Chumash	—	C šuma, co?o	—	—	T tu
Salina	S stikʷaw	CM mak, ɟep	—	—	—
Guaicura	—	T didi	—	—	—
Chontal	S ɟee?	- ñikáta	- redóndo	Q xulk̓uk̓	W úftiñe
Jicaque	S sašsway	- uk	—	P pa	N la
Campa	N troákera	M kaméɟa	P -pánkati	P pirihátahi	W -wáhiro
Nahua	- yankʷi-k	Q kʷal-	Y yawal-tik	W waaki	T -tookaa
Subtiaba	N nuši	M -hña	—	- šo	N gi-nihka
Common	N *new S *s'e	Q *qʷel T *ter M *qhame C *cew	Y *yewl T *tol P *pali	W *we P *pe Q *kʷol	T *tew N *ne W *?ewe

REFERENCES

Arana Osnaya, 1959a, 1959b, 1964, 1966
Bright, 1956
Dixon and Kroeber, 1919
Escalante and Faier, 1959
Fernández de Miranda, 1956
Greenberg and Swadesh, 1953
Gudschinsky, 1958a, 1959c
Hale, 1958, 1959
Hattori, 1960
Hymes, 1960
Kroeber and Chrétien, 1937
Lees, 1953
Longacre, 1957, 1961a, 1961b, 1966

McQuown, 1956
Manrique Castañeda, 1958
Newman, 1964
Olson, 1964, 1965
Radin, 1916
Sapir, 1916, 1917, 1920, 1925
Schmidt, J., 1872
Schuchardt, 1900
Swadesh, 1951, 1953, 1954b, 1954c, 1956, 1959a, 1959b, 1959c, 1959d, 1960a, 1960b, 1960c, 1960d, 1960e, 1960f, 1962, 1964a, 1964b, 1966
Weitlaner, Fernández de Miranda, and Swadesh, 1959, 1960

5. Systemic Comparison and Reconstruction

ROBERT LONGACRE

0.   Introduction
1.   Comparative method (as illustrated with Mixtecan materials)
1.1. Sound correspondences (Mixtec:Cuicatec:Trique)
1.2. Reconstruction
1.3. Apparent exceptions
1.4. Patterns of phonemic substitution in the proto-language
1.5. Analogical change
1.6. Lexical borrowing
1.7. *Wörter-und-Sachen* analysis of the reconstructed corpus
2.   Phonological systems reconstructed for Otomanguean language families
2.1. Proto-Mixtecan
2.2. Proto-Popolocan
2.3. Proto-Chiapanec-Manguean
2.4. Proto-Otopamean
2.4.1. Proto-Otomian
2.4.2. Proto-Otomí-Mazahua
2.4.3. Proto-Otomí-Pame
2.5. Proto-Zapotecan
2.6. Proto-Chinantecan
2.7. Proto-Otomanguean
2.8. Proto-Popo-Manguean
2.9. "Macro-Mixtecan"
2.10. Proto-Otomanguean *m*
3.   Phonological systems reconstructed for other Middle American language families
3.1. Proto-Uto-Aztecan
3.2. Proto-Zoquean
3.3. Proto-Mayan
3.4. Proto-Totonacan
4.   Diffusion phenomena and linguistic family trees
4.1. Mayan sub-families
4.2. Popolocan sub-families
4.3. Uto-Aztecan sub-grouping
4.4. Zoquean sub-classification
4.5. Mazatec dialects
4.6. Mixtecan sub-grouping
5.   Summary and implications for classification of Middle American languages

APPENDICES:
A. Proto-Mixtecan *am*
B. Proto-Otomí-Mazahua tones
C. Pre-Proto-Popolocan-Mixtecan deictics
D. Proto-Zapotec geminate clusters
E. Proto-Otomanguean isoglosses
F. Linguistic Map of Middle America

0. INTRODUCTION. The systemic comparison of languages and reconstruction of earlier stages has been pre-eminently successful in the field of Indo-European studies. In spite of limited application to other language groups (noticeably Semitic, Finno-Ugric, Bantu, Sino-Tibetan, and Algonquian), the accomplishment of Indo-European comparative reconstruction still remains unparalleled. Nevertheless, over the past several decades the comparative reconstruction of American Indian languages, especially those of Middle America, has gone forward at an ever accelerating rate. Whorf's Uto-Aztecan reconstruction of 1935 was not only the first piece of systemic reconstruction involving Middle American languages, but remains a model of craftsmanship in respect to its sensitivity to basic

117

considerations of linguistic structure. Its only defect is its brevity. Other serious comparative studies did not follow until the latter part of the next decade when Swadesh's article on Proto-Zapotecan (1947) and Wonderly's article on Proto-Zoquean (1949) appeared. The Newman and Weitlaner articles on Proto-Otomí and Proto-Otomí-Mazahua (1950) provided an auspicious start for the past decade which saw the appearance of Arana's article on Proto-Totonac-Tepehua (1953), McQuown's tentative sketch of Proto-Mayan (1956), and volumes by Longacre (1957) and Gudschinsky (1959c) on Proto-Mixtecan and Proto-Popolocan. In this decade has appeared a sketch on Proto-Mixtec by Mak and Longacre (1960), an article of Bartholomew's revising Proto-Otomian consonants (1960), and an ethnolinguistic article of Millon and Longacre which incidentally sketches a few features of Proto-Amuzgo-Mixtecan (1961). The present backlog of unpublished studies includes: Arana's sketch of Proto-Amuzgo-Mixtecan; Fernández de Miranda and Weitlaner's volume on Proto-Chiapanec-Manguean (1961); a very brief sketch of Smith and Weitlaner (1957) on Proto-Chinantecan; and an article of Bartholomew's (1959) on Proto-Otomí-Pame. A significant study now in progress is Fernández de Miranda's (1960) revision and amplification of Proto-Zapotec which was first reconstructed by Swadesh almost a quarter of a century ago.[1]

---

[1] In the five years since this article was written, further comparative studies have appeared (not included in the main bibliography of this volume): C. F. Voegelin, F. M. Voegelin, and Kenneth Hale, *Typological and comparative grammar of Uto-Aztecan I* (phonology) (*IJAL*, Memoir 17, 1962); Calvin Rensch, *Proto - Chinantec phonology* (master's thesis, Univ. Pennsylvania, 1963); Terrence Kaufman, *Mixe-Zoque diachronic studies* (unpublished, 1963); Allan Wares, *A comparative study of Yuman consonantism* (doctoral dissertation, Univ. Texas, 1964): Burton W. Bascom, Jr., *Proto-Tepiman* (Tepehuan-Piman) (doctoral dissertation, Univ. Washington, 1966); Paul Kirk, *Proto-Mazatec* (doctoral dissertation, Univ. Washington, 1966); Calvin Rensch, *Proto-Otomanguean*

All told, the above makes an imposing tally. Notice that all branches of the so-called 'Mexican Penutian' (excluding Huave whose affinities to Zoquean, Mayan, and Totonac-Tepehua are doubted by both McQuown and Swadesh) have been subjects of some systemic comparison and recon-

---

phonology, (doctoral dissertation, Univ. Pennsylvania, 1966).

The following articles have appeared (also not included in the main bibliography of this volume): Maurice Swadesh, "The Oto-Manguean hypothesis and Macro-Mixtecan" (*IJAL*, 26: 79–111, 1960); Longacre, "Swadesh's Macro-Mixtecan hypothesis" (*IJAL*, 27: 9–29, 1961); Wigberto J. Moreno, "Estudios Mixtecos" (reprinted from the introduction to the facsimile edition of *Vocabulario en Lengua Mixteca* of Fray Francisco de Alvarado, Mexico City, 1962); Longacre, "Amplification of Gudschinsky's Proto - Popolocan - Mixtecan" (*IJAL*, 28: 227–42, 1962); Norman Nordell, "On the status of Populuca in Zoque-Mixe" (*IJAL*, 28: 146–49, 1962); Longacre, "Progress in Otomanguean reconstruction" (*Proc. Ninth Int. Cong. Linguistics*, Cambridge, Mass., 1962 [1964]); Ronald Olson, "Mayan affinities with Chipaya of Bolivia I: correspondence" (*IJAL*, 30: 313–24, 1964); "Mayan affinities with Chipaya of Bolivia II: cognates" (*IJAL*, 31: 29–38, 1965); Kaufman, "Materiales lingüísticos para el estudio de las relaciones internas y externas de la familia de idiomas mayanos" (in *Desarrollo cultural de los Mayas*, pp. 81–136, E. Z. Vogt and A. Ruz L., eds., Mexico City, 1964); Longacre, "On linguistic affinites of Amuzgo" (*IJAL*, 32: 46–49, 1965); B. W. Upson and Longacre, "Proto-Chatino phonology" (*IJAL*, 31: 312–22, 1965).

It is evident that the volume of study completed since I wrote this article considerably exceeds the work summarized here. To take account of the recent work would require rewriting the entire article. A recent summary which takes account of most of the above is found in Longacre, "Comparative reconstruction of indigenous languages" (*Current Trends in Linguistics*, vol. 4).

One important shift in my own position is that I now regard Amuzgo as constituting a seventh language family within Otomanguean. This is reflected in the classification embodied in the linguistic map (App. F), but is not reflected elsewhere in this article.

Some other articles of possible relevance here but not mentioned in the body of this article are: Bright, 1956; Ecker, 1939; Fernández de Miranda, 1951; Greenberg and Swadesh, 1953; Hale, 1958; 1959; McQuown, 1942; Mason, 1952; Mayers, 1960; Radin, 1916; Ravicz and Romney (unpublished MS); Swadesh, 1956; Weitlaner, 1942; Wonderly, 1953. To these can be added an unpublished file of Uto-Aztecan cognates prepared by Wick J. Miller.

struction. The time would soon be ripe, it seems, for comparing Proto-Zoquean, Proto-Mayan, and Proto-Totonac-Tepehua, and demonstrating the assumed relationship of the three to each other—if, indeed, it be demonstrable.[1a] The chief difficulty at present would seem to be the lack of extensive published ensembles of cognate sets in each of these language families. A further consideration will then be the possible affinity of the Mexican stock to Penutian of California. Each of the six branches of Otomanguean (Mixtecan, Popolocan, Chiapanec-Manguean, Otomí-Mazahua-Pame, Zapotecan, and Chinantecan) has been reconstructed either in published or unpublished studies. Some of these reconstructions (noticeably Chinantecan) are indeed most sketchy. Two others (Mixtecan and Popolocan) are extensive. For Chiapanec-Mangue we have all we can ever hope for, because the two languages are extinct and exist only in rather fragmentary records. Although Swadesh's Zapotecan sketch does not give a very extensive body of cognate sets, the present studies of Fernández de Miranda should supply what is lacking here. The combined efforts of Newman and Weitlaner plus Bartholomew readies Otomí-Mazahua-Pame for comparison with other branches of Otomanguean. The time is therefore very near when Proto-Otomanguean may itself go onto the drafting-board, if Otomanguean proves to be a valid genetic grouping.[2]

[1a] Terrance Kaufman has assembled evidence (unpublished cognate sets) to substantiate this grouping.

[2] With the completion of Rensch's dissertation (of footnote 1) Otomanguean is now firmly established. In this massive work (427 cognate sets), every phase of comparative Otomanguean phonology (consonants, vowels, laryngeals, tones, consonantal alternations) is carefully considered. Every constituent family of Otomanguean is given chapter length treatment. This study modifies some details of my Proto-Mixtecan reconstruction and replaces entirely my speculations regarding the probable structure of Proto-Otomanguean. In particular, Rensch reduces drastically the number of vowels reconstructed for Proto-Otomanguean and for Proto-Mixtecan as well. The latter reduction is made possible by the reconstruction

Meanwhile Gudschinsky's comparison of Popolocan and Mixtecan (1959c) and the Fernández-Weitlaner common reconstruction of Popolocan-Mixtecan with Chiapanec-Mangue (1961) amount, in effect, to two approximations to Proto-Otomanguean. When reconstructed with detail and care, the latter may give us a piece of Middle American linguistic reconstruction approaching in depth and diversity the accomplishment of Indo-European scholarship, although the work will long be hampered by the skeleton crew manning Middle American comparative studies as compared to the more favorable number of scholars in Indo-European.

In this article we sketch (1) the operation of the comparative method (as illustrated by Mixtecan materials) along with factors obscuring regular sound change, with mention of some important ethnolinguistic byproducts of the comparative method; (2) reconstructed phonological systems involving Otomanguean languages with mention of any grammatical features that have also emerged in the course of such work, and with attention to approximations already made to the reconstruction of Proto-Otomanguean itself; (3) reconstructed phonological systems involving other Middle American languages; (4) problems arising from "diffusion" versus "family tree" concepts.

1. The comparative method as worked out on the terrain of Indo-European studies is "comparative" in a very specialized sense of that term. We are not here comparing gross similarity of shape and function (as in, say, comparative anatomy). Linguistic typology in the latter sense has been slow developing, although this may be a fruitful development in this decade. Rather we are concerned with the discovery of systematic

of two laryngeals for Proto-Mixtecan rather than my one laryngeal (*?). Kirk in Proto-Mazatec and Bartholomew in Proto-Otopamean likewise reconstruct systems of but four vowels. Rensch also rejects the whole system of postposed deictic particles first suggested by Gudschinsky (1959) and further developed in Longacre 1962 and 1964.

sound correspondences between languages.

In the application of the comparative method several stages may be noted: (a) By systemic comparison regular sound correspondences are noted. (b) An attempt is then made to discover which sets of sound correspondences are in contrast in the same or similar phonological environments, and which sets are in noncontrastive distribution (i.e., occur in mutually exclusive environments or in free variation). In this fashion the number of reconstructed phonemes is ascertained. (c) The reconstructed phonemes are then assigned symbols according to phonetic plausibility, i.e., in terms of the phonetic nature of the reflexes (the present-day phonemes which have developed from the reconstructed sounds), in terms of the geographical distribution of those reflexes, and according to their possible placement in the emerging phonological system. (d) Once the phonological system is tentatively worked out for a proto-language (i.e., a "parent" language), we are in a position to recognize other features (grammatical and lexical innovations) which in part obscure the regularity of appearance of the postulated reflexes. These latter features may have considerable ethnolinguistic import.

These stages in the application of the comparative method are illustrated with some detail in the following section. Illustrative data are drawn from the reconstruction of Proto-Mixtecan (by comparison of Mixtec, Cuicatec, and Trique). But here let it be noted that, beginning in the most pedestrian fashion with a search for regular sound correspondences, systemic reconstruction eventually leads to the uncovering of facts which relate not only to the phonological history of a language family but also to its grammatical and lexical history as well.

1.1. SOUND CORRESPONDENCES. For Mixtec (of San Miguel el Grande), Cuicatec (of Concepción Pápalo), and Trique (of San Andrés Chicahuaxtla) the following sound correspondence is observed before front vowels:

(1) M *š* ~ C *d* ~ T *c* as in M *vĭšĭ* 'sweet', *ndùšī* 'honey'; C *nā-dī²ī* 'honey', *čyāādē* 'sugar'; T *zĭ³cǐ²ĭ⁴³* 'candy', *ga³cǐ²ĭ⁴³* 'honey'.

There is also a further sound correspondence observed before back vowels and *a*:

(2) M *s* ~ C *d* ~ T *t* as in M *tï-sàà*, C *²yáádá*, T *ža³taha⁴³* 'bird'.

These two sound correspondence are partially similar in that the Cuicatec reflex is identical in both cases while Mixtec *š* and Trique *c* could be considered to be palatalizations of Mixtec *s* and Trique *t* respectively. Since reflexes Mixtec *š* and Trique *c* occur in environments which may exert palatalizing influence (before front vowels) while Mixtec *s* and Trique *t* occur in nonpalatalizing environments, it seems plausible that we have here not two contrasting reconstructed phonemes but simply one such phoneme with reflexes distributed in mutually exclusive and noncontrasting environments.

However, in contrast to these two sound correspondences the following sound correspondences occur:

(3) M *t* ~ C *t* ~ T *č* as in M *kātā*, C *kāātā*, T *ga³ča²¹* 'to sing'.
(4) M *č* ~ C *t* ~ T *č* as in M (*kōò*) *yúčǐ* 'alligator', C *²yááté* 'lizard', T *če³⁴³* 'scales'.

These latter two sound correspondences are also found to be in complementary distribution relative to one another: (4) is found in ultima syllables before front vowels in all three languages; and in Mixtec before *a* and after *i* or *u*; (3) is found elsewhere.

1.2. RECONSTRUCTION. From the above sound correspondences in which (1) and (2) contrast as a pair with (3) and (4) we reconstruct two phonemes. What phonetic values may be assigned to them? For sets (3) and (4) we assume a Proto-Mixtecan voiceless alveolar stop, viz. **t*. For sets (1) and (2) we need to reconstruct another sound which is presumably also alveolar; **s*, **đ* and **θ* are likely choices. The first option **s* is not so likely in view of the Mixtec dialect evidence summarized in section 4.5. Choice of symbol for our reconstructed Proto-Mixtecan phoneme is arbitrary as to $*\theta$ or $*\check{d}$. I have chosen the former in that two other spirants, $*x$ and $*x^w$, seem to be witnessed to in the three languages. By choosing $*\theta$ we obtain a series $*\theta$, $*x$, $*x^w$ which parallels the $*t$, $*k$, $*k^w$ stop series, and the $*^nd$, $*^ng$, $*^ng^w$ prenasalized series.

1.3. APPARENT EXCEPTIONS to the appearance of regularly postulated reflexes may be occasioned by various features. Some such aberrances may indicate the need for reconstructing another phoneme or may indicate a previously postulated phoneme in a hitherto unsuspected position (i.e. forming a consonant cluster, a vowel cluster, or some post-vocalic consonantal element coloring the quality of the preceding vowel). Thus, from the following frequently encountered sets of sound correspondences six Proto-Mixtecan vowels are reconstructed (a number of specially conditioned reflexes are omitted here; but some alternative reflexes are indicated below without statement of conditioning factors):

	M	C	T	PMx
(1)	i	$\sim i$	$\sim i$	$*i$
(2)	i/e	$\sim e$	$\sim e$	$*e$
(3)	$\ddot{i}$	$\sim i/e$	$\sim i$	$*\ddot{i}$
(4)	a	$\sim a$	$\sim a$	$*a$
(5)	u/o	$\sim u/o$	$\sim o$	$*o$
(6)	$u/\ddot{i}$	$\sim u/e$	$\sim u$	$*u$

Nevertheless, having reconstructed these Proto-Mixtecan vowels on the basis of the above sound correspondences, there yet remains a further sound correspondence:

(7) $M\ u/o \sim C\ u/o \sim T\ a$

While this further sound correspondence is partially similar to numbers (4) to (6), it apparently contrasts with all three.[3] It would seem, therefore, that the only course open to us is that of reconstructing a further

[3] Swadesh and Arana's attempt to dispose of this as an assimilation of Proto-Mixtec $*u/o \ldots a > u \ldots u$ or $o \ldots o$ ignores a mass of data.

vowel phoneme, e.g. $*\mathfrak{o}$. Such a phoneme was reconstructed in my Proto-Mixtecan study. At the same time I reconstructed a post-vocalic $*-m$, which evidently occurred with considerable frequency, which was the main source for nasalized vowels in the Mixtecan languages, and which survives to this day in closely related Amuzgo as well as in Mixtec dialect forms that have added a final vowel. Apparently this $*-m$ patterned as some sort of suffixal element. Consequently the occurrence of a given vowel reflex colored by old post-posed $*-m$ versus reflex uncolored by $*-m$ is largely unpredictable. Thus in the same language may occur nasalized and unnasalized vowel reflexes in etymological doublets that seem to stem back to the same Proto-Mixtecan root plus or minus $*-m$. I had also realized that on occasion, the $*-m$ not only resulted in nasal coloring of the vowel, but in raising and backing of the vowel as well (e.g. PMx $*nam > M\ nu$). What I failed to realize was that the raising and backing influence of the post-posed bilabial nasal was general enough to account entirely for the aberrant set of reflexes, M $u/o \sim C\ u/o \sim T\ a$. It now seems plausible that every instance of reconstructed $*\mathfrak{o}$ vowel may be reconstructed simply as $*am$. In brief, instead of reconstructing a further vowel phoneme, we simply expand the distribution of post-vocalic bilabial nasal to a number of sets where its presence was previously unsuspected.

Thus, sets 167 and 222 of my Proto-Mixtecan study are remarkably parallel, but for the former set I reconstructed $*ya^2na^2\mathfrak{?}$ 'network bag', whereas for the latter set I reconstructed $*k^wa^2n\mathfrak{o}^2\mathfrak{?}$ 'to weave'. The latter we now reconstruct simply as $*k^wa^2na^2m\mathfrak{?}$. Thus, set 167 represents a Proto-Mixtecan noun built on the root 'to weave' and not characterized by post-posed $*-m$, while the root 'to weave' has the post-posed nasal. Notice that both the Proto-Mixtecan noun and verb correspond as to the vowel of their first syllables, as to tone class $*22$ and as to presence of final glottal stop. Similarly, my set 223, formerly thought to witness to *nɔ in its last syllable, is seen to witness to *nam instead.

Such a restatement typically leads to adjustments all along the line. However, the postulation of *am rather than *ɔ not only obeys the law of parsimony in avoiding reconstruction of further phonemes, but constitutes a more adequate explanation for several apparent anomalies of phonological development (see Appendix A).

1.4. PATTERNS OF PHONEMIC SUBSTITUTION IN THE PROTO-LANGUAGE. Another factor apparently interfering with regular appearance of postulated reflexes may consist of patterns of phonemic substitution in the proto structure. Once such patterns are recognized, it is seen that they do not constitute exceptions to regularity of sound development; the developments are regular enough, but a cognate in one language may not hark back to exactly the same form as does a cognate in another language. Granted slightly different starting points, it is not surprising that the end points differ also. Thus, in Indo-European languages vowel gradation has played an important part and results in apparent anomalies of phonological development until its role is understood. In the Mixtecan languages consonant gradation of a systematic sort may be postulated for the parent structure. The patterns of consonant gradation were primarily of two sorts, with Proto-Mixtecan *kʷ-, *y-/*w-/*x-, *k-, and *ⁿd-/*n- marking verb paradigms with four tense-aspects (and various allomorphs of the second and fourth aspects), and *t-/*θ-, *y-, *ⁿd-, and *n- marking nouns. Possibly the *y- of the noun paradigms indicated *indefinite* (which became Trique unpossessed and Amuzgo plural), whereas *t-/*θ- marked *definite* (which became Trique possessed and Amuzgo singular). A given noun reconstructs with *either* a paradigm involving *t- *or* with a paradigm involving *θ-. In the cognate sets of my Proto-Mixtecan study there is almost no overlap (total of only four cases) of these

122

two paradigms. Such overlap as occurs presumably reflects a mixture of nouns harking back to *t- versus *θ- paradigms but built on the same Proto-Mixtecan root.

The scheme of Proto-Mixtecan consonantal gradation sketched above is, of course, an end product of comparative reconstruction. It affords a systematic explanation of many apparent exceptions and anomalies of phonological development. Therefore, we summarize and illustrate here some of the problems encountered at this point in the course of reconstructing of Proto-Mixtecan.

In reconstructing *CVCV forms, both of the vowels as well as the second consonant reconstruct quite regularly—although not without problems of the sort illustrated above in reference to the reconstruction of *am versus *ɔ. In the second consonantal position phonemes *θ and *t are reconstructed from the sound correspondences already presented and exemplified. In this second consonantal position we also catalogue such additional correspondences as:

$$\begin{array}{cccc} \text{M} & \text{C} & \text{T} & \text{PMx} \end{array}$$
$$(1) \qquad y/\tilde{n} \sim y \sim y/zero < {}^{*}y$$

(with Mixtec ñ reflex conditioned by occurrence of another nasal in the Proto-Mixtec form, and Trique zero reflex conditioned by following i).

$$(2) \qquad n \qquad \sim n \sim n < {}^{*}n$$
$$(3) \qquad \check{c}(<\text{PM}{}^{*}t) \sim n \sim n < {}^{*n}d$$

(Mixtec reflex č occurs intervocalic; other conditioned reflexes, including ⁿd occur elsewhere.)

But although these reflexes and reconstructions are clearly established in reference to the second consonant of *CVCV forms, they do not seem directly applicable to the first consonantal position. Furthermore, we experience the same difficulty in reconstructing the consonant of some *CV forms. Evidently something has disturbed the regularity of anticipated reflex for the first consonant of many forms, whether disyllabic or monosyllabic. Thus, from such sets as 97, 98, and 171, we can abstract the sound correspondence:

$$M \ \tilde{n} \ (PM \ *y) \sim C \ y \sim T \ t;$$

from such sets as 277 we can abstract

$$M \ \tilde{n} \ (PM \ *y) \sim C \ d \sim T \ t;$$

and from set 178 we can abstract

$$M \ \tilde{n} \ (PM \ *y) \sim C \ t \sim T \ n.$$

Taking these sets at their face value, we could reconstruct three additional Proto-Mixtecan phonemes—albeit phonemes of very limited distribution: t^y, d^y, and $^nd^y$. But positing these three additional phonemes would be but a beginning, in that inspection of further sets would necessitate the reconstruction of more such phonemes of restricted distribution. This would be especially true in regard to sound correspondences abstracted from the first consonantal position of *CVCV* forms. Here, for example, Arana and Swadesh reconstruct *r from $M \ y \sim T \ d$ (with inconsistency of C d versus t^y reflex; why not postulate r versus $ɼ$?). In brief, postulation of such further phonemes on the basis of these apparent irregularities in the first consonants of forms rapidly works in the direction of reducing our proto structure to the status of a phonological wastebasket choked with an abundance of phonemes of very restricted distribution. However, consonantal gradation may be posited as lying back of all these apparently irregular and haphazard sound correspondences. It then becomes unnecessary to posit a host of further phonemes of restricted distribution.[4]

1.5. ANALOGICAL CHANGE. A factor which

[4] Telltale traces of the old alternation survive in the form of etymological doublets in all three languages. Thus we find Cuicatec *náʔá* 'firewood' side by side with *yáʔá* 'stick' as are Mixtec *vīšì* 'sweet', and *ⁿdùšī* 'honey'; Cuicatec *dà-kààčī* 'to boil' and *ʔyūūcī* 'to fry'; Cuicatec (*dāīyā*) *déénó* 'granddaughter' and (*dāīyā*) *híínó* 'grandson'; Mixtec *ʔīnī* 'afternoon, early evening', and *šīnī* 'supper'; Trique *ga³naʔ²h* 'to weave' and *ži³naʴ²¹* 'loom'.

often obscures regular sound correspondences between languages may be analogical change in one language. In such circumstances we suppose the phonological development to have been originally quite regular, but subsequent grammatical and/or lexical developments have obliterated the regular reflex (as "foots" may be substituted for "feet" in a child's language).

In Trique the fortis phonemes t and k are restricted to word-final syllables where they contrast with lenis d and g. In non-word-final syllables this contrast does not occur; rather there occur somewhat colorless alveolar and velar stops (varying to spirants) which we assign to the lenis phonemes. In that word stress typically falls on the word-final syllable, it seems possible that the fortis-lenis contrast in alveolar and velar stops was originally a phonetic distinction correlating with onset of stress or lack of onset of stress. However, some instances of d and g in word-final syllables do occur and the phonemic contrast is not to be doubted in modern Trique. Spanish loans such as *na²du³* 'soldier' are possibly too few to have played a very significant part in the lenis stops becoming phonemic. A few native roots display g in second syllable—perhaps in forms that hark back to Proto-Mixtecan *x^w or *$^ng^w$. But it is striking that the clearest fortis-lenis contrasts in word-final syllables involve a morpheme d- (replacive of first consonant) and g- (likewise replacive) with the former indicating POSSESSED status on nouns and the latter indicating PUNCTILIAR aspect of verbs. Note, e.g. the following minimal pairs:

$$tu̧³ \ ni³ \text{ 'their blood'}$$
$$du̧³ \ ni³ \text{ 'their palm-trees'}$$

(with $yu̧³$ 'an unpossessed palm-tree')

$$ka̧³ \text{ 'squash'}$$

$$ga̧³ \text{ 'she dug (it)'}$$

(with $wa̧³$ CONTINUATIVE ASPECT, 'she's digging it')

In this first pair, presumably Proto-Mixtecan *θom lies back of the Trique form POSSESSED PALM. However, the regular reflex of Proto-Mixtecan *θ in ultimate syllables is not d, but t. Nevertheless, since bisyllabic stems with initial y- alternate to d- in the possessed forms of such nouns, it seems plausible here to believe that (a) regular development of Proto-Mixtecan *θ to Trique t took place in an earlier stage of Trique; but (b) analogical extension of d- SIGN OF POSSESSED to monosyllabic nouns has obliterated this earlier t reflex. Similarly, in respect to the second pair, we assume that regular development of Proto-Mixtecan *k to Trique k first took place, but that this regular reflex was obliterated by later extension of g- morpheme for PUNCTILIAR aspect.[5]

1.6. LEXICAL BORROWING. Other apparent exceptions to regular sound development may be attributed to lexical borrowing at a time when certain sound developments had already taken place and were no longer operative. Thus, as we have stated, M $s/\check{s} \sim$ T $t <$ PMx *θ, but there is no regular correspondence M $s \sim$ T s. Nevertheless, a set occurs exhibiting this apparently anomalous correspondence: M $s\bar{o}^?\bar{o}$ 'ear', $s\acute{o}^?\acute{o}$ 'deaf' $\sim$ T $zo^{3?}o^3$ 'deaf'. In that the Mixtec and Trique forms are so very similar (T has z as lenis phoneme in penultimas, and z versus fortis s only in ultimas) we suspect here a Mixtec loan word in Trique. This suspicion is reinforced by noting another set: M $^nd\bar{u}\check{c}\bar{\imath}$ 'beans', 'eyes' $^nd\acute{u}\check{c}\acute{\imath}$ 'blind' $\sim$ regularly to T ru^3ne^{43} 'beans', ru^3ne^4 yq^{43} 'eyes' ($<$PMx *$^ndu^3ndi^4$, set 16). But there is a Trique form $du^3\check{c}i^3$ 'blind' which is phonologically quite different from the inherited item ru^3ne^{43} 'beans', 'eyes'. Again it

seems best to assume that $du^3\check{c}i^3$ 'blind' is a Mixtec loan word in Trique. We note that both these items presumed to be Mixtec loan words refer to pathology. Knowing that the Mixtecs were culturally dominant over the Triques before and after the conquest, we might wonder if these two borrowings (and a few other items) do not reflect a cultural situation involving Mixtec shamans and Trique clients.[6]

1.7. WÖRTER-UND-SACHEN ANALYSIS OF THE RECONSTRUCTED CORPUS. In the above sections we have illustrated the nature of systemic comparison and reconstruction by use of Mixtecan data. We have noted that apparent exceptions to regular phonological developments do not lead us to abandon the assumption of regular sound change. On the contrary, by taking account of these exceptions we bring into better focus the reconstructed phonological system with possible discovery of some facts about the grammar as well. We may also uncover some lexical borrowings that can be recognized as such only by the application of systemic reconstruction. Nevertheless, analysis of such borrowings may have considerable ethnolinguistic value.

---

[5] This assumption is not wholly gratuitous. An old Proto-Mixtecan root meaning 'hard' and later 'metallic' is seen in Trique $zi^5ka^{5?}$ 'hard' and zi^3-$ka^{34}h$ 'rattle (of rattlesnake)'. But in a stressless syllable following a syllable with phrase stress we find forms with k weakened to g: du^3kwa^3-$ga^?a^{43}$ 'jail' (=‘house of iron’)' and $\check{z}u^3kwa^{21}$-ga^{12} 'rattlesnake'.

[6] In this respect it is interesting to note two other Trique lexical items which may belong to the same lexical domain: la^3kwq^3 'lame' from my set 142 and la^3kwe^3h 'mucus' from set 127. These items involve the only occurrences in our cognate sets of penultimate l- in Trique forms; penultimate l- is somewhat more common in Mixtec dialects. Furthermore, we can in set 127 match the Trique form la^3kwe^3h 'mucus' with Mixtec $l\bar{a}k^w\bar{a}$ 'pus'—although we have no Mixtec form with initial l- to match the Trique word $^wla^3kwq^3$ 'lame' (and, in fact, the Mixtec cognate yak^wa simply means 'crooked'). However, it is not impossible that these two Trique terms might also be Mixtec loans. If so, then Trique has borrowed them from Mixtec at a comparatively early period—earlier than the Trique shift of $(k^w)a(h)$ to e. Moreover, we have evidence that the Triques—who are rather conservative about linguistic borrowing—borrowed the Spanish word cojo 'lame' in the form $ga^3\check{c}o^2$ some time in the past when they (or their Mixtec overlords) were in contact with a Spanish dialect in which j was pronounced as an alveopalatal sibilant (no such Spanish dialect exists in the region today).

One further possible ethnolinguistic by-product of systemic reconstruction consists in the application of a *Wörter-und-Sachen* analysis to the reconstructed corpus. Thieme (1958) has done some work of this sort in Indo-European studies. Millon and Longacre (1961) have made such a cultural analysis of the reconstructed Proto-Mixtecan and Proto-Amuzgo-Mixtecan vocabularies. In attempting to guard against some of the pitfalls inherent in a *Wörter-und-Sachen* approach, we sought for evidence of the existence of whole cultural complexes rather than merely isolated traits. Thus, on the Proto-Mixtecan horizon (some 3000 years ago?) there seems to be clear evidence for the following cultural complexes: maize complex, masa preparation complex, agricultural complex, maguey complex, and weaving complex.

2. PHONOLOGICAL SYSTEMS RECONSTRUCTED FOR BRANCHES OF OTOMANGUEAN. In this section we present in summary form phonological systems reconstructed for the six language families comprising what used to be called 'Macro-Otomanguean' but what we will refer to here simply as Otomanguean. These six families are Mixtecan, Popolocan, Chiapanec-Manguean, Otopamean, Zapotecan, and Chinantecan.

2.1. PROTO-MIXTECAN, used illustratively in the preceding sections, has the following phonological system:

Consonants

*t	*k	*k^w	*$ʔ$
*θ	*x	*x^w	
*nd	*^ng	*$^ng^w$	
*n		*m	
*y		*w	

Vowels

*i	*$ï$	*u
*e	*a	*o

Tones

*1 high register (restricted to tone sandhi variants)

*2 mid-high register

*3 mid-low register

*4 low-register

Of the consonant phonemes only *$ʔ$ and *m occur final in forms; *$mʔ$ could occur final as well. The glottal stop *$ʔ$ could occur in medial or initial cluster with possibly any consonant. Aside from these considerations the canonical forms are *$CVCV$ and *CV with no other consonant clusters, and no vowel clusters.

The semi-vowel *y apparently had a variety of allophones. A lateral allophone *$[l]$ occurred before *i and *u but its occurrence is partly conditioned there by distribution of *$ʔ$. It is possible that a phoneme *l of limited distribution (as I posited in 1957) should be retained.[7] A further nasalized allophone of *y, i.e. *$[ỹ]$ occurred at least in the Proto-Mixtecan dialects that became Mixtec and Cuicatec; occurrence of the allophone was contingent on occurrence of a nasal consonant (often final *-m) somewhere in the form.

Of the last vertical column of consonants, only *k^w and *w occurred in penultimate syllables. Furthermore, *m is extremely rare in pre-vocalic (but frequent in post-vocalic) except in the cluster *$ʔm$. Of all the consonants the alveolars *θ, *nd, and *n are the least restricted in distribution.

Of the vowels, *e and *o do not occur in penultimate syllables nor before post-posed *-m.

In regard to the tones: One tone or two non-identical tones occurred on *CV forms, while two tones, identical or non-identical, occurred on *$CVCV$ forms. Basic tone pattern *4(4) did not occur, while tone patterns involving tone *1 were restricted to sandhi variants. The occurring basic tone patterns and tone sandhi variants are here listed:

$$\left.\begin{array}{c} *22 \\ *24 \end{array}\right\} \sim *21$$

[7] At any rate *l was apparently phonemic in Proto-Mixtec from which Trique possibly borrowed such l- initial forms as are mentioned in 1.6.

$*33 \atop *23$ $\Big\} \sim *11$

$*34 \sim *14$

$*43 \sim *13$

$*42 \sim *41$

$*32 \sim *31$ (in the dialect which became Mixtec)

$*32 \sim *12$ (in the dialects which became Cuicatec and Trique)

2.2. PROTO-POPOLOCAN, as reconstructed by Gudschinsky (1959c) has the following phonological system:

Consonants

$*t$	$*t^y$	$*k$	$*k^w$	$*\textit{?}$
$*c$	$*\check{c}$			
$*s$	$*\check{s}$	$*h$	$*h^w$	
$*n$	$*\tilde{n}$		$*m$	
$*y$	$*l$ (?)		$*w$	

Vowels

$*i$		$*u$
$*e$		$*o$
	$*a$	

Tones

*1 high register (restricted to tone sandhi variants)

*2 mid-high register

*3 mid-low register

*4 low register

Clusters of two and three consonants occurred, but no vowel clusters. Since these clusters occurred initial in forms, and display some phonological variety, no sequence of nasal plus stop need be interpreted as a single prenasalized phoneme (as is, by contrast, necessary in Proto-Mixtecan). Gudschinsky lists (1959c, p. 21) *l as a Proto-Popolocan phoneme but this phoneme does not appear on any subsequent chart nor come in for comment in any of her expository paragraphs—although her statement to the effect that Proto-Popolocan has one liquid is probably a reference to *l.[8]

[8] In her set 248 Gudschinsky reconstructs *la as a further alternate along with *na, *nta, *ya 'tree', 'stick', 'wood'; the *la form is witnessed to

For Proto-Popolocan, unlike Proto-Mixtecan, no regular patterns of consonantal alternation may be posited in reconstructed nouns. Rather, various elements occur which Gudschinsky considers remnants of a former system very similar to that found in Proto-Mixtecan. The various preposed elements in both nouns and verbs are, on the whole, similar to preposed elements (consonantal alternates) in Proto-Mixtecan with the striking exception of Proto-Popolocan *t-, *tV-, and *c- which are alveolar elements of a sort not found in Proto-Mixtecan verb paradigms (although t- occurs in verb paradigms of Amuzgo).

Regarding the reconstructed Proto-Popolocan tones, Gudschinsky remarks, "*1 was almost certainly always a sandhi variant rather than a 'basic' tone," and "a disproportionately large number of items are reconstructed with *4 as one alternant, possibly because *4 was also a sandhi variant."[9]

Apparently the labiovelar and labial consonants $*k^w$, $*h^w$, *m and *w, did not occur before *o and *u. Among the vowels *o is apparently rare (reconstructed in three sets on the basis of the correspondence $u \sim o \sim u \sim o$ and in three other sets on the uniform o reflex, Gudschinsky, 1959c, p. 38).

In monosyllabic reconstructed items Gudschinsky reconstructs forms on all four contrasting pitch levels. But while Proto-Popolocan items on pitch level *2 reconstruct solidly enough, such items do not

by Chocho only. In set 354 she reconstructs *lihi, *nt^{y}ihi 'pasture', 'grass' with only the Huautla dialect of Mazatec witnessing to *lihi. In set 355 she reconstructs *la$\textit{?}$a 'dancer, singer' with Ixcatec and Huautla Mazatec witnessing to the initial *l.

[9] Gudschinsky cautions: 'A tentative reconstruction of PPn tone structure is postulated in spite of severe difficulties' (p. 38). These difficulties arise from the fact that only for two dialects of Mazatec have definitive tone analyses been published. Tones are not recorded on the Chocho forms and tone analyses of Ixcatec and Popoloca are 'in tentative phonemicization' (p. 38).

seem to have been involved in tone sandhi variation. Furthermore, pitch levels *1 and *4 are suspect of being only tone sandhi variants. I therefore venture to suggest that in Proto-Popolocan all monosyllables sort essentially into two broad tone classes: (1) those with invariable tone *2; and (2) those with basic tone *3 which varied to *4 and/or to *1. However, the latter broad tone class may possibly have had three sub-classes: (a) those varying only to *4; (b) those varying only to *1; and (c) those varying to both *4 and *1 (Gudschinsky, 1959c, pp. 39–40).

In disyllabic reconstructed items Gudschinsky reconstructs five basic patterns (including *44) with sandhi variants (p. 40). Actually, I believe that the underlying picture is simpler than her summary might indicate. I therefore venture to restate Proto-Popolocan tone in disyllabics as follows: (1) Basic tones *42 and *32 are witnessed to by one set each with *42 ∼ *44 ∼ *14, and *32 without sandhi variation. (2) Aside from these rare reconstructed patterns there are four tone classes determined by types of possible sandhi variation to higher and lower pitch levels. Common to all these tone classes are *33 and *44:

(3) Class A: *33 ∼ *34 ∼ *44 ∼ *13
(4) Class B: *33 ∼ *34 ∼ *44 ∼ *31 ∼ *11
(5) Class C: *33 ∼ *43 ∼ *44 ∼ *13
(6) Class D: *33 ∼ *43 ∼ *44 ∼ *31 ∼ *41

Conspicuously lacking in the above are *21, *22, *23, and *24, all of which are possible in a four-level system (cf. 2.7. below).

2.3. Proto-Chiapanec-Manguean, as reconstructed by María Teresa Fernández de Miranda and R. Weitlaner on the basis of written records of these two extinct languages, has the following phonological system:

Consonants

*p	*t	*k	*ʔ
	*s	*h	*hʷ

*ᵐb	*ⁿd		*ⁿg	
*m	*n	*ñ(?)		*M
*w	*y			
	*l(?)			
	*r			

Vowels			Vowel Clusters		
*i	*ị	*u	*ii		*uu
*e	*a		*ee	*aa	
			*ai		*au

Proto-Chiapanec-Manguean *ñ and *l are reconstructed by Fernández de Miranda and Weitlaner with some hesitation. Reflexes of *ñ overlap with reflexes of *n; the former may be posited only on the strength of four sets. Reflexes of *l overlap with reflexes of *r in such a fashion so as to suggest that these two were the same phoneme at an earlier stage. Fernández de Miranda and Weitlaner also characterize the vowel clusters as being somewhat dubious. The consonants *t and *ⁿd had palatalized allophones *[ts] and *[nz] before *u, while *s is considered to have had an allophone *t before *u also.[10] The velar stop *k had a palatalized allophone before *i and *e. The phoneme *M is posited rather than consonant group *hm. Presence of phonemic pitch seems probable but the sources do not mark this feature well enough to permit even the most general sort of speculation. Nasalization is marked in some of the sources but was probably conditioned by contiguous nasal consonant.

2.4. Proto-Otopamean as such has not been reconstructed at the present time. Instead we have: (1) Proto-Otomí, first reconstructed by Newman and Weitlaner (1950) and recently revised by Doris Bartholomew. (2) Proto - Otomí - Mazahua ('Primitive Central Otomian') by Newman and Weitlaner (1950); (3) Proto-Otomí-Mazahua tone tentatively reconstructed in an unpublished paper of Stewart (1957);

[10] The seeming overlap between phonemes *t and *s is not serious in that *[tV] (not *u) contrasted with *[sV] (not *u) while *[tsu] contrasted with *[tu].

127

and (4) Proto-Otomí-Pame (not taking into account Mazahua) by Bartholomew.

2.4.1. PROTO-OTOMIAN. Bartholomew's revision of Proto-Otomí consonants[11] gives us the following system; postulated phonetic qualities of consonants are indicated in brackets in that phonetic features cannot be readily inferred from the phonemic symbols:

*p [hp]	*t [ht]	*c [hts]
*b [p]	*d [t]	*z [ts]
*m [ᵐb]	*n [ⁿd]	*y

Proto-Otomí vowels are reconstructed as follows according to Newman and Weitlaner:

*i	*ə	*u	*i̧	*u̧
*e	*a	*o	*ȩ	*o̧
*ɛ	*a	*ɔ		*a̧

2.4.2. PROTO-OTOMÍ-MAZAHUA. Mazahua and Otomí are closely related. It may therefore be expected that most or all of the revisions of the sort that Bartholomew made in the Newman-Weitlaner inventory of Proto-Otomí consonants might hold as well for Otomí-Mazahua. We omit here the Newman-Weitlaner line-up of Otomí-Mazahua consonants pending re-examination by Bartholomew or someone else. The Proto-Otomí-Mazahua vowel inventory is identical with that reconstructed for Proto-Otomí.

Newman and Weitlaner also reconstruct a considerable number of diphthongs for Proto-Otomí-Mazahua. Some of these diphthongs they reconstruct simply as a device to handle certain Otomí-Mazahuan vowel correspondences. In respect to these 'diphthongal formulas' they comment: 'In view of the progressive assimilatory influences that have operated upon Mazahua it is likely that this type of diphthong formula represents an assimilatory factor, giving a

*k [hk]	*kʷ [hkʷ]	*ʔ
*g [k]	*w [kʷ]	
*s		*h

high or front vowel reflex in PMz, rather than a genuine diphthong in the parent language. But, because the conditioning factor cannot be determined from the data ... we must symbolize these special Otomí-Mazahua correspondences as distinctive vowel combinations at the PCO level.' (p. 78)[12]

For another sort of diphthong more historical reality is claimed by Newman and Weitlaner. This latter sort of diphthong is posited on the basis of such correspondences as POt $V_1V_2 \sim$ PMz V_1mV_2, e.g. *ȩi is posited as the basis of POt *ȩi $\sim$ PMz *ȩme; *ɔi, on the basis of POt *ɔi $\sim$ PMz *ɔmə; and *u̧i, on the basis of POt *u̧i $\sim$ PMz *umə. Similar are cases with *h interposed between the two members of the posited cluster: *a̧hi is reconstructed from POt *a̧hi $\sim$ PMz *ahma. Commenting on these cases Newman and Weitlaner write: 'Since most of these diphthongs have a nasal vowel as the first element in PCO and POt, the PMz *m in such cases is obviously a reflex of the vowel nasalization' (1950, p. 77). I suggest here an alternative hypothesis, viz. that the Mazahua -m- is not an innovation but an archaism, and that the nasal vowel quality in corresponding Otomí forms is a vestige of the older post-posed nasal. It seems quite plausible to take the

[11] Consonant clusters are of four sorts (Bartholomew, p. 327); (a) *p, *t, *c, *k, *kʷ, *m, *n, *y, or *w in cluster with *h, which follows the stops, but precedes the other consonants. (b) The same consonants listed above in cluster with *ʔ, which follows the stops, but precedes the other consonants. (c) *m or *n preceding any other consonant (but not in cluster with each other); *m preceded *p and *b, while *n preceded all others. (d) Clusters of three consonants involving combinations of (a) or (b) with (c), such as *mph, *nhy, *nkʔ, *nʔn and an additional two clusters *ʔtʔ and *ʔcʔ. Bartholomew discusses some systematic features in the patterning of these clusters in reference to the concept of phonetic rank (Eunice Pike, 1954) and simulfixation in Otomí (Wallis, 1956).

[12] Newman and Weitlaner abbreviate Proto-Mazahua as PMz, and Proto-Otomí-Mazahua—which they term 'Primitive Central Otomian'—as PCO.

Mazahua witness here as basic and explain the Otomí form by loss of *m* with resultant development of diphthong. Furthermore, such a suggestion is in line with the role of *m* in other branches of Otomanguean (cf. 2.10.). If my explanation of the Otomí-Mazahuan reflexes is correct we can probably assume (a) no vowel clusters in Proto-Otomí; and (b) Proto-Otomí-Mazahua postposed *-mV* and *-hmV* elements similar to certain postposed deictics suggested by Gudschinsky for Proto-Popolocan-Mixtecan.

Proto-Otomí-Mazahua tones as reconstructed by Stewart on the basis of three Otomí dialects and one Mazahua dialect include high, low, rising, and falling tones (Appendix B).

2.4.3. PROTO - OTOMÍ - PAME. Bartholomew's unpublished reconstruction of Proto-Otomí-Pame presumably has to do with an earlier layering than does the reconstruction of Otomí-Mazahua. As such, Otomí-Pame probably is more indicative of the structure of Otopamean as a whole—although definitive statements regarding the latter must await the common reconstruction of Otomí-Mazahua, Matlatzinca-Ocuilteco, Chichimeca, and Pame.

The inventory of consonant phonemes for Otomí-Pame is a small one (noticeably absent are semi-vowels).

*p	*t	*c	*k	*ʔ
*m	*n	*s		*h

But these nine consonants occur as geminate clusters and in clusters with *h*, *m*, and *ʔ* :[13]

*pp	*tt	*cc	*kk	*ʔʔ
*mm	*nn	*ss		*hh

[13] Pame has other consonant clusters not indicated here; some such clusters occur word-final as well. Some of these clusters correspond to *CV* elements in Otomí. Thus Otomí *-di* or *-de* ∼ Pame *-dn* in several sets while Otomí *gi* ∼ Pame *-gɲ* in two sets. Bartholomew gives no source for Pame *d* or *g*; I conjecture that these correspondences may hark back to Proto-Otomí-Pame *-tVn* and *-kVn* elements.

*ph	*th	*ch	*kh
*mh	*nh	*lh[14]	
	*tʔ	*cʔ	
*ʔm	*ʔn	*lʔ	
*mʔm	*nʔn		

Proto-Otomí-Pame vowels are likewise fewer in number than Proto-Otomí-Mazahua vowels: *i*, *e*, *ɛ*, *a*, *o* with the corresponding nasalized phonemes. Bartholomew comments: 'A number of cognate sets indicate proto vowel clusters. These clusters are the probable source of the Otomí extra vowels. Though the data enable us to make this basic assumption, the actual correspondences do not permit us to trace the precise development from the proto clusters to Otomí' (Bartholomew, 1959, p. 30).

Pame has three phonemic tones which occur on stressed syllables: high, low, falling. It is evident here that we have a tone system which invites comparison with the four tones reconstructed by Stewart for Otomí-Mazahua.

2.5. PROTO-ZAPOTECAN as reconstructed by Swadesh (1947) and currently under modification by Fernández de Miranda has the following inventory of consonants:

*p	*t	*k	*kʷ	*ʔ
	*c	*č		
	*s	*š		
*m	*n			
	*l			
	*r			
*w	*y			

These consonants may appear geminated with the exception of *kʷ*, *ʔ*, *r*, *w*, and *y*.

Vowels, as reconstructed by Swadesh

[14] Notice that a further consonant *l* is reconstructed as occurring in clusters *lh* and *lʔ*. In that *sh* and *sʔ* do not occur, *l* and *s* are in complementary distribution. Underlying the *lh* reconstruction is Otomí *th* ∼ Pame *lh*; and underlying the *lʔ* reconstruction is Otomí *tʔ* ∼ Pame *lʔ*. The possibility of considering *s* and *l* to be but one Otomí-Pame phoneme should be considered.

are:

$$*i \qquad\qquad *u$$

$$*e \qquad *a \qquad *o$$

The pairs of contrasting phonemic entities reconstructed here as single consonants versus geminates could alternatively be reconstructed as lenis versus fortis consonants. But Swadesh's arguments in favor of the former reconstruction appear on the whole to be valid. He argues that there is some evidence that other clusters existed of a non-geminate variety in Proto-Zapotecan. In addition, some present-day dialects have phonetically geminated versus phonetically single consonants. In the materials of Fernández de Miranda there is considerable phoneme substitution between a reconstructed single consonant and its corresponding geminate (for a possible historical explanation, see §2.10).

Swadesh does not reconstruct *m and *mm for Proto-Zapotecan. In view of the fact that apparent reflexes of bilabial nasal are very rare, he states: 'Since we have no evidence that necessarily points to an *m in Proto-Zapotec, we have to assume a secondary development of mm from *np in cases like 40 (*cunpi), even though mm or m is found in all the dialects.' (p. 223). Fernández de Miranda reconstructs *mm and *m as rare Proto-Zapotecan phonemes.

2.6. PROTO - CHINANTECAN. The preliminary reconstruction of Proto-Chinantecan made by Smith and Weitlaner (1957) exhibits the following inventory:

Consonants

*p	*t	*k	*ʔ
	*c		
*b	*d	*g	
	*s		*h
	*l		
	*r		
*m	*n	*ŋ	

Vowels

$$*i \qquad *ï \qquad *u$$

$$*e \qquad *a \qquad *o$$
$$*a$$

(with all corresponding nasalized vowels as well).

Noteworthy in the above is the reconstruction of *ŋ, in that a velar nasal is reconstructed for no other branch of Otomanguean.

Consonant clusters with *ʔ and *h are posited: *hg, *ʔg, *hl, *ʔl, *hm, *ʔm, *hn, *ʔn, *hŋ, *ʔŋ. The restriction of these clusters to those with *g, *l, or a nasal consonant as a second member is a curious feature here; it leads one to suspect that Proto-Chinantec *g in such clusters (where no other stop occurs) is a reflex of some Proto-Otomanguean semi-vowel such as *y or *w.

A quantity of vowel clusters is posited. In Proto-Chinantec, the absence of semi-vowels together with the presence of many vowel clusters—the bulk of which involve *i or *u (whether nasal or oral)—make it probable that Proto-Chinantec vowel clusters arose from *VyV and *VwV sequences in Otomanguean.

2.7. PROTO - OTOMANGUEAN. A first approximation to Proto-Otomanguean has been made by Gudschinsky (1959c) in her reconstruction of 'Proto-Popotecan,' i.e. Proto - Popolocan - Mixtecan. She reconstructs the following phonemes[15] for Proto-Popolocan-Mixtecan (abbreviated PPMx):

Consonants

*t	*tʸ	*k	*kʷ	*ʔ
*θ		*x	*xʷ	

[15] I have modified Gudschinsky's reconstructed system slightly here by subtracting *ɔ—which was reconstructed for Proto-Popolocan-Mixtecan largely on the supposed strength of my reconstruction of such a vowel in Proto-Mixtecan. Proto-Popolocan-Mixtecan *tʸ is rare; Gudschinsky, in fact, reconstructs it from but three sets in which PPn *tʸ ~ PMx *t (her sets 34, 36, and 42). She mentions in a footnote (p. 44) a number of residue sets in which PPn *č or *tʸ corresponds to PMx *θ. It is possible that both Proto-Popolocan-Mixtecan *tʸ and *θʸ should be reconstructed. Gudschinsky is uncertain about the status of *ny as a phoneme or cluster in Proto-Popolocan-Mixtecan.

$*n$ $*n^y$ $*m$

$*l$ $*y$ $*w$

Vowels

$*i$ $*ï$ $*u$

$*e$ $*o$

$*ë$ $*a$

Some of the more noteworthy phonological developments from Proto-Popolocan-Mixtecan to Proto-Popolocan are (1) PPMx $*yk$ or $*ky >$ PPn $*t^y$ (before PPMx $*ë$), thus augmenting distribution of this presumably rare phoneme; while before other reconstructed vowels the PPn reflex was $*č$. (2) A three-way split of PPMx $*\theta$ into PPn $*s$, $*š$, and $*c$. It seems to me to be plausible that $*s$ and $*š$ were freely varying allophones in early Proto-Popolocan, but that contrast arose in late Proto-Popolocan when considerable dialect difference had already arisen. The third Proto-Popolocan reflex of Proto-Popolocan-Mixtecan $*\theta$, viz. Proto-Popolocan $*c$, occurred in cluster with $*h$ or $*n$—but these latter two elements, especially $*n$, have been in many instances lost in all Popolocan languages except Mazatec. Gudschinsky posited $*č$ as another Proto-Popolocan reflex of Proto-Popolocan-Mixtecan $*\theta$ but possibly Proto-Popolocan-Mixtecan $*\theta^y$ might be reconstructed here instead. (3) Proto-Popolocan-Mixtecan $*mn$ cluster was reduced to Proto-Popolocan $*m$ by loss of second member (unpublished Popolocan-Mixtecan sets).

Some noteworthy phonological developments from Proto-Popolocan-Mixtecan to Proto-Mixtecan are: (1) Unconditional merger of Proto-Popolocan-Mixtecan $*t$ and $*t^y$ into Proto-Mixtecan $*t$. (2) Development of a Proto-Mixtecan prenasalized series $*^nd$, $*^ng$, $*^ng^w$ from fusion of stop and/or spirant with preposed nasal. This development came about by reduction of other Proto-Popolocan-Mixtecan clusters in initial position (exclusive of $*?C$), so that the three surviving clusters were reinterpreted as unit phonemes. (3) PPMx $*mw >$ PMx $*m$.

In tone systems Proto-Popolocan and Proto-Mixtecan are very similar. Both are four-level systems with $*1$ restricted to sandhi variants. Either tone pattern $*44$ did not occur at all in Proto-Popolocan-Mixtecan (it is clearly witnessed to in Proto-Popolocan but absent in Proto-Mixtecan), or it was possibly restricted to tone sandhi variants. A portion of Gudschinsky's summary of this and related considerations follows:[16] 'For PPtn, I postulate the occurrence of all the possible sequences, with loss of $*44$ in PMx, and the augmenting of the frequency of $*44$ in PPn by special sandhi development. The sequences with $*2$ on the initial syllable may have been lost in PPn, but it is more likely that they are hidden by the inadequate analyses of the living languages. This hypothesis is supported by the fact that PPn has a much larger inventory of alternations and variants than PMx, and it seems probable that some of these should rather be reconstructed as basic sets with $*2$. For example, PMx has $*43 \sim *13$ and $*42 \sim *41$. PPn has $*43 \sim *13$ in some sets, and $*43 \sim *41$ in others. The obvious conclusion is that $*43 \sim *41$ reflects PPtn $*42 \sim *41$. Unfortunately it has not been possible to match the majority of the PMx reconstructions in this fashion, and exact correspondences are too few for any definite conclusions' (Gudschinsky 48-9).[17] It also

---

[16] Gudschinsky labels what I here term Proto-Popolocan-Mixtecan as 'Proto-Popotecan' and abbreviates to PPtn.

[17] But just as Gudschinsky conjectures that one class of Proto-Popolocan $*43$ stems could actually reflect Proto-Popolocan-Mixtecan $*42$, it could similarly be suggested that one class of Proto-Popolocan $*34$ could be Proto-Popolocan-Mixtecan $*24$ (PPn $*34 \sim *13$ versus PPn $*34 \sim *31$; see Section 2.2.). Similarly there are classes of Proto-Popolocan $*33$ stems which may possibly mask $*22$ versus $*23$. Gudschinsky reconstructs Proto-Popolocan $*32$ in one set with no witness to sandhi variant. Proto Mixtecan $*32$ is peculiar as well, in that it has two sandhi variants: $*31$ in the late Proto-Mixtecan dialect that became Mixtec, and

seems plausible, by way of more general observation, that Proto - Popolocan - Mix - tecan had sandhi variation both to higher and lower tone patterns. The latter sort of sandhi variation was dropped in the transition to Proto-Mixtecan (with concomitant disappearance of pattern *44 in Proto-Mixtecan as well).

Gudschinsky reconstructs for Proto-Popolocan-Mixtecan two noun declensions very similar to those I posit for Proto-Mixtecan:

> *t declension: *t, *y, *n, *nt, *x
> *θ declension: *θ, *y, *ny, *nθ

These noun declensions with some modifications survive as declensions in Proto-Mixtecan, but only as fragments in Proto-Popolocan. Possibly the three-way split of Proto-Popolocan-Mixtecan *θ into late Proto-Popolocan *s, *š, and *c (not to mention *č)—which shattered the *θ declension into bits—had something to do with the disappearance of neatly delineated noun declensions in Proto-Popolocan. On the Mixtecan side, where *θ does not undergo split and merger with other phonemes, the declensions were retained.

Items preposed to verbs are more varied on the Proto-Popolocan-Mixtecan horizon than on the Proto-Mixtecan horizon. Even on the Proto-Popolocan horizon we do not find anything as neat and regular as the four tense-aspects of Proto-Mixtecan. Noticeably, *t and *θ figure in Proto-Popolocan-Mixtecan and Proto-Popolocan verb forms, but not in Proto-Mixtecan verb forms (Gudscinsky p. 58).

Gudschinsky reconstructs postposed deictics for Proto-Popolocan-Mixtecan. An outer layer deictic has survived only as Proto-Mazatec *-V^3/*-V^4 marking end of noun phrase and slightly deictic in function,

and as Proto-Trique *-a^3 end of noun phrase. But she postulates that this deictic particle is a Proto-Popolocan-Mixtecan development antedated by an older deictic layer which was already losing deictic significance and fusing with the Proto-Popolocan-Mixtecan stems. These 'inner layer' deictics she reconstructs as: *xmV, *ʔmV, *xV, and *ʔV. It seems likely that these reduce essentially to two forms plus or minus *m, i.e. either to *xV(m) and *ʔV(m) or to *x(m)V and *ʔ(m)V.[18]

As a first approximation to Proto-Otomanguean, Gudschinsky's 'Proto-Popotecan' may prove to be (a) actually on the Proto-Otomanguean horizon of reconstruction, as a reconstruction based upon but two language families and needing to be amplified by taking account of further language families; or (b) slightly more recent than the Proto-Otomanguean horizon of reconstruction, in that these two families may prove to constitute a group more closely related to each other than to other Otomanguean languages.

2.8. PROTO-POPO-MANGUEAN. A second approximation to Proto-Otomanguean has been made by Fernández de Miranda and Weitlaner in their reconstruction of 'Proto-Popo-Mangue' on the basis of Popolocan, Mixtecan, and Chiapanec-Manguean (1961). The following phonological system is

---

*12 in the late Proto-Mixtecan dialects that became Cuicatec and Trique. It is therefore possible that Proto-Popolocan-Mixtecan *32 was rare and had no sandhi variant, and that such variants developed only in later Proto-Mixtecan dialects.

[18] Furthermore it seems plausible to me that it will also eventually be necessary to reconstruct either *-m or *-mV (possibly *-Vm) in sets that possibly show influence of a bilabial nasal but no evidence of *x or *ʔ. Thus, *ɔ on the Proto-Mixtecan horizon has been eliminated in favor of *am. But Proto-Popolocan a versus u reflexes of my formerly postulated *ɔ are similar to a versus u reflexes of Proto-Popolocan-Mixtecan *am versus *am. Furthermore, Gudschinsky has expressly formulated that "*a has reflex *u before *m or *w in some dialects of PPn' (p. 46). If we eliminate *ɔ on both Proto-Mixtecan and Proto-Popolocan-Mixtecan horizons, then it seems simplest to attribute Proto-Popolocan reflex *u of reputed *ɔ to *a plus postposed bilabial nasal which disappeared early and without trace (except vowel nasalization?) in Proto-Popolocan. Gudschinsky attributes reflex *u of reputed *ɔ to a preceding nasal.

reconstructed for Proto-Popo-Manguean:

*t	*t^y	*k	*k^w	*$ʔ$
*c		*h	*h^w	
*n			*m	
*l	*y		*w	

Vowels

*i	*$ï$	*u
*e		*o
*$ë$	*a	

The reconstructed consonants comprise a system which resembles that projected for Proto-Popolocan-Mixtecan in respect to absence of *p and presence of series *c, *h, and *h^w which resembles the Proto-Popolocan-Mixtecan series of spirants (*$θ$, *x, *x^w). However, it is within the realm of possibility that Proto-Popo-Manguean *p could be reconstructed rather than *k^w. The latter is attested to in but one set where on the Mixtecan side presence of consonantal alternation (PMx *w/*$^ng^w$) further weakens the witness to the postulated *k^w. Furthermore, on cursory examination it appears to me to be possible that some of the Fernández-Weitlaner reconstructions with Chiapanec-Manguean *p may prove to be cognate with sets with Proto-Mixtecan *k^w.

Fernández de Miranda and Weitlaner reconstruct consonant groups *kh and *kh^w in contrast with *k and *k^w on the one hand and with *h and *h^w on the other hand. Leaving aside the more dubious reconstruction *k^w just discussed, the pertinent sound correspondences are:

(1) PChM *k ∼ PPMx *k < PPM *k
(2) PChM *h ∼ PPMx *x < PPM *h
(3) PChM *h^w ∼ PPMx *x^w < PPM *h^w
(4) PChM *p/*^mb ∼ PPMx *x^w < PPM *$h^w(i)$
(5) PChM *h ∼ PPMx *k
(6) PChM *h^w ∼ PPn *k/zero ∼ PMx *k^w

For correspondences (5) and (6) Fernández de Miranda and Weitlaner reconstruct *kh and *kh^w respectively. This is a plausible reconstruction in the light of Gudschinsky's Popolocan-Mixtecan reconstructions which indicate a considerable number of consonant clusters. However, a possibility suggested by Swadesh (1960a, p. 96) should be investigated here, viz. the possible presence of front versus back velars. For the moment the presumption is against this suggestion in view of the fact that clear evidence has not yet been presented to substantiate presence of this sort of phonemic contrast in Otomanguean. Nevertheless, the presence of two k-positions in Mayan and Totonacan should alert us to the fact that contrasts of this sort are found in Middle America as a possible areal feature of the sort sometimes found to transcend genetic groupings.

Besides the clusters *kh and *kh^w just discussed, Fernández de Miranda and Weitlaner posit *nt, *nt^y, *nk, and *hm. It seems to me that their data also suggest *mw, *mn, *mp, and/or *nk^w. Furthermore, there is some evidence that the forms with a preposed nasal alternated grammatically with forms without a preposed nasal. Perhaps Proto-Popo-Manguean *hm harks back to an earlier *mh. The following Pre-Popo-Manguean scheme might be suggested:

t/nt
t^y/nt^y
k/nk
c/nc
n/mn
w/mw

To this we could probably add *y/*ny (as underlying PChM *$ñ$) and either *p/*mp or *k^w/*nk^w (or both?). To this general pattern of consonant alternating with nasal plus consonant, might be added a more specialized alternation *t^y/*y of which there appear to be traces.

Certain preposed elements in Proto-Popo-Manguean verbs are similar to those posited for Proto-Popolocan-Mixtecan verbs (especially if PChM *p ∼ PMx *k^w). Preposed *ti-/*tu- for Proto-Chiapanec-Manguean past tense and *ta- for future tense have similar *tV- elements in Proto-Popolocan

133

and in Amuzgo, but no parallels in Proto-Mixtecan. For discussion of some postposed Proto-Popo-Manguean elements see Appendix C.

2.9. MACRO-MIXTECAN. Swadesh has recently made several suggestions concerning what I continue here to call Otomanguean phonology in spite of his attempt to expunge Chiapanec and Manguean from this group and to rename the whole Macro-Mixtecan. One suggestion of his—that possibly Mixtec is the most typical language of this family—must await evaluation until we have a better picture of Otomanguean structure. However, two suggestions of Swadesh seem to me to be worthy of special mention: (a) Both *p and *kʷ may need to be reconstructed for Proto-Otomanguean with these both falling together as *kʷ in Proto-Mixtecan and Proto-Popolocan. Note the possibility that these both fell together as *p in Proto-Chiapanec-Manguean. (b) It may eventually prove necessary to reconstruct front versus back velar positions.

2.10. PROTO-OTOMANGUEAN *m. One of the most interesting features of Otomanguean structure may well prove to be the consonant *m.[19] While possibly somewhat rare in stems, this phoneme was apparently quite frequent as a preposed and postposed element (possibly with an associated vowel). (1) In Proto-Mixtecan stems, *m is rare but *ʔm/*m is fairly frequent. It is possible that ultima *-ʔmV syllables in Proto-Mixtecan may hark back to a Proto-Otomanguean postposed deictic *-ʔmV which eventually became part of the stem (cf. various *-ʔV and *-hV elements in Proto-Popolocan). (2) In the Popolocan languages, incidence of m in stems has been augmented by the development of older *mn cluster (from preposed *m- plus initial *n-) to *m in Proto-Popolocan. Similarly, some cases of Proto-Mixtecan *m in stems hark back to older cluster *mw (from preposed *m-

plus initial *w-). (3) Proto-Mixtecan and Proto - Chiapanec - Manguean prenasalized stops originated from such clusters as *mt, *mθ, *mtʸ, *mk, *mx, *mkʷ, and *mxʷ which fell together in various ways with concomitant reduction of other *-mC- or *-mC- clusters. (4) As postposed *-mV and *-ʔmV elements that fused into the stem (with loss of *m in Otomí leading to development of vowel clusters), the phoneme *m played an important role in Otomí-Mazahua phonology and possibly in general Otopamean phonology as well. (5) In the development of Proto-Zapotecan from Proto-Otomanguean it is possible that *m—which all but disappeared in that branch—played a crucial role. I offer here somewhat diffidently a hypothesis which is outlined below.

Many Proto-Otomanguean *mC clusters became Proto-Zapotecan *CC (geminate) by assimilation of the *m to the following consonant. Thus, the Proto-Zapotecan geminate clusters developed from what seems to be a prevailing type of Proto-Otomanguean non-geminate cluster, viz. *mC. The fact that the 'fortis and lenis' (i.e. geminate versus simple) are often somewhat confused in Zapotecan reflects Proto-Otomanguean *mC versus *C, pursuant to a frequent pattern of consonantal alternation testified to in such an early layer as Proto-Popo-Mangue (cf. under 2.8). Thus, such forms as *CVCV and *CVmCV, as well as *CV and *mCV existed side by side for many Proto-Otomanguean roots; haphazard survival of forms with or without *m- accounts for a certain inconsistency in 'fortis versus lenis' (i.e. geminated consonant versus single consonant) reflexes in Proto-Zapotecan. The fact that *m is very scarce in Proto-Zapotecan is due precisely to this wholesale assimilation of that consonant.

A detail of Isthmus Zapotec morphophonemics is possibly explained by such a hypothesis, viz. Ci- or Ca- prefix before a lenis consonant alternates to Cu- prefix

---

[19] Cf. Appendix D.

before a fortis consonant in causative paradigms. We may assume here that the *Ci*- and *Ca*- basic forms of the prefixes hark back to Proto-Otomanguean **CV*- syllables not followed by **m*- of the succeeding syllable, while the *Cu*- forms of these same prefixes hark back to Proto-Otomanguean **CV*- syllables followed by **m*- in the succeeding syllable. The bilabial **m* presumably leaves a trace in labializing *i* and *a* to *u*.

Note the following Isthmus Zapotec data:[20]

giǰuʔuni	'It's going to be fried'
gučuʔuni	'Fry it'
riziʔidé	'I learn'
rusiʔidé	'I teach'
niziʔidikabe	'they did not learn'
nusiʔidu	'you do not teach'
riǰiʔicibě	'she gets angry'
ručiʔime	'he makes (me) angry'
(naʔa)	
nižaleʔ	'this did not come open'
nušalétú	'you (pl.) did not open it'
zadoʔoni	'it will sell'
zutoʔolu	'you will sell (something)'

In the last two examples we suggest the following development: Proto - Otomanguean **θat-* > PZ **sat* > IZ *zad-*; Proto-Otomanguean **θamt* > PZ **sutt* > IZ *zut*.

We hasten to add that it is by no means true, either internally in Isthmus Zapotec or in Proto-Zapotec, that instances of fortis consonants are regularly preceded by vowel *u*. Nevertheless, we have cited a tendency in this direction. Our observation offers an explanation of occurrences of *i* and *a* alternating with *u* where observed; it does not attempt to explain parallel cases where such a development might be expected but does not occur. For further Zapotec data of possible relevance here see appendix D.

3. Phonological systems reconstructed for other Middle American language families. With various systems reconstructed for branches of Otomanguean and with Proto-Otomanguean itself beginning to take shape, I now turn to the summary of reconstruction in other Middle American linguistic stocks. There first follows a sketch of Proto-Uto-Aztecan of the Aztec-Tanoan phylum; then follow Proto-Zoquean, Proto-Mayan, and Proto-Totonacan, which are usually considered to be related to each other and have sometimes been termed 'Mexican Penutian'. We do not have materials available for Proto-Hokaltecan (or for Hokaltecan plus Jicaque and Yurumangui).[21]

3.1. Proto - Uto - Aztecan. In a pithy little nine-page article written in 1935 Whorf gave us an excellent sketch of Proto-Uto-Aztecan phonology with some attention to structural features of the reconstructed language as well. In Whorf's words: 'The comparative linguistics of the Uto-Aztecan stock is now entering upon its second stage. . . . This first stage may be described as finding out what we had to deal with. One of its leading ideas was classification of the stock into sub-groups and attempts to grade degrees of linguistic kinship. . . . If the key word of the first stage was classification, that of the second stage has become structure. In the first stage we compared words willy-nilly, looking for resemblances to appear. On the basis of much rough and quick comparison we attempted to arrange our hodge-podge of facts into something like order. Eventually a feeling for the basic structure of Uto-Aztecan speech emerged; these languages had a characteristic structure of word and stem, as Semitic and Bantu have' (p. 600). The above quotation describes well the genesis and growth of a comparative reconstruction project, which begins with desultory comparisons and ends with systemic comparisons, reconstruction of proto-forms, and some awareness of the structure of the reconstructed layer.

[20] From a problem of Velma Pickett's included in Nida's Morphology (1949, p. 262 ff.).

[21] Cf. Greenberg and Swadesh, 1954; Bright, 1956.

Whorf gives the following inventory of Proto-Uto-Aztecan phonemes:

Consonants

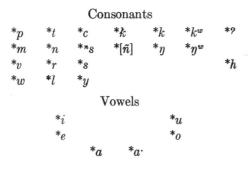

*p	*t	*c	*k̯	*k	*kʷ	*ʔ
*m	*n	*ⁿs	*[ñ]	*ŋ	*ŋʷ	
*v	*r	*s				*h
*w	*l	*y				

Vowels

*i			*u
*e			*o
	*a	*a·	

In setting up the Proto-Uto-Aztecan consonants Whorf postulated *p/*v, i.e. *p as a stop phoneme and *v as a spirant overlapping distributionally with the stop to such an extent that it is very difficult to separate with certainty reflexes of the one versus reflexes of the other. Whorf similarly postulated a relationship of *m/*ŋʷ ('ŋʷ, related in some similar but not quite the same way to *m' p. 606). Regarding *ñ Whorf commented 'Possibly ñ should be added to the list' (p. 606).

Several morphophonemes are reconstructed which can be better summarized by first sketching briefly Whorf's picture of Proto-Uto-Aztecan structure. Stems are primarily of *CVCV* structure with a small minority of *CV* stems. *CVCV* stems occurred in patterns of derivation and inflection that involved suffixes, a limited number of prefixes, 'changes in and apocopation of the second stem vowel', and reduplication. In addition to these grammatical devices, Proto-Uto-Aztecan was also characterized by the alternations *p/*v and *m/*ŋʷ.

Whorf appears to have felt that alternation between *p and *v in Proto-Uto-Aztecan stems involved interchange of full phonemes harking back to an earlier period when *p had a stop allophone *[v] occurring in intervocalic position. But apparently Proto-Uto-Aztecan stops in general had spirant allophones in intervocalic position; in many of the daughter languages the

136

conditioning factor or factors disappeared with the result that the stop/spirant alternation became phonemic. There are, however, certain Uto-Aztecan stems with medial consonant which appear to be resistant to spirantization. Whorf shrewdly reasoned that such consonants were not originally intervocalic, but that another consonant occurred in cluster before the consonants that proved resistant to spirantization—so that no spirant allophone occurred in these Proto-Uto-Aztecan stems. Whorf further noticed that there was a nasalizing influence associated with some instances of occurrence of consonants resistant to spirantization. Putting all these and other data together, Whorf formulated the hypothesis that the medial clusters in which spirant allophones did not occur consisted of stop preceded by nasal consonant or by a limited class of other consonants 'perhaps *l, *r, possibly no more.' (p. 606). His 'spirant-proof unnasalized set' *ˣp, *ˣt, *ˣc, *ˣk̯, *ˣk, and *ˣkʷ—presumably are clusters consisting of stop preceded by *l or *r; while his nasalized set *ᵐp, *ⁿt, *ⁿc, *ᵑk̯, *ᵑk, *ᵑkʷ are to be interpreted simply as nasal plus stop clusters.

Furthermore, Whorf seems to indicate that *l, *r, and nasals could also appear as final consonants in a *CVCVC* sub-type of the broad *CVCV* pattern. In short, syllable patterns *CV* and *CVC* occurred; when *CVC* occurred the final *C* was *l, *r, or a nasal. Combinations of these two syllable patterns give *CVCV*, *CVCVC*, and *CVCCVC*.

In regard to the relative chronology of the above, Whorf is somewhat vague. He seemed to hint that these clusters existed in Pre-Proto-Uto-Aztecan, in that he reconstructed Proto-Uto-Aztecan morphophonemes with antispirantizing and nasalizing tendency rather than the consonant clusters as such—which he may have wanted to relegate to an earlier stage. But this hardly seems possible. Either the clusters still existed in Proto-Uto-Aztecan, and spirant allophones were in complementary distribution with stops; or the clusters had already disappeared from Proto-Uto-Aztecan, and the spirant allophones were already separate phonemes. There scarcely seems to be room for an intermediate stage when 'anti-spirantizing and nasalizing influences' existed, while the clusters had nevertheless disappeared and the spirant allophones were not yet phonemic.

Whorf seems to feel that vowel length characterized Proto-Uto-Aztecan, but reconstructs only $*a$ versus $*a\cdot$ with the comment 'Varied reflexes of other vowels may also be a function of length but this has not yet been worked out' (p. 606). Here we probably would do well to trust Whorf's appraisal of the situation. Nevertheless, as his reconstruction of vowels now stands, it could be restated as follows: Converting Whorf's $*e$ to $*\ddot{\imath}$ (by far the commonest reflex is $\ddot{\imath}$), and interpreting his $*a$ as $*\ddot{a}$ and his $*a\cdot$ simply as $*a$ we obtain:

$$*i \qquad *\ddot{\imath} \qquad *u$$
$$*\ddot{a} \qquad *a \qquad *o$$

The only regrettable feature of Whorf's study is its brevity. We could wish for a catalogue of cognate sets appended to this most useful and provocative article, but this apparently was beyond the scope of Whorf's intentions.

3.2. PROTO-ZOQUEAN. Wonderly has reconstructed Proto-Zoquean by the comparison of Zoque (4 dialects), Tapachulteca, Sierra Popoluca, and Mixe (1949). In regard to Tapachulteca, Wonderly comments: 'Materials on the extinct or nearly extinct Tapachulteca are scanty and not too reliable, but are included where possible' (p. 2). He postulates the following reconstructed system:

Consonants[22]

$*p$	$*t$	$*c$	$*k$	$*k^w$	$*\text{?}$
	$*s$				$*h$

[22] Wonderly does not reconstruct an alveopalatal series $*t^y$, $*\check{c}$, $*\check{s}$, $*\tilde{n}$ for Proto-Zoquean (in

$*m$	$*n$		$*\eta$		
$*w$	$*y$				$*W$

Vowels

$*i$	$*a$	$*u$
$*e$		$*o$
$*\ddot{a}$		$*a$

Of the above phonemes, $*k^w$ is set up on the basis of the correspondence Zoque and Popoloca $k^w \sim$ Tapachulteca and Mixe p in one set; it is thus not well attested. The vowel $*\ddot{a}$ is set up on the basis of correspondence Mixe-Zoque-Popoluca $a \sim$ Tapachulteca e. Although its reconstruction might be questioned in view of the poor quality of the Tapachulteca data, it can probably be regarded as solid.

Wonderly reconstructs a morphophoneme $*W$ which deserves special comment. It is reconstructed on the basis of Zoque morphophoneme $X \sim$ Sierra Popoluca morphophoneme V. In Central Zoque, X has the following phonological characteristics: (1) $-hC + X > -CX > C$ since X itself is phonologically zero. (2) $-V\eta + X > -Vw$. (3) $-Vh + X > -Vy$ (if V is a, e, i, or a) and $-Vw$ (if V is u). In Northern Zoque, morphophoneme X does not include $h > y$ when preceded by a, e, i, or a as in (3) above, but includes the other morphophonemic changes. In Sierra Popoluca—in suffixes cognate with Zoque suffixes containing morphophoneme X—there occurs a morphophoneme V which is actualized phonologically as follows:

(1) CVC- stem + morphophoneme $V >$ $CV\cdot C$-

(2) $CV\text{?}C$- stem + morphophoneme $V >$ $CV\text{?}VC$-

spite of its well-nigh universal presence) in that he feels there is ample cause to believe that these phonemes have arisen 'from an alveolar phoneme palatalized by a contiguous y or i'. It seems safe to infer that palatalized allophones were present in Proto-Zoquean, and have independently become phonemic in the various languages and dialects by break-downs in the pattern of complementary distribution.

(3) $CVCC$- or $CVCCC$- + morphophoneme V > no change

Wonderly's choice of symbol *W is based on the following argument: (a) The Proto-Zoquean phonological feature here symbolized seems to have been a semi-vowel. Thus, PZoq *W > SP V which acts like a vowel in that Sierra Popoluca V > V· while V? > V?V; but acts like a consonant in that, given a CC or CCC cluster in Sierra Popoluca, this V morphophoneme is not actualized at all (thus V figured as a consonant which is eliminated in reduction of certain clusters). On the Zoque side, Proto-Zoquean *W > X which acts like a semi-vowel in that it conditions h to w apparently in most if not all Zoque dialects; and conditions h to y as well after certain vowels in Central Zoque. But, again, Zoque X acts like a consonant in that its presence results in loss of h from final -hC clusters. (b) But if this Proto-Zoquean morphophoneme were a semi-vowel, a bilabial semi-vowel seems indicated. Crucial here is the fact that in Central Zoque and in Sierra Popoluca w 'does not appear in word-final position, and appears in syllable-final position in a very limited number of intervocalic -CC- clusters most of which are Spanish loans.' But *W as set up in Proto-Zoquean is apparently syllable-final or at least post-vocalic. Wonderly suggests that possible his Proto-Zoquean *w and *W were in complementary distribution. His only hesitation seems to be as to whether Proto-Zoquean *w was actually lacking in syllable final. Nevertheless, in the data of his article, post-vocalic *w is clearly lacking, and Wonderly apparently knew of no exceptions or he would have included them. Furthermore, *h, *$?$, *s, *y, *m, *n, and *$ŋ$ all appear in syllable final, i.e. every non-stop phoneme except *w; while in postvocalic position preceding a final C, both *h and *y occur but not *w. The apparent phonetic similarity of *w and *W, their situation in complementary distribu-

tion in available reconstructions, and the curiously defective distribution of *w as just mentioned all combine to make it seem very plausible that *W was simply an allophone of Proto-Zoquean *w.

3.3. PROTO-MAYAN, as reconstructed by McQuown (1955) has the following phonological system:

Consonants

*p	*t	*c	*$č$	*k	*$ḳ$	*$?$
*'p	*'t	*'c	*'$č$	*'k	*'$ḳ$	
		*s	*$š$	*x		*h
*m	*n			*$ŋ$		
*w			*y			
	*l					
	*r					

Vowels

*i		*u		*i·		*u·
*e	*a	*o		*e·	*a·	*o·

A slightly more recent work of McQuown's (1956) posits not five but six Proto-Mayan vowel positions, posits presence of two contrasting pitch-accents, and adds *$ç$ to the reconstructed consonants.

The consonant system exhibits symmetrical series of stops and glottalized stops including the affricates *c and *$č$ (and *'c and *'$č$) as well as fronted and backed velars *k and *$ḳ$ (and *'k and *'$ḳ$). As less extensive series occur spirants, nasals, semi-vowels, and liquids. Consonant clusters occurred as follows: C_1C_2, with C_2 consisting of the semi-vowels *y and *w; and C_1 consisting of any consonant except: the bilabials *p, *'p, *m, the liquids *l, *r, and the semi-vowels themselves.

3.4. PROTO-TOTONACAN, as reconstructed by Arana (1953) on the basis of three Totonac dialects and one Tepehua dialect, has the following phonological system:

Consonants

*p	*t	*c	*$č$	*$tł$	*k	*$ḳ$	*$?$
		*s	*$š$	*$ł$	*x		
*m	*n						
*w			*y				
	*l						

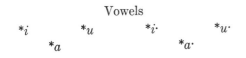

Vowels

$*i$ $\quad$ $*u$ $\quad$ $*i\cdot$ $\quad$ $*u\cdot$

$\quad *a$ $\quad\quad\quad\quad *a\cdot$

Initial clusters of spirant plus stop occurred: $*sk$, $*šk$, $*st$, $*šḳ$, $*lk$, $*lt$. In medial position, syllable-final consonants (e.g. $*t$, $*k$, $*s$, $*n$, and $*y$) followed by syllable-initial consonants or clusters constituted clusters of two or three members.

Proto-Totonac was characterized by consonantal alternation in the following patterns: $*k/*ḳ$; $*c/*č/*tl$; $*s/*š/*l$. There is also some suggestion of vowel alternation.

In the list of phonemes, $*ʔ$ is included in the stop series, perhaps for want of a better place. Arana actually reconstructs glottalized vowels in preference to either a separate glottal stop phoneme or a series of glottalized consonants.

As a whole, phonological developments from Proto-Totonacan to Totonac and Tepehua are rather regular and pedestrian. Evidently the dialects have not diverged far from each other. There is clear evidence in the Totonac dialect of San Pedro Petlacotla of considerable lexical borrowing from adjacent Tepehua.

4. DIFFUSION PHENOMENA AND LINGUISTIC FAMILY TREES. Against the background of the above summary of reconstructed systems in Middle America I now discuss certain matters having to do with diffusion of features versus 'family tree' relationships, and with classification into subgroups within a language family.

The position here taken is that an intelligible and useful concept of language relationship must retain the notion of linguistic 'family' in the sense of (a) an internal relationship of peculiar relevance for the languages included within a family; (b) external relationships of less relevance with languages of related families; and (c) related versus non-related languages and language families. This we explain in a hypothetical situation below:

Linguistic groups X, Y, Z, and W each contain a small number of related languages which may be symbolized as l, m, n, and o respectively. The l languages which comprise group X are related primarily to each other, as are the m languages of group Y, the n languages of group Z, and the o languages of group W. The linguistic groups X, Y, and Z (but not including group W) comprise a broader grouping, and are mutually related in a fashion analogous to that in which l languages of Y are related (or the languages of group Y, Z, or W). There is a given language α among the l languages of group X, and a given language π among the m languages of group Y. Relationship of α to π is by virtue of the broader relationship of group X to group Y rather than by direct relationship of α to π as such.

In keeping with the above assumptions, we entertain the following questions: (1) Since in group X, languages α, β, γ, and δ are found, what are the internal relationships of the four languages? Are they four coordinate off-shoots of one parent stock, or do two or three of the languages constitute a sub-group? (2) Is a language ϵ—reputedly of group X—actually found to belong to group Y or Z? Similarly in keeping with our assumptions, we consider the following to be non-fruitful lines of inquiry: (3) Which language, α or β, of group X is the most closely related to language π of group Y? (4) May not the linguistic divergence between α and γ of group X be greater than the divergence between γ of group X and π of group Y? To answer the last question affirmatively seems to this writer to lead either to combining groups X and Y, or to scrapping the very concept of linguistic family. Therefore, if we grant the validity of group X versus group Y this question may not be answered affirmatively.[23]

[23] The above attempt to make explicit what we mean by linguistic 'family' is not simply a theoretical construct. It attempts to give weight to some known facts of language history and development. For example, we know that the Romance languages have developed from a somewhat

However, the family-tree concept may be criticized on the grounds that it does not permit us to give adequate weight to resemblances between certain languages. What if, e.g., a given language σ assigned to group R does as a matter of fact appear to be very resemblant to a language of group T? What of resemblances between apparently unrelated languages? Or to ask another question of a slightly different sort: Why are family-tree genealogical schemes *within* a language family or among major branches of a stock often so indeterminate?

Resemblances between languages can be from one of three sources: (1) genetic relationship; (2) chance parallelism of development; and (3) diffusion from one language or language group to another. In respect to the third consideration, several conclusions seem possible. First of all, it seems that borrowing is on the whole most frequent and uninhibited between two mutually intelligible dialects of the same language. But borrowing may take place between any two languages granted a situation of contact with some bilingualism. Finally, languages in the same geographical area tend to become similar (e.g. note common

---

homogeneous vernacular Latin spoken in the first few centuries of the Christian Era. We also have documents to substantiate earlier stages of Greek, Indic, Germanic, and Slavic—so that we can with considerable assurance speak of Germanic, Slavic, and Indic (or Indo-Iranian) as language families. But these families and others are considered to be related qua families in the Indo-European stock. We entertain questions concerning internal relationships within, say, Germanic or Romance. We entertain similar questions about mutual relationship among the branches of IE. We may also entertain questions concerning the linguistic family into which some poorly attested language fits. But we have not entertained questions such as: Which Germanic language is most closely related to French? Nor are we accustomed to considering that the distance between two Germanic languages could be greater than the distance between some Germanic language and some Slavic language. We do not attend to the last two considerations simply because we believe in the historical validity of language families within Indo-European.

grammatical features in the Balkans; French-like phonemic systems in the Breton dialects of France; and presence of domal stops in the Indo-Pakistan subcontinent).

On finding a language σ of genetic group R which is resemblant to another language τ of genetic group T, we can assume one of two things (other than fortuitous coincidence) and maintain the concept of language family: (a) We can assume a strong diffusion of σ to τ, e.g. influence of French on English; or (b) we may re-examine the scheme of genetic relationship itself. We may, e.g., find that language σ forms a one-language group Q which is coordinate with groups R and T. Or we may find in structural resemblances between supposedly unrelated languages significant clues to unsuspected genetic affinities which are nevertheless demonstrable by the comparative method. We may, finally, find that the resemblance is simply an areal feature of no relevance to genetic grouping.

Some Middle American problems of this general nature (i.e. problems in sub-grouping and considerations of diffusion) are now discussed here.

4.1. MAYAN SUB-FAMILIES. Reconstructing Proto-Mayan on the basis of Mam, Huastec, and Yucatec, McQuown (1956) classified the Mayan languages on the basis of shared retention of seven features assumed to be Proto-Mayan.

McQuown points out that Huastec (isolated from the rest of Mayan and lying to the northwest), Yucatec (in the Yucatan peninsula), and the Highland Guatemalan languages form three points of a triangle which 'may be thought of as long established differentiated blocks' to which may be added the somewhat central-western Mayan languages of Tabasco and Chiapas (Chontal, Chol, Tzeltal-Tzotzil), Chicomuceltec and Motocintlec (towards the Pacific Coast) and Chorti (southeast of the Highland Group). He points out that there are special connections between Huastec and Chicomuceltec (which share particular lexical items found only in them), between Mam and Chuh (which share survival of *ŋ although they differ sharply in most other aspects), and between Chol and Chorti (which are separated phonologically only by the line between a six-vowel and a five-vowel system).

Against this general schematized background McQuown notes: (1) Certain isolated archaisms survive at the points of the triangle: (a) lexical tones (high and low) in Yucatec; (b) k versus k^w in Huastec; and (c) k versus $ḳ$ in the Guatemalan highlands. In addition, $č$ versus $ç̌$ survives in some of the Highland languages (Mam, Aguacatec, Ixil, and Kanhobal). On the western edge of the Highlands n versus $ŋ$ survives 'in a fully exploited form' only in Chuh but is also present word-final in Mam. In the central-western belt the old six-vowel system survives in Chol and Chontal—which are in this respect western outliers in reference to the languages of Highland Guatemala and Yucatec. To this picture of scattered archaisms surviving at the fringes of the Mayan region may be added the common survival of vowel quantity in Huastec, Yucatec, and Highland Guatemala. Thus, in terms of dialect geography, the general picture of surviving archaisms is a plausible one, with the Guatemalan highlands (especially Mam, Aguacatec, and Ixil) emerging as the most conservative block of languages.

The languages found along the northwest edge of the Guatemalan highlands and in the Chiapas highlands extending on down to the coast (i.e. Chuh, Toholabal, Tzotzil, Tzeltal, Chol, Chontal) are the more innovating. To these could be added Chorti—which has a special affinity with Chol although found at the eastern fringe of the Mayan region. Kanhobal shares some characteristics both of the conservative block (retains k versus $ḳ$ and $č$ versus $ç̌$) and also of the innovating block (loss of quantity).

Combining the above insights with 'an impressionistic sampling of the lexical material' (p. 194), McQuown emerges with the following 'cautious sub-grouping of the Mayan languages' (our summary here omits a few details): (1) Huastecan; (2) Cholan (Chontal, Chol, Chorti); (3) Tzeltalan (Tzeltal, Tzotzil, Toholabal); (4) Chuh; (5) Kanhobalan; (6) Motocintlec; (7) Mamean (Mam, Aguacatec, Ixil); (8) Quichean (Rabinal, Uspantec, Quiché, Cakchiquel, Tzutuhil); (9) Kekchian (Kekchí and Pocomam - Poconchi); (10) Mayan proper (Yucatec, Lacandone). He mentions that by 'less cautious sub-grouping' we could combine Cholan and Tzeltalan, Chuh and Kanhobalan, Motocintlec and Mamean, Quichean and Kekchian.

4.2 POPOLOCAN SUB-GROUPING. Using at first the Proto-Popolocan reconstruction of Fernández de Miranda and later Gudschinsky's more extensive treatment of the same, Hamp has attempted to clear up certain problems in the mutual degrees of affinity within the Popolocan family. Hamp at the outset of his first treatment of the subject (1958) makes very clear the principle on which he feels genetic proximity should be based: 'The only criterion for genetic proximity consists in the recognition of a decisive set, whether in number or in structural placement, of shared structural innovations; and these must be innovations by addition or replacement, rather than by loss.' (p. 150). On these grounds he rejects both Fernández de Miranda's belief that Popoloca and Ixcatec are especially closely related and Gudschinsky's belief that Popoloca, Chocho, and Ixcatec are coordinate, in favor of a belief that Chocho and Popoloca are especially closely related. (See fig. 1, which reproduces these alternative stemmata from Hamp, 1958.)

In his more recent treatment of the problem Hamp (1960) abandons five of the seven significant Chocho-Popoloca common innovations that he at first posited. However, he adds two more shared innovations involving these two languages; and further

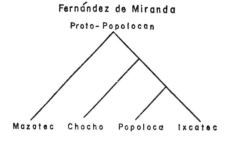

Fernández de Miranda
Proto-Popolocan

Mazatec   Chocho   Popoloca   Ixcatec

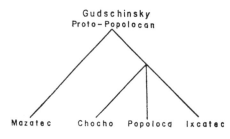

Gudschinsky
Proto-Popolocan

Mazatec   Chocho   Popoloca   Ixcatec

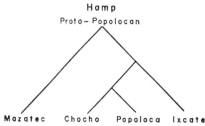

Hamp
Proto-Popolocan

Mazatec   Chocho   Popoloca   Ixcatec

FIG. 1—THREE PROPOSALS REGARDING AFFINITY IN POPOLOCAN. (From Hamp, 1958.)

clarifies and strengthens one of the shared innovations at first posited. By comparison with these Chocho-Popoloca shared innovations, the Ixcatec-Popoloca and Chocho-Ixcatec agreements do not seem to Hamp to carry so much import in that these latter agreements are fewer and not so strategically placed structurally.

The Chocho-Popoloca shared innovations that Hamp considers of abiding importance are: (1) loss of *s and *š from clusters *št, *šk, *škh, šh, and *sk (as opposed to retention of reflexes of *s and *š in Ixcatec). (2) parallel treatment of allophones of *c including a three-way split into Chocho and Popoloca c, č, and r. (3) parallel merger of *tᵛ before *h with *t in Chocho-Popoloca (and with r as well in Chocho). (4) parallel

142

treatment of *š before back vowels (> Popoloca ş and Chocho š and r).

Hamp closes with the caution: 'Finally, it is worth pointing out how misleading it would be if one were to classify languages on the basis of mere appearances; a glance at the superficial agreements between Ixcatec and Chocho in Gudschinsky's chart 11 should satisfy anyone on the futility of such an approach' (p. 62).

4.3 UTO-AZTECAN SUB-GROUPING. In concluding his sketch of Proto-Uto-Aztecan, Whorf was pessimistic about the validity of sub-grouping within that family: 'In time past some of us hoped that the stock could be classified in such a way that we could summarize the situation by stating generalized reflexes for sub-groups such as "Shoshonean", "Piman", "Sonoran", from which the reflexes of the individual tongues in these groups could be derived as a second step. This hope is vain. No such groups exist. The nearest thing to one is Piman, but it is unsafe to generalize about even so small and compact a group of dialects as Piman.' (p. 606).

In such a classification as McQuown's (1955), Uto-Aztecan languages of Mexico are divided into three groups: (1) Taracahitian (including Mayo-Yaqui, Tarahumara, and a host of extinct languages); (2) Aztecoid (including Aztec, Cora-Huichol, Pipil of Guatemala, and a number of extinct Mexican and Central American languages); (3) Piman (Papago, Tepecano, Northern Tepehuan, Southern Tepehuan, and a number of extinct languages). The first group may be largely a grouping of geographic convenience; the large number of extinct languages in it makes extensive investigation of the group qua group impossible. But it would be worthwhile to inspect Mayo-Yaqui and Tarahumara to see what, if any, common innovations are shared by them. In terms of Whorf's reconstruction of Uto-Aztecan along with his listed reflexes in eight languages, it is difficult to make out a good case for special Cora-Huichol and

Aztec affinities (Cora and Huichol admittedly are close but the question here is relation of the two to Aztec). Thus, if Whorf's Proto-Uto-Aztecan *e be reconstructed as *$ɨ$ (which seems probable) we note that Cora and Aztec share a common innovation (> A e, Cora e, i). But, unfortunately, Tarahumara also shares reflex e so we do not have here an exclusively shared Aztec-Cora innovation. Slightly better is Aztec-Cora treatment of *u which goes to i only in these two languages in the eight languages for which Whorf lists reflexes. It perhaps does not detract too greatly from the evidential value of this that Cora also has a reflex v (of *u) shared with Southern Paiute. Lastly, Aztec and Cora possibly share a similar handling of the bilabial phonemes *p and *v: PUA *p > Aztec p or $zero$, and to Cora p and $h/zero$; while PUA *v > Aztec w or $zero$, and to Cora w, v, or $zero$. Whorf does not give us the data to discover whether the $p/zero$ and $w/zero$ reflexes are phonemic splits under parallel conditions in Aztec and Cora.

For Piman we get somewhat better results—as Whorf's comments might lead us to believe in spite of his pessimism regarding sub-grouping. Thus, for the two Piman languages (Tepecano and Papago) whose reflexes are listed by Whorf we note that: (1) PUA *c > T,P $s/š$ (split under same conditions?). (2) PUA *k^w > T,P b. (3) PUA *^ns > T,P $h/ʔ$. (4) PUA *s > T,P $h/ʔ$ (thus merging with *^ns). (5) PUA *y > T,P d. (6) PUA *w > T,P g. Note that peculiar reflexes of *k^w, *y, and *w apparently yield a Proto-Piman voiced stop series *b, *d, *g not found in Proto-Uto-Aztecan (but data should be checked from other Piman languages).

4.4. ZOQUEAN SUB-CLASSIFICATION. In the last section of his Proto-Zoquean study Wonderly (1949) draws some Zoquean isoglosses that deserve extended comment. Zoquean is not internally as diversified as, e.g. Mixtecan. Indicative of this is the fact that phonological developments from language to language are rather pedestrian. For example, Wonderly writes, "PZoq stops in word initial position remain unchanged in all dialects, except that *c > $č$ before *i in Popoluca, and before *i, *$ä$ in Tapachulteca" (p. 3). The relative closeness of Zoquean languages is indicative of the fact that they are relatively less removed from the period when they were mutually intelligible dialects than are languages of families that show greater diversity. Two things therefore may be expected: (1) Extensive dialect borrowing in late Proto-Zoquean and in early stages of each language may leave its trace in a web of mutually inconsistent isoglosses that may even cut across language boundaries. (2) Many loans—even of fairly recent date—may be indistinguishable from inherited stock in view of the rather non-distinctive nature of Zoquean phonological developments.

Considering the last point first, it is instructive to note a comment of Wonderly's: "In SP, M,[24] there is a tendency toward intervocalic voicing of stops, with at least traces of 'Verner's law' in M. In NeZ, the stops *$-p$-, *$-t$- become $-b$-, $-d$- ($-r$- in Chapultenango) in most words; there is a residue of apparent exceptions which may be due to dialect borrowing or other factors" (p. 3). In other words, while $-b$- and $-d$- are reflexes of *$-p$- and *$-t$- in Northeast Zoque, borrowings from adjacent dialects with reflexes $-p$- and $-t$- may be one factor obscuring this picture.

Notice that this tendency towards voicing of intervocalic stops is found at three of the extremities of the Zoquean area, viz. Sierra Popoluca at the north, Mixe on the west, and Northeast Zoque on the east; its distribution is that of an archaism rather than that of an innovation. Probably, therefore, Proto-Zoquean stops had voiced allophones in intervocalic and the loss of these voiced

[24] Abbreviations: SP: Sierra Popoluca; M: Mixe; CZ: Central Zoque; NZ: Northern Zoque; SZ: Southern Zoque; WZ: West Zoque; NeZ: Northeast Zoque; T: Tapachulteca.

allophones in the rest of Zoque and in Tapachulteca is an innovation.[25]

A similar Zoquean phenomenon is voicing of stops after nasals; Wonderly summarizes this as follows: 'In SP and WZ, stops remain voiceless after nasals. In CZ, NZ, NeZ, stops are voiced after nasals. In M, stops are voiced after nasals except when the cluster is word final. In T and SZ, stops are voiced after nasals in some words and voiceless in others. (In some of the dialects, the voicing is probably allophonic rather than phonemic.)' (p. 6). Since voiced allophones of intervocalic stops seem to have been a Proto-Zoquean feature, it seems probable that voiced allophones of stop after nasal were also Proto-Zoquean and that Sierra Popoluca and West Zoque reflect an innovation by which voiced allophones were eliminated. This same innovation has spread to South Zoque and Tapachulteca but has affected only certain morphemes; as such this may be a result of dialect borrowing. Thus South Zoque *cintak* 'pine forest' exists side by side with *cindak* which may be a borrowing from Central Zoque. Mixe shares the unvoicing innovation to the extent that word-final consonants preceded by nasals are voiceless. Figure 2 summarizes unvoicing of old stop allophones.

One type of palatalization sketched by

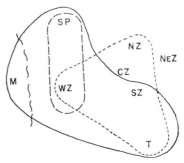

Fig. 2—MAP OF UNVOICING OF OLD VOICED STOP ALLOPHONES. Broken line (short dashes): area where voiced stop allophones in intervocalic are completely eliminated. Broken line (long dashes): area where there is complete elimination of voiced allophones after nasals. Solid line: area where there is partial or complete elimination of voiced stop allophones after nasals. Line of ʃ's: area where unvoicing occurs only following nasals in word final.

Wonderly is entitled: 'Metathesis of *y with a following consonant' (p. 7). That the metathesis of *yC > Cy is in reality an end-product of palatalization is seen in the varied Zoquean developments: PZoq *yC > M yCy when word-medial and Cy when word-initial. In CZ, NZ, NeZ, *yC > Cy but traces of an earlier *yCy occur in CZ where *yt > yty. I assume, therefore, that PZoq *yC was phonetically *[yCy], that in many areas the palatalized allophones became phonemic, and that in some areas the preceding *y was entirely lost. In still other areas the palatalized allophone after *y did not become phonemic (and possibly disappeared).[26] This is summarized in figure 3.

Loss of *h* in word-final cluster is described as follows by Wonderly: "Word-final PZoq *-hC always loses the *h* in CZ, NZ, SZ, WZ,

---

[25] Another probable archaism found only in Northeast Zoque is indicated by some puzzling reflexes of the nasals. Wonderly says 'In intervocalic position the picture is somewhat confused: in the NeZ dialects, *m, *n, *ŋ appear in some words as nasals, in others as voiced stops, in still others as voiceless stop + nasal; the conditioning factors can probably be found only after more work is done on the structure of the NeZ dialects, and in some of these cases the PZoq form will probably have to be set up with an intervocalic consonant cluster' (p. 5). In reference to the same phonemes in word-final Wonderly continues: 'In certain words in the NeZ dialects, they correspond to -p, -t, -k; in certain other words of the same dialect they correspond to -m, -n, -ŋ. The correspondences are not all the same for all NeZ dialects, but the tendency is for the correspondences with -p, -t, -k.' (p. 5). These peculiar correspondences of Northeast Zoque are as a whole unparalleled in any of the other languages and dialects.

[26] Palatalization of *c to č before *i takes place in Sierra Popoluca and in Tapachulteca but nowhere else in the Zoquean area. In Sierra Popoluca this type of palatalization extends to other alveolar phonemes. In Tapachulteca palatalization of *c occurs not only before *i but also before *e. Wonderly correctly infers that the two developments are independent of each other. However, it is possible that Proto-Zoquean *c had a palatalized allophone before front vowels and that this allophone has become phonemic in Sierra Popoluca and Tapachulteca independently and in different manners.

144

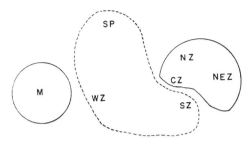

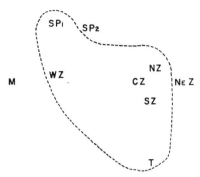

FIG. 3—Solid line: areas where yC^v and/or C^v are found. Broken line: area where $*[yC^v]$ remains phonemically yC with loss of $*[C^v]$ allophone.

FIG. 4—STAGE I. Broken line incloses central area where late PZoq $*h$ was lost from $*-hC$ in at least some words.

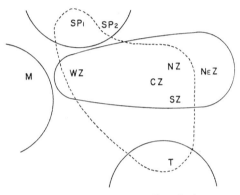

FIG. 5—STAGE II. Broken line incloses area where loss of $*h$ from $*-hC$ clusters continued to be extended until all such clusters were affected. Solid line indicates bundles of isoglosses which came to distinguish early stage of SP, M, Z, and T. These latter isoglosses are at cross purposes to the earlier isogloss, which represents an early dialect boundary which later became of less importance.

T, SP. In certain words the $*h$ is also lost in M. In certain other words the $*h$ is also lost in the Chapultenango dialect of NeZ ... Map IV leaves part of the Popoluca area outside the main isogloss, as preliminary data collected by Elson indicates that the $*h$ is not lost in the Texistepec dialect of Popoluca" (p. 8).

In accounting for the loss of $*h$ the following scheme seems plausible: (1) Proto-Zoquean $*h$ was not lost from word-final clusters in such late Proto-Zoquean fringe dialects as those which eventually became Northeast Zoque, and in a part of the dialects which became Sierra Popoluca. (2) Proto-Zoquean $*h$ was lost from word-final clusters in central late Proto-Zoquean dialects (including what became West Zoque, Central Zoque, North Zoque, South Zoque, and Tapachulteca as well as part of what later became Sierra Popoluca)—but probably only in certain words at first. (3) Loss of $*-h$ from such clusters was universalized in the central dialects which now were split, along with the contiguous fringe dialects, into early stages of the four languages. The progressive elimination of $*h$ could now proceed somewhat independently in the four proto-languages following the drift that set in late Proto-Zoquean—but loans from language to language could still have figured in the process. (4) Elimination of $*h$ from final clusters then spread sporadically into Mixe and into Northeast Zoque as well. In that the words affected are different in Mixe and in Northeast Zoque, it

seems that the two developments do not represent archaisms (as their fringe position might indicate) but rather a late spread from the central innovating area. This development is sketched in three stages in figures 4–6.

Plotting all the above features on the same map-like figure we obtain figure 7. which represents the late Proto-Zoquean dialect situation in reference to the central innovating area (involving loss of voiced allophones, loss of palatalized allophones, and loss of h) versus east and west fringe conservative areas.

145

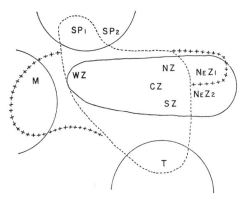

FIG. 6—STAGE III. Line of crosses: later extensions of area in which *h* was lost from *-hC* in some words. Broken line and solid line as in Stage II (fig. 5).

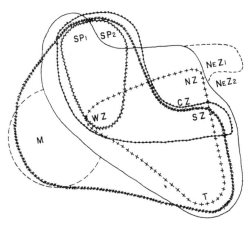

FIG. 7—Line of crosses: 1, area in which intervocalic voiced stop allophones are completely eliminated. Line of ſ's: 2, area in which voiced stop allophones after nasals are completely eliminated. Line of X's: 2A, area in which voiced stop allophones after nasals are completely or partly eliminated. Dotted line: 3, area where *[yCʸ] remained phonemically *yC* with loss of *[Cʸ] allophone. Solid line: 4, area where *h* is completely lost from *-hC* clusters. Broken line: 4A, later extensions of the area in which *-hC* was lost (but only in certain words).

In terms of the isoglosses plotted in the accompanying figure, we note the primary character of isoglosses 1, 2, 3, 4, and the secondary character of 2A and 4A which represent later extensions of 2 and 4 respectively. We can obtain a coefficient of innovation by scoring each dialect as follows: (a) 2 points for participation in any isogloss

146

of primary character; (b) one point for participation in an isogloss of secondary character. We will not score both participation in a primary isogloss and participation in its corresponding secondary isogloss for the same language, since this would amount to scoring the same feature twice. Scores follow:

WZ participates in 1, 2, 3, 4 and scores 8.

SZ participates in 1, 2A, 3, 4 and scores 7.

SP₁ participates in 2, 3, 4 and scores 6.

T participates in 1, 2A, 4 and scores 5.

SP₂ participates in 2, 3 and scores 4.

CZ participates in 1, 4 and scores 4.

NZ participates in 1, 4 and scores 4.

M participates in 2A, 4A and scores 2.

NeZ₁ participates in 4A and scores 1.

NeZ₂ participates in no innovations and hence scores zero.

West Zoque seems to represent the center of innovation in late Proto-Zoquean. South Zoque represents an area very close to the center of innovation, with Sierra Popoluca (exclusive of Texistepec) only slightly less removed and Tapachulteca still further removed. Sierra Popoluca (Texistepec), Central Zoque, and North Zoque are about equally innovating, but even further removed from the center of innovation than Tapachulteca. The conservative areas are: Mixe (on the west) and Northeast Zoque on the east, with the latter almost completely insulated from the innovation center. Notice that in terms of the features here considered Central Zoque and North Zoque are one dialect area.

The late Proto-Zoquean dialect situation is represented in figure 8. in which the concentric circles represent units on an eight-point scale which marks off the coefficient of innovation.

4.5. MAZATEC DIALECTS. Gudschinsky (1958a) has given us a careful study of Mazatec dialect history. She constructs a plausible family tree for Mazatec dialects. Dividing High Mazatec (HM) from Low

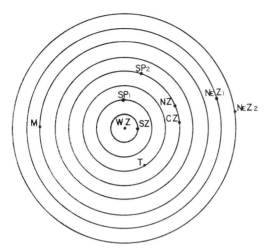

F<small>IG</small>. 8—SCHEMATIC REPRESENTATION OF LATE PZoq DIALECT SITUATION IN REGARD TO LINGUISTIC DISTANCE FROM CENTER OF INNOVATION IN WEST ZOQUE (WZ).

Mazatec (LM) (with common HM innovation *$t^y k$ > $šk$ and common LM innovation *$t^y(i/e)$ > t) she then further subdivides HM into Western (common innovation: *tk > sk) and Eastern (common innovation: *tk > hk); while LM divides into San Miguel and Valley Mazatec (common innovation of Valley Mazatec: *$Vhna/u$ > $Vhña/u$). Valley Mazatec in turn divides into Southern (common innovation: *$t^y k$ > tk) and Northern (common innovation: *$čha$ > $čha$). Further subdivisions occur: (1) eastern High Mazatec divides into Huautla (*$t^y h \check{V}$ > $š\check{V}$) and Jiotes (*k^w > k). (2) Low Southern Valley Mazatec divides into Mazatlán (*tk > hk) and Jalapa (*$hñá/ú$ > hya/u). (3) Low Northern Valley Mazatec divides into Soyaltepec and Ixcatlán (*$t^y k$ > tik; *tk > tuk).

The picture thus obtained is a plausible one both in terms of present day geographical distribution (valley versus highlands, and dissection of area by rivers) and in terms of what is known of Mazatec history. In respect to the latter, Gudschinsky points out that from around A.D. 1300 on, the Mazatec area—either under native rulers or under Mixtecs or Aztecs—was divided into Lowland and Highland 'kingdoms'. Furthermore, at an earlier period (ca. 890–1170) there was a single Mazatec nation concentrated apparently in what is now Valley Mazatec—which would account well for the unity of Valley Mazatec.

Nevertheless, as Gudschinsky points out, there was some spread of innovations across dialect boundary with occasional consequent shift of dialect boundary. Noticeable here is the spread of features from High Mazatec into contiguous portions of Low Mazatec. Thus, the dialect of San Miguel can be classified as Low Mazatec in that it shares the typical *$t^y(i/e)$ > t innovation of that dialect group. But the dialect of San Miguel is also characterized by the *$t^y k$ > $šk$ innovation which is diagnostic of High Mazatec. Here we have an apparent option; in that either isogloss can be considered to be the older development, it could be argued (1) that the Mazatec of San Miguel is a High dialect that was invaded by spread of an innovation from Low Mazatec; or (2) that it is a Low dialect that was invaded by spread of an innovation from High Mazatec. Gudschinsky adopts the latter alternative in that there are other clues (lexical isoglosses) which seem to indicate spread from such High Mazatec dialects as Huautla to San Miguel. Furthermore, this is supported by what is known of the present cultural situation (Huautla is a dominant center) and past history (formerly the Valley dialects were culturally dominant; later two centers of cultural dominance emerge in Low and High Mazatec respectively). The Mazatec dialect of Mazatlán reflects a similar spread of a High Eastern Mazatec feature (*tk > hk) into a Low Southern Valley dialect.

Gudschinsky also traces a number of lexical isoglosses. She writes: 'A number of the lexical isoglosses closely approximate the dialect boundaries established by the phonological isoglosses, except that there is more diffusion of lexical items especially from the High dialect to Mazatlán and San Miguel' (p. 474). The reference to diffusion of High

147

Mazatec lexical items to Mazatlán and San Miguel correlates with shifting of dialect boundaries noticed above whereby each of these dialects came to share a phonological isogloss with High Mazatec (or at least with Eastern High Mazatec).

There is another phonological isogloss which Gudschinsky mentions but does not put on her maps: '*sh* in the dialects of Huautla and Jiotes (of the High dialect) and of San Miguel, Jalapa, and Ixcatlán (of the Low Dialect) corresponds to *ch* in the dialects of Tecoatl, Eloxochitlán, and San Mateo (of the High dialect) and of Mazatlán and Soyaltepec (of the Low dialect).' (p. 474). Gudschinsky comments that this isogloss 'seems to contradict the family tree just outlined'. She mentions that both *sh* and *ch* are reflexes of Proto-Popolocan **ch* but does not describe for us the situation in Proto-Mazatec as such. But, considering the geographical distribution of **c(h)* (on the Western and Northeast fringes of Mazatec speaking territory) she recognizes this as an archaism as opposed to the Central area where passage of **c* to *s(h)* is an innovation 'spreading from a central area and leaving conservative islands on the margins'.[27] Figure 9 illustrates this central innovating area as well as the shifting of the boundary of High Mazatec as illustrated above.

[27] Gudschinsky's projected course of development for Proto-Popolocan **c* as posited in her Proto-Popotecan does not agree with the development as sketched in her Mazatec Dialect History. On chart 15 (p. 28) of Proto-Popotecan she traces Proto-Mazatec reflexes as follows: PPn **c* > PMaz **s(h)* and to PMaz **c* elsewhere. On charts 3, 4, 5 (pp. 8–10), she projects the following developments in Jiotes, Mazatlán, and Soyaltepec: PMaz **s(h)* > *c*—thus making PPn **c(h)* develop to PMaz **s(h)* and then, in turn, to *c(h)* once more. Furthermore, the projected PMaz **s(h)* reflex of Proto-Popolocan **c(h)* is, as we have seen, found only in central dialects where it looks like an innovation rather than an archaism. I, therefore, suggest the following reformulation: (1) PPn **c* > PMaz **c* everywhere (including clusters with *h*). Gudschinsky's chart 15 needs to be modified by striking out the special reflex PMaz **s(h)*. (2) PMaz **c* remained *c* in certain archaizing fringe dialects, and (3) PMaz **c(h)* went to *s(h)* in the central dialects.

148

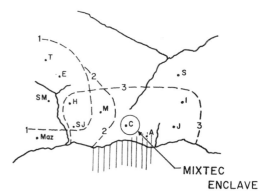

FIG. 9—T (Tecoatl); E (Eloxochitlán); SM (San Mateo); H (Huautla); SJ (Jiotes); Maz (Mazatlán); M (San Miguel); S (Soyaltepec); I (Ixcatlán); J (Jalapa). 1____1 Boundaries of High Mazatec according to primary dialect differentiation. 2____2 Later extension of certain High Mazatec features (but Mazatlán shares more features with Low Mazatec than does San Miguel). 3____3 Central innovating area where PMaz **c (h)* > *s (h)*. Vertical lines: Mazatec-speaking region from which no data are available.

Among the lexical isoglosses other instances occur which, in common with the above phonological isogloss, show survival of archaisms on margins as opposed to an innovating central area. Thus, Gudschinsky (p. 477) notes the following restricted distributions of lexical items which are presumably archaic survivals:

(1) Mazatlán, Soyaltepec, and Ixcatlán
(2) Mazatlán, Tecoatl and Soyaltepec
(3) Mazatlán and Jalapa
(4) Tecoatl and Eloxochitlán
(5) Tecoatl, Eloxochitlán, and Mazatlán
(6) Tecoatl, Eloxochitlán and Ixcatlán
(7) Soyaltepec
(8) Tecoatl and Eloxochitlán

These dialects may be arranged as follows in order of decreasing frequency of mention in the above list: Tecoatl, Mazatlán, Eloxochitlán, Soyaltepec, Ixcatlán, Jalapa. The four most frequently mentioned dialects are also within the archaizing area defined by retention of **c*. With less frequency do Ixcatlán and Jalapa align themselves with the western archaizing fringe along with Soyaltepec. An eastern fringe including Tecoatl, Mazatlán and Eloxochitlán is apparently a more extensive and better defined archaizing area.

In summary, Gudschinsky's study of Mazatec dialects is an excellent example of the manner in which insights of the comparative method may be combined with those of dialect geography. We need not oppose the 'family tree' concept of linguistic relationship to 'wave' phenomena of dialect diffusion. We need not deny the second in order to establish the first, nor need we abandon the first in order to do justice to the second.

4.6. MIXTECAN SUB-GROUPING. In reference to shared innovations, the isoglosses plotted for the Mixtecan family (exclusive of Amuzgo whose precise placement is still doubtful)[28] pattern as follows: (a) strong Mixtec-Cuicatec isoglosses; (b) strong Cuicatec-Trique isoglosses; (c) weak Mixtec-Trique isoglosses. Nevertheless, in spite of the relative weakness of the Mixtec-Trique isoglosses, they are important as vestiges of a former dialect division not correlating well with the subsequent (and more relevant) separation into the three languages.

The shared Mixtec-Cuicatec innovations are: (1) $*x^wa > vaa$. (2) $*^ng^wa > vaa$. (3) $*k^wV > ku$ (with loss of vowel and vocalization of labial component) under varying conditions. (4) Mixtec and Cuicatec eliminate w from present-day verb paradigms but preserve reflex of pardigmatic $*w$ in fossilized fragments (while Trique preserves $*w$ in present-day verb paradigms). (5) Mixtec and Cuicatec merge Proto-Mixtecan tones $*2$ and $*3$—thus becoming three-level tone systems. (6) Proto-Mixtecan $*o >$ Mixtec and Cuicatec o/u (versus consistent reflex o in Trique). The first four isoglosses group together; thus Mixtec and Cuicatec show parallelism in the treatment of labialized phonemes, as well as

in the elimination of bilabial $*w$ from verb paradigms.

The shared Cuicatec-Trique innovations are: (1) After $*^nd$, PMx $*i >$ C e/i, T e. (2) After $*n$, PMx $*i >$ C o/u, T $ï$ (C has no $ï$ phoneme). (3) After $*n$, PMx $*e >$ C, T i. (4) After $*w$, PMx $*e >$ C a, T i (also after $*x^w$ and $*^nd$, $*e >$ C a). (5) Before labials, PMx $*i >$ C, T u. (6) It is of some interest also that Cuicatec and Trique share a reconstructed $*12$ sandhi variant of basic tone pattern $*32$, while Mixtec reflexes seem to indicate a $*31$ sandhi variant.[29] Notice that Cuicatec-Trique isoglosses (1)–(5) indicate a common Cuicatec-Trique treatment of front vowels, just as the Mixtec-Cuicatec isoglosses (1)–(4) indicate a common Mixtec-Cuicatec treatment of labial consonants.

By contrast the shared Mixtec-Trique innovations are but two: (1) Proto-Mixtecan $*t$ is palatalized in Mixtec and Trique (> T $č$ uniformly; > M dialect reflexes, such as t^v, $č$, c, $š$ or modification of following vowel $*a$ to e—with a few Mixtec dialects showing none of these developments). (2) Proto-Mixtecan $*θ$ splits into two reflexes conditioned by front versus back vowels (T everywhere; M in all but fringe dialects). Both the above reflexes are peculiar in that each of them divides the Mixtec-Trique area in two in such a way so as to include Trique with some Mixtec dialects but not with others. This is reminiscent of the Zoquean isoglosses presented above in that the isoglosses fail to conform neatly to the language boundaries. However, we need to examine in detail the Mixtec dialect evidence:[30] (1) Proto-Mixtec $*t(i)$ is palatalized all over the Mixtec region except for a block of coastal dialects in the southwest corner of

---

[28] Swadesh (1960) has argued in favor of retaining Amuzgo as Mixtecan. I have raised the possibility that Amuzgo may form along with Mixtecan proper a broader 'Amuzgo-Mixtecan' grouping (Longacre, 1961a; Longacre-Millon, 1961). But, cf. note 1.

[29] The Popolocan evidence suggests that in Proto - Popolocan - Mixtecan (= Otomanguean also?) basic form $*32$ had no sandhi variants. We suggested above in Sec. 2.7. that possibly $*32$ also had no sandhi variants in early Proto-Mixtecan, but that these variants developed in late Proto-Mixtecan dialects. If so, then the Cuicatec-Trique sharing of variant $*12$ of basic $*32$ is another shared Cuicatec-Trique innovation.

[30] As summarized by Mak and Longacre, 1960.

149

Oaxaca. (2) Proto-Mixtec *t(ɨ) is palatalized only on the northern and northeastern fringes (dialects of Puebla, and Mixtec enclaves in Mazatec) plus the somewhat northwestern dialect of Juxtlahuaca, Oax. (3) Proto-Mixtec *t(a) remains unpalatalized in the southwest coastal block noted above; goes to te (with *t unaffected but with palatal influence on the vowel) in northern and northeastern fringes and in a sizeable block of north-central dialects; and goes to ča or tya in the intervening region. (4) Proto-Mixtec *θ apparently goes to d in fringe dialects on the north, northeast, and east as well as in one dialect of the southwest coastal block. Elsewhere, apparently *θ split into s/š according to back versus front vowels.

To summarize, note that (a) There is a southwest coastal block enclosed by isoglosses (1) and (3) above with one dialect of this block involved in isogloss (4) as well. (b) There is a northern innovating area as seen in palatalization of *t(ɨ), in *ta > te (as distinct from *t itself being palatalized), and in palatalization of *t(i). In that the palatalization of *t(ɨ) occurs in the northern and northeast fringes plus Juxtlahuaca, while *ta becomes te in these fringes plus part of the central area, and palatalization of *t(i) occurs everywhere except in the southwest conservative coastal block, these isoglosses show a common tendency in that they inclose the northern and northeast fringes plus varying amounts of the central area. (c) There is a central innovating area in which *t(a) is palatalized to ty or ča (and in which take place other varied developments beyond the scope of this paper). Development of s/š reflexes of Proto-Mixtecan and Proto-Mixtec *θ patterns as one of these central innovations which has spread over much of the area and leaves reflex d only in northern, northeastern, eastern, and southern fringes.

Trique, which palatalizes all *t to č and splits *θ to t/c (before back and front vowels respectively in a manner quite parallel to Mixtec) shares the first innovation with the

Mixtec northern innovating area and the second innovation with the Mixtec central innovating area. It seems plausible to assume that in late Proto-Mixtecan there were two isoglosses delimiting areas where Proto-Mixtecan *t and *θ had palatalized allophones (possibly at first only before front vowels). The isogloss for *[tʸ] included what became Trique and some adjacent northern Mixtec dialects (assuming that Mixtec did not extend as far north as at present). From this view, Mixtec palatalization of *ta to ča or tya in the central innovating area is more recent than *ta > te, which is more characteristically northern. The isogloss for *[θʸ] included late Proto-Mixtecan dialects that became Trique and certain adjacent western and central Mixtec dialects (assuming that Mixtec did not extend westward into Guerrero as at present).

It is probably best to assume that Proto-Mixtecan *θ was phonetically [θ] and [θʸ] in late western Proto-Mixtecan dialects that became Trique and west-central Mixtec, but was phonetically [d] in the late eastern Proto-Mixtecan dialects that became Cuicatec and the present Mixtec non-western fringes. On this assumption the phonological developments in the various languages and dialects are most easily explained. Thus, western Proto-Mixtecan *[θ] gives Trique t and Mixtec s, while its palatalized allophone *[θʸ] gives Trique c and Mixtec š. Eastern Proto-Mixtecan *[d] gives Mixtec and Cuicatec d. It seems clear that but one Proto-Mixtecan phoneme is involved, while it also seems plausible that it varied phonetically from west to east in late Proto-Mixtecan dialect areas.

The above postulated development divides late Proto-Mixtecan into two dialect areas (West PMx versus East PMx) delineated according to distribution of variants of *θ. Division according to distribution of variants of *t yields further dialect areas in which Pre-Proto-Cuicatec and a portion of southern Pre-Proto-Mixtec pattern as fringe areas while Pre-Proto-Trique and northern Pre-Proto-Mixtec pattern as an innovating central region. Both isoglosses draw a line of separation between dialects that eventually became Cuicatec versus those that eventually became Trique. But within what eventually became Mixtec, the dialects are variously grouped, some with what eventually became Cuicatec, others with what eventually became Trique.

It is postulated here that the two innovations common to Trique and some Mixtec dialects reflect an earlier period of dialect divergence than do the Mixtec-Cuicatec and Cuicatec-Trique shared innovations, which appear to be more numerous and carry greater weight. In that the Mixtec-Trique shared innovations are few and do not correlate well with the present boundary between the two languages it is assumed that (a) Trique, while maintaining contact with Cuicatec, separated geographically from Mixtec at a relatively early period— possibly at a time when early Proto-Trique and early Proto-Mixtec were still mutually intelligible dialects. (b) This separation created a Trique-Cuicatec-Mixtec dialect chain. Consequently, shared innovations between Trique-Cuicatec and Cuicatec-Mixtec continued to develop while shared Mixtec-Trique innovations ceased to develop. It is necessary to carry out the above scheme further by taking into account present-day separation of Trique from Cuicatec, as well as the present-day position of Trique as a language island surrounded by Mixtec. In doing this I assume (c) that Trique and Cuicatec lost mutual contact some time *after* they had ceased to be mutually intelligible dialects while Mixtec and Cuicatec continued to maintain contact in spite of the continued eastward drift of Cuicatec; and (d) that Mixtec, in its period of expansion finally flowed around the Trique-speaking area and engulfed it on all sides. In reference to (c) it may be noted that development of an effectual language barrier between Cuicatec and Mixtec finally checked further development of common

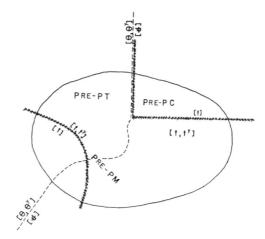

FIG. 10—STAGE 1. The late Proto-Mixtecan dialect situation shows no Mixtec-Trique dialect boundary according to the two isoglosses plotted, but delineates Cuicatec from Trique. Line of X's: presence of allophones *[t] and *[tᵛ] of *t versus presence of only allophone *[t]. Broken line: presence of allophones *[θ] and *[θᵛ] of *θ versus presence of allophone *[d].

shared innovations—which do not appear to be of any more consequence than the Cuicatec-Trique shared innovations. Nevertheless, the continued Mixtec-Cuicatec contact may be reflected in the Mixtec-Cuicatec lexicostatistic count which is apparently consistently higher than that for Mixtec-Trique or for Cuicatec-Trique.[31] In reference to (d) it may be noted that the belated renewal of Mixtec-Trique contact did not result in further shared phonological isoglosses, but is nevertheless reflected in presence of Mixtec loans in Trique.

These four hypothetical stages of development are illustrated in figures 10–14.

5. SUMMARY AND IMPLICATIONS. Systemic comparison and reconstruction of Middle American Indian languages has been carried forward to the point where there is promise of considerable pay-off in the near future. Part of this pay-off will consist in the evolution of

[31] For lexicostatistic counts involving Mixtec-Cuicatec, Cuicatec-Trique, and Mixtec-Trique, see Swadesh, 1960 (which evaluates previous counts by Gudschinsky and Arana); Longacre 1961a; Millon and Longacre, 1961.

151

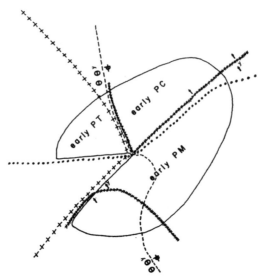

FIG. 11—STAGE 2. Mixtec-Trique isoglosses cease to develop after Trique pulled away from Mixtec. Mixtec-Cuicatec and Cuicatec-Trique isoglosses continue to develop. Line of crosses: separates early Proto-Trique from early Proto-Mixtec and early Proto-Cuicatec which share a common treatment of labials. Line of circles: separates early Proto-Mixtec from early Proto-Cuicatec and early Proto-Trique which share a common treatment of front vowels. Line of X's and broken line: as in fig. 10.

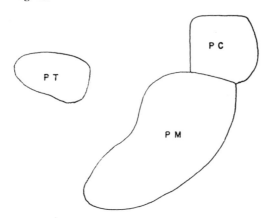

FIG. 12—STAGE 3. Effectual contact between Proto-Trique and Proto-Cuicatec is severed. Proto-Cuicatec and Proto-Mixtec are now mutually unintelligible; most further isoglosses developed between the two are lexical. Proto-Cuicatec is pulling off eastward.

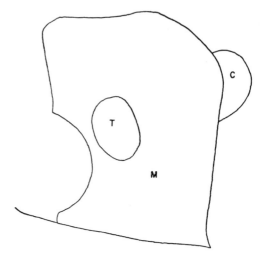

FIG. 13—STAGE 4. Period of Mixtec expansion results in Trique being engulfed by Mixtec on all sides with consequent cultural domination (late Mixtec loans in Trique). Cuicatec is off to the east but still in contact with Mixtec.

a more satisfactory classification of Middle American Indian languages. For example, careful reconstruction of Proto-Otomanguean will make possible some careful judgments as to relative degrees of affinity between Mixtecan, Popolocan, Chiapanec-Manguean, Zapotecan, Chinantecan, and

Otopamean; for some preliminary speculations along this line see appendix F. Meanwhile, a somewhat agnostic classification of these languages that simply lists them as related families is preferable to one that at-

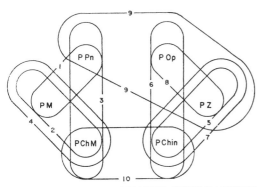

FIG. 14—INFERRED SHARED INNOVATIONS IN OTOMANGUEAN AS NUMBERED IN THE TEXT. Abbreviations: PPn (Proto-Popolocan); PMx (Proto-Mixtecan); PChM (Proto-Chiapanec-Manguean); POp (Proto-Otopamean); PZ (Proto-Zapotecan); PChin (Proto-Chinantecan).

tempts to sub-group them—as, e.g. the dubious sub-grouping 'Otomanguean' (Popolocan, Mixtecan, Otopamean, Chiapanec-Manguean) versus 'Macro-Otomanguean' ('Otomanguean' plus Zapotecan and Chinantecan). Such a classification as Lamb's (1959) is, therefore, quite satisfactory in this respect. Within each family comprising Otomanguean, systemic comparison will eventually elucidate the relationships in terms of such schemes as those here sketched for Mixtec, Cuicatec, and Trique in 4.5. above. Some detailed problems which should be cleared up in the near future are: (a) precise position of Amuzgo (within Mixtecan proper or in some more remote relationship to Mixtecan within Otomanguean?); (b) sub-groupings within Otopamean; (c) position of Chatino (assumed to be Zapotecan).

For criticism of existing classifications within Uto-Aztecan, see Section 4.3. above. In view of the perennial interest in this language family, it is hoped that someone will soon take up Whorf's work where he left off and give us a basis for clarifying problems that he raised.

'Mexican Penutian' is still largely in the speculative stage. While it is generally assumed that Zoquean, Mayan, and Totonac-Tepehua go together, little systemic re-construction has yet been offered to validate this.[32] Nevertheless, if this grouping be valid such work is entirely possible and needs to be undertaken.

Two languages—Huave and Tarascan—remain mavericks. Hauve was classified by Radin (1916) with Zoquean-Mayan-Totonac, but this relationship is now separately questioned by McQuown and Swadesh. Swadesh (1960) has in turn suggested that Huave fits into his 'Macro-Mixtecan' (i.e. Otomanguean minus Chiapanec-Mangue). But, here again, his evidence, like Radin's for Mayan-Huave affinities, is not conclusive. Swadesh also cites resemblant forms between Tarascan and other American Indian languages involved in vague, quasi-universal relationships.

The above considerations are embodied in a linguistic map of Middle America which is presented in Appendix F. On this map Hokaltecan, Uto-Aztecan, Mayan-Zoquean-Totonacan, and Otomanguean are posited as broad groupings, each involving a number of languages. The reality of the Uto-Aztecan grouping has been demonstrated. Current work in various branches of Otomanguean brings ever nearer the day when the reality of this grouping (plus or minus a few languages or language families) will be demonstrated. The other two groupings—Hokaltecan and Mayan-Zoquean-Totonacan—may be regarded simply as probable. Tarascan, Huave, and Xinca-Lenca are considered to constitute three further groups of limited membership. Extinct languages are included in the classification whenever identification of the affinities of such a language seems to be probable; otherwise, extinct languages are plotted geographically without inclusion in the classification.

Systemic reconstruction, vigorously pur-

[32] Swadesh's 'proto-Penutioid' sketch (1956) is on much too broad a front (his 'Penutioid' includes, among other languages and families, Zuni, Totonac, Huave, Tarascan, and Quechua-Aymara) to afford systemic and detailed validation of such a less ambitious (but still problematical) grouping as 'Mexican Penutian.'

sued, will be successful in demonstrating some relationships, but will have to leave other relationships unproven or doubtful, i.e. thresholds will be encountered beyond which systemic reconstruction does not yield results. But, far from being a drawback, this will constitute a criterion for identifying relevant and demonstrable relationships. Within the proper sphere of application the comparative method will lay a basis for sub-grouping and proper evaluation of the results of such methods as glottochronology which are in danger of being run into the ground by free-lance practitioners. Ethnolinguistic implications in terms of related languages, in terms of identification of the nature and direction of diffusions versus inherited items, and in terms of *Wörter-und-Sachen* interpretation of reconstructed vocabularies, will probably be forthcoming as well. Some such preliminary results are already in (Longacre-Millon, 1961). In brief, systemic comparison and reconstruction of Middle American Indian languages is about to put into orbit a satellite or two with considerable pay-load. This is, therefore, no time to discourage, or discontinue, research.

APPENDICES

A. Some apparent anomalies of phonological development resolved by positing Proto-Mixtecan *am* rather than *ɔ*.

I had postulated a special Trique reflex *e/i* of *a* after *w* (giving sound correspondence M *a* ∼C *a* ∼ T *e/i*) in my sets 179–87. I had also postulated a special Cuicatec reflex *i* of *ɔ* after *w* (thus giving sound correspondence M *a* ∼ C *i* ∼ T *a*) in sets 226–8. These sets may now all be considered to be reflexes of Proto-Mixtecan *wa(m)*. It is not at all strange that reflexes of *wam* are rare in that there is a tendency in this language family to avoid two bilabials in the same form. Therefore we have more sets witnessing to *wa* (sets 179–87) than to

154

wam (sets 226–8). Furthermore, in set 183 I had a troublesome residue which is now seen to be perfectly regular. This set apparently was to be reconstructed as a set with ultimate *wa* in that the Mixtec vowel reflex was *a* and the Trique vowel reflex was *i*. Nevertheless, there was a possible Cuicatec cognate with vowel reflex *i*. Leaving aside the Trique reflex, I could have reconstructed *ɔ* on basis of M *a* ∼ C *i*. The Cuicatec and Trique reflexes offered contrary witness in regard to *a* versus *ɔ*, and yet I had no evidence anywhere in Mixtecan of vowel gradation in general, nor of vowel gradation *a*/*ɔ* in particular. Now, however, by recognizing that *wa(m)* underlies this set we may attribute the Cuicatec form to *wam* and the Trique form to *wa* without the least difficulty, in that presence versus absence of *-m* is a familiar phenomenon. Furthermore, I had another such anomaly in my set 188 where apparently the correspondence M *a* ∼ C *a* ∼ T *a* appeared after *w* but where the Trique reflex 'should' have been *e/i*. Here we now attribute the Trique reflex to *am* which regularly gives Trique a after *w*.

B. Otomí-Mazahua tone correspondences and Proto-Otomí-Mazahua tones (as reconstructed by Donald Stewart).

(1) Two Otomí dialects cited have tone systems with high pitch, low pitch and rising pitch; a third Otomí dialect has high, low, and falling pitches. (2) These reconstruct as follows:

O₁	O₂	O₃	POt
high	high	rising	*high (disyllabic)
high	high	low	*high (monosyllabic)
low	low	falling	*low
rising	rising	low	*rising

(3) Mazahua has high, low, rising and falling pitches. (4) These Mazahua pitches reconstruct with the Proto-Otomian pitches as follows:

POt	Mz	POMz
*high	high	*high (before Mz h or vl. cons.)
*high	low	*high (elsewhere in Mz)
*low	low	*low
*rising	high	*rising (before Mz h or vl. cons.)
*rising	falling	*rising (elsewhere in Mz)
*high	falling	*falling

C. Possible Proto-Chiapanec-Manguean reflexes of 'deictics' posited by Gudschinsky for Pre-Proto-Popolocan-Mixtecan.

Postposed elements *-me and *-mu, which appear with great frequency in Proto-Chiapanec-Manguean form an interesting parallel with Proto-Popolocan-Mixtecan *-m or *mV (see above, Sec. 2.7.); and may constitute archaic survivals of a similar early feature in Proto-Otomanguean. Gudschinsky's Pre-Proto-Popolocan-Mixtecan deictics *-xV and *-ʔV (plus or minus *-m) seem witnessed to as well. Thus, postposed -hV elements are fairly common in Chiapanec-Mangue where their archaic nature is seen in the fact that they have often come to function as stems or parts of stems. Such a Proto-Chiapanec-Manguean form as *ai 'sick, pains' seems to be cognate with Proto-Mixtecan *(k)aʔi (Mak-Longacre, p. 38). The state of the Chiapanec-Mangue recorded data is such that nothing can be inferred as to presence or absence of Chiapanec and Mangue ʔ. At any rate, whether or not ʔ was found in Chiapanec and Mangue forms for 'sick', it is possible that Proto-Chiapanec-Mangue *ai witnesses to an earlier *a plus postposed *-ʔi (Gudschinsky's *-ʔV deictic?). In one of the sets of Fernández de Miranda and Weitlaner there is a postposed Proto-Chiapanec-Manguean *-Mi (PPM *hmi) while in other sets this element seems to have become part of the stem. Putting together these various scattered clues, it appears possible that Chiapanec-Mangue witnesses to *-mV, *-hV, *-ʔV and *hmV postposed elements all of which figure prominently in Popolocan-Mixtecan as well.

D. Further Zapotec data of possible corroborative value in reference to the posited development: Proto-Otomanguean *mC cluster > Proto-Zapotec *CC (geminate) cluster.

Another datum further points in the direction of supposing that Zapotec geminated consonants came from Pre-Proto-Zapotec (presumably Proto-Otomanguean) *mC clusters. Fernández de Miranda reconstructs *ll and *l for Proto-Zapotecan. It may be significant, however, that while there is a uniform reflex l for *l in all dialects, there is the following set of reflexes for *ll (abbreviations A, VA, M, Cu, Co, R, and I are for Zapotec dialects cited in Fernandez's study; I represents Isthmus dialect of Zapotec): ll in A, VA, M corresponds to l in Cu, Co, and R; and corresponds to nd in I. (e.g. 'stinky': A rillàaʔ, VA ǰlla-, M lla-, te-laʔ, Co laaʔ, R rilaʔ, I rindaʔ; and 'snake' A bèllà, VA bèll, M bäll, Cu mbelʔ, Co ᵐbälʔ, R bála, I beʔendaʔ. Here it seems plausible to suppose that the Proto-Zapotecan opposition was not *ll versus *l (the latter is mentioned above without illustrative cognate sets), but rather *nl versus *l. Swadesh (1947) posited cluster *nl as well as *ll, but both do not seem to be necessary in the light of further data. Thus, while most Otomanguean *mC clusters were reduced to geminates in the transition to Proto-Zapotecan, at least *nl (originally *ml) was not so reduced, and remains as an indication of the original state of affairs.

Another isolated datum occurs to lend plausibility to the above hypothesis: Thus, Fernández de Miranda reconstructs Proto-Zapotecan /ttuttu ca ∼ *ttatta wica 'daily' on basis of A tutu cá, VA toto zá, and R tutuǰa versus Cu atata wiz and Co tä wiž?. It seems clear from other Otomanguean language families that there is a definite tendency toward dissimilation of labial consonants in

155

the same form. Supposing, therefore, a final *-*m* on the Proto-Otomanguean form lying behind Proto-Zapotecan *ttatta* (probably itself a reduplication) we obtain *ttuttu ca* from a Proto-Otomanguean form with final *-*m* and *ttatta wica* from a Proto-Otomanguean form with final *-*m* reduced to zero before following *w*.

E. Some possible isoglosses conjectured for Proto-Otomanguean.[33]

It is not possible yet to draw definitive isoglosses for Otomanguean as a whole in that shared innovations can not unambiguously be distinguished from shared retentions until Proto-Otomanguean itself is reconstructed in some detail. Nevertheless, we here suggest a few possible shared innovations obtained on comparing qua systems, the six phonological systems reconstructed for the various families of Otomanguean. Consequently, these inferred shared innovations are not based on systemic reconstruction of Proto-Otomanguean itself, but on extrapolation from reconstruction in less depth. As such, the suggestions of this section involve considerable speculation and conjecture.

Some inferred Otomanguean shared innovations are:

(1) Disappearance of *p* in Proto-Mixtecan and Proto-Popolocan (by merger with *kʷ*?).

(2) Development of a prenasalized series of consonants in Proto-Mixtecan and Proto-Chiapanec-Manguean (by reduction of other *mC* and/or *nC* clusters).

(3) Development of *ny* or *ñ* in Proto-Popolocan and Proto - Chiapanec - Manguean (may be simply a shared retention?).

(4) Merger of *tʸ* and *t* in Proto-Mixtecan and Proto-Chiapanec-Manguean.

(5) Disappearance of *xʷ* in Proto-Zapotecan and Proto-Chinantecan (cf. also the disappearance of *x* in Proto-Zapotecan).

[33] cf. note 1.

(6) Disappearance of *w* and *y* in Proto-Chinantecan and Proto-Otopamean with consequent development of a considerable number of vowel clusters.

(7) Development of *r* (in contrast with both *l* and *y*, or with a phoneme of which *[l]* and *[y]* are allophones) in Proto-Zapotecan and Proto-Chinantecan. (Swadesh, 1960, reconstructs Proto-Otomanguean *r* on what seem to me to be insecure data.)

(8) Development of contrasting geminated consonant versus single consonant (by assimilation of *mC* > *CC*?) in Proto - Zapotecan and Proto - Otopamean. Possibly parallel is development of voiced versus voiceless consonant series in Proto-Chinantecan. (Swadesh, 1960, posits Proto - Otomanguean geminated consonants; I do not believe that this will prove to be valid.)

(9) Disappearance of *ɨ* (assuming its existence in Proto-Otomanguean) in Proto-Popolocan, Proto-Zapotecan, and Proto-Otopamean.

(10) Disappearance of *kʷ* in Proto-Chiapanec-Manguean and Proto-Chinantecan. (Swadesh, 1947, does not reconstruct *kʷ* in Proto-Zapotecan, but this phoneme is reconstructed by Fernández de Miranda.)

It is interesting to note that inferred Proto-Otomanguean isoglosses (1)–(4) apparently group Proto-Mixtecan, Proto-Popolocan, and Proto-Chiapanec-Manguean while (5)- (8) apparently group Proto-Zapotecan, Proto-Chinantecan, and Proto-Otopamean. Number (9), however, groups Proto - Popolocan with Proto - Zapotecan and Proto-Otopamean; while number (10) groups Proto - Chiapanec - Manguean and Proto-Chinantecan. This preliminary exploration suggests the possibility that Proto - Popolocan, Proto - Mixtecan, and Proto-Chiapanec-Manguean may form a group as over against Proto-Zapotecan,

Proto-Chinantecan, and Proto-Otopamean. But the latter two isoglosses listed, if reinforcable by other similar features, could result in a pattern of mutually conflicting isoglosses which would make any such dichotomy artificial. The isolation of Chiapanec-Manguean from the rest of Otomanguean within historic times, i.e. at least from 1525 on, is at all events, not to be considered as indicative of any necessary remoteness of relationship within Otomanguean. Otopamean lies to the northwest of the mass of Otomanguean languages. It is therefore plausible to expect that Otopamean is more closely related to the Mixtecan and Popolocan languages which lie geographically nearer, than to Chinantecan and Zapotecan which lie more to the east (with Mixtecan and Popolocan intervening). Nevertheless, we must follow the evidence wherever it leads—when that evidence is finally in. It may eventually be established that the placement of Otopamean is with the eastern rather than with the western languages. Resolution of this problem must await detailed reconstruction of Otomanguean. We have gone about as far as we can go until this further step be taken. At any rate, we must be prepared for some surprises. Thus, while I would personally be inclined to consider Zapotecan closer to Mixtecan and Popolocan than to Chinantecan or Otopamean, nevertheless it may be that the extensive cultural contact of Mixtec and Zapotec has resulted in certain diffusions which obscure the original picture of dialect split and development.

F. Linguistic map of Middle America. The accompanying map indicates the probable distribution of speakers of various Indian languages as spoken in Middle America at the time of the conquest. It is based on the previous linguistic maps of Mendizábal and Jiménez (1936, 1941), Frederick Johnson (1940), and McQuown (1955). Johnson's map is accompanied by a helpful discussion of the sources for such a map and of the problems encountered in drawing it.

McQuown's maps treat not only Mexico and Middle America but South America as well; like Johnson's map they are accompanied by a helpful discussion. All three maps embody linguistic classifications which agree in broad outline and diverge in details.

The map here presented includes most languages referred to in any source as spoken in the area at the time of the Conquest. It includes more languages than are found on either the Mendizábal-Jiménez map or the Johnson map. McQuown lists along with his map some additional extinct languages not included here, while Arana and Swadesh (1959) in their series of linguistic maps (based on glottochronology as well as on former classifications) list still more languages than McQuown. The sources contain, in fact, a welter of names and labels for various peoples and languages. It is by no means uncommon to find the same language or dialect referred to by several names or to find the same name apparently applied to quite unrelated languages. In letting the map reflect a level of medium complexity we have hoped to avoid the diminishing returns which might result from further cluttering with names of doubtful linguistic import. In deciding which 'languages' to include we have followed the rule of requiring inclusion on two of the previous maps on which the present map is based. Practically, this has meant inclusion of any 'language' mentioned by either Mendizábal-Jiménez or Johnson since McQuown's rather full listing scarcely ever omits what either of the other maps mention.

The geographical limits of the map are meant to correlate roughly with the geographical delimitation of Mesoamerica as a cultural entity. A broken line is given on the map to indicate the northern frontier of Mesoamerica as indicated some time ago by Kirchhoff (1943). On the south, the frontier of Mesoamerica seems to be at once a linguistic and a cultural line of demarcation. Beyond the Maya, the Lenca, and the southern outliers of Otomanguean are groups

157

which seem to have South American affinities both linguistically and culturally. Beyond this line the only linguistic group which we indicate on the map is the Jicaque which we include because they seem to be related linguistically (but not culturally) to Hokaltecan. On the north, the cultural line delimiting Mesoamerica cuts across linguistic lines. Thus, while most of Otomanguean lies in Mesoamerica, Otopamean splits with Pame and Chichimeca-Jonaz lying outside Mesoamerica. Each of the main divisions of Uto-Aztecan (Piman, Taracahitian, and Aztecoidan) are found on both sides of the boundary. Of the Hokaltecan languages, Yuman, Serian, and Coahuiltecan are found outside the northern boundary of Mesoamerica, while Tequistlatecan and Supanecan are found well to the south within Mesoamerica. Because of the linguistic relations involved we have, therefore, included on the map the area up to the Mexican-United States border.

In plotting the languages geographically we have followed Mendizábal-Jiménez more closely than the other two previous maps but have occasionally modified Mendizábal-Jiménez in the direction of distributions indicated by the other two cartographers. Methodologically, the present map is a compromise between Mendizábal-Jiménez and McQuown. The former attempt to mark boundaries not only between language families and stocks but between the individual languages as well; the latter indicates no boundary lines as such but simply plots languages on the map by means of code numbers. In the present map I use hatchings, lines, and shadings to mark off languages of different stocks and families but use only code numbers to indicate individual languages within a family (parentheses inclose code numbers referring to extinct languages). It is hoped that the boundaries shown—even if often arbitrarily drawn—and groupings indicated will contribute to the intelligibility and usefulness of the map; while it is also hoped that absence

158

of boundary lines between individual languages of each family will not only spare my making further arbitrary decisions but will amount to an overall simplification.

A few specific points in which the present map differs from one or more of the previous maps are here mentioned: (1) Classificationwise I leave Guaycuran unclassified; refer to Mayan-Zoquean-Totonacan as Macro-Mayan rather than as 'Mexican Penutian' or as 'Macro-Penutian'; reject the sub-grouping 'Otomanguean' within 'Macro-Otomanguean' in favor of a more agnostic grouping of the six families[34] concerned into a stock termed simply Otomanguean; retain Coca and Tecuexe as Aztecoidan (Mason and Johnson) in spite of the doubts of Mendizábal-Jiménez and McQuown; do not attempt to set up sub-groupings within Mayan; classify Jicaque as Hokan; consider the 'Mazatec' of Jalisco, Guerrero, and Tabasco to be three unclassified languages which possibly share only a name in common with Mazatec within Otomanguean; consider the 'Chontal' of Guerrero to be an unknown language not necessarily related to the Chontal of Oaxaca (Tequistlatecan); consider Tapuchultec I and Aguacatec II to be Zoquean; follow Mendizábal-Jiménez in leaving Pison-Janambre unclassified rather than as Coahuiltecan (McQuown and Johnson, but see Mason's accompanying discussion of the problem, 1940, pp. 62–63); reject Mendizábal-Jiménez's classification of Guachichil as Coahuiltecan but follow Johnson and McQuown in classifying it as Uto-Aztecan (Aztecoidan). (2) Apache, Toboso, and Olive are eliminated from the map of Mexico on the supposition that they came into Mexico after the conquest (Mason, 1940, pp. 60, 62). (3) A few Mendizábal-Jiménez distributions are modified as follows: (a) The area of Tepehuan-Tepecan is

[34] As stated in note 1, I now regard Amuzgo as constituting a seventh branch of Otomanguean. Although Amuzgo is so represented on the map I have not tried to bring the body of the article in line with the map in this regard.

enlarged somewhat at the expense of Cozcan (following Johnson) on its southern boundary. (b) The Guachichil enclave in Tamaulipec, a Southern Tepehuan enclave in Cora, and a Chiapanec enclave in Zapotec are omitted following Johnson. (4) A few John-

son distributions are modified also: (a) Maribichicoa is put in Salvador (following McQuown) rather than in Nicaragua.

A complete key for the map is given in the caption to figure 15.

REFERENCES

Arana Osnaya, 1953, 1957
Arndt, 1959
Bartholomew, 1959, 1960
Bernal and Dávalos Hurtado, *see* Huastecos, Totonacos y sus Vecinos
Bright, 1956
Dahl, 1953
Ecker, 1939
Ellegard, 1959
Fernández de Miranda, 1951, 1960
—— and Weitlaner, 1961
Gamboa, 1942
Greenberg and Swadesh, 1953
Gudschinsky, 1955, 1958a, 1959c
Haas, 1959
Hale, 1958, 1959
Hall, 1958
Hamp, 1958, 1960
Hay, *see* The Maya and their Neighbors
Hoeningswald, 1960
Hymes, 1959, 1960
Johnson, F., 1940
Kirchhoff, 1943

Kroeber, 1960a
Lamb, 1958, 1959
Longacre, 1957, 1961a, 1961b
McQuown, 1942, 1955a, 1956
Mak and Longacre, 1960
Mason, 1940, 1952
Mayers, 1960
Millon and Longacre, 1961
Newman and Weitlaner, 1950a, 1950b
Pike, E. V., 1954
Radin, 1916
Ravicz and Romney, n.d.
Smith, P., and Weitlaner, 1957
Stewart, 1957
Swadesh, 1947, 1956, 1959b, 1959e, 1960a
Tax, 1960
Thieme, 1958
Vivó, 1941
Wallis, 1956
Weinreich, 1958
Weitlaner, 1942
Whorf, 1935
Wonderly, 1949, 1953

6. Environmental Correlational Studies

SARAH C. GUDSCHINSKY

1.   Introduction
2.   Middle American studies
2.1. Geographical dialects
2.2. Languages in contact
2.3. Nongeographical dialects
3.   Strategy of environmental correlational studies
3.1. Geographical-historical dialects
3.1.1. Identification of innovations
3.1.2. Mapping of innovations
3.1.3. Interpretation of isoglosses as indicating dialect history in terms of splits and contacts
3.1.4. Interpretation of isoglosses in terms of diffusion, resistance, and migration
3.2. Nongeographical dialects

1. INTRODUCTION. Since environmental correlational studies do not constitute a traditional field of research, it is necessary to begin this article by delimiting the scope of its subject matter and defining its aims. The term 'environmental correlational' implies the entire gamut of 'speech varieties' or 'dialects' or 'styles' in their correlations with geography, history, social class, age, sex, role, cross-cultural or cross-language contacts. Such a broad definition poses a severe problem, however, in that it overlaps—if indeed it does not include—the material of the other chapters of this volume: descriptive studies include special styles, men's and women's speech, baby talk, and the like; lexicostatistical and genealogical classifications deal with his-torically and geographically conditioned dialects; and any study of language-in-culture must deal with at least some kinds of environmental correlation. The problem is complicated by the paucity of specifically correlational studies in the literature on Middle American languages.

I have chosen to solve the problem by focusing on two unifying topics: geographical dialects and nongeographical dialects. I see these as ideally two complete studies, each drawing on the full range of recent theoretical and technical advance.

The geographical-historical study of any language group would include the interior history of its linguistic structure through successive dialect splits and regroupings, and its modifications by borrowed elements; an exterior history of its geographical locations, its various centers of prestige, its shifting lines of communication, and its contacts with other languages; and a cultural history of its speakers in terms of cultural traits that can be reconstructed at each horizon, and in terms of the weakening and restructuring of various aspects of the culture, especially under pressure from outside sources.

Goals similar to these have been proposed before, but they contrast sharply with much of the present emphasis in historical studies on the larger classifications and on statistical

161

or computer-programmed methods for proving relationship, sub-grouping, and estimating time depth. The two points of view are complementary rather than mutually exclusive, however. The classificatory studies might be expected to provide both the basis for choosing particular language groups for detailed study, and also the initial working hypotheses. Conversely, a carefully planned detailed study of this kind should serve to confirm or modify the larger hypotheses and to refine and develop theory and technique.

The nongeographical dialect study of any speech community would include the synchronic description of all the various sub-dialects, styles, or varieties whether conditioned by social class, role, or special literary use—and a correlation of these with the total socio-cultural environment.

These goals contrast with the tendency of some descriptive studies to attain rigor or elegance of statement at the cost of restricting the data to a single speech variety, perhaps even one particular speech style of a single informant.

Although there are no complete studies of either type in any Amerindian language, there are a number of articles illustrating individual facets of the problems.[1] Section 2 provides a survey of selected source material from the Middle American languages, loosely grouped under the headings 'Geographical dialects,' 'Languages in contact,' and 'Nongeographical dialects.' The purpose, conclusions, and method of each article are briefly described. Section 3 presents the proposed studies as a series of procedures for research. A selected bibliography of theoretical articles and data-oriented examples is included with each procedure.

[1] The most extensive dialect study in Middle America is a part of the 'Man-in-Nature' project of the University of Chicago. As reported by McQuown (1959a) it includes interlocking studies of geographical and nongeographical dialect with reference to historical and cultural features and language contact. Each aspect of the study is reviewed separately where it is relevant.

2. MIDDLE AMERICAN STUDIES.

2.1. GEOGRAPHICAL DIALECTS. Included within this survey of Middle American studies of geographical dialects is a variety of articles which make some correlation of linguistic variation with geography.

The most extensive dialect survey is that of the Tzeltal-Tzotzil area in Chiapas, Mexico, made as a part of the 'Man-in-Nature' project of the University of Chicago.[2] (For a preliminary report, see McQuown, 1959a.) This study establishes the major dialect areas and correlates them with geographical, ecological, cultural, and historical features.

The data include word-lists collected from 139 informants in 19 communities (now 480 informants, 47 communities; see McQuown, 1962). The large number of informants from each community permitted the analysis of internal divergence and social dialect which is discussed in §2.2, as well as the external divergence discussed here.

Phonemic analyses are made of the data from each local community, and some of the grammatical features are noted. There are not yet (1960) complete structural analyses of the entire speech of any of the communities (see now, however, Berlin, 1962a; Hopkins, 1962a; Kaufman, 1961, 1962; Radhakrishnan, 1962; Robles, 1962; Sarles, 1962), but the materials so far available have proved sufficient for the preliminary study. (See Mayers, Hajda, and McQuown, 1959.)

Lexicostatistical counts are recorded for each pair of word-lists. For the geographical dialect study, lexicostatistical distances, expressed as centuries of divergence between communities, are marked on a schematic map with dialect distance rather than geographic distance indicated by space. (See Mayers, 1959; Mayers and McQuown, 1959a,b.) This initial mapping is used as the basis of a dialect classification, and is

[2] See note 1.

also used, in its implication of actual time, to confirm or modify hypotheses made from archeological and historical data. (See Adams and McQuown, 1959.) The phonological, grammatical, and lexical isoglosses are plotted on the basic lexicostatistical diagram to show the types of dialect variation. As might be expected, there is little concordance in the occurrence of the various isoglosses. In general the grammatical and phonemic isoglosses are taken to reflect the older divisions and historical dialects. The phonetic and lexical isoglosses represent newer trends and the results of contact. (See Nash and others, 1959; Hajda, 1959a, b, c, d, e; McQuown, 1959c).

Gudschinsky's study of the Mazatec dialects (1955, 1958a) is on a much smaller scale, but includes considerable detail. The ultimate purpose of both articles is to reconstruct linguistic history on a family-tree model. The basic data are a reconstruction of Proto-Mazatec, and a lexicostatistical comparison of 13 Mazatec dialects. In the earlier article the historical development of the existing local varieties of Mazatec, as implied by the lexicostatistical counts, is mapped as successive stages of differentiation from a postulated homogeneous beginning. This is then compared with a somewhat different order of development implied by the sound changes. It is concluded that the phonological history indicates the basic dialect development, and that the lexical history—where it differs— indicates a more recent cross-dialect contact.

This history of split and regrouping is further developed in the second article by the careful mapping of the phonological innovations and a small group of lexical innovations. From this mapping a detailed linguistic history is deduced and correlated with what is known of the political history of the tribe.

McQuown's classification of Mayan languages (1956) uses mapping of shared features to give historical implications, but

differs from the Mazatec studies in using shared *retentions* rather than innovations.

The paper presupposes at least a tentative comparative reconstruction of Proto-Mayan; seven of the reconstructed elements are used by McQuown as diagnostic. He maps the areas which retain these elements. He then superimposes on the map dotted arrows, indicating three closer relationships based in part on other criteria which he assumes may indicate immigration. From the resulting map, he deduces a tripartite grouping, but his proposed classification is somewhat more conservative than this, having ten major divisions. The point of particular interest here is his use of mapping and geography to postulate immigration lines that simplify his ultimate classfication and make it more plausible geographically and historically.

Wonderly's Zoque article (1949) is basically a historical study. His §1 is wholly historical, dealing with the reconstruction of the proto-Zoquean stops based on data from five dialect areas of Zoque and one each of Popoluca, Mixe, and Tapachultec.

It is the second section that has relevance for this article. In it Wonderly arrives at historical-geographical conclusions as to the innovating centers and areas of resistance of certain morphophonemic alternations. He does this by mapping (1) the larger area in which the morphophonemic alternation (voicing of stops following nasal, metathesis of y, loss of h from clusters, palatalization of c) occurs in any form; (2) the two areas within (1) in which the alternation is partial occurring only in some words, or only in some phonological environments. He then assumes that the area of (1) which is excluded from (2) marks the area of innovation where the new morphophonemic alternation first occurred and from which it spread to the other areas, and that the areas of (2) are peripheral areas where the phenomenon has not yet been carried to completion.

163

Key (1952-53) has made a preliminary study of four dialects of Nahuatl. It is very tentative both in its historical aspect (he notes the phonological correspondences but does not attempt to reconstruct the proto-forms) and in its dialectal aspect. The sets of correspondences, with accompanying comments, provide descriptions of the various dialects studied. Three of the sets are mapped to show their geographical distribution, but this is too few to show bundling of isoglosses from which dialect boundary evidence could be deduced. Nor is there any clear evidence of innovating versus resisting areas.

Hasler (1954-55a, b, c) has also made a preliminary contribution toward the dialect study of Nahuatl. His article includes a brief note on the method of ascertaining dialects by the use of sets of correspondences from the historical study.[3]

Holland (1959) has made a brief study of Mixtec and Cuicatec dialect variation based on lexicostatistics. He correlates the lexicostatistical groupings with the geographic facts, and adduces evidence as to the place of origin and migrations of the Mixtec, dating these with reference to the Conquest.

Aschmann (1956) has provided comparative word lists of two dialects of Totonac, with preliminary comments on the dialect differences.

2.2. LANGUAGES IN CONTACT. In the usage of Weinreich (1953) languages are 'in contact' if they are used alternately by the same person. This contact may range from the unique bilingualism of a single individual in a community, to widespread bilingualism of a large group with resulting modification of linguistic and socio-cultural patterns. Although there are a number of ways in which these phenomena might be studied, only a few of them have been attempted in Middle American languages.

They include bilingualism in its social setting, modification of linguistic structure by loanwords, and the historical and cultural implications of loanwords.[4]

There are two authors whose work has emphasized especially bilingualism in its social setting. Waterhouse (1949a) has provided us with a brief note concerning the rather special case of the Oaxaca Chontal who as children are monolingual speakers of Spanish, but learn their 'native' Chontal in adolescence and use it as their preferred language as adults. She cites reasons for this order of language learning, and describes the language behavior of individuals of various ages.

In addition to the social factors, there is brief mention of the linguistic effects of the bilingualism, notably the loss of a phoneme in the speech of the younger people causing a change from phonologically conditioned to morphologically conditioned allomorphs in certain classes of verb stems. The final paragraph indicates some reciprocal modification of the Spanish used with and by the children.

K.L. Pike, in a series of four text studies illustrates the problems of partial bilingualism as seen by the Mixtec themselves. In each of the four articles he presents a Mixtec text with English translation. His introductory remarks and appended comments explain the nature of the conflict between the Mixtec and Spanish systems, and its relevance to the point of the text. Two of the texts (1945a, 1946b) involve Spanish speakers whose intonation distorted the lexical tone of their Mixtec utterances so that they were misunderstood. Another (1945b) involves the mimicking of Spanish

---

[3] This article was completed in Brazil without access to some of the relevant literature. Hasler's materials in particular are inadequately reported from secondary sources.

[4] The studies reviewed here are all drawn from the past two decades or so. Among the older materials there are a large number of etymological studies of Indian loans in Spanish, a smaller number of studies of loan words from Spanish to the Indian languages, some studies of place-names, and a few comparative word lists. These are omitted here as peripheral to the main point of the chapter; additional bibliography may be found in Marino Flores (1957).

intonation by a monolingual Mixtec in order to impress his neighbors. The fourth (1947) relates the predicament of two Mixtec men who got themselves into trouble by using a few mechanically learned Spanish phrases without understanding either the questions which they were asked or their own replies.

There are three studies that deal with the theoretical and descriptive problems of a phonological structure modified by loanwords from another language.

Wonderly (1946) deals with a problem of partially assimilated Spanish loans in Zoque. The body of his paper consists of a comparison of two alternative ways of handling this data. The first is separate analyses of the native Zoque vocabulary and the lexicon of Spanish origin. He demonstrates that the two bodies of data differ in both phonemic inventory and distribution of phonemes, but that there is some ambiguity in assigning specific words to one category or the other. The second alternative is a single analysis of all the data. This yields a large inventory of phonemes and a more complicated distribution pattern than either of the separate analyses. Comparing these results, Wonderly concludes that: (1) the separate analysis of native Zoque elements is useful for historical and comparative purposes in that it conserves the basic phonological structure and distribution; (2) the separate analysis of Zoqueized Spanish is useful for showing the extent of assimilation to the Zoque pattern, but that (3) the single analysis of both sets of data fits the language as a whole best, as it avoids the ambiguities permitted by the double analysis, and also because it reflects the genuine assimilation of the Spanish loans to the new Zoque patterns.

Garvin (1947) restates Wonderly's materials in terms of the occurrence of distinctive features in Zoqueized Spanish, in native Zoque, and in the total Zoque system. He notes that the Zoqueized Spanish has some contrasts that do not occur in normal Spanish, but no distinctive features that are not used also in Spanish. The total system draws its distinctive features and its contrasts from both sub-systems so that it has some new pairs of contrasting phonemes that do not occur in either sub-system.

Fries and Pike (1949) reach quite a different solution to a similar problem in Mazatec—the occurrence of [nt] in unassimilated loans in contrast with the normal [nd] in native words. Since their paper is theory rather than data oriented, they deal with only this one facet of the Mazatec bilingual problem as a part of the larger problem of coexisting systems. Arguing primarily from the evidence of native reaction they conclude that two or more conflicting systems or parts of systems may coexist in the speech of a single monolingual individual. They suggest detailed procedures for discovering such systems, or demonstrating their occurrence.

There are three languages, Yaqui, Tzeltal-Tzotzil, and Huichol, in which loanwords have been studied specifically to discover historical and/or cultural correlations.

There are two studies of linguistic acculturation in Yaqui (J. B. Johnson, 1943; Spicer, 1943). Spicer uses loanwords to gain an insight into the nature of Yaqui acculturation in general. He first culls from the total Yaqui vocabulary the names of cultural items not native to preconquest Yaqui culture. He notes that this list of words consists almost entirely of loans from Spanish; there are few invented words without at least one element of foreign origin and few non-Spanish loans. To find cultural correlations, he calculates the percentages of loanwords in each of several cultural classifications such as household items, ritual vocabulary, kinship terms, sponsor terms, and names and titles in ceremony. He finds that Spanish loans in Yaqui are, for the most part, terms for material items new to the culture, or they correlate with areas of the culture where the old system was dislocated under Spanish pressure, as was the kinship system, the political organization, etc.

To find historical correlations, he dates the loanwords as old and new. This is done on the basis of a phonological comparison of the original word in the lending language with the new form in Yaqui. The forms showing certain regular phonetic and morphological modification are assumed to have entered Yaqui prior to the 19th century and to have become fixed before the majority of Yaqui speakers had occasion to learn Spanish phonetics. It is noted that not all words can be so dated, as many entered Yaqui without modification and that there has been some recent replacing of old loans with new ones. The various loans are tentatively correlated with the known periods of historical Spanish contact and domination.

J. B. Johnson (1943) adduces evidence that the whole of Yaqui linguistic structure has been affected by Spanish loans. He gives the evidence from vocabulary, phonology, and grammar. He finds these elements to be more recent than the 16th century since they do not occur in early grammars. (For a comparison of Yaqui acculturation with Tewa acculturation see Dozier, 1956.)

Loanword studies in Tzotzil and Tzeltal are used by McQuown (1959a) to discover the degree of acculturation at different historical periods. The loans, especially the Spanish loans, are divided into historical groups—largely on the basis of phonemic accommodation to Tzeltal and Tzotzil. This first assumption of chronological layers of loans is supported by the fact that some communities have lost old Spanish loans that are current in other communities, and reborrowed a newer layer of Spanish loans with less phonemic accommodation. Scales of the percentage of each kind of loan in each community provide indices of acculturation at different historical periods. There is a high degree of correlation (shown by mapping) between these linguistic indices

and the borrowing, or resistance to borrowing, of other culture items at each period. These are mapped as follows: (1) the smallest percentages of old loans are mapped against the retention of preconquest culture traits; (2) the percentages of later loans are mapped against cultural borrowings that date from the early colonial period; (3) recent Spanish loans are correlated with the current Mexican cultural borrowings. (See Nash and others, 1959; Mayers, Hajda, and Mc-Quown, 1959; Hajda, 1959f; Hajda and Verbitsky, 1959a, b, c.)

Grimes' *Spanish-Nahuatl-Huichol Monetary Terms* (1960) is a very brief note, but it has importance as an example of the tracing of loans through an intervening language. His data include comparable lexical items from Huichol, Nahuatl, and Spanish. Huichol has two sets of monetary terms. The older terms, now going out of use, are nontransparent phrases in Huichol. On analysis with reference to current Nahuatl dialects they turn out to consist of Nahuatl numbers combined with the old Spanish *tomin* 'real' or 'bit'. This fact suggests that the money system was first adopted by the Nahuatl from Spanish and taken over bodily into Huichol from Nahuatl. The newer set of monetary terms consists of Huichol numbers with Spanish coin names, showing direct borrowing from recent Spanish contact.

2.3. NONGEOGRAPHICAL DIALECTS. The term nongeographical dialect is used here to cover all the speech varieties that correlate with features of the sociocultural environment rather than with geographical distribution. This includes the phenomena which are discussed by Sapir (1915) under the title 'abnormal speech types', as well as the social dialects discussed by Bloomfield under the label 'non-local' (1933, ch. 3).

The studies surveyed here fall into three groups: studies of status dialect, of baby talk, and of social dialect. The status dialects are special usages conditioned by the status or rank of the person addressed, or more accurately, by his status relative to the speaker. Three of these illustrate something of the range of possibilities.

Jane Nellis' study of Sierra Zapotec (1947) is primarily a listing of the greetings, titles, and endearments used in the village of Atepec. The social conditions in which each of these is used are briefly described.

Law (1948) similarly describes the greeting forms of Gulf Aztec. This system appears to be more extensive than that of the Zapotec, with different greeting phrases specified for a large number of relationships. The most unusual feature is the use of formal dialogues as greetings between persons of certain special relationships (e.g. the ceremonial co-parent relationship of natural parents to godparents or godparents of the same child to each other). The formal linguistic behavior is accompanied by special handclasps.

Pittman (1948) reports the complex system of honorifics used in the Nahuatl of the village of Tetelcingo, Morelos, Mexico. The article constitutes a morphological analysis of the affixes belonging to this system. They include an honorific noun suffix, second and third person possessives, second and third person pronominal forms, and several devices for distinguishing honorific verbs from their nonhonorific counterparts, with further complexity resulting from the combination of honorific and nonhonorific subjects and objects. These honorifics may be combined to give exceptionally reverential forms. The article closes with a glossary of affixes.

There are two articles on baby talk that deal, not with the imperfect control of the adult code incidental to speech development, but rather with the special speech style used by adults in talking to babies, and in teaching them to talk. Such baby talk may differ from 'normal' adult speech in lexicon, in phonemic pattern, or both.

K. Larson's study of Huastec baby talk (1949) focuses on the lexical aspect. She presents a list of special words used by parents in talking with their children, and analyzes some of the more interesting ones.

Grimes (1955), on the other hand, is primarily concerned with style and its place in the linguistic system. He begins with a phonemic analysis of Huichol as a whole, including phonemes (first noted by McIntosh, 1945, notes 2, 3, 4) that occur only in words which were felt by the informant to be the 'same' as corresponding words with different phonemes. A study of these extra phonemes revealed that they occur only in baby talk, songs, or in a context involving diminution, endearment, or cuteness. In an attempt to fit the phenomenon into the structural system of the language, four hypotheses were rejected: style as a nonstructural feature; style as part of the phoneme system; conditioning by a styleme; phonemic contrast. The hypothesis accepted by Grimes is that of coexistent phonemic systems, based on the theoretical materials of Fries and Pike (1949). He includes as coexistent systems two other speech styles, used for secrecy and excitement, which are characterized respectively by special phonetic qualities of breathiness and falsetto articulation of the voiced sounds.

Social dialect, in the sense of local dialect vs. standard language, has been under attention for a long time and has provided much of the impetus for the early dialect geography work in Indo-European languages. More recently there has been emphasis on the direct tie of dialect with status or role.

The outstanding study of this kind in Middle America is a part of the 'Man-in-Nature' project of the University of Chicago (McQuown, 1959a). The data for this study consist of the word lists collected from 139 informants in 19 dialects which were also used for the study of geographical dialects. The informants were carefully chosen to represent a variety of social class and role, as well as a geographical spread of communities. The internal diversity of each community is studied by much the same techniques as the external diversity.

First lexicostatistical distance is computed and mapped for the individual informants on charts in which space indicates lexical difference.[5] Then the phonemic and the lexical isoglosses are mapped on the lexicostatistical charts showing the complicated picture of the relative closeness of the idiolects within the communities. The idiolects are grouped on the basis of quantity of shared features. These idiolect groups are compared with cultural phenomena in order to find correlations (see McQuown and others, 1959). There is not the close agreement of linguistic clustering with socio-cultural clustering that had been hoped for, but some interesting results are reported: (a) There tends to be idiolect clustering within barrios of the various communities. At least one apparent exception to this turned out to be a case of informants who had changed barrio in young adulthood. (b) The difference between core and periphery of the social group has its origin in ethnic difference, so that it correlates closely with linguistic difference. (c) There is correlation of dialect with kin group through the mother's line, demonstrated by a mapping of lexical divergence against surnames of mothers of informants. (d) People who have held political office (but not religious office) in their local community tend to be linguistically more like each other across community boundaries than people who have not (see McQuown, 1959b).

3. THE STRATEGY OF ENVIRONMENTAL CORRELATIONAL STUDIES. In the preceding

[5] This is a useful way of quantifying lexical difference. It seems to the reviewer, however, that the notion of time depth is out of place in discussing completely mutually intelligible varieties within a single community. More appropriate might be some non-temporal unit, as for example the 'dip' of Gudschinsky (1955) or even the raw percentage scores.

It would also seem a bit dangerous to compute lexical distance on the basis of single lists, since the competing forms almost certainly occur in the understanding vocabulary of each informant, and may even occur in his speaking vocabulary on other occasions.

section, we have looked briefly at the various kinds of environmental correlational studies to be found in the literature on Middle American Indian languages. The studies are in general fragmentary, tentative, or preliminary in nature, and much of the newer theoretical advance, based on research in other parts of the world, has not yet effectively touched Middle America.

It seems appropriate at this point, therefore, to suggest a program of further research. The wide variety of theory and method can be unified into two main topics: (1) geographical-historical dialects, and (2) nongeographical dialects. Included under each of these headings are a discussion of the aims of such a study, a set of suggested procedures for a unified program of planned research, and selected bibliographical references to theoretical materials and examples of studies.

No attempt is made here at a rigorous definition of 'dialect'. It is used in the very loose sense of any speech variety that is structurally different from other speech varieties under consideration. The notions of structure and system are basic to the discussion, however, and unstructured etic variations in speech are not considered. (For discussion of the place of structure in dialectology, see Weinreich, 1954. For the problem of terminology, see Martinet, 1954. For dialect definition by quantification of lexical resemblance, see Swadesh, 1954b. For a test of mutual intelligibility, see Voegelin and Harris, 1950; but see Wolff, 1959a, for a critique of the test.)

3.1. GEOGRAPHICAL-HISTORICAL DIALECTS. It is the purpose of this section to suggest briefly procedures for recovering the history of a language, and of the people who spoke it. This requires the exhaustive application of the techniques of dialect geography and loan word study to data obtained from comparative as well as descriptive study.

Such an historical study includes both the successive splits of the original genealogical stock, and the various contacts with other languages or dialects. These data are mapped to show the geographical location of the earlier stages of the language, the lines of diffusion, and the direction of migrations. The relative time of various changes and contacts can be ascertained, and all of this can be correlated to give a history, not only of the language itself, but also of the culture, the movements, and the cultural contacts of its speakers. (For discussion of the relationship of geneological development and diffusion, and their relationship to classification, see McQuown, 1955b; Hymes, 1959, pp. 57–59. For the relationship of linguistics to prehistory, with special reference to Indo-European, see Tovar, 1954. See Swadesh, 1952, for an example of the interplay of inheritance and diffusion.)

The proposed procedures for a historical-geographical study are: (1) identification of innovations with reference to a reconstructed proto-language, (2) mapping of the innovations, (3) interpretation of the isoglosses as indicating dialect history in terms of successive splits and renewed contacts, and (4) interpretation of the isoglosses as indicating dialect history in terms of centers of diffusion, areas of resistance, and extent and direction of migrations.

This set of procedures presupposes an adequate body of data of two kinds: descriptive studies of the relevant languages, and a reconstruction of the proto-language of the languages or language groups under attention. It is the possibility of reconstructing a proto-language that may determine the size of group chosen for an initial study, though two or more such studies may provide the basis for later investigation of more remote layers.

Ideally the descriptive data should include complete descriptions of all of the languages presumed to belong to the given language family, with at least their principal local variations, and also of all the presumably nonrelated languages found in the same area. Care must be taken, however, to eliminate aberrant idiolects, which can be more effectively studied as nongeographical dialects. In practice, first approximations may be obtained with less than the ideal quota of data; these may then be used as a guide for further more detailed studies. (See Swadesh, 1954a, for a description of a method for the rapid collection of preliminary data.) Since the specific techniques of both descriptive studies and historical reconstruction may be found elsewhere in this volume they are not discussed here.

3.1.1. IDENTIFICATION OF INNOVATIONS. The first procedure is the identification of innovations in the grammatical, phonological, and lexical structure. In general any item or any feature that cannot be reconstructed for the proto-language may be taken to be an innovation.

In the grammar, the more regular features are apt to be recent levelings or analogic changes, whereas the irregular forms are likely to be relics of an older layer of structure. Plausibility in the order of development may also be helpful in screening out the grammatical retentions.

In the phonology, the phonemes that are most like the environments in which they occur are most apt to be recent developments, since phones tend to become more like their environments. If, for example, in a voiced environment, a voiced phone in one language corresponds to a voiceless phone in another language, it is most plausible to reconstruct a voiceless proto-phone, and to posit the voicing as an innovation, since voicing is a far more likely development in such an environment than unvoicing.

If there appear to be two different groups of internally consistent sets of correspondences that conflict with each other, it is possible that one group represents the inherited material, and that the other represents material borrowed at a very early stage, so that the modifications in the different dialects correspond to each other in much the same way as the sound changes in the inherited material. One criterion for deciding that one group of sets is inherent rather than borrowed is its occurrence in a large part of the core vocabulary—that part of the vocabulary that is least subject to loss. (See Dyen, 1956a, for an example of the application of this principle.)

Lexical innovations may be borrowings from another language or dialect, or they may be neologisms or semantic shifts within the inherited material. Borrowings that are transparently similar to the lending language may be recognized easily. Older borrowings may be sufficiently acculturated as to be nearly unrecognizable, except that they do not fit the reconstructed patterns of the more remote proto-language. Neologisms may be reconstructable for the more recent proto-language of a group of dialects, but not for the more remote layer. In this case, it may be almost impossible to guess which of apparently competing reconstructed forms was the original and which was the innovation (if indeed they were not co-existing forms with different meanings in the original language). Decisions in such cases must often be delayed until after the mapping, when the older form may be found occupying 'relic areas' and the newer forms showing a typical pattern of recent diffusion. (See Salzman, 1954, for a suggestion for a uniform test list for eliciting loanwords, so that cross-cultural studies of resistance to or acceptance of loans can be made. See Chrétien, 1956, for a study in which borrowings are separated from inherited material.)

3.1.2. MAPPING OF INNOVATIONS. The second procedure is a mapping of the innovations, by enclosing within a single line on a geopolitical map all the communities which share one specific feature (one sound change, one grammatical feature, one lexical item). There will be a separate isogloss for each feature mapped. (For examples of such mapping in Middle American languages, see Wonderly, 1949; Gudschinsky, 1955, 1958a; McQuown, 1959a.)

One of the most striking features of al-

most any set of isogloss maps is the lack of congruence of the individual isoglosses. Except in the presence of the most formidable natural or political barrier, there are few if any really sharp dialect boundaries. If every shared innovation implies shared history, there must have been in most languages, shifting groupings at different points in history and/or there must have been transition areas receiving traits by diffusion from two or more innovating centers. It is probable in most cases that both of these hypotheses fit some part of the history, and the problem becomes one of dating the isoglosses and turning the apparent confusion into a record of consecutive events. (See Davis and McDavid, 1950; Reed and Spicer, 1952, for special methods of mapping and interpreting the confused isoglosses of a complex transition area.)

3.1.3. INTERPRETATION OF ISOGLOSSES. The third procedure is the interpretation of the isoglosses as indicating dialect history in terms of successive splits and renewed contacts. Such a history of splits is usually diagrammed as a family tree, although it is trite to note that no perfect family tree exists in languages—development by successive dialect splits is always accompanied by continued or renewed contact which blurs the dialect boundaries and give rise to the "mesh" described by Swadesh (1959e).

A quantification of features shared by two or more speech communities may be used at an early stage of research to provide an estimate of dialect subgrouping, which would in turn be useful as a guide for further studies. Lexicostatistics uses a quantification of shared lexical retentions to arrive at sub-grouping with estimated time depth of separation. This may not always provide the best possible guess as to historical sub-groupings of dialects for two reasons: first, the lexicon is the part of the linguistic structure most subject to chance change and, second, as Brugmann pointed out as early as 1884, retentions are often shared by widely scattered dialects, whereas shared

170

innovations of a nontrivial character strongly imply a period of common history or close contact. (See Hymes, 1960, for a complete discussion of lexicostatistics and bibliography. See Gleason, 1959, for a somewhat different way of arriving at a family tree by counting likenesses.)

Sub-groups may also be arrived at by a detailed chronological ordering of the periods of common history implied by the shared isoglosses. A useful initial hypothesis is that, other things being equal, the bundling of grammatical and phonological isoglosses represents older developments, and the lexical isoglosses represent the more recent developments. This is due to the fact that borrowings and diffusion in general affect the vocabulary of a language most easily and the grammatical structure least easily. 'Other things' are seldom equal, however, and it becomes necessary to look for other ways of dating the isoglosses. The following is a suggestive list of techniques by which relative chronology can be assigned to specific innovations. As can be seen, there is considerable interplay between the lexical, grammatical, and phonological developments, so that it is not profitable to discuss these separately.

(a) A sound change involving modification by its linguistic environment must be presumed to be older than the loss of the modifying environment.

(b) In a series of sound changes such that a becomes b, and b becomes c, and the contrast between a and b is replaced by a contrast between b and c, the change from b to c must be presumed older than the change from a to b, or the contrast would have been lost. (Such a change in all the allophones of two phonemes would be a trivial phonetic shift, if not accompanied by related effects in the phonological structure.)

(c) The borrowing of lexical items from other languages may be judged as early or recent according to the degree they have been modified by the borrowing language.

This is not, of course, an infallible test, as some words require little or no modification to fit the system of the borrowing language.

(d) Borrowed lexical items may be roughly dated by what is known of cultural, political, or linguistic history from outside sources. Direct loans from Spanish, for example, could not include in the same period both *tomin* 'real', 'bit' and *radio*, since the former term had disappeared from Mexican Spanish usage before the invention that gave rise to the latter term.

(e) Lexical items having their origin in close-knit phrases may sometimes be roughly dated by the degree of fusion or internal sound change; transparent compounds or locutions are usually of more recent origin.

(f) The borrowing of lexical items may be judged as early if the modified form presupposes the phonologic system of an earlier stage of the lending language.

In sub-grouping the assumption is made that larger groupings are older than smaller ones unless there is clear evidence that the isoglosses marking the smaller grouping are older than those marking the larger grouping. When a given speech community shares features with more than one postulated dialect group, the older features are taken to indicate the original affinity; the newer features are taken to indicate a later contact across old dialect lines. (For a discussion of sub-grouping, see Dyen, 1953; for a sample study in Polynesian, see Grace, 1959.)

It is convenient to reconstruct intermediate stages in the language history (i.e. the proto-language of the major dialect groupings) so that changes can be discussed in terms of system. A vital part of the structural change is the effect of contact with other languages. The most obvious effect of borrowing is in the lexical structure; as new words are added, old words are dropped, or there is a shift in their area of meaning. Grammatical changes may be traceable to borrowings, either to the direct borrowing of morphemes with grammatical function, or to analogical restructuring triggered by

171

the borrowing of a large number of items with a similar structure, or the breakdown of older patterns due to the influx of new forms that do not fit. In phonological change, it is often the sounds of unassimilated loans which provide new contrasts and give phonemic status to earlier phonetic shifts. (For the whole problem of bilingualism, including a consideration of both the social and the linguistic factors, see the theoretical formulations of Weinreich, 1953, 1957a; Haugen, 1949, 1950. For the details of structural change, see especially Vogt, 1954. Examples of studies of bilingualism may be found in Weinreich, 1957b; Haugen, 1953, 1954; Casagrande, 1954–55. For a bibliography and for suggestions for research in the Americas, see Haugen, 1956.)

The effect of language contact is not all in one direction, and a study of the lending language as also a borrowing language would be in order here. In Middle America this would involve the study of local varieties of campesino Spanish, and the comparison of these with each other and with the Indian languages. Then a study of regional dialects might answer the question of which Indian language was the most influential in the area as a whole—not just in terms of loans, but in terms of phonetic and phonemic influence.

It might be noted, parenthetically, that area studies are one way of describing this interaction of various languages across linguistic borders. These constitute descriptions of language typologies occurring in a specific geographic area of linguistic diversity. (See Emeneau, 1956, for an example of this kind of study. For area study and its relation to genetic studies and dialect geography see Voegelin, 1945. Wolff, 1959b, provides a sample from Nigerian languages, and discusses the relationship of area studies to typology. For various theories of typology, see Ullmann, 1953; Wells, 1954; Hockett, 1955; Voegelin, 1956; Greenberg, 1957b, 1960; Kroeber, 1960a, 1960b; Householder, 1960.)

172

3.1.4. INTERPRETATION OF ISOGLOSSES. The fourth procedure is the interpretation of the isoglosses as indicating dialect history in terms of centers of diffusion, areas of resistance, and the extent and direction of migrations. This is in the nature of an explanation of the isogloss divergence which mars the perfection of the family tree study. In general an innovating area will appear on the map as the center of concentric isoglosses, and the most resistant areas will appear bounded by a crosshatch of isoglosses that center elsewhere—though the facts are seldom quite that simple.

The spread from the innovating centers may be by migration or by diffusion. In general, spread by migration results in more or less homogeneous groups with fairly sharp borders, while a long history of spread by diffusion results in series of concentric isoglosses. Further, the innovating center from which migration came is likely to be more diverse dialectally, whereas the area settled by migration tends to be linguistically rather uniform, with new dialects only beginning. (See Dyen, 1956b, for a statement of migration theory; Sapir, 1916, for the older concepts on which he built; Diebold, 1960, for an application of this theory to Mayan and Salish; see Pulgram, 1956, for a contrast of migration with diffusion or 'infiltration'; Chrétien, 1956, for a migration inferred from word distribution.)

Reference to the relative chronology of the isoglosses that indicate diffusion or migration, will establish the relative dates at which the various centers of innovation were expanding and important.

Toponymy might also be expected to give a clue to migration according to the following hypotheses: (a) one would not expect that a place name would spread by diffusion to a location where the lending language had never been spoken. Presumably, then, the language of origin of a traditional place-name was at one time spoken in that place; (b) one would expect the speakers of a language to have had at some time at least some contact with every place for which they use a native name; (c) place names which are clear loan-translations of names originating in another language, indicate that the contact of the borrowing language with this place is more recent than that of the lending language. None of these hypotheses has been thoroughly tested.

From the total material on diffusion and migration, it should be possible to chart a history of the movements of the early speakers of the language, the periods of prominence and prestige of various areas, and the shifts in the lines of communication and resistance. The information about innovating centers and shifting lines of communication can be correlated with a history of contacts with other language groups. The direct contacts can be seen by the geographical distribution of direct loans at each level, either in terms of the dialects sharing such loans or the location of centers from which the loan words diffused. These data will indicate whether there was widespread contact in a large area, or a small point of contact from which loans spread. (This technique, however, cannot recover contact which involved little or no borrowing.)

Indirect cultural diffusion across language boundaries may sometimes also be inferred from the shape of loan words, if they can be demonstrated to have passed through an intervening language or languages. In order to demonstrate that a word passed from language a to language b, and subsequently from b to c, it is necessary to discover three sets of modifications: that of loans from a to b, that of loans from a to c, and that of loans from b to c. Presumably then, some items in c that do not fit the patterns of direct loans from a to c can be reconstructed as having come from a given form in b, which in turn is the normal correspondence to a source word in a.

Not only a history of cultural contacts, but something of the culture itself can be recovered from linguistic study. In each

proto-language, for example, there are some cultural terms that can be reconstructed with considerable certainty. These give an insight into the nature of the cultural horizon under attention. This is not infallible, of course, since the meanings of words may change with the changing culture in such a way that the original forms may have had quite a different meaning from that which they bear in all of the daughter languages. (See Millon and Longacre, 1961).

Something of the history of the culture can be known by the nature of the loan words from outside languages that can be ascribed to each layer. This lexicon represents cultural change or accretion and so also implies the weakening or restructuring of earlier culture patterns. The adoption of new kin words, for example, suggests a breakdown in the older social structure; the adoption of new religious terms suggests a restructuring of the religious system; the adoption of new political terms suggests the adoption with it of elements of a new political system. If the outside forces which caused these weakenings and breakdowns are known (as for example in the case of the Spanish conquest), the loans and the structural changes which accompanied them can be dated. (For discussions of language and cultural change see Hoijer, 1948; Herzog, 1941.)

3.2. NONGEOGRAPHICAL DIALECTS. It is the purpose of this section to outline the content of a complete synchronic description of the speech of a given community, including a description of all the various subdialects, styles, or types—whether conditioned by social class, sex, age, community role, or special literary use—and a correlation of these with the total sociocultural environment.

The existence of such sub-dialects becomes evident early in the descriptive study as the researcher finds that he has conflicting data from different informants, or that in the speech of a single informant there are elements that do not fit neatly in a single

173

system. It is customary to handle this problem in descriptive statements either (1) by normative analysis with aberrant detail relegated to footnotes, (2) by limiting the description to one style of one informant, or (3) by concentrating on one of the less "normal" dialects.

The dialects proposed for study are highly complex with interlocking distributions, since a single individual may control a number of sub-dialects and use them interchangeably or with special conditioning factors and since in a society of any great complexity, no two informants may be presumed to use precisely the same group of subdialects. (See K. L. Pike, 1960, ch. 15 on interlocking systems.)

The method of study, however, is basically simple. It consists of plotting the dialectal differences against the possible conditioning factors. This plotting may be either a mapping on a geographical map or stylized chart, or it may consist of statistical correlation. (See McQuown, 1959a, for charting and mapping of lexical distance as measured by lexicostatistics; Fischer, 1958, as an example of statistical method; Fries and Pike, 1949, for procedures for discovering coexisting systems in the speech of a single informant.)

The completeness of the study depends on the amount of data plotted, and the variety of hypotheses considered. The basic data are of two kinds: (a) descriptive studies, with copious text, of the speech of a large number of informants drawn from a wide variety of social levels and cultural roles within a single community, and (b) comparable studies of the speech of the same informants on a wide variety of occasions, including the more highly structured events in the culture.

This provides two dimensions so that it is possible to compare the speech of different informants in comparable social context, and also the speech of the same informants in different social contexts. Both sets of comparisons should be made, to discover

the structural differences in phonology, grammar and lexicon between the dialects. Once a fairly full list of dialect differences is available, it is possible to augment the data readily by eliciting crucial test items and text from additional informants in additional contexts.

The speech varieties may be correlated with classes of informants based on social class, status, age, sex, kinship, occupation, etc. (For studies correlating speech phenomena with social class or status see: McDavid and McDavid, 1952; Atwood, 1953; Ferguson and Gumperz, 1960; Klausner, 1955. For a study correlating speech phenomena with socio-economic factors, see Sapon, 1953. For dialect correlated with sex, see Sapir, 1929b.)

Speech variety may also be correlated with cultural occasions such as religious ceremonial, political gathering, or recreational event, or with cultural activities such as storytelling, education of children, singing, etc. These are not rigid categories, but have considerable overlap. (For dialects used in ceremonial or myth, see White, 1944; Newman, 1955; French, 1958; Hymes, 1958. For dialect used by parents to babies, and by babies in learning to talk, see Casagrande, 1948; Voegelin and Robinett, 1954; Ferguson, 1956. For linguistic play, see Conklin, 1956, and 1959. For warpath language, see Opler and Hoijer, 1940. Ferguson, 1959, discusses the cultural setting for the use of prestige and nonprestige dialects by informants who control both.)

A large number of correlations should be used to be sure that no useful ones are overlooked. As in the case of the geographical mapping described in §3.1 it is unlikely that the isoglosses, whether drawn on a map or implied by statistical measurement, will be exactly congruent. Therefore, the dialects implied by bundling of isoglosses must be described in terms of an obligatory core and permitted variation, and the exact range of their occurrence stated in socio-cultural terms. Unexpected deviation should be in-

174

vestigated for interfering factors such as recent change of status of an informant or a previously unexplored correlation. It is to be expected that some of the 'dialects' may be fragmentary rather than complete systems. They may, for example, consist of a special set of lexical items whose phonology and grammar are like that of the more casual language used for everyday purposes. Such sub-dialect fragments might be described as deviations from the more "normal", or statistically more frequent dialects. (See also K. L. Pike, 1960, pp. 75–76, for a discussion of systems as topologically related.)

REFERENCES

Adams and McQuown, 1959
Aschmann, 1956
Atwood, 1953
Berlin, 1962a, 1962b
Bloomfield, 1933
Casagrande, 1948, 1954–55
Chrétien, 1956
Conklin, 1956, 1959
Davis and McDavid, 1950
Diebold, 1960
Dozier, 1956
Dyen, 1953, 1956a, 1956b
Emeneau, 1956
Ferguson, 1956, 1959
—— and Gumperz, 1960
Fischer, 1958
French, 1958
Fries and Pike, 1949
Garvin, 1947
Gleason, 1959
Grace, 1959
Greenberg, 1954, 1957b, 1960
Grimes, 1955, 1960
Gudschinsky, 1955, 1958a
Hajda, 1959a, 1959b, 1959c, 1959d, 1959e, 1959f
—— and Verbitsky, 1959a, 1959b, 1959c
Halle and others, 1956
Hasler, 1954–55a, 1954–55b, 1954–55c
Haugen, 1949, 1950, 1953, 1954, 1956
Herzog, 1941
Hockett, 1955
Hoenigswald, 1960
Hoijer, 1948
Holland, 1959
Hopkins, 1962a, 1962b
Householder, 1960
Hymes, 1958, 1959, 1960
Johnson, J. B., 1943
Kaufman, 1961, 1962
Key, 1952–53
Klausner, 1955
Kroeber, 1960a, 1960b
Larson, 1949

Law, 1948
McDavid, 1946, 1951
—— and McDavid, 1952
McIntosh, 1945
McQuown, 1955b, 1956, 1959a, 1959b, 1959c, 1962
—— and others, 1959
Mandelbaum, 1949
Marino Flores, 1957
Martinet, 1954
Mayers, 1959
——, Hajda, and McQuown, 1959
—— and McQuown, 1959a, 1959b
Millon and Longacre, 1961
Nash and others, 1959
Nellis, 1947
Newman, 1955
Opler and Hoijer, 1940
Pike, K. L., 1945a, 1945b, 1946b, 1947, 1960
Pittman, 1948
Pulgram, 1956
Radhakrishnan, 1962
Reed and Spicer, 1952
Robles Uribe, 1962
Salzmann, 1954
Sapir, 1915, 1916, 1929b
Sapon, 1953
Sarles, 1962
Spicer, 1943
Spier, Hallowell, and Newman, 1941
Swadesh, 1952, 1954a, 1954b, 1959e
Tovar, 1954
Ullmann, 1953
Voegelin, 1945, 1956
—— and Harris, 1950
—— and Robinett, 1954
Vogt, 1954
Waterhouse, 1949a
Weinreich, 1953, 1954, 1957a, 1957b
Wells, 1954
White, 1944
Wolff, 1959a, 1959b
Wonderly, 1946, 1949

Type Linguistic Descriptions

7A. Classical Nahuatl

STANLEY NEWMAN

INTRODUCTION
1.   Sources

PHONOLOGY

2.   Phonemic units
2.1.   Vowels
2.2.   Consonants
2.3.   Stress
3.   Distribution of Phonemes
4.   Morphophonemics
4.1.   Automatic changes
4.2.   Selective changes
4.2.1. In prefixes
4.2.2. In suffixes
4.2.3. In stems

MORPHOLOGY

5.   Types of processes
6.   Morphological categories
6.1.   Inflectional word classes
6.2.   Derivations
6.3.   Stem types
7.   Nominals
7.1.   Nouns
7.1.1. Stem modifications and the possessive singular
7.1.2. Reduplication
7.1.3. Inflectional prefixes
7.1.4. Inflectional suffixes
7.1.5. Noun-forming derivations
7.2.   Pronouns
7.3.   Postpositions
8.   Verbs
8.1.   Stem modifications and the preterit
8.2.   Reduplicated stems
8.3.   Inflectional prefixes
8.4.   Inflectional suffixes

8.5.   Irregular verbs
8.6.   Verb-forming derivations
8.6.1. Derivational suffixes
8.6.2. Compounding
9.   Particles

SYNTAX

10.   Utterance types
10.1   Non-verbal utterance
10.2.   Verbal utterance
11.   Components of the sentence
11.1.   Predicate
11.2.   Substantive

INTRODUCTION

1. SOURCES. The first grammar of Nahuatl, that of Padre Fray Andrés de Olmos (1547), was published only 26 years after Cortés shattered the power of the Aztec empire by capturing the city of Tenochtitlan. During the century that followed, four more Nahuatl grammars were composed by Spanish friars who were serving their church in the New World.

This linguistic activity stemmed from a European tradition which was scarcely a half-century old. Antonio de Nebrija's Gramática Castellana (1492) was the first treatment of any European vernacular. Only Latin, Greek, and Hebrew had previously been worthy of the attention of grammarians. So unprecedented a venture as Nebrija's needed justification. When Queen Isabella, on being presented with the Gramática Castellana, inquired with some puzzlement what its purpose was, Nebrija is said to have replied that language was always "the companion of rule"; foreign peoples under Spanish rule must be given the language of Spain along with its laws (Trend, 1953, p. 118). To this political argument was added a humanistic one, potent at a time when Spain was seething with patriotic and religious zeal. Nebrija's grammatical procedure of comparing Spanish with Latin, point for point, was an attempt to determine wherein the language of his country had resources comparable to Latin and wherein it lacked the expressiveness of the Roman tongue. Only by being measured against the Latin standard could a vernacular be sufficiently ennobled and enriched to make it a worthy vehicle for the expression of lofty thoughts.

It was in this linguistic climate that the friars dedicated their grammatical efforts to the glory of Spain and the spread of the faith. Even before the first grammar appeared, some Nahuatl sermons had already been published.[1] The guidance of a grammar, wrote Molina, would enable other servants of the church to learn the language of the aborigines and thus to confess them, to preach to them, and to administer the holy sacraments to them. He also gave recognition to the humanistic motive. Like any other vernacular, he stated, the Nahuatl language was spoken badly by some natives and perfectly by others; his grammar, based on the speech of the most learned Aztecs, presented a language that was rich and eloquent (Molina, 1571a, p. 222). When he and other grammarians discussed the Nahuatl principles in -dus (i.e., Nahuatl forms functioning somewhat like Latin amandus, etc.), they were following the humanistic precept of measuring the Indian vernacular against the Latin standard (Olmos, 1547, p. 53; Molina, 1571a, p. 189; Galdo Guzmán, 1642, p. 355).

[1] Sahagún's Sermones en Mexicano were published in 1540, according to Viñaza (1892, p. 3).

From the point of view of modern linguistics, the early grammars of Nahuatl were most deficient in their treatment of phonology. Sounds were conceived in terms of orthography. Nearly all the discussions of Nahuatl sounds began with a list of the letters missing in the language of the Aztecs, and careful attention was paid to the spelling rules derived from Spanish orthography. The few attempts to describe sounds were largely based on likenesses to other languages: Nahuatl tz was like the Hebrew Tzade; Nahuatl -ll- was like the Latin rather than the Castillian -ll-. Fortunately, the sound system was relatively simple and transparent. The Spanish orthography, though not an ideal script for Nahuatl, conveyed most of the phonemically relevant distinctions, and the combined efforts of several missionaries served to direct attention even to such unfamiliar features as vocalic quantity and the glottal stop. From their discussions of spelling and pronunciation, and from the modern dialect data, it has been possible to arrive at a fairly reliable picture of Classical Nahuatl phonology.

Morphology was treated more adequately. It was presented, of course, in terms of a preconceived scheme. For example, the entire morphological description was organized by discussing in turn each of the eight parts of speech. Similarly, the conjugation of the verb tended to follow the classical categories: in order to tailor Nahuatl to fit such categories as the future perfect or the present subjunctive, the grammarian might state that the future perfect was the same as the preterit perfect, or he might illustrate the present subjunctive paradigm with a phrase containing the present indicative verb forms preceded by a particle meaning "if." Despite these and other reflections of a classical model, the outlines of Nahuatl morphology, particularly its inflectional system, could not fail to emerge. Most of the grammarians knew the language through long and intimate contact. With a laudable respect for examples they provided copious illustrative material. Most of them, also, tried conscientiously to convey the fine shades of meaning expressed in the examples, for such nuances were matters of primary importance to the writers of the early grammars.

They did not regard the mechanics of sentence building as a rubric of grammar. Forms larger than words or phrasal inflections were discussed in terms of idioms and styles of expression, in brief chapters entitled "On the Mexicanisms Which Are Some Ways of Speaking the Language Properly" or "On Some Ways of Common Speech." Up to the present time the syntactic structure has been given less attention than the other aspects of the language. The body of Classical Nahuatl texts still remains to be analyzed syntactically.

From the middle of the 17th century until nearly the end of the 19th, this grammatical tradition continued with little change, though with diminishing activity. Beginning in 1885 the re-publication in Mexico of the early Nahuatl grammars was symptomatic of a new and revitalized interest in *la lengua mexicana.* The European tradition of literary scholarship, primarily in its French version, became merged with the older grammarian tradition. The new approach produced Nahuatl specialists whose broad field of interest encompassed Nahuatl antiquities, history, and literature as well as language. This trend is represented in the twentieth century scholarship of Dávila Garibi (1938, 1948) and Garibay (1940a).

Finally, the tradition of structural linguistics was brought to the study of Nahuatl in Whorf's sketch of the Milpa Alta dialect (1946). Other structural descriptions of modern dialects are those of Croft on Matlapa (1951, 1953a, 1954), Harold and Mary Key on Sierra Nahuat (1953, 1960), Pittman on Tetelcingo (1954), Hasler on dialectology (1954–55a,b,c), and Law on Isthmus Nahuat (1958).[2]

[2] The basic sources used for the present article were the dictionary of Molina (1571b) and the five grammars written between 1547 and 1645—Olmos

PHONOLOGY

2. PHONEMIC UNITS. The following symbols are employed to represent the 23 segmental phonemes of Classical Nahuatl: *a, a·, ch, cu, e, e·, i, i·, k, l, m, n, o, o·, p, s, t, tl, tz, w, x, y, ?.* The heavy stress is indicated by *'* only when it occurs on the final syllable of the word, but it is unmarked when it falls on the penult; the weak stress is always unmarked.

2.1. VOWELS. The eight vowel phonemes were patterned in a system of four positions, each containing a short and a long vowel: high front position, short *i* and long *i·*; mid front, *e* and *e·*; low central, *a* and *a·*; and mid back, *o* and *o·*.

Apparently the quality of most of these vowels fluctuated only slightly or not perceptibly. The *i* and *i·* were both close vowels, having the quality of Spanish *mi* or English *meet.* The short *e* may have varied between a close vowel, as in French *fée,* and the more open sound of English *bet*; but *e·* was always close. Both the *a* and *a·* were unvarying open vowels in the low central position, as in Spanish *lana.* The *o* and *o·* probably fluctuated between the close mid quality of the vowel in French *beau* and the open high vowel of English *put.*[3]

(1547), Molina (1571a), Rincon (1595), Galdo Guzmán (1642), and Carochi (1645). These materials were supplemented by modern studies, both of the classical language and the present-day dialects, and my own work with a Nahuatl dialect of central Mexico during the 1940's.

[3] Olmos and Molina employed the five vowel letters of the Spanish alphabet in writing Nahuatl. Both noted that the Indians made very little differentiation between the *o* and the *u,* sometimes confusing these letters in the same word. But these two earliest grammarians of Nahuatl undoubtedly contributed to the confusion by using the letter *u* to represent, not only *o* and *o·* on occasions, but the *w* consonant phoneme as well. Their practice, however, suggests that the *o* and *o·* vowels must have been higher than the Spanish *o* phoneme. Whorf described the short *o* in the Milpa Alta dialect, one of the dialects presumably close to the classical language, as sometimes "open, but less open than [ɔ]"; he indicated that both *o* and *o·* were close vowels, under some conditions *o* being "very close, practically [u]" (1946, p. 372).

The phonemic distinctiveness of the two quantities is illustrated in the following word pairs: *xiwitl* 'year', *xi·witl* 'comet'; *metztli* 'leg', *me·tztli* 'moon'; *tlatia* 'to burn', *tla·tia* 'to hide'; *toka* 'to follow', *to·ka* 'to bury'.[4]

2.2. CONSONANTS. Among the stop consonants the bilabial *p*, alveolar *t*, and velar *k* were unaspirated voiceless sounds, like the Spanish *p*, *t*, *k* in *pelo*, *tiro*, *kilo*. Following *n*, *k* was sometimes voiced to [*g*]. The labialization of the phoneme *cu* was voiced or partially voiced in syllable initial position, like the Spanish *cu* in *cuarto*. But in syllable final position *cu* was pronounced as a voiceless labialized stop, paralleling the pattern of *w*. The pronunciation of *ʔ*, the glottal stop, when it appeared within the word, seems to have been a glottal closure followed by an aspirated release. But in word final and especially in utterance final position the glottal catch was only partially actualized or was omitted entirely, leaving the aspiration as the main perceptible feature of this phoneme.[5]

The fricatives and affricates were consonants with no clearly variant pronunciations. The *s* was an alveolar fricative, as in English *see*; the *x* was an alveo-palatal, pronounced like the *sh* in English *she*. Corresponding to these fricatives in position were the alveolar affricative *tz*, like the *ts*

in English *cats*, and the alveo-palatal affricate *ch*, like the *ch* in English *church*. The *tl* was always a voiceless lateral affricate.

The nasal consonants were invariably voiced. The *m* was always bilabial. The *n* was articulated as a velar [ŋ] before *k* or *cu*, like the first-syllable *n* in Spanish *cinco* or *cincuenta*; it was alveolar elsewhere. The *l* was a lateral consonant, voiced in syllable initial position, like the *l* of Spanish *lana*; but it was voiceless when it appeared in syllable final position preceding a consonant other than *l*. Similarly, the semivowel *w* was voiced at the beginning of a syllable, as in English *water*, but it was voiceless in syllable final position. There appears to have been a difference between men's and women's speech in the syllable initial actualization of *w*: men pronounced it as a bilabial, women as a labio-dental.[6] The semivowel *y* was invariably voiced.

---

[4] Rincon was the first to report the quantitative distinctions in Nahuatl vowels. Although he did not mark these distinctions in his transcription, the final chapter of his grammar contained a list of word contrasts, illustrating forms which, though spelled identically, differed in "accent." Rincon's five accents attempted to cover the phenomena of stress and the glottal stop as well as quantity. Carochi provided a much clearer treatment of vowel quantity. His accents, recorded in his transcription, were confined to showing quantity and the glottal stop. For a recent discussion of the accent problem, see Barrett (1956) and Bright (1960).

[5] There can be little doubt concerning the phonetic character of the glottal stop in Classical Nahuatl, for nearly all of the early grammarians attempted to describe the sounds of this phoneme, which became known as the *saltillo*. Some of the writers, like Olmos, treated it as a consonantic phenomenon; others, like Rincon and Carochi, included it among the syllabic accents.

Olmos used the letter *h* for this phoneme, apparently perceiving the aspiration of the preconsonantal *ʔ* as its most characteristic feature. He related this phonetic feature to the voicelessness of preconsonantal *l* and *w*, which he wrote *lh* and *uh*. He also added an *h* at the end of certain plural forms, in most cases where the plural morpheme -*ʔ* (§8.42c) would be expected; but he stated that he followed this practice in order to distinguish the plurals from the singulars, even though the natives might not pronounce the *h*. With evident asperity he observed that the Indians sometimes pronounced this letter forcefully and at other times seemed to swallow it (1547, p. 107).

Rincon reported that the *saltillo* was pronounced differently in various parts of Mexico; he noted that the Tlaxcalans gave it a particularly strong and harsh pronunciation (1595, p. 264). Carochi, phonetically the most perceptive of the early grammarians, used the grave accent to indicate the distinct closure of the *ʔ* in word medial position; he wrote the circumflex accent for the pre-pausal *ʔ* to indicate its weaker closure and more aspirated pronunciation (1645, p. 402). These were essentially the phonetic features of the glottal stop phoneme in the Milpa Alta dialect, as described by Whorf (1946, p. 372).

[6] The first of the Nahuatl grammarians, Olmos, reported the difference between men's and women's pronunciation of *w* (1547, p. 107), an observation repeated by the remaining early writers. His *lh* spelling of the voiceless allophone of *l* was not followed by subsequent grammarians, but his convention of writing *w* as syllable initial *hu*

182

2.3. STRESS. Except for nouns in the vocative (see §7.1.5.2a), which were stressed on the final syllable, words of more than one syllable took the heavy stress on the penult. A weaker degree of stress characterized the remaining syllables.

3. DISTRIBUTION OF PHONEMES. Only the following four combinations of consonant (C) and vowel (V) formed the syllable unit.

V: *a* 'ah!' the first syllable of *i·a·maw* 'his book'

VC: *ok* 'yet'; the first syllable of *ompa* 'there'

CV: *ka* 'with'; the first syllable of *teo·tl* 'god'

CVC: *wa·n* 'and'; the first syllable of *tlaxkalli* 'bread'

Words were composed of any combination of these syllabic structures. The word unit, consequently, could begin in a consonant or a vowel and could end in a consonant or a vowel. Sequences of vowels could occur anywhere in the word, each vowel counting as a syllable. The combination of syllables permitted no more than two consonants to be juxtaposed within the word; elsewhere, in word initial or final position, consonants appeared singly, never in clusters.

On the basis of the consonant allophones determined by syllable position, such as the voiceless *l* or *w* in syllable final position, it is possible to describe the division of the word into structural syllables. When two consonants were juxtaposed, the syllable division was always made between them. A consonant occurring intervocalically belonged with the following syllable. When two vowels appeared in sequence, a syllable division was made between them.

In word initial position any phoneme could occur except *l* or *ꞌ*. In word final position any phoneme but *m* was permitted.

_____

(sometimes merely *u* between vowels) and syllable final *uh* has become part of the literary tradition of Nahuatl.

4. MORPHOPHONEMICS. Several types of phoneme changes took place. Only a few changes were automatic throughout the language (§4.1). Others were applied selectively to the phonemes of certain prefixes (§4.2.1), suffixes (§4.2.2), or stems (§4.2.3). There were also unique changes affecting only one morpheme; these will not be discussed here but will be described under the appropriate morpheme. Besides these phonologically determined changes, stems underwent additional alterations determined by morphological conditions (§6.3).

4.1. AUTOMATIC CHANGES. The nasals, *m* and *n*, were in contrast only before vowels. Under other conditions *n* became *m* before *p*, and *m* became *n* before all other consonants and in word-final position: *i·m-* 'their' in *i·m-a·maw* 'their book' but *i·n-tlan* 'near them'; *nemi* 'to live' in *ni-nemi* 'I am living' but *o·-nen* 'he lived'.

The sequence *l* and *tl* became *l* and *l*: *tlachia* 'to see' in *ni-tlachia* 'I see' but *xi-wa·l-lachia* 'look this way'.

4.2. SELECTIVE CHANGES. More common than automatic changes were the changes which, under given phonological conditions, selectively affected certain morphemes but not others. For example, many prefixes ending in a vowel elided their final phoneme before the initial vowel of the following morpheme (§4.2.1). But the vowel of *ki-*, 3rd person object, was dropped under unique conditions (§8.3.5), and *tla-* 'something, things' did not undergo elision under any conditions (§8.3.1).

4.2.1. IN PREFIXES. In some prefixes having the shape CV-, the vowel was dropped before a following vowel. This change applied to the possessives (§7.1.3), the subject prefixes (§8.3.6), and the reflexives (§8.3.2): *no-* 'my' in *no-tlatki* 'my household goods' but *n-iꞌiyo* 'my breath'; *mo-*, reflexive for second and third persons in *tik-mo-machiltia* 'you know it' (reverential) but *o·ti-m-aꞌxitiko* 'you arrived' (reverential). The elision of the prefix vowel was cancelled, however, before a stem beginning in *i-* followed by two consonants, for under these conditions the stem vowel was dropped (see §5.2.3a).

The *i* vowel of subject prefixes was assimilated to *ø* before *on-* 'thither': *ni-*'I' in *ni-kochtika* 'I am sleeping' but *no-k-on-ittatiw* 'I am coming to visit him'.

4.2.2. IN SUFFIXES. Some suffixes beginning in *y-* assimilated their initial consonant to *l* after a stem terminating in *l* (§7.1.5.2d, 7.1.5.2f, 7.1.5.3c): *-yo·*, abstract noun, in *ta⁹-yo·-tl* 'paternity' (*ta⁹* 'father') but *tlakael-lo·-tl* 'anxiety'.

4.2.3. IN STEMS. In contact with certain prefixes or suffixes, the initial or final phonemes of the stem underwent the following types of change:

(a) *-VizCC*. The stem-initial *i* was zeroed if it was followed by a consonant cluster. This change took place after prefixes which dropped their final vowel (see §4.2.1) in contact with other types of vowel-beginning stems. Examples of this process of stem elision are: *no-sti* 'my fingernail' (*isti* 'fingernail'), *tik-mo-tztili⁹tika* 'you are looking at him' (reverential) (*itztili⁹tika* 'to be looking at').

(b) *VVz-*. Before certain suffixes the final stem vowel in a two-vowel cluster was zeroed: *-lis*, abstract noun, in *tla⁹cuilo-lis-tli* 'writing' (*tla⁹cuiloa* 'to write, to paint'), *tla⁹tla·tlawti-lis-tli* 'an oration' (*tla⁹tla·tlawtia* 'to orate').

(c) *V·-*. The final vowel of the stem was lengthened before certain suffixes: *-ni*, imperfective agent, in *tlacua·-ni* 'one who is eating' (*tlacua* 'to eat'), *tla⁹tlakoa·ni* 'sinner' (*tla⁹tlakoa* 'to make a mistake, to commit a sin').

(d) *V·Vz-*. In a two-vowel cluster at the end of a stem the final vowel was zeroed and the preceding vowel lengthened before certain suffixes: *-s*, future, in *ni-te·machti·-s* 'I will preach' (*te·machtia* 'to preach'); *-skia*, conditional, in *mokoko·-skia* 'he would be sick' (*mokokoa* 'to be sick').

(e) *CyVi-*. Before certain suffixes the final vowel of the stem was changed to *i*, and a preceding *tz* or *t* was palatalized to *ch*, a

preceding *s* to *x*: *-lia*, applicative, in *nik-wetzki-lia* 'I am laughing at it' (*wetzka* 'to laugh'), *tine·ch-no·chi-lia* 'you are calling him for me' (*no·tza* 'to call'), *nimitz-machi-lia* 'I know about you' (*mati* 'to know').

MORPHOLOGY

5. TYPES OF PROCESSES. Classical Nahuatl was primarily a suffixing language. A large part of the inflectional system (§7.1.4, 8.4) and most of the huge derivational apparatus (§7.1.5.1–7.1.5.4, 8.6.1) were controlled by suffixes. Prefixes also carried part of the inflectional load (§7.1.3, 8.3): pronominal inflections, both for noun and verb, were expressed by prefixing techniques. Compounding (§7.1.5.5, 8.6.2) was extensively used; it was one of the formal resources of the language which became elaborated in the poetic style of religious discourse that flourished in early post-conquest times.

Besides these additive processes, reduplication of stems (§7.1.2.1, 8.2) and of one group of suffixes (§7.1.2.2) was also employed. All reduplicative patterns repeated the initial consonant, if any, and the first vowel of the morpheme.

Internal change was another process affecting stems. Contraction and augmentation produced modified stem types which, though distinctive in function for the noun (§7.1.1) and the verb (§8.1), were somewhat alike in form for the two word classes (§6.3).

6. MORPHOLOGICAL CATEGORIES.

6.1. INFLECTIONAL WORD CLASSES. On the basis of their inflections, words could be classed as nominals, verbs, or particles. Depending on their subclass, nominals were inflected for number (singular or plural), or status (absolutive or possessive), or both. Verbs were inflected for tense, aspect, mode, and subject or subject-object. Particles were uninflected words.

The inflections were formed by prefixes and by those suffixes on the outermost layers of the inflected word.

6.2. DERIVATIONS. In contrast to inflections, the derivations were inner formations,

184

produced by the compounding of stems or by the attachment of suffixes close to the stem. The addition of one or more derivational layers resulted either in a complete word of the particle class or in a noun or verb stem which required the necessary inflectional treatment for completion as a word.

Derivations were often marked by the inclusion of *-ti* or *-ka·*, termed "ligatures" in the grammatical tradition of Classical Nahuatl. The conditions determining the usage of these morphemes cannot be precisely defined, for in some derivations the ligatures were among the optionally varying elements in Nahuatl morphology: *tla·l-pan* or *tla·l-ti-pan* 'on the ground'. In other derivations, however, they appeared consistently. They were employed in derivations of all kinds— those formed by suffixation or by compounding, and those resulting in derived nouns, verbs, or particles.

The ligature *-ti* was used in verb compounds before certain stems, such as *ka* 'to be' or *nemi* 'to go about', which were highly frequent and sometimes semantically specialized as second-position stems: *koch-ti-ka* 'to be sleeping' (*kochi* 'to sleep'), *patlan-ti-nemi* 'to go about flying' (*patlani* 'to fly'), *ki·s-t-e·wa* 'to start to leave' (*ki·sa* 'to leave', *-t* contracted from *-ti*, *e·wa* 'to start, to rise'). The same ligature appeared between a noun stem and certain derivational suffixes, as in *te-ti-k* 'hard' (*te* 'stone', *-k*, qualitative). It also occurred before certain postpositions when they were combined with noun stems though not with pronominal elements: *tepe·-t-ikpak* 'on top of the mountain' (*tepe·* 'mountain') but *no-kpak* 'on top of me' (*no-* 'my'), *xa·l-ti-pan* 'on the ground' (*xa·l* 'ground') but *i·-pan* 'on it' (*i·-* 'its, his, her').

The *-ka·* ligature joined two verb stems in which the first functioned as a modifier of the second: *cuala·ni-ka·-itta* 'to look at ... angrily' (*cuala·ni* 'to be angry', *itta* 'to look at'), *tlatziw-ka·-ka·wa* 'to leave ... through negligence' (*tlatziwi* 'to be negligent', *ka·wa*

'to leave'). The non-final alternants of some noun-forming suffixes required the addition of *-ka·*: *-e?* varied with non-final *-e?-ka·* 'possessor of,' as in *to·pil-e?* 'constable' (*to·pil* 'the staff of office'), *to·pil-e?-ka·-tla·lia* 'to appoint ... as constable' (*tla·lia* 'to place, to appoint'), *to-to·pil-e?-ka·-w* 'our constable' (*to-* 'our', *-w*, augment for possessive); *-wa?* varied with non-final *-wa?-ka·* 'owner of', as in *a·xka·-wa?* 'person of property' (*a·xka·* 'property'), *a·xka·-wa?-ka·-tzin-tli* 'the person of property' (reverential) (*-tzin*, reverential, *-tli*, singular absolutive), *a·xka·-wa?-ka·-ka·wa* 'to leave ... as a person of property' (*ka·wa* 'to leave'). Other noun-forming suffixes had non-final allomorphs manifesting a fusion with the *-ka·* ligature: *-k* varied with non-final *-ka·*, qualitative, as in *chipa·wa-k* 'clean (thing, person)' (*chipa·wa* 'to clean'), *chipa·wa-ka·-yo·-tl* 'cleanliness' (*-yo·*, abstract noun, *-tl*, singular absolutive); *chika·wa-k* 'strong' (*chika·wa* 'to strengthen'), *chika·wa-ka·-tlaso?tla* 'to love deeply' (*tlaso?tla* 'to love'); *-ki* varied with non-final *-ka·*, perfective agent, as in *teo·-pix-ki* 'priest' (*teo·* 'god', *pix-*, modified stem of *pia* 'to have'), *no-teo·-pix-ka·-w* 'my priest' (*-w*, augment for possessive).

6.3. STEM TYPES. An inflected word was built upon any one of the four structural types of stem, as illustrated in the following table.

	SIMPLE	MODIFIED[7]
Basic	*pa·ki* 'to be happy' *teo·* 'god'	*pa·k-* *teo·w-*
Thematic	*pa·k-tia* to make happy' *teo·-pia* 'to have god'	*pa·k-ti?-* *teo·pix-*

The basic stem, or base, contained only one morpheme; the thematic stem, or theme, was polymorphemic. Either of these stem types could occur in the simple (unmodified) form or in the modified form proper for that

---

[7] In the presentation of stems throughout this grammatical description, a modified stem will be identified by the terminal hyphen. A stem presented without a hyphen will be the simple stem.

base or theme. The modifications added no increments of meaning to the stem: the simple stem was used for certain inflections and derivations, the modified stem for others. Some modified stems were formed by contraction, as *pa·k-* from *pa·ki*; others were augmented, as *teo·w-* from *teo·*; and others underwent more complex types of change, as *pa·k-ti⁷-* from *pa·k-tia* or *teo·-pix-* from *teo·-pia*. The forms of the modified stem will be described separately for the noun (§7.1.1) and the verb (§8.1.1).

7. NOMINALS. Of the three subclasses of nominals (nouns, pronouns, and postpositions), nouns had the most extensive set of inflections. The following forms of *petla* 'mat' will illustrate the four inflectional categories of the noun:

	SINGULAR	PLURAL
Absolute	*petla-tł* 'mat'	*petla-me⁷* 'mats'
Possessive	*no-petł* 'my mat'	*no-petla-wa·n* 'my mats'

Nouns, then, were inflected for number and status, the possessive status being further inflected for the person of the possessor.[8] Independent pronouns were inflected for number only in the absolute. Some pronominal forms took singular and plural endings similar to those of the noun. Postpositions, expressing relational concepts primarily, had only the possessive inflection. The pronominal elements prefixed to postpositions were the same as those appended to the possessive stems of nouns.

7.1. NOUNS. Among the selective, or variable, features of noun inflection were those affecting the stem: vowel-ending nouns formed various types of modified stem for

---

[8] Olmos and subsequent grammarians noted that in some provinces, though not in others, nouns referring to inanimate objects lacked the plural (Olmos, 1547, p. 20). Such forms should be classed as defective nouns, in that they did not take plural suffixes. However, these nouns did not lack the number category, for they carried the formal mark of singular number: to illustrate the absence of a plural noun in a context requiring a plural meaning, Olmos used the example *wapalli* 'board,' which contained *-li*, one of the singular absolute suffixes.

the singular possessive (§7.1.1), and some nouns underwent reduplication for the plural absolute (§7.1.2.1). Also selective were the singular (§7.1.4.1) and the plural (§7.1.4.2) absolute suffixes.

Other inflectional features of the noun were uniform. All consonant-ending nouns appeared in the simple stem for the singular possessive. To form the plural possessive, one plural suffix was added to the simple stem of all nouns (7.1.4.2e). And the same set of possessive pronouns was prefixed to all nouns (7.1.4.1).

7.1.1. STEM MODIFICATIONS AND THE POSSESSIVE SINGULAR. Noun stems underwent the following two types of modification for the possessive singular:

(a) The contracted stem. Some vowel-ending nouns dropped their final vowel: *amo-cuik* 'your (plural) song' (*cuika* 'song'), *i·m-pan* 'their flag' (*pani* 'flag'), *i·-toka* 'his name' (*tokai* 'name').

(b) The augmented stem. Other nouns ending in a vowel were augmented by *-w* to form the possessive singular stem: *no-tew* 'my stone' (*te* 'stone'), *to-teo·w* 'our god' (*teo·* 'god'), *te·-tla·kaw* 'someone's slave', literally 'someone's man' (*tla·ka* 'man').

Some vowel-ending nouns and all consonant-ending nouns used the simple unmodified stem for the possessive singular: *mo-chi⁷chi* 'your (singular) saliva' (*chi⁷chi* 'saliva'), *no-tlaxkal* 'my bread' (*tlaxkal* 'bread').

7.1.2. REDUPLICATION. Initial reduplication could be applied to basic stems of the noun or to one group of derivational suffixes occurring in thematic stems of the noun. This process expressed either the plural or the distributive.

7.1.2.1. Two reduplicative patterns affected noun stems:

(a) *(C)V·-*. Repetition of the initial consonant, if any, and the first vowel of the stem, with lengthening of the vowel, formed the plural absolute stem of some nouns. To this stem was added one of the plural absolute suffixes (§7.1.4.2). In most instances the reduplicated stem took the plural -*ʔ*: *cue·cueya-ʔ* 'frogs' (*cueya* 'frog'), *mo·mo·yo·-ʔ* 'mosquitoes' (*mo·yo·* 'mosquito'). In some instances this formation was a variant plural of the simple stem with the suffix form -*me*ʔ: *ko·koyo·-ʔ* or *koyo·-me*ʔ 'coyotes' (*koyo·* 'coyote'), *o·ose·lo·-ʔ* or *ose·lo·-me*ʔ 'ocelots' (*ose·lo·* 'ocelot'). The reduplicated stem occurred with other plural suffixes, which also formed variant plurals with simple stems: *i·ichka-me*ʔ or *ichka-me*ʔ 'sheep' (plural) (*ichka* 'sheep', singular), *cua·cuaw-tin* or *cuaw-tin* 'eagles' (*cuaw* 'eagle'), *ka·kalpix-ke*ʔ or *kalpix-ke*ʔ 'majordomos' (*kalpix-ki* 'majordomo').

(b) (*C*)*Vʔ*-. Repetition of the initial consonant, if any, and the following vowel, with shortening of the vowel and insertion of a glottal stop, formed a special derivation expressing the distributive. This type of reduplicated stem was inflected only in the singular, for both the absolute and the possessive: *aʔa·wil-li* 'various acts of levity' (*a·wil* 'act of levity, frivolity', -*li*, singular absolutive), *kaʔkapollaʔ-Ø* 'cherry orchards here and there' (*kapollaʔ* 'cherry orchard', -*Ø*, singular absolutive), *mo-xiʔxicuinyo* 'your various gluttonies' (*mo-* 'your', *xicuinyo* 'gluttony'), *i·n-chaʔcha·n* 'their separate houses', i.e., each of the houses belonging to each one of them (*i·n-* from *i·m-* 'their', *cha·n* 'house').

7.1.2.2. In thematic noun stems containing one of the affective suffixes, the suffix itself was reduplicated as part of the plural formation. The reduplicative pattern, *CV*-, involved repetition of the first consonant and vowel of the suffix, with shortening of the vowel. Of the four affectives, two could appear with or without the absolutives, -*tli* in the singular and -*tin* in the plural. The reverential -*tzin* or -*tzin-tli*, expressing respect, affection, or compassion, was pluralized as -*tzitzin* or -*tzitzin-tin*: *ilama-tzitzin*, plural of *ilama-tzin* 'respected old lady', *tla·ka-tzitzin-tin*, plural of *tla·ka-tzin-tli* 'poor little man'; reduplication of the stem as well as the suffix could take place, as in

pi·pil-tzitzin-tin, plural of *pil-tzin-tli* 'dear little boy'. The diminutive of scorn or contempt, -*to·n* or -*to·n-tli*, had the plural form -*toto·n* or -*toto·n-tin*: *chichi-toto·n*, plural of *chichi-to·n* 'puppy', *atoya-toto·n-tin*, plural of *atoya-to·n-tli* 'rivulet', *pi·pil-toto·n-tin*, plural of *pi·pil-to·n-tli* 'mischievous little boy'.

The other two affectives occurred without the absolutive suffixes. The pejorative -*po·l* appeared as -*popo·l* in the plural: *tlaweli·loka·-popo·l*, plural of *tlaweli·loka·-po·l* 'rogue'. The diminutive of approval, -*pil*, was reduplicated to -*pipil* for the plural: *siwa·-pipil*, plural of *siwa·-pil* 'beautiful woman, fine woman'.

7.1.3. INFLECTIONAL PREFIXES. Only one group of inflectional prefixes was employed with nouns. The singular (§7.1.1) and plural (§7.1.4.2e) possessives were formed with prefixes indicating the person and number of the possessor: *no-* 'my', *mo-* 'your (singular)', *i·-* 'his, her, its', *to-* 'our', *amo-* 'your (plural)', *i·m-* 'their', and *te·-* 'someone's'. These prefixes were also appended to postpositions (7.3).

7.1.4. INFLECTIONAL SUFFIXES. The suffixes marking noun inflections indicated the singular (§7.1.4.1) absolutive and the plural (§7.1.4.2) absolutive and possessive.

7.1.4.1. The following suffixes of the singular absolutive, added to the simple stem, were selectively distributed among nouns:

(a) -*li* (after *l*), -*tli* (after other consonants), -*tl* (after vowels). Examples are: *kal-li* 'house', *tla·koʔ-tli* 'slave', *siwa·-tl* 'woman'.

(b) -*in*, as in *to·tol-in* 'hen', *mich-in* 'fish', *to·ch-in* or *to·ch-tli* 'rabbit'.

(c) -*Ø*. The absence of an overt suffix was characteristic of the singular absolutive of a few noun bases, especially quantifiers such as *miek-Ø* 'much' or *we·y-Ø* 'large'. This inflectional category was also marked by the zero suffix in noun themes derived by certain suffixes: -*k*, qualitative, as in *toma·wa-k-Ø* 'fat (animal, person)' (*toma·wa* 'to fatten'); -*wa*ʔ 'owner of', as in *a·xka·-waʔ-Ø* 'person of property' (*a·xka·* 'property'); -*e*ʔ 'possessor of', as in *kal-e?-Ø* 'one who possesses a house' (*kal* 'house'); *-ki*, perfective agent, as in *kokox-ki-Ø* 'sick person'; *-tzin*, reverential, as in *ta?-tzin-Ø* 'father' (reverential) (*ta?* 'father'). Although these words were not overtly identified for the absolutive singular, they were marked like other nouns for the possessive and plural inflections (§7.1.4.2d).

7.1.4.2. Plural suffixes could be attached either to the reduplicated stem (§7.1.2.1a) or to the simple stem. Like the singular absolutive suffixes, the plural absolutives were selectively distributed among nouns:

(a) *-?*, as in *tla·ka-?* 'men', *siwa·-?* 'women', *po·chte·ka-?* 'merchants'. This plural occurred only with vowel-ending stems.

(b) *-me?*, as in *pitzo-me?* 'pigs', *ichka-me?* 'sheep (plural)', *cui·cui·tzka-me?* 'swallows'. This suffix was attached primarily to vowel-ending stems.

(c) *-tin*, as in *ta?-tin* 'fathers', *okich-tin* 'males', *cuaw-tin* 'eagles'. Principally consonant-ending stems took the *-tin* plural. Some nouns had variant plurals with either *-me?* or *-tin*: *to·tol-me?* or *to·tol-tin* 'hens', *tepotzo?-me?* or *tepotzo?-tin* 'hunchbacks'.

(d) *-ke?*, as in *toma·wa-ke?* 'fat (animals, people)', *a·xka·wa?-ke?* 'people of property', *kale?-ke?* 'people who have houses', *kokox-ke?* 'sick people'. This plural was used with derived nouns whose singular absolutive was *-Ø* (§7.1.4.1c). Somewhat like the *-ka·* ligature (§6.2), the *-ke?* plural was fused with derivatives in *-k*, qualitative, and *-ki*, perfective agent; it was simply added to other derivational suffixes.

Only one unvarying suffix, attached to the simple stem of nouns, was employed for the plural possessive:

(e) *-wa·n*, as in *mo-to·tol-wa·n*, 'your hens', *i·m-pil-wa·n* 'their sons'. Some derived nouns took the ligature *-ka·* before *-wa·n*: *no-cua·cuawe?-ka·-wa·n* 'my cows' (*cua·cuaw-e?* 'cow', literally 'one who possesses horns').

7.1.5. NOUN-FORMING DERIVATIONS. Suffixes which formed nouns could be added to verb stems (§7.1.5.1), to noun stems (§7.1.5.2), to either verb or noun stems (§7.1.5.3), and to either nominal or particle stems (§7.1.5.4). Derived nouns were also produced by compounding (§7.1.5.5).

7.1.5.1. The following suffixes converted verbs into nouns:

(a) *-ni*, imperfective agent, as in *kochi-ni* 'one who is sleeping' (*kochi* 'to sleep'), *tla·ka-wapa·wa-ni* 'one who rears human beings' (*tla·ka* 'person, man', *wapa·wa* 'to rear, to nourish').

(b) *-?*, imperfective agent, as in *tla?cuilo-?* 'one who is writing' (*tla?cuilo-*, *VVz-* stem (4.2.3b) of *tla?cuiloa* 'to write', to paint'), *te·-yo·lla·li-?* 'that which consoles people' (*te·-*, indefinite personal object, *yo·lla·li-*, *VVz-* stem of *yo·lla·lia* 'to console').

(c) *-ki*, perfective agent. This suffix indicated the agency of a completed action or the habitual agency of the specialist; it also referred to the quality or result of a completed action. Examples are: *pala·n-ki* 'rotten, that which is rotten, that which has rotted' (*pala·n-*, modified stem of *pala·ni* 'to rot'), *mik-ki* 'corpse' (*mik-*, modified stem of *miki* 'to die'), *kak-chi·w-ki* 'shoemaker' (*kak* 'shoe', *chi·w-*, modified stem of *chi·wa* 'to make').

(d) *-l* (after some stems ending in a vowel) or *-Ø*. Because this morpheme expressed the passive agent, or recipient, of the verb action, it was added only to transitive verbs. Most of these formations contained one of the indefinite object pronouns, either the personal *te·-* or the non-personal *tla-* (§8.3.1). Examples are: *pixki-Ø-tl* 'the harvest' (*pixki-*, *CyVi-* stem of *pixka* 'to gather the harvest', *-tl*, singular absolutive), *tla-i·-l-li* or *tla-i·-Ø-tl* 'a drink', such as pulque or wine (*i·* 'to drink', *-li* or *-tl*, singular absolutive), *te·machti·-l-li* 'that which is taught to people' (*machti·-*, *V·Vz-* stem of *machtia* 'to teach'), *tla-ke·n-Ø-tli* or *tla-ke·mi-tl* 'clothes' (*ke·n-*, modified stem of *ke·mi* 'to put on clothes'), *tla-i·na·x-Ø-tli* or *tla-i·na·ya-l-li* 'that which is hidden' (*i·na·x-*, modified stem of *i·na·ya* 'to hide').

(e) *-ka*, verbal noun, as in *i·-tzope·li·-ka* 'its

sweetness' (*i·-* 'its, his, her', *tzope·li-*, *VVz-* stem of *tzope·lia* 'to sweeten'), *to-pala·n-ka* 'our rottenness, our corruption' (*to-* 'our', *pala·n-*, modified stem of *pala·ni* 'to rot').

(f) *-ya*, instrumental, as in *no-tlachia-ya* 'my vision' (*no-* 'my', *tlachia* 'to look at'), *no-tla-teki-ya* 'my knife' (*tla-*, indefinite non-personal object, *teki* 'to cut').

(g) *-lis*, abstract noun, as in *yo·li-lis-tli* 'life' (*yo·li* 'to live', *-tli*, singular absolutive), *tla-cua-lis-tli* 'the act of eating' (*tla-*, indefinite non-personal object, *cua* 'to eat').

(h) *-ya·n*, locative, as in *no-kochi-ya·n* 'my sleeping place' (*no-* 'my', *kochi* 'to sleep'), *tlaxkal-chi·wa-lo·-ya·n* 'place where bread is made' (*tlaxkal* 'bread', *chi·wa* 'to make', *-lo·*, passive).

7.1.5.2. The following derivational suffixes were added to noun stems:

(a) *-é*, vocative. This morpheme, always the final syllable of the word, was given the heavy stress.[9] Examples are: *siwa·-tl-é* 'woman!' (*siwa·* 'woman', *-tl*, singular absolutive), *te·machtia·ni-me?-é* 'preachers!' (*te·machtia·ni* 'preacher', *-me?*, plural absolutive). The vocative suffix could fuse with the absolutives *-li* or *-tli* to form *-lé* or *-tlé*, and with the reverential *-tzin* to become *-tzé*: *pilto·n-tlé* 'boy!' (*pilto·n* 'mischievous boy'), *no-pil-tzé* or *no-pil-tzin-é* 'my son!' (*no-* 'my', *pil* 'boy, son').

(b) *-e?* 'possessor of', as in *yo·li-lis-e?* 'one who has life' (*yo·li* 'to live', *-lis*, abstract noun), *tla·ltikpak-e?* 'the one who possesses the earth', one of the names given to Our Lord (*tla·ltikpak* 'the surface of the earth').

(c) *-wa?* 'owner of, possessor of', as in *ilwika-wa?* 'owner of the sky', one of the names given to Our Lord (*ilwika* 'sky'), *tilma?-wa?* 'one who owns a cloak' (*tilma?* 'cloak').

(d) *-lo?* (after *l*), *-yo?* (elsewhere), intensive descriptive. This suffix indicated a

quality or an entity characterized to an intensive degree by the reference of the underlying noun: *si·tlal-lo?* 'starry, something full of stars' (*si·tlal* 'star'), *a·-yo?* 'watery, something which contains much water', such as soup (*a·* 'water'), *ti-naka-yo?-ke?* 'we (are) things made of flesh' (*ti-* 'we', *naka* 'meat', *-ke?*, plural absolutive).

(e) *-tla?*, intensive locative, as in *te-tla?* 'stony place' (*te* 'stone'), *xo·chi-tla?* 'flower garden' (*xo·chi* 'flower'), *xal-la?* 'sandy place' (*xal* 'sand').

(f) *-lo* (after *l*), *-yo* (elsewhere), inalienable. This element was used only with the possessive forms of nouns: *no-naka-yo* 'my flesh', i.e., the meat of my body, in contrast to *no-nak* 'my meat' (*no-* 'my', *nak-*, modified stem of *naka* 'meat'), *i·-xo·chi?cual-lo* 'its (the tree's) fruit' (*i·-* 'its, his, her', *xo·chi?cual* 'fruit').

(g) *-tika*, distributive, as in *se·sen-metz-tika* 'every month' (*se·sen-*, reduplicated stem of *sem-* 'one', *metz* 'month'), *ma·ma·cui·l-ilwi-tika* 'every five days' (*ma·ma·cui·l-*, reduplicated stem of *ma·cui·l* 'five', *ilwi* 'day').

(h) *-ko* (after consonants), *-k* (after vowels) 'in, into', as in *a·kal-ko* 'in the boat' (*a·kal* 'boat'), *ko·mi-k* 'inside the pot' (*ko·mi* 'pot').

(i) *-tew* 'in the manner of', as in *cha·lchiw-tew* 'in the manner of jade' (*cha·lchiwi* 'jade'), *ketzal-tew* 'in the manner of beautiful feathers' (*ketzal* 'beautiful feather').[10]

7.1.5.3. Only a relatively few suffixes could be added to either noun or verb stems.

(a) *-ka·n*, locative, as in *mich-wa?-ka·n* 'place where people have fish' (*mich* 'fish', *-wa?* 'owner of'), *ye·k-ka·n* 'a good place'

---

[9] Because the vocative was loosely attached to the outer layer of nouns, following the inflectional suffixes, it could be classed as an enclitic rather than a suffix. However, no other morpheme seems to have behaved in this enclitic manner.

[10] In the traditional treatments of Classical Nahuatl, *-ko* and *-tew* were classified with the postpositions (§ 7.3), which they resembled in being attached to noun stems and in expressing relational, or "prepositional," meanings. The present classification, however, is based upon inflectional features: the postpositions took the prefixed pronouns to form the same possessive inflection as nouns; *-ko* and *-tew*, on the other hand, manifested the structural characteristics of suffixes, in that they formed words in conjunction with noun stems, not with pronominal or other prefixes.

(*ye·k* 'good (thing)'), *te·-pa'pa·kilti'-ka·n* 'place which brings happiness to various people' (*te·-*, indefinite personal object, *pa'pa·kilti'-*, modified reduplicated stem of *pa·kiltia* 'to cause . . . to be happy'), *ko·n-chi·w-ka·n* 'pot-making place' (*ko·n-*, modified stem of *ko·mi* 'pot', *chi·w-*, modified stem of *chi·wa* 'to make').

(b) *-k*, qualitative, as in *tlil-ti-k* 'black' (*tlil* 'dye', *-ti*, ligature), *ista-k* 'white' (*ista* 'salt'), *chipa·wa-k* 'clean' (*chipa·wa* 'to clean'), *tla-namaka-k* 'one who sells things' (*tla-*, indefinite non-personal object, *namaka* 'to sell').

(c) *-lo·* (after *l*), *-yo·* (elsewhere), abstract noun, as in *tlil-lo·-tl* 'blackness' (*tlil* 'dye', *-tl*, singular absolutive), *teo·-yo·-tl* 'divinity' (*teo·* 'god'), *yo·l-ka·-yo·-tl* 'the sustenance necessary for living' (*yo·l-*, modified stem of *yo·li* 'to live', *-ka·*, ligature), *teo·pix-ka·-yo·-tl* 'priesthood' (*teo·pix-*, modified stem of *teo·pia* 'to have god').

7.1.5.4. The reverential *-tzin* was distinctive in its distribution, for it could be attached to particles and independent pronouns as well as to nouns: *ke·ma'-tzin* 'no' (reverential) (*ke·ma'* 'no'), *te'wa-tzin* 'you' (singular, reverential) (*te'wa* 'you', singular), *ame'wa·n-tzitzin* 'you' (plural, reverential) (*ame'wa·n* 'you', plural), *ikno·-tzin* 'orphan' (reverential) (*ikno·* 'orphan'). For additional examples, see §7.1.2.2 and 9.

7.1.5.5. Derived nouns could be formed by combining noun stems; in noun compounds the final stem functioned as the head term, the preceding stems operating as modifiers. Compounds consisting of two nouns were extremely common: *tepos-meka-tl* 'iron chain' (*tepos* 'metal', *meka* 'chain, rope', *-tl*, singular absolutive), *teo·-tla'tol-li* 'divine word' (*teo·* 'god'. *tla'tol* 'word', *-li*, singular absolutive). In the elaborate religious style developed after the conquest, longer compounds were favored: *tla·ka-tzintilis-tla'tlaso·l-li* 'the original sin' (*tla·ka* 'man, person', *tzintilis* 'beginning', *tla'tlaso·l* 'sin'), *xiw-tlapal-la'cuilo·l-a·mox-tli* 'a book painted in colors' (*xiw-*, modified stem of

190

xiwi 'green', *tlapal* 'red', *tla'cuilo·l* 'painted', with automatic change of *tl* to *l* after *l*, *a·mox* 'book', *-tli*, singular absolutive).

7.2. PRONOUNS. The independent personal pronouns were inflected for number in the absolutive. The pronouns included abbreviated or short forms which lacked the inflectional suffixes of number. But the full form for each person carried the singular *-tl* or the plural *-tin*, which were among the absolutive suffixes also appended to nouns.

ne', *ne'wa*, or *ne'wa·tl* 'I'
te', *te'wa*, or *te'wa·tl* 'you' (singular)
ye', *ye'wa*, or *ye'wa·tl* 'he, she, it'
te'wa·n or *te'wa·ntin* 'we'
ame'wa·n or *ame'wa·ntin* 'you' (plural)
ye'wa·n or *ye'wa·ntin* 'they'

Using different absolutive plural suffixes, the indefinite and interrogative pronouns were also inflected for number: *aka'* 'someone', *aka'me'* 'some people'; *a·kin* 'who?' (singular), *a·ki'ke'* 'who?' (plural).

7.3. POSTPOSITIONS. Limited to the possessive inflection, postpositions employed the same set of pronominal prefixes as nouns. Some postpositions could appear either with these prefixes or, as second-position stems, in composition with nouns: *to-tza·lan* 'between us', *kal-tza·lan* 'between the houses'; *i·-pan* 'on it', *tla·l-pan* 'on the ground'; *amo-tlan* 'near you' (plural), *a·-tlan* 'near the water'; *i·m-i'tik* 'inside them', *teo·pankal-i'tik* 'inside the church'. Other postpositions occurred only with the possessive prefixes: *no-pal* 'for my benefit', *mo-tlok* 'near you', *te·-ikampa* 'behind somebody'.

8. VERBS. The selective features of the verb, like those of the noun, included inflectional modifications of the stem (§8.1); for the verb these modifications were primarily associated with the preterit. In addition, the verb was selectively identified as either transitive or intransitive: the intransitive was limited in its pronominal inflection to the subject prefixes (§8.3.6); the transitive was inflected for object (§§8.3.1., 8.3.4.,

8.3.5), or reflexive (§8.3.2) as well as for subject pronouns.

Most of the inflectional machinery of the verb, however, revealed a striking uniformity. All verbs took the same pronominal paradigm of subject prefixes. There was only one set of object pronouns and one of reflexives. With the exception of the preterit, all tense, aspect, mode, and subject-number inflections (§8.4) were constructed in the same manner for all verbs.

8.1. STEM MODIFICATIONS AND THE PRETERIT. Unlike the noun, whose simple stem could end in either a vowel or a consonant, the simple stem of the verb always terminated in a vowel. The verb underwent modifications of contraction and augmentation which were comparable, therefore, only to those of the vowel-ending noun. For the noun these modifications formed the stem of the possessive singular; for the verb they resulted in the stem of the preterit; and the possessive singular and preterit functions, associated with the modified stem of some nouns and verbs, were performed by the simple stem of other nouns and verbs (§7.1.1).

8.1.1. Verb stems underwent the following types of modification:

(a) The contracted stem. To form the modified stem, the final vowel of some verbs was zeroed: *o·-ni-kis* 'I left' (*o·-*, past, *ni-* 'I', *kisa* 'to leave'), *o·-n-a·n* 'I hunted' (*a·mi* 'to hunt').

(b) The contracted sibilant stem. Some verbs whose simple stem ended in *-ya* or *-ia* dropped the final syllable—the total syllable *-ya*, the final *-a* of *-ia*—and added *s* or *x*: *o·-istas* 'it became white' (*istaya* 'to become white'), *o·-ni-k-yo·kox* 'I invented it' (*k-*, 3rd person object, *yo·koya* 'to invent'), *o·-ti-sis-keʔ* 'we agreed' (*ti-* 'we', *sia* 'to agree', *-keʔ*, preterit subject plural), *o·-ni-k-pix* 'I held it' (*pia* 'to hold, to have').

(c) The contracted glottal stem. Some verbs with their simple stem ending in two vowels dropped the final vowel and added *ʔ*: *o·-ti-te·-machtiʔ-keʔ* 'we taught people' (*te·-*, indefinite personal object, *machtia* 'to teach, to cause . . . to know'), *o·-ni-tekipanoʔ* 'I worked' (*tekipanoa* 'to work').

(d) The augmented stem. Some verbs augmented the simple stem with *ʔ* to form the modified stem: *o·-tla-cuaʔ-keʔ* 'they ate something' (*tla-*, indefinite non-personal object, *cua* 'to eat'), *o·-ni-no-somaʔ* 'I frowned' (*no-*, 1st person reflexive, *soma* 'to frown').

8.1.2. For some verbs the preterit was formed from the simple stem, to which was added *-k*, preterit subject singular (§8.4.1b), or *-keʔ*, preterit or future subject plural (§8.4.2b). Alternative preterit formations occurred for some verbs: from *selia* 'to sprout', preterits could be based on the contracted sibilant stems, *selis-* or *selix-*, or the suffixed simple stem, *selia-k*; from *toto·nia* 'to become hot', preterit formations could be constructed from the contracted sibilant stem, *toto·nix-*, or from the suffixed simple stem, *toto·nia-k*; from *no·tza* 'to shout at', preterits could be formed from the contracted stem, *no·tz-*, or from the suffixed simple stem, *no·tza-k*.

8.1.3. In addition to the preterit formation, the modified stem was used in several derivational formations. The perfective agent, *-ki* (§7.1.5.1c), was added to modified verb stems: *ichtek-ki* 'thief' (*ichtek-*, contracted stem of *ichteki* 'to rob'), *teo·pix-ki* 'priest' (*teo·pix-*, contracted sibilant stem of *teo·pia* 'to have god'), *te·-yo·lla·liʔ-ki* 'one who gives people consolation' (*te·-*, indefinite personal object, *yo·lla·liʔ-*, contracted glottal stem of *yo·lla·lia* 'to give consolation').

Before the ligatures *-ka·* or *-ti* (§6.2), the modified stem of verbs having such a stem was employed in derivations formed either by suffixation or compounding: *koch-ka·-yo·-tl* 'supper, that which permits sleep' (*koch-*, contracted stem of *kochi* 'to sleep', *yo·-*, abstract noun, *-tl*, singular absolutive), *ni-no-kokox-ka·-neki* 'I imagine myself sick' (*ni-* 'I', *no-*, 1st person reflexive, *kokox-*, contracted sibilant stem of *kokoa* 'to be sick', *neki* 'to imagine, to want'), *xi-k-mo-cui·liʔ-ti-wetzi* 'take it quickly' (reverential) (*xi-*, imperative subject, *k-*, 3rd person object, *mo-*, 2nd or 3rd person reflexive, *cui·li?-*, contracted glottal stem of *cui·lia* 'to take', reverential, *wetzi* 'to do quickly, to attack'), *tla-sese·x-ti-mo-tla·lia* 'it is getting cool' (*tla-*, indefinite non-personal object, *sese·x-*, contracted sibilant stem of *sese·ya* 'to become cool', *tla·lia* 'to put'). Similar derivations were constructed with the simple stem of those verbs which, lacking a modified stem, formed their preterit with the simple stem and *-k* or *-ke?*: *tla-yowa-ti-mo-mana* 'it is getting dark' (*yowa* 'to become night', *mana* 'to lie on the ground').

8.2. REDUPLICATED STEMS. Reduplication of the verb stem, like that of the noun, involved the repetition of the initial consonant, if any, and the first vowel. Unlike the noun, which used reduplication for the plural inflection, the verb employed reduplication solely for derivational functions. The following reduplicative patterns were applied to verb stems:

(a) $(C)V$-. Simple reduplication of the first consonant and vowel of the stem occurred only in conjunction with the frequentative suffixes, *-ka* and *-tza* (§8.6.1.1): *popolo-ka* 'to speak barbarously' (*polo* 'to stutter'), *kokomo-tza* 'to clatter with one's feet' (*komo* 'to fall with a thud').

(b) $(C)V$·-. Verbs with this reduplicative pattern, which included vowel lengthening, expressed an intensive, habitual, or continuative action: *cho·cho·ka* 'to weep loudly' (*cho·ka* 'to weep'), *i·ichteki* 'to rob a place habitually' (*ichteki* 'to rob'), *te·teki* 'to slice' (*teki* 'to cut with a knife'), *mo-no·no·tza* 'to consult with one another' (*mo-*, reciprocal, *no·tza* 'to shout at').

(c) $(C)V?$-. Reduplication with an inserted glottal stop indicated a distributive or interrupted repetitive action: *i?ichteki* 'to rob several places' (*ichteki* 'to rob'), *te?teki* 'to cut something up into pieces' (*teki* 'to cut with a knife'), *cho?cho·ka* 'to weep repeatedly' (*cho·ka* 'to weep').

(d) $(C)V?(C)V?$-. A doubling of the glottal reduplicative pattern expressed an intensification of the repetitive notion: *ne?ne?nemi*

192

'to walk up and down, stopping intermittently' (*nemi* 'to walk'), *m-a?a?a·wiltia* 'to amuse oneself in various places' (*m-*, contracted from *mo-*, 2nd or 3rd person reflexive, *a·wiltia* 'to pass the time in levity').

8.3. INFLECTIONAL PREFIXES. Verb inflections expressed by prefixes were concerned primarily with pronominal references; they included, in addition, one tense element and two morphemes indicating direction. This system of prefixes occupied seven positions.

8.3.1. In the first position adjacent to the stem were two indefinite object pronouns: the personal *te-* 'someone, people' and the non-personal *tla-* 'something, things.' These indefinites were either used in place of the definite objects of the fifth position (§8.3.5), or, with verbs taking two objects, they functioned as secondary objects in conjunction with the definites: *ni-te·-a?wa* 'I am scolding someone' (*a?wa* 'to scold, to quarrel with'), *ni-tla-cua* 'I am eating something' (*cua* 'to eat'), *ni-k-te·-maka* 'I am giving it to somebody' (*k-* 'it, him, her', *maka* 'to give'), *ni-k-tla-maka* 'I am giving something to him', *ne-tla-cuitlawi·-lo* 'one is on one's guard against things' (*ne-*, indefinite reflexive, *cuitlawi·-*, $V·Vz$- stem of *cuitlawia* 'to guard', *-lo*, passive).

8.3.2. The following reflexive or reciprocal pronouns comprised the prefixes of the second position: *no-*, first person singular, *to-*, first person plural, *mo-*, second or third person singular or plural, and *ne-*, indefinite singular or plural. Examples are: *ni-no-cuepa* 'I am turning around' (*cuepa* 'to turn'), *ti-to-tlaso?tla-?* 'we love one another' (*tlaso?tla* 'to love', *-?*, general subject plural), *ne-po·walo* 'one becomes proud of oneself' (*po·walo* 'to become proud). Besides conveying a reflexive or reciprocal meaning, these pronouns were also used with reverential forms (§8.6.1.2c): *o·-mo-mikili?* 'he died' (reverential) (*o·-*, past, *mikili?-*, modified stem of *mikilia*, reverential of *miki* 'to die'), *ti-m-a·miki·tia* 'you are thirsty' (reverential) (*a·miki·tia*, reverential of *a·miki* 'to be thirsty'). As the examples indicate, subject pronouns (§8.3.6) accompanied reflexives referring to the first or second persons.

8.3.3. The third position was filled by the directionals, *on-* 'thither, away, go and do' and *wa·l-* 'hither, come and do': *no-k-on-itta* 'I am visiting him' (*no-*, from *ni-* 'I' (§4.2.1), *itta* 'to see'), *xi-wa·l-lachia* 'look this way' (*xi-*, imperative subject, *lachia*, from *tlachia* 'to look').[11]

8.3.4. The plural third person object, *im-*, was the sole member of the fourth position slot. When the verb had only one object, *im-* was attached to a preceding *k-* (§8.3.5) to form the plural of the third person object: *k-im-pa·ktia* 'he makes them happy' (*pa·ktia* 'to cause . . . to be happy'). When two objects occurred, one could be expressed by *im-* and the other by any fifth position pronoun: *xi-ne·ch-in-maka* 'give them to me' (*ne·ch-* 'me', *maka* 'to give'), *ni-mitz-im-pialia* 'I am keeping them for you' (*mitz-* 'you', singular object, *pialia* 'to keep for').

8.3.5. The fifth position from the stem was occupied by the definite object prefixes: *ne·ch-* 'me'; *mitz-* 'you', singular; *te·ch-* 'us'; *ame·ch-* 'you', plural; *ki-* (preconsonantal in either word initial or in postconsonantal position), *k-* (elsewhere), third person. Examples are: *o·-ti-ne·ch-cui·li?* 'you took it away from me' (*o·-*, past, *cui·li?-*, modified stem of *cui·lia* 'to take away from'), *n-ame·ch-miktia* 'I am beating you' (plural) (*miktia* 'to beat, to kill'), *an-ki-miktia-?* 'you (plural) are killing it' (*-?*, general subject plural).

8.3.6. In the sixth position were the subject pronouns: *ni-* 'I', *ti-* 'you', singular, *ti-* 'we', *am-* 'you', plural, and *xi-*, imperative subject. The absence of a pronoun in this slot indicated a third person subject. Sub-

---

[11] Although Carochi included examples to illustrate the directional meaning of *on-*, he noted that in some expressions it merely "serves as an ornament and adds a certain gravity to one's speech" (1645, p. 445). Wherever this prefix is found in modern dialects, it most commonly carries a directional denotation (Croft, 1953, p. 275; Whorf, 1946, p. 384). In Sierra Nahuat, however, Key identifies *on-* as a prefix indicating respect (1960, p. 139).

ject plural was indicated by suffixes: *ti-tlapo·wa* 'you (singular) are counting' (*tlapo·wa* 'to count'), *ti-tlapo·wa-?* 'we are counting' (*-?*, general subject plural), *tlapo·wa* 'he is counting', *tlapo·wa-?* 'they are counting', *xi-tlapo·wa* 'count!' (singular imperative), *xi-tlapo·wa-ka·n* 'count!' (*-ka·n*, imperative subject plural).

8.3.7. The outermost prefix position, the seventh from the stem, contained only one morpheme, the past tense *o·-*. This prefix was used most frequently with the preterit formations (§8.1) and the remote past suffix, *-ka* (§8.4.1a): *o·-ni-tlapo·w* 'I counted' (*tlapo·w-*, modified stem of *tlapo·wa* 'to count'), *o·-ni-tlapo·w-ka* 'I had counted, I used to count'. The past prefix also occurred, though rarely, with the imperfective *-ya* (§8.4.1d): *o·-ni-tlapo·wa-ya* or *ni-tlapo·wa-ya* 'I was counting.'

8.4. INFLECTIONAL SUFFIXES. The verb complex ended in two inflectional layers of suffixes.

8.4.1. The first position after the verb stem was filled by suffixes of tense (remote past, preterit, future), aspect (imperfective), or mode (conditional). The absence of a first-position suffix indicated the present tense, the simple stem of the verb being employed for this function: *ki-paka* 'he is washing it' (*paka* 'to wash'), *ni-nemi* 'I am living' (*nemi* 'to live').

(a) *-ka*, remote past, attached to the modified stem, if the verb possessed this stem type: *o·-nen-ka* 'he lived long ago' (*o·-*, past, *nen-*, modified stem of *nemi* 'to live'), *o·-ni-tlacua?-ka* 'I had eaten, I had been eating' (*tlacua?-*, modified stem of *tlacua* 'to eat'), *o·-cuicawitz-ka* 'he came to sing' (*cuicawitz-*, modified stem of the compound *cuica* 'to sing' and *witze* 'to come'), *o·-ni-k-paka-ka* 'I used to wash it' (*paka* 'to wash', the simple stem of a verb having no distinctive modified stem form).

(b) *-k*, preterit, with the simple stem of verbs which had no modified stem: *o·-ni-k-itta-k* 'I saw it' (*itta* 'to see'), *o·-se·wa-k* 'it was cold' (*se·wa* 'to be cold'). For verbs having

193

a modified as well as a simple stem, the preterit was constructed with the modified form instead of the preterit suffix (§8.1).

(c) *-s*, future: *tlapo·wa-s* 'he will count' (*tlapo·wa* 'to count'). Verbs ending in two vowels used the *V·Vz-* stem with the future suffix (§4.2.3d): *ni-tlatekipano·-s* 'I will work' (*tlatekipanoa* 'to work').

(d) *-ya*, imperfective, referring to an incompleted or durative action in the past: *ni-nemi-ya* 'I was living, I have been living' (*nemi* 'to live'), *ti-no·tza-ya-ʔ* 'we were calling' (*no·tza* 'to call', *-ʔ*, general subject plural).

(e) *-skia*, conditional: *aya·k miki-skia* 'nobody would die' (*miki* 'to die'). Like the future, the conditional was suffixed to the *V·Vz-* stem of verbs terminating in two vowels (§4.2.3d): *ni-mitz-tlaxtla·wi·-skia* 'I would pay you' (e.g., if you would serve me), 'I would have paid you' (e.g., if you had served me) (*tlaxtla·wia* 'to pay'). Although this suffix expressed a conditional event in the past or present, the prefixing of *o·-*, past, resulted in an unambiguous past conditional: *o·-ni-mitz-tlaxtla·wi·-skia* 'I would have paid you'.

8.4.2. The second and final position of the inflected verb was occupied by suffixes expressing plurality of the subject; each of these suffixes was associated with certain tense, aspect, or mode categories of the verb.

(a) *-ka·n*, imperative subject plural: *xi-no·tza-ka·n* 'call!' (plural imperative) (*no·tza* 'to call'). The *V·Vz-* stem of verbs ending in two vowels was employed with this suffix: *xi-te·machti·-ka·n* 'preach!' (plural imperative) (*te·machtia* 'to preach'). The suffix *-ka·n* always formed the plural of verbs containing *xi-*, imperative subject, but it was also used with other subject prefixes to convey a hortatory force as well as to denote a plural number: *ti-tlapo·wa-ka·n* 'we must count' (*tlapo·wa* 'to count').

(b) *-keʔ*, preterit and future subject plural: *o·-an-tlapo·w-keʔ* 'you (plural) counted' (*tlapo·w-*, modified stem of *tlapo·wa* 'to

count'), *tlapo·wa-s-keʔ* 'they will count' (*-s*, future). When added to verbs which formed their preterit with the simple stem and *-k* (§8.4.1b), this suffix coalesced with *-k* to result in *-keʔ* rather than the expected **-k-keʔ*: *o·-ti-k-to·ka-keʔ* 'we buried it' (*to·ka* 'to bury').

(c) *-ʔ*, general subject plural, added to verbs in the present, remote past, imperfective, or conditional: *t-a·miki-ʔ* 'we are thirsty' (*a·miki* 'to be thirsty'), *o·-ti-k-pix-ka-ʔ* 'we used to have it' (*pix-*, modified stem of *pia* 'to have', *-ka*, remote past), *an-po·walo·-ya-ʔ* 'you (plural) were being counted' (*po·walo·* 'to be counted', *-ya*, imperfective), *no·tza-skia-ʔ* 'they would call' (*no·tza* 'to call', *-skia*, conditional).

8.5. IRREGULAR VERBS. A few verbs had stems and inflectional formations which did not follow the prevailing patterns. The verb 'to be' was inflected with the suppletive stems *ie-* and *kat-*, the latter giving rise to several irregular variations: *n-ie-s* 'I will be', *katki* 'he is', *ti-kate-ʔ* 'we are', *an-katka-ʔ* 'you (plural) are'. Other irregular verbs had unique though obviously related stem forms, such as *iʔka-* and *iʔkak* 'to be standing', *iaʔ-*, *ia·-*, *iaw-*, and *wia-* 'to go'.

With the irregular verbs should be classed the two directional auxiliaries, which were employed only as final-position stems in verb compounds. A defective paradigm of inflections as well as unique stem forms characterized these auxiliaries; the present tense was based on *ti-* 'to go in order to' and *ki-* 'to come in order to', the preterit on *to-* and *ki-*, and the future on *ti·w-* and *ki·w-*, singular subject, and *ti·wi-* and *ki·wi-*, plural subject. The general subject plural, *-ʔ*, was used in all inflections of the auxiliaries: *ti-tlapo·wa-to-ʔ* 'we went to read' (*tlapo·wa* 'to read, to count'), *ti-tlapo·wa-ki·wi-ʔ* 'we will come to read'.

8.6. VERB-FORMING DERIVATIONS. Verb themes could be constructed by the addition of suffixes to verb stems (§8.6.1.1– 8.6.1.3) and to noun or particle stems

(§8.6.1.4). In addition, compounding (§8.6.2) was a productive process in the formation of verb themes.

8.6.1. DERIVATIONAL SUFFIXES. Of the enormous range of suffixing processes which produced derived verbs in Classical Nahuatl, only a highly selected sample can be presented. Many of these processes were clustered into derivational subsystems.

8.6.1.1. One subsystem was composed of the following three suffixes, added to verb stems which referred to specific kinds of sounds and movements:

(a) *-ni*, medio-passive momentaneous, attached to a *V·-* form of the stem: *tecui·-ni* 'to burst into flame', *tzaya·-ni* 'to rip' (of cloth), *polo·-ni* 'to stutter'.

(b) *-ka*, medio-passive frequentative, added to a reduplicated stem (§8.2a): *tetecui-ka* 'to rush noisily' (of a river), 'to make the noise of a blazing fire', *chichipi-ka* 'to fall in a large quantity of drops' (of any liquid) (*chipi* 'to fall in drops').

(c) *-tza*, active frequentative, added to the same type of reduplicated stem as *-ka*: *tetecui-tza* 'to make a clattering noise with one's feet'. Of the three suffixes, *-tza* was the only one forming transitive verbs which required an object: *xi-k-kakapatz-ti-wetzi* 'make the tortillas rapidly', literally 'make frequent slapping sounds on it rapidly' (*xi-*, imperative subject, *k-*, 3rd person object, *kakapatz-*, modified stem of *kakapa-tza*, containing the reduplicated stem of *kapa* 'to make a slapping sound', *-ti*, ligature, *wetzi* 'to do . . . rapidly, to fall').

8.6.1.2. Several sets of transitivizing suffixes comprised another subsystem of verb derivations. This was a formally intricate subsystem. Each transitivizing morpheme had several allomorphs: e.g., the causative was formed by *-a*, *-wia*, *-tia*, or *-ltia*. Similar allomorphic forms overlapped different morphemes: e.g., *-wia* was one of the allomorphs of the causative, the applicative, and the reverential. Although the suffix allomorphs were selectively distributed among most

verbs, and although the simple unchanged stem of the verb was employed most commonly, many verbs had optionally variant forms of stem and suffix entering into the transitivizing derivations: e.g., the causative *-tia* was suffixed to the unchanged stem of *yo·li* 'to live' in *yo·li-tia* 'to give life', to the *CyVi-* stem of *icusi* 'to get cooked' in *icuxi-tia* 'to cook', and to the modified contracted stem of *pa·ki* 'to be happy' in *pa·k-tia* 'to cause . . . to be happy', the latter varying optionally with *pa·ki-ltia* as a causative.

(a) *-a*, *-wia*, *-tia*, *-ltia*, causative: *koto·ni-a* or *koto·n-a* 'to break' (*koto·ni* 'to be broken'), *temo-wia* 'to take down' (*temo* 'to go down'), *pa?i·-tia* 'to give medicine to drink' (*pa?i·* 'to drink medicine'), *chi·wa-ltia* 'to cause . . . to make' (*chi·wa* 'to make'), *miki-tia* or *mik-tia* or *miki-ltia* 'to kill' (*miki* 'to die'), *itti-tia* or *itta-ltia* or *itzti-ltia* 'to make . . . see' (*itta* 'to see').

(b) *-lia*, *-wia*, *-lwia*, *-alwia*, *-ilwia*, applicative. This morpheme, when added to an intransitive verb, produced a transitive which demanded an object; when suffixed to a transitive verb, it directed the verbal predication to a second object. Examples are: *miki-lia* 'to die for' (*miki* 'to die'), *chi·wi-lia* 'to make . . . for' (*chi·wa* 'to make'), *tla?cuil-wia* 'to write to' (*tla?cuiloa* 'to write'), *tlapo-lwia* 'to open . . . for' (*tlapoa* 'to open'), *i?t-alwia* 'to talk about' (*i?toa* 'to talk'), *pach-ilwia* 'to press . . . for' (*pachoa* 'to press').

(c) *-a*, *-lia*, *-wia*, *-tia*, *-ltia*, *-alwia*, reverential. The reverential formation always included the reflexive prefixes (§8.3.2), a pattern indicated by *mo-*, second or third person singular or plural reflexive, in the illustrative examples below. Apparently the transitivized manner of expression, "you cause yourself to do so-and-so" or "you do so-and-so for yourself," conveyed respect for the person addressed or spoken about. Examples are: *mo-kalaki-a* 'to enter' (reverential) (*kalaki* 'to enter'), *mo-cho·ki-lia* 'to weep' (reverential) (*cho·ka* 'to weep'), *mo-chi·walti-lia* 'to cause ... to make' (reverential) (*chi·walti-*, modified stem of *chi·waltia*, composed of *chi·wa* 'to make' and *-ltia*, causative), *mo-chi·wili-lia* 'to make ... for' (reverential) (*chi·wili-*, modified stem of *chi·wi-lia*, composed of the *CyVi-* stem of *chi·wa* and *-lia*, applicative), *mo-tła?pal-wia* 'to greet' (reverential) (*tła?paloa* 'to greet'), *mo-nemi-tia* 'to live' (reverential) (*nemi* 'to live'), *mo-tolo-ltia* 'to swallow' (reverential) (*toloa* 'to swallow'), *on-m-e·wi-tia* or *on-m-e·wa-ltia* 'to depart' (reverential) (*on-* 'thither', *e·wi-*, the *CyVi-* stem of *e·wa* 'to rise'), *i?t-alwia* 'to talk' (reverential) (*i?toa* 'to talk').

(d) *-tzinoa*, reverential for reflexive verbs: *mo-teo·chi·w-tzinoa* 'to pray' (reverential) (*mo-teo·chi·wa* 'to pray'), *mo-tłalo?-tzinoa* 'to run' (reverential) (*mo-tłaloa* 'to run'). Unlike the other suffixes of the transitivizing subsystem, *-tzinoa* occurred as a single allomorph and it was consistently added to the modified stem form of the verb. In phonemic shape it also differed from the other reverential suffixes, which it resembled in function. It constituted a minor subsystem with *-po·loa*, pejorative, which was likewise added to modified verb stems: *i?to?-po·loa* 'to confess one's sins' (*i?toa* 'to talk'). Both *-tzinoa* and *-po·loa* had a formal resemblance to two of the affective suffixes added to nouns (§7.1.2.2).

8.6.1.3. Somewhat like the transitivizing elements, a set of passivizing allomorphs, *-o·*, *-lo·*, *-wa*, was suffixed to variable verb stems to form derived verbs: *te·x-o·* 'to be ground' (*te·si* 'to grind'), *machti-lo·* 'to be taught' (*machtia* 'to teach'), *a·xi-wa* 'to be reached' (*a·si* 'to reach'), *a·n-o·* or *a·na-lo·* 'to be taken' (*a·na* 'to take'), *itk-o·* or *itki·-wa* 'to be raised' (*itki* 'to raise'), *so-lo·* or *so-wa* 'to be punctured' (*so* 'to puncture').

8.6.1.4. Verbalizing suffixes were attached to nouns or particles to form either intransitive or transitive verbs.

(a) *-a*, *-ti*, *-tia*, intransitive verbalizer: *te·nyo-a* 'to become famous' (*te·nyo·* 'fame'), *tła·ka-ti* 'to be born' (*tła·ka* 'man'), *ne·n-ti* 'to be frustrated' (*ne·n* 'in vain'), *te-tia* 'to become hard' (*te* 'stone').

(b) *-lia*, *-tia*, *-wia*, transitive verbalizer: *o·me-lia* 'to make two from' (*o·me* 'two'), *tła·ka-tia* 'to give birth to' (*tła·ka* 'man'), *po?-tia* 'to make ... similar' (*po?* 'like'), *ista-wia* 'to salt' (*ista* 'salt'), *achtopa-wia* 'to be first in doing' (*achtopa* 'first').

8.6.2. COMPOUNDING. A compound was identified as a verb by the presence of a verb stem in the final stem position. In special usages, certain verbs required inflectional affixes between the compounded stems: verbs preceding *neki* 'to want' took the future suffix, *-s*, as in *ti·tłani-s-neki* 'to want to send' (*ti·tłani* 'to send'); when employed as final-position stems with specialized meanings, some half-dozen verbs, among them *tła·lia* 'to put', were inflected with reflexive prefixes, as in *sese·x-ti-mo-tła·lia* 'to get cool' (of the weather) (*sese·x-*, modified stem of *sese·ya* 'to get cool', *-ti*, ligature, *mo-*, reflexive second or third person singular or plural). Outside of these special instances compound verbs were inflected as units, the prefix inflections appearing before the first stem and the suffix inflections after the final stem, as in *o·-ni-mitz-mik-ka·-toka-ka* 'I had imagined that you were dead' (*o·-*, past, *ni-* 'I', *mitz-* 'you', singular object, *mik-*. modified stem of *miki* 'to die', *-ka·*, ligature, *toka* 'to imagine', *-ka*, remote past).

In verb compounds the final stem could be preceded by a verb, a noun, or a particle. Verb-plus-verb combinations were freely formed: *cuika-witze* 'to come to sing', *tłaokox-cuika* 'to sing sadly' (*tłaokox-*, modified stem of *tłaokoya* 'to be sad'). Some verb stems assumed specialized meanings as second-position elements in compounds: *mati* 'to know' meant 'to think that, to seem' in compounds; *wetzi* 'to fall' took on the meaning 'to do ... rapidly'; *e·wa* 'to rise' could mean 'to try' as a second-position stem.

Noun stems were incorporated within the verb compound. Before transitive verbs the incorporated noun stem functioned as an object or as a verb modifier: *xo·chi-pe?pena* 'to pick flowers' (*xo·chi* 'flower', *pe?pena* 'to pick, to select'), *tle-watza* 'to roast, to dry (e.g., meat) in the fire' (*tle* 'fire', *watza* 'to dry'). With intransitive verbs the noun stem acted either as subject or as verb modifier: *kech-koto·nalo·* 'to be beheaded' (*kech* 'neck', *koto·nalo·* 'to be cut'), *tle-watzalo·* 'to be roasted' (*tle* 'fire', *watzalo·* 'to be dried').

Particles having a modifying function were also compounded with verbs: *a?kopa-tlachia* 'to look upward' (*a?kopa* 'upward, above', *tlachia* 'to look'), *ne·m-pe·waltia* 'to abuse without cause' (*ne·m-* from *ne·n* 'in vain, without cause', *pe·waltia* 'to abuse').

9. PARTICLES. The lexicon of Classical Nahuatl was rich in particles, whose nuances of meaning intrigued the early grammarians (Olmos, 1547, pp. 98–106; Carochi, 1645, pp. 493–529). The expressive force of the numerous particles was augmented by the stylistic device of using clusters of them in syntactic combination (§10.2).

Among their derivational potentialities, particles shared only a few of the derivational suffixes which formed nouns (§7.1.5.4) and verbs (§8.6.1.4). They had no unique derivational morphemes of their own. Reduplication was applied to some particle stems: *se·sen-yowal* 'every night' (*se·sen-*, from *se·sem-*, reduplicated form of *sem-*, combining stem of *se* 'one', *yowal* 'night'). The particle *we?kaw* 'a long time' occurred in a reduplicated form in *we·we?kawtika* 'from time to time'.

Particles were profusely compounded. Two particles with similar meanings were often joined: *ok* 'yet', *no?ma?* 'yet', *okno?ma?* 'yet'. Modifications of meaning were conveyed by the compounding of particles: *intla·-k-ay-ai·k* 'if never until now' (*intla·* 'if', *-k*, elided from *-ka·*, ligature, *ay-*, elided from *aya* 'not yet', *ai·k* 'never'). Some particles appeared either in compounds or in syntactic combinations of the same type, such as *ka*, a particle having reverential force, in *ke·ma?-ka* or *ke·ma? ka* 'no' (reverential) (*ke·ma?* 'no'), *ka a?mo·* or *ka a?mo·-*

tzin 'yes' (reverential) (*a?mo·* 'yes', *-tzin*, reverential), *achti?-tzin-ka* 'in a little while' (reverential). The analysis of many derived particles was obscure, particularly the groups of particles which were formally related and had similar meanings, such as *achto, achtopa, akachto, akachtopa, akatto, yakatto, yakattopa,* all meaning 'first'.

SYNTAX

10. UTTERANCE TYPES. In Classical Nahuatl an utterance could be formed with or without a verb.

10.1. NON-VERBAL UTTERANCE. A noun in the vocative (§7.1.5.2a) or a single particle, such as *iyo* 'alas' or *ke·ma?* 'no', constituted a complete utterance. Morphemes or words joined in a copular relationship also formed utterances without verbs. One of these constructions was the combination of a subject pronoun prefixed to a noun: *ni-tla·ka* 'I am a man' (*ni-* 'I', *tla·ka* 'man'), *ti-no-pil-tzin* 'you are my son' (reverential) (*ti-* 'you', singular, *no-* 'my', *pil* 'son', *-tzin*, reverential). Another type of copular utterance was the sequence of two or more nouns, with or without modifying particles: *nakatl in i·tlacual cuawtli* 'meat is the food of the eagle', literally 'meat the its-food eagle'.

10.2. VERBAL UTTERANCE. A sentence was an utterance containing a verb. The minimal simple sentence was composed of an independent clause expressed by a single verb (§11.1). When two or more independent clauses were closely linked, they comprised a compound sentence. The complex sentence was made up of one or more dependent clauses in addition to the independent clause or clauses.

In the great majority of instances the status of the clause was overtly marked by a particle functioning as an introducer. Among the many particles signalizing the independent clause were: *aw* 'and', *axka·n* 'now', *kil* 'it is said that', *ma·*, affirmative with the imperative form of the verb, *ma·ka* or *ma·kamo·*, negative with the imperative, *ni·man* 'then', *san* 'only, but', *ye* 'certainly, already'. Some of the subordinating particles which introduced dependent clauses were: *inik* 'in order that', *intla·* 'if', *intla·ka* or *intla·kamo·* 'if not', *i[?]cua·k* 'whenever, at the time that', *i·man* 'when', *i·pampa* 'because', *ma·nel* 'though', *okik* 'while'. Each of these particles had a wide range of meanings and usages, which were further extended by their frequent occurrence in compounded forms (see §9) and in syntactic sequences, such as *san achi[?]ton* 'nearly', *san cue·l* 'in a very short time', *san ika in* 'in a short time, presently', *san i·pan* 'moderately', *san mach* 'not only that', *san sen* 'together', *san wel achi·k* 'almost', *san ye* 'on the contrary', *sa san* 'anyhow', *sa sankenin* 'more or less'.

Although the clause was often formally labeled as dependent or independent by the introducing particle, it could also appear with no formal indication of its status. Juxtaposed clauses might be implicitly independent or dependent: *mesentlalike[?] mononotzke[?] in teteo·* 'the gods assembled; they deliberated', literally 'they-assembled they-deliberated the gods'; *awel onmomomayaw in tleko* 'he was unable to throw himself into the fire', literally 'he-was-unable he-threw-himself the into-fire'.

11. COMPONENTS OF THE SENTENCE. The sole obligatory component of the sentence was the predicate. The substantive, functioning as a subject or an object, was an optional unit of sentence structure. A predicate or a substantive occurred either in the simple form of a single word or in the expanded form of several words. The words of an expanded unit were linked either in a parallel construction or in a complex construction made up of a nuclear term with its modifyng satellites.

11.1. PREDICATE. The minimal sentence was the independent clause containing a one-verb predicate: *o·chika·wak* 'it was strong', *o·nikcuik* 'I took it'. In such sentences the subject and the object could be expressed by inflectional prefixes (§8.3) or by incorporated noun stems (§8.6.2).

Parallel predicative constructions, particularly those composed of a redundant sequence of verbs with similar meanings, were a favorite stylistic device of Classical Nahuatl: *wewenton i·pan mocuep i·pan mixew i·pan mokixti o·welkoliw o·welkaistak o·mocuastapon* 'he changed himself into an old man, he transformed himself into one, he took on the appearance of one, he became completely bent, he became completely white-headed, he became completely gray-headed'. Parallel verbs were sometimes linked with the conjunctive particle *i·wan* 'and': *intla· tikmi·ti·s motech kisas i·wan kiyamawili·s in monakayo* 'if you will drink it, it will enter and heal your flesh', literally 'if-you-will-drink-it into-you it-will-enter and it-will-heal the your-flesh'.

In addition to parallel linkages, the predicate was also expanded by subsidiary modifying words and by complementing words or phrases. Innumerable particles and particle combinations functioned as adverbs of time, place, and manner: *ya·lwa* 'yesterday', *awi·k* 'here and there', *iw* 'thus', *iw in* 'in this way', *iw on* 'in that way', *wei iwi* 'in an extreme manner', *san ye no·iw* 'in the same way'. Another form of adverbial modifier was composed of a noun, usually a noun having a qualitative reference, followed by the particle *ik*: *cualli ik* 'in a good manner, well' (*cualli* 'good, good thing'). Many kinds of complementive expansions could be formed. One commonly used type was the secondary verb which followed the nuclear verb: *o·nipe·w nitlacua* 'I began to eat', literally 'I-began I-eat'; *nikmati nitla[?]cuilo·s* 'I know how to read', literally 'I-know-it I-will-read'. When the complement followed a nuclear verb of thinking or believing, or when it was a direct quotation after a verb of saying, it was introduced by the linking particle *ka* 'that': *sekintin momatke[?] ka miktlampa in kisaki·w* 'some thought that it (the sun) rises in the north', literally 'some they-thought that from-the-north the it-comes-to-rise'; *kilwi in wewenton ka nika·n* *katki in pa?tli* 'the old man said, "Here is the medicine" ', literally 'he-said the old-man that here it-is the medicine'.

11.2. SUBSTANTIVE. Independent personal pronouns were employed as substantives with subject or object functions, but their occurrence was rare. They appeared primarily in copular expressions, with or without verbs: *cuix a?mo· te?* 'might it not be you?' literally 'maybe? not you'; *ka? ne?wa·tl* 'it-is I'. Elsewhere they served to emphasize the pronominal references expressed in the verb complex: *ka a?mo· o·nimitzmikti? ye? te?wa·tl o·tine·chmikti?* 'I certainly did not hit you; it was you who hit me', literally 'certainly not I-hit-you it you you-hit-me'. The interrogative and indefinite pronouns also functioned as substantives: *a·ki?ke? o·wa·lla?ke?* 'who came?' literally 'who-(plural)? they-came'.

In most instances the simple substantive was a noun in the role of subject or object. Although word order was flexible, a subject substantive usually followed the predicate verb and preceded an object substantive: *kicuito in askatl in tlaolli* 'the ant came to take the maize kernel', literally 'it-came-to-take-it the ant the maize-kernel'.

Nouns in parallel construction, representing a type of expanded substantive, were either linked with *i·wan* 'and' or were merely juxtaposed: *i·a·matzon i·wan i·a·maneapanal* 'his-paper-mitre and his-paper-stole'. The juxtaposition of two nouns was a metaphorical device, which produced new lexemes by attaching extended meanings to certain combinations: *noma· noksi*, literally 'my-hand my-foot'. meant 'my body'; *in xo·chitl*

in cuikatl, literally 'the flower the song', meant 'the poem'.

Expanded substantives were also composed of a nuclear noun with its modifier or its complement. The head noun usually followed its modifying term, which was a particle or another noun: *wel a?mo· cualli* 'it's not a very good thing', literally 'very not good-thing'; *in cualtin tla·ka?* 'the good men', literally 'the good-ones men'. The sequence of a nuclear term preceding the modifying noun, however, was the normal possessive construction. In this type of syntactic construction a possessed noun or postposition was followed by a noun functioning as the possessor: *i·tzacual tonatiw* 'the pyramid of the sun', literally 'its-pyramid sun'; *i·nmasawa·n in te·teo·?* 'the gods' deer', literally 'their-deer the gods', a metaphor meaning 'the Spaniards' horses'; *i·kampa in tepe·tl* 'in back of the mountain', literally 'its-rear the mountain'; *i·pan kalli* 'inside the house', literally 'its-interior house'. The complementive type of expanded substantive was composed of a nuclear noun followed by a relative clause, usually with the intervening particle, *in* 'the, this': *totechiwka·wa·n in o·nemiko? in tla·ltikpak* 'our ancestors who came to live on the earth', literally 'our-ancestors this they-came-to-live the on-earth'. A relative clause could also function as the complement of a subject or object expressed, not only by a noun, but also by a pronominal prefix: *kinmotlaso?tilia in tote·cuiyo dios in kimotlayekoltilia* 'Our Lord God loves those who serve him', literally 'he-loves-them-(reverential) the our-lord god this they-serve-him- (reverential)'.

REFERENCES

Barrett, 1956
Bright, 1960
Carochi, 1645
Col. de gramáticas, 1904
Croft, 1951, 1953a, 1953b, 1954
Dávila Garibi, 1938, 1948
Galdo Guzmán, 1642
Garibay K., 1940a
Hasler, 1954–55a, b, c
Hoijer and others, 1946
Key, 1960

—— and Key, 1953
Law, 1958
Molina, 1571a, 1571b
Nebrija, 1492
Olmos, 1547
Pittman, 1954
Rincón, 1595
Schoembs, 1949
Trend, 1953
Viñaza, 1892
Whorf, 1946

7B. Classical Yucatec (Maya)

NORMAN A. McQUOWN

0.	Introduction
1.	Phonology
1.1.	Phoneme inventory
1.1.1.	Consonants
1.1.2.	Vowels
1.1.3.	Prosody
1.1.3.1.	Tones
1.1.3.2.	Junctures
1.1.3.3.	Intonations
1.1.3.3.1.	Levels
1.1.3.3.2.	Terminal contours
1.2.	Orthography
1.2.1.	Consonants
1.2.2.	Vowels
1.2.3.	Prosody
1.2.3.1.	Tones
1.2.3.2.	Junctures
1.2.3.3.	Intonations
1.3.	Phoneme variants (allophones)
1.3.1.	Consonants
1.3.2.	Vowels
1.3.3.	Prosody
1.4.	Phoneme distribution
1.4.1.	Initial consonants
1.4.2.	Initial consonant clusters
1.4.3.	Medial consonant clusters
1.4.4.	Final consonant clusters
1.4.5.	Vowel clusters
1.4.6.	Tone sequences
1.4.7.	Morphophonemic alternation
2.	Morphology
2.1.	Morpheme shapes
2.1.1.	Types
2.1.2.	Examples
2.2.	Morpheme classes
2.3.	Verbs
2.3.1.	Intransitive verbs (roots and stems)
2.3.2.	Transitive verbs (roots and stems)
2.3.3.	Voice
2.3.4.	Aspect
2.3.5.	Mood
2.3.6.	Verb complex
2.3.6.1.	Conjunct I
2.3.6.2.	Conjunct II
2.3.6.3.	Auxiliary I
2.3.6.4.	Auxiliary II
2.3.6.5.	Subject pronouns
2.3.6.6.	Reduplication
2.3.6.7.	Root II
2.3.6.8.	Root I
2.3.6.9.	Stem formatives
2.3.6.10.	Statuses
2.3.6.11.	Voices
2.3.6.12.	Aspects
2.3.6.13.	Moods
2.3.6.14.	Object pronouns
2.3.6.15.	Subject pronouns I
2.3.6.16.	Subject pronouns II
2.3.6.17.	Terminals
2.4.	Nouns
2.4.1.	Noun roots
2.4.2.	Compound stems
2.4.3.	Complex stems
2.4.3.1.	Deverbative noun stems
2.4.3.2.	Desubstantive noun stems
2.4.4.	Noun inflection
2.4.4.1.	Nominal possessive affixes
2.4.4.2.	Suffix -*il*
2.4.4.3.	Suffix -*ak*
2.4.4.4.	Attributives
2.5.	Particles
2.5.1.	Particle conjugation
2.5.2.	Particle compounding
2.5.3.	Prepositional particles

2.5.4.   Demonstrative particles
2.5.5.   Adverbial particles
2.5.5.1.   "Partículas del presente"
2.5.5.2.   "Partículas del pretérito imperfecto"
2.5.5.3.   "Partículas del pluscuamperfecto"
2.5.5.4.   "Partículas del futuro imperfecto"
2.5.5.5.   "Partículas del futuro perfecto"
2.5.5.6.   "Partículas del imperativo futuro"
2.5.5.7.   "Partículas del optativo"
2.5.5.8.   "Partículas del subjuntivo"
2.5.5.9.   "Partículas del futuro"
2.5.5.10.   Particles of time and place
2.5.5.11.   Particle *tak* 'al punto'
2.5.5.12.   Particle *to* 'en haciendo,' etc.
2.5.6.   Conjunctional particles
2.5.6.1.   Dubitative particles
2.5.6.2.   Modal particles
2.5.6.3.   Causal particles
2.5.6.4.   Instrumental particles
2.5.6.5.   Particles of quantity
2.5.6.6.   Negative particles
2.5.6.7.   Others
2.5.7.   "Partículas intensivas"
2.5.8.   "Partículas disyuntivas"

0. INTRODUCTION. Classical Yucatec Maya was the language spoken by the inhabitants of the peninsula of Yucatan from the middle of the 15th to the middle of the 17th centuries. Conquered in the middle of the 16th century by the emissaries of the Spanish crown, the speakers of this language were provided with an alphabet based on the contemporary Spanish usage of the Latin letters. The literature which constitutes our corpus of Classical Yucatec was written down by a few gifted native speakers trained in the use of the alphabet by members of the Roman Catholic clergy. The same alphabet and derivatives of the same written tradition survive to the present day; Modern Yucatec, differing minimally from the language of the classical period, survives as one fairly uniform language with but minor dialect variations. It is spoken at the present time by several hundred thousands of modern Maya in the states of Campeche, Yucatan, and Quintana Roo in the peninsula of Yucatan in Mexico, in portions of neighboring British Honduras (Belice), and in the Department of the Peten in Guatemala. Close linguistic relatives of the Yucatec Maya are the Lacandones, who still live in the jungles of the Mexican states of Chiapas and Tabasco. The Yucatec Maya numbered among them the Itzaes who were long resistant to the Spanish conquest, who fled from Chichen Itza in Yucatan to Tayasal on the Lago de Flores in the Peten, and who there maintained their independence for more than a century after the conquest.

The speakers of Yucatec are surrounded by speakers of other languages of the Mayan family (McQuown, 1956): by the Chontal of Tabasco, the Chol, the Tzeltal and the Toholabal, the Kekchi, and the (Cholti-) Chorti. They came under the influence of Nahua-speaking Toltecs and Aztecs in the millennium preceding the Spanish conquest, and under the influence of Spanish-speaking priests, soldiers, and landlords thereafter. The Yucatec language is genetically related to Huastec, and to other Mayan languages spoken in the Mexican state of Chiapas and in the highlands of Guatemala. Although the time-depth within the Yucatec branch of the Mayan family is only about 1200–1500 years, the family as a whole began to diverge 4000–4500 years ago. The identity of the nearest relatives of Yucatec within the family is uncertain.

The language of the Yucatecs constituted the medium for the culture of the ancient Maya (Morley-Brainerd, 1956)—both Old and New Empires, both in the Peten and in Yucatan. Its earlier stages undoubtedly survive in copious glyphic materials, for the most part in stone inscriptions, but also in three known fig-bark-paper codices (the Madrid, the Paris, and the Dresden) (Brasseur de Bourbourg, 1869–70, and Rada, 1892; Rosny, 1887; and Förstemann, 1880, 1892, respectively). The glyphic materials have as yet only in small part been deciphered (Thompson, 1962). Its later stages survive in numerous chronicles, set down in Latin letters after the conquest, but recording in fair part preconquest events. Some aspects of the preconquest culture of the Maya may be studied in lexica of the type of the Motul dictionary. Present-day literature is living, both *viva voce* and in print, and constitutes an inexhaustible source of Yucatec linguistic and cultural materials.

Information on the Yucatec language of the classical period is available in the *Arte de Lengua Maya* by Fray Juan Cornel (Martínez Hernández, 1929) printed in Mexico for the first time in 1620, and in the *Diccionario de Motul* written in the last quarter of the 16th century in all likelihood by Fray Antonio de Ciudad Real and printed for the first time in Mérida, Yucatan, in 1929. Other grammars bearing on the language of the classical and later periods, as well as other dictionaries, both published and unpublished, are listed in the References at the end of this article.

Texts in Yucatec are to be found in the *Book of Chilam Balam of Chumayel* (edited in original Maya and English translation by Ralph L. Roys; (1933) and in numerous other *chilam balames* available in manuscript collections and in photocopies of such manuscripts. Modern Yucatec texts and vocabularies are available in the University of Chicago collection. These were gathered between 1930 and 1940 by Manuel J. Andrade, in part in phonetic transcription and in part phonographically recorded on aluminum disks, and in 1949 by Norman A. McQuown. The phonetically transcribed Chicago materials are in part available (Lacandone) in No. 10 of the University of Chicago's Microfilm Collection of Manuscripts on Middle American Cultural Anthropology. For Modern Yucatec we have a grammar by Manuel J. Andrade (1940) as No. 41 (1956) of that series. The grammar contains numerous fully analyzed short utterances, these being extracted from modern texts not yet incorporated into the microfilm series. Other sources of text materials, both classical and modern, are listed in the References.

This outline is to be viewed as a guide to the Motul dictionary, to the Coronel grammar for Classical Yucatec, to Andrade's grammar for Modern Yucatec, with the categories rearranged in such a manner as to make the gaps in these treatments more apparent, and to make the rich content of all three sources more readily available to the serious student. A grammar in conformity with the norms of modern descriptive linguistics has yet to be written.

References to the Motul dictionary (M)

1.   Phonology
1.1.   Phoneme Inventory
1.1.1. Consonants

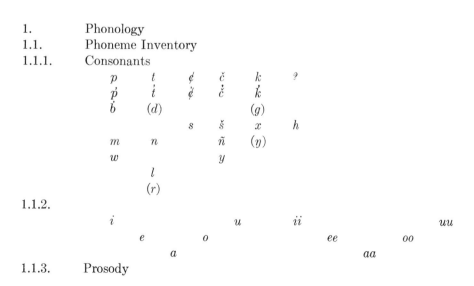

1.1.3. Prosody

1.1.3.1.   Tones
$$\grave{a} \qquad \acute{a}$$

1.1.3.2.   Junctures
$$\wedge \qquad - \qquad \neq \qquad \#$$

1.1.3.3.   Intonations

1.1.3.3.1. Levels
$$3 \qquad 2 \qquad 1$$

1.1.3.3.2. Terminal Contours
$$\rightarrow \qquad \smile \qquad \curvearrowright$$

1.2.   Orthography

1.2.1.   Consonants

p	t	tz	ch	c	$(\ )$, ', $(V)V$, ', j, -
pp	th	$\mathfrak{z}$	$c\hbar$	k	
b	(d)			(g)	
		ς, z x	$\hbar, h$	h	
m	n	$(\tilde{n})$	(n)		
v, u		y, i			
	l				
	(r)				

1.2.2.   Vowels

i		u	ii, ij		uu
	e	o		ee	oo
		a		aa	

1.2.3.   Prosody

1.2.3.1.   Tones
$$a \qquad \acute{a}$$

1.2.3.2.   Junctures

(no space)   (medial space)   (medial space)
(initial space)   (final space)
(after punctuation)

1.2.3.3.   Intonations

$-$,   .   ¿?   ¡!   (marks of punctuation)

1.3.   Phoneme Variants (Allophones)

1.3.1.   Consonants

are to folios, except where pages are specified. The latter are to the pages of the Coronel grammar. References to Andrade's grammar (A) are to paragraphs.

The voiceless stops and affricates (except $\mathfrak{z}$) are slightly aspirated prevocalically and before open junctures ($- \neq \#$). The second series ($\acute{p}\ \acute{t}\ \acute{\phi}\ \overset{\cdot\cdot}{\check{c}}\ \acute{k}$) are glottalized in all positions, are lenis medially between vowels, fortis elsewhere. The voiced pre-glottalized stop allophone of $\dot{b}$ occurs after the four

junctures and before close ($\wedge$) juncture. Before the open junctures ($- \neq \#$) $\dot{b}$ occurs in its pre-glottalized voiced nasal followed by voiceless nasal allophone. d and g occur only in words of Spanish origin and in those only in their stop allophones. The sibilant s is dental and apical, the shibilant $\check{s}$ is palatal, the x is a velar fricative, and the h a voiceless frictionless vocalic sound identical in timbre with the voiced vowel which follows it. The m is bilabial, the n is dental (except, in

Classical Yucatec? before velars, where it is velar [ŋ]). The ŋ occurs in Modern Yucatec in pre-junctural position in contrast with n in this position. The w and y are high-back and high-front semivowels respectively, tending to devoice before ≠, but voiced elsewhere. The lateral l is palatal. The tap r is dental.

1.3.2. VOWELS. The simple vowels have the values of the syllabics of English BEAT, BET, BOT (fly), BOAT, BOOT (or Spanish TIRO, PERO, PARO, TORO, PURO), except that the vowel a tends occasionally to rise to the position of the vowel in English BUT, and the vowel e before the semivowel y to the position of the syllabic of the first syllable

of English LATER. The double vowels represent elongations of the simple vowels if they are alike in tone, rearticulations if they differ.

1.3.3. PROSODY. Except for the tones (low unmarked, high with the acute ′ accent occasionally marked in the Classical Yucatec texts) (both well established in Modern Yucatec), the other prosodic features are for Classical Yucatec conjectural and for Modern Yucatec as yet not definitively established. The distinctions here indicated (four junctures, three pitch levels, and three terminal contours) are not unlikely.

1.4. PHONEME DISTRIBUTION.[1]

1.4.1. INITIAL CONSONANTS.

	i	e	a	o	u	ïi	ee	aa	oo	uu
p										
p̓										
t										
t̓										
¢										
¢̓										
č										
č̓										
k										
k̓										
ʔ										
b̓										
d										
g										
s										
š										
x										
h										
m										
n										
w										
y										
l										

[1] The blanks in the grids which follow may be (in part) filled in as the particular combinations are encountered in lexical materials. There will, of course, be systemic gaps in distribution, but these will not appear until the grids have been reasonably well filled out.

1.4.2. INITIAL CONSONANT CLUSTERS. Initial consonant clusters in Classical Yucatec are extremely rare. Noted are initial geminates *čč* in *ččaki* 'hábil' and *ččanuuk* 'conjeturar' (Motul 151r) and initial *kʔ* in *kʔotoč* 'nuestra casa' (Motul 58r) alternating with *kaʔotoč* 'id.' In Modern Yucatec initial clusters of *h* or *š* (from Classical Yucatec *ʔax* or *ʔiš*) and stem-initial consonant occur.

1.4.3. MEDIAL CONSONANT CLUSTERS.

Some clusters (the geminates) are extremely common, others less so. Parallel to the vocalic clusters with smooth transition, hiatus, or rearticulation are sequences of *VʔV*. Whether the latter are ever in free variation with the former, either in Classical or in Modern Yucatec, is uncertain.

1.4.6. TONE SEQUENCES.

$C\acute{V}$

$C\grave{V}$

	p	ṗ	t	ṫ	ȼ	ȼ̇	č	č̌	k	k̇	ʔ	ḃ	s	š	x	h	m	n	w	y	l
p																					
ṗ																					
t																					
ṫ																					
ȼ																					
ȼ̇																					
č																					
č̌																					
k																					
k̇																					
ʔ																					
ḃ																					
s																					
š																					
x																					
h																					
m																					
n																					
ŋ																					
w																					
y																					
l																					
r																					

1.4.4. FINAL CONSONANT CLUSTERS. Final consonant clusters are likewise rare. Noted are *kš* in *makš* (Motul 281) '¿quién?' and *nš* in *kunš* (Motul 90) 'pues'.

1.4.5. VOWEL CLUSTERS.

	i	e	a	o	u	ʔi	ʔe	ʔa	ʔo	ʔu
i										
e										
a										
o										
u										

$C\acute{V}\acute{V}$

$C\grave{V}\grave{V}$

$C\acute{V}\grave{V}$

$C\grave{V}\acute{V}$

$C\acute{V}C$

$C\grave{V}C$

$C\acute{V}\acute{V}C$

$C\grave{V}\grave{V}C$

$C\acute{V}\grave{V}C$ *šúùš*

$C\grave{V}\acute{V}C$

$C\acute{V}C\acute{V}$

$C\grave{V}C\grave{V}$

206

CV́CV̀	kími		CV́CCV̀V̀	
CV̀CV́			CV́CCV́V̀	
CV́V́CV́			CV́CCV̀V́	
CV̀V̀CV̀			CV̀CCV́V̀	
CV́V́CV̀			CV́CCV̀V̀	
CV̀V̀CV́	pèèró		CV́CCV́C	
CV́V̀CV̀			CV̀CCV́C	kàštál
CV́V̀CV́			CV́CCV̀C	sástàl
CV̀V́CV̀			CV̀CCV̀C	
CV̀V́CV̀			CV́V́CCV́C	
CV́CV́V́			CV̀V̀CCV̀C	
CV̀CV̀V̀			CV́V́CCV̀C	
CV́CV́V̀			CV́V̀CCV́C	
CV́CV̀V́			CV́V̀CCV̀C	
CV̀CV́V̀			CV̀V́CCV́C	
CV̀CV̀V́			CV̀V́CCV̀C	
CV́CV́C			CV́CCV́V́C	
CV̀CV̀C			CV̀CCV̀V̀C	
CV́CV̀C	'ú?ùn (Motul 209r)		CV́CCV́V̀C	kánhóòl
CV̀CV́C	kìmén		CV́CCV̀V́C	
CV́V́CV́C			CV̀CCV̀V́C	
CV̀V̀CV̀C			CV̀CCV́V̀C	
CV́V́CV̀C			CV́CCV́CV́	
CV̀V̀CV́C	màaké?		CV̀CCV̀CV̀	
CV́V̀CV̀C	náàkàl (Motul 316)		CV́CCV́CV̀	
CV́V̀CV́C			CV́CCV̀CV̀	kámpànà
CV̀V́CV́C			CV́CCV̀CV́	
CV̀V́CV̀C	čàákàl((Motul 150r)			etc.
CV́CV́V́C				
CV̀CV̀V̀C				
CV́CV́V̀C				
CV́CV̀V́C				
CV̀CV́V̀C	lùbáàn			
CV̀CV̀V́C				
CV́CCV́				
CV̀CCV̀				
CV́CCV̀	hántò			
CV̀CCV́	lìbró			
CV́V́CCV́				
CV̀V̀CCV̀				
CV́V́CCV̀				
CV̀V̀CCV́				
CV́V̀CCV̀				
CV̀V́CCV́				
CV̀V̀CCV̀				
CV̀V́CCV̀				
CV́CCV́V́				
CV̀CCV̀V̀				

Those sequences which appear in Classical Yucatec grammars, texts, and dictionaries (and even a thorough search will reveal only a small functionally loaded sample) will need to be completed by a thoroughgoing investigation of living Modern Yucatec in order to make a beginning toward filling out the above chart. Portions of the chart will remain blank even after such investigation, since there will be systemic gaps in distribution. The examples listed are illustrative only. Among minimally different pairs might be listed xàwán 'cosa que está boca arriba' and xáwàn 'suegra (madre del yerno ó de la nuera)'.

1.4.7. MORPHOPHONEMIC ALTERNATION. Morphophonemic alternation is of relatively minor importance. It is treated for the most part under the heading of particular morpheme combinations in the morphology. Alternation of vowels (which may reflect dialect variation) is to be found in some forms:

$i \sim a$ siya$b$ $\sim$ saya$b$ (Motul 103)
$a \sim e$ xa¢im $\sim$ xe¢im (Motul 171)
$a \sim o$ màsón $\sim$ mòsón (Motul 285)
$o \sim e$ k̇oyem $\sim$ k̇eyem (Motul 250r)
$u \sim o$ kučom $\sim$ kočom (Motul 87)

2. MORPHOLOGY.

2.1. MORPHEME SHAPES.

2.1.1. TYPES.

A. C — derivational (and inflectional) prefixes
B. $C_1(V_1)$ reduplication (with vowel syncope)
C. C_1V_1 reduplication
D. CV — N, V, P; $\sqrt{N}$, $\sqrt{V}$, $\sqrt{P}$; inflectional prefixes
E. CVC — N, V, P; $\sqrt{N}$, $\sqrt{V}$, $\sqrt{P}$; inflectional prefixes
F. C — derivational suffixes
G. VC — derivational (and inflectional) suffixes
H. C — derivational suffixes

2.1.2. EXAMPLES.

2.1.2.A. DERIVATIONAL AND INFLECTIONAL PREFIXES. The prefixes of the C-type are few in number. We list:

š (Modern Yucatec from Classical Yucatec ʔiš) 'hembra' (derivational) (Motul 227)
h (Modern Yucatec from Classical Yucatec ʔax) 'varón' (derivational) (Motul 3r)
w (Classical Yucatec) 'mi' (inflectional) (Motul 426)
y (Classical Yucatec) 'su' (inflectional)

2.1.2.B. REDUPLICATION (with vowel syncope). The $C_1(V_1)$-type is also rare. Already cited are ččaki (from čačaki) (Motul 151r).

2.1.2.C. REDUPLICATION. The C_1V_1-type is quite common. We might cite papaal 'andar entre muchachos, muchacheando' (Motul 367) based on paal 'muchacho o muchacha de poca edad' (Motul 366).

2.1.2.D. WORDS (N V P), ROOTS (N V P), INFLECTIONAL PREFIXES. The V in the CV-type may be simple (V) or complex (VV).

208

The CV shapes are common, the CVV shapes much less so. Examples, by way of illustration are (numbers refer to folios in the Motul dictionary):

	i	e	a	o	u	ii	ee	aa	oo	uu
p				162r	162r					
$\dot{p}$		226r								
t			395	424r						
$\dot{t}$										
$¢$		129	113							
$\dot{¢}$			√122							
$č$		138r		146r						
$\dot{č}$			√150							
k	70r		58r	74r	83r	70r				
$\dot{k}$			230r	249	251r					
$ʔ$	221r	160r	1	340	436					
b	51	49r	38	√53r			49r			
s	101r		91r							
$š$		456								
x	184r	180	170	188	193					
h		205								
m			277r							
n			314r							
w			436r							
y		217r	210							
l		264	256r	231						

2.1.2.E. WORDS (N V P), ROOTS (N V P) INFLECTIONAL PREFIXES. Of 4200 possible monosyllabic morphemes of the shape CVC, 1279 actually occur in the citation entries in the Motul dictionary. Of these 1279, 1038 contain simple vowels, although 2100 CVC shapes are possible, and only 241 contain vowel clusters, although 2100 $CVVC$ shapes are likewise possible. The 1279 occurring shapes follow:[2]

---

[2] The numbers refer to folios of the Motul dictionary. They are set in positions in a frame which correspond to the positions occupied by the consonant phonemes in the chart in § 1.1.1. The letter r following a folio number here indicates the reverse side of the folio, which in ordinary bibliographical practice is shown by v, verso. Folio 376r, for example, represents the syllable pip, 377r the syllable $piš$, and so on. The blanks may be filled in from sources other than the Motul in so far as the morphemes occur.

pi

376r	376r		375r	374r
		375r	376	376
374r				
		375	377r	
376r	376r			

pii

pe

	374		373	369r	369r
		372	373	373	
357r					
	373r				

pee

373r			
		372	
		371r	
374r			

pa

367	367	357r	358	354r	353r
		357r	359	363r	
		357	369	359	359
	366r		360		

paa

				354
		360		
	366			

po

381	381		379r	378r
		379	379r	380
		379	382r	
380r				
	380r			

poo

381			
		382	
380r			

pu

	386	383	383r	
		383	383r	384
		382r		
	384r			

puu

	386		383r	382r
				384

ṗi

	390r			389r	
389r	391	390			
390					
390					

ṗii

ṗe

				387r	
389					
	388				
389					
388					

ṗee

| | 388 | |
| 388 | |

ṗa

	387			386	386
	386	387r			
387					
	386r				
386r					

ṗaa

ṗo

	392		391r	391r	391
				391r	
392					

ṗoo

| 391r |

ṗu

394r	395		393	392r	
	393	395	393		
394r					
	394				
394					

ṗuu

			392r	
	393			
394r				
394¹				

¹ Also ṗuˀul.

210

ti

	423r	421	421	420r	418r
423r		421	421r		
420					
		424	422		
422r	423r				
	422				

tii

(grid, no labels)

te

417	417r			415r	
417r					
		415r			
416	416r				
	416				

tee

	416				

ta

414	414		402r	397r	395¹
		402		404	
395r					
		401r	414r	402r	
408r	410				
	406				

taa

			402r		
		402			
395r					
	410				
414r					

to

426r	427		425	424r	424r
426r				425r	
			427	425	
426	426				

too

426r				424r	
426r					
		424r			
		425r			

tu

429r	430r		428r	427r	427r²
430r		428r	428r		
427					
		428	431		
424	429r				
	428r				
	429				

tuu

				428	
		428r			
427r					
	428				

¹ Also 395r.
² Also 118r.

211

tí

		432r			
	433				
432r					
		432r			
	432r				
	433				

tii

ie

	432r				
	432r				
	432r				

iee

ia

		431			
	432r				
431					
			431r		
	431r				

iaa

io

		433r	433r		
	434r				
433r					
		434r	433r		
	434r				
	434	434			

ioo

		433r			
434					

iu

435r		435			
	435r				
435					
	435r				
	435r				
	435r				

iuu

⊄i

119 118

118r

118r

⊄ii

⊄e

118 117 116r

117

117r 118

117

⊄ee

117

117r

⊄a

116 114 113r

115r

113r

114

116

116r 114r

115r

⊄aa

114

116

116

⊄o

120 30r

119r

119

119r

⊄oo

119

⊄u

121r 120r

120[1]

121r

121r

⊄uu

121r

[1] Also 120r.

ȼi

131	131		130	131
129r				
	131			
	130r			

ȼii

| | | | 130 |

ȼe

	129	128r
	128r
128r		
128r

ȼee

ȼa

127r		123r
123		
126	126r	
	125	
125r

ȼaa

ȼo

| 132r | | 131r |
| 132r | |
| 131r |
| 132 | 132 | |
| | 132 |
| 132 |

ȼoo

ȼu

| 133 | | 132r |
| 133 | |
| 132r |
| 133 | 133 | |
| | 132r |
| 133 |

ȼuu

| 183 | |
| 133 |
| 132r |

či

				142	141r	140r
					144	
141						
				143r		
144	144r					
	144					

čii

				142r	141r
140r					

če

				138r	138r
				139r	
				139	
140					
	139r				

čee

				138r
138r				
			139	
	138r			
	139r			

ča

			135	133r	133r
				136	
133r					
			135r		
137	137				
138		136			
	136r				

čaa

					133r
				135r	
137	137				
	136r				

čo

			145		145
			146		
			145r		
146r					
	146				

čoo

				145
145				
	146r			

ču

149r			147r	146r	146r
				148r	
				148¹	
149	149				
		148r			
	148r				

čuu

				147
				148

¹ Also 148r.

či

			228	156	
			156		
155r					
					156r
	156r				
		156r			
	156r				

čii

				156	

če

	155r			
		154		
153r				
		154		
154r	155			
	154r			

čee

154r				

ča

153			150r	
153		151r	152	
150				
			151r	
152r	152r			
153r		151r		
	152[1]			

čaa

152r	152r			
	152[2]			

čo

157r	158		157	157
		157		
		158	157r	
157r	157r			
		157r		

čoo

			157	

ču

160			158r	
		158r		
158r				
		160r	159	
		159		
	160			

čuu

[1] Also 152r.
[2] Also 152r.

216

ki

74		74r	72	70r[1]	70r
		74r			
70r					
		71r	74r		72r
73	73r				
	72r				

kii

					71r
72r					

ke

70	70	70	69	68r	
			69	69	
	69r				
	69				

kee

68r					
	69r				
	69				

ka

66r	67r		60r	60	59
67			60r		
69					
			68r	61	
64r	65				
68			62		
	63				

kaa

		68			60
	65				
			62		
	69r				

ko

82	82r	83	77r	75	75
82r		83r			
75					
		77r	83r	78	
81	81				
			79		
	80				

koo

	82r	83			
75					
		77r		78	
	81				
	80r				

ku

90r	90r	90r	85r	83r	
		85	89r		
89r	90				
			88		
	88				

kuu

	90r		85r	83r	
	90				

[1] Also 71.

217

k̇i

248r	248r	248r	246		
				246	
		245r			
	246r				
	246				

k̇ii

			246		
			249		
	246r				

k̇e

244r			243r	249r	
243					
		243r	245		244
245	244r		244		
	244r				

k̇ee

k̇a

239	239				230r
				234r	
231					
		232r	241	233r	
236r	238				
240r			234r		
	235r				

k̇aa

239	239		232	232	
231					
		241	233	233	
	237r				
		234r			

k̇o

	251r		249		
				250r	
249					
		249	251r	250	
251	251				
251r			250r		
	250r				

k̇oo

251r		283			
	251				

k̇u

255			252r	252r	252
				253	
252					
		255	255r		
254r					
			253		
	253r				

k̇uu

254	254r				
	254				

ʔi

226r	227	222	223	221r	221r
226r		222	224r	224r	
221r					
		222	227	224r	
226r					
	225r				

ʔii

ʔe

165r	165r		162r	161	161
		161r		162r	
161					
		161r	170	162r	
164					
	163r				

ʔee

			162r
164r			

ʔa

37	37r		3r	1r
37			3r	33
1:				
		3	38	3r
36r	36r			
		33		
	34r			

ʔaa

	33	
1		

ʔo

351r	352	344r	345	340
351r	352r	345		347
		344	353	345r
350r	350r			
352r		346		
	349			

ʔoo

	352	345r
350r		
	349r	

ʔu

	452	443	444	
451r		444	445	449r
443				
		443	452	
		447		
	450r			

ʔuu

	444	
	447r	

¹ Also 1r.

219

ḃi

	53			51	51
	53	53	52	52	
51					
		51r	53	52	
	52r				
	52				

ḃii

	52r				
	52				

ḃe

				49r	49r
			49r	50	
49r					
	50r				
	50				

ḃee

49r					
	50				

ḃa

	48r			40	
	48r	44		43	
38					
			49	40r	
	49		41r		
	43r				

ḃaa

	48r		40r	39r	
		49		43	
		40r			
	44				

ḃo

	56	56		53r	
	56		54	54r	
53r					
		54	56r	54	
55r	55r				
56					
	55				

ḃoo

	56				
			56r		
55r	55r				
			54r		
	54r				

ḃu

			57	56r	
	58	58r		57	
56r					
			58r	57	
			57		
	57r				

ḃuu

				57r	
	57r				

si

104r				102	101r
104r	105r	105r		103	
101r					
		102		102r	
104	104				
			103		

sii

			105r		
101r					
		102			
	103r				

se

101r					100r
100r					
		101			
	101r				
		101			

see

		101			

sa

98r	99r			91r	91r
99		100		96r	
91r					
		94		95	
97r					
100			95r		
	96r				

saa

	99r				
			94		
	96r				

so

107	107r				
107		107r			
106					
		106			
107	107				
106			106r		
	107				

soo

	107r			107	
		106		106r	
	107				
107r			106r		

su

112	112			108r	108
112		110		111	
108					
		109r		110r	
111r					
		110r			
	111				

suu

	113			108r	
		110			
		109r		110r	
	111r				
	111				

221

ši

459r[1]	460			458r	
	460		458r	459	
458					
			460	459	
459	459r				
460					
	459				

šii

	460		458	
	460			

še

456r			456r	456	456
456r	457			456r	
456					
				457r	
	456r				

šee

ša

				454	453r
455r				454r	
453					
				456	
455	455				
455r			454r		
	455				

šaa

					453r
					230

šo

	462			460r	
	463		460r	461r	
460r					
				463r	460r
462					
			461		
	461r				

šoo

šu

465			463r	463r	
465			464	464	
463r					
			465r		
	464				

šuu

[1] Also 460.

222

xi

	186r		185r	185	184
	187	185	185r	185	
184r					
	186r				

xii

		187r	186		

xe

	183r	180	180r	180	
183r	183r	180r	181	181	
180					
			184	181	
183	183r				
183[1]					
	181r				

xee

xa

	178	171	171r	170	
178	178	171	171r	170	
170					
			179	172	
176r	176r				
178			173		
	176				

xaa

170					
		170r			

xo

	193		188r	188r	
			189r	190	
188					
		188r	193	189r	
192					
188			189r		
	190r				

xoo

		188r			
		188r			
		188r			
193					
	191				

xu

202	202	193r		193r	
	202r	193r	193r	194	
			202r		
195	195				
			193r		
	194				

xuu

[1] Also 183r.

hi

207

207

hii

207 207

he

206r 206 205r 205
206 r 206 206 206
205r
206

206r

hee

206
205r

ha

204r 204r 202r
203r 203r
203

203r
204

haa

205
203
202r 203

203r

ho

208 207r 207r 208r
208 208r 207r
207
208
207r
208

hoo

207r

208

hu

209r
208r
209

209

huu

209r

209r

mi

	306			
			306	
		306		
306				

mii

me

	305r		303	303
	305r		303	303r
				303r
304r	305			

mee

		306		

ma

	209	285	285r	281
	302	285r	285r	289
278r				
		285	302r	286
292	293			
	291		287	

maa

			285r	281r
		285r		289
287r				
		302		
	294r			

mo

		308r	307	306	306
	308r		307		
306					
		306r			
308			307r		
	307r				

moo

			306r	
	308			

mu

	313r		310r	309	308r
		314	310r	311	
		310r	314	311	
313	313r				
			311		
	312r				

muu

				309
				312
	313r			

ni

				327r	326r
328r	328r	328	328	328r	
326r					
			328r		
	328r				
	328r				

nii

(no entries)

ne

		325[1]	325r	325	225
	326r	325r	325r	325r	
325					
				325r	
325r	326				

nee

(no entries)

na

323r		316r	317	315r	314r
324	324r	317	318r	321r	
315					
			325	319	
323	323				
325			321		
	322r				

naa

	324r				
315					
	323			318r[2]	

no

	332		330	329	
	332		330	331	
				330	
331r	331r				
	331				

noo

				331	
			332		
	331				
	331				

nu

338		334r	335	332r	
339	339r	335			
335r	337r				
	335r				

nuu

	334r		332r	
339r	334r			
335r				

[1] Also 325r.
[2] Also 230.

226

wi

		449r		448
	449r			
		448	449r	
	448r			
	448			

wii

448				
			449r	448
	448r			

we

			446	445r
	447			446r
		446		446
	446r			
		446		
	446r			

wee

wa

442	442	438r	438r	437r
		438r	438r	440r
437				
		438	442r	438r
442r				
	440r		439	

waa

	442			
			439[1]	

wo

				451
	451			

woo

			451	

wu

		444		

wuu

				443

[1] Also 439r.

yi

219r					
				219	
218r					
		219		219	
	219				

yii

			219		

ye

	218r				217r
		218r		218	
217r					
			218		

yee

ya

	216r	216r		211	210[1]
		217	212		
211					
			217	212	
214r	214r				

yaa

211				212	
214					
	213				

yo

220			219r	219r	
	220			220	
285					

yoo

yu

	221r			220r	
				220r	
220r					
221					
			220r		
	221				

yuu

[1] Also 216.

li

		267r	267r	267	
				268	
	269r				

lii

le

265r		266r	265	264r	264
266		266r			
264					
		264r			
265					
	265				

lee

		266r			
		265r			

la

262				257	
262r	263			261	
256r					
				258r	
261r			260		
	261r				

laa

262			258r	257	
				259r	
	261				

lo

273	273	271	271	271	272
273	273r			271r	
270					
		238r	274	271r	
272r	273r				
	272				

loo

273				271r	
	273r				
				274	

lu

277		275	275	275	
	277			275r	
274					
	276r				

luu

277					

2.1.2.F. DERIVATIONAL SUFFIXES. The C-type of derivational suffix is not common. The following have been noted: p (Andrade 3.37), t (A 3.26), $č$ (A 3.27), $k(\ )$, $\dot{k}$ (A 3.37), s (A 3.25), n (A 3.24), l (A 3.34).

2.1.2.G. DERIVATIONAL (AND INFLECTIONAL) SUFFIXES. The VC-type is common. Examples follow:

i	e	a	o	u	ii	ee	aa	oo	uu	
	117r	64	64r	113						p
										$\dot{p}$
105	68r	98r	132r	111r						t
										$\dot{t}$
										$ȼ$
		262								$\dot{ȼ}$
	75r	64r	192	254						$č$
										$\dot{č}$
71	265r	91r		109						k
105		264	192							$\dot{k}$
		111								$ʔ$
	68r	68	146	90r	253					$\dot{b}$
241	119			133						s
	244r	146								$š$
		65	261							x
160	110r	63r	62r	111r						m
71r	73	65r	192	109			107			n
222		134								w
		75r		110r						y
66	68r	65	100	91r						l

2.1.2.H. DERIVATIONAL SUFFIXES. Word- (or utterance-) final C-type derivational suffixes are very rare. Only $-y$ (from xi°) has been noted (Motul 260).

2.2. MORPHEME CLASSES. There are three major morpheme classes: verbs, nouns, and particles. Verbs are distinguished from nouns by the fact that there is a special set of verbal derivational suffixes followed by special verbal inflectional suffixes. The derivational suffixes mark the status, the inflectional suffixes mark the voice, aspect, and mood. Nouns take neither of these sets of suffixes. Particles take no suffixes or prefixes for person and number, whereas both verbs and nouns take both. Those of the verb mark its subject or object. Those of the noun mark its possessor.

2.3. VERBS. Verbs are divided into two major classes, intransitive and transitive. Intransitive verbs take pronominal subject endings:

Sg. 1) en Pl. 1) oon
     2) $eč$ 2) $eeš$
     3) $Ø$ 3) $oo\dot{b}$

Transitive verbs take pronominal subject affixes (prefixes for person and number) (suffixes for number):

Sg. 1) $^{\circ}in$ before C, w before V (Modern Yucatec $^{\circ}iŋw$)
     2) $^{\circ}a$ $^{\circ}aw$
     3) $^{\circ}u$ y (Modern Yucatec $^{\circ}uy$)
Pl. 1) $k(a)$ $k(a)$
     2) $^{\circ}a$ . . . . . $^{\circ}aw$ . . . . $eeš$
     3) $^{\circ}u$ . . . . . y . . . . $oo\dot{b}$

Transitive verbs take pronominal object suffixes identical in form with the subject suffixes of intransitive verbs (. . . en, . . . $eč$, . . . $Ø$, . . . oon, . . . $eeš$, . . . $oo\dot{b}$), but preceding the subject suffixes within the verb complex. Examples:

     $náak$-**en** 'I went up'
     $^{\circ}in$-$kambesax$-$Ø$ 'I taught him'
     $^{\circ}u$-$xa\dot{ȼ}$-**en**-$oo\dot{b}$-e° 'they hit ME'
     yan $^{\circ}a$-$ȼentik$-**oon**-$eeš$ 'you (pl.) have to feed US'

Intransitive verbs in conjunct constructions require the transitive set of affixes, and transitive verbs in conjunct constructions, since they already have the transitive set of affixes, add the suffix $-ik-$:

     (intr.) tan $^{\circ}unoxočtal$**$oobe^{\circ}$** 'THEY are getting large'
     (tr.) $ȼook$ $^{\circ}imbeet$**ik** 'I had done it'

2.3.1. INTRANSITIVE VERBS (ROOTS AND STEMS). Some verb roots are inherently INTRANSITIVE: xan 'eat (in general)', $čex$ 'laugh', $si\dot{t}$ 'jump', kim 'die' (Motul 177, 139, 105r, and 73 respectively). Some intransitive verb stems are desubstantive:

     $winik$ 'hombre': $winikxal$ 'hacerse hombre'

néǵan 'cerca': *neǵanxal* 'acercarse'

nač 'lejos': *načxal* 'alejarse'

seb́ 'presto': *seb́xal* 'hacerse presto'

These make use of the intransitivizing suffix *-xal*. Others are deverbative (?): *lemba(n)* 'shine', *kilba(n)* 'thunder', *ʔalba(n)* 'soften up (in the heat)', *kulukb́a* 'be seated', *lelemankil* 'lighten' (Motul 265r, 72r, 35 [Solís 520], 265 respectively) (based on verb [?] roots *lem, kil, ʔal, kul(uk),* and *lem).* These make use of the suffixes *-b́a-n-, -(uk)-b́a-,* and *-an-k-il,* the latter in combination with reduplication *(le)* in this example. All of these are complex and the verbal nature of the roots *(lem, kil, ʔal)* or of the stems *(kul-uk*: possibly nominal? from the verb root *kul* 'sit') is in doubt. Examples:

kat xan-aken 'después comeré'

winik-x-i ʔumexen dyos 'se hizo hombre el hijo de Dios'

lemb́a-n-i ʔukukutil kaxloxil 'resplandeció el cuerpo de nuestro redentor'

2.3.2. TRANSITIVE VERBS (ROOTS AND STEMS). Some verb roots are inherently TRANSITIVE: *kuč* 'carry', *čuk* 'seize', *pul* 'throw' (Motul 85r, 146r, and 384r respectively). Some transitive verb stems are desubstantive:

b́uk 'ropa de vestir': *b́ukin(t)* 'vestirse ropa'

maldisyon '(a) curse': *maldisyont* 'curse (someone)'

nombrar 'appoint(ment)': *nombrart* 'appoint (someone)'

These make use of the suffixes *-in-* (Classical) with *-t-* (Modern), or of *-t-* alone (this latter for incorporating Spanish verbs in the infinitive and for making Yucatec verbs from Spanish nouns). Others are deverbative:

xan 'eat (in general)': *xan-t-* 'eat (something)'

puǵ 'flee': *puǵ-es-* 'cause to flee'

These make use of the suffixes *-t-,* and *-es-* which here transitivize intransitive verb roots. Examples:

b́ukin ʔanoḱ '¡vístete tu ropa!'

ʔu-puǵes-axen 'he chased me away'

2.3.3. VOICE. Transitive verbs (whose use in the active voice and indicative mood is indicated by the suffix *-ax-*) may shift from active to PASSIVE voice by replacing *-ax-* with the suffix *-aab́* (Andrade 3.9).

ʔinkaxoltax ʔinsuyem 'conocí mi capa'

kaxolt-aab́-i 'it was recognized'

Transitive verbs (whose use in the active voice and indicative mood is indicated by the suffix *-ax-*), when used in conjunct constructions, replace the *-ax-* by *-ik* (with no shift of function).

ʔučuukaxen Juan 'cogióme Juan'

kooš čuukik 'vamos a cogerle'

2.3.4. ASPECT. Both intransitive and transitive verbs manifest two aspects, COMPLETIVE *(-Ø)* and INCOMPLETIVE *(-Vl* and *-al)* (for the intransitives):

(intr.) *xan-Ø*	*xan-al*	'eat'
(intr.) *čeex-Ø*	*čeex-el*	'laugh'
(intr.) *winik-x-Ø*	*winik-x-al*	'become a man'
(intr.) *kulukb́a-Ø*	*kulukb́-al*	'be seated'
(intr.) *puǵ-Ø*	*puǵ-ul*	'flee'

and completive *(-Ø)* and incompletive *(-—)* (for the transitives) (Type I):

(tr.) *kučax-Ø*	*kuč-—*	'carry'
(tr.) *čukax-Ø*	*čuk-—*	'seize'
(tr.) *pulax-Ø*	*pul-—*	'throw'

and completive *(-Ø)* and incompletive *(-Ø)* (for the transitives) (Type II):

(tr.) *kamb́esax-Ø*	*kamb́esax-Ø*	'teach'
(tr.) *b́ukin(t)ax-Ø*	*b́ukin(t)ax-Ø*	'dress'

and completive *(-Ø)* and incompletive *(-——)* (for the transitives) (Type III):

(tr.) *kanántax-Ø*	*kanán-——*	'protect'

The passives follow the intransitive pattern for the incompletive (in Modern Yucatec the ending appears as *-aal* [*-aʔal*] rather than *-ab́-al* which appears in Classical Yucatec).

Transitives occasionally have a PERFECTIVE in *-ma* (A3.21) (Motul 278):

ʔinkub-ma 'I have delivered it'

Since this suffix is not obligatory, and since it does not always occur in the position in which the completive and incompletive occur, it may be derivative rather than aspectual in nature.

2.3.5. MOOD. Intransitive verbs in the IMPERATIVE mood add the suffix -*en* to the root or stem:

xan-en! 'eat!'

čuyl-en! 'hang!'

The personal pronominal suffix for the second singular is -*Ø*. The second plural adds -*eeš* after the modal suffix:

kul-en-eeš! 'sit down (all of you)!'

Transitive verbs in the IMPERATIVE mood add the suffix -*Ø* to the root or stem (occasionally followed by the terminal -*iʔ*) when it ends in a single *C*, or -*e* when the stem ends in two *C*:

¢ik-Ø! 'obey!'

kanant-e! 'protect!'

Intransitive (and passive) verbs form their OPTATIVE mood by adding the suffix -*Vk* (or -*ak*) (the first after roots, the second after stems):

(*bin*) *kimik* 'he (will) die'

ka ¢ikbanakoon 'we will talk'

ken čilakooḃ 'when they (will) lie down'

nakakoon '¡subamos nosotros (luego)!'

Transitive verbs form their optative mood in three ways. Some replace the active voice indicative mood marker (*ax*) by -*Vḃ*, some by -*Ø*, some by -*e* (of these three apparently only the last has survived in Modern Yucatec) (A 3.21):

(*bin*) *ʔin¢ikiḃ* 'I (shall) obey'

(*bin*) *ʔinkambes-Ø* 'I (shall) teach'

(*bin*) *ʔinkanante* 'I (shall) protect'

wa ʔukate 'if he wants it' (Modern Yucatec)

bin ʔaxante 'you will eat it' (Modern Yucatec)

The passives follow the intransitive pattern for the optative (in Modern Yucatec the ending appears as -*aak* [-*aʔak*] rather than -*aḃ-ak* which appears in Classical Yucatec).

2.3.6. VERB COMPLEX. The following positions are recognizable in the verb complex:

1) CONJUNCT I

2) CONJUNCT II

3) AUXILIARY I

4) AUXILIARY II

5) SUBJECT PRONOUNS

6) REDUPLICATION

7) ROOT II

8) ROOT I

9) STEM FORMATIVES

10) STATUSES

11) VOICES

12) ASPECTS

13) MOODS

14) OBJECT PRONOUNS

15) SUBJECT PRONOUNS I

16) SUBJECT PRONOUNS II

17) TERMINALS

2.3.6.1. CONJUNCT I. Among the PARTICLES which appear in this position are the following:

k A 2.13 (plus -*ik*- in position 11) '(habitual action)'

ma(ʔ) A 4.24, M 277 and 277r (plus -*ik*- in position 11) '(negative; prohibitive)'

he A 2.14, M 205 (plus -*ik*- in position 11, and -*eʔ* in position 17) 'certainly'

kooš (*kooneeš*) (morphologically not a particle, but a verb form) A 4.21 (plus -*ik*- in position 11) 'let's'

ʔutiʔal A 4.23, M 419 (morphologically not a particle, but a noun form) 'in order that, so that' (plus -*ik*- in position 11)

tuyoʔlal A 4.23, M 220 (morphologically not a particle, but a noun form) 'in order that, so that' (plus -*ik*- in position 11)

Of these only *ma(ʔ)* occurs regularly in Classical Yucatec.

2.3.6.2. CONJUNCT II. Among the PARTICLES which appear in this position are the following:

t A 2.9 (not really conjunct, since it does not require -*ik*-, but it is limited to use with transitive verbs) '(past completed)' (Modern Yucatec only)

(*ti*)*lik* M pp. 31–2 (plus -*ik*- in position 11) 'while . . . ing'

2.3.6.3. AUXILIARY I.

tan A 2.10 (plus *-ik-* in position 11)
'(continuing action)' A 4.14 (incompletive indicative)

hoop̓ A 2.11, (plus *-ik-* in position 11)
'(action which began in the past)'
A 4.17 (incompletive indicative)

ȼook A 2.12 (plus *-ik-* in position 11)
'(action which was, is, or will be over)'
A 4.15 (incompletive indicative)

bin A 2.16 '(action which may occur)'
A 3.18, A 3.11, A 3.12, A 3.49 (incompletive optative)

Of these verbal auxiliaries, *tan*, *hoop̓*, and *ȼook* are used only in Modern Yucatec, are conjunct (that is, require *-ik-* in transitive main verbs and transitive subject pronouns for intransitive main verbs), and require the simple incompletive indicative form of the main verb. Only *bin* is found both in Classical and in Modern Yucatec, is not conjunct, and requires the optative forms of the main verb.

2.3.6.4. AUXILIARY II.

(*bin*) *ʔinkax* A 2.15 (plus optative forms of transitive main verbs, preceded by the transitive subject pronouns, the simple incompletive indicative forms of intransitive main verbs with no subject pronouns, and the passives in *-bil*) A 4.56, A 4.55 'be going to . . . .'

This construction is found only in Modern Yucatec. Other inflected auxiliaries also occur in this position:

hop̓en M 208r, p. 30 (plus optative etc. as above with *ʔinkax*) 'began to . . . .'

ȼoken M 131r, p. 30 (plus optative etc. as above with *ʔinkax*) 'finish . . . .ing'

These constructions are found very rarely in Modern Yucatec, having been replaced by the conjunct forms in position 3 (Auxiliary I) (Classical Yucatec *hop̓i*, *ȼoki*).

2.3.6.5. SUBJECT PRONOUNS. The subject pronouns for transitive verbs (see 2.3. above) or for conjunct intransitives occur in this position. Occasionally subject pronouns in this position (5) are omitted when pre-

ceded in position (4) by other verb forms provided with such subject pronouns. Examples:

ʔinkat (ʔim)p̓átal wayeʔ 'I wish to stay here'

náaken (ʔiŋ)wenél 'I climbed up to sleep'

Sometimes position 5 pronouns are omitted after forms in preceding positions even when these latter are not verb forms or are not provided with subject pronouns. Examples:

ma (ʔu)kaštik 'he can't find it'

ten (ʔin)hantaal 'it is I who am being eaten'

ȼook (ʔu)b̓eetaal 'it was done'

2.3.6.6. REDUPLICATION. Occasional C_1V_1-reduplication of the first part of the verb root is found (see 2.1.2.C.).

2.3.6.7. ROOT II. In position 7, one of two roots (either verbal or nominal) may occur. With the root appearing in position 8, it may form a compound stem:

ȼib̓ 'paint, write' (with *ʔol* 'heart') (plus *-t-* in position 10) *ȼib̓ʔolt-* 'imagine'

2.3.6.8. ROOT I.

(with *men* 'work') *yax* 'abundant' (plus *-n-* in position 10) *menyax* (Modern Yucatec *meyah*) 'work' (*menyaxn-*) (Modern Yucatec *meyahn-*)

(with *p̓uk* 'bend over') *lah* 'all' (plus *-Ø-* in position 10) *p̓uklah-* '(all) bend over'

In position 8, if position 7 contains a verbal root, a nominal root may appear. If nothing appears in position 7, then position 8 is occupied by a verbal root, or by various stems, verbal or nominal. The types are the following:

CV *ȼa* 'give', *ča* 'take, bring', *b̓o* 'satisfy oneself', *še* 'vomit', *xo* 'grind (fine)', *xu* 'fall (on one's face)', *xe* 'abrir (puerta o ventana)', *wa* 'mentir, trampear', *le* 'engañar'

CVC *wiʔ* 'comer (generalmente)', *ʔuk̓* 'be thirsty', *šol* 'poner firme, apoyar', *čeex* 'laugh', *xan* 'eat', *čak* 'cocer en agua', *kim* 'die', *lop* 'double up' *xak̓* 'comer con golosina', *čuk* 'seize', *sit̓* 'jump', *ča⁹* 'let go', *hok̓* 'come out', *⁹em* 'come down', *xa¢̓* 'strike', *kuč* 'carry', *pul* 'throw', *lom* 'stab', *kon* 'sell', *⁹ok* 'enter', *sut* 'return', *keb̓* 'belch', *⁹uč* 'happen', *kub̓* 'deliver', *b̓in* 'go', *⁹aal* 'say', *kuš* 'live', *mek̓* 'hug', *k̓at* 'want', *luk̓* 'leave', *loč* 'twist', *lub̓* 'fall'

CVC (*<CV⁹C*) *⁹i(l)* 'see' (*<⁹i⁹-l-*), *tu(b̓)* 'spit' (*<tu⁹-b̓-*) (complex bases)

CV(C) (*<CVn, CVl*) *b̓i(s)* 'take' (*<b̓in-s-*), *ta(s)* 'bring' (*<tal-s-*) (complex bases)

CVV(C) (*<CVVl*) *b̓ee(t)* 'do' (*<b̓eel-t-*) (complex base)

C(VC) (*<Cal*) *t(ak)* 'come (optative)' (*<tal-ak*)

CVVC (*<CVC*) *k̓uub̓(ul)* 'be delivered' (*<k̓ub̓* 'deliver') (passive stem, A 3.48)

CVC-aan (past participle, A 3.47) *hul-aan* 'that which has arrived', *kim-en* 'that which has died', *čaan* 'that which is carried'

CVC-b̓il (supine, A 4.55) *xa¢̓-b̓il* 'to be flogged', *b̓eet-b̓il* 'to be done'

Other nominal stems: *⁹ok̓-ot* 'dance', *⁹aw-at* 'cry', *⁹ak̓ab̓* 'night'

Spanish roots: *⁹enkantar* 'enchant', *segir* 'follow', *maldisyon* 'curse'

2.3.6.9. STEM FORMATIVES. In position 9 verb-stem formatives appear, some deverbative (to transform simple verb roots into derived verb stems), others desubstantive (to transform nouns appearing in position 8 into verbs).

-Ø- (most frequent desubstantive suffix) (*⁹ok̓-ot-Ø-n-ax-Ø-i>*) *⁹ok̓otnaxi* 'he danced', *tan ⁹uy(ak̓ab̓-Ø-t-al>*) *ak̓ab̓-tal* 'it is becoming night', *tan ⁹in-(noxoč-Ø-t-al>)noxoč̓tal* 'I am getting big' (A 3.28, 38, 40)

-in- (desubstantive suffix) (base for transitive stems) *ka ⁹ič-in-sab̓* 'and he was bathed', *⁹uti⁹al ⁹ub̓uk-in-t* 'so that he puts on clothes', *kooš han-in-tik* 'let's make him our son-in-law' (A 3.22)

-an- (deverbative suffix) (verb root fre-

quently reduplicated, see 2.3.6.6) (base for intransitive stem) *tan ⁹u-si-sit-an-k-il* 'he is jumping' (A 3.16)

-Vk- (deverbative suffix) (base for intransitive stem) *kul-uk-b̓a-l* 'he is seated' (A 4.49 Form 7)

-el- (derverbative suffix) *w-oxel-maxeč* 'téngote conocido':*mamak ⁹ox-maik* 'ninguno lo sabe' (M 345r, 346)

-b̓(e)- (deverbative suffix) (base for transitive stems) *ma sah-b̓-esken* 'don't frighten me', *⁹uti⁹al ⁹akin-b̓-es* 'so that you may hurt him'; (desubstantive suffix) (base for intransitive stems) *kuči(⁹)-b̓-al* 'it is barking', *tan ⁹utu(⁹)-b̓-aal* 'it was being spat out' (A 3.29)

-b̓(a)- (deverbative suffix) (base for intransitive stems) *kuluk-b̓a-* 'be seated', *⁹al-b̓a-n-ak* 'is soft', *¢ik-b̓a-nakoon* 'so that we can converse'; (base for transitive stems) *¢ik-b̓a-t-ab̓* 'he was notified'

-kin- (-kun-) (deverbative suffix) (base for transitive stems) *ku ¢ookol ⁹ukuš-kin-tike⁹* 'after he revived him', *tanili ⁹uč̓il-kun-taal* 'immediately he was caused to lie down' (A 3.23)

-ka(b̓)- (deverbative suffix) (base for intransitive stems) *k ukul-ka(b̓)-t(i)k ⁹ub̓a* 'at once she sat down' (A 3.33)

-lan- (deverbative suffix) (base for transitive stems) (A 3.36) *t uk̓eš-lan-tax* 'they exchanged (clothes) with one another'

2.3.6.10. STATUSES. In position 10, status markers (transitive or intransitive) and status changers appear.

-n- (intransitive marker) (with Spanish stems, and with some monosyllabic, and nearly all polysyllabic Maya stems) (A 3.24) *b̓inak pribar-n-aki* 'maybe she will faint', *⁹awat-n-axi* 'it cried out', *k̓op-n-axen* 'I knocked' (A 3.53)

-(e)s- (transitive marker) (changes monosyllabic stems (intr.) into transitives) (A 3.25) *xok̓sab̓i* 'they were brought out', *han ȼookes* 'hurry up and finish it'

-*p*- (intransitive marker) (A 3.37, 3.31, 4.49) *tan k kin-p-axal* 'we are getting hurt', *ioč-p-axen* 'I tripped', *iok-p-alak* 'it is fragile'

-*č*- (intransitive marker) (A 3.27, 3.31, 3.54, 4.49) *koxaan-č-axen* 'I got sick', *noxoč-č-axi* 'he grew large', *binak sas-č-axaki* 'perhaps it will dawn', *ʔot-č-alak* 'is dropping'

-*k̇*- (intransitive marker) (A 3.37, 3.31, 4.49) *ioč-k̇-axen* 'I tripped', *kuk-k̇-alak* 'turns over repeatedly in bed'

-*l*- (intransitive marker) (A 3.34, 3.52, 4.49) *hek-l-axi* 'he rode', *kuš-l-aki* 'he will live', *tan ʔušimba-l* 'he is walking', *kaxakba-l* 'he resides in a village'

-*k*- (intransitive [?] marker) (A 3.16, 4.54) *tan ʔukak̇atan-k-il* 'he is crossing (the street)'

-*t*- (transitive marker) (with Spanish stems, and with some monosyllabic and most polysyllabic Maya stems) (bound to some roots) (required with some compound stems) (A 3.26, 4.50) *tin nombrar-t-ax* 'I appointed him', *ka maldisyon-t-aboob* 'and a curse was uttered against them', *wa ka ʔinxan-t-e* 'if I eat it', *ček-t-abi* 'he was stepped on', *ʔan-t-* 'help', *bee-t-* 'do', *tu činpol-t-ax* 'he bowed his head', *kaxetčin-t-ik* 'you throw it with all your might'; (intransitive marker) (A 3.26, 3.51, 4.49) *tan ʔusas-t-al* 'it is becoming dawn'

2.3.6.11. VOICES. In position 11, voice markers (active and passive) and the conjunct transitive status marker appear.

-(*a*)*x*- (active voice marker) (transitives A 4.9) (intransitives A 3.51 ff.) (A 3.10, 4.66, 3.47) *t ubeet-ax* 'he did it', *t apul-ax-eʔ* 'you threw it', *t ulomxoob* 'he stabbed them', *t ubeet-( )oob* 'they did it', *kain-ax-i* 'he sang', *hekl-ax-eni* 'I rode', *wal-ax-i (wal-x-i)* 'he stood up', *ka t uȼuȼ-ax-oob* 'and they kissed him', *t apul-x-en ȼonoteʔ*

'you threw me into the cenote', *ka t ukublant-ax* 'and he delivered them', *ʔinwil-ax-ma* 'I have seen it', *bin-ax-aan* 'he has gone', *ʔuk-ax-en* 'I was thirsty', *wiʔ-x-en* 'I was hungry', *ka segirn-ax ʔubin* 'and he kept on going', *yanč-ax-i* 'it came to pass', *t uyub-ax* 'he felt it'

-(*a*)*b*- (passive voice marker) (A 3.9, 3.49, 4.10) *bis-ab tiʔ* 'it was taken to him', *kaxolt-ab-i* 'he was recognized', *ka ȼa-b-al* 'it is given', *ka xant-ab-ak* 'it will be eaten', *kub-ab* 'it was delivered', *ka maldisyont-ab-oob* 'and a curse was uttered against them'

-(*i*)*k*- (conjunct transitive marker) (A 2.10, 11, 12, 3.20, 4.13 ff.) (A 2.13, 14) *tan ʔimbeet-ik* 'I was (am, will be) doing it', *hoop ʔubeet-ik-oob* 'they began to do it', *ȼook ʔabeet-ik* 'you had (have, will have) done it', *kbeet-ik-eeš* 'we (you plur. and I) do it time after time', *he ʔintas-ik-eʔ* 'I will (certainly) bring it', *kooš beet-ik* 'let us do it', *yan ʔuxant-k-oonoob* 'they will surely eat us up'

2.3.6.12. ASPECTS. In position 12, aspect markers (completive, incompletive, and perfective) appear.

-*Q*- (completive marker) (A 2.9, 4.9) (A 3.9, 10, 4.10) *t abeetax-Q-eeš* 'you did it', *lub-Q* 'he fell', *ʔilab-Q-eč* 'you are seen', *tuštab-Q-eč ʔakinsen* 'you were sent to kill me', *t inȼonax-Q xuntul kex* 'I shot a deer', *tal-Q-eč* 'you came'

-*Vl*- (incompletive marker) (A 3.48, 3.14, 3.57, 4.13, 4.49, 4.52) (with intransitive stems) *tan ʔinlub-ul* 'I am falling', *tan ʔintal(el)* 'I am coming', *kabet ʔinnáak-al* 'I need to climb'

-—- (incompletive marker) (with transitive stems) (Type I) *tan ʔabis-(—)ik teloʔ* 'you are taking it there', *yan ʔukins-(—)ik* 'she has to kill it', *ka yanxi ʔuča-(—)ik* 'and he happened to pick it up'

-*Q*- (incompletive marker) (with transitive stems) (Type II) *kambesax-Q*

ʔinkax 'yo enseño', xantantax-Q ʔukax t uniḃ 'pagado va lo que ha merecido (he is eating his just deserts)' menyax xanal ʔinkax 'estoy guisando de comer'

- - - (incompletive marker) (with some transitive stems) (Type III) kanan - - - ʔinkax 'yo guardo', payalči ʔinkax 'I am praying' (M p. 16)

-al- (incompletive marker) (A 3.14, 3.49, 4.52) (with complex intransitive bases) čen ṗelak ʔučanačt-al-e ʔ 'as soon as he retires', tanili ʔukult-al 'first he sits down'

-Vl- (incompletive marker) (A 3.9, 14, 49, 4.13) (with passive roots which have high tone on the root, and frequently double the root vowel) ȼaaḃ-al (or better -al below?), ƙuuḃ-ul 'it is delivered', k upuuƙ-ul 'it is stirred up'

-(a)-al) (incompletive marker) (A 3.9, 14, 15, 49, 4.13) (with passive stems) (Classical Yucatec -aḃ-al is Mod. -a-al) ȼa-aḃ-al 'it is given', ʔutiʔal ʔument-a-al 'in order that it be made', k uyens-a-al 'it is being brought down', k uyant-a-al 'he is being helped', ten xant-a-al 'it is I who am being eaten', tan ʔabis-a-al teloʔ 'you are being taken there'

-ma(x)- (completive [?] perfective marker) (with transitive stems or roots) (sometimes follows active voice -ax-, sometimes is attached directly to the base) (A 3.21, M 278) (A 4.66) ʔinwilax-ma 'I have seen it', k ḃeet-ma 'we have made it', kuyilik ʔumuȼ-ma ʔuyičeʔ 'when he sees that her eyes are closed', woxel-ma 'sabido lo tengo', ten ʔox-ma-ik 'yo lo sé (tengo sabido)', le suuk ʔukuč-ma-x-oʔ 'the hay he has carried'

2.3.6.13. MOODS. In position 13, mood markers (imperative and optative) appear.

-Q- (imperative mood marker) (A 2.18, 4.37, 38) (with transitive stems) ȼa-Q tiʔ 'give it to him!', ča-Q-eeš 'you (pl.) turn it loose!', mas k akuḃ-Q 'you

had better deliver it', le kan ɩ́anakeʔ, k anukik-Q 'when she speaks, answer her!', ma (ʔa)xantik-Q 'don't eat it!', ʔuƙ-Q xunṗit haʔ 'drink a little water!'

-e (imperative mood marker) (A 2.18, 4.37, 38) (with transitive stems of Type III in Classical Yucatec, and with all stems in utterance final in Modern Yucatec) ȼa-e 'give it!', xant-e 'eat it!', keč haʔ ka ʔawuƙ-e 'drink at least some water', xoyat-e ʔinway '¡riega mi celda!' (M p. 16)

-(V) (imperative mood marker) (M pp. 16–17) (with transitive stems of Type I in utterance final, that is, after simple roots with -Vḃ optative mood) (in Classical Yucatec only) ȼɩ́k-i '¡obedece tú!', ƙúp-u '¡córtalo!', mól-o '¡júntalo!'

-a (imperative mood marker) (M p. 17) (with complex transitive bases) (Classical Yucatec form surviving in Mod.?) ʔil-á '¡mira!' (Solís 398)

-en(-) (imperative mood marker) (A 2.18, 4.37, 38, 57) (with intransitive stems or roots) ʔem-en-eeš 'you (pl.) come down!', xoƙ-en-Q 'come out!', š-en 'go!', kot-en 'come!', kul-en-eeš 'you (pl.) sit down!' (A 3.19)

-Vḃ (optative mood marker) (M pp. 14-15) (with transitive verb roots of Type I) (Classical Yucatec only) bin ʔinȼɩk-iḃ 'yo obedeceré', bin ʔamol-oḃ 'tú juntarás', ḃin katúp-uḃ 'apagaremos'

-Q- (optative mood marker) (M pp. 9, 14, 25, 26) (A 2.15, 16, 18, 20, 21, 23, 3.18, 49, 4.37 ff.) (both Classical and Modern Yucatec) (with transitive stems of Type II in Classical, and with those of Types I, II, and III in Modern) bin ʔakambes-Q-eeš 'vosotros enseñaréis', ḃin ʔinkušba-Q 'lo aborreceré', lay kučiyo bin ʔakims-Q-ik ƙeƙen 'este es el cuchillo con que has de matar el puerco', ḃin ʔinkax ʔinkuḃ-Q teč 'I am going to deliver it to you', mas k akuḃ-Q 'you had better deliver it', *ka hokok ʔuyuk-Q-ooḃ* 'they come out in order to drink', *ḃaaš k awaal tieʔ* 'whatever you tell him', *ʔahančak-Q ʔasieeš* 'you will cut your wood in a hurry', *ʔakat ka ʔinɖa-Q tečʔ* 'do you want me to give it to you?'

-e (optative mood marker) (M 12, 14, 16) (with transitive stems of Type III in Classical Yucatec, and with all stems in utterance final in Modern Yucatec) (A 3.18, 50, 4.40, 4.41) *ḃin ʔaxant-e* 'you will eat it', *ḃin ʔin-kanant-e* 'yo guardaré', *ḃin ʔintoxl-e* 'lo desterraré', *ʔutiʔal yaal-e* 'in order that he may say it', *ʔinkat ka ʔuxant-e* 'I want him to eat it', *ka ḃin teloʔ ʔukašt-e* 'and he went there to look for it', *ka ḃin ʔučukte-e ʔutiʔal ka yil-e wa k upahtal ʔuɖonik* 'and he went to lie in ambush to see whether it was possible to shoot it'

-Vk- (optative mood marker) (M pp. 8–9, 13) (with intransitive roots) (A 2.16, 18, 20, 23, 3.11. 49, 4.41) (A 3.11) (also with passive stems with double vowel and high tone) *ḃin kim-ik-eč* 'you will die', *ḃin luḃ-k-eeš!* 'don't you (pl.) fall!', *wa ka t-ak (tal-ak)* 'if he had come (and he had not)', *ken t-ak-eneʔ (tal-ak-en-eʔ)* 'when I come', *waalen teloʔ, ka ɖikḃan-ak-oon* 'stop there so that we may talk', *ka hok-ok ʔukikel* 'so that the blood may come out', *ka kuuḃ-uk* 'that it may be delivered'

( )-ak (optative mood marker) (A 3.11, 49) (A 3.12, 13) (A 4.41) (with intransitive and passive stems, these high-toned) *ka kóntestart-ak* 'she will be answered', *ka kins-á-ak* 'he will be killed', *wa ka ḃis-a-ak-en* 'if I had been taken', *ka manlah-ak* 'that all be bought', *tooneʔ, ma kkat ka kins-a-ak-ečiʔ* 'we did not want you to be killed', *tu yoʔlal ka tas-á-ak* 'so that he would be brought', *ḃik ʔalkaḃn-ak-eeš* 'don't you (pl.) run!'

2.3.6.14. OBJECT PRONOUNS. The object pronouns (A 2.5, 3.8) appear in position 14 (see 2.3. above). The third person object is always -Q. The marking of plurality in the third person object is optional: *ča-Q-e* 'take him (them)'.

2.3.6.15. SUBJECT PRONOUNS I. The subject pronouns appear in position 15 (see 2.3. above). In Modern Yucatec in the first person plural (A 2.5) subject pronoun for intransitives and passives the form *-oon* either excludes the listener or includes only one listener (?). A plurality of listeners requires a second suffix in position 16. The third person subject pronoun is always -Q. The marking of plurality in the third person subject is optional: *ʔu-ɖonik* 'he (they) shoot(s) it'.

2.3.6.16. SUBJECT PRONOUNS II. The only element to appear in position 16 is *-eeš* added after *-oon* of the first plural to indicate a plurality of listeners:

luḃ-oon-eeš 'you (pl.) and I fell'

2.3.6.17. TERMINALS. In position 17 various terminal suffixes appear:

-eʔ, -aʔ, -oʔ (terminals suffixed to the final element of a phrase introduced by *ḃei* 'thus, just like', *he(l)* '(demonstrative)', *te(l)* 'here (there)' *wai* 'here (abouts)') (A 4.51)

-aʔ (nearer to the speaker) (A 3.5) *ḃey-aʔ* 'in this manner, like this', *ḃei kuḃeetaal-aʔ* 'this is the way it is done', *heel-aʔ* 'here it is, here they are', *he le ṗok t immanax-aʔ* 'here is the hat I bought', *lel-aʔ* 'this (one)', *le peḱ-aʔ* 'this dog', *teel-aʔ* 'here', *way-aʔ* 'this way', *le ha-aʔ* 'this water', *hel ʔimmačma( )* 'look I am holding it' (-aʔ omitted)

-oʔ (nearer to the listener) (A 3.5) *ḃey-oʔ* 'in that manner, like that, by so doing, that being the case', *ḃei kan ʔaḃeet-oʔ* 'that is the way you are going to do it', *heel-oʔ* 'there it is, there they are', *heleč-oʔ* 'there you are!', *leel-oʔ* 'that (one)', *le peḱ-oʔ* 'that dog', *le peḱ ʔamačma-oʔ* 'that dog you are holding', *teel-oʔ* 'there'

-eɂ '(in the neighborhood of or toward the speaker)' (A 3.6) *heel-eɂ* '(it will) certainly (be done)', *way-eɂ* 'here', *koten way-eɂ* 'come here!', *wai čemaš-eɂ* 'here in Chemax', *beorita-eɂ* 'right away', *wai banda-eɂ* 'in this region'

-eɂ '(clause terminal)' (A 3.6, 4.16, 4.44, 4.58) *he ɂawilik-eɂ* 'ya verás', *he ɂubeetaal samal-eɂ* 'it will be done tomorrow', *wa k awolt-eɂ*, *he ɂatal ɂa-čanɂanten-eɂ* 'if you were willing, you would come and help me a little', *wa ka kinsaak-eɂ* 'if he had been killed', *le ka kuč-eɂ* 'when he arrived'

-i(ɂ) '(utterance terminal)' (A 3.7, 4.59) *kimi* 'he died', *lúkoobi* 'they left', *ma bineči?* 'you did not go', *ma ɂilabeni* 'I was not seen', *ma ɖaab teni?* 'it was not given to me', *ma ɂiŋwohli* 'I don't know', *ti? k uɂenkantartal maki?* 'there is where people are enchanted', *čaooni?* 'turn us loose', *xokok xun tuli* 'let one come out', *maš tuuni?* 'who, then?', *ɂadyoseeši?* 'goodbye, you-all!', *dyos bootik teči?* 'thank (God reward) you!', *xun puli* 'at once', *tanili?* 'first', *ka kinsabi—le ɂokolo?* 'and the thief was—finally—killed', *hélili k tal ɂokkiné?* 'we will surely come this evening'

When the constructions in an utterance (a complex verb form alone or with satellites) require more than one terminal, *-aɂ* takes precedence over all others, *-eɂ* takes precedence over *-oɂ*, and all three of these take precedence over *-iɂ*.

le naoɂ (that house': *ka ɂok ɂičil le nae?* 'when he went into the house'

ma ɂičkinaki? 'they have not bathed': *he ken ma ɂičkinake?* 'those who have not bathed'

All may be omitted under certain conditions (*le libro* 'that book', *he ɂinčama* 'here I have fetched it', *le bakooɓ* 'those bones', omitting *-oɂ* after *o*, *-aɂ* after *a*, and *-oɂ* after *-ooɓ* respectively).

2.4. Nouns.
Nouns are of three kinds (1) roots, (2) compound stems, and (3) complex (derived) stems. Derived or complex stems, in turn, may be divided into two major classes, the desubstantives, and the deverbatives.

2.4.1. Noun roots.
There is a great variety of noun roots: *kax* 'village', *kin* 'day', *na* 'house', *mak* 'person', *kab* 'hand', *paal* 'child', *kak* 'fire', *če?* 'tree', *kiiš* 'thorn(s)', *kiwik* 'market', *yum* 'father', *ko* 'belly', *luum* 'earth', *ɂoč* 'opossum', *ni?* 'nose', *meeš* 'beard', *hool* 'head', *poop* 'mat', *ɖuk* 'gizzard', *kop* 'hoop', *ha?* 'water', *kal* 'throat', *bub* 'tadpole'

Most of these are monosyllables. Some are unanalyzable polysyllables.

2.4.2. Compound stems.
Nouns combine with nouns to form compound noun stems: *kan* 'four', *tiɖ* 'corner': *kantiɖ* 'cosa cuadrada' *yaš* 'green', *če?* 'tree': *yašče?* 'ceiba (bombax ceiba)', *kik* 'blood', *čoč* 'tripe': *kikčoč* 'piles', *luum* 'tierra': *luumluum* 'cosa terregosa (llena de tierra)', *poop* 'mat', *te?'* tree': *poopte?* 'bridge', *toos* 'dust', *ha?* 'water': *toosha?* 'mist'.

Some of these initial elements may not be substantives in the narrow sense (that is, may not accept the possessive affixes nor the plural suffix), and yet be subject to some type of derivation associated neither with verbs nor with particles (such as the ability to combine with classifiers, characteristic of the numerals).

2.4.3. Complex stems.
Complex noun stems may be deverbative or desubstantive.

2.4.3.1. Deverbative noun stems.
Deverbative noun stems may be divided into two groups, (1) those which function as nouns of action (or, with *ɂax-* . . . , as agents), as nouns results of action ('that which has . . .', 'that which has been . . . ed'), or nouns of future action ('that which is to be . . . ed', 'that which may be . . . ed, is worthy of being . . . ed'), and (2) those which function in a variety of other ways (adding a number of different *-VC* suffixes). Deverbative nouns of

group (1) may be formed freely from any verb. Those of group (2) tend to be frozen forms, and their suffixes (except for *-il*) to be limited in the number of verb roots to which they are applied.

2.4.3.1.1. DEVERBATIVE NOUN STEMS (PRODUCTIVE).

(-*Vl*)-Q (based on the intransitive active incompletive) *kím-il-*Q 'dying', *ti kímil* 'to (be) dy(ing)', *ʔax-kímil* 'person (who is) dying'; *ʔém-el-*Q 'descending', *ti ʔémel* 'to (be) descend(ing)', *ʔax-ʔémel* 'person (who is) descending'; *xán-al-*Q 'eating', *šen ti xánal* '¡véte a comer! (to be eating)'—(or on the transitive passive incompletive stem) *lóx-ol-*Q 'being rescued', *ti lóxol* 'to be (being) rescued', *ʔax-lóxol* 'person (who is) being rescued'; *kúub-ul-*Q 'being delivered', *ti kúubul* 'to be (being) delivered', *ʔax-kúubul* 'person (who is) being delivered'

(-*al*)-Q (based on the intransitive active incompletive stem) *čánačt-al-*Q 'retiring', *ti čánačtal* '(be) retir(ing)' *ʔax-čánačtal* 'person (who is) retiring'

(-*á-al*)-Q (based on the transitive passive incompletive stem) *ment-á-al-*Q 'being made', *ti mentáal* 'to be (being) made', *ʔax-mentáal* 'person (who is) being made' (Modern Yucatec only) (A 3.15, 49, 4.13)

(-*áb-al*)-Q (based on the transitive passive incompletive stem) *kambes-áb-al-*Q 'being taught', *ti kambesábal* 'to be (being) taught', *ʔax-kambesábal* 'person (who is being) taught' (Classical Yucatec) (M p. 11)

(-*íil*)-Q (based on the intransitive active perfective stem)(?) *nak-í-il-*Q 'having gone up', *ti nakíil* 'to have gone up', *ʔax-nakíil* 'person (who is) having gone up' (M p. 9 **nacijl** only occurs, other forms analogical?) (Classical Yucatec only?)

(-*áx-il*)-Q (based on the transitive active perfective stem)(?) *kambesáxil* 'hav-

ing taught (it)' (M p. 11) (Classical Yucatec only?)

(-*áb-il*)-Q (based on the transitive passive perfective stem)(?) *kambesábil* 'having been taught' (M pp. 18-19) (Classical Yucatec only)

-*bíl* (based on any transitive verb stem) (A 3.17, 4.55) (with a variety of meanings, most of them projective, *not* retrospective) (Modern Yucatec) *kat-bíl-oobeʔ* 'they should be asked', *bin ʔukax xant-bíl* 'it is going to be eaten', *kaštbíl* 'it should be looked for', *xač bíl* 'he should be flogged', *bin ʔukax beet-bíl* 'it is going to be done', *tin tuštah čá-bíl-eč* 'I sent for you (I sent someone you were to be fetched)', *čam-bíl bálčeʔ* 'soaked BALCHE', *hum-pel mentbíl číč* 'an artificial bird'

(-—)-Q (based on transitive active incompletive stems, Type I) (M p. 12) *čik-—-*Q 'obeying (him)', *ti čik* 'to (be) obey(ing) (him)', *ʔax-čik* 'hombre cortés y cortesano (person (who is) obeying) (him)'

(-*ax*-Q)-Q (based on transitive active incompletive stems, Type II) (M p. 11) (A 3.10, 4.9) *kambes-ax-Q-*Q 'teaching (him)', *ti kambesáx* 'to (be) teach(ing) (him)', *ʔax-kambesáx* 'person (who is) teaching (him)'

(-— —)-Q (based on transitive active incompletive stems, Type III) (M p. 12) (Solís 312) *kanáan-— —-*Q 'guarding (him)', *ti kanán* 'to (be) guard(ing) (him)', *ʔax-kanán* 'person (who is) guarding'

(-*ik*-Q)-Q (based on transitive active (in)completive stems in conjunct construction) (see 2.3.6.11 and 2.3.3 above) (M p. 12) (Type I) *čik-ik-Q-*Q '(while) obeying (him)', *ti čikik* '(while in a position) to (be) obey(ing) (him)'

(-*ik*-Q-)-Q (based on transitive active (in)completive stems in conjunct construction) (see 2.3.6.11 and 2.3.3 above) (M p. 11) (Type II) *kambes-*

ik-Q̱-Q̱ '(while) teaching (him)', *ti kambesik* '(while in a position) to (be) teach(ing) (him)'

(*-ik-Q̱*)*-Q̱* (based on transitive active (in)completive stems in conjunct construction) (see 2.3.6.11 and 2.3.3 above) (M p. 12) (Type III) *kanant-ik-Q̱-Q̱* '(while) guarding (him)', *ti kanantik* '(while in a position) to (be) guard(ing) (him)'

(*-a(lʔ)*)*-an* (based on intransitive active incompletive stems) (M pp. 9, 18) (A 3.45, 4.53) 'that which is . . . ed' *nak-á-an* 'cosa que está subida (levantada)' (M p. 9, 316), *em-á-an* 'cosa que se ha abajado' (M 164), *bin-án* 'el que es (ó ha) ido' (M. p. 18, 52r), *man-á-an* 'cosa que ya ha pasado' (M p. 18, 294r), *kim-én* 'cosa muerta'

(*-ax*)*-an* (based on (in)transitive active (in)completive stems) (M p. 11, 18) (A 3.47, 4.53) 'that which is . . . ed' *kambesá-an* 'lo enseñado' (cf. *kambes-ab-ax-án* 'cosa enseñada', (M p. 18) (?), *binah-áan* 'he has gone' (A 3.47), *lilatax-áan* 'cosa que está rociada', *nuȼáan* 'cosa que está cumplida', *kal-áan-eč* 'you are drunk', *kal-áan-en* 'I am locked up', *lub-áan* 'cosa que está caída' (M 274r) 'it is fallen' (A 4.53), *le mak koh-áan-oʔ* 'the man who is sick', *koh-áan le makóʔ* 'that man is sick', *ȼik-áan* 'cosa obedecida', *ken-aan* 'cosa adornada', *čel-a(a)n-tak* 'cosas echadas'

(*-V́l*)*-Q̱* (based on transitive passive incompletive stems) (M p. 19) 'that which is . . . ed' *lub-úl-Q̱* 'cosa caída', *xut-úl-Q̱* 'cosa despegada', *čax-ál* cosa contrahecha', *wak-ál* 'cosa hendida',

paʔ-ál 'quebrado', *ȼik-íl* 'lo obedecido', *mal-él* 'cosa que ya ha pasado'

-íil 'worthy of' (A 3.45) *ȼik-ȼil* 'worthy of respect' (M 118r)

-ben 'worthy of, -able, -ible' (A 3.41) *ȼik-ben* 'worthy of respect', *ča -ben* 'acceptable'

2.4.3.1.2. DEVERBATIVE NOUN STEMS (NON-PRODUCTIVE).

-Vb *xaȼ-ab* 'stick, club', *čuy-ub* 'hanger, rack'

-íl *kuč-íl* 'burden', *kim-íl* 'death'

-ál *xan-ál* 'food'

-úl *meyh-úl* 'task'

2.4.3.2. DESUBSTANTIVE NOUN STEMS.

-Vb *ʔak-ab* 'night'

-Vm *ʔul-um* 'turkey', *kit-ám* 'wild boar', *ȼel-ém* 'hornet'

-Vč *ʔot-oč* 'house', *tun-ič* 'stone', *bek-eč* 'lizard'

-el *bak-el* 'bones', *ȼoȼ-el* 'hair', *bak-el* 'meat'

2.4.4. NOUN INFLECTION. Nouns are optionally inflected for plural (suffix *-oob*) and may be possessed (affixes are the same as the subject pronouns for transitive verbs, see 2.3 above). Some nouns are inherently possessed, that is, do not appear in their simple form without the possessive affixes. When such nouns stand alone, they take the suffix *-il* as a mark of their independent status. Nouns in *-il* have many other functions. Some derived nouns are frequently used in attributive function. Of these, those in *-ak* have special functions.

2.4.4.1. NOMINAL POSSESSIVE AFFIXES. Before stems beginning in infirm *ʔ* (Spanish vowel-initial loans have firm *ʔ*) and in infirm *h* (not all instances of *h* are infirm) the following set appears:

Sg.	Pl.				
1) *w* . . .	1) *k(a)* . . .	*wok* (*ʔiŋwok*)	*kaʔok*	*ʔok* 'foot'	
2) *ʔaw* . . .	2) *ʔaw* . . . *eeš*	*ʔawok*	*ʔawokeeš*		
3) *y* . . .	3) *y* . . . *oob*	*yok* (*ʔuyok*)	*yokoob*	(*ʔuyokoob*)	
		weʔ (*ʔiŋweʔ*)	*kaheʔ*	*heʔ* 'egg'	
		ʔaweʔ	*ʔawaʔeeš*		
		yeʔ (*ʔuyeʔ*)	*yeʔoob*	(*ʔuyeʔoob*)	

Before stems beginning in any other consonants the following set appears:

Sg. 1) *ʔin* . . .	Pl. 1) *ka* . . .	*ʔinyum*	*kayum*	*yum* 'father'
2) *ʔa* . . .	2) *ʔa* . . . *eeš*	*ʔayum*	*ʔayumeeš*	
3) *ʔu* . . .	3) *ʔu* . . . *ooḃ*	*ʔuyum*	*ʔuyumooḃ*	

The possessive affixes, when attached to the stem *ḃa* 'person', form combinations which serve as pronominal objects which are (in Classical Yucatec) independent of the verb. In Modern Yucatec these objects are usually phonologically fused with the verb.

Sg. 1) *ʔimḃa*	Pl. 1) *kaḃa*
2) *ʔaḃa*	2) *ʔaḃaeeš*
3) *ʔuḃa*	3) *ʔuḃaooḃ*

For the fused form note:

ku wálkatkuḃa 'right away he stopped (himself)' (*wal-ka(ḃ)-t-(i)k-Ǫ ʔu-ḃa*)

2.4.4. SUFFIX *-il*. This suffix has a wide variety of uses:

(1) possession by a thing (rather than by a person): *ʔintása* 'mi taza': *ʔutasa-il refektoryo* 'la taza del Refectorio'; *ʔimpoop* 'mi petate': *ʔupoopil ʔinkama* 'el petate de mi cama'; *ʔušiwil ḱaknab* 'la yerba del mar'; *ʔuyaweil ʔinway* 'la llave de mi celda'

(2) what is proper to someone: *yuʔun pádre* 'la carta del Padre': *yuʔunil pádre* 'la carta del Padre (la que envían a él)'; *ʔusaxal xwan* 'el temor el que tiene Juan': *ʔusaxalil xwan* 'el que se tiene de él'; *ʔuyail dyos yetel lakḃil* 'el amor que se tiene a Dios y al prójimo'

(3) specified object of possession: *ʔinyamexenil* 'mi amado hijo', *ʔinɟikɟilyumil* 'mi reverenciable Padre', *ʔimmatánhúunil* 'mi recibida carta'

(4) specified object among others: *¿ḃal ti čeʔil loʔʔ* 'what tree is that?'

(5) abstract characteristic: *winik* 'hombre': *winikil* "humanidad" (*kawinikil* 'nuestra h.'); *ɟeem* 'cosa flaca': *ɟeemil* 'la flaqueza';

loḃ 'cosa mala': *loḃil* 'maldad'; *ʔuɟ* 'cosa buena': *ʔuɟil* 'bondad'

(6) characteristic illness: *ya ʔokil ʔinkax* 'tengo enfermedad de pies'; *ya ʔičil ʔukax pádre* 'está enfermo de los ojos el Padre'; *ya ɟémil ʔinkax* 'tengo mal de pecho'

(7) proper for . . ., characteristic of . . .: *ʔuɟ nok ti ʔéešil* 'buena manta para pantalones'; *manán ʔišɨm ti mánil* 'no hay maíz para comprar'; *mataḃ ʔúlum ti šáčeil* 'no se hallan gallinas en parte alguna'; *ʔoki ti winikil* 'entró en ser hombre (hízose hombre)'; *ʔoki ti tuničil ʔučuplil lot* 'hízose piedra la mujer de Lot'

(8) material of which something is made: *maskaḃil* 'cosa de hierro', *ḱatil* 'cosa de barro', *maskaḃil ḃat* 'hacha de hierro', *ʔaseroil ḃat* 'hacha de acero'

(9) from such and such a place: *kaknaḃil čič* 'pájaros de la mar'; *wiɟil tunič* 'piedra de la sierra'; *náčil winik* 'hombre de lejos, extranjero'; *káxil winik* 'hombre del pueblo'

2.4.4.3. SUFFIX *-ak*. This suffix (A 3.12, 4.48, 49) characterizes past or present result: *luḱak* (*luḱuk*) 'he has left', *ʔučak* (*ʔučuk*, *ʔučik*) 'it has (had) happened', *sábadoak* 'last Saturday', *talak* 'he has come', *sistak* 'it has subsided', *hehetek* 'it is cracked in several places', *sahak* 'he is afraid', *ḱušuk* 'it burns', *ṗoolak* 'it is full of blisters', *lelemnak* 'it is brilliant', *ṗučalak* 'it is shredded', *kušlik* 'he is alive', *tokpalak* 'it is fragile', *ʔakaknak* 'it is slimy', *kopokḃal* 'it is coiled', *takaanak* 'it is stuck', *čukaantakooḃ* 'they are trapped', *wai kaxakḃalen* 'I live here', *maʔ sahaken tiiʔ* 'I am not afraid of him', *tiʔ tučaanak le čan kuukóʔ tu ḱaḃ čeʔ* 'there was

241

the little squirrel sitting up on the branch of the tree'

2.4.4.4. ATTRIBUTIVES. Some nominal derivatives (as well as some nominal roots) are used primarily in attributive function.

> le **noxoč** kaxá^ʔ 'this LARGE town'
> le he^ʔ **kačalé^ʔ** 'the BROKEN egg'
> le **čakḃil** kašó^ʔ 'the COOKED chicken'
> le **hac** ^ʔolȼil 'the POOREST one'

2.5. PARTICLES. Although particles are not inflected as verbs and nouns are, they may be conjugated (with an intervening zero copula), and they may be compounded, often multiply.

2.5.1. PARTICLE CONJUGATION. The independent pronominal subjects or objects contain a particle (*t-* or *l-*, *la-*) combined with the intransitive subject pronouns:

Sg. 1)	*ten(i)* 'yo (soy)'	Pl. 1)	*toon* 'nosotros (somos)'
2)	*teč* 'tú (eres)'	2)	*teeš* 'vosotros (sois)'
3)	*lay* 'él (es)'	3)	*looḃ* 'ellos (son)'

¿*makš ḃataḃ wayé^ʔ*? '¿quién es gobernador aquí?', *teni* 'yo soy', *ten t inxaȼax* 'a mí me herí', *teč k impayik* 'a ti te debo'

2.5.2. PARTICLE COMPOUNDING. Numeral particles may be compounded with numeral classifiers (possibly to be considered as nouns?) and with other particles: *xumṗel* 'one (piece)', *ka^ʔṗel* 'two (piece)', *^ʔošṗel* 'three (piece)', *xunxuntul* 'de uno en uno', *ka^ʔka^ʔtul ^ʔušimḃal pádreooḃ* 'de dos en dos andan los Padres', ¿*xaytenxi ^ʔapočik mísa^ʔ* '¿cuántas veces menospreciaste la misa?', *ka^ʔtenxi ^ʔinḳasik suḳin* 'dos veces he quebrantado el ayuno'

2.5.3. PREPOSITIONAL PARTICLES. The only prepositional particle is *ti*. It has multiple meanings: *ti ^ʔu taatá* 'to the father', *ti xumpel ḳánče^ʔ* 'on a stool', *ti le ḳaanó^ʔ* 'in the hammock', *t(i l)e ḃeó^ʔ* 'by the road', *tálen ti yotoč ḳu* 'vengo de la Iglesia', *ȼa ti pádre* 'dálo al Padre', *ḃenel ^ʔinkax ti na* 'voy a casa', *ti če^ʔ* 'con palo', *máni ti wotoč* 'pasó por mi casa', *t intan* 'según mi parecer (por mi palabra)', *ti nač táli* 'viniendo de lejos', *ti*

242

neȼan 'estando cerca', *ti loḃ ^ʔuḃeel* 'siendo malas sus obras', *ti yan* 'habiendo', *ti kulán* 'estando en casa', *ti ya ^ʔupol* 'doliéndole la cabeza', *ti kimil ^ʔinkax* 'estando yo enfermo', *ti tox yol* 'estando sano', *ti čapaxán* 'estando enfermo', *máni t uyam winikooḃ* 'pasó por entre la gente', *ka ian t umen le ḃašal takinó^ʔ* 'she was called by the gambler', *t inwiknál* 'near me'

Other prepositional expressions are derived from nouns or verbs, although they may be used analogously as particles: *^ʔičíl le ḳáako^ʔ* 'into the fire', *yokol le pílao^ʔ* 'over the basin', *ka ḃin yétel pédro* 'and they went with Pedro'

2.5.4. DEMONSTRATIVE PARTICLES. Demonstrative particles are various. Some are independent. Others are linked to an enclitic which marks clause-end: **he** *lik ^ʔutanlik dyose^ʔ*, *lay ḃin ḃootaḃak* **lo^ʔ** 'EL QUE sirve a Dios, ÉSE será pagado', *layla^ʔ* 'ESTO es', **he** *lae^ʔ* 'él', **he** *ḃe^ʔ* 'eso'

The function of the **-i(^ʔ)** is to mark utterance (clause?) final: *méntax ^ʔinkáxi* 'ya lo hago', *ma^ʔ ^ʔimméntei* 'aún no lo he hecho', *téni lo^ʔ* 'yo soy ése de quien se trata', *ma^ʔ ḃay* 'no es así', *ḃay ḃe^ʔ* 'así es eso', *^ʔaxkími-looni* 'cierto es que hemos de morir', *la^ʔi lo^ʔ* 'aquél es', *hooni ha^ʔ t ule^ʔ makal* 'somos como el agua en la hoja del macal'

The particle **le** functions together with the terminals *-a^ʔ* 'this' and *-o^ʔ* 'that' with the noun and its modifiers in between: **le** *hač ḳaasó^ʔ* 'the worst one'

The particle **^ʔu**—formally identical with the third person (singular) possessive prefix—functions as a kind of weak demonstrative in a fashion similar to that of the articles in English or Spanish: *^ʔu núukul* 'the tool', *^ʔu hóol* 'the head', *^ʔu kal* 'the neck', *^ʔu y ok* 'the foot', *^ʔu laḳ (^ʔu hel)* 'the one, the other, another'

Together with the *-il* of proper possession

(see 2.4.4.2 above), it has a similar function: *ʔu kašiloob́* 'the chickens'

Occasionally the numerals function in a manner similar to that of the indefinite articles in English or Spanish: *humṕel kax* 'a village', *huntul čan paaleʔ* 'a little boy'

The particle *tax* (Classical Yucatec, M 402r, 403) (Modern Yucatec *tahtiali, letiʔ,* Solís 179) serves as a demonstrative with relative function equivalent to English 'whose' or Spanish 'cuyo': *lay tax grásya yának t apišaneeš* 'éste es cuya gracia more en vuestras ánimas', *lay tax nok̓ loʔ* 'aquél es cuya es la ropa', *makš tax ȼimin loʔ* '¿cuyo es este caballo?', *maʔ mak tax tiʔali* 'no tiene dueño (no hay quien cuyo dueño aquel)', *¿makš tax kaxloxil xesukrístoʔʔ* '¿cuyo hijo es nuestro Redentor Jesucristo? (preguntando por su madre)'

2.5.5. ADVERBIAL PARTICLES. Among adverbial particles are these:

tiʔ, laʔ, tun 'then, there' (Modern Yucatec) (*tiʔ* and *tun* also Classical)

napulak 'right away', *sam* 'a while after', *tak* 'until', *nač* 'far', *naȼ* 'near', *seb́* 'soon', *seb́ táakene* 'I will come soon' (Classical *napul,* M 324, *sam,* 98r, *tak,* M 397r, *nač,* M 317, *naȼ* ibid., *seb́,* M 100r)

Among adverbial particles there are those which are associated specifically with verbs in conjunct form (see §2.3, 2.3.3, 2.3.6.11), those which are incorporated into the verb complex (position 7), and those which require no specific linkage with the verb but are associated in phrase construction with it.

2.5.5.1. "PARTÍCULAS DEL PRESENTE."

2.5.5.1.1. CONJUNCT.

(li)k 'suélese': *lik yalik sam páblo* 'dice San Pablo', *lik yálab́al* 'dícese', *ximak lik ʔusukintik xanáleʔ, ʔusukinte ʔub́a ti sípileʔ* 'el que ayuna la comida, que se abstenga de pecar', *ʔinkeb́an lik wok̓tik* 'lloro (actualmente) mi pecado', *b́al k awok̓tik* '¿qué lloras?', *teč k impayik* 'a ti te llamo'

taač 'tener costumbre': *maʔ taač ʔim-*

b́eeltik 'no lo suelo hacer', *taač ʔinkantik xalač winik* 'acostumbrado estoy de hablar con el gobernador'

latulax 'hasta que': *maʔ ʔab́enél latulax walik teč* 'no te vayas hasta que te lo diga'

ʔučeb́al 'para que, en que, con que': *tánle dyos ʔučeb́al ʔab́enél ti kaan* 'sirve a Dios para que vayas al cielo'

xunak 'infinitas veces': *xunak walik tiʔ* 'dígoselo infinitas veces'

ʔamal 'todas las veces que': *ʔamal wub́ik ȼeʔ, wok̓tik ʔinkeb́an* 'todas las veces que oigo sermón, lloro mis pecados'

b́aili 'ordinariamente': *b́aili ʔuxaȼiken wičan* 'ordinariamente me azota mi marido'

b́ay 'así': *b́ay bin ʔukib́ik dyos teeš* 'así lo hará Dios con vosotros'

2.5.5.1.2. INCORPORATED.

yaš 'primero': *ʔinyašb́eeltik loeʔ* 'ésta es la primera vez que hago eso', *maʔ ʔayašʔilikeeš* 'no es la primera vez que veis' (requires conjunct *-ik-*)

susu 'a menudo': *bin ʔasusub́eelte* 'haráslo con continuación' (does not require conjunct *-ik-*)

2.5.5.1.3. OTHERS.

k(ax) 'actualmente': *halmax ʔinkax teeš* 'os estoy diciendo', *xanal ʔukib́ax* 'estaba (estuve) comiendo', *xanal bin ʔukib́* 'estaré comiendo', *kambes ʔink̓ib́ax ti paalalooб́* 'enseñando estuve a los muchachos' (this is actually a verb used in a phrasal construction)

b́al 'estar a pique': *talb́alooб́* 'ya quieren venir', *kučb́aloon ti kax* 'ya queremos llegar al pueblo'

2.5.5.2. "PARTÍCULAS DEL PRETÉRITO IMPERFECTO."

kači 'el mismo día': *¿tab́eč yan kači?* '¿dónde estabas?'

kuči 'antes del día': *woxel kuči* 'sabíalo (pero se me ha olvidado)'

2.5.5.3. "PARTÍCULAS DEL PLUSCUAMPERFECTO."

ʔili . . . kuči 'ya': *bin ʔili pádre kuči, ka*

luk̇en 'ya se había ido el Padre, cuando me partí', *kimén ʔili kuči, ka luk̇oon* 'ya se había muerto, cuando partimos'

2.5.5.4. "Partículas del futuro imperfecto."

bin '(verb 'go'): *bin nakaken* 'yo subiré', *bin ʔinkambes-Q* 'yo lo enseñaré'

2.5.5.5. "Partículas del futuro perfecto."

ʔili . . . kučom (kočom) 'ya': *ʔokán ʔili kin kočom, ka bin lukukoon* 'ya se habrá puesto el sol, cuando nos partamos', *bin wuȼkin kočom* 'yo lo haré (habré hecho) (si no hay algo que lo impida)'

2.5.5.6. "Partículas del imperativo futuro."

kat 'después': *kat nakaken* 'suba yo después', *kat kakambes* 'enseñemos nosotros después'

2.5.5.7. "Partículas del optativo."

kaxi 'ojalá': *káxi tibilak ʔabeeleeš* 'ojalá que sea buena (la manera en que) caminéis'

kayna 'ojalá': *kayna ʔatanleeš dyos* 'ojalá sirvieseis a Dios', *ʔiná* 'ojalá y': *yolte ʔiná dyos ʔuȼaab ʔatoxʔ ólal* 'ojalá y te ayude Dios que dé que tengas salud'

2.5.5.8. "Partículas del subjuntivo."

xii '(would . . .)': *xii šiiken ti xoʔ, ka yának ʔinȼimin* 'yo iría a Mérida, si tuviese caballo (hubiera mi caballo)'

xii wil '(would . . .)': *xii wil ʔimmánab ʔišim, ka yának ʔintakin* 'yo compraría maíz, si tuviera dinero'

wil '(would . . .)': *binéči wil metnál, ka kímikeč ʔičil ʔakéban* 'hubieras ido al infierno, si hubieras muerto en tu pecado'

2.5.5.9. "Partículas del futuro."

ʔiwal(eʔ) 'hoy mismo': *kato šiikeč ʔiwaleʔ* 'te irás todavía hoy mismo', *bik wa bin manébal kin ten ʔiwal loeʔ* '(como tal vez ir a pasar el día yo este mismo de hoy) no sé cómo me irá este día'

2.5.5.10. Particles of time and place.

bikin 'cuando': *bikin ʔabootik ʔapaš*

¿cuándo pagarás tu deuda?', *bikini huluk pédro* '¿cuándo vino Pedro?' *tab(š)* 'donde': *tabš ʔinȼaik ʔišim* '¿dónde he de poner el maíz?'

Among the answers to these questions are: *kabxa* 'antes de ayer', *kabeš* 'después de mañana', *ʔošex* 'de aquí a tres días', *ʔošxe* 'tres días ha', *koneš* 'de aquí a cuatro días', *konxe* 'cuatro días ha', *hobiš* 'de aquí a cinco días', *hóbiši* 'cinco días ha', *xólxe* 'ayer', *same* 'rato ha', *heleben paal* 'muchacho de hoy (que nació hoy)' *xolxeben* 'cosa de ayer', *tiʔ* 'allí', *wayéʔ* 'aquí'

2.5.5.11. Particle *tak* 'al punto.'

šen tak '¡véte al punto!', *tiʔ tak ʔuxaȼax* 'luego allí al punto lo azotó', *maʔ tak ʔukambesiken pádre* 'nunca me enseña el Padre', *may tak baxún ʔuyakunkioon dyos* 'ámanos Dios sin número'

2.5.5.12. Particle *to* 'en haciendo, hecho que sea; aún.'

huluk to pádre 'viniendo (venido que sea) el Padre', *ʔinȼokes to láyeʔ* 'en acabando esto (hecho esto)', *maʔto šiik pádre* 'aún no se ha ido el Padre', *ʔúbi to* 'aún oye', *ʔintúkle to* 'pensarlo hé'

2.5.6. Conjunctional particles. Under this head, we find dubitative, modal, causal, instrumental, and negative particles, particles of quantity and price, and others.

2.5.6.1. Dubitative particles.

wa '¿quién sabe cómo? ¿acaso? ¿tal vez? (follows *bik* 'cómo', *bal* 'qué', *baxún* 'cuánto', *bikin* 'cuándo', *mak* 'no') *ʔbik bin ʔabenébalʔ* '¿cómo vas a ir?': *bik wa* 'no lo sé (¿quién sabe cómo?)', *¿makš bin šiik?* '¿quién va a (ha de) ir?': *mak wa* 'no lo sé (¿quién sabe quién?)', *¿ti biní wa ʔayumʔ* '¿(que) se fué tal vez tu padre?': *bik wa* 'no lo sé (¿quién sabe cómo?)', *¿teč wa* '¿eres tú?', *¿la wa loʔʔ* '¿es aquél?', *¿teč wa la šin?* '¿eres tú ó es aquel?'

wa . . . (preceding *bikin* 'cuándo', *baxún* 'cuánto', *bik* 'cómo', *bal* 'qué', *tab* 'dónde') '¿ . . . ?', *maʔ woxél wa bikin*

ʔutálel pádre 'no sé cuándo viene el Padre', *maʔ woxél wa baxun wayéʔ* 'no sé cuánto (dista) de aquí'

ʔebaláʔ 'no sé si ...': *ʔinȼibtax húʔun teč' ȼaabi ʔebaláʔ* 'te escribí una carta, no sé si te la dieron'

xi 'no sé ...': *xitab ti biní pédro* 'no sé dónde se fué Pedro', *xibik teč ʔiwaléʔ* 'no sabes qué será de ti hoy', *ȼokes xi bal (wa bal) yálax pádre teč* 'haz lo que te mandó el Padre'

xiš 'quizás': *xiš tečaki* 'quizás eres tú', *xiš maʔaki tan ʔabenél* 'quizás no irás'

wil 'debe de': *tiʔ wil yáni* 'allá debe de estar', *laʔ wil šiikie* 'aquél debe de ir allá', *maʔ wil húluki* 'no debe de haber venido'

ʔol 'casi': *ʔol kímil ʔukax xwan* 'casi se está muriendo Juan', *ʔol kími xwan* 'ahinas murió (poco faltó que muriera) Juan', *ʔol ʔubenel* 'ahinas no se fuera', *ʔolak kímiken* 'ahinas me muero'

2.5.6.2. MODAL PARTICLES.

bik(š) '¿cómo?': *¿bikš ʔamentiki?* '¿cómo lo haces?' '¿cómo lo hiciste?', *¿bikš bin ʔamentik?* '¿cómo lo has de hacer?', *¿bikš ʔabinki?* '¿cómo te fuiste?', *¿bikš ʔakimsiki tul?* '¿cómo mataste el conejo?', *xulbil ʔinkimsiki* 'flechado lo maté'

bay 'así': *ma bay ʔukáti* 'no quiere eso así', *čuybil ʔukáti* 'cosido lo quiere'

2.5.6.3. CAUSAL PARTICLES.

bal ʔučun '¿porqué?': *¿bal ʔučun ʔaxaȼki?* '¿porque (lo) azotaste?', *¿bal ʔučun ʔapuȼul?* '¿porqué te huyes?' *bal tax ʔoklal* '¿por qué motivo?': *¿bal tax ʔoklal kimki ʔumexén dyos?* '¿por qué motivo murió el hijo de Dios?'

bal ʔuwilal '¿para qué?': *¿bal ʔuwilal ʔakimsik ʔúlum?* '¿para qué matas las gallinas?' *xanal ʔuwilal* 'para comer', *bal ʔuwilal ka ʔinkimsax* 'para comer la maté'

2.5.6.4. INSTRUMENTAL PARTICLES.

-il 'donde ...': *yanil* 'donde hay', *ma-náanil* 'donde falta'; 'con que ...': *ʔučukil ʔabootik ʔapaš* 'con que puedes pagar tu deuda'; 'donde ...': *ʔuȼ ulúumil yólaxil kaxtal ʔinyum* 'buena es la tierra donde quiere morar mi padre'; 'por ...': *lay ʔokomil wol* 'por esto estoy triste'; 'es ... que': *lay ʔučun ʔunaxil benél* 'por esta causa es conveniente que te vayas'; 'como ... do': *bay halanil* 'como está mandado'

2.5.6.5. PARTICLES OF QUANTITY.

baxún '¿por cuánto?': *¿baxún ʔamánki ʔasuyem?* '¿por cuánto compraste tu manta?', *¿baxún winik yan ti yotoč ku?* '¿cuántos hombres hay en la Iglesia?'; '¿de qué tamaño': *¿baxún ʔukax ʔamexén?* '¿de qué tamaño es tu hijo?'

ba 'como': *ba ʔukax paal loe?* 'como del tamaño de aquel niño'

2.5.6.6. NEGATIVE PARTICLES.

maʔ (ma)(maa) 'not': *maʔ ʔilaabi* 'he was not seen', *ma teč* '(emphatically) not (lit. not, you!)', *ma teč ʔukímil* 'he is NOT dead', *¿baaš ten maa t abeetik?* 'Why don't you do it?'

mabaxún 'nunca' (plus optative): *mabaxún ʔinčóčob ʔinsípil* 'nunca me desato mis pecados', *mabaxún wilábeč* 'nunca te he (has sido) visto (por mí)', *mabaxún šiiken kampéč* 'nunca he ido a Campeche'; 'infinitos, -as': *mabaxún ʔunúmyail mitnal* 'infinitas son las penas del infierno'

maxaykún 'sin duda' (plus optative): *xač yaab ʔimpáyma teč, maxaykún ʔimbooteʔi* 'muy mucho te debo, no es posible que yo lo pago'

baš maʔ '¿por qué no?': *¿baš maʔ tan ʔabenel?* '¿por qué no vas?', *¿baš maʔ ʔawálax ten?* '¿por qué no me lo dijiste?'

ti maʔ 'sin que': *maʔ ʔabenél ti maʔ ʔawálik ten* 'no te vayas sin que me lo digas'

maʔil 'antes que': *háleeš ti pádre maʔil*

245

šiik 'decidlo al padre antes de que se vaya'

ti ma? 'que (comparative)':paynum ?inyamaileč, ti ma? ?immexén 'más yo te amo que (no) a mi hijo'

masamak 'en ninguna manera':masamak puɟuken 'en ninguna manera me huiré'

xik ma? 'mira no dejes de ...' (plus optative):xik ma? ?awalab ti pádre 'imira, no dejes de decirlo al Padre!'

ka(iš) ma?ak 'por que no':lik yilɩk dyos ?utumtum ?óltabal winikoḃ tumén kisin, ka ma?ak ?úɟik ?uḃaoob, kaiš ma?ak ?unoxkink(i) ?uḃaoob 'permite Dios que sean tentados los hombres por el Demonio, por que no se mejoren, por que no se ensoberbezcan'

ḃakak 'aunque' (plus optative):ḃakakiš šiik 'aunque se vaya'

xik 'mira no, aun no' (plus optative): xik lúḃukeč 'aun no caigas'

¿kunš k? '¿no será bueno?':¿kunš k awalaḃ ti pádre? '¿no será bueno que lo digas al Padre?'

čan ti 'no':čan ti ?okol 'no llores', čan ?awalaḃ ti pádre 'no lo digas al Padre'

ḃaki (no):ḃaki ?aḃenel 'no te vayas', ḃakitó 'déjalo por ahora', ḃakiló? 'déjalo del todo—no lo hagas'

?áčak 'sin que':ma? ?aḃenél, ?áčak ?awálab ti pádre 'no te vayas, sin que lo digas al Padre'

?áčak 'sin':?áčaken 'sin mí', ?áčakeč 'sin ti', ma?ḃaloon ?áčak dyos 'no somos nada sin Dios'

?ačak 'si no':ḃin xaɟak, ?áčak ?upúɟul 'fuera azotado, si no se huyera'

kaiš ?áčak 'no':wa ma? ?akáti ḃenel, kaiš ?áčak 'si no quieres irte, no te vayas'

miš mak 'no one, nobody'

miš ḃaal 'nothing'

miš ḃikin 'never'

minaan 'not to have; not to exist'

2.5.6.7. OTHERS.

ka 'and'

šan 'also, and'

leilɩ 'still, and'

yetel 'y':pay pédro yetel xwan 'llama a Pedro y a Juan', šen yetel 'véte con él', wétel 'conmigo', ?awétel 'contigo', yétel xwan 'con Juan', šen yeteloob 'véte con ellos'

yetun 'con él':wetun 'conmigo', ?awetun 'contigo, en tu casa', yétun ḃátaḃ 'en la casa del cacique', yétun krus 'junto a la cruz'

kaiš 'y':?ukéyaxen xwan kaiš ?uxáɟaxen 'riñóme Juan y azotóme'

katun 'y después:?ukéyaxen wičam, kaiš ?uxáɟaxen, katun púɟitun 'riñóme mi marido, y azotóme, y después se huyó'

k 'y':?ukéyaxen pádre ken ?uxáɟax 'riñóme el Padre y me azotó'

k 'cuando':kon ḃinɩ 'cuando me fuí'

kunš '¿y?':¿tox wa ?awol? '¿estás bueno?', tox wol 'bueno estoy', ¿kunš ?ayum? '¿y tu padre?', ¿kunš ?ana?? '¿y tu madre?'

ma?iš 'tampoco':ma? ?aḃenél ma?iš ?uḃenel ?alak 'no te vayas ni tampoco se vaya tu compañero'

kun 'pues':kuneč 'pues tú', ¿kunen wa ma? tan ?intálel? '¿pues yo no he de ir?'

t umen 'because':t umen ?áalab tené? 'because I have been told'

2.5.7. "PARTÍCULAS INTENSIVAS".

xumbaḃ 'four hundred', xunket 'juntamente', xunmol 'juntos', ket 'juntamente', t ulakal 'todo', paḃté 'todo junto':?uɟ yuɟkinki t ulakal 'bene omnia fecit', ḃinón ti paḃteil 'fuímonos juntos'

2.5.8. "PARTÍCULAS DISYUNTIVAS".

wa 'whether, or, if':wa ?a?íxo wa ?awatán 'whether your son or your wife', wa kawólte 'if you wish'

lak, lawak 'ó, ú':šen ča ?úlum, lak he?, lak wax, lawak 'vé, trae gallina, ó huevo, ó pan, ú otra cosa'

ḃaš, ḃašan 'ó, ú':tak he?, ḃaš wax, ḃašan 'vengan huevos, ó pan, ú otra cosa'

lawak, lawkinak ti 'ó, otra cualquiera':

šen pay pédro, lawak xwan, lawak law-kinak ti winikil 've, llama a Pedro, ó a Juan, ó a otro cualquiera hombre'
lawak ti 'cualquier': *šen ča lawak ti lakil* 've, trae cualquier plato'
ʔukinaki 'cualquiera que sea': *ʔukinaki čeʔ ʔačabi* 'toma de ahí un palo cualquiera que sea'

lakeč 'ó':maʔ taač ʔinkol, lakeč tumén ʔimbenel ti xoʔ, lakeč tumén ʔimmáxantabal, tumén batab, lakeč ʔinkanán mesón 'no suelo hacer milpa, ó por ir a la ciudad (de Mérida), ó porque me ocupa el cacique, ó porque soy mesonero'

REFERENCES

Andrade, 1940
Beltrán de Santa Rosa, 1746, 1859
Brasseur de Bourbourg, 1869–70
Cacalchen, Libro de, 1647–1826
Calkini, Chilam Balam de
Chicxulub, Crónica de, 1542–62
Ciudad Real, 1600, 1929
Coronel, 1620
Förstemann, 1880, 1892
Gates, 1938
Izil, Chilam Balam de
López Otero, 1914
McQuown, 1956
Martínez Hernández, 1926, 1929
Maya Society, 1937
Mediz Bolio, 1943
Mena, n.d.
Morley and Brainerd, 1956
Nah, Chilam Balam de, n.d.
Nida and Moisés Romero, 1950

Pacheco Cruz, 1920, 1939, 1948
Pérez, n.d., 1866–67, 1898
Pike, K. L., 1946a
Rada y Delgado and López de Ayala, 1892
Romero Fuentes, 1910
Rosny, 1887
Roys, 1933, 1939, 1944
San Buenaventura, 1684, 1888
San Francisco, Diccionario de, n.d.
Seler, 1887, 1902
Solís Alcalá, 1949
Sotuta, Libro de, n.d.
Thompson, J. E. S., 1962
Ticul, Documentos de, 1642–1761
Tizimin, Chilam Balam de, 1870
Tozzer, 1921
Vienna, Diccionario de, n.d.
Xiu Chronicles, 1608–1817
Zavala, 1898
—— and Medina, 1898

7C. Classical Quiche

MUNRO S. EDMONSON

0.	Introduction
1.	Phonology
1.1	Phoneme inventory
1.1.1.	Consonants
1.1.2.	Vowels
1.1.3.	Prosody
1.2.	Orthography
1.2.1.	Consonants
1.2.2.	Vowels
1.2.3.	Prosody
1.3.	Phoneme variants
1.3.1.	Consonants
1.3.2.	Vowels
1.3.3.	Prosody
1.4.	Phoneme distribution
1.4.1.	Initial consonants
1.4.2.	Consonant clusters
1.4.3.	Vowel clusters
1.4.4.	Morphophonemic alternation
2.	Morphology
2.1.	Morpheme shapes
2.2.	Morpheme classes
2.3.	Verbs
2.3.1.	Intransitive verbs
2.3.2.	Transitive verbs
2.3.3.	Mode
2.3.3.1.	Modal deverbatives
2.3.4.	Aspect
2.3.5.	Mood
2.3.6.	Verb complex
2.3.6.1.	Aspect
2.3.6.2.	Mood
2.3.6.3.	Object
2.3.6.4.	Subject
2.3.6.5.	Root II
2.3.6.6.	Root I
2.3.6.7.	Intensive
2.3.6.8.	Status
2.3.6.9.	Mode
2.3.6.10.	Adverbials
2.4.	Nouns
2.4.1.	Noun roots
2.4.2.	Compound stems
2.4.3.	Complex stems
2.4.3.1.	Deverbative noun stems
2.4.3.2.	Desubstantive noun stems
2.4.3.3.	Phrase-compound noun stems
2.4.4.	Noun inflection
2.4.4.1.	Pronominal nouns
2.4.4.1.1.	Polite usage
2.4.4.1.2.	Reflexive
2.4.4.2.	Nominal prefixes *ax*- and *(i)š*-
2.4.4.3.	Reduplication
2.4.4.4.	Plural
2.4.4.5.	Suffixes -*al* and -*il*
2.4.4.6.	Suffix -*ax*
2.4.4.7.	Adjectival suffixes
2.4.4.7.1.	Suffix -*a*
2.4.4.7.2.	Suffixes -*ik* and -*ak*
2.4.4.7.3.	Suffix -*Vlax*
2.4.4.8.	Restricted noun suffixes
2.5.	Particles
2.5.1.	Particle inflection
2.5.2.	Particle compounding
2.5.3.	Prepositional particles
2.5.3.1.	Postpositions
2.5.4.	Pronominal particles
2.5.4.1.	Interrogative pronouns
2.5.4.2.	Demonstrative pronouns
2.5.4.3.	Pronominal compounds
2.5.5.	Adverbial particles
2.5.5.1.	Conjunctive particles
2.5.5.2.	Temporal particles
2.5.5.3.	Modal particles
2.5.5.4.	Particle complex
2.5.5.5.	Locative particles
2.5.5.6.	Quantitative particles
2.5.6.	Interjectional particles

0. INTRODUCTION. Classical Quiche[1] was spoken in highland Guatemala, principally in the departments of Totonicapan, El Quiche, and parts of Baja Verapaz, Solola, and Quezaltenango in the centuries preceding and following the Spanish conquest in the 16th century. Modern Quiche, differing mainly in its incorporated neo-Nahuatl and Spanish elements and in the degree of its municipal differentiation into dialects, is still spoken by nearly half a million Indians in the same area. Apart from municipal differentiation, which dates largely from the last four centuries, Classical Quiche was a quite homogeneous language, most of the speakers of which were unified around the 14th to the 16th centuries in the most important native state in the highlands, with its capital at Gumarcaah (Utatlan), near the modern Santa Cruz del Quiche. The Quiche lineages disputed control of the central highlands with those of the Tzutuhil and Cakchiquel, who are also the closest linguistic relatives of the Quiche, and they never completely subjugated the Rabinal lineage of Baja Verapaz. Rabinal is the most divergent of the Quiche dialects, and has often been considered a separate language. The expansion of the Quiche state pushed westward the Mam-speakers in the areas of Quezaltenango and Huehuetenango to about the present linguistic boundary (a north-south line about 10 miles west of the former city). Northern neighbors of the Quiche are Aguacatec (in Aguacatan), Ixil (in Nebaj and Chajul), and Uspantec (San Miguel Uspantan). Historically the Quiche were also in contact with the Kekchi and Pokomam to the north and east. To the south they colonized the Pacific slopes to the vicinity of Retalhuleu and Mazatenango, but they never settled the coastal plain.

All the neighbors of the Quiche were thus speakers of highland Mayan languages, which diverged from the lowland ones at about the beginning of the great lowland Maya civilization in the last centuries B.C. By around the 5th A.D. they had further separated into eastern (Kekchi, Pokonchi, Pokomam), central (Quiche, Cakchiquel, Tzutuhil, Uspantec) and western (Mam, Aguacatec, Ixil) groups. Uspantec diverged from the other central highland languages around the 13th century, and Cakchiquel-Tzutuhil from Quiche in the 15th. In the central highlands the lineage wars of the ruling dynasties were probably a decisive factor in these subdivisions. During the period prior to the Spanish conquest (perhaps in the 14th century) the central highlands were exposed to extensive Nahuatl-Pipil influence, possibly by conquest, since the leading lineages of the Quiche state appear to be at least partly identified with the Aztecs, and personal names of some of the Quiche kings were Nahuatl. This influence is in any case reflected in a sprinkling of naturalized loan words of Nahuatl origin. A larger number of Nahuatl words was introduced after the conquest, mainly via Spanish.

Missionaries early trained Indian assistants to write Quiche, a tradition which then became partly autonomous until at least the 19th century, and the most valuable part of our corpus of Classical Quiche materials comes from this source. The most outstanding document in this corpus is the *Popol Vuh*, the longest and one of the best preserved of nearly a dozen lineage histories known to have been written in the 16th

---

[1] As an amateur in what is perhaps the most technical of the fields of anthropology, I should like to acknowledge the generous assistance of Dr. Norman A. McQuown in furnishing me an advance draft copy of his "Outline of Classical Yucatec," on which I have leaned very heavily in preparing this corresponding sketch of Quiche. I have even made a deliberate attempt to parallel his text in the hope that this would illuminate similarities and differences between two well-known related languages. I am also indebted to Dr. McQuown for access to Theodore Ebneter's "Report on Classical Quiche" (mimeographed) and other materials. I am indebted to Prof. Adrián I. Chávez, President of the Academia Maya-Quiché of Quezaltenango, Prof. Aníbal R. García of Cantel, and Mr. Antonio Saquic of San Andrés Xecul for their patience in instructing me in Modern Quiche.

century in a modified Spanish alphabet. Three more of these are published in Quiche and Spanish (Recinos, 1957). One or two more may be extant in manuscript collections. The others are lost or known only in Spanish translation. Post-16th century documents almost invariably reflect the massive influence of Spanish which justifies their classification as Modern Quiche. A noteworthy and puzzling exception is the 19th-century *Rabinal Achi*, which is remarkably close to the *Popol Vuh* in language and in style. Partial exception may also be made of a manuscript divining calendar of the 18th century from Quezaltenango (*Chol Poval—Ahilabal Q'ih*). Three missionary grammars of the 16th century by Fathers Vico, Anleo and Martínez, and other works by Father Vico are extant in manuscript and are useful for the study of Classical Quiche.

Textual materials for the study of Modern Quiche include the books of at least two 17th-century and one 18th-century *cofradia*, a collection of 18th-century wills and land titles that appears to come from Rabinal or vicinity, some late 18th-century "documents" from Totonicapan, a calendar from Santa Catarina Ixtahuacan, and the *Zaqi Q'axol* (a play about the conquest of Mexico), both of 19th-century date. Important 20th-century materials in Quiche include the publications of Father Teletor from Rabinal, Schultze Jena from Chichicastenango, and the Burgesses from Quezaltenango, as well as the extensive recordings and transcriptions of Andrade in manuscript at the University of Chicago (see References). Nothing of consequence appears to have been written by the Indians themselves in this century.

The principal grammars of Quiche are those of Ximénez (?1722), Brasseur de Bourbourg (1862), and Friedrich (1955). The principal dictionaries and vocabularies are Basseta's (?1698), the Anonymous Franciscan's (1787), Brasseur de Bourbourg's (1862), Schultze-Jena's (1933), Teletor's (1959) and Xec and Maynard (1954). The primary collections of Quiche manuscript materials are at the universities of Chicago, Princeton, Tulane, and California.

1. PHONOLOGY.

1.1. PHONEME INVENTORY.

1.1.1. CONSONANTS.

p	t	ȼ	č	k	q	'
ṗ	ṭ	ȼ̇	č̣	ḳ	q̇	
		s	š		x	
m	n					
w			y			
	l					
	r					

1.1.2. VOWELS.

i		u	ii		uu
e	o		ee	oo	
a			aa		

1.1.3. PROSODY. No close study has been made of Quiche prosody. The following features may be considered plausible guesses.

1.1.3.1. TONES. Quiche does not appear to use tone segmentally.

1.1.3.2. JUNCTURES. Close juncture is distinguished from open by a strongly marked stress accent on all syllables preceding open juncture. Intermediate and terminal open junctures are probable.

1.1.3.3. INTONATION. There is extensive suprasegmental use of tone in Modern Quiche, probably involving at least four phonemes: steady, rising, falling and steady-falling: *a, á, à, aà*.

1.1.3.3.1. LEVELS. This would imply three levels: *3 2 1*.

1.2. ORTHOGRAPHY. Although it is clear that both Classical and Modern Quiche had both short and long vowels, as well as a glottal stop, since neither of these features is consistently indicated in the orthography, we can here only note the fact, and shall be unable to write these features in this grammar.

1.2.1. CONSONANTS.

p	t	tz	ch	k	k, q	( ), h, '
b	th	tz	ch	g	g	
		z, s, ç	x		h	
m	n					
v, u			y, i, j			
	l					
	r					

251

1.2.1.1. ALPHABETIC VARIANTS. Several other orthographies have been used for Quiche, differing mainly in their treatment of the consonants. Principal of these are Father La Parra's (16th century), Schultze Jena's, that of the Institute Indigenista de Guatemala and that of the Academia Maya-Quiché. The following table summarizes their correspondences.

	ACADEMIA MAYA-QUICHÉ	INSTITUTO INDIGENISTA	LA PARRA	SCHULTZE-JENA
k	c, qu	c, qu	c, qu	k
q	λ	k	3	g
'		'		?
ṗ	ɓ	b	b	b
ṭ	ḓ	t	th	
ȼ	ŧ	tʒ	4,	tŝ
č	*	ch	4	ch'
ḱ	γ	c', qi	g	x̌
q̇	◇	ḱ	3,	k̲
š	sh	x	x	š'
x	j	j	h	h
w	gu, w	w	v	w

Publications of the Instituto Bíblico de Quezaltenango use the orthography of the Instituto Indigenista, but substitute gk for ḱ to mean q̇.

1.2.2. VOWELS.

i		u	ii, ij, iy	uu, uv, vv
e	o		ee	oo, ou, ov
	a			aa

1.2.3. PROSODY. Prosodic features are quite irregularly represented in Classical Quiche documents, most of which are characterized by somewhat erratic word division and little or no punctuation. Later documents or published texts apply the canons of Spanish punctuation in a manner which may have little to do with Quiche prosody, Classical or Modern.

1.3. PHONEME VARIANTS.

1.3.1. CONSONANTS. The unglottalized stops and affricates (except ') are aspirated before open junctures, and there is particularly strong aspiration of w, y, l and r in the same position. Articulation of the glot-

talized series is often lenis intervocalically and often fortis in initial and final positions. Palatalization of the palatal stops occurs before at least a and e in some words and may be both modern and dialectic. The sibilant s is apical and alveolar; the shibilant š is palatal; the x is a strong-velar fricative. The m is bilabial; the n is alveolar, shifting morphophonemically to m before close junctures followed by bilabials and phonetically to ŋ before palatal stops. The w is a high back semi-vowel; the y is high front; both tend to be devoiced under the strong prejunctural aspiration already noted. The lateral l is palatal, and is also markedly devoiced in prejunctural aspiration. The r is an alveolar tap intervocalically, becoming devoiced and aspirated pre- and postjuncturally. In this position the r becomes almost a shibilant.

1.3.2. VOWELS. The simple vowels correspond well to those of English beat, bet, bot (fly), boat, boot or Spanish tiro, pero, paro, toro, puro. The double vowels are simple elongations of them, normally with smooth articulation. All single vowels are markedly weakened when occurring in unstressed syllables and may be heard as shwa (ə, English thus). The diphthongs implied by the orthography of Classical Quiche (in cases in which a CV_1 element is followed by a V_2C one) are not heard in the modern language, in which the first vowel is always assimilated to the second.

1.3.3. PROSODY. Except for the primary distinction between close and open juncture by a very marked prejunctural stress accent, the prosodic features of Classical and Modern Quiche remain to be established.

1.4. PHONEME DISTRIBUTION.

1.4.1. INITIAL CONSONANTS.

	a	e	i	o	u	aa	ee	ii	oo	uu
p	63*	35	38	41	38	1	2	1	1	--
ṗ	58	19	41	39	42	1	1	4	—	1
t	68	32	69	44	55	—	1	2	1	
ṭ	5	1	3	5	9	1	1	—	—	—
ȼ	32	10	23	22	21	1	2	—	—	—
ȼ̇	17	—	12	5	7	—	—	—	—	—
č	45	15	51	32	25	2	4	1	—	—

252

	a	*e*	*i*	*o*	*u*	*aa*	*ee*	*ii*	*oo*	*uu*
č	30	2	14	14	17	1	—	—	—	—
k	87	21	29	47	46	—	2	—	—	1
k̇	21	5	7	5	5	—	—	—	1	—
q	37	6	14	35	27	—	—	—	—	—
q̇	46	10	19	39	18	1	1	—	2	—
'	9	—	5	2	5	—	—	—	—	—
s	47	27	60	36	41	1	1	—	1	—
š	40	18	28	24	32	—	1	1	—	—
x	53	21	30	45	54	5	1	2	—	2
m	58	25	18	26	42	—	1	—	—	1
n	54	18	33	15	17	—	1	1	—	1
w	45	11	25	19	4	—	—	2	2	—
y	49	17	14	39	38	2	—	—	—	—
l	39	18	27	29	18	—	1	—	2	1
r	20	22	21	22	18	—	—	—	—	—

* Numbers refer to frequency of occurrence of these CV combinations in Edmonson, 1965.

1.4.2. CONSONANT CLUSTERS. Consonant clusters occur in Quiche only as a result of close juncture between separable morphemes. In initial position this is almost exclusively a matter of the use of the completive particle *š*, which can be followed by any other consonant.

In medial position (-*C* close juncture *C*-) it is probable that all combinations occur, though not all can be readily documented.

Final consonantal clusters do not occur.

1.4.3. VOWEL CLUSTERS. Vowel clusters are very rare in Classical Quiche orthography, and are articulated in Modern Quiche as a single elongated vowel assimilated to the value of the second of a given pair. It is not impossible that the original form of these clusters was that of diphthongal $V_1'V_2$ sequences; such articulation of the morphemes involved is occasional in Modern Quiche. Geminate clusters are perhaps historically long vowels; diphthongal clusters appear to result only from the combination of separable morphemes, e.g., *ka-ip'* 'two'.

1.4.4. MORPHOPHONEMIC ALTERNATION. Alternation of vowels is found in some words and may be dialectic:

i - a	*sinik - sanik*	'ant'
e - a	*senayep' - sanayep'*	'sand'
o - a	*mop - map*	'palm tree'
e - i	*mep' - mip'*	'poor'
o - u	*ox - ux*	'we'

Examples of inversion of both consonants and vowels can be found in Modern Quiche: *n oroxel* - (for Classical:) *r onoxel* 'all (of it)' *kixap'* - (for Classical:) *kaxip'* 'four'

2. MORPHOLOGY.
2.1. MORPHEME SHAPES.
2.1.1. TYPES.

A. *C* — P; suffixes (rare)
B. *V* — P; suffixes (rare)
C. *CV* — N, V, P; $\sqrt{N}$, $\sqrt{V}$; (about 10 per cent)
D. *VC* — N, V, P; $\sqrt{N}$, $\sqrt{V}$; prefixes (about 5 per cent)
E. V_1C_1 — reduplication (about 4 per cent)
F. V_1C_2 — reduplication (rare)
G. $C_1V_1C_2$ — reduplication (very rare)
H. *CVC* — N, V, P; $\sqrt{N}$, $\sqrt{V}$ (about 65 per cent)
I. *VCVC* — N, V; $\sqrt{N}$, $\sqrt{V}$ (about 5 per cent)
J. *CVCVC* — N, V; $\sqrt{N}$, $\sqrt{V}$ (about 5 per cent)
K. Foreign Loan Words (about 5 per cent)
   činamital 'lineage' (Nah. chinamitl)
   tekpanir 'multiply' (Nah. tecpan)
   kašlan 'Spanish' (Sp. castellano)
   animá 'soul' (Sp. ánima)
L. Unanalyzed Compounds (rare)
   waxšak 'eight'

2.2. MORPHEME CLASSES. Quiche morphemes may be broadly classified as nouns, verbs and particles. All three classes may be compounded. Nouns and verbs may take prefixed pronouns indicative of number and persons and denoting possession in the case of nouns, subject and object in the case of verbs. Nouns may additionally be combined with a particular set of affixes, and verbs with a different set of suffixes.

2.3. VERBS may be transitive or intransitive. Intransitive verbs take the prefixed pronouns:

Sg. 1) *in*		Pl. 1) *ox*	
2) *at*		2) *iš*	
3) *Ø*		3) *e*	

Transitive verbs beginning with a consonant take the prefixed pronouns:

Sg. 1) *nu*   Pl. 1) *qa*
  2) *a*   2) *i*
  3) *u*   3) *ki*

Transitive verbs beginning with a vowel take the prefixed pronouns:

Sg. 1) *w*   Pl. 1) *q*
  2) *aw*   2) *iw*
  3) *r*   3) *k*

Transitive verbs may take both subject and object prefixes, in which case the object prefixes are identical with the subject prefixes of intransitive verbs, and always precede the regular transitive subject prefixes. (For numerals see §2.3.6.)

Examples:

^{1} *k²* *iš³* *qa⁴* *sač⁶* *wi¹⁰* *iw onoxel* 'we shall forget about all of you'

š¹ *(Ø)³* *r⁴* *il⁶* *o⁸* 'he saw it'

š¹ ^{2} *e³* *al⁶* *aš⁸⁹* *ik⁸⁹* 'they were born'

^{1} *č²* ^{2} *oq̇⁶* *ik⁸⁹* 'he had to cry'

The suffix -*V*- serves as a transitive marker for transitive verb stems and roots, a transitivizer for intransitive verb stems and roots, and a transitive desubstantivizer for noun stems and roots. The suffix -*i*- is the corresponding intransitive marker.

Examples:

pet 'come' : *petex* 'to come through (something)'

ṗan 'do'   : *ṗanox* 'to do, act of doing'
           ṗanoš 'to be done'
           ṗanik 'to be acting'

ȼix 'word' : *ȼixox* 'speak'

kam 'die' : *kamiṗex* 'to kill'

2.3.1. INTRANSITIVE VERBS. Some verb roots are inherently intransitive: *q̇uš* 'eat', *ȼe* 'laugh' *oq̇* 'weep', *kuṗ* 'sit', *kam* 'die'. These require the intransitive suffix -*i-k* when they are utterance terminal, but may stand alone when followed by other elements within the utterance.

Examples:

š¹ *in³* *ul⁶* *pa xa* 'I arrived at the house'

š¹ *in³* *ul⁶* *ik⁸⁹* 'I arrived'

š¹ *e³* *kam⁶* *ik⁸⁹* 'they died'

Some intransitive verb stems are desubstantive:

Examples:

ȼiṗ 'writing' : *ȼiṗanik* 'to be writing'
ȼix 'word'   : *ȼixonik* 'to be speaking'
winaq 'man'   : *winaqirik* 'become a man'
naxt 'distant' : *naxtirik* 'recede'

These make use of the desubstantivizing infix -*V*-, and require the intransitive terminative -*i-k*, whatever the intervening inflection. Transitive verbs may also form intransitives by means of the intransitivizing suffix -*i-k*.

Examples:

loq 'love (something)' : *loqonik* 'be in a loving state'
čuč 'soften' : *čučunik* 'become soft'
ṗan 'make, do' : *ṗanolik* 'having acted'
tis 'sew' : *tisominik* 'be sewn'
kol 'rescue' : *kolotaxik* 'escape'
iq̇ 'surpass' : *iq̇owik* 'be excessive'

All complex intransitive verb stems, whether desubstantive or detransitive, require the intransitive terminative -*i-k* when they are employed as verbs, though they may omit this suffix with or without the substitution of others when used participially. The suffix -*i-k* is occasionally found as an intransitivizer of simple transitive verb roots.

Examples:

ṗan 'make, do' : *ṗanik* 'act'
q̇ot 'cut' : *q̇otik* 'be cutting'

2.3.2. TRANSITIVE VERBS. Some verb roots are inherently transitive: *qam* 'take', *eq* 'carry', *moq* 'seize', *čay* 'hit', *tik* 'plant'. These require the transitive suffixes -*V*-(*x*) or -*a* when they are utterance terminal, but may stand alone when they are followed by other elements within the utterance.

Examples:

š¹ ^{3} *u⁴* *ṗan⁶* ^{8} *ri čak* 'he did the job'

š¹ ^{3} *u⁴* *ṗan⁶* *o⁸* 'he did it'

^{1} *k²* ^{3} *u⁴* *tik⁶* *a⁸* 'he will plant it'

š¹ *e³* *tix⁶* *čik¹⁰* 'they tried it again'

Some verb stems are desubstantively transitive:

Examples:

aȼ'iyak 'clothes' : *aȼ'iyakix* 'to clothe'
ȼip 'writing' : *ȼipax* 'to write'
saq 'white' : *saqix* 'to whiten'
ȼix 'word' : *ȼixox* 'to say'

These make use of the desubstantive transitive suffix -*V*-, and require the transitive marker -*x*. The same forms appear as transitivizers of intransitive verb stems with a variety of stem inflections:

Examples:

šaxowik 'dance' : *šaxowisax* 'to cause to dance'
čutinik 'dwindle' : *čutinarisax* 'to cause to become small'
kamik 'die' : *kamipex* 'kill'
anik 'run' : *anomax* 'flee from'

Some complex transitive stems ending in -*V*-*p*- require the transitive terminal -*a*; all other complex transitive stems require the transitive terminative -*V*-*x* when they are used as verbs, though they may omit this suffix and substitute others when used participially. The suffix -*V*-*x* is occasionally found as a transitivizer of simple intransitive verb roots.

Examples:

pet 'come' : *petex* 'come through (something)'
pe 'go' : *peex* 'go along (something)'

2.3.3. Mode. Various distinctions equivalent to voice, aspect, mood, tense and participial construction in other languages are expressed in the Quiche verb by what may be called MODE. At least six modes are common to transitive and intransitive verbs (roots and stems): PURPOSIVE (-*p*-), INDEFINITIVE (-*n*-), DEFINITIVE (-*m*-), INFINITIVE (transitive -*x*, intransitive -*k*), CAUSATIVE (transitive -*t*-, intransitive -*s*-) and EXTENSIVE (transitive -*w*-, intransitive -*x*-). Intransitive verbs (roots and stems) form deverbatives with the suffix -*e*- in the AGENTIVE (-*l*) and ABSTRACTIVE (-*m*) modes. Transitive stems in -*p*- and transitive verb roots may additionally form an INCEPTIVE with the suffix -(*a*)-*Ø*, and all transitive stems an INCHOATIVE (-*r*-), PROGRESSIVE (-*y*-), PASSIVE (-*š*-) and ACTIVE (-*l*-) mode. All of the transitive stem suffixes except -*m*- (definitive) may be followed by intransitive suffixes in -*i*- and -*e*-. The transitive stems in -*w*-, -*n*-, -*m*-, -*p*- and -*t*- may take other transitive suffixes. All intransitive suffixes may be followed by transitive suffixes in -*V*-. The intransitive stems in -*p*- and -*n*- may also take intransitive suffixes in -*i*- and -*e*-. Combinations using up to five successive modal suffixes are found. (See §2.3.6.9.)

Examples:

panopex 'to (intend to) do' (transitive purposive: transitive)
koȼapa 'put to bed' (transitive purposive-inceptive: transitive)
petipex 'to (intend to) come' (intransitive purposive: transitive)
ȼipanik 'to be writing' (transitive indefinitive: intransitive)
xunamatax 'to equalize' (transitive definitive-causative: transitive)
qatox 'to cut' (transitive infinitive)
pinik 'to walk' (intransitive infinitive)
panatanik 'to be having things done' (transitive causative: intransitive)
kamisax 'to cause to die' (intransitive causative: transitive)
šaxowik 'to be dancing' (transitive extensive: intransitive)
pinixeyik 'to be walking along' (intransitive extensive-progressive: intransitive)
axawax 'to need' (transitive extensive: transitive)

2.3.3.1. MODAL DEVERBATIVES. A great wealth of participial deverbatives is generated by the system of modal suffixes in Quiche. All transitive verb stems ending in consonants other than -*p*-, -*w*- and -*t*- may be used as nouns. The intransitive indicative in -*i*-*k* may also be employed as an infinitive. Any intransitive verb (stem or root) may take the deverbative suffixes -(*e*)-*l* (agentive) and -(*e*)-*m* (abstractive). A few transitive roots also form an agentive-abstractive in -(o)-m. Transitive and intransitive purposive stems (ending in -$\dot{p}$-) form a present participle in -a-l which has instrumental meaning. Intransitive indefinitives (in -i-n-) form a past participle in -a-k.

Examples:

$\dot{p}anox$ 'to do' (infinitive)

$winaqir$ 'becoming a man' (inchoative)

$\dot{c}i\dot{p}am$ 'written' (definitive)

$tana\dot{p}ay$ 'stopping' (progressive)

$loqo\check{s}$ 'loved' (passive)

$\dot{p}anol$ 'doer' (active)

$\dot{p}olon$ 'rolled' (indefinitive)

$ulik$ 'to arrive' (infinitive)

$\dot{t}isominel$ 'one who is sewing things up' (agentive)

$axawarem$ 'government' (abstractive)

$iyom$ 'grandmother' (abstractive)

$o\dot{q}e\dot{p}al$ 'lamentation' (purposive participle)

$kaminak$ 'dead' (indefinitive participle)

Deverbatives are subject to normal noun inflection (see §2.4.3.2).

2.3.4. ASPECT. All finite verbal phrases (transitive roots in -$\emptyset$ and transitive roots and stems in -V-x, -V, and -a, intransitive roots in -$\emptyset$ and intransitive roots and stems in -i-k) require introductory particles of aspect, mood subject and (in the case of transitive verbs) object. The aspective particles are $\check{s}$, COMPLETIVE and $\emptyset$, INCOMPLETIVE.

Examples:

$\check{s}^1$ $\emptyset^2$ $\emptyset^4$ kam^6 ik^{89}　$\emptyset^1$ ka^2 $\emptyset^4$ kam^6 ik^{89}
'he died'　　　　　:　'he is dying'

$\check{s}^1$ $\emptyset^2$ $\emptyset^3$ u^4 ya^6　$\emptyset^1$ k^2 $\emptyset^3$ u^4 ya^6
'he gave it'　　　　:　'he gives it'

2.3.5. MOOD. The mood particles are $k(a)$, INDICATIVE, $\check{c}(i)$, NECESSITATIVE and, very rarely $m(a)$, NEGATIVE, all alternating with $\emptyset$, DECLARATIVE. A finite verb may not take the zero forms for both aspect and mood. In Classical Quiche aspect and mood particles were frequently compounded; in Modern Quiche they are not and have

therefore come to resemble tense prefixes; $\check{s}$, past, $k(a)$, present and $\check{c}(i)$, future, probably as a result of Spanish influence. The primary expression of negation in Classical Quiche employed the particle $m(a)$ alone or compounded with other adverbial particles preceding the aspective particle. In Modern Quiche this has become a conjunct construction, the negative particle before the verb complex requiring the negative (formerly optative) particle tax among the terminal adverbials.

Examples:

$\check{s}^1$ ^{2} $\dot{q}o^6$ 'it was'

ma^0 $\check{s}^1$ ^{2} $\dot{q}o^6$ 'it wasn't' (Classical Quiche)

k^2 in^3 $\dot{p}in^6$ ik^{89} 'I am walking'

ka^2 nu^4 $\dot{p}an^6$ o^8 'I am doing it'

ma^0 na^0 ^{1} ka^2 nu^4 $\dot{p}an^6$ o^8 tax^{10} 'I am not doing it' (Modern Quiche)

$\check{c}i^2$ ki^4 $\dot{p}an^6$ o^8 'they must do it'

$\check{s}^1$ ma^2 $wa\check{c}^6$ il^{89} 'blindness'

$\check{s}^1$ k^2 el^6 ik^{89} 'he was going along'

$\check{s}^1$ $\check{c}^2$ in^3 $\dot{p}is^6$ on^{89} ik^{89} 'I must have been singing'

2.3.6. VERB COMPLEX. The following positions are recognizable in the verb complex:

(1) ASPECT

(2) MOOD

(3) OBJECT

(4) SUBJECT

(5) ROOT II

(6) ROOT I

(7) INTENSIVE

(8) STATUS

(9) MODE

(10) ADVERBIALS

2.3.6.1. ASPECT. The only particle which can occur in position 1 is $\check{s}$, indicating the COMPLETIVE aspect. Its alternative is $\emptyset$, INCOMPLETIVE. (See §2.3.4.)

2.3.6.2. MOOD. The particles which can occur in position 2 are $k(a)$, INDICATIVE, $\check{c}(i)$, NECESSITATIVE and very rarely $m(a)$, NEGATIVE, all alternating with $\emptyset$, DECLARATIVE (which requires the completive $\check{s}$ in position 1). (See §2.3.5.)

2.3.6.3. OBJECT. The intransitive subject (and transitive object) pronouns occur in position 3. (See §2.3. For polite usage see §2.4.4.1.2.)

2.3.6.4. SUBJECT. The transitive subject pronouns occur in position 4. (See §2.3. For polite usage see §2.4.4.1.2.)

2.3.6.5. ROOT II. Compound verbs are created by the appearance of simple verb and noun roots in position 5 in combination with inflected ones in position 6. In Modern Quiche the second verb is frequently the Spanish infinitive.

Examples:

$\emptyset^1$ k^2 $\emptyset^3$ u^4 $xal\text{-}^5$ $wa\check{c}^6$ ip^{89} ex^{89} 'he transfigures it'

$\emptyset^1$ ka^2 $\emptyset^3$ nu^4 $\dot{q}a\check{s}\text{-}^5$ $qoop^6$ it^{89} ax^{89} 'I endure it'

$\emptyset^1$ ka^2 $\emptyset^3$ $\dot{\phi}al\text{-}^5$ qat^6 ik^{89} 'it wobbles'

$\check{s}^1$ $\emptyset^2$ in^3 $(u)^4$ $\dot{p}an^6$ $suprir$ 'it pained me' (Modern Quiche)

2.3.6.6. ROOT I. The primary verbal root occurs in position 6. A noun root may also occur in this position provided it is followed by the transitive desubstantive $-V-$ in position 8. Inflected nouns are also occasionally found as verb roots.

Examples:

$\check{s}^1$ $\emptyset^2$ ox^3 u^4 $\emptyset^5$ war^6 at^{89} is^{89} ax^{89} 'he put us to sleep'

$\emptyset^1$ k^2 ox^3 $\emptyset^4$ $\emptyset^5$ $winaq^6$ $i\check{s}^{89}$ ik^{89} 'we are enslaved'

$\emptyset^1$ ka^2 $\emptyset^3$ $\emptyset^4$ $\emptyset^5$ zaq^6 ir^{89} ik^{89} 'it is brightening' ('good morning' in Modern Quiche)

$\emptyset^1$ ka^2 $\emptyset^3$ u^4 $\emptyset^5$ $\check{s}axap^6$ ix^{89} 'he is making shoes'

$\emptyset^1$ k^2 $\emptyset^3$ $\emptyset^4$ $\emptyset^5$ kap^6 iy^{89} ax^{89} ik^{89} 'he is repeating'

2.3.6.7. INTENSIVE. Three types of reduplication may occur in position 7 as INTENSIVE markers. The commonest type is $-V_1C_1$. Somewhat rarer is the form $-V_1C_2$. Very rarely one encounters syllabic reduplication: $-C_1V_1C_2$.

Examples:

$\dot{p}it$ 'break' : $\dot{p}it^6$ $i\dot{p}^7$ $o\check{s}^{89}$ ik^{89} 'broken to bits'

$\dot{p}u\dot{q}$ 'belch' : $\dot{p}u\dot{q}^6$ $u\dot{q}^7$ 'growl (of stomach)'

nus 'slither like a snake' : $nus\text{-}^6$ nus^7 'whoosh like a rocket'

2.3.6.8. STATUS. The suffixes occurring in position 8 are transitive ($-V-$, $-a-$ and $-o-$) and intransitive ($-i-$ and $-e-$) markers. A $-\emptyset$ suffix in this position serves to leave intransitive verb roots intransitive and transitive ones transitive. The suffix $-V-$ is occasionally found as a transitivizer of intransitive verb roots, and the suffixes $-i-$ and $-e-$ are occasionally found as intransitivizers of transitive verb roots. The suffixes $-V-$ (commonly) and $-i-$ (rarely) are encountered as transitive and intransitive desubstantivizers, respectively. The position 8 suffixes are also extensively used in conjunction with those of position 9 in the composition of complex verbals.

Examples:

$\dot{\phi}al^6$ ex^{89} 'to return (something)'

$\dot{\phi}ix^6$ a^8 'is about to ignite'

$\dot{q}in^6$ om^{89} 'rich'

$\dot{q}ol^6$ ik^{89} 'to be'

$\dot{k}as^6$ il^{89} em^{89} 'life'

k^2 ^{3} u^4 $\dot{q}am^6$ 'he takes it'

k^2 ox^3 ox^6 'we go'

$\dot{p}in^6$ ix^{89} 'to walk (something)'

$\dot{q}am^6$ ik^{89} 'to be taking'

$\dot{p}an^6$ el^{89} 'doer'

al^6 ax^{89} 'to bear a child'

$\check{c}ut^6$ ik^{89} 'to be small'

2.3.6.9. MODE. Seventeen consonantal suffixes of MODE occur in position 9. They stand in a complex relationship to the position 8 suffixes which they follow, because they serve as stem-formatives which can then go back and take a fresh position 8 suffix and a new suffix from position 9. Examples are found in which this derivational process may take place up to five times. The relationship of the evolving stem to the status suffixes of position 8 which can precede and follow the modal indicators is indicated in the following table.

The suffix -(V)-Ø may only follow transitive verb roots. Its meaning is FINITIVE and it

STEM	8	9	8	MODE	FUNCTION
(S)/TV	-a-	-k		perfective	N
√V	-Ø-	-Ø		inceptive	V
		-Ø		finitive (utterance medial)	V
		-Ø		finitive (utterance terminal)	V
		-l-		active	N, S/IV
		-y-		progressive	N, S/IV
		-r-		inchoative	N, S/IV
(S)/TV		-š-	-i-	passive	N, S/IV
(S)/N	-V-	-x-	-e-	infinitive	N, TV, S/IV
		-t-		causative	S/V
		-w-		extensive	S/V
(S)/IV	-i-	-ṗ-	-a-	purposive	S/TV
		-n-	-V-	indefinitive	N, S/TV
		-m-		definitive	N, S/TV
		-s-		causative	S/TV
		-x-		extensive	S/TV
		-k		infinitive	N, IV
(S)/IV	-e-	-l		agentive	N
(S)/TV	-o-	-m		abstractive	N

The suffix -(a)-k (PERFECTIVE) may only follow the suffix -(i)-n-, thus forming an INDEFINITIVE-PERFECTIVE deverbative frequently described as a "past participle." It cannot be further inflected except as a noun.

Examples:

kam⁶ in⁸⁹ ak⁸⁹ il⁸⁹ 'death'

pet⁶ in⁸⁹ ak⁸⁹ 'come'

ṗan⁶ at⁸⁹ ax⁸⁹ in⁸⁹ ak⁸⁹ 'done, arranged'

ṗe⁶ in⁸⁹ ak⁸⁹ 'gone'

iq́⁶ ow⁸⁹ in⁸⁹ ak⁸⁹ 'surpassed, excessive'

The suffix -(a)-Ø may only follow certain common transitive verb roots, and stems ending in the suffix -(V)-ṗ-. Its meaning is INCEPTIVE and it may not take further inflection.

Examples:

k² ³ u⁴ q́am⁶ a⁸⁹ 'he is about to take it'

k² ³ a⁴ tis⁶ a⁸⁹ 'you are going to sew'

The suffix -(Ø)-Ø may only follow transitive and intransitive verb roots. Its meaning is FINITIVE and it cannot stand as utterance terminal nor be further inflected.

Examples:

ka² ³ k⁴ ax⁶ ⁸⁹ ki wa 'they want their tamales'

k² iš³ ṗe⁶ ⁸⁹ pa ri ṗe 'you (pl.) are coming down the road'

may be utterance terminal. It may not be further inflected.

Examples:

k² ³ u⁴ xuš⁶ u⁸⁹ 'he is igniting it'

ka² ³ nu⁴ yuq⁶ u⁸⁹ 'I am stretching it'

The suffix -(a)-l (ACTIVE) must follow the purposive -ṗ- to create an ACTIVE-PURPOSIVE deverbative which has frequently been called "instrumental."

Examples:

kun⁶ aṗ⁸⁹ al⁸⁹ 'cure, medicine'

čuč⁶ uṗ⁸⁹ al⁸⁹ 'step-mother'

teweč⁶ iṗ⁸⁹ al⁸⁹ 'blessing'

war⁶ aṗ⁸⁹ al⁸⁹ 'blanket, bedroom'

The suffixes -(V)-l-(ACTIVE), -(V)-y- (PROGRESSIVE), -(V)-r- (INCHOATIVE) and -(V)-š- (PASSIVE) may follow the roots or stems of transitive verbs or transitivized nouns. As terminals they are deverbatives, and they may further take the -i- and -e- suffixes of position 8 and the corresponding modals of position 9.

Examples:

keel 'grinder'

ṗanolik 'act'

kamisay 'killing'

ṗinixeyik 'walk along'

q́equmar 'darkening'

oxoṗarik 'cough'
axawaš 'needed'
loǧošik 'be purchased'
tixošel 'student'

The suffix -(V)-x- is employed and inflected in the same manner as the preceding suffixes. It has both FINITIVE and INFINITIVE functions, and may stand as utterance terminal. It is mandatory for verbalized noun roots used as finite verbs, optional for transitive verb roots and rare as a transitivizer of intransitive verb roots. As the infinitive of simple transitive verbs, it is rarely further inflected, but as a suffix to more complex stems it is very commonly so, employing the -i- and -e- suffixes. Extremely rarely it may be found compounded with a -V- suffix.

Examples:

k^2 ^{3} u^4 *ȼix*^{6} *ox*^{89} 'he says it'
kumaȼ^6 *ix*^{89} 'to bewitch'
xaq^6 *at*^{89} *ax*^{89} *in*^{89} *ak*^{89} 'opened, cleared'
rix^6 *ow*^{89} *ox*^{89} *ik*^{89} 'finish off, become obsolete'
ṗan^6 *at*^{89} *ax*^{89} *el*^{89} 'something that must be done'

The suffixes -(V)-t- (CAUSATIVE) and -(V)-w- (EXTENSIVE) follow transitive or transitivized stems and roots, and require further inflection in -V-, -i- or -e-. The latter inflections are, however, very rare with the causative -t-.

Examples:

ṗan^6 *at*^{89} *ax*^{89} *ik*^{89} 'to have something done'
šax^6 *ow*^{89} *ik*^{89} 'to be (or go on) dancing'
ax^6 *aw*^{89} *ax*^{89} 'to need'
te^6 *et*^{89} *ik*^{89} 'to open'
na^6 *ot*^{89} *is*^{89} *at*^{89} *ax*^{89} 'to have someone enlightened'
ǧaš^6 *ow*^{89} *em*^{89} 'suffering, pain'

The suffixes -$ṗ$- (PURPOSIVE) and -n- (INDEFINITIVE) may follow either transitive -V- stems or intransitive -i- ones. Stems in -$ṗ$- rarely and those in -n- rather commonly occur as deverbatives. Both suffixes may be further inflected by suffixes in -V-, -i- or -e-. The purposive -$ṗ$- may also take the special suffix -a-l to form the "instrumental" (purposive-active), and the indefinitive -n- may take the special suffix -a-k to form the "past participle" (indefinitive-perfective). Stems in -$ṗ$- may also take the inceptive suffix -a-$\emptyset$.

Examples:

xor^6 *oṗ*^{89} *is*^{89} *ax*^{89} 'to chill, cool'
kam^6 *iṗ*^{89} *ex*^{89} 'to intend the death of'
čut^6 *in*^{89} *ar*^{89} *is*^{89} *an*^{89} *em*^{89} 'humility'
ox^6 *oṗ*^{89} 'a cough'
ȼix^6 *on*^{89} 'speech'
ȼiṗ^6 *an*^{89} *ik*^{89} 'to be writing'
xol^6 *ox*^{89} *oṗ*^{89} *ik*^{89} 'give up the ghost'
pet^6 *iṗ*^{89} *ex*^{89} *ik*^{89} 'to be coming'
koȼ^6 *aṗ*^{89} *a*^{89} 'to be about to put (someone) to bed'
ǧet^6 *on*^{89} *el*^{89} 'choker'
tas^6 *oṗ*^{89} *al*^{89} 'savings'
tix^6 *oš*^{89} *in*^{89} *ak*^{89} 'taught'

The suffix -m- (DEFINITIVE) is usually based on a -V- transitive stem, but also occurs occasionally on an -i- intransitive one. It may stand as a deverbative without further inflection, but may also occasionally take transitive suffixes in -V-.

Examples:

čun^6 *am*^{89} 'whitewashed'
xun^6 *am*^{89} *at*^{89} *is*^{89} *ax*^{89} 'to have something equalized'
xi^6 *im*^{89} 'groaned'
il^6 *om*^{89} 'seen'
an^6 *im*^{89} 'hastened'
tis^6 *om*^{89} *in*^{89} *ik*^{89} 'to be sewing'

The suffixes -(i)-s- (CAUSATIVE) and -(i)-x- (EXTENSIVE) are formed from intransitive roots and stems. Both require additional inflection in -V-.

Examples:

ṗin^6 *ix*^{89} *ey*^{89} *ik*^{89} 'to be walking on and on'
ǧak^6 *at*^{89} *is*^{89} *an*^{89} *ik*^{89} 'to be adjusted'

The suffix -(i)-k is both FINITIVE and INFINITIVE of intransitive verbs. It can stand as utterance terminal and may take no further verbal inflection.

Examples:

$\check{s}^1$ ^{23} $\dot{q}o^6$ ol^{89} ik^{89} 'it was'
u $\dot{p}an^6$ ik^{89} 'his action'
$\dot{\rlap{/}c}il^6$ ox^{89} ik^{89} 'get dirty'
$\check{s}i\dot{p}^6$ $i\check{s}^{89}$ ik^{89} 'be threatened'

The suffixes -(e)-l (AGENTIVE) and -(e)-m (ABSTRACTIVE) occur with intransitive roots and stems. Occasionally the -e- in position 8 detransitivizes a transitive root. Further verbal inflections of these forms are extremely rare, though they may be inflected as nouns. Transitive verbs may form an abstractive in -(o)-m.

Examples:

$\check{s}im^6$ on^{89} el^{89} 'jailer'
ya^6 $a\check{s}^{89}$ el^{89} 'receiver'
yat^6 em^{89} 'tied bundle'
kik^6 ot^{89} em^{89} al^{89} 'happiness'
$\dot{q}axol^6$ om^{89} 'man who has engendered sons'

2.3.6.10. ADVERBIALS. A number of modal adverbial particles appear in position 10 in the verb complex. Some of these also function as independent adverbial particles, though some of them do not. They are structurally unusual in that they are in close juncture with the preceding verb (the stress accent normally shifts to them from the preceding syllable), but commonly bring about vowel or consonant clusters, an otherwise rare phenomenon in Quiche. Most of these particles have been discarded or considerably modified in Modern Quiche.

Examples:

-wi 'then'
-na 'still' ('necessarily' in Modern Quiche)
-ok 'accordingly'
-la 'indeed'
-on 'already'
-lo 'perhaps'
-ta(x) 'possibly' ('not' in Modern Quiche)
-an 'meanwhile'
-čik 'again'

2.4. NOUNS. Nouns are of three kinds (1) roots, (2) compound stems, and (3) complex (derived) stems.

2.4.1. NOUN ROOTS. There is a great variety of noun roots:

ax 'ear of corn', xa 'water', xaa 'house', $\dot{q}a\dot{q}$ 'fire', $\dot{p}aa\dot{\rlap{/}c}$ 'spider-monkey', $ulew$ 'earth', $winaq$ 'person', $anim\acute{a}$ 'soul (Sp. ánima)', $tinamit$ 'town (Pipil chinámit)'.

The great majority of Quiche noun roots are of the type CVC. Some proportion of the remainder are probably unanalyzed compounds. Numerals, colors and similar elements may not behave as typical nouns (for example in relation to pronominal possession), but are subject to inflection of nominal type in one or another connection (plural $-V\text{-}\dot{p}$ for numerals above one, or generalizing $-a\text{-}l$ for colors, for example).

2.4.2. COMPOUND STEMS. Noun roots may combine to form compound noun stems, but the process seems to be very rare:

waxšak 'eight', laxux 'ten'	: waxšak-laxux 'eighteen'
al 'woman's child', qaxol 'man's son'	: al-qual 'child'
ġan 'yellow', xa 'water'	: ġan-a 'bile'
ač 'fellow', aliṗ 'in-law'	: ač-aliṗ 'co-parent-in-law'
isumal 'hair', či 'mouth'	: isuma-či 'beard '

2.4.3. COMPLEX STEMS. Most complex noun stems are deverbative. A very few may be desubstantive. A quite exceptional one or two are apocopated phrases.

2.4.3.1. DEVERBATIVE NOUN STEMS. Twelve suffixes serve as the terminations of deverbative noun stems. All of them may occasionally be inflected as nouns. (See §2.3.6.9.)

$-(V)\text{-}x$ (transitive infinitive)
$a\dot{p}^6$ $i\check{s}^{89}$ ax^{89} 'plant corn', muq^6 ux^{89} 'to bury', $atin^6$ is^{89} ax^{89} 'to have (someone bathed)'

$-(i)\text{-}k$ (intransitive infinitive)
r ul^6 ik^{89} 'his arrival', w ax^6 aw^{89} $a\check{s}^{89}$ ik^{89} 'my need', qa loq^6 on^{89} ik^{89} 'our loving'

-(V)-r (inchoative)

kaq⁶ er⁸⁹ 'reddening', kex⁶ ur⁸⁹ 'becoming (or imitating) a deer', čut⁶ in⁸⁹ ar⁸⁹ 'becoming smaller'

-(V)-l (active)

pač⁶ al⁸⁹ 'leaning', r ax⁶ il⁸⁹ 'the price', tux⁶ ul⁸⁹ 'sweat-bather'

-(V)-m (definitive)

e ȼap⁶ im⁸⁹ 'captives', ȼal⁶ am⁸⁹ 'plank', q̇ox⁶ om⁸⁹ 'drum, marimba'.

-(V)-y (progressive)

u tan⁶ ap̓⁸⁹ ay⁸⁹ 'his stopping', r ul⁶ iy⁸⁹ 'the overthrowing', al⁶ ay⁸⁹ 'bearing, giving birth'

-(V)-n (indefinitive)

kol⁶ on⁸⁹ 'saved', uč⁶ an⁸⁹ 'oration', mes⁶ on⁸⁹ swept'

-(Vp̓a)-l (purposive active)

p̓⁶ in ip̓⁸⁹ al⁸⁹ 'gait, walk', čap̓⁶ op̓⁸⁹ al⁸⁹ 'fastening', q̇ol⁶ ip̓⁸⁹ al⁸⁹ 'cauldron'

-(ina)-k (indefinitive perfective)

xaq⁶ at⁸⁹ ax⁸⁹ in⁸⁹ ak⁸⁹ il⁸⁹ 'clearing of the land', k̓is⁶ in⁸⁹ ak⁸⁹ 'finished', et⁶ am⁸⁹ in⁸⁹ ak⁸⁹ 'known'

-(e)-l (agentive)

wor⁶ el⁸⁹ 'hole', tix⁶ on⁸⁹ el⁸⁹ 'teacher', teweč⁶ in⁸⁹ el⁸⁹ 'blesser'

-(e)-m (abstractive)

axaw⁶ ar⁸⁹ em⁸⁹ 'government', ok⁶ em⁸⁹ 'entrance', xa⁶ ar⁸⁹ iš⁸⁹ an⁸⁹ em⁸⁹ 'irrigation'

-(o)-m (abstractive)

al⁶ om⁸⁹ 'bearer, mother', ap̓⁶ iš⁸⁹ om⁸⁹ 'corn farmer', q̇in⁶ om⁸⁹ al⁸⁹ 'wealth'

2.4.3.2. DESUBSTANTIVE NOUN STEMS. It is possible that a desubstantive noun stem formation is indicated by the suffixes -(i)-x and -(i)-r in certain temporal expressions:

Examples:

ip̓ir 'yesterday'

kap̓ix 'day after tomorrow'

kap̓ixir 'day before yesterday'

ošip̓ix 'three days hence'

xunap̓ir 'last year'

Two apparently inflected particles in -(e)-r may be related. (See §2.5.1.)

oxer 'formerly'

mier 'formerly'

2.4.3.3. PHRASE-COMPOUND NOUN STEMS. An interesting and exceptional compound in Modern Quiche has been formed from elements which are neither substantival nor inflective:

pa 'on', u 'his', wi 'head': nu pu-u-wi 'my hat' (the form nu pa-nu-wi can also be heard)

A similar formation is indicated by the Classical Quiche:

či 'by', u 'his', wi 'head': č-u-wi 'tribute, load of cacao'

2.4.4. NOUN INFLECTION. Nouns are optionally inflected for plural (suffix -V-p̓) and may be possessed (prefixes are identical with the subject pronouns for transitive verbs; see §2.3). Since the copulative verb is commonly omitted, nouns may also stand in copula construction with the intransitive pronouns (in ačiy 'I am a man'). In this usage the demonstrative pronominal particle (are 'that one, he') takes the place of the Ø form in the third person singular. Nouns are additionally inflected by means of two prefixes (ax- and iš-); they may be reduplicated, and they may take one or more of thirteen suffixes (-Vp̓, -el, -cm, -en, -um, -Vm, -Vlax, -al, il, -ax, -a, -ik and -ak).

2.4.4.1. PRONOMINAL NOUNS. Three nouns have essentially pronominal use: la(l) 'you (polite singular)', alaq 'you (polite plural)' and ip̓ (self).

2.4.4.1.1. POLITE USAGE. Polite usage is well established in both Classical and Modern Quiche. It employs the normal third person singular forms of verbs with the following (grammatically singular) nouns la(l) or alaq in the normal position of nominal subjects, immediately following the verbal complex. Polite form possession of nouns is indicated without pronominal prefixes.

Examples:

š¹ ²³ pet⁶ ik⁸⁹ alaq 'you (pl.) came'

¹ ka² ³ kam⁶ la(l) 'you will die'

lal axaw 'you are the lord'

ulew la(l) 'your land'

Polite usage in Quiche is found from inferiors to superiors and is almost never mutual. In Modern Quiche younger brothers employ polite usage to older ones.

2.4.4.1.2. REFLEXIVE. The noun *iṗ* 'self' is used to express reflexive action. It follows the verb but precedes a nominal subject, a departure from normal word order (verb, subject, object).

Examples:

š¹ ² w⁴ at⁶ in⁸⁹ w iṗ 'I bathed myself'

¹ k² u⁴ sik̓⁶ r iṗ r išoq 'the woman called to herself'

š¹ ² e³ ča⁶ či k iṗil k iṗ 'they spoke to each other'

2.4.4.2. NOMINAL PREFIXES *ax-* and *(i)š-*. The prefixes *ax-* and *(i)š-* indicate respectively the masculine and feminine agentive or possessive: 'one of ... ' or 'one who ... '. They appear before both simple and complex noun stems. In Classical Quiche the prefix *(i)š-* carried implications of diminution; in Modern Quiche it has lost even its femininizing and agentive-possessive function and appears as a largely meaningless element in archaic compounds.

Examples:

ax-Miq̇in A 'person from Totonicapán'
ax-pop 'king'
ax-puṗ '(blowgun) hunter'
ax-ṗeyil 'traveller'
Iš-Kanul 'Santa María Volcano'
iš-kaqaṗ 'rainbow'
iš-koloṗ 'guts'
š-qaq 'claws'
š-pač 'lizard'
š-čoṗ 'colander (strainer for leaching corn dough)'

2.4.4.3. REDUPLICATION. Reduplication of noun roots takes the same forms as the reduplication of verb roots and has the same intensivizing function. It is particularly common in relation to nouns of adjectival quality. The types are: *-V₁C₁*, *-V₁C₂* and *-C₁V₁C₂*.

Examples:

tipit 'bitter'
qečeč 'strutter (bird)'
saq-saq 'very white'

A special case of reduplication of the third type is characteristic of numerals:

xun 'one' : *xuxun* 'each one', *či xuxunal* 'individually'
kaṗ 'two' : *kakaṗ* 'each of two'
oš 'three' : *ošoš* 'by threes'
r oš 'third': *r oš r oš* 'three times'

2.4.4.4. PLURAL. A number of nouns may form plurals in *-V-ṗ*. Never universal, this usage is somewhat less common in Modern than in Classical Quiche. It may be followed by the additional abstractive suffix *-a-l*.

q̇axolaṗ 'men's sons'
kuṗuleṗ 'people of Cubulco'
kaxiṗ 'four' (Modern Quiche: *kixaṗ*)
ooṗ 'five' (Rabinal dialect: *xooṗ*)
wukuṗ 'seven'
xuyuṗal 'mountain range'

A rare suffix *-om* is used to pluralize a few nouns.

Examples:

alaṗom 'boys'
alitom 'girls'

Certain nouns, usually of adjectival quality, distinguish singular from plural by the suffixes *-i-* and *-a-* respectively. (See §2.4.4.7.2.)

Examples:

ȼipiȼik 'one sharp-pointed thing'
ȼipiȼak 'two or more sharp-pointed things'

2.4.4.5. SUFFIXES *-al* and *-il*. The suffixes *-al* (ABSTRACTIVE) and *-il* (GENERALIZER) are the commonest and most characteristic of noun derivations. They are closely related in form and function and may be compounded in either order.

Examples:

nimal 'size'
alal 'weight'
q̇owil 'strength'
winaq̇il 'population'
uȼilal 'goodness'
qiṗalil 'spirit'

2.4.4.6. SUFFIX *-ax*. The suffix *-ax* serves (1) as an indicator of MEASURE, and (2) as a GENERALIZER for nouns referring to body parts. The second usage, relatively rare in

Classical Quiche, has largely disappeared from the modern language. In both uses the suffix may be compounded with the following suffix -*il*.

Examples:

xu perax 'a sheet of'
xu qolax 'a cake of'
xu čolax 'a row of'
xu ǵetax 'a pinch of'
¢amax 'nose'
pamax 'belly'
ǵataxil 'a minute'
komaxil 'blood, serum'

2.4.4.7. ADJECTIVAL SUFFIXES. Nouns of adjectival quality cannot normally be possessed nor pluralized. They will usually take the typical nominal suffixes -*al* (abstractive), -*Vx* and -*Vr* (desubstantive) and -*il* (generalizer). In addition, however, they may be derived by the suffixes -*a*, *ik*, -*ak*, and -*Vlax*. Only the last of these finds any extensive use in relation to non-adjectival nouns.

2.4.4.7.1. SUFFIX -*a*. The suffix -*a* is commonly appended to many of the more frequent adjectival nouns when they stand in the normal position immediately preceding the noun they modify and when the noun begins with a consonant. The suffix may also be combined with the generalizer -*il*. Its inflective meaning is not clear.

Examples:

ǵana poot 'a yellow blouse'
raša ¢el 'the blue bowl (heaven)'
meṗa 'poor'
meṗail 'poverty'

2.4.4.7.2. SUFFIXES -*ik* and -*ak*. The suffixes -*ik* (singular) and -*ak* (plural) occur with great frequency as adjectival forms, particularly with reduplicated stems. More occasionally they may occur in relation to simple adjectival nouns, or rarely in the composition of desubstantive verbals. They may be followed by the generalizing suffix -*il*.

Examples:

a¢ik 'older brother'
čomak 'thick'
teṗetik 'coarse' (singular)

teṗetak 'coarse' (plural)
¢a¢akirinik 'crow (of a cock)'
nimakil 'enormity'

2.4.4.7.3. SUFFIX -*Vlax*. The *intensive* suffix -*Vlax* occurs commonly with both adjectival and non-adjectival nouns. Like plurals in -*Vṗ*, this form may also be serve as a base for verbs.

Examples:

kiǵelax 'bloody'
¢ailax 'salty'
nimalax 'lordly, grand'
tewilax 'cool'
pokolax[6] *ix*[89] 'make dusty'
pokolax[6] *ir*[89] 'crumble to dust'
qečelax 'forest'

2.4.4.8. RESTRICTED NOUN SUFFIXES. A number of noun suffixes are apparently restricted to certain classes of nouns. Most of them are sufficiently rare to render an interpretation of their structure and function difficult. These include the suffixes -*Vl*, -*el*, -*um*, -*it*, -*Vy*, -*on* and *?*-*Vm*.

Examples:

isumal 'hair'
ǵequmalax 'very dark'
kaley 'pebble'
kačay 'incense'
tiyoxital 'fleshly'
laxuxitakil 'one tenth'
ǵeǵel 'avarice'
kiǵel 'pool of blood'
'aǩel 'chickenish'
rašon 'blue-winged dove'
'akem (*'aǩam*) 'squash'

2.5. PARTICLES. Particles are not inflected as verbs and nouns are, but they may be compounded. They may be classified as pronominal, prepositional, adverbial or interjectional in function.

2.5.1. PARTICLE INFLECTION. A few particles have forms suggestive of inflection, but may equally well be archaic compounds.

Examples:

waral 'here'
kamik 'now'
oxer 'formerly'
mier 'formerly'

upik 'there'

xanik 'how much?'

tasek 'even if'

2.5.2. PARTICLE COMPOUNDING. Adverbial and certain pronominal (demonstrative and interrogative) particles are commonly compounded (in close juncture).

Examples:

(x)a(n)-pa-činaq 'who?'

xa-wi 'where?'

naki-la-lo 'who might it be that ...?'

wa-kamik 'today, now'

we-ta 'if'

ma-xa 'there isn't one which ...'

ma-na 'not (yet)'

va-e 'that one, this one'

la-e 'that one, this one'

2.5.3. PREPOSITIONAL PARTICLES. There are two prepositional particles: *či* and *pa*. Both have multiple meanings and there is no clear contrast in their usage.

Examples:

pa tinamit 'in the town'

či xuyup 'in the country, on the mountain'

š in ul pa r očoč 'I reached the house'

pa niqaxaripal qix 'at noon'

č u ka xunap 'two years later'

2.5.3.1. POSTPOSITIONS. Precise positional relationships are expressed by a limited number of postpositional nouns. Most of these may function in this connection only as objects of the preposition *či*.

Examples:

či 'mouth'	:*či nu či* 'before me'
wa(č) 'eye, face'	:*č a wa(č)* 'in front of you'
ix 'back'	:*či r ix šan* 'behind the wall'
wi 'head, tip'	:*či ki wi e xuyup* 'on top of the mountains'
pa(m) 'belly, womb'	:*č u pam tinamit* 'inside the city'
šol 'space'	:*či qa šol* 'among us, between us'
še 'root, base'	:*č u še čee* 'under the tree'
e(č) 'eat,	:*či r e(č)* 'by means of it'

possess' (in Modern Quiche this often takes the form *č e*)

šmut '(?)'	:*č u šmut kax č u šmut ulew* 'between heaven and earth' (rare)

Of these elements, *e(č)* often and *še* rarely may appear without the preposition *či*.

Examples:

w eč 'mine'

še tinamit 'below the town, Lower Town'

q eč 'ours'

eč la(l) 'yours (polite singular)'

Certain postpositional nouns never appear in conjunction with prepositions.

Examples:

uq 'friend'	:*iw uq* 'with you (plural)'
umal 'source'	:*r umal* 'through it, because of it'
ušlep '(?)'	:*r ušlep kex* 'under the deer' (rare)

A similar construction representing non-positional relationships occurs with certain nouns.

Examples:

r onoxel 'all of it'

u tukel 'by itself'

2.5.4. PRONOMINAL PARTICLES. The uses of pronominal particles in relation to verbs and nouns have already been treated (see §2.3, 2.4.4). A certain number of other particles function as interrogative or demonstrative pronouns.

2.5.4.1. INTERROGATIVE PRONOUNS. The principal interrogative pronouns are *xa* 'what?', *sa(č)* 'what?', *čin(aq)* 'who?' and *naki* 'who?'.

Examples:

(x)a-pa-činaq k u pano? 'who is doing it?'

naki-pa š petik? 'who came?'

(x)a-sa k i biix? 'what are you (plural) saying?'

2.5.4.2. DEMONSTRATIVE PRONOUNS. The principal demonstrative pronouns are: *are* 'that one', *la-e* 'that one', *wa-e* 'this one' and *r(i)* 'the'.

Examples:

are ri w aqan 'that is my foot'

r u ġaṕ r ačiy 'the man's hand'
are ri š ki ṗano 'that's what they did'
r ax-čoǵe ri xaa 'the owner of the house'
wa-e r išoqil ax-ġix 'that is the wife of
   the sun-priest'

The particle *r(i)*, in addition to serving as a weak demonstrative rather like the definite article in English or Spanish, may also function as a relative pronoun.

Examples:

are ri ri š ki ṗano 'that's what they did'
r ačiy ri ġo čila 'the man who is there'

2.5.4.3. PRONOMINAL COMPOUNDS. Pronominal particles may be compounded with each other and with other particles.

Examples:

(x)a(n)-čin(aq) 'which?, who?'
xa-sa(č) 'what?'
ri xa 'that one'
are la-e 'there'
naki-tak 'whichever'
xa-ta 'perhaps'
are-ta 'hence'
xa-ni 'when?'
či-nu 'similarly'
či-ġu(t) 'after'
wa-kamik 'today'
xa-pa 'whither?'
xa-wi 'whither?'
xa(n)-pa 'how much? when?'
xa-na 'perhaps'
(ka)t-ok 'then'
naki-pa 'what is?, who knows?'
xa-nik 'how far?'
xa-qin 'often'
xa-la 'what's that? somewhere'
naki-la 'who?, someone'

2.5.5. ADVERBIAL PARTICLES. Adverbial particles are conjunctive, temporal, modal, locative and quantitative. The first three classes can occur almost exclusively as part of a preverbal complex in which they may be compounded in that order (except that the negative modal precedes the negated element and certain modals may also be used as verb-terminal particles. (See §2.3.6.10.) Elements of each class of adverbials may be compounded with one another as well, and pronominal particles may precede adverbial ones of any class. Particles of location and quantity are not bound to any particular position, and frequently occur postverbally. Of the major classes of morphemes in Quiche, it is the adverbial particles which have suffered the greatest change and differentiation since Classical times. In many modern locutions they are almost wholly replaced by Spanish phrases, conjunctions and adverbs.

2.5.5.1. CONJUNCTIVE PARTICLES. The principal conjunctive particles are: *ša* 'only, but', *kate* 'so, then', *ġa* 'since', *ta* 'if, when', *lal* 'like', *kexe* 'like, as', *ġu(t)* 'and, so', *we* 'if, whether', *(nay)-pu(č)* 'and, or', *ni* 'thus', and *nox-ne* 'whether'. Except when preceded by pronouns, they stand in the initial position in a clause. They may be compounded with one another and with other adverbial elements.

Examples:

ša-ta 'whatever'
ša-ṗa 'wherever'
ša-et 'a little'
ša-wi 'truly'
ša-tax 'soon'
ni-ġut 'this way'
kate-na 'later'
ta-ki 'when'
ta-zek 'if ... then'
ta-ġu 'and then'
ta-on 'well'
ta-na 'first'
ta-la 'whither away?'
kexe-wa 'at this time'
kexe-ta 'thus'
kexe-ġut 'so'
kexe-wi 'thus'
ġut-wa-e 'now this'
ġu-ri 'now then'
ġu-la 'this way'
we-pu 'or'
we-ta 'whether, perhaps'
we-pa 'some'

2.5.5.2. TEMPORAL PARTICPES. The principal temporal particles are: *kamik* 'now', *mier* 'formerly', *oxer* 'formerly', *naṗe* 'at first', *mi* 'already', and *kan* 'then'. In the absence of preceding pronouns or conjunctives, these frequently initiate clauses. They may occasionally be compounded with following modals.

Examples:

wa-kamik 'today'
oxer-ok 'before'

2.5.5.3. MODAL PARTICLES. The modal particles include negatives, affirmatives, interrogatives, dubitatives, continuatives (and discontinuatives). Those in commonest use are: *ma* 'not', *pa* 'interrogative', *či* ''ever', *xu* 'how', *na* 'yet', *xe* 'indeed', *šaš* 'absolutely', *le* 'perhaps', *ok* 'still', *wi* 'then (Spanish pues)', *čik* 'again', *an* 'meanwhile', *ki* '(?)', and *on* '(?)'. Most of them are subject to compounding with one another and with preceding conjunctive particles. Most of them (*na, lo, ok, wi, čik* and *on*) are also used as verbal terminals. (See §2.3.6.10.)

Examples:

pa-či 'where?'
pa r(i) 'where?'
pa-su 'what for?'
na-či 'always'
ma-xa (ma-xi) 'without, before, lest'
akan-ok 'hereon'
apon-ok 'finally, enough'
pa-wi 'where?'
či-lo 'more or less'
xu-pa 'how?'
xu-ča 'how?'
xu-čin 'often'
xe-la 'that way'
pa-la 'which'
xu-la 'how?'
xu-max 'everywhere'
apan-ok 'directly'
šaš ... wi 'absolutely'
ma-wi 'not'
ma-na 'not yet'
kan-ok 'still'
kan-na 'yet'
(ša)š-ma 'not at all'

2.5.5.4. PARTICLE COMPLEX. The elements in the particle complex which typically initiates a Quiche utterance may combine to form phrases of considerable complexity.

In addition to combinations of pairs of elements, prepositional and adverbial particles may combine with other morphemes or with each other. We may distinguish (1) preverbal phrases composed exclusively of particles from (2) those in which nouns or verbs also enter. Particle phrases appear to be the more characteristic.

Examples:

pa-sa la 'what!'
pa-su waral 'what?'
oxer kan-ok 'formerly'
ma ša-ki 'than not?'
ša-ta pa 'maybe, still then, in a moment'
š-ta wi 'then ... please'
ša-pa wi 'wherever'
šaš ma-wi 'absolutely not'
šaš pa-su wa č wi 'it is something'
šas kexe-wi 'it must be thus'
kexe-q̇ut we 'so if'
naki-la lo 'perhaps something, who might it be that ... ?'
xan-čin la lo 'who might it be that ...?'
ma-wi naki-la 'nothing'
ma nay puč- 'neither'
xa-nik an 'how far?'
či ma-xa ok 'before'
ma-xa na 'not yet'
ma-xa ni 'not the ... '
(x)a tak ta-on 'whichever'
ta-na pa-la 'at long last'
ša-ta pa 'still then'
pa-la činaq 'whichever'
we pa-la 'someone'
či-la apon-ok 'farther on'
(x)a-pa činaq 'which?'
ša-et na 'somewhat later'
xa-ni pa 'when?'
xa-wi či 'where?'
xa-la sač 'something else'
xa-la wi 'sometime, someplace'
xa-sa lo 'what might it be that ... ?'
xa-činaq a xe tak 'each one'
ma-xa ṗi či 'there's nothing that ... '
š xa-nik pa 'in what condition?'
xu-la ča 'how?'
xu-pa ča 'how?'
ma ta-q̇u wi 'not already'

may kan-ok 'formerly'

la ... nox-ne 'whether ... or'

nox-ne ... mi 'whether ... or not'

nox-ne ... nox-ne 'either ... or'

we... nox-ne mi 'either...or not'

pa-su wa č 'what's that?'

pa-su wa lo 'what might it be that ... ?'

pa-su wa ri 'what is it that ... ?'

are ta-la 'wherefore'

are ġu-la 'that's what it was'

ġut wa-e 'now this'

ma ša-ki 'than not?'

xa ri pa 'how much?'

pa-su ġu ri 'why, then?'

xe (a)re ri 'that is, quite'

la ki ta 'however'

ma are la 'I don't know what ... '

In a few cases nouns or verbs enter intimately into these combinations: even though the structure then changes, some of uses are of interest in this syntactic context.

Examples:

či k ix kan-ok 'back then'

na xun čik 'not another one'

kiy ȼix 'really'

ġas ȼix 'really'

ma-wi hun 'not one'

xa-čin r uq 'with whom?'

š ka ġin činaq 'in a little while'

xa r(i) mul 'how many times?'

nox ȼi(x) 'truly'

nox r e 'whether, all the more'

pa-su r umal 'what for?'

pa-su wa r umal 'what for?'

č u wi či-ġut 'after'

2.5.5.5. LOCATIVE PARTICLES. The principal locative particle is *la* 'here, there'. Others appear to be compounds: *či-la* 'here, there', *či-ri* 'here', *waral* 'here', *upik* 'here, there, outside', *ulok* 'there, hither'.

Examples:

ġo la 'there are'

či-la pa tinamit 'there in town'

ma n(a) ġo tax či-ri 'there aren't any here'

š el ulok 'he went there'

k in pet upik 'I'm going out'

2.5.5.6. QUANTITATIVE PARTICLES. One somewhat rare particle expresses quantity: *šo* 'very, much'. Other quantitative expressions employ nouns or verbs.

Examples:

šo ġatan 'it is very hot'

kiy kiy 'very sweet'

nim ri ġaš 'it is a bad pain'

2.5.6. INTERJECTIONAL PARTICLES. Principal interjections include: *o* 'ouch!', *a* 'aw!', *i* 'hey!', *oy* 'psst!', *ay* 'ow!', *er* 'uh!', and *ow* 'hi!'. Classical Quiche also includes others: *yexa*, *ula*, *ax-kar-rok*, all with the meaning 'hail!'.

REFERENCES

Andrade, 1946
Alemán, 1884
Anleo, 1865
Anonymous, 1838, 1902, 1950
Barberena, n.d.
Barrera Vásquez, 1940
Basseta, ?1698
Blomme, 1884
Brasseur de Bourbourg, 1861, 1962
Burgess, D. M., 1946
—— and Xec, 1955
Burgess, P., n.d., *a–d*, 1924, 1925
Cadena, 1892
Charencey, 1883
Ebneter, 1960
Edmonson, 1965
Fernandez Ferraz, 1902
Friedrich, 1955
Gates, 1920

Goubaud Carrera, 1946a, 1946b
Halpern, 1942
Hernández Spina, 1932
Lewy, 1937
López, 1892
McQuown, n.d., 1956
Mason, 1940
Recinos, 1916, 1917, 1957
Rodas, n.d.
Scherzer, 1855
Schuller, 1920
Schultze-Jena, 1933, 1944
Squier, 1861, 1865
Stoll, 1884, 1913
Teletor, n.d., 1942, 1943, 1949, 1959
Villacorta C., 1934
Wick, 1951
Xec and Maynard, 1954
Ximénez, ?1722

7D. Sierra Popoluca

BENJAMIN F. ELSON

0.	Introduction
1.	Phonology
1.1.	Segmental system
1.2.	Intonational system
1.3.	Phoneme distribution
2.	Morphophonemics
2.1.	Within the phonemic phrase
2.2.	Within words
3.	Syntax
3.1.	Clause types
3.1.1.	Independent clauses with verbs
3.1.1.1.	Intransitive declarative clauses
3.1.1.2.	Transitive declarative clauses
3.1.1.3.	Intransitive indefinite clauses
3.1.1.4.	Transitive indefinite clauses
3.1.1.5.	Intransitive imperative clauses
3.1.1.6.	Transitive imperative clauses
3.1.2.	Stative clauses
3.1.3.	Interrogative clauses
3.1.4.	Relative dependent clauses
3.1.5.	Time dependent clauses
3.1.6.	General dependent clauses
3.2.	Phrases
3.2.1.	Substantive phrases
3.2.1.1.	Simple phrases
3.2.1.2.	Count phrases
3.2.1.3.	Modified phrases
3.2.1.4.	Stative noun phrases
3.2.1.5.	Nominal participle phrases
3.2.1.6.	Verbal participle phrases
3.2.1.7.	Possessed noun phrase
3.2.1.8.	Coordinate phrase
3.2.1.9.	Appositional phrases
3.2.1.10.	*he?m iga*
3.2.1.11.	*méš·, máske*
3.2.1.12.	Locational noun subject tagmeme
3.2.2.	Comment phrases
3.2.3.	Location phrases
3.2.4.	Temporal phrases
3.2.5.	Instrumental phrases
3.2.6.	Accompaniment phrases
3.2.7.	Simile phrases
3.2.8.	Endocentric verb phrases
3.2.9.	Interdependent verb phrases
4.	Morphology
4.1.	Inflection
4.1.1.	Inflection of substantives
4.1.1.1.	Subjects or objects
4.1.1.1.1.	Nouns
4.1.1.1.2.	Pronouns
4.1.1.1.3.	Numerals
4.1.1.1.4.	Adjectives
4.1.1.1.5.	Location substitutes
4.1.1.1.6.	Nominal and verbal participles
4.1.1.2.	Comments of stative clauses
4.1.1.2.1.	Nouns
4.1.1.2.2.	Pronouns
4.1.1.2.3.	Numerals
4.1.1.2.4.	Adjectives
4.1.1.2.5.	Location substitutes
4.1.1.3.	Location tagmemes
4.1.1.3.1.	Nouns
4.1.1.3.2.	Pronouns
4.1.1.3.3.	Location substitutes
4.1.1.3.4.	Possessed directionals
4.1.1.4.	Time tagmemes
4.1.1.5.	Instrumental tagmemes
4.1.1.6.	Verbal number tagmemes
4.1.2.	Negatives
4.1.3.	Inflection of verbs
4.1.3.1.	Intransitive declarative predicates
4.1.3.2.	Intransitive indefinite predicates
4.1.3.3.	Transitive declarative predicates
4.1.3.4.	Transitive indefinite predicates

4.1.3.5. Intransitive imperative predicates
4.1.3.6. Transitive imperative predicates
4.1.3.7. Time subordinate clause predicates
4.1.3.8. *mu* 'when'
4.1.3.9. General subordinate clause predicates
4.1.3.10. Intradependent verb phrases
4.1.4.   Suffixed universally (except to particles in §4.1.5)
4.1.5.   Uninflected particles
4.2.   Derivation
4.2.1.   Substantives
4.2.1.1. Substantive stems
4.2.1.2. Compound stems
4.2.2.   Verbs
4.2.2.1. Transitive and intransitive stems
4.2.2.1.1. Affixation
4.2.2.1.2. Derivation
4.2.2.2. Intransitive stems
4.2.2.2.1. Affixation
4.2.2.2.2. Compounds
4.2.2.3. Transitive stems
4.2.3.   Temporals
4.2.4.   Nominal participles
4.2.5.   Verbal participles

0. INTRODUCTION. Sierra Popoluca (SP) is spoken by approximately 10,000–12,000 people in southeastern Veracruz, Mexico. SP is the most northern dialect of the Zoquean family, which includes Zoque and Mixe.

The purpose of this article is to present a balanced picture of the phonology, morphology, and syntax of SP, but, obviously, is not exhaustive for any of these aspects of SP grammar. There is only a limited statement of phonemic distribution. Clause and phrase structure have been presented in the main, but practically nothing has been indicated of sentence structure. Emphasis in the morphology section is on inflectional affixes; the methods of stem formation have been illustrated rather than discussed in detail. In addition, many SP-speakers are quite bilingual and frequently introduce Spanish words and phrases into their speech. I have included only those Spanish borrowings which are used by monolinguals as well and thus have become a part of general SP structure.

The descriptive model used for the analysis and presentation of the syntax (thus

influencing the morphological section as well) is the tagmemic model originally formulated by K. L. Pike (1954, 1955, 1960). Pike's formulation has been revised somewhat by R. L. Longacre (1960). In emphasizing clause structure and using it as the beginning point of analysis and description, I have followed Longacre rather than Pike. The tagmemic model has not, however, been used for discussing the morphology.

1. PHONOLOGY. SP contains two phonological subsystems: segmental and intonational.

1.1. THE SEGMENTAL SYSTEM consists of 30 phonemes. Of these 21 are consonants, 6 are vowels, and 3 are suprasegmental phonemes. The suprasegmental phonemes are closely related to the vowels.

The 21 consonants are presented in the following chart.

p	t	t^y	k
b	d	d^y	g
	c	$č$	
	s	$š$	
m	n	$ñ$	$ŋ$
		y	w	h
l			
r			

The principal allophonic variations of the consonant are given in the following statements:

(1) Voiceless stops are unaspirated when immediately followed by a vowel or by another consonant of the same point of articulation (except nasals), otherwise they are aspirated: *pétkuy* [*pét^hkuyY*] 'broom', *ikébakpút káwah* [*ikébak^hpút^hkáwah*] 'he chased away the horse', *hú·t^y* [*hú·t^yh*] 'where', *t^yú·ki* [*t^yú·ki?*] 'turtle', *ikká* [*ikká?*] 'he killed it'.

When voiceless stops are followed by nasals of the same point of articulation, the aspiration is released through the nose and has the phonetic character of a voiceless nasal: *wít^yñé* [*wít^yÑñé?*] 'he has walked', *pétné* [*pétNné?*] 'it is swept', *iñép mé·me* [*iñépMmé·me?*] 'he stepped on a butterfly'.

(2) Nasals and *y* have voiceless off-glides in phrase-final position: *kóm* [*kómM*] 'corner post', *pón* [*pónN*] 'soft', *cá·ñ* [*cá·ñÑ*] 'snake', *ká·ŋ* [*ká·ŋ Ŋ*] 'jaguar', *kúy* [*kúyY*] 'tree, wood'.

(3) The phoneme *h* has the voiceless character of the preceding nasal or *y* when immediately following these: *ká·mhó·m* [*ká·mMó·mM*] 'in the cornfield', *anhá·tuŋ* [*anNá·tuŋŊ*] 'my father', *iñhón* [*iñÑónN*] 'your bird', *sáŋhó·m* [*sáŋŊó·mM*] 'fiesta time'.

The six vowels form a three by two system.

i	*ɑ*	*u*
e	*a*	*o*

The high vowels are quite high, while the low vowels are relatively low, approximating [*ɛ*], [*a*], and [*ɔ*]. The range of phonetic variation for the vowels is relatively small.

The three suprasegmental phonemes function (morphophonemically) with the vowels and may be said to constitute a part of the vowel system. They are length /·/, glottal catch /ʔ/, and secondary stress /'/: *pók* 'tecomate', *pó·k* 'cornstalk', *kútᵛu* 'person with a harelip', *kú·šuh* 'lame person', *ipétpa* 'he sweeps it', *ipéʔtpa* 'he places them side by side', *ikapún* 'he castrated it', *ikápun* 'his barrow'.

Although glottal catch occurs (phonetically) in various positions, it is contrastive only after vowel and before consonant in the same syllable. It will be indicated in the phonemic transcription only at this point. Glottal catch occurs noncontrastively in the following environments: phrase finally after short vowels *ági šútᵛu* [*ágišútᵛuʔ*] 'it is very small'; between vowels phrase medially *káak* [*ká·ʔakʰ*] 'huarache'; and, optionally, phrase initially before vowels *iká* [*ʔikáʔ*] or [*iká·ʔ*] 'his hand'.

Length and glottal catch may not occur with the same vowel at the same time.[1]

---

[1] Elsewhere (Elson, 1961a), I proposed a phonemic interpretation of glottal catch and vowel length similar to the one presented here, but which was inconsistent in its treatment of the phonetic material. That treatment allowed glottal catch and length to occur together as features of

1.2. THE INTONATIONAL SYSTEM consists of 9 phonemes: primary stress /"/; four pitches, from low to high /1/, /2/, /3/, /4/; three terminals /↓/, /↑/, /|/; and a feature of fade or final voicelessness /ᵛ/.

An intonation contour defines the limit of a phonemic phrase. It consists of a minimum of primary stress, one pitch, and one terminal: *i"kɔ3↓* 'his hand' (matter-of-fact answer to a question). The maximum number of phonemes in an intonation contour is five: primary stress, two pitches, a terminal, and fade. These are distributed as follows: primary stress and one pitch occur early in the phrase; the second pitch occurs on the last stressed syllable (i.e., the last syllable with secondary stress); the terminal, which is rising, falling, or steadiness of voice, follows the last stress; and fade, which involves an unvoicing of the final syllable or syllables, is phrase final. Primary stress usually occurs on vowels that otherwise have secondary stress, but may also occur on vowels that would not carry secondary stress in that morpheme sequence. Examples are: *he"m"pa·šiñ3|* *i"haʔmpa-heʔmipóopo33↓ᵛ* *"nakpaiáʔm23|* *i"tᵛucikúʔ-dayñéum31↓ᵛ* 'The man set his shrimp trap. He went to look at it; someone else had eaten their tails'.

In the above examples the first number indicates the pitch that occurs on the vowel with primary stress, the second number indicates the pitch that occurs on the last vowel with secondary stress. Between these two points the pitch may (nonsignificantly) either be sustained, or may drop or rise.

1.3. PHONEME DISTRIBUTION will be dis-

---

the same vowel: /páʔ·tɑ/ [*páʔatɑʔ*] 'find it!' Although this analysis allowed concise morphophonemic statements, in certain cases the phonetic material was treated inconsistently. In this paper, we treat all instances of vowel-glottal catch-vowel as vowel clusters. This will necessitate additional morphophonemic statements, but will give consistency to the phonemic interpretation of the phonetic facts. This interpretation also coincides with the practical orthography currently in use.

cussed in terms of the occurrence of phonemes within the phonemic phrase.

(1) After silence and before the first vowel all consonant phonemes occur except *ŋ*. Voiced stops, except *dᵛ*, occur in this position only in relatively recent Spanish loan words. Also, except for recent Spanish loan words, no consonant clusters occur in this position except *tr* and *kr*; words with these clusters are rare.

(2) All vowels occur initially.

(3) After vowel and before silence all consonants have been observed except voiced stops, though *w* is exceedingly rare in this position. Even recent Spanish loan words do not retain voiced stops in this position. Two phrase-final consonant clusters occur: *ks* and *ps*.

(4) All vowels, long and short, stressed and unstressed, occur in phrase-final position.

(5) Between vowels, consonant clusters usually consist of two consonants. Where three consonants are found, the first is *p* or *k* and the second *s* or *š*. Voiced stops *b* and *d* have not been observed in clusters except in Spanish loan words, though *dᵛ* and *g* occur as the final member of clusters. Clusters of four consonants are possible but the first member will be *p* or *k*, the second *s*, the third *t* or *k*, and the fourth *r*.

(6) Clusters of up to four vowels have been observed. Only short, stressed or unstressed, vowels may occur initially and medially in clusters, though long vowels may occur as the final member.

Vowel plus glottal catch occurs only immediately preceding a consonant.

When a vowel is long, secondary stress also occurs. There is no limit on the number of secondary stresses that may occur within a phonemic phrase.

2. MORPHOPHONEMICS. As morphemes follow one another, some morphemes have different phonemic shapes in different occurrences depending upon the phonemic environments in which they occur.

2.1. WITHIN THE PHONEMIC PHRASE the

272

following rules apply regardless of word boundaries.

(1) When any morpheme which ends (otherwise) *VT* (where *V* is any vowel and *T* is any voiceless stop) precedes a morpheme which begins *V*, the phonemic form of the sequence is *VDV* (where *D* is the voiced counterpart of the voiceless stop):[2] *ipak itᵛuhkuy* /*ipágitᵛúhkuy*/ 'he took his gun', *huˑtᵛ iʔñiš* /*húudᵛiʔñíš*/ 'where did you see it', *iñip.aʔy* /*iñibáʔy*/ 'he planted it for him'.[3]

(2) When a morpheme which ends (otherwise) *VL* (where *V* is any short vowel, and *L* is any voiced consonant) precedes a morpheme beginning *V*, the phonemic form is *VʔLV*: *kuy.aʔy* /*kuʔyáʔy*/ 'he has wood', *hon ihap* /*hóʔniháp*/ 'bird's bill'.

(3) When a morpheme which ends (otherwise) *Vˑ L* (where *Vˑ* is any long vowel and *L* is any voiced consonant) precedes a morpheme beginning *V*, the phonemic form of the sequence is *VVLV* (where *VV* is a sequence of identical short vowels): *maˑl iwat* /*máaliwát*/ 'he did wrong', *caˑñ itᵛuʔc* /*cáañitᵛúʔc*/ 'snake's tail', *kaˑm.aʔy* /*káamáʔy*/ 'he has a cornfield'.

(4) When a morpheme which ends (otherwise) *Vˑ T* (where *Vˑ* is any long vowel and *T* is any voiceless stop) precedes a morpheme beginning *V*, the phonemic form of the sequence is *VVDV*: *poˑp.aˑp* /*póobáˑp*/ 'it whitens', *ihaˑk ikawah* /*iháagikáwah*/ 'he pulled his horse along', *huˑtᵛ iaŋ* /*húudᵛiáŋ*/ 'where did he go'.

(5) When a morpheme which ends (otherwise) *Vˑ* precedes a morpheme beginning *V*, the phonemic form of the sequence is *VV*: *anakpaˑ.aʔypa* /*anakpaáʔypa*/ 'I'll fatten it for him'.

[2] Four suffixes -*i*, -*a*, -*a*/-*a*, and -*um* do not follow this and the other statements of this section.

[3] For illustrating morphophonemic changes, we separate words by spaces and morphemes within words by dots on the line. The morphophonemic rules being stated apply at those points. The phonemic form follows between solidi.

Phonemic forms will be cited without the phonemes of the intonation system, since many alternative contours would be possible.

(6) Morphemes having the shape *CV* have alternants with the shape *CVV* when stressed and occurring before a consonant: *he nakpa* /héenákpa/ 'he is going', *ca.yukma* /cáayúkma/ 'upon a rock', *naknakne.ba* /náknáknéeba/ 'he goes over and over'.[4]

2.2 WITHIN WORDS the morphophonemic rules listed below apply:

(1) When a morpheme ending with an alveopalatal consonant *tʸ, dʸ, č, š, ñ, y*, the vowel *i*, or the sequence *ih* precedes a morpheme beginning (otherwise) with an alveolar consonant *t, c, s, n*, in the phonemic form the alveolar consonant is palatalized: *kuy.cecpa* /kuyčécpa/ 'he planes wood', *witʸ.ne* /wítʸñé/ 'he has walked', *iñ.sospa* /iñšóspa/ 'you cook it', *či.ta·* /čťitʸá·/ 'it was given to him', *iñčih.taʔmpa* /iñčihtʸáʔmpa/ 'you are hitting it'.

(2) Suffix morphemes, indicated by hyphens preceding them, whose vowel nuclei contain length or glottal catch when stressed, occur without length when unstressed, and without glottal catch when unstressed except when a vowel follows: *ammac-aʔy-taʔmpa* /ammácaytʸáʔmpa/ 'we grabbed it for him', *anak-tam-to-ba* /anáktamtóoba/ 'we want to go', *koʔc-ta·-taʔp* /kóʔctatáʔp/ 'someone hit him without result', *imak-oʔy-aʔy* /imágoʔyáʔy/ 'he lied to him'.

(3) Suffix morphemes ending *V·* occur without length if the next following syllable begins with a consonant: *yo·š-a·-p-tʸim* /yó·šáptʸim/ 'he is working also', *koʔc-ta·-tʸim* /kóʔctátʸim/ 'he was hit too'.

(4) Prefix morphemes ending (otherwise) *n* have alternants ending *m* when a bilabial follows, *ñ* when an alveopalatal follows, and *ŋ* when a velar follows: *an-petkuy* /ampétkuy/ 'my broom', *an-yo·mo* /añyó·mo/ 'my wife', *an-kawah* /aŋkáwah/ 'my horse'.

(5) Prefix morphemes ending (otherwise) *ñ* have alternants ending *m* when a bilabial follows, and *ŋ* when a velar follows: *iñ-*

petkuy /impétkuy/ 'your broom', *iñ-way* /iŋwáy/ 'your hair'.

(6) When the person prefixes co-occur with prefixes *ak-, aŋ-*, and *na-* a number of variations result. These are presented in the following chart.

PERS. PREFIXES	*ak-*	*aŋ-*	*na-*
an-	*anak-*	*anaŋ-*	*ana-*
tan-	*tanak-*	*tanaŋ-*	*tana-*
iñ-	*inik-*	*iniŋ-*	*ini-*
i-	*ik-*	*iŋ-*	*ini-*
a-	*ak-*	*aŋ-*	*ana-*
ta-	*tak-*	*taŋ-*	*tana-*
mi-	*mik-*	*miŋ-*	*mini-*

Where *n* occurs in the above combinations, it alternates freely with *r*: *anahó·ypa* or *arahó·ypa* 'I take him for a walk'.

Where they are pertinent, other morphophonemic changes will be discussed as the morphemes are considered.

In the examples cited throughout the rest of the paper, except where otherwise indicated, spaces occur between words and the phonemic form of each word is given as it would be pronounced in isolation. This is done as a convenience to the reader in following the examples. Intonation phonemes, however, are not included since for almost any sequence of morphemes several combinations of intonations phonemes are possible. In order to approximate the pronunciation of most of the examples, the reader should apply the morphophonemic rules of §2.1. and use a *31↓ˇ* intonation contour.

3. SYNTAX. A sentence in SP is defined by a combination of phonological and grammatical criteria. An independent sentence contains at least one independent clause and usually contains an intonation contour of the final type. A dependent sentence does not contain an independent clause.[5]

SP clauses are defined as any sequence

---

[4] The morpheme *-ne* optionally, in some situations, does not occur in the shape *-nee*: /naknétʸim/ or /naknéetʸim/ 'he went too'.

[5] I am indebted to Viola Waterhouse for the terms "independent" and "dependent" sentences.

which upon analysis consists of or contains a predicate or predicate-like tagmeme. Items which function as predicates, i.e., words and phrases which manifest predicates, are verbs. In other words, each verb or verb phrase taken together with the non-verbal elements related to it constitute a clause. There are also independent clauses which do not contain verbs. In such clauses nouns and adjectives function as a kind of predicate.

An independent clause is one which contains no subordinating verb affixes or particles, while dependent clauses do contain such subordinating elements.

When one or more clauses occur in sequence an independent sentence is formed (1) if there are one or more independent clauses, and (2) if there is a final intonation contour which coincides with the end of the clause. It is possible for more than one final intonation contour to occur within a single clause, but only one sentence if formed if there is only one clause: *hésagam i ″koᵓc3*↓˅ *kon heᵓm ″čikščay3*↓˅ 'Then he hit him with the thorn-vine'. The opposite is true as well: *i ″nakpa iáᵓm23 │ ″tumtum kuké·ha23 │ ″kuᵓtnetáwom heᵓm cás21*↓˅ 'And he goes to look at it each morning; someone has eaten the shrimp'. Here two independent clauses occur but only one final intonation contour is present, consequently, only one sentence is formed.

Dependent sentences are responses, greetings, and the like: *″dᵘa2*↓˅ 'no'.

This section is limited to the discussion of clauses and phrases. The description is in terms of the constituent tagmemes found at these levels.

3.1. CLAUSE TYPES. We recognize 13 basically different clause types: eight are independent and five are dependent. The criteria used for distinguishing these are primarily internal, i.e., differences in the structure of words functioning as predicates and differences in tagmemes which may co-occur with these different predicates. It is assumed that these different types will also function in different ways in forming sentences.

These criteria include independent vs. dependent clauses, intransitive vs. transitive clauses, declarative vs. imperative vs. indefinite vs. interrogative clauses, clauses with verbs vs. clauses without verbs. Obviously, these criteria crisscross with one another.

Clause-level tagmemes are the constituent units of the clause. A discussion of the morpheme classes which give substance to the structure is given later.

3.1.1. INDEPENDENT CLAUSES WITH VERBS. Clauses of this type consist of a predicate tagmeme around which other tagmemes nucleate. Although we consider these tagmemes to be all on the same level, future analysis may show groupings which will cause some of these tagmemes to be subordinated, i.e., included in the analysis of phrases rather than clauses.

3.1.1.1. INTRANSITIVE DECLARATIVE CLAUSE (IDC). The minimum structure of IDC consists of a single intransitive declarative predicate tagmeme manifested by an intransitive declarative verb (§4.1.3.1) or verb phrase (§3.2.8): *anákpa* 'I'm going', *póypa híkskay* 'he runs fast'. Other tagmemes which may occur with the predicate tagmeme are: subject, location, time, instrument, accompaniment, simile, verbal number; sequence, introducer, exclamatory, vocative. The predicate is the nucleus of the clause; the first seven tagmemes mentioned above are central, while the last four are peripheral.

The subject tagmeme is manifested by a substantive (§4.1.1.1) or a substantive phrase (§3.2.1). The subject may either precede or follow the predicate; a subject pronoun almost always precedes: *míñpa heᵓm pé·toh* 'Peter is coming', *hé čokoᵓyá·p imíñ* 'he is coming slowly'.

The location tagmeme is manifested by a locational word (§4.1.1.3) or locational phrase (§3.2.3). The location tagmeme may either precede or follow the predicate, though a location substitute usually precedes the predicate. When the predicate is first the location tagmeme follows the subject if both are present: *hémak nákpa he?m šíwan* 'John is going over there', *áč aóy ká·mhó·m* 'I have been to the cornfield', *nákpa šíwan á·tébet* 'John is going to Soteapan'.

The time tagmeme is manifested by a heterogeneous class of substantives (§4.1.1.5), temporal particles (§4.1.4.6), and special idiomatic time clauses (§3.2.4.3). These may be grouped together into phrases (§3.2.4). In addition, certain subordinate clauses may manifest the time tagmeme. In general, the time tagmeme precedes the predicate, though it may follow as well: *yá?p há·ma tanákpa* 'today we will go', *pos he?m pá·šiñ cúuyt*im pútum it*ákkáam* 'well, the man very early left his house', *d*á móy mú·macúu* 'he didn't sleep all night'.

The instrumental tagmeme is manifested by instrumental nouns (§4.1.1.4), and in the intransitive clause by a few otherwise locational nouns (with the suffix *-yukma* §4.1.1.3), or by instrumental phrases (§3.2.5.1). The instrumental tagmeme usually follows the predicate: *nák púyma* 'he went on foot', *nák iká·mhó·m káwahyúkma* 'he went to his cornfield on horseback'.

The accompaniment tagmeme is manifested by an accompaniment phrase (§3.2.6). The prefix *waga-* 'together with' is often present in the verb when the accompaniment tagmeme occurs: *áč anákpa kon šíwan* 'I am going with John', *hé nák tú·hi kon ičímpa* 'he went hunting with his dog', *awáganákpa kon pé·toh* 'I am going with Peter'.

The simile tagmeme is manifested by a simile phrase (§3.2.7): *aywéhpa kómo yó·ya* 'he made a noise [shouted] like a pig', *wít*pa húuc pá·šiñ* 'it walks like a man', *wít*pa húuc íga pá·šiñ yó?ypa* 'he walks like a man jumping'.

The verbal number tagmeme is manifested by verbal numbers (§4.1.1.6): *aóy túmkay* 'I went twice'.

The above seven tagmemes each have a corresponding interrogative form: *í· nákpa* 'who is going?' *hú·t* nákpa* 'where is he going?' *húčaš nákpa* 'when is he going?' *t*í·yúkma nákpa* 'on what is he going'? *húuc wít*pa* 'how does he walk?' *hú·té·n oyyáh* 'how many went?'

The following four peripheral tagmemes are not manifested by interrogatives.

The sequence tagmeme is manifested by a small class of Spanish conjunctions (§4.1.4.1): *i nák* 'and he went', *péro sé·t* 'but he returned'.

The introducer tagmeme is manifested by a small subclass of temporal substitutes (§4.1.1.5): *hésak nák* 'then he went', *ókma pút it*ákhó·m* 'later he went out of his house'.

The exclamatory tagmeme is manifested by a small number of SP words plus several Spanish loan words (§4.1.4.9): *bwéno áč anákpa* 'Well, I'm going', *yúli wasté·n óy* 'I think two went'.

The vocative tagmeme is manifested by an appropriate uninflected noun: *šíwan áč anákpa* 'John, I'm going'.

The IDC may be said to consist of a predicate tagmeme plus one or more of the above mentioned optional tagmemes. An examination of 200 typical IDCs selected at random from text material recorded by tape recorder indicates that two or three tagmemes are the usual number per occurrence of this clause type; instances of more than four tagmemes occurring are rare. The subject tagmeme is present approximately 50 per cent of the time, the location tagmeme about 40 per cent, the introducer about 15 per cent and the sequence tagmeme about 10 per cent. All other tagmemes were present less than 10 per cent of the time.

3.1.1.2. TRANSITIVE DECLARATIVE CLAUSE (TDC). The minimum structure of TDC consists of a single predicate tagmeme manifested by a transitive declarative verb (§4.1.3.3), or verb phrase (§3.2.8): *aykó?cpa* 'I am hitting him', *pá·mi it*áypa* 'he chops it rapidly'. In addition to differences in the

275

predicate, TDCs are also distinguished by the potential occurrence of object tagmemes. Three different objects are recognized: direct object, indirect object, and causative object. All of these tagmemes are manifested by appropriate substantives.

The direct object may occur with any transitive verb: *aŋkóʔcpa šíwan* 'I hit John', *itʷáŋpa kúy* 'he is cutting wood', *šíwan ihókspa heʔm ká·ma* 'John is hoeing the cornfield'.

The indirect object may occur when the predicate tagmeme is manifested by *či* 'to give something to someone' or by certain transitive stems with the suffix *-aʔy* 'indirective-benefactive': *añčíiba šíwan yáʔp túmiñ* 'I'll give John this money', *míč manamíʔñáʔy yáʔp pá·suŋ* 'I brought you this squash'.

Although *-aʔy* functions as an indicator of the indirect object in a few situations, its normal function is to indicate that the direct object is possessed by someone other than the subject: *ikóʔc ikáwah* 'he hit his (own) horse', *ikóʔcáʔy ikáwah* 'he hit his (the other's) horse'.

The causative object may occur with transitive stems which are further derived by the causative prefixes *ak-* 'causative' or *na-* 'associative-causative' (4.2.2.3.2): *sámñi ikkúʔt heʔm yó·mo* 'he fed the woman bananas', *heʔm šíwan anakčíiba iháʔyuk heʔm kúy* 'I'll cause John to give his brother the stick', *anahókspa šíwan heʔm ká·ma* 'I'll cause John to hoe the cornfield with me'. Although the above is observed SP, normal style is to have fewer subjects and objects (usually only one) present in a clause.

In addition to the three object tagmemes discussed above, all of the central and peripheral tagmemes which are found in the IDC also occur with TDC. However, with certain tagmemes there are differences in the manifesting class.

The instrumental tagmeme is manifested by instrumental nouns (§4.1.1.4) and by certain accompaniment phrases (§3.2.6, subclass b): *ikóʔc heʔm ikáwah kúyma* 'he hit his

horse with a stick', *antáŋpa heʔm kúy kon aʔná·čah* 'I'll chop the tree with my ax'.

The accompaniment tagmeme is manifested by only certain accompaniment phrases (§3.2.6, subclass a). Usually the prefix *waga-* 'together with' is present in this situation: *aŋwágakóʔc heʔm pa·šiñ kon šíwan* 'I hit the man with John, John and I hit the man'. It should be pointed out that this construction is fairly rare in this clause type, and is definitely the result of Spanish influence. The normal SP method of encoding the same message is: *šíwan anakóʔc heʔm pá·šiñ* 'I caused John to hit the man with me'.

TDCs may be said to consist of a transitive predicate tagmeme plus any of the above mentioned optional tagmemes. The average number of tagmemes occurring in a TDC is three to four, though up to seven have been observed.

An object (usually the direct object) occurs most frequently of the optional tagmemes. In a random count an object was present 60 per cent of the time, while the subject was present only 17 per cent of the time. Other optional tagmemes occurred less often. The location tagmeme, which was present frequently in IDC occurs here less than 10 per cent of the time. Some optional tagmeme accompanied the predicate about 88 per cent of the time.

As with IDC the order of tagmemes is not fixed, though peripheral tagmemes and tagmemes manifested by substitutes usually precede the predicate. When both subject and object are present the subject tends to precede the predicate and the object to follow. Otherwise the central optional tagmemes tend to follow the predicate: *i hésak heʔm šíwan ikóʔc heʔm itʷá·wa kúyma* 'and then John hit his brother with a stick'.

3.1.1.3. INTRANSITIVE INDEFINITE CLAUSE (IIC). IIC is manifested by an intransitive indefinite verb. Such verbs always contain the suffix *-na·m* 'intransitive indefinite' (§4.1.3.2): *čí·ŋnená·m* 'someone has been bathing, there has been bathing'. A subject tagmeme is not possible with IIC and other optional tagmemes occur rarely. Possible optional tagmemes are: sequence, introducer, exclamatory (rare), location, and time: *péro yáʔm pú·tná·mpa* 'but someone appears here', *bwéno cúʔmak wá·nná·m* 'well, last night there was singing'.

3.1.1.4. TRANSITIVE INDEFINITE CLAUSE (TIC). TIC consists of a transitive indefinite predicate tagmeme manifested by a transitive indefinite verb. Such verbs always contain the suffix *-ta·* 'transitive indefinite' (§4.1.3.4): *kóʔctá·* 'someone hit him, he was hit'. The subject tagmeme is not possible in TIC, though object tagmemes occur frequently. Other tagmemes observed are: sequence, introducer, exclamatory (rare), location, and time: *i hésak heʔm šiwan kóʔctá· ká·mhó·m* 'and then John was hit in the cornfield, and then someone hit John in the cornfield'.

The TIC occurs frequently since it seems to be a feature of SP style to have only one subject or object tagmeme per clause. Since the order of tagmemes in TDC is not fixed, ambiguity may arise. This ambiguity is resolved by subsequent occurrences of TIC and IDC. For example the clause *i hémak heʔm šiwan ikoʔc pé·toh* may either mean 'and there John hit Peter' or 'and there Peter hit John'. The ambiguity is resolved by *koʔcóʔy pé·toh, kóʔctá· šiwan* 'Peter did hitting; John was hit'.

In addition to the tagmemes discussed in the above clause types, there appears to be a position of emphasis or focus. When the subject, object, time, or location is manifested by a noun or noun phrase and occurs first in the clause, it is emphasized or in focus: *heʔm pá·šiñ nák péʔmam pláya* 'the man [what follows is about him] went to the beach', *kuyyúkma cénné* 'to the tree it was tied', *heʔm káwah šiwan ipáʔt* 'the horse, John found it'.

Besides the position of emphasis for the various central tagmemes of the clause, there appears to be an emphasis-referent tagmeme which is manifested by substantives, but

these substantives are not directly related to the predicate as subject or object: *heʔm pá·šiñ tóbaʔyaytᵛá· heʔm iwačó·mo* 'as for the man, someone took his wife from him', *i heʔm šiwan dᵛá nák hé* 'and as for John, he did not go'.[6]

3.1.1.5. INTRANSITIVE IMPERATIVE CLAUSE (IMC). The minimum form of IMC consists of an intransitive imperative predicate tagmeme manifested by an intransitive imperative verb. Verbs manifesting IMC predicates always contain the imperative morpheme *-a* (§4.1.3.5): *pó·ya* 'run! flee!' *pú·ta* 'go out!' Other tagmemes which may accompany the intransitive imperative tagmeme are: introducer, exclamatory, vocative, location, time, and the auxiliary imperative. The only word which manifests the latter tagmeme is *impá·mi* 'hurry' [lit. 'your strength, might']. The auxiliary imperative may sometimes occur in place of the predicate tagmeme: *šiwan impá·mi* 'John, hurry up'. Examples are: *hésak míč ná·ka ká·mho·m hóyma* 'then you go to the cornfield tomorrow', *kó·na kó·ñkuyyúkma* 'sit on the chair', *sáap mí·ña mihé·hi kómpa* 'now come and rest compadre'.

3.1.1.6. TRANSITIVE IMPERATIVE CLAUSE (TMC). The minimum form of TMC consists of a transitive imperative predicate tagmeme manifested by a transitive imperative verb. Verbs manifesting TMC predicates always contain the imperative morpheme *-a* (§4.1.3.6): *kóoca* 'hit him'. Other tagmemes which may accompany the transitive imperative predicate tagmeme are: introducer, exclamatory, vocative, direct object, indirect object, causative object, time, location, and the auxiliary imperative: *sáap aŋmííča iʔñíškuy* 'now close your eyes', *kómpa nanagáaya šiwan yáʔp túmiñ* 'compadre take John this money', *akkúuta heʔm yó·ya* 'cause the pig to eat it'.

3.1.2. STATIVE CLAUSES. There is one

---

[6] This tagmeme, if it is the same, has also been observed following the clause: *hé kúkma nákpa heʔm pá·šiñ dᵛápak waá·p* 'he went in the middle, the one who couldn't do it'.

independent clause type which does not contain a verb: the stative clause. It consists of two principal tagmemes, a subject (which is optional) and a comment tagmeme. Classes which manifest the comment tagmeme are discussed in §4.1.1.2. Other observed optional tagmemes are sequence, introducer, and location: *káwah* 'it is a horse', *áč ašútʸupak apá·šíñ* 'I am a little person', *péro ikó·bak pá·šíñ* 'but his head was [that of] a man', *cá·m mišútʸu* 'you are very small', *húuma antákma* 'my country is far away', *yáʔm dʸá húuma antákkáam* 'at my house is not far from here'.

The stative clause may also be subordinated with a clause subordinator (§4.1.4.7): *anhúypa heʔm káwah pórke wá·* 'I'll buy the the horse because it is good', *pút íga pá·ho* 'he came out in order to be a coyote [i.e., he became a coyote].'

3.1.3. INTERROGATIVE CLAUSES. As mentioned above, there are interrogative substitutes which may manifest the central tagmemes of the clause. When these are present in a single, sentence-forming clause, the result is an interrogative clause: *í· nákpa* 'who is going?' *tʸí· ítʸ* 'what is there?' *hú·tʸ miñákpa* 'where are you going?' *húčaš mimíñpa* 'when are you coming?' *húuc iŋwát* 'how did you do it?' *tʸíiga mióy* 'why did you go?' *tʸí·ma ikóʔc* 'with what did he hit him?' *kon í· mióy* 'with whom did you go?' *kon tʸí· iŋkóʔc* 'with what did you hit him?' *húʔcaŋ ičó·wa* 'how much is the price?'

3.1.4. RELATIVE DEPENDENT CLAUSES. Four of the above-mentioned interrogative words are also used to introduce relative clauses. Relative clauses always manifest clause-level tagmemes: *anákpa hú·tʸ ítʸ anhá·tuŋ* 'I am going where my father is', *anhúypa tʸítʸam iwáaŋhá·m* 'I'll buy him whatever he wants', *anákpa húčaš kéh* 'I'll go anytime [lit. I'll go when it appears]', *ananákpa ítʸam nákpa* 'I'll take whoever wants to go'.

3.1.5. TIME DEPENDENT CLAUSES. There are two types of time dependent clause, one in which the particle *mu* occurs in the predi-

278

cate and the other in which the verb manifesting the predicate contains suffixes *-pa·m* or *-wa·m* (§4.1.3.7).

Verbs manifesting IDC, TDC, or TIC predicates may occur with a preceding particle *mu* 'when'. The result is that the entire clause is subordinate and manifests the time tagmeme of the adjacent clause. Intransitive verbs and transitive indefinite verbs are inflected only with set II person prefixes (§4.1.3.7). The tagmemes already discussed may occur with the three subtypes of this clause: *hésak mu aʔnóy á·tébet, ampákcóŋ heʔm túmiñ* 'then when I went to Soteapan, I received the money', *mu iíš itʸáwa, dʸá iháypáʔt* 'when he saw his brother he didn't speak to him', *mu ikóʔctá·, aktáŋ* 'when he was hit, he fell down'.

The second type of time subordinate clause functions similarly. Verbs manifesting IDC, TDC, or TIC predicates may occur with the subordinating suffixes *-pa·m* or *-wa·m*. The entire clause is subordinate and manifests the time tagmeme of the adjacent clause. Intransitive verbs and transitive indefinite verbs are inflected only with set II person markers (§4.1.3.7). Most of the clause-level tagmemes already discussed may occur with the three subtypes of this clause: *hésak annákpá·m, aʔñíš máa* 'as I was going along, I saw a deer', *ikóʔcwá·m itʸá·wa iíš ihá·tuŋ* 'when he was hitting his brother he saw his father', *ikóʔctawá·m, aktáŋ* 'when he was being hit, he fell down'.

3.1.6. GENERAL DEPENDENT CLAUSE. There are two types of general dependent clauses: one in which the verb inflection is the same as that of independent clauses, and the other in which the verbs are inflected with *-iñ* 'obligatory'. Both types follow subordinating particles (§4.1.5.7).

The first type includes subordinate varieties of IDC, TDC, IIC, and TIC which manifest the object tagmeme, or add statements of cause or purpose. The constituent tagmemes are as described above. Such clauses may manifest one object tagmeme: *aʔñíšpa íga póypa heʔm pá·šiñ* 'I see that the man is running'; or may add a statement of cause or purpose: *anákpa íga anhúypa ampuktú·ku* 'I'm going so that I can buy my clothing', *apóy pórke hémagam pú·tná·mpa* 'I ran because there is appearing there [i.e., spirits appear]', *póy he⁷m šïwan pórke kó⁷ctá·* 'John ran because someone hit him'.

The second type includes subordinate varieties of IDC, TDC, and TIC, but the verb is inflected by *-iñ* (§4.1.3.9), and the negative particle used is *ódoy* rather than the normal *dʸá*. Otherwise the clause functions as the one above described: *ananákpa yá⁷p cá·ši íga ičígiñ mók* 'I'm taking this child so he can pick corn', *wá· íga miñágiñ* 'it would be good if you could go', *išúnpa íga čïitʸáiñ há⁷yaŋ* 'he wants a lot to be given him', *námpa íga ódoy miñágiñ* 'he said for you not to go'.

The second type is much less used than the first type, and probably has stronger force.

3.2. PHRASES. In general, phrases are expansions of words which manifest clause-level tagmemes. A phrase is considered to consist of two or more words.[7]

3.2.1. SUBSTANTIVE PHRASES. Substantive phrases are those phrases which manifest subject or object tagmemes.

All phrases which manifest subject or object tagmemes may contain the determiner as one constituent. The determiner is manifested by an article (*he⁷m* 'the') or by a subtype of pronoun (*pé⁷m* 'that', *yá⁷p* 'this').[8]

3.2.1.1. THE SIMPLE PHRASE consists of the determiner plus a head tagmeme which is manifested by a noun, numeral, or nominal participle: *yá⁷p pá·šiñ* 'this man', *he⁷m wasté·n* 'the two', *pé⁷m máhpak* 'that big one'.

3.2.1.2. THE COUNT PHRASE consists of a number plus a small subclass of nouns which are in some way receptacles. As will be seen

below this count phrase functions as a numeral: *tú·m kárga* 'one load', *síŋkoh hé·pe* 'five cups'. The determiner may also occur: *he⁷m dyés kúštʸat* 'the ten sacks'.

3.2.1.3. THE MODIFIED PHRASE consists of three tagmemes, all of which are optional, but two of which must occur for the modified phrase to be present. The tagmemes are count, quality, and specific. The count tagmeme may be manifested by a numeral, a simple numeral phrase, or by a count phrase. The quality tagmeme may be manifested by a nominal participle (see §3.2.1.5) or a simple nominal participle phrase. The specific tagmeme is manifested by a noun or simple noun phrase. The theoretical maximum, i.e., a simple phrase (see §3.2.1.1) manifesting each tagmeme, has not been observed. Rather when the quality and specific tagmemes are both present the determiner occurs preceding the combination no matter which is first. Examples are: *tú·m máhpak pá·šiñ* 'a big man', *he⁷m wasté·n he⁷m pók* 'the two tecomates', *tú·m kárga sák* 'one load of beans', *he⁷m ká·ŋ máhpak* 'the big jaguar', *wasté·n he⁷m máhpak* 'two big ones'.

3.2.1.4. THE STATIVE NOUN PHRASE consists of a noun plus an adjective modified by an adverb (usually *cá·m* 'very'). This phrase has been observed only at the end of a clause:[9] *kúuta yá⁷p kú·ma cá·m wá·* 'eat these very good plam nuts', *iníitʸ ikučí·yu cá·m cú·pa* 'he has his very sharp knife'.

3.2.1.5. NOMINAL PARTICIPLE PHRASES are derived phrases for which see §4.2.4. Such phrases occur with the determiner tagmeme: *he⁷m cá·m pá·mi máhpak* 'the very, very big one', *he⁷m ká·mhó·mpak* 'the one from the cornfield', *he⁷m dʸápak húuma* 'the one not from away'.

3.2.1.6. VERBAL PARTICIPLE PHRASES are derived clauses for which see §4.2.5. Such phrases occur with the determiner tagmeme:

---

[7] This differs from Longacre's definition of phrase. For him one word may constitute a phrase if it is expandable.

[8] There are two rare forms which apparently substitute for *he⁷m*: *hére* 'that', *hí·* 'the'.

[9] It should be noted that this sequence could be considered as a stative clause with the noun in double function as object of one clause and subject of another.

heʔm óywáap húuma 'the one who went far away', *heʔm dᵘápak ikóʔc itᵘá·wa* 'the one who did not strike his brother'.

3.2.1.7. THE POSSESSED NOUN PHRASE consists of noun inflected by set II person markers (§4.1.1.1.1) and usually preceded, but occasionally followed, by a noun or pronoun or any of the above phrases (except §3.2.1.4), or by another noun inflected by set II (i.e., a possessed noun): *heʔm máhpak pá·šiñ iyó·ya* 'the big man's pig', *heʔm óywáap húuma· ikáwah* 'the horse of the one who went far away', *heʔm aʔnokhá·tuŋ ibú·roh* 'my god-father's burro'.

3.2.1.8. THE COORDINATE PHRASE consists of a list of nouns or simple noun phrases each of which refers to different things. Coordinators may or may be present: *anhúypa ampuktú·ku ancúhmitᵘ ammačí·tᵘi* 'I'll buy my clothing, my blanket, my machete', *nákpa šiwan éntre pé·toh* 'John and Peter are going'.

3.2.1.9. APPOSITIONAL PHRASES consists of a series of nouns, or simple noun phrases, all referring to the same thing. They are similar to coordinate phrases but coordinators do not occur: *hémagam ipáʔt heʔm pá·šiñ hámñapá·šiñ higánteh* 'there he found the man, a mountain man, a giant'.

3.2.1.10. *heʔm íga*. Occasionally, a subordinate clause containing the subordinator *iga* may occur with *heʔm* resulting in a kind of substantive phrase: *nákpa tancéʔk heʔm íga mitᵘápné* 'we will go and pay back that you were shot'.

3.2.1.11. *mé·š, máske*. Certain emphasis particles (§4.1.4.4) may precede some of the phrases above described: *mé·š heʔm šiwan nákpa* 'John, too, is going', *máske á·ñi ikúʔtpa* 'he eats only tortillas'.

3.2.1.12. LOCATIONAL NOUN SUBJECT TAGMEME. In addition to the phrases indicated above, the subject tagmeme may in restricted circumstances be manifested by locational nouns, for which see §4.1.1.3: *aŋká·mhó·m itᵘ húuma* 'my cornfield is far'.[10]

[10] Certain phrases, particularly of the modified

3.2.2. COMMENT PHRASES are those substantive phrases which manifest the comment tagmeme in the stative clause.

(1) Noun comment phrases contain the elements of the modified phrase (§3.2.1.3) without, however, the determiner: *heʔm šiwan máhpak pá·šiñ* 'John is a big man', *yáʔp káwah ičó·wa tú·m kárga sák* 'the price of this horse is a load of beans'.

(2) Adjective and directional phrases manifesting the comment tagmeme consist of adverbs (§4.1.4.5) plus adjective or directional: *cá·m yágac* 'he is very tall', *heʔm á·tébet cá·m húuma* 'Soteapan is far away'.

3.2.3. LOCATION PHRASES are those phrases which manifest the location tagmeme. These phrases are similar in structure to phrases discussed in §3.2.1. Place names and location nouns (§4.1.1.3) may occur in possessed, modified or simple phrases: *heʔm pláya* 'the beach', *heʔm máhpak tákkáam* 'at the big house', *šiwan iká·mhó·m* 'in John's cornfield'.

There is a group of direction words that always occur possessed: *ták iwé·ñtᵘaŋ* 'beyond the house,' *káwah ikunášwiñ* 'below the horse'.

There is a morpheme *heʔp* which occurs with location substitutes: *héʔp yáʔm* 'nearby here'.

Appositional phrases usually involve a location substitute or a directional plus a word or phrase, or clause introduced by *hú·tᵘ*: *hé·m á·tébet* 'there in Soteapan', *hémum iká·mhó·m* 'there in his cornfield', *húuma hú·tᵘ iwát iká·ma* 'far away where he made his cornfield'.

Any of the above may occur with *ásta* 'as far as' or *dénde* 'from': *ásta hé·m hú·tᵘ óy sé·tᵘi* 'as far as there where he turned and came back', *amíñ dénde šiwan iká·mkutúŋ* 'I came from the road to John's cornfield'.

and possessive types, which contain two "major" elements, may occur split or in reverse order. Such arrangements usually coincide with features of emphasis within the clause: *piyu anaitᵘ béynte* 'I have twenty chickens,' *áros antúk tú·m kárga* 'I harvested a load of rice', *heʔm pá·šiñ nák ibúroh* 'the man's burro went away', *nák ibúroh heʔm pá·šiñ* 'the man's burro went away'.

3.2.4. TEMPORAL PHRASES manifesting the time tagmeme are modified phrases consisting of a time noun modified by an article or numeral: *yá²p há·ma* 'today', *túmtum kuké·ha* 'each morning'. A second type are appositional phrases consisting of an SP time indicator plus a Spanish one: *hésak kómo a las kwátro* 'then about four o'clock', *sáabam el dós de nobyémbre* 'now the second of November'; or two or more SP elements: *sá·bay hésak cúuyam* 'later when it is dark'.

Certain clauses seem to have solidified as time idioms: *ikukéh há·ma* 'at dawn' [lit. 'the sun made it all appear'], *kugáp cú* 'midnight' [lit. 'the night halves'], *kugáp há·ma* 'noon' [lit. 'the sun halves'].

3.2.5. INSTRUMENTAL PHRASES manifest the instrumental tagmeme.

(1) In IDC the instrumental phrase is the same as the location phrase except that only the suffix *-yukma* 'upon' occurs with the noun: *anákpa káwahyúkma* 'I'm going on the horse', *óy šiwan ikamyónyúkma* 'he went in John's truck'.

(2) In TDC the instrumental phrase consists of a phrase introduced by kon 'with' and with nouns referring to things: *ikká he²m máa kon itᵛúhkuy* 'he killed the deer with his gun'.

3.2.6. ACCOMPANIMENT PHRASES are substantive phrases introduced by *kon* 'with': *anákpa kon he²m šiwan imáat* 'I am going with John's son-in-law'. There are two subclasses of accompaniment phrases (a) those with nouns referring to persons: *kon šiwan* 'with John'; and (b) those with nouns referring to things: *kon itᵛúhkuy* 'with his gun'. These manifest different tagmemes in TDC.

3.2.7. SIMPLE PHRASES are substantive phrases introduced by *húuc* or *kómo*: *witᵛpa húuc tú·m kú·šuh* 'he walks like a lame man'.

3.2.8. ENDOCENTRIC VERB PHRASES consist of verb plus an immediately following (usually) or preceding adjective, adverb or negative. The negative always precedes the verb: *ikyó²npa yágac itᵛóc úšpiñ* 'the alligator

stuck out his tongue a long way', *ana²ŋá·katá úšaŋ he²m pó·ktak* 'we fought some over the unused field', *ikó²c wá·wá·* 'he hit him really well', *pá·mi nákpa he²m cá·ši* 'the child is going very fast', *éybaktᵛim nákpa* 'he is going again', *dᵛá aóy* 'I didn't go'.

A second type of verb phrase consists of a verbal particle plus a verb: *anákpa ídᵛak* 'I was going to go', *wáap pútpa* 'he might get out', *máam nanáktá·* 'suddenly he was taken'.

3.2.9. INTERDEPENDENT VERB PHRASES are composed of two verbs. Their structure is discussed in detail in §4.1.3.10.

4. MORPHOLOGY. In the presentation of the morphology, inflection is discussed first and then derivation. The discussion of inflection, and to some extent that of derivation, shows the relation between the syntactic function and the form of the word or morpheme classes.

4.1. INFLECTION. Although the decision as to whether certain individual morphemes are derivational or inflectional is difficult, there is clearly a difference between the two systems in SP.

4.1.1. INFLECTION OF SUBSTANTIVES. Substantives constitute a large group of words which exhibit certain similarities of inflection, derivation, and syntactic function.

4.1.1.1. SUBJECTS OR OBJECTS. The inflection of substantives functioning as subject or object.

4.1.1.1.1. NOUNS functioning as subjects or objects may be inflected with the following affixes:

an- '1st per.'		-*tam* '1st and 2nd pl.'	-*tᵛim* 'just'
tan- '1st and 2nd'	Stem		
iñ- '2nd per.'		-*yah* '3rd pl.'	
i- '3rd per.'		-*aŋhoh* 'mass pl.'	-*gaktᵛi* 'again'

CHART I

The prefixes mark possession. Without the possessive markers the noun may function as specific in the modified phrase, and with the possessive markers in the possessive

281

phrase: *tákgaktⁿi* 'a house again', *káwahyah* 'horses', *yó·mtam* 'women', *antáktam* 'our house', *iñyó·motⁿim* 'just your wife', *iñyó· yayah* 'your pigs', *caáŋhoh* 'a pile of rocks'.

4.1.1.1.2. PRONOUNS functioning as subjects or objects may be inflected as follows:

itⁿúmpay 'all of them' have somewhat different syntactic possibilities: *há⁷yaŋtⁿim* 'many also'.

Numerals inflected in this way manifest the count tagmeme in the modified phrase (3.2.1(3)), except inflection with possessive

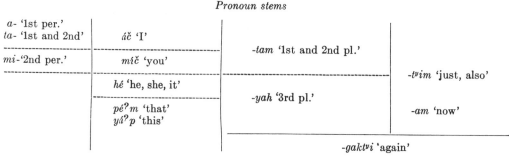

Pronoun stems

a- '1st per.' ta- '1st and 2nd'	áč 'I'		
mi-'2nd per.'	mič 'you'	-tam '1st and 2nd pl.'	-tⁿim 'just, also'
	hé 'he, she, it'	-yah '3rd pl.'	-am 'now'
	pé⁷m 'that' yá⁷p 'this'		
		-gaktⁿi 'again'	

CHART II

The chart includes all SP pronouns as well as pronoun inflection. *pé⁷m* 'that one' and *yá⁷p* 'this one' have certain differences of syntactic function. Examples are: *aáčⁿam* 'we, us' (exclusive), *taáčⁿam* 'we, us' (inclusive), *mimíčⁿam* 'you all', *áčgaktⁿi* 'I, too,' *yá⁷bam* 'this one now', *héeyah* 'they'.

4.1.1.1.3. NUMERALS functioning as subjects or objects are inflected as follows:

| an- '1st per.' tan- '1st and 2nd' | | | -tⁿim 'just, also' -nam 'still' |
| iñ- '2nd per.' i- '3rd per.' | Stem | -te·n | -gaktⁿi 'again' |

CHART III

The suffix *-te·n* is obligatory with numbers two through five and with the word for 'how many': *wasté·ngaktⁿi* 'two also', *tukuté·nnam* 'three still'. Other numerals are not inflected with *-te·n*. The possessive prefixes occur with some numerals: *aŋwasté·n* 'my two'. The number 'one' is inflected by *-tⁿim* and *-nam* only: *tú·mtⁿim* 'just one', *tú·mnam* 'one still'. Spanish numbers are inflected occasionally: *siŋkohtⁿim* 'just five'. Two non-count numerals *há⁷yaŋ* 'many' and

prefixes has not been observed in this position,

4.1.1.1.4. ADJECTIVES may function as subjects or objects when they are inflected by possessive prefixes: *wá· ičábac* 'its redness is nice'.

4.1.1.1.5. LOCATION SUBSTITUTES may function as subjects or objects when they are inflected by possessive prefixes: *tóypa anyá⁷m* 'I hurt right here' [lit. 'my here hurts'], *ikó⁷cá⁷y ihé·m* 'he hit him right there' [lit. 'he hit his there'].

4.1.1.1.6. NOMINAL AND VERBAL PARTICIPLES also function as subjects and objects. Nominal participles may be inflected by *-tⁿim*, *-nam*, and *-am*: *he⁷m máhpagam* 'the one now big'. Nominal participles may, with these affixes, manifest the quality tagmeme in the modified phrase.

Verbal participles have been observed only with *-tⁿim* 'just': *he⁷m ikó⁷cwáaptⁿim* 'just the one who hit him'.

The formation of nominal and verbal participles will be discussed in §4.2.

4.1.1.2. COMMENTS OF STATIVE CLAUSES. The inflection of substantives functioning as the comment of the stative clause.

4.1.1.2.1. Nouns functioning as comments may be inflected as follows:

a- '1st per.' ta- '1st and 2nd' mi- '2nd per.' an- '2nd to 1st' man- '1st to 2nd'	Stem	-tam '1st and 2nd pl.' -yah '3rd pl.'	-tᵛim 'just' -am 'now' -nam 'still'

CHART IV

Examples are: *apá·šiñtᵛam* 'we are men', *mičá·šitᵛamnam* 'you are still children', *káwahyah* 'they are horses', *yó·yatᵛim* 'it is just a pig', *manhá·tuŋ* 'you are my father'.

4.1.1.2.2. Pronouns functioning as comments may be inflected as indicated in Chart II, with the following revisions: -*gaktᵛi* does not occur, and *a-* and *mi-* may occur with *hé*: *aáčam* 'it is I', *dᵛá ahé* 'I am not he'.

4.1.1.2.3. Numerals functioning as comments are inflected as follows:

a- '1st per.'			-tam '1st and 2nd pl.'
ta- '1st and 2nd'	Stem	-na·	
mi- '2nd per.'			-yah '3rd pl.'

CHART V

Examples are: *awasná·tam* 'we are two', *tukuná·yah* 'they are three'.

Spanish numbers and *há?yaŋ* 'many' follow the same pattern but -*na·* is never present: *mihá?yaŋtam* 'you are many', *séysyah* 'they are six'.

Numerals *tú·m* 'one' and *itᵛúmpay* 'all' do not function in this way.

4.1.1.2.4. Adjectives functioning as comments may be inflected as follows:

a- '1st per.' ta- '1st and 2nd' mi- '2nd per'	Stem	-tam 'plural'	-tᵛim 'just' -am 'now' -nam 'still'

CHART VI

Examples are: *máham* 'it is big now', *mišútᵛutamnam* 'you are still small', *cábactamtᵛim* 'they are just red'.

4.1.1.2.5. Certain location substitutes also function as comments and may participate in the inflectional system set forth

in Chart VI: *áč dᵛá ahémak* 'I am not there', *húumatamnam* 'they are still far away'.

4.1.1.3. Location tagmemes. The inflection of substantives manifesting the location tagmeme.

4.1.1.3.1. Nouns manifesting the location tagmeme may be inflected as shown in Chart VII, page 284.

Locative suffixes are normally obligatory; the other affixes are optional: *aŋká·mhó·m tam* 'in our cornfield', *náakáamgak* 'at the next river', *itᵛákkáamyah* 'at their house', *mé·sahkukáam* 'under the table', *kuyyúkma* 'in the tree', *káwahaŋhó·m* 'among the horses', *pá·ši?ŋaŋkú?k* 'in the midst of the people', *tágaŋná·ka* 'beside the house'.

In a few cases the plural indicator may precede the locative suffix: *itᵛá·wata?maŋhó·m* 'among his brothers'.

Certain place nouns do not occur obligatorily with locative suffixes when manifesting the location tagmeme: *á·tébet* 'Soteapan, city', *pláya* 'beach', *lú·muh* 'hill'.

Certain noun-like formations occur with -*ma* to manifest the location tagmeme: *antákma* 'my country', *aŋwá·šá·wma* 'north'.

4.1.1.3.2. Pronouns may occur with one of the locative suffixes to manifest the location tagmeme: *áčkáam* 'at my place', *míčtᵛa? maŋhó·m* 'among you'.

4.1.1.3.3. Location substitutes may be inflected with -*tᵛim* 'just', -*am* (now', -*nam* 'still': *hémagam* 'right over there', *hé·mtᵛim* 'just there'.

4.1.1.3.4. Possessed directionals. There is a group of possessed directionals which are always inflected by possessive prefixes: *ikusáŋwiñ* 'above it', *iŋkunášwiñ* 'below you'.

4.1.1.4. Time tagmemes· Inflection of substantives manifesting the time tagmeme. Such substantives are nouns and time sub-

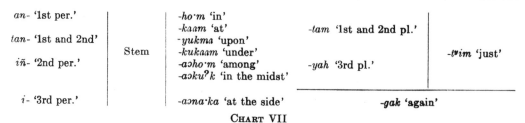

an- '1st per.'		*-ho·m* 'in'	*-tam* '1st and 2nd pl.'	*-tʸim* 'just'
tan- '1st and 2nd'	Stem	*-kaam* 'at' *-yukma* 'upon'		
iñ- '2nd per.'		*-kukaam* 'under' *-aoho·m* 'among' *-aoku²k* 'in the midst'	*-yah* '3rd pl.'	
i- '3rd per.'		*-aona·ka* 'at the side'		*-gak* 'again'

CHART VII

stitutes. These are inflected with *-tʸim* 'just', *-am* 'now', and *-nam* 'still': *sá·bɑyñam* 'still later', *sáɑptʸim* 'right now'. The time tagmeme is also manifested by temporals for which see §4.2.3.

4.1.1.5. INSTRUMENTAL TAGMEMES. Inflection of substantives manifesting the instrumental tagmeme. Such substantives are nouns. They participate in the inflectional system presented in Chart VII except that *-ma* occurs instead of the locatives suffixes: *ikúyma* 'with his stick', *púyma* 'on foot, with his foot'.

4.1.1.6. THE VERBAL NUMBER TAGMEME is manifested by verbal numbers. These are inflected by *-tʸim* 'just', *-am* 'now', and *-nam* 'still': *tú·mkɑytʸim* 'just once', *wáskɑ²yam* 'twice'.

4.1.2. NEGATIVES are inflected with *-tʸim* 'just', *-am* 'now', and *-nam* 'still': *dʸánam* 'not yet', *ódoytʸim* 'don't'. Negatives occur in endocentric verb phrases.

4.1.3. INFLECTION OF VERBS. Verbs constitute a large class of words which exhibit certain similarities of inflection, derivation and syntactic function.

We first present a composite chart of verbal inflection, then each kind of verb is discussed. Morphemes which change intransitive verbs to transitive and vice versa are considered to be derivational rather than inflectional.

The meaning of the morphemes below is as follows: Order I prefixes indicate person but, as will be seen, have different functions when occurring with different verb types; *waga-* 'together', *ca·m-* 'very'. Suffixes are: *-a²y* 'benefactive-indirective', *-ne* 'durative, *-ta²m* ist and 2nd pl., *-yah* '3rd pl., *-ta* 'transitive indefinite', *-na·m* 'intransitive indefinite', *-gak* 'repetitive', *-to* 'desiderative', *-ta²p* 'frustrative', *-pa* 'incompletive', *-um* 'definite completive', *-a* 'imperative', *-iñ* 'obligatory', *-pa·m* 'incompletive time subordinate', *-wa·m* 'completive time subordinate', *-tʸim* 'just, also', *-am* 'now', *-nam* 'still', *-i* meaning undetermined.

I	II		I	II	III	IV	V	VI	VII	VIII
set-1										
a-										
ta-										
mi-										
set 2								*-to*	*-pa*	
an-	*waga-*				*-ta²m*	*-ta·*		*-ta²p*	*-um*	
tan-		Stem	*-a²y*	*-ne*¹¹			*-gak*			*-tʸim*
iñ-										
i-	*ca·m-*				*-yah*	*-na·m*		*-a*		*-am*
set 3								*-iñ*		
								-pa·m		*-nam*
man-								*-wa·m*		
an-								*-i*		

CHART VIII

¹¹ These suffixes have been previously considered derivational. Both participate in certain idiomatic formations.

284

4.1.3.1. INTRANSITIVE DECLARATIVE PREDICATES. Verbs functioning as intransitive predicates may be inflected as follows:

I	II		II	III	V	VI	VII	VIII
a- ta- mi- —	waga- ca·m-	Stem	-ne	-ta²m -yah	-gak	-to	-pa	-tʸim -nam -am
						-ta²p	-um	-tʸim -nam

CHART IX

Examples are: *awáganaktá²mpanam* 'I'm still going with him', *mióyñeyahtá²p* 'you all went in vain', *cá·m hó·yyahtóobam* 'they like to walk a lot', *poyñéum* 'he fled', *nakgákpa* 'he is going again'.

4.1.3.2. INTRANSITIVE INDEFINITE PREDICATES. Verbs functioning as intransitive indefinite predicates are inflected always with the suffix *-na·m*. Other affixes which may occur are *-ne*, *-pa*, and *-um*: *čí·ŋnená·m* 'someone is bathing', *pú·tná·mpa* 'someone comes out'.

4.1.3.3. TRANSITIVE DECLARATIVE PREDICATES. Verbs functioning as transitive declarative predicates may be inflected as follows:

(b) is possessed and the possessor is someone other than the subject: *aŋkó²cá²y šiwan ikáwah* 'I hit John's horse', *šiwan ikó²cá²y ikáwah* 'John hit someone else's horse', but *šiwan ikó²c ikáwah* 'John hit his own horse', *šiwan anami²ñá²y yá²p kóoŋ* 'John brought me this basket'.

Other affixes function as illustrated for intransitive declarative verbs.

4.1.3.4. TRANSITIVE INDEFINITE PREDICATES. Verbs functioning as transitive indefinite predicates are inflected always with *-ta·*. Set I person markers occur, but not sets II and III. Other affixes of the transitive declarative system occur except *-to* and *-ta²p* have not been observed: *akó²ctamtá·* 'someone hit me', *kó²cayñetá· ikáwah* 'someone hit his horse'.

4.1.3.5. INTRANSITIVE IMPERATIVE PREDICATES.

I	II		I	II	III	V	VI	VII	VIII
a- ta- mi- an- tan- iñ- i- man- an-	waga- ca·m-	Stem	-a²y	-ne	-ta²m -yah	-gak	-to	-pa	-tʸim -am -nam
							-ta²p	-um	-tʸim -nam

CHART X

Set II prefixes indicate subject: *aŋkó²cpa* 'I hit him', *i²ñišgákum* 'you saw him again', *išunyáhpa* 'they want it'. Set I prefixes indicate object: *šiwan akó²cpa* 'John is hitting me', *miišgákpa* 'he sees you again'. Set III prefixes indicate both subject and object: *maŋkó²cpa* 'I hit you', *míč aŋkó²c* 'you hit me'.

The suffix *-a²y* indicates that the object of focus either (a) is an indirect object, or

CATES. Verbs functioning as intransitive imperative predicates are always inflected with *-a*. Other affixes which may occur are: *waga-*, *-ne* (with certain stems only), *-ta²m*, *-gak*, *-tʸim*, *-am*, *-nam*: *mí·ña* 'come!' *wágapoytʸáama* 'run away together!' *wó·néatʸim* 'just lie down!'

4.1.3.6. TRANSITIVE IMPERATIVE PREDICATES. Verbs functioning as transitive imperative predicates are always inflected with

-*a*. Other affixes which may occur are as follows:

I	II			I	II	III	V	VI-VII	VIII
						-*ta²m*			-*tⁿim*
a-	*waga-*		Stem	-*a²y*	-*ne*		-*gak*	-*a*	-*am*
						-*yah*			-*nam*

CHART XI

Examples are: *ayó·špáata* 'help me!' *wágakó²c yá·ha* 'both of you hit them!' Other morphemes function as illustrated in the above sections.

4.1.3.7. TIME SUBORDINATE CLAUSE PREDICATES. Verbs functioning as predicates of time subordinate clauses (when *mu* is not present) are inflected always with either -*pa·m* or -*wa·m*. Set II person markers occur when intransitive stems are used. There is no restriction on affixes except as presented in Chart VIII: *iñakwá·m* 'when he went along', *ansé·tpá·m* 'as I return', *aŋko²cwá·m* 'when I was hitting him'.

4.1.3.8. *mu* 'when'. When *mu* is present, intransitive verbs are inflected with set II prefixes, and suffixes beyond Order V do not occur (see Chart VIII): *mu a²nóy* 'when I went', *mu ikó²cyáh* 'when they hit him'.

4.1.3.9. GENERAL SUBORDINATE CLAUSE PREDICATES. Verbs functioning as the predicate tagmeme in a general subordinate clause may be inflected with -*iñ*. Other affixes occur except for the restrictions indicated in Chart VIII, and as discussed in the sections above: *wá· íga miñágiñ* 'it is good that you go'.

4.1.3.10. INTRADEPENDENT VERB PHRASES. Certain modifications of inflection take place in intradependent verb phrases. There are two types of such phrases. One type consists of a small class of auxiliary verbs (about 6) plus main verb. When the main verb is intransitive and the phrase manifests a declarative tagmeme, then suffixes of Orders II, IV, V and VI occur with the auxiliary verb and the person prefixes, Order III suffixes, and -*i*, which is obligatory in this situation, occur with the main verb:

móhum wé·hi 'he began to weep', *óyñe hó·yi* 'he went for a walk'. The plural indicating suffixes occur after -*i*: *óy mihó·yitⁿam* 'you went for a walk'.

This set of auxiliary verbs functions similarly with transitive declarative verbs, except that -*i* is not present on the main stem: *óy iá²m* 'he went to look at it', *móhpa antúk* 'I began to pick it'.

When a member of this set of auxiliaries occurs with a transitive indefinite main verb, the same suffixes occur with the auxiliary and set II person prefixes occur with the main stem: *miñpa ikó²ctá·* 'someone is coming to hit him'.

When a member of this set of auxiliaries occurs with intransitive imperative verbs, -*a* occurs with the auxiliary and -*i* occurs with the main verb which is also inflected by the person marker *mi-*: *mí·ña miwtiki* 'come and eat!' *ná·ka mihó·yitⁿam* 'you all go take a walk!'

When a member of this set of auxiliary verbs occurs with a transitive imperative verb, -*a* occurs with both verbs: *ná·ka áama* 'go and look at it!' The verbs may be further inflected as discussed above.

There is a hortatory phrase which consists of one of the auxiliary verbs with no inflection plus a main verb (transitive or intransitive) inflected by *tan-* or *ta-*: *miñ taŋkú²t á·ñi* 'come let us eat tortillas,' *nák tahó·yi* 'let us go for a walk'.

In the second type of verb phrase, a fully inflected intransitive verb may function as an auxiliary followed by a main verb inflected only for person and number. Main verbs which are intransitive occur only with set II person markers. When -*pa* does not occur with the auxiliary verb, *mu* occurs between the auxiliary and the main

286

verb: *wéhpa išé·t* 'he returns weeping', *wánpa itᵛúk kápel* 'he sings as he picks coffee', *wéh mu išé·t* 'he returned weeping, he wept as he returned'.

4.1.4. SUFFIXED UNIVERSALLY. There is a set of inflections that occurs with all words, except some of those mentioned in §4.1.5.: *-wey* 'I said', *-un* 'he said', *-hak* 'Oh, I see', *-kip* 'you see': *nákpaun* 'he is going he said', *káwahwey* 'horse I said', *cábachak* 'Oh, I see, red', *dᵛágip tᵛí·* 'you are welcome'.[12]

4.1.5. UNINFLECTED PARTICLES. These are classified in terms of their syntactic function.

(1) Coordinators: *éntre* 'and', *ni* 'nor', *i* 'and'.

(2) Conjunctions: *i* 'and', *péro* 'but', *héetᵛim* 'and'.[13]

(3) Articles: *he²m* 'the', *yâ²p* 'this', *pé²m* 'that', *hére* 'that', *hi·* 'the' (the last two are very rare).

(4) Emphasizers: *mé·š* 'also', *máske* 'only', *sólo* 'only'.

(5) Adverbs: *cá·m* 'very', *ági* 'very'.

(6) Time particles: *yákiñ* 'just now', *agoríta* 'right away', *indenánte* 'this morning', *má²k* 'a bit ago', *máaksi* 'earlier today', *má²kmáagam* 'a bit ago'.

(7) Clause subordinators: *íga* 'that,[14] in order that', *pórke* 'because', *kómo* 'since', *aúŋke*[15] 'even though', *méiga* 'if'.

(8) Exclamatory particles: *yúli* 'I think so', *bwéno* 'good', *yabés* 'you see'.

(9) Pseudo-verbs: *téh* 'let's go', *táamu*[16] 'let's go'.

(10) Verbal particles: *wáap* 'possibly', *máam* 'suddenly'.

(11) Contrary-to-fact particle: *ídᵛak*.

(12) Time subordinator: *mu*.

(13) Locative particles: *ásta* 'as far as', *dénde* 'from'.

4.2 DERIVATION. There are two major methods of deriving stems: affixation and compounding.

4.2.1. SUBSTANTIVE DERIVATION.

4.2.1.1. SUBSTANTIVE STEMS. Affixes occur with various kinds of roots to form substantive stems.

(1) Two suffixes are used to derive place names: *-ko·m* 'place of', *-pak* 'arroyo': *táškó·m* 'Ocosotepec', *šútᵛučiŋkó·m* 'Ocotal Chico'; *ká·ŋpak* 'Tilapa River', *é·špak* 'Sochapan River'.

(2) There are three suffixes which occur with nouns to form other nouns: *-tu·ku* 'old, valueless', *-tᵛa·ka* 'without', *-te·ro* 'pertaining to' (*-te·ro* also occurs with verb stems). Examples are: *taktú·ku* 'an old house', *yuktú·ku* 'orphan', *puktú·ku* 'clothing', *káatᵛá·ka* 'armless person', *yó·yaté·ro* 'hog dealer'.

(3) There are six suffixes which occur with verb stems to form nouns: *-kuy* 'instrument', *-i* 'resultant', *-a/-a* 'resultant',[17] *-kaawiñ* 'plural actors', *-te·ro* 'actor', *-pay* meaning undetermined. The latter also occurs with a numeral. Examples are: *pétkuy* 'broom', *háykuy* 'writing instrument', *pí·hi* 'heat', *háapi* 'corn dough', *ákši* 'shelled corn', *mó·ya* 'flower' (cf. *moy* 'to foam), *púuka* 'tropical ulcer' (cf. *pu²k* 'to rot'), *kuyú·hkáawiñ* 'learners', *yó·šakáawiñ* 'workers', *yó·šaté·ro* 'a good worker', *haytᵛé·ro* 'one who talks a lot', *té·ñpay* 'the height of a man' (cf. *te·ñ* 'to stand'), *itᵛú·mpay* 'all of them' (cf. *tú·m* 'one').

(4) There is a suffix *-aŋ* which occurs with one verb and two neutral stems to form substantives: *hípsaŋ* 'live coal', *yáksaŋ* 'like this', *hésaŋ* 'like that'.

(5) There are five prefixes which occur with noun stems to form other stems, *ku-*, *aŋ-*, *na-*, *ak-*, and *waga-*: *kutó·tᵛi* 'brains',

---

[12] Two other morphemes have been observed that are perhaps part of the system: *-saŋ* and *-koy*. They are both very rare.

[13] *héetᵛim* is an inflected form but functions idiomatically as 'and'.

[14] *íga* may function as an inflected particle in response to the sentence *tᵛíiga miñákpa* 'why are you going?' *ígatᵛim* 'just because'. Elsewhere it is not inflected.

[15] This Spanish particle does not have glottal catch between the vowels.

[16] *táamu* occurs with the suffix *-am*.

[17] There is a possibility that *-i* and *-a/-a* are allomorphs.

287

kukú·ma 'ring', *kupóʔk* 'runt', *kuá·ši* 'foolish', *aŋwí·ši* 'beard', *aŋtác* 'tooth of a comb', *aʔŋáy* 'page of a book', *inimí·šitᵛá·wa* 'his fellow Oaxaqueño', *akcá* 'testicles', *wágayó·mo* 'twin girls'. *ku-* also occurs with numerals to form nouns which are always possessed: *ikutᵛú·m* 'by himself, he alone,' *ikuwástak* 'both of them', *ikusíŋkoh* 'the five of them'.

(6) There is a prefix-suffix combination, *ku-..-aŋ*, which occurs with some verbs to form nouns; such nouns are always possessed: *ikuhágaŋ* 'a broken piece of it' (cf. *hak* 'to break'), *ikucáʔyaŋ* 'what remains of it' (cf. *caʔy* 'to remain').

4.2.1.2. COMPOUND STEMS. Substantive stems are also formed by compounding other stems. There are two types of compounds: normal and loose. The first involves a shift of stress, the second does not.

Examples of normal compounds: *nuʔnkúypak* 'needle' (cf. *núʔnkuy* 'sewing instrument', *pák* 'bone'), *iškúypak* 'eyelash' (cf. *íškuy* 'eye', *pák* 'body hair'), *sutúkuy* 'small sticks' (cf. *šútᵛu* 'small', *kúy* 'wood), *nápsna* 'pure water'.

Examples of loose compounds: *hámñapá·šiñ* mountain man', *šútᵛuták* 'small house'.

There is a prefix-suffix-root combination, *ku-..-aŋ-root*, that occurs with verb stems to form noun stems: *kučiʔŋáŋna* 'water that has been bathed in' (cf. *čiŋ* 'bathe', *na* 'water').

4.2.2. VERB DERIVATION.

4.2.2.1. TRANSITIVE AND INTRANSITIVE STEMS. Derivation common to both transitive and intransitive stems.

4.2.2.1.1. DERIVATION BY AFFIXATION.

(1) There are two prefixes used to derive verb stems without regard to whether they are transitive or intransitive, *ku-* and *aŋ-*. These occur with some roots that are not otherwise stems: *kunu·m* 'to stalk something', *kučo·n* 'to swing', *aŋmat* 'to speak', *aŋyaʔk* 'to be sad'. They occur with many other roots which are also stems: *kumoŋ* 'to sink' (*moŋ* 'to sleep'), *kupak* 'to believe

something' (*pak* 'to take something'), *kupuh* 'to defend someone' (*puh* 'to come out in large numbers'), *aŋweh* 'to shout' (*weh* 'to weep'), *aŋhay* 'to make a loud noise' (*hay* 'to speak'), *aŋpah* 'to close the door of something' (*pah* 'to pen something up').

(2) Practically every SP verb root, as well as some larger forms, may occur with the reduplicative suffix. Stems with the reduplicative suffix must be immediately inflected by *-ne*, or they must have a derivational affix or another root following. Examples are: *náknaknéeba* 'he goes again and again', *išišóʔypa* 'he is able to see', *itᵛáŋtaŋhákpa* 'he cuts it all apart by chopping' (cf. *taŋ* 'to chop something', *hak* 'to break something'), *tᵛékšektᵛékšeknéeba* 'he wiggles his lower jaw', *póytᵛakpóytᵛagóʔypa* 'he runs about the village' (cf. *poy* 'to run, flee').

4.2.2.1.2. DERIVATION BY COMPOUNDING. In addition to the compounds of root plus reduplicative affix plus root (an example is given above), there are four types of compounds distinguished.

(1) Enclosing compounds involve a prefix-root combination occurring with another root: *kunagáyyah* 'they all went away', *aŋmeesnuʔk* 'to close it by making a wall' (cf. *mees* 'to make a wall', *aŋnuʔk* 'to close something'), *aŋhayhak* 'to calm someone down' (cf. *hay* 'to speak', *aŋhak* 'to lead').

(2) Regular compounds involve two verb stems. The meaning of the first stems appears to precede the meaning of the second stem in time or is "logically" prior to it: *išpak* 'to be acquainted with someone' (cf. *iš* 'to see something', *pak* 'to take something'), *aʔmkiʔm* 'to look up' (cf. *aʔm* 'to look at something', *kiʔm* 'to go up'), *hiʔkka* 'to drown' (cf. *hiʔk* 'to choke', *ka* 'to die').

(3) Substantive-verb compounds: *wa·cak* 'to fix something' (cf. *wa·* 'good', *cak* 'to leave something'), *ko·bakpih* 'to annoy someone' (cf. *ko·bak* 'head', *pih* 'to heat, heat something'), *kaaput* 'to escape' (cf. *ka* 'hand', *put* 'to go out').

(4) Special compounds involve a small

number of verb stems which occur with large numbers of roots and stems, including other compounds. When so used they frequently have a slightly different meaning than when occurring alone: *wiʔknas* 'to eat first' (cf. *nas* 'to go by'), *hoksket* 'to finish hoeing' (cf. *ket* 'to go down'), *nuʔnmagoʔy* 'to nail temporarily' (cf. *magoʔy* 'to lie').

4.2.2.2. INTRANSITIVE STEMS. Derivation which results in intransitive stems.

4.2.2.2.1. AFFIXES.

(1) There is a suffix *-aʔy/-aʔyaʔy* 'directional' which occurs with a few stems involving motion: *héˑm nágaʔyáʔy* 'he went that way'.

(2) There are two suffixes which occur with nonverbs to form intransitive stems, *-aˑ* 'factive', *-aʔy* 'possessive': *kuaˑšaˑ* 'to act foolishly' (*kuaˑši* 'foolish'), *hoogaˑ* 'to smoke' (*hóˑko* 'smoke'), *tagaʔy* 'to have a house' (*ták* 'house'), *hemagaʔy* 'to go there' (*hémak* 'over there'), *kuʔyaʔy* 'to have wood' (*kúy* 'wood'). Some verb stems derived by *-aʔy* are also transitive: *ikuʔyáʔypa* 'he puts wood on it'.

(3) There is a suffix *-oʔy* which occurs with transitive stems to form intransitive ones: *cagoʔy* 'to shake' (*cak* 'to touch something'), *koʔcoʔy* 'to hit, be wont to hit' (*koʔc* 'to hit something').

4.2.2.2.2. COMPOUNDS. Many transitive-verb-direct-object combinations may be transformed into intransitive stems by compounding the noun object with the transitive verb stem: *amokméʔcpa* 'I am looking for corn' (cf. *amméʔcpa mók* 'I am looking for corn'), *mišakñíppa* 'you are planting beans' (cf. *iññíppa sák* 'you are planting beans').

4.2.2.3. TRANSITIVE STEMS. Derivations which result in transitive stems.

(1) There is a suffix *-ka* instrumental which occurs with intransitive stems to form transitive ones: *imáˑčkáaba* 'he plays with it', *antéˑñkáaba* 'I stand on it', *antáʔŋoykáaba* 'I chop with it'.

(2) There are two prefixes that occur with

intransitive verb stems to form transitive ones, *ak-* 'causative', and *na-* 'associative-causative': *aknak* 'to send something' (*nak* 'to go'), *aktogoy* 'to lose something' (*togoy* 'to be lost'), *akka* 'to kill something' (*ka* 'to die'), *nanak* 'to take something', *natogoy* 'to be lost with someone'.

4.2.3. DERIVATION OF TEMPORALS.

(1) There is a prefix *ma-* 'past': *matak* 'yesterday', *mawáški* 'two days ago', *maáˑm-tᵛayma* 'last year'.

(2) There is a suffix *-ma* 'future': *hóyma* 'tomorrow', *wastákma* 'day after tomorrow'.

(3) There is a prefix-suffix combination: *kuháˑmsaŋ* 'dry season' (cf. *háˑma* 'sun') *kutúhka* 'wet season' (cf. *túh* 'rain'), *kusagáŋka* 'time of beans'.

(4) There is a special compounding form *muˑma-* 'all': *múˑmaháˑma* 'all day', *múˑmacúu* 'all night'.

4.2.4. NOMINAL PARTICIPLES are words or phrases which, when *-pak* is affixed to the head word, function as substantives. Nominal participles also manifest the quality tagmeme of the substantive modified phrase (§3.2.1.2). Certain nouns (especially place nouns), pronouns, adjectives, classes which manifest the location tagmeme, and certain items which manifest the time tagmeme may occur with *-pak* resulting in a nominal participle: *heʔm áˑtébetpak* 'the one from Soteapan', *heʔm áčpak* 'the one that belongs to me', *heʔm cáˑm páˑmi yágacpak* 'the very, very long one', *heʔm húumapak* 'the one far away', *heʔm šiwan ikáˑmhóˑmpak* 'the one from John's cornfield', *heʔm sáappak* 'the right now one'.

4.2.5. VERBAL PARTICIPLES are clauses, IDC, TDC, and TIC, which, when *-waap* or *-paap* occur on the verb instead of the tense-mode inflection, function as substantives manifesting subject or object tagmemes. If there is already a noun subject or object then the verbal participle is in apposition to it: *heʔm nakwáap aktáŋ tuŋhóˑm* 'the one who went fell in the road', *amméʔcpa amméʔcpáap* 'I'm looking for the one I'm looking for', *he?m iko?cwáap ihá·tuŋ tak hó·m sé·t* 'the one whose father hit him in the house returned'. When the negative is pres-

ent in the verb phrase *-pak* occurs with the negative: *he?m dʸápak óy yá?m ítʸ* 'the one who did not go is here'.

REFERENCES

Elson, 1947a, 1947b, 1948, 1951, 1954, 1960a, 1960b, 1961a
Foster, G. M., 1943, 1949
Foster, M. L., and G. M. Foster, 1948

Hockett, 1947
Longacre, 1960
Pike, K. L., 1954, 1955, 1960
Wonderly, 1949

7E. Isthmus Zapotec

VELMA B. PICKETT

0.	Introduction
0.1.	Language and dialects
0.2.	Method of presentation
1.	Phonological hierarchy
1.1.	Phonemes
1.1.1.	Consonants
1.1.1.1.	Fortis consonants
1.1.1.2.	Lenis voiced-voiceless consonants
1.1.1.3.	Lenis voiced consonants
1.1.1.4.	Lenis voiceless consonants
1.1.2.	Vowels
1.1.3.	Tone phonemes
1.2.	Syllables
1.2.1.	Syllable-initial margin
1.2.2.	Syllable-final margin
1.2.3.	Syllable nucleus
1.2.4.	Rare syllable patterns
1.2.5.	Consonant and vowel restrictions
1.3.	Phonological words
1.3.1.	Consonant cluster distribution
1.3.2.	Vowel cluster distribution
1.4.	Phonological phrases
1.5.	Phonological sentences
1.6.	Hesitation pauses
2.	Grammatical hierarchy
2.0.	Introduction
2.0.1.	Hierarchy
2.0.2.	Limitation of scope
2.0.3.	Identification of terms and symbols
2.0.3.1.	Slot, filler, and tagmeme
2.0.3.2.	Formulaic representation
2.1.	Morpheme-cluster level
2.1.1.	Plural imperative cluster
2.1.2.	Ambulative cluster
2.1.3.	Causative cluster
2.2.	Word level
2.2.1.	Declarative verbs
2.2.2.	Stative verbs
2.2.3.	Imperative verbs
2.3.	Phrase level
2.3.1.	Noun phrases
2.3.2.	Independent pronoun phrase
2.3.3.	Verb phrases
2.3.4.	Other major phrases
2.3.5.	Minor phrases
2.4.	Clause level
2.4.1.	Independent clauses
2.4.1.1.	Declarative clauses
2.4.1.2.	Imperative clauses
2.4.1.3.	Minor clauses
2.4.2.	Dependent clauses
2.5.	Sentence level
2.5.1.	Independent sentences—nonclause
2.5.2.	Independent sentences—clause
2.5.2.1.	Independent sentence type 1
2.5.2.2.	Independent sentence type 2
2.5.2.3.	Independent sentence type 3
2.5.2.4.	Independent sentence type 4
2.5.3.	Dependent sentences—nonclause
2.5.4.	Dependent sentences—clause
3.	Lexical hierarchy
3.1.	Morphemes and morphophonemics
3.1.1.	Morpheme classes
3.1.1.1.	Bound roots
3.1.1.2.	Prefixes
3.1.1.3.	Clitics
3.1.1.4.	Free roots
3.1.2.	Morphophonemics
3.2.	Words
3.2.1.	Words and word classes
3.2.1.1.	Independent and dependent words
3.2.1.2.	Distribution classes

3.2.2.   Words and tagmamorphemics
3.3.   Word clusters
4.   Text

0.1. LANGUAGE AND DIALECTS. The presentation of the structure of any one of the so-called dialects of Zapotec cannot fully represent the language group as a whole, for it includes at least seven mutually unintelligible "dialects," more properly called different "languages." In an article of this nature, therefore, it is impossible to do more than cover in broad scope the structure of only one of these languages. The present sketch is of Isthmus Zapotec, which is spoken in an area bordering the Pacific coast in the Isthmus of Tehuantepec, and specifically of the dialect spoken in the largest town of the area, Juchitan. In a few details in the phonemics and lexicon, the dialect differs somewhat from those spoken in other towns of the area. For greater detail on the structure of Isthmus Zapotec, and for comparison with other Zapotec languages, the reader may consult the monographs and articles included in the bibliography.

0.2. METHOD OF PRESENTATION. Zapotec grammar is here presented in terms of three interlocking hierarchies[1] — phonological, grammatical, and lexical — each with its levels of structure ranging from the lowest (least inclusive) to the highest (most inclusive). The hierarchies are interlocking in that they are dealing with the same body of data, but they are distinct in that each has its own separate set of criteria for distinguishing contrastive units. Even units given similar names (words, phrases, and sentences) are distinguished differently in each hierarchy, with criteria which relate only to the particular hierarchy under attention. The phonological hierarchy presents the material related to the traditional "phonological

level"; the grammatical hierarchy includes both morphology and syntax; the lexical hierarchy singles out those parts of morphology and syntax which treat morpheme classes, word classes, and morphophonemics.

1. PHONOLOGICAL HIERARCHY. The phonological system of Isthmus Zapotec is viewed as composed of at least five levels ranging from lowest to highest as follows: phonemes, syllables, phonological words, phonological phrases, phonological sentences.

1.1. PHONEMES. Isthmus Zapotec phonemes include fortis and lenis consonants, simple and rearticulated vowels, and three tones.

1.1.1. CONSONANTS. The consonants are divided into two major contrastive groups: fortis and lenis. The fortis group comprises stops and fricatives which are always voiceless (p, t, $č$, k, s, $š$). The lenis group is further divided into those which freely vary from voiced to voiceless (stops and fricatives b, d, $ǰ$, g, z, $ž$) and those which are regularly voiced (resonants m, n, $ŋ$, l, w, y, flap r, and apical trilled $r̃$). In addition, there is a glottal stop phoneme and two rare voiceless consonants, f and h, all of which have limited distribution.

In other Zapotec languages there are both fortis and lenis resonants. In Isthmus Zapotec the resonants have a phonetic difference between short and long, but the long resonants are more limited in distribution than they are in the other languages of the family. The phonetically long resonants have previously been analyzed as fortis consonants in Isthmus Zapotec, but the description is somewhat simplified by considering them to be clusters of like consonants. Note the following contrastive pairs: /'šonŏ/ ['šo·nŏ²] 'eight':/'čonnă/ ['čon·ă] 'three'; /'gela/ ['ge·la] 'new corn plants':/'belle/ ['bel·e] 'flame'.

1.1.1.1. FORTIS CONSONANTS. Fortis con-

[1] The model used is based on the trimodal structure theory set forth by Kenneth L. Pike (1954, 1955, 1960). There are some differences, however, in the application of the theory as to details and terminology.

[2] Except in the section dealing specifically with tone (§1.1.3), phonetic illustrations are written with phonemic tones.

sonants are always voiceless. Of these, the stops are frequently slightly aspirated and the fricative *š* is slightly retroflexed, varying to clearly retroflexed in some idiolects. Illustrations in initial position: /'pe^ʔpe^ʔ/ 'a wild fruit'; /'tappa/ 'four'; /'čii/ 'ten'; /'ko^ʔ/ 'no'; /'saa/ 'music, fiesta'; /'šo^ʔ/ 'odor'.

1.1.1.2. LENIS VOICED-VOICELESS CONSONANTS. Lenis consonants which vary from voiced to voiceless are the stops and fricatives corresponding to the fortis series. The stops *b*, *d*, and *g* tend to vary slightly toward a more fricative articulation in medial position and are more frequently voiced than the affricated stop *ǰ* and the fricatives *z* and *ž*. Velar stop *g* is especially fricative and somewhat fronted before high front vowel *i*.

Illustrations in initial position: /'be/ 'mold'; /'daa/ 'mat'; /'ǰi/ 'day'; /'gu/ 'sweet potato'; /'gi/ ['ǥi] 'fire'; /'zee/ 'fresh corn'; /'ža^ʔna^ʔ/ 'underneath'.[3]

1.1.1.3. LENIS VOICED CONSONANTS. The series of lenis voiced consonants comprises three nasals (bilabial, alveolar, and velar), an alveolar lateral, two semi-vowels (*w* and *y*), flap *r*, and apical trilled *r̃*. The trilled *r̃* and the velar nasal are both rare phonemes and have limited distribution. The two *r* phonemes are in contrast in utterance initial and medial positions only. In final position they do not contrast but vary from flap to trill and from voiced to voiceless. In this position, only the symbol *r* is used. In utterance-initial position the flap *r* is accompanied by a vocalic onset. The velar nasal occurs only utterance medial and final and contrasts with /n/ only in medial position and in very limited distributions.

Illustrations (in initial position where possible): /'maní^ʔ/ 'animal'; /'naa/ 'me'; /'páŋ/ 'bread'; /'lari/ 'cloth'; /'waga/ 'rat'; /'ya/ 'yes'; /ru'zaa/ [ⁱr̃u'zaa] 'passes (something) through'; /r̃u'zàá/ 'medium ripe'.

---

[3] Certain subdialects, for example speakers from Tehuantepec, do not seem to have a contrast between *š* and *ž*. But compare the following contrast in the Juchitán dialect: /ru'šiǰi/ 'plays': /ru'žiǰi/ 'laughs.'

1.1.1.4. LENIS VOICELESS CONSONANTS. Three phonemes of limited distribution are lenis and voiceless: *f*, *h*, and glottal stop. When *h* precedes vowels it varies freely with a light velar fricative. When in clusters (preceding *m*, *n*, or *l*), it has allophones of voiceless nasals and lateral, corresponding to the contiguous voiced phonemes, e.g., /'hmá/ ['Mmá] 'more'; /'hneza/ ['Nne·za] 'fine'; /'hluuna bě/ ['Lluuna bě] 'his/her bed'.

Glottal stop occurs only following vowels, e.g., /'ko^ʔ/ 'no'; /'bi^ʔku^ʔ/ 'dog'.

Illustrations of *f* and *h* in initial position: /'féw/ 'ugly'; /'hánna/ 'let's'.

1.1.2. VOWELS. Vowel phonemes are of two types: simple and rearticulated. Each type has five qualities; high front *i*, mid front *e*, low central *a*, mid back *o*, and high back *u*. /e/ and /o/ freely vary from open to close. /i/ and /a/ have rare nasalized allophones which occur immediately following /nw/, or as phonetic manifestations of /Vn^ʔ/, e.g., /nan'wí/ [nan'wĩ] 'in very small pieces'; /'špán^ʔ/ ['špą̃^ʔ] 'my bread'.

Simple vowels have lengthened allophones which occur in the nuclear syllable of phonological phrases, under the following conditions: in open syllables and syllables closed with /ʔ/ but which have an up-glide tone. Rearticulated vowels are always stressed and are long.

Rearticulated vowels freely vary from rearticulation with no glottal closure to weak glottal closure in normal speech and heavy glottal closure in special emphatic style. The rearticulated vowel, although a single phonemic unit, is symbolized in this paper by a digraph of two like vowels.

Illustrations of both simple and rearticulated vowels: /″bi/ [″bi·] 'wind'; /″de/ [″de·] 'ashes'; /″na/ [″na·] 'says'; /″ro/ [″ro·] 'eats'; /″ru/ [″ru·] 'a cough'; /″rii/ 'water jug'; /″zee/ 'fresh corn'; /″naa/ 'me'; /″doo/ 'rope'; /″čùú/ 'let's go'.

1.1.3. TONE PHONEMES. Phonemic tones are high (written with acute accent), low (unmarked), and up-glide (written with a wedge /ˇ/ on single vowels and with grave plus acute accent /ˈ/ on rearticulated vowels).

Illustrations: /ti'léžu/ 'a rabbit'; /ne 'béénda²/ 'and snake'; /ti'neza/ 'a road'; /ne 'bèélǎ/ 'with meat'.

High tone has three allophones: high, slightly lowered, and high-gliding-down (written [ˆ]). In a series of high tones, the last is slightly lowered. High tone tends to glide down when it occurs on the nuclear syllable of a phonological phrase (§1.4), especially when these syllables are open or are closed with a resonant consonant.

Illustrations: /i'rútti²/ (last tone slightly lowered) 'no one'; /'čuppa "zá/ ['čùppà "zâ·] 'two clouds; /"léžu/ ["lê·žù] 'rabbit'; /ne "bénnye/ [nè "bên·yè] 'with mud'.

Low tone has three allophones: mid (written with a macron), low, and mid-gliding-down (written ⌐). Like the high tone allophones, their distribution relates to the nuclear syllable of the phonological phrase. The nuclear syllable itself has a down glide when the word including it is final before pause and alternates freely between downglide and low when medial. The low tones preceding such a low tone nucleus are phonetically mid; those following such a nucleus and those in other distributions are low.

Illustrations: /'giǰi la"yu/ ['gíǰì lā"ȳù·] 'world'; /"laadu 'lá/ ["lāādù 'lá] ~ ["làâdù 'lá] 'us?'; /'biku "wiini 'yaase²/ ['bīkū "wìīnì 'yààsè²] 'little black dog'.

The glided allophones of both high and low tones are very short in closed syllables. In syllables closed by a resonant, the glide ends on the consonant.

Illustration: /"čonnǎ/ ["čon̄·ā] 'three'.

Resonant consonants carry the pitch of surrounding vowels: syllable-final they have the pitch of the preceding vowel with glides ending on them as illustrated above; syllable-initial they have the pitch of the following vowel.

Illustration: /kán'dáánà²/ [káń'dáánà²]

294

(last tone slightly lowered) 'I'm hungry'.

1.2. SYLLABLES. There are four common syllables patterns: CV, CCV, CCCV, and CVC. Each of these is divided again into those which may occur in either stressed or unstressed position—those with simple vowels—and those which occur in stressed position only—those with rearticulated vowels.

1.2.1. SYLLABLE-INITIAL MARGIN. In the single C syllable-initial position, any consonant may occur except glottal stop. Consonant clusters which may occur in syllable-initial position are listed individually and illustrated under two headings: major and minor, according to their frequency of occurrence.

Major monosyllabic consonant clusters:

šp: /'špiini²/ 'servant'
št: /'štaanǐ/ 'her blouse'
šk: /'škaanda²/ 'dream'
mb: /'mbòótǎ/ 'very big'
nd: /'ndǐ²/ 'this'
ŋg: /'ŋgǎ/ 'that'
by: /'byaǰi/ 'plum'
dy: /'dyaga/ 'ear'
gy: /'gyá²/ 'above, north'
ny: /'nyee/ 'foot'
ry: /'rye/ 'goes'

Minor monosyllabic consonant clusters:[4]

šl: /'šlužu/ 'maguey fiber'
šn: (idiolectal variant of hn, but in some idiolects contrasts with hn) /'šneza/ 'his road'
fl: /'flùúčǐ/ 'loud whistle'
hl: /'hlaza/ 'scales'
py: /'pyú²/ 'a very little bit'
sy: /syá'do²/ 'morning'
šy: /'šyaa/ 'his wing'
zy: /'zya²/ 'deep, much (liquids)'
žy: /'žyàá/ 'cotton'
my: /'myatti²/ 'unidentified person, one's self
ǰy: /'ǰya/ 'griddle'

[4] In addition to those listed, there are a few minor clusters found only in unassimilated Spanish loans, e.g., /tr/ and /yn/ in /'tréynta/ 'thirty'.

tw: /na'twi 'lu/ 'is embarrassed'

kw: /'kwe^ʔ/ 'next to, side'

bw: /'bwi^ʔ/ 'guava'

dw: /laǰi'dwá^ʔ/ 'my heart'

gw: /'gwe^ʔ/ 'drank'

šw: /'šwaa 'liǰi/ 'daughter-in-law'

sw: /ru'swi^ʔ/ 'extinguishes'

zw: /ru'zwi^ʔ 'lu/ 'imagines'

žw: /'žwaana^ʔ/ 'person in charge of a fiesta'

čw: /na'čwi^ʔ/ 'slippery'

ǰw: /ri'ǰwi^ʔ/ 'burns oneself'

rw: /'rwa^ʔ/ 'carries'

nw: /'nwă^ʔ/ 'is carrying'

yw: /ka'ywi^ʔ/ 'is being extinguished'

mp: /'bladú 'sa^ʔmpa^ʔ/ 'clay plate'

The clusters of three consonants are likewise considered to be minor, since they are of limited distribution in terms of dictionary count. The following combinations have been noted:

str: /strom'pi^ʔpi^ʔ/ 'fruit of the kapok tree when still green'

špr: /'šprímu/ 'his/her cousin'

špy: /'špyaani^ʔ/ 'his/her intelligence'

šty: /'štyá^ʔya^ʔ/ 'my aunt'

hny: /hnyàá/ 'his/her mother'

stw: /stwi/ 'embarrassment (a sickness)'

škw: /'škwassa/ 'temples'

ryw: /rywi^ʔ/ 'is extinguished'

byw: /'bywi^ʔ/ 'was extinguished'

nyw: /'nywi^ʔ/ 'should have been extinguished'

gyw: /'gywi^ʔ/ 'let it be extinguished'

zyw: /'zywi^ʔ/ 'it will be extinguished'

The 'extinguished' verb has the only occurrence of the *Cyw* clusters listed above.

1.2.2. SYLLABLE-FINAL MARGIN. In syllable-final position, only the following single consonants may occur: lenis voiced consonants (*m, n, ŋ, l, w, y, r*), fortis stops and fricatives (*p, t, č, k, s, š*), and glottal stop. The fortis consonants occur final only in stressed syllables which are simultaneously the nuclear syllable of a phrase. Glottal stop most frequently occurs in this same distribution.

1.2.3. SYLLABLE NUCLEUS. Most syllable nuclei contain only a single vowel. There are also six vowel clusters, all of rare occurrence, all including an /i/ or /u/, and all having a limited tonal pattern. The six clusters are /ɨu/, /ɨaa/, /ɨee/, /ɨuu/, /úaa/, and /iǎ/. These are in contrast with the combination /yV/ and are also in contrast with the two-syllable combination /CVyV/, as seen in the following illustrations: /'ryaa/ 'feels at home'; /ne'ríaa/ 'and feels at home'; /'nyàá^ʔ/ 'I should have gone'; /'niǎ/ 'I have with me'; /bi'yaa/ 'danced'.

1.2.4. RARE SYLLABLE PATTERNS. In addition to the patterns thus far presented, there are the following rare patterns: those which include a final consonant cluster and those which are composed of or begin with a vowel.

The syllable-final consonant clusters are limited to /w^ʔ/, /l^ʔ/, and /ŋ^ʔ/, and these are very limited in occurrence. Only the following syllables of this type have been noted: *Cow^ʔ*, *Cal^ʔ*, *Caŋ^ʔ*, and *CCaŋ^ʔ*.

Illustrations: *w^ʔ* syllable final: /'tŏw^ʔ/ 'turkey'; *l^ʔ* syllable final: /'šál^ʔ/ 'my shawl'; *ŋ^ʔ* syllable final: /'špáŋ^ʔ/ 'my bread'.

Syllables consisting of or beginning with a vowel are very rare in words of native origin; they occur principally in free alternation with the syllable *gV*, e.g., /gi'rǎ^ʔ/ ∼ /i'rǎ^ʔ/ 'all'; /genda'ro/ ∼ /enda'ro/ 'dinner'. This alternation occurs only on unstressed syllables. Stressed vowel syllables occur in Spanish loan words such as /'óra/ 'hour, when (relative)'; /'ána/ 'Anna'.

1.2.5. CONSONANT AND VOWEL RESTRICTIONS. A few restrictions have been noted on the occurrence of specific vowels and of tone in relation to specific syllable patterns. Syllables including a rearticulated vowel are either open syllables or are closed with a glottal stop. When closed with glottal stop, only the up-glide tone occurs, as in /'čàá^ʔ/ 'I'm going'. Unstressed syllables closed by a glottal stop have only high or low tone, not the up-glide tone, e.g., /'ǰiinya^ʔ/ 'work'; /'nappá^ʔ/ 'I have'.

295

1.3. Phonological words.[5] The phonological word includes an obligatory stressed syllable (indicated by ′ preposed to the syllable) and optionally one or more unstressed syllables. (The maximum number noted is six.) Illustrations: /ˈgyeʔ/ 'flower'; /rakaˈlaʔ-ǰikabeni̯/ 'They want it'.

The placement of the stressed syllable is contrastive.[6] Note, for example, the following contrastive pairs: /ˈriga/ 'shell, rind': /riˈga/ 'is cut'; /ˈnagá/ 'twisted': /naˈgáʔ/ 'green'; /ˈbigu/ 'turtle': /biˈgŭ/ 'crumbs'.

The obligatory feature of the stressed syllable of a word is greater intensity than that of the unstressed syllables. In addition, there are certain optional features which, when present, help to identify the stressed syllable, since these features occur only in a stressed syllable: presence of a glottal stop in utterance-initial or medial position and presence of a rearticulated vowel.

1.3.1. Consonant cluster distribution. Certain of the monosyllabic consonant clusters listed above may also be ambisyllabic when medial in a phonological word. These are /tr/, /mb/, /nd/, /ŋg/, and /ny/.

Other consonant clusters are only ambisyllabic. They include the following:

n.ny: /ˈbennye/ 'mud'

n.w: /nanˈwi̯/ 'in very small pieces'

n.dr: /berenˈdrú/ 'ant lion' (This /drú/ syllable, which occurs only in this one word, varies phonetically to [dr̃] and [b̌], a voiced bilabial trill, but even in these forms it is stressed and carries a high tone.)

---

[5] For the relationship of phonological words to gammatical words, see §3.2.1.1.

In the analysis of the higher levels of phonology, consultation with Eunice Pike has been very helpful.

[6] As indicated above, the stressed vowels in open syllables are phonetically long. An alternate analysis (Pickett, 1951) considers vowel length to be phonemic and makes nonphonemic stress dependent partially on this length. The present analysis is preferable because it more easily includes the rapidly increasing Spanish loan-word list and is in more accord with the description of the higher phonological levels.

296

n.t: /riginyenˈtáá/ 'throws or drops on the floor'

ŋ.k: /ˈřĕŋkĕ/ 'a turn on the heel'

n.č: /ninˈčaa/ 'large jar'

n.ǰ: /žinˈǰáʔ/ 'fever'

Glottal stop plus consonant or consonant cluster, e.g., ʔ.k: /ˈbiʔkuʔ/ 'dog'; ʔ.nd: /baˈkáʔndaʔ/ 'shade'. These clusters occur only between a stressed and unstressed syllable and occur most frequently when the stressed syllable coincides with the nuclear syllable of a phonological phrase.

1.3.2. Vowel cluster distribution. A few vowel clusters occur between syllables within the phonological word which do not occur within the syllable. Since syllable-initial vowels are very uncommon in words of native origin (see §1.2.4), only a few random clusters have been observed, including the following:

e.u: /neúˈnaakă/ 'with that woman'

a.u: /laúˈkaa/ 'write (plural imperative)'

a.i: /žaiˈbaʔ/ 'sky, heaven'

e.a: /neáˈǰe/ 'and different'

i.u: /tiuˈnaa/ 'a woman'

e.i: /neíˈră ʔ/ 'and all'

a.a: /paáˈǰe/ 'if different'

e.e: /neéndaˈro/ 'and dinner'

e.o: /neˈórakĕ/ 'and at that time'

1.4. Phonological phrases. The phonological phrase has an obligatory nuclear syllable (indicated by ″ preposed to the syllable), which coincides with the stressed syllable of a phonological word. In addition, it may include one or more optional words. The number of words included in a single phrase varies with the speed.

Illustrations: /″gidi/ 'skin'; /ˈgidi ˈladi ″yaga/ 'skin body tree (=bark)'; /ˈgĕdá ˈtúžá gú″naa/ '(each time) comes some woman'.

The features described (§1.3) as sometimes present in the stressed syllable of a phonological word are intensified here, and in addition there is increased length on the vowel (§1.1.2).

In song, where musical rhythm is substituted for the spoken phonological phrase, these identifying features are eliminated. Even songs of native origin are sung without glottal stops and without rearticulated vowels. Any vowel length which is present is determined by the rhythm of the music rather than by the place of the syllable in the corresponding spoken phrase unit.

There are two contrastive features of the spoken phrase which include more than the nuclear syllable: (1) presence of geminate consonant clusters at the border between the nuclear syllable and the one following and (2) allophonic tone distribution.

Geminate consonant clusters occur only in this position in the phonological phrase, and they include only fortis consonants and resonants. Illustrations: /″gittu ′ngǎ/ 'That's a squash'; /′stĭ ″binninĭ/ 'It belongs to the people'.

The phrase nuclear syllable carries the phonetic down-glide of high and low tones, and the mid and low allophones of low have their distribution in relation to this syllable. The details of these alternations and illustrations have been given above.

The placement of the phrase nuclear syllable is contrastive. When it is in the first word of the phrase, the identifying features of a stressed syllable are more frequently retained on the nonnuclear words than when the nuclear syllable is in a later word.

Illustrations: /″baˀdu ′laadŭ/ 'We were children'. (Here the rearticulated vowel is retained in the nonnuclear word.) /′ǰapa ″wiiniˀ/ 'little girl' (Here the nonnuclear word /′ǰapa/ has an oral vowel instead of the rearticulated vowel it has in nuclear position. Compare /′badu ″ǰaapaˀ/ 'young lady', in which nonnuclear /′badu/ has lost the stress-identifying medial glottal stop, but nuclear /″ǰaapaˀ/ retains the stress-identifying rearticulated vowel not present in the above illustration.)

Phonological phrases are frequently equivalent to grammatical phrases, but they may also include more than one grammatical phrase and are often a full grammatical clause. Only one grammatical phrase, the noun compound, includes more than one phonological phrase. Each co-ordinate part of the compound phrase may be a complete phonological phrase.

1.5. PHONOLOGICAL SENTENCE. A phonological sentence is composed of one or more phonological phrases bounded by pauses. Within a running text, the phonological sentence frequently coincides with grammatical sentence boundaries, but it may include more than one grammatical sentence, and in one instance—dependent clause followed by pause—it is part of a grammatical sentence.

There are at least three ways of ending sentences. These are a combination of grammatical form and a pitch contour which affects the pitch of the tone system. These are listed and illustrated below.

(1) Sentences ending with the dependent marker /′lá/ (closing certain grammatical dependent clauses and sentences) usually maintain their regular tone relationships. The pitch of the /′lá/ morpheme coincides with the height of the regular high tone or (freely variant) the up-glide tone. Illustrations: /pa″gèèdábé ′lá/ 'if he comes, . . .' (dependent clause); /′kumu ″rĭkku ′laabe ′lá/ 'Since he is rich' (dependent sentence).

(2) Sentences ending with the interrogative marker /′lá/ or the parenthetical interrogative marker /″hánˀ/ have an extra-high pitch on these morphemes, a pitch which does not correlate with the high of the tonal system. Sometimes the interrogative /′lá/ tends also to gradually raise the "key" of the tones of preceding words, but without affecting the relative pitch of the tones themselves. Illustrations: /nan″dáˀ ′lá/ (the /′lá/ is higher than the /áˀ/) 'Is it hot?; /nan″dáˀ ″hánˀ/ (the /″hánˀ/ is higher than the /áˀ/ 'It's hot, isn't it?

(3) Phonological sentences which are grammatically independent and declarative

297

tend to have a general down-drift of pitch, lowering the key of the tone registers gradually but leaving the relative pitches of the tones unaffected. Accompanying the down-drift of pitch there is also a tendency toward a relaxed quality, a fade in intensity, sometimes even to voicelessness—completely unvoiced unstressed syllables, voiceless off-glide on the vowel of final stressed syllables. (This relaxed quality is less, however, if the sentence ends with a syllable including $V?$ with high tone.) Frequently such declarative sentences are followed by a step-up in pitch at the beginning of the next sentence unit. Both the down-drift and the step-up in pitch are more frequent on longer sentences than on shorter ones.

1.6. HESITATION PAUSE. Extra-systemic to the phonological hierarchy described above is the hesitation pause. This pause may break into any of the above-described groupings (word, phrase, or sentence). It is marked by tenseness of quality, change of tone, and some lengthening of otherwise short syllables.

Illustrations (hesitation pause marked with #): /en"tónses # "ndi? #/ 'So then, this, . . .' The /e/ of the final syllable of the first word is lengthened; the phonemic up-glide tone of /"ndi?/ is kept phonetically at a level mid; /'beda "nda tier"mánu "este # "de # "méhiko/ 'Arrived a brother uh # from # Mexico City'. The two low tones of /"este/ (hesitation word) are maintained phonetically low-low rather than the expected mid-low; the final /e/ of this word is lengthened somewhat, as is the /e/ of /"de/ before the next pause.

2. GRAMMATICAL HIERARCHY. In this section, the same data are divided into grammatical functional parts rather than phonological parts.

2.0.1. HIERARCHY. The grammatical system of Isthmus Zapotec is viewed as composed of at least seven structural levels, ranking from the highest to the lowest as follows:

298

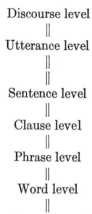

Discourse level
‖
Utterance level
‖
‖
Sentence level
‖
Clause level
‖
Phrase level
‖
Word level
‖
Morpheme-cluster level

The constructions represented by each level contain one or more units which function as nucleus, and one or more modification forms, which are here labelled satellites. The kind of structure at one level is differentiated from that at another level by the functional relationship of nucleus and satellite constituents, by their potential complexity, and by their potential distribution is larger matrices.

Within the general kind of structure represented by each level, there are further divisions into construction "types" which differ from one another in their composition or in their composition and external distribution.

Each higher-level construction is potentially composed of a sequence of constructions of the level next lower in the hierarchy, as indicated by the connecting lines in the diagram above. The diagram is presented with the levels in schematic, sharply differentiated form for introductory purposes. The description of the various levels must likewise be presented in order, as though they were completely mutually exclusive units with step-by-step inclusiveness. The facts presented in the description, however, will reveal that a particular text cannot necessarily be successively segmented into sublevel layers; i.e., not all sentences of any one utterance can be directly segmented into successive layers of clause, phrase, and word. Clauses, for example, are determined not simply by the fact that they are composed of phrases and are the basic components of sentences but also by their particular kind of internal structure. In terms of their distribution, certain types of clauses may occur as part of another clause construction or even as part of a (lower-level) phrase construction.

2.0.2. LIMITATION OF SCOPE. The various levels in the grammatical hierarchy provide a framework for a complete description of the grammar of the language. Lack of space in the present paper, however, precludes a thorough, detailed description of all of the levels. Morpheme-cluster-level and word-level constructions, since they relate to only one word type and since they have not been previously described in tagmemic terms, are described completely with formulas to show their tagmemic structure. At phrase, clause, and sentence levels, however, only representative patterns are described and presentation is in summary statement form. Utterance and discourse levels are not included. A brief survey of these two higher levels and details of phrase, clause, and sentence levels are given in Pickett, 1960.

2.0.3. IDENTIFICATION OF TERMS AND SYMBOLS. In addition to those which are considered to be traditional, the following terms and symbols are used.

2.0.3.1. SLOT, FILLER, AND TAGMEME. The constructions at each level of the hierarchy are viewed as composed of a sequence of tagmemes, i.e., a sequence of emic units composed of a functional "slot" and the class of forms which "fill" that slot. A clause construction, for example, includes a predicate slot filled by a verb phrase, and hence a predicate tagmeme. The phrase filler is likewise composed of tagmemes (e.g., the head slot filled by a verb) but at the next lower level. The terms used here are taken from Kenneth L. Pike, but with certain differences of interpretation. (See Pike, 1954, 1960; Longacre, 1964; Pickett, 1960.)

2.0.3.2. FORMULAIC REPRESENTATIONS. The following conventions are used to represent tagmemes and morphemes.

(1) Tagmemic formulas include the following representation for each tagmeme: Slot-name:Slot-filler name, e.g., +asp:asp +nucl:v-stem, to be read "plus (obligatory) aspect slot filled by aspect prefixes, plus nucleus slot filled by verb stems." Explanation of the abbreviations and details regarding the fillers are given in paragraphs labelled "slot fillers" below each formula.

(2) Braces { } are placed around a name-form of morphemes which have more than one allomorph of nonautomatic alternation.

2.1. MORPHEME-CLUSTER LEVEL. Slots in word-level constructions are filled either by single morphemes or by clusters of morphemes which function as units. These clusters of morphemes, although below word level, have their own tagmemic structure.

2.1.1. PLURAL IMPERATIVE CLUSTER. The plural imperative morpheme cluster is composed of two obligatory tagmemes: +imper: *la-* +asp:{*gu-*}.

Slot fillers. Each of the two slots is filled by only one morpheme. The prefix *la-* occurs only in this construction. The aspect prefix {*gu-*} is the potential aspect, which may also occur alone in the verb aspect slot of verb words.

Illustration[7] *la—gú* ('*kaa*) 'plural-imperative—potential (write)'.

2.1.2. AMBULATIVE CLUSTER. The ambulative morpheme cluster has a meaning of movement or repetition in performing an action. It is composed of two obligatory tagmemes: +amb:*ka-* +sta:*na-*.

Slot fillers. The *ka-* prefix which fills the

---

[7] In §2 and 3, the tagmemes of the level under discussion are separated by dash—, both in citation form and English literal translation. Spaces between words in the citations indicate grammatical word boundaries. Phonologically, words are written as in slow speech, i.e., as though each word were the center of a phonological phrase. The nuclear syllable is indicated by the word-stress symbol ´.

ambulative slot is one specific allomorph of the continuative-aspect prefix. The *na-* prefix which fills the stative slot is one specific allomorph of the stative prefix. An alternate form (depending partially on the verb stem class, partially on idiolect) adds the potential aspect prefix in the second slot. Illustrations: *ka—na ('yubi)* 'continuative—stative (search)' ~ *ka—na-u ('yubi)* 'continuative—stative-potential—(search) (=goes around searching)'.

2.1.3. CAUSATIVE CLUSTER. The nuclear slot of verb words may be filled by single-morpheme stems (roots) or by morpheme clusters. The causative cluster is composed of two obligatory tagmemes: +caus:{*si-*} +core:v-root C.

Slot fillers. The prefix {*si-*} has a meaning of causative action. Verb roots which fill the core slot are those of the C class—causative-forming roots (see §3.1.1.1).

Illustrations: *(ru-) si—'žoonyeʔ* '(habitual aspect) causative—run (=makes run)'. (Compare *ru'žoonyeʔ* 'runs'.)

2.2. WORD LEVEL. Grammatical words are single morphemes or combinations of bound and free morphemes which fill slots within constructions at phrase (the most common distribution), clause, or sentence level. Words are of two major classes: independent (minimum free forms) and dependent (enclitics and proclitics). The latter are discussed further in §3.1.1.3.

There is very little word-level structure (morphology) in Isthmus Zapotec, since most of the bound morphemes are enclitic or proclitic. In this section we deal with the tagmemic structure of the only words which include affixes—a class of verb-like words. The remaining words are treated as distribution classes (based on external distribution) and are described under the lexical hierarchy (§3.2).

There are three word types,[8] but these are joined as a class named verbs because of overlap of fillers in some of their slots. These

are: declarative verbs, stative verbs, and imperative verbs. Another classification, based primarily on external distribution, crisscrosses this classification and the classification of verb stems—that of transitive vs. intransitive. Since the transitive-intransitive distribution does not parallel either the stem classification or the word-level tagmemic structure, it is treated in the lexical hierarchy under distribution classes.

2.2.1. DECLARATIVE VERBS. Declarative verbs include two obligatory tagmemes: a satellite tagmeme of aspect and a nuclear tagmeme.

Formula. +asp:asp +nucl:v-stem

Slot fillers. The verb stems which fill the nucleus slot include verb-stem clusters and active-verb roots. The aspect slot is filled by a class of seven aspect prefixes and the ambulative morpheme cluster.

Habitual aspect {*ru-*}	: *ru— 'dii* 'gives'
Completive aspect {*bi-*}	: *bi— 'dii* 'gave/will have given'
Incompletive aspect {*zu-*}	: *zu—'dii* 'will give'
Continuative aspect {*ku-*}	: *ku—'dii* 'is/was giving'
Potential aspect {*gu-*}	: *gu—'dii* 'will give/ should give'
Unreal aspect {*nu-*}	: *nu—'dii* 'if only would give' *(ké) nu—'dii* '(not) unreal—give (didn't give)'
Perfective aspect {*wa-*}	: *wa—'dii* 'has given'
Ambulative aspect *ka- na(u-)*	: *kanau—'dii* 'goes around giving'

2.2.2. STATIVE VERBS. Stative verbs differ from declarative in both of their two obligatory tagmemes.

Formula. +sta-asp:{*na-*} +sta-v-nucl: sv-root/n-root

Slot fillers. The stative aspect slot is filled by only one prefix, the stative prefix {*na-*}. The stative verb nucleus is filled by stative verb roots or a small subclass of noun roots.

Illustrations: *na—'lĕ* 'stative-aspect—hol-

---

[8] Structural types are contrastive structures within the general kind at any one level, contrastive in their internal tagmemic composition or in a combination of internal composition and external distribution.

low' (stative verb root) (= 'is hollow'); *na—'bennye* 'stative-aspect—mud' (noun root) (= 'is muddy').

2.2.3. IMPERATIVE VERBS. Imperative verbs differ from declarative verbs in their aspect tagmeme and their external distribution.

Formula. +imper-asp:imper-asp +nucl: v-stem

Slot fillers. The nucleus slot-fillers are the same as those in the declarative verbs. The imperative-aspect fillers comprise one prefix (second-singular imperative) and one morpheme cluster (plural imperative). The filler of the imperative-aspect slot is in agreement with the person filler of Imperative Dependent Subject slot in the clause-level constructions.

Illustrations: Singular imperative {*bi-*}: *bi—'dii (ni)* 'imperative-aspect—give (it)'. The singular imperative prefix is homophonous in most cases with the completive aspect prefix. In rare instances, the choice of allomorph is different in the two morphemes, however. Note, for example, *'b—eedă* 'came' (*b-* completive-aspect allomorph):*gu–'da?* 'come!' (*gu-* imperative prefix allomorph).

Plural imperative {*la- gu-*}:*lagú—'dii (ni)* 'imperative-aspect—give (it) (second plural)'; *lagú—'dii (nu ni)* 'imperative-aspect give (we it) (first plural)'.

2.3. PHRASE LEVEL. The phrase is a potential sequence of two or more words[9] which function as a unit of other than predicate-subject relationship. Phrases fill slots within constructions at clause (the most common distribution) or sentence levels or within another phrase construction.

There are at least seventy different phrase types in Isthmus Zapotec. The large number is due partially to extensive borrowing of Spanish prepositions but is primarily due to the analytical inclusion of clitics as (dependent) words.

Space prohibits presenting the formulas

[9] A phrase construction may be represented by only one word provided it is potentially expandable.

and illustrations of even all the major types. Only samples are chosen to indicate some of the varying types of constructions included at this level.

2.3.1. NOUN PHRASES. Phrases which have nouns as fillers of the head slot include a head-modification phrase, three kinds of possessive phrases, and a compound phrase. Noun phrases are all endocentric. They fill the Independent Subject or Object slot in clauses.

Head-modification phrase: *'štalle—'bére—'wiini?* 'many—chicken—little'; *'čuppa—'bá?du—'skwéla* 'two—child—school (= two school children)'.

Possessive noun phrase-1: *ka—'š— pi?ku—'wiini—be—kě* 'plural—possession marker—dog—little—his/her—that (= those little dogs of his/hers)'.

Possessive noun phrase-2 (obligatorily possessed nouns): *ti—'benda—'wiini—bě* 'a—sister—little—hers'.

Possessive noun phrase-3: *ka—'gi?ri—'wiini—'š ti—'bě* 'plural—candle—little possession marker one—his/her (= his/her little candles)'. In phrase-1 the possession marker *š* is preposed to the head word; in phrase-3 it is part of a possession-marking phrase *š ti*, which is postposed to the head word.

Compound phrase: *'lari—ga'miža?—kal-'són para 'ngiiw* 'clothes—shirt—pants for man'; *'za—bi'zaa—ka'fé—ne—'késu* 'lard—beans—coffee—and—cheese'.

2.3.2. INDEPENDENT PRONOUN PHRASE. This phrase, like the noun phrases, fills the Independent Subject or Object slot in clauses. It has a nuclear slot filled by an independent word, but the remaining (satellite) slots are filled by dependent words.

Illustrations: *'laa—bě* 'person base—he/she (= he/she or him/her)'; *'laa—sí—ka bě* 'person base—only—plural he/she (= only they/them)'.

2.3.3. VERB PHRASES. There are at least nine different verb phrases, filling predicate slots in clauses. Three basic types (classes of types) are differentiated by internal composition criteria: stative, auxiliary aspect, and verb-modification phrases. The latter two are further divided according to the fillers of the head slots and correlation with external distribution in the clause structure: transitive-declarative, intransitive-declarative, transitive-imperative, and intransitive-imperative. Verb phrases are endocentric. Illustrations are given for each of the three basic types.

Stative phrase: *na'čonga—'gye* 'is-hard—rock (= as hard as a rock)'.

Auxiliary aspect phrase: *ze—'topa* (*be 'yága*) 'went—gather (he wood)'.

Verb-modification phrase: *má—ké—'zuni—rú*(*be nĭ*) 'already not—will-do—still (he/she it) (= He/she won't do it any more.)'; *ri'naba—'diĭǰa?* 'asks—word (= inquires)'; *'bi?ni—ga'nár* 'did win (= won)'.

2.3.4. OTHER MAJOR PHRASES. Phrases which fill other clause-level slots include time phrases, location phrases, manner phrases, and purpose phrases. These phrases are all exocentric. Each includes a minimum of an orientation tagmeme and a focus tagmeme, in that order. One illustration for each of these four phrase types follows.

Time phrase: *'má — 'bya? — 'čupa — sé'mána* 'already—about—two-week'.

Location phrase: *'ike—'danĭ* 'head—hill (= at the top of the hill)'.

Manner phrase: *'kasi—ti 'téku* 'like—a Teco (= in a manner befitting a loyal native of Juchitán)'.

Purpose phrase: *para—'laa bĕ* 'for—person him/her'.

2.3.5. MINOR PHRASES. Minor phrases include others filling clause-level slots, interrogative phrases filling sentence-level introducer slots, some which occur as complete sentences (e.g., vocative phrases), and some which fill slots within other phrases (e.g., the possessive relation phrase referred to under possessive noun phrase-3). A few illustrations follow.

Phrases with pause markers. Nearly all clause-level slots include a filler which is composed of any other filler of that slot

plus the dependent or pause-marking word *lá* referred to as a "comma" by one bilingual speaker. Illustration, filler of Time slot: *'óra ke—lá* 'hour that—,'.

Content-question introducer phrase (sentence-level slot filler): *'ži—'módo* 'what—manner'.

Vocative phrase (complete sentence): *'ba? du—ka?* 'child—plural (= Children!)'.

Quantifier phrase (filler of modification slot in a noun phrase): *'tobi—sĭ* 'one—only'.

2.4. CLAUSE LEVEL. The constructions labeled "clause" fill slots within constructions at the sentence level (the most common distribution) or within phrases or other clauses. A clause may be equivalent to a complete sentence (i.e., forming the sentence nucleus, with no satellites), or it may form a sentence nucleus which is accompanied by satellite forms, or it may be one of two clauses in a compound-nucleus sentence. Internally, the clause is a unit of predication which has as minimum form some kind of predicate tagmeme and some kind of subject tagmeme.

Clause types are of two major classes: dependent and independent. Dependent clauses fill optional slots in sentences or slots included within another clause or a phrase. They are marked as dependent by one or more of the satellite forms included. Independent clauses fill the obligatory nuclear slot of sentences.

2.4.1. INDEPENDENT CLAUSES. Independent clauses include four major types and three minor types. Each type is contrastive with the others in terms of the basic nuclear tagmemes—Predicate, Dependent Subject, Independent Subject, Object. Two types (the declaratives) have the same satellite tagmemes; the others have few or no satellite tagmemes.

2.4.1.1. DECLARATIVE CLAUSES. There are two declarative clause types, differentiated by the presence or absence of the Object tagmeme and a corresponding difference of choice of verbs as fillers of the predicate slot. In addition to the predicate, the nucleus of each includes an obligatory Dependent Subject and an optional Independent Subject. Optional satellite tagmemes in each are: Time, Location, Manner, Purpose.[10] The satellite tagmemes vary in order as they orbit around the nuclear tagmemes, and no more than three satellite tagmemes have been observed in any one clause occurrence. The most frequent distribution (about 85 per cent) is that of only one satellite.

Intransitive declarative: *za'ka—rí'ni?—bĕ* 'thus — speaks — he' (Manner — Predicate —Dependent Subject); *des'pwés lá—gu 'dinde—'nézu 'čéle—'laaka 'pór te'r̃éno* 'afterward,—fought—Nezuchele—also for land' (Time—Predicate—Independent Subject—Purpose).[11]

Transitive declarative: *'ǰi gu'la?ki 'stǐ 'dyúǰi 'gíǰi la'yu—gu'la?ki—be—'díiǰa 'za* 'day set up God world—set—he—word Zapotec (= When God made the world, He also made the Zapotec language.)' (Time—Predicate—Dependent Subject—Object); *ye 'tawá ny—á—'laa ka be—rá 'liǰi ka bĕ* 'went eat with—I—person plural she—location home plural she (= I went to eat with them at their house.)' (Predicate—Dependent Subject—Object—Location).

2.4.1.2. IMPERATIVE CLAUSES. Imperative clauses, like the declarative, are both transitive and intransitive. They differ from the declarative types in that they do not include an Independent Subject tagmeme, the Predicate slots are filled by imperative verbs, the Imperative Dependent Subject slot is filled only by imperative dependent pronouns, and satellite tagmemes are rare and are always postposed to the nucleus tagmemes.

Transitive imperative: *lagú'kaa—nǐ* 'write —it' (Predicate—Object); intransitive imperative: *la'kwǐ — nú — 'yánna* 'sit-down

[10] There is in addition a Predicate Specifier tagmeme, but its occurrence is rare, and its fillers are nearly all Spanish loan expressions; hence it has been left out of this presentation.

[11] In this illustration the Dependent Subject tagmeme has a zero manifestation.

— we — now' (Predicate — Imperative Dependent Subject—Time).

2.4.1.3. MINOR CLAUSES. Minor clause types include three equational clauses. Two of these have three obligatory tagmemes; the third has two, but one of them may be repeated. No satellite tagmemes have been observed in equational clauses.

Equational-1 clause includes an Equational Predicate slot filled by a verb phrase with only one verb as head—the verb meaning 'to be' or 'to become'—, Dependent Subject, and an Equational slot filled by a subclass of noun phrases. Illustrations: *'nakka—be—'máystru de 'skwéla* 'is—he—teacher of school'.

Equational-2 clause includes Independent Subject, an Equational Predicate slot filled by a single word *ngă* 'that' (which in this slot carries the meaning of 'is'), and an Equational slot filled by noun phrases, independent pronoun phrases, or the nucleus of certain clauses. Illustrations: *'ngă—'ngă —'laa nǐ* 'that—that—person it' (= 'That's it.'); *'naa—ngá—'bìt é 'beenda kĕ* 'I—that —killed I snake that' (= 'I am the one who killed that snake'.)

Equational-3 clause has only two obligatory tagmemes, but the Independent Subject tagmeme may be repeated. Its Equational Predicate slot is filled by noun phrases or attributive phrases.

Illustrations: *'ba?du—'laa bĕ* 'child—person he/she' (= 'He/she is just a child'); *'ómbre rí lá—'póbre—'laa* 'man this ,—poor —person he' (= 'This man was poor') (repeated subject tagmeme).

2.4.2. DEPENDENT CLAUSES. Dependent clauses comprise a class of clause types which are differentiated from independent clauses, and in detail from one another, by their external distribution and by the internal feature of dependent-marking tagmemes. Postposed markers indicate only dependence; preposed markers also indicate the distribution of the clause as a whole, i.e., as to whether it is a filler of a Time slot, Location slot, etc. The nucleus of dependent

303

clauses may be the nucleus of any independent clause except one of the imperative types. Satellite distribution is limited, but those satellite tagmemes which do occur are the same as those of independent clauses.

In addition to differences as to transitive and intransitive predicates, there are ten basic dependent clause types: location, relative subject, relative object, relative manner, purpose, manner, two time clauses, object clause, and sentence-slot clause. Only a few of these will be illustrated.

Time clause: *'óra—ibi'gett—á—de ra 'nyaa* 'hour—return—I—from location field' (= 'When I return from the field'.) (Time introducer — Predicate — Dependent Subject—Location).

Location clause: *ra—'nùú—bé—kĕ* 'where —is—he—that' (= 'there where he is') (Location Introducer—Predicate—Dependent Subject—Demonstrative Closer).

Relative Subject clause: *('zyaba) ni— 'nùú — rá'kĕ* '(will-fall) which — is — place that' (Relative Introducer, functioning also as subject—Predicate—Location). This whole relative clause functions as subject of the clause 'will-fall. . . . '

Sentence-slot clause: *pa—'lĭi—ni'kòó—w —'lari—lá* 'if—you—had-accepted—you—clothes—,' (Introducer—Independent Subject—Predicate—Dependent Subject—Object—Dependent Closer).

2.5. SENTENCE LEVEL. Grammatical sentences are constructions which potentially occur alone as complete utterances. They may range in length from a single word (as in dependent response sentences or vocative sentences) to a lengthy coordinate structure or pyramiding structure of clause within clause. The sentence-level overlaps at certain points with the clause-level in that an independent clause may also be a complete sentence. The two kinds of constructions differ, however, in the type of potential expansion and in the fact that certain phrases or words may be sentences but not clauses.

In terms of their specific internal structure and their distribution in larger matrices,

304

sentence types are of two classes: independent and dependent. Independent sentences frequently begin a discourse unit. Dependent sentences most commonly do not begin a discourse unit; when they do, they are dependent on the presence of some form of nonverbal behavior.

Each of these two classes is divided into subclasses, based on whether the sentence types are clause constructions or nonclause (phrase or word) constructions.

2.5.1. INDEPENDENT SENTENCES — NON-CLAUSE. Independent sentences whose slots are filled by phrases and words are of three types: vocative, interrogative, and exclamation.

Illustrations: *'baʔdu kaʔ* 'child vocative-plural' (= 'Children!'); *u'nă 'márko* 'which Mark' (= 'Where is Mark?'); *'áy 'nána* 'Oh!'

2.5.2. INDEPENDENT SENTENCES—CLAUSE. Clause independent sentences include four major types or classes of types. Type 1, the declarative-imperative subordinating, is basic to the others.

2.5.2.1. INDEPENDENT SENTENCE TYPE 1. Declarative-imperative subordinating. This sentence type has an obligatory nuclear slot filled by an independent clause which is preceded optionally by a satellite slot filled by a sentence-slot dependent clause.

Illustration: *pa 'lĭi zu'syand u 'ngiiw ke lá—zuni ga'nár lu 'stalle bí'ǰičči* 'if you will-heal you man that,—will gain you much money'.

2.5.2.2. INDEPENDENT SENTENCE TYPE 2. Declarative compound. This sentence is composed of a series of independent declarative clauses optionally connected by the link word *nĕ* 'and'.

Illustrations: *bi'ree be—'zĕ bĕ* 'went-out he—went he'; *'ryuu-nissa ni pri'méru— 'ryaya ni—ne—rí'biibi 'ndaani ti 'lari na 'lassé* 'gets-rinsed it first—gets-dissolved it —and—gets-strained it inside a cloth thin'.

2.5.2.3. INDEPENDENT SENTENCE TYPE 3. Yes-or-no interrogative. This sentence type adds an optional Question Introducer tagmeme and an obligatory Yes-or-no Closer tagmeme to the basic form of sentence type 1.

Illustrations: *'čě wʔ lu'gyaa—lá* 'going you market —?'; *'nyée—'čě wʔ lu'gyaa—lá ?—* 'going you market—?'

2.5.2.4. INDEPENDENT SENTENCE TYPE 4. Class of interrogative sentences—clause content-information. Clause content-information sentences are a class of six sentence types, differentiated by the function of their introductory tagmemes. Most of the introductory tagmemes have a double function of indicating question and functioning in the place of some clause-level tagmeme in the basic clause, e.g., Subject, Object, Location, Time.

Illustrations. *'ži—'ráka 'laʔ ǰi bě* 'what—wants he' (the interrogative *ži* functions as Object filler in the clause); *pa'ǰi—'čě bě* 'what day—going he' (the interrogative phrase *pa 'ǰi* functions as Time slot filler in the clause).

2.5.3. DEPENDENT SENTENCES — NON-CLAUSES. Nonclause dependent sentences are responses, dependent on an utterance of another speaker (or occasionally on one of the same speaker) or on some nonverbal behavior.

Illustrations: Two answers to the question *'čě wʔ lu'gyaa lá* 'going you market ?': *koʔ* 'no'; *stí 'r̃áttu sǐ* 'another little-while yet' (= 'A little later'.)

2.5.4. DEPENDENT SENTENCES — CLAUSE. Class of sequence types. Sequence sentences are composed of the basic independent sentence type 1 accompanied by one or two introductory tagmemes which connect sentences together in sequence. One of the introductory tagmemes has a double function of introducer and some other function within the main clause.

Illustrations: *'pwe—'čùú nǔ* 'well—go we' (= 'Well, let's go'.) (only one introducer tagmeme); *'peru—'daʔgu 'yoo san an'tónyo* 'but—closed house Saint Anthony' (= 'But Saint Anthony was locked up'.) (only one introducer tagmeme); *'bwéno pwes—ra 'kě—* *riza be i'r̃ǎ ǰi* 'okay well—location that—walked he all day' (= 'Okay, well, he went there every day'.) (two introducer tagmemes, the second of which also functions as location marker).

3. LEXICAL HIERARCHY. In this section we view the fillers of the slots of the grammatical hierarchy as lexical forms and classes —the morphemes and words in terms of their distribution classes and their phonemic shapes.

3.1. MORPHEMES AND MORPHOPHONEMICS. Morphemes are viewed first as to their classification, second as to their phonemic shapes.

3.1.1. MORPHEME CLASSES. In terms of their general distribution, morphemes are of four major classes: bound roots, prefixes, clitics, and free roots.

3.1.1.1. BOUND ROOTS are verb roots only. These are of two subclasses, based on their distribution in verb or causative-cluster structures: causative-forming roots (class C) and neutral roots (class N). Class C roots may fill the core slot of the causative cluster (§2.1.3) or may directly fill the nuclear slots of verb (word) structures. Class N roots fill only the nuclear slots of the word structures. Illustrations: Class C root *-ra* 'be used up', as in *bi'ra* 'was all used up' and *bisi'ra* '(he) used (it) all up' (including causative prefix {*si-*}); Class N stem *-e* 'go' as in *'rye* 'goes'.

Verb roots are also divided into two major classes which crisscross the above grouping: active and stative verb roots. Active verb roots directly or indirectly (via the causative cluster) fill the nuclear slot in declarative or imperative verbs; stative verb roots fill the nuclear slot of stative verbs. There is some overlap of membership between the two classes. The root *-kiččiʔ* 'white', for example, may fill either the stative-verb nucleus or the declarative verb nucleus slot, as in *bi'kiččiʔ* 'became white', but the root *-biidiʔ* 'dirty' fills only the stative-verb nucleus slot. The external distribution of those which may occur in the stative-verb

305

nucleus slot, however, differs from those which do not. Stative-verb roots (occasionally the whole stative verb word) may occur in the Modification slot of noun phrases, as in *'yoo 'kičǐ?* 'house white'.

Verb roots vary in length from one syllable to three, with two syllables as the most common shape.

3.1.1.2. PREFIXES comprise a small class of morphemes which fill the aspect slots of verb structures and an even more limited class of morphemes which fill slots in morpheme clusters. These are listed in §2.1. and 2.2.1.

Prefixes are of three canonical forms: C, CV, and V.

3.1.1.3. CLITICS are dependent forms, both proclitic and enclitic, which have a more free distribution in phrase and clause than affixes. These morphemes are treated as dependent words rather than as affixes. Most clitics are of one-syllable length, but there are a few composed of two syllables.

3.1.1.4. FREE ROOTS are root morphemes which are uninflected and which are isolatable grammatical words. The free-root class includes nouns and a number of smaller distribution classes. They include canonical shapes of one, two, or three syllables, with two syllables as the most common shape.

3.1.2. MORPHOPHONEMICS. Morphophonemic alternations include both automatic and nonautomatic types. Automatic alternations include the following three kinds:

Loss of glottal stop. Morphemes composed of or ending with an unstressed *V?* syllable or a stressed *V?* syllable with up-glide tone, have an alternant without the glottal stop when in utterance medial position. Morphemes ending with a stressed *V?* syllable have an alternant without the glottal stop when the syllable is not in the nuclear slot of the phonological phrase. Illustrations: *"ba?du?* 'child':*"ba?du kǎ* 'that child'; *i"rǎ?* 'all':*i"rǎ kabě* 'all of them'; *'badu "wiini?* 'child little' (= 'baby').

Tone alternations. Morphemes composed of or ending in an unstressed syllable with

306

up-glide tone when in utterance final position have two tone alternants when in medial position: a low tone and a high tone, depending on the basic tone and stress pattern of the word which precedes it. Morphemes which follow such a syllable may have alternant tones, depending on their own basic tone and stress pattern. For example, a word with all low tones has an alternant with the first tone high when following the above type syllable.

Illustrations: (1) up-glide alternates with low: *"ratti bě* (as complete utterance): *"nissa* (as complete utterance):*"ratti be 'nisa* 'he is always thirsty'; (2) up-glide alternates with high: *ka"yǎttí bě* (as complete utterance):*ka "yǎttí bé 'nisa* 'he is thirsty'.

There are more than a dozen word types with different basic tone and stress patterns, each one having its own pattern of tone alternation and effect on the surrounding tones.

Clusters of *š* or *s* plus consonant. There are no clusters of *š* or *s* plus lenis stop or plus *č*, *š*, or *s* (except ambisyllabic clusters *šš* and *ss*). When morpheme combinations would result in one of these clusters, morphemes beginning with lenis consonants *b*, *d*, or *g* have alternants beginning with the corresponding fortis consonant *p*, *t*, or *k*, and morphemes beginning with *r* have alternants beginning with *t*. Combinations with other consonants are most easily described in process terms of consonant cluster reduction, as follows: *š* or *s* + *č*, *j*, *ž*, or *š* > *š*; *š* or *s* + *z* or *s* > *s*. Illustrations, using the possessive marker proclitic {*š*}: *'š pere bě* 'his/her chicken' (basic form *'bere*); *'š tii bě* 'his/her water jug' (basic form *'rii*); *'šál bě* 'her shawl' (basic form *'čal*); *'sidi bě* 'his/her salt' (basic form (*'zidi*).

Nonautomatic alternations are of two types: morphemically conditioned and phonemically-conditioned. It is the verb prefixes, the verb roots, and dependent pronouns which are most commonly affected by these alternations. The aspect prefixes have morphemically - conditioned alternations which can be described by means of distributional sets, and within these sets there are phonemically-conditioned alternations and subsets of morphemically-conditioned alternations. The causative prefix {si-} has seventeen morphemically-conditioned allomorphs. Verb root alternations are only morphemically conditioned. Allomorphs of the dependent pronouns are principally phonemically conditioned. For details of these alternations, see Pickett 1953, 1955.

In addition to the segmental alternations, there is a complex system of tonal alternations in verbs, depending on the verb class, the person, and the aspect.

3.2. WORDS. Grammatical words are here described in terms of their distribution classes and their co-occurrence restrictions as fillers of slots.

3.2.1. WORDS AND WORD CLASSES. Words may be divided by two different types of classification: (1) independent vs. dependent, based on their distribution in utterances, and (2) smaller distribution classes, based on distribution in specific slots.

3.2.1.1. INDEPENDENT AND DEPENDENT WORDS. Independent words are isolatable units which can compose a whole sentence, at least as response to the question "How do you say X?" or "What do you call this?". Independent words are also phonological words, but a phonological word may include two independent words and several dependent words. Illustrations: 'ba?du? 'child' (can be a vocative sentence); 'ndi? 'this' (can be a response sentence); 'beedă 'came' (can be a complete clause sentence).

Dependent words are proclitic and enclitic forms, which are not isolatable in the way independent words are but which have a freer distribution than affixes. Dependent words, like independent words but unlike affixes, fill slots on higher levels than the word level itself. Illustrations: 'lu 'wiini bě 'face little his/her', in which the enclitic bě fills a phrase level slot. Compare the same bě morpheme at clause level in 'beeda bě 'came he/she'.

Dependent words are usually unstressed parts of phonological words, but a few are themselves centers of phonological words, e.g., 'gupa "ga nĭ 'keep meanwhile it', in which "ga 'meanwhile' is a dependent grammatical word but is stressed and thus is the center of a phonological word and phrase.

3.2.1.2. DISTRIBUTION CLASSES. Word classes defined by their differing distribution in slots at the various levels include a list of more than fifty basic classes and three types of subclasses. Only the major classes will be listed here, i.e., those which are frequent in occurrence either in text count (the independent and dependent pronouns) or in both text count and membership list.

(1) Nouns occur in head slots of noun phrases in Object and Independent Subject slot in clauses: gu'naa 'woman'.

(2) Dependent pronouns occur in Dependent Subject slot in clauses. The total list follows: {a?} 'first person singular'; {lu?} 'second person singular'; bě 'third person singular human'; mě 'third person singular animal'; nĭ 'third person singular inanimate'; dŭ 'first person plural exclusive'; nŭ 'first person plural inclusive'; tŭ 'second person plural'.

(3) Independent pronouns occur in Object and Independent Subject slots in clauses. The total list follows: 'ndĭ? 'this'; 'ngă 'that' 'ngě 'that over yonder'; 'naa 'first person singular'; 'lii 'second person singular'; nĭ 'third person singular inanimate'. Other persons are indicated by independent pronoun phrases composed of person base word 'laa and dependent pronouns (§2.3.2).

(4) Intransitive declarative verbs occur in Intransitive Declarative Predicate slot in clauses: 'beedă 'came'. It should be noted that verbs as a unit do not form one single distribution class but four different classes, because of their relationship to other clause-level tagmemes. The transitive-intransitive distinction was not discussed in the word-level description of the grammatical hierarchy because it is not paralleled by the

307

internal structure of the verb words. Of the verbs formed from Class N (neutral) stems, some are transitive, some intransitive. Of the verbs formed from Class C (causative-forming) stems, there are various criss-crossing combinations. In some cases, a verb formed from a simple stem will be intransitive but its corresponding causative form will be transitive, e.g., *bin'dá?* 'was heated': *bisin'dá? be nǐ* 'he/she heated it'. In other cases both are transitive (or optionally members of the intransitive class as well), e.g., *bi'ziidi be (nǐ)* 'he/she learned (it)':*bi'siidi be (nǐ)* 'he/she taught it (causative form)'.

(5) Intransitive imperative verbs occur in Intransitive Imperative Predicate slot in clauses: *gu'da?* 'come'.

(6) Transitive declarative verbs occur in Transitive Declarative Predicate slot in clauses: *'bi?ni (be nǐ)* 'did (he/she it)'.

(7) Transitive imperative verbs occur in Transitive Imperative Predicate slot in clauses: *'bi?ni (nǐ)* 'do (it)'.

3.2.2. WORDS AND TAGMAMORPHEMICS. The term tagmamorphemics is used to describe those variants in tagmemic structure which are conditioned by the specific slot fillers. A number of co-occurrence restrictions exist in Zapotec between the fillers of one slot and those of another. Here we simply summarize the types of variants. Details are given in Pickett, 1960.

(1) Co-occurrence of specific fillers in phrase slots. This type of variation occurs in the exocentric location, time, and manner phrases and in the head-modification noun phrase. The location phrase, for example, has a Location Orientation slot filler *ra* 'location indicator', which co-occurs with only certain fillers of the Location Focus slot: *ra—'giigu?* 'at river' but not **ra—'giǰi* 'at town'.

(2) Limitations in agreement between the Independent and Dependent Subject tagmemes of both declarative and imperative clauses. The two subject tagmemes must agree in number and person. In addition, in the declarative clauses there are certain

co-occurrence restrictions related to the position of the Independent Subject when it is filled by a noun. For details, see Pickett, 1960, pp. 58, 69.

(3) The verb 'to say' as Transitive Predicate slot filler. When a form of the verb 'to say' fills a predicate slot, the Object slot filler may be one or more sentences, and may include single words or phrases other than nouns or independent pronouns, is more frequently preposed to the predicate than with other fillers, and is often split in two parts. Illustration: *pa'rá '—čé w?—'na bě* 'where go you—says—he' (interrogative sentence in preposed Object slot).

3.3. WORD CLUSTERS. A thorough study of levels of groupings of lexical units, as distinct from grammatical structure, remains to be done. There are, however, certain idiomatic clusterings of words which are worthy of note as a beginning study of levels of lexical structure.

In one type, the two grammatical slots involved are Head and Modifier of the stative verb phrase, but there is a one-to-one co-occurrence restriction between the fillers of the slots, and the total meaning is simply 'extremely X'. Illustrations: *na'nanda 'giiba?* 'is-cold metal'. This same order of words could well fill predicate and subject slots, with meaning 'The metal is cold', but this particular combination is so frequently used idiomatically that the first of the two ambiguous meanings to be understood is not the predicate - subject relationship but the phrasal relationship of 'cold metal', or 'very cold'; *na'kiči 'be* 'is-white mold' (= 'very white'); *na'ya 'gyé?* 'is-clean flower (= 'very clean'); *na'ǰaa 'dútu?* 'warm' plus a unique constituent (= 'comfortably warm').

A second lexical word cluster is composed of certain fillers of one of the transitive predicate slots combined with certain fillers of the Object slot. Illustrations: *ru'yubi* 'looks for' + *'diiǰa?* 'word' = 'picks a fight'; *ru'kaa* 'fastens' in various combinations with Object words, e.g., *ru'kaa 'dyaga* 'fastens ear' (= 'listens'); *ru'kaa 'riǰi* 'fastens noise' (= 'screams, calls loudly'); *ru'kaa 'nă^ʔ* 'fastens hand' (= 'pushes').

A third cluster includes certain fillers of one of the predicate slots and certain fillers of the Location slot. Illustration: *'ratti* 'dies' + *'giigu^ʔ* 'river' = 'drowns' (not necessarily in the river).

4. TEXT. The following short text is given

Phonological sentence borders are marked by diagonal /. Grammatical sentences are indicated by periods: one period for independent sentences, two for dependent. In addition, there is one instance of a sentence fragment, a portion of a sentence which was left incomplete as the speaker interrupted herself with a different sentence. The end of this fragment is indicated by dash —.

″bwéno / .. 'čĭ-'gwě-nĭ-á   ″lii | či-″hmá ná'wíín-é-'lá / | ..
okay   going-speak-with-I you   day more was-little-I,

″káda 'gĕdá bĭ″síta ra-'liǰ-é-lá / | 'gĕda 'tŭžá gú″naa |
each come visitor to-home-my-,   come some woman

'gĕdá 'gwĭ 'nĕ 'hnyă ″diiǰa^ʔ | 'zĕdá man'dádu-lá / | —
come speak with mother-my word come errand-,

″napp-á ti-'bangú ″wiini či-'kĕ |. na'wiini^ʔ / |.
have-I a-bench   little day-that was-little

kasi-″gùúy-á ka-bi″síta | ″gyuu-ke-lá / | 'máká
when see-I pl.-visitor   enter-that-,   already

'zi-u″žoony-é |. zi-″kàá ″bángú^ʔ / |. gu″ry-ĕ ga″lawwĭ
went-run-I   went-get-I bench   sat-I center

de-″laa-ka^ʔ / |. ″hnyàá kasi-″gúuya 'naa | 'máká
of person-pl.   mother-my when-see me   already

ka″gĭru 'nyèé | 'para-″gyasá-^ʔ / | 'para 'ké-u'kaá
was-pinching leg-my for get-up-I   for not-fasten

″dyá^ʔga-^ʔ | 'ži ká″nĭ^ʔ-ka-bĕ / |.   'peru ″naa 'ké-″rúná-^ʔ |.
ear-my   what was-saying-pl.-she but I not-hear-I

ri″niib-é ″nyèé-sy-á^ʔ / |.
move-I leg-only-my

to show some of the relationships between groupings of the phonological and grammatical hierarchies.

Phonological word centers (stressed syllables) are marked by '. Borders are indicated by spaces. These spaces coincide with the borders of independent grammatical words. Dependent grammatical word borders are marked by hyphen.

Phonological phrase centers (nuclear syllables) are marked by ″. Grammatical borders are marked by a vertical line |.

Free translation. Okay, I'll tell you about when I was little. Each time a visitor came to my home, some woman came to chat with my mother or came on an errand— I had a little bench at that time, a little one. Whenever I would see visitors coming, right away I would run and get the bench and sit down right in the middle of them. When my mother saw me, she immediately started pinching my leg to make me get up, so I wouldn't hear what they were saying. But I paid no attention. I simply moved my leg.

REFERENCES

Angulo, 1925, 1926a, 1926b
—— and Freeland, 1935
Córdova, 1578a, 1578b
Henestrosa, 1933
Leal, 1950, 1954
Longacre, 1964
Mason, 1939
Nellis, 1947

Pickett, 1951, 1953, 1955, 1960
—— and Elson, 1962
Pike, E. V., 1948
Pike, K. L., 1954, 1955, 1958, 1960
Radin, 1930, 1935, 1946
Swadesh, 1947
Vivó, 1941

7F. Huautla de Jiménez Mazatec

EUNICE V. PIKE

0.	Introduction
1.	Phonome
2.	Syllable
3.	Phonological word
4.	Phonological phrase
5.	Phonological sentence
6.	Relationship between phonology and grammar
6.1.	Minimal pairs
6.2.	Phonological phrases which end in the middle of a grammatical phrase
7.	Monologue
7.1.	Official speech
7.2.	Christian prayer
7.3.	Pagan prayer
7.4.	Narrative monologue
7.5.	Non-monologue speech
8.	Grammatical sentence
8.1.	Declarative sentences
8.2.	Imperative sentences
8.3.	Equational sentences
8.4.	Demonstrative sentences
8.5.	Interrogative sentences
9.	Clause
9.1.	Types of clause
9.1.1.	Declarative clauses
9.1.1.1.	Declarative transitive clauses
9.1.1.2.	Declarative intransitive clauses
9.1.1.3.	Declarative impersonal clauses
9.1.2.	Imperative clauses
9.1.3.	Equational clauses
9.1.4.	Demonstrative clauses
9.1.5.	Interrogative clauses
9.2.	Dependent clauses
9.2.1.	*nka*-clause
9.2.2.	Time clause
9.2.3.	Result clause
9.2.4.	*but*-clause
9.2.5.	Purpose clause
9.2.6.	Limiting clause
9.2.7.	Manner clause
9.2.8.	*if*-clause
9.2.9.	*although*-clause
9.2.10.	Secondarily dependent clauses
10.	Grammatical phrase
10.1.	Predicate phrase
10.1.1.	Transitive verb phrases
10.1.2.	Intransitive verb phrases
10.1.3.	Impersonal verb phrases
10.1.4.	Adjectival phrases
10.1.5.	Appearance verb phrases
10.1.6.	Numerative verb phrases
10.1.7.	Copulative verb phrases
10.1.8.	Demonstrative verb phrases
10.2.	Types of subject and/or object fillers
10.2.1.	Noun phrases
10.2.2.	Pronoun phrases
10.2.3.	Possessive pronoun phrases
10.2.4.	Demonstrative clauses
10.2.5.	Demonstrative noun phrases
10.2.6.	$\check{s}i^3$ plus declarative phrase
10.2.7.	$\check{s}i^3$ plus possessive pronoun or possessed noun
10.2.8.	Relative phrases
10.3.	Instrumental fillers
10.4.	Independent recipient fillers
10.5.	Specifier phrases
10.6.	Manner fillers
10.7.	Types of location slot fillers
10.8.	Interrogative slot fillers
10.9.	Time slot fillers
11.	Grammatical word

311

11.1.   Independent grammatical words
11.1.1. Verbs
11.1.2. Nouns
11.1.3. Pronouns
11.1.4. Possessive pronouns
11.1.5. Adjectives
11.1.6. Time words
11.1.7. Manner words
11.1.8. Specifier words
11.1.9. Clause fillers for grammatical phrases
11.2.   Dependent grammatical words
11.2.1. Optional slot fillers
11.2.2. Obligatory slot fillers

0. INTRODUCTION. This article is an attempt to describe some of the units of Mazatec[1] speech. Those included of the phonological hierarchy[2] are: (1) the vowel phoneme with its types, *i, e, o, a,* etc.; (2) the consonant phoneme with it types, *t, k, m,* etc.; (3) the syllable with its types contrasting by tone; (4) the phonological word with its types contrasting by the placement of an obligatory syllable; (5) the phonological phrase with its types contrasting by a combination of fade or lack of fade in intensity or pitch on a lengthened syllable; (6) the phonological sentence with its types contrasting by breathiness, or downdrift of pitch on a ballistic syllable, or by a ballistic syllable followed by length.

The units in the grammatical hierarchy[3] described here are: (1) the grammatical sentence which occurs in the body of a monologue with its types contrasting by the kind and number of clauses of which it is composed; (2) the independent clause with its types contrasting by the kind of grammatical phrases of which it is composed and by the verb; (3) the dependent clause with its types contrasting by the introducer; (4) grammatical phrases contrasting (a) by their function in the clause, (b) by the words in the obligatory slot and (c) by the parts which modify those words; (5) words separated into various parts of speech according to their distribution in the various phrases.

1. PHONEME. The vowel phonemes are *i, i̧, e, ȩ, a, a̧, o, o̧.* Following a sequence of consonant plus glottal stop, a vowel is laryngealized. Allophones of *o* and *o̧* vary from high back rounded to low rounded. The length of the individual vowel varies in accordance with its place in the syllable, word, or phrase.

The consonant phonemes are: stops *p, t, k* (voiced after *m* or *n* unless followed by *h*); affricates *c, č, c̣* (retroflexed *č*); glottal stop *ʔ*; sibilants *s* and *š* (retroflexed especially before vowels); the phoneme *h* (voiceless nasal before nasals, a light fricative—bilabial after *v*, alveopalatal before *y*, and velar elsewhere); voiced nasals *m, n* (velar before *k*), *ñ*; voiced fricative *v* (voiceless before *h*); the glide *y*; the lateral *l*; the flap *r* (rare); and occasionally from Spanish loan words, *b, d, g, rr.*

2. SYLLABLE. The nucleus of the syllable always follows the margin. It may contain one, two, or three vowels. The clusters are composed either of all oral vowels, or of all nasal vowels. The clusters of two are: *ao, ai, ia, io, ie* (rare), *oi, oe, oa.* The clusters of three are: *iai, iao, oia, oai, oao, ioa,* and *ioi.* Nasalized vowels cluster in the same way.

The length of a syllable with one vowel is approximately the same as a syllable with three vowels. The vowels in a syllable with three are extremely short. For conditions under which the length of the syllable varies, see §3.

The margin of the syllable may contain one, two or three consonants. Except for *st, sk, št,* and *šk,* all clusters must contain *h, n,* or *ʔ*. They are as follows: *ht, hk, hc, hč, hc̣, hm, hn, hñ, hv, hy; th, kh, ch, čh, c̣h; mh, nh, vh, sh, šh; tʔ, kʔ, cʔ, čʔ, c̣ʔ; mʔ, nʔ, ñʔ, yʔ, vʔ, lʔ, sʔ, šʔ; ʔm, ʔn, ʔñ, ʔv, ʔy; mp, nt, nk, nc, nč, nc̣.*

[1] There are about 90,000 speakers of "Mazatec," most of them living in the northern part of the state of Oaxaca, Mexico. There are numerous dialects, differing from one another in varying degrees. This is a study of the Huautla de Jiménez dialect, which has an estimated 30,000 speakers. For information on other dialects, see Gudschinsky, 1955, 1958a, 1959c; E. V. Pike, 1954, 1956; Villa Rojas, 1955.

[2] This study is an outgrowth of the theory presented in K. L. Pike, 1954, 1955, and 1960.

[3] Discussions with Velma Pickett about the grammatical hierarchy in relation to Mazatec grammar proved to be very helpful.

312

Clusters of three are as follows: *hnt, hnk, hnč, hnč̣; ʔnt, ʔnk, ʔnc, ʔnč, ʔnč̣; ntʔ, nkʔ, ncʔ, nčʔ, nč̣ʔ; nth, nkh, nch, nčh, nč̣h; hcʔ, hčʔ; skʔ, štʔ, škʔ*.

The nucleus of the syllable may contain a single tone, or a cluster of two or three tones. There are four contrasting heights, and these may combine into the following clusters. Considering tone [1] to be high, and tone [4] to be low, they are: [13], [14], [23], [24], [34], [43], [42], [32], [21], [424], and [423].

There is no relationship between the number of tones and the number of vowels in a syllable. There may be a cluster of two tones on a syllable with one vowel (*ti[42]* 'a jar'), or just one tone on a syllable with two or three vowels (*koai[4]* 'he will go').

For a more complete description of the phonemes, and for a discussion of the immediate constituents of a syllable, see Pike and Pike, 1947. The glide [21] was not listed in that article. Usually the phonetic pitch seems to be a level half way between tone [2] and tone [1], but it has been interpreted as a [21] cluster. Examples of it contrasting with tone [1] and tone [2] are: *si[1]če[21]* 'he steals', *si[1]te[2]* 'he spins', *si[1]he[1]* 'he asks'. Morphemes with the cluster [21] have allomorphs with tone [1] which occur when preceding tone [1]. In some other environments it varies to tone [2].

3. PHONOLOGICAL WORD. Each phonological word has one and only one obligatory syllable. That syllable is the phonological word center, and the placement of it is contrastive. In §3–6 I have indicated that syllable by bold face. Examples: *ša[4ʔ]nta[4]**na[4]** 'mother hen,' *ša[42]**nta[4]na[4]** 'my hen' *ya[1]ši[2]le[4]* 'chair', *ya [1]**ši** [2]le[4]* 'his dry stick'.

This obligatory syllable has a number of allos: (1) relatively loud; (2) relatively long; (3) combination of both; (4) loud fading quickly to soft sometimes even to voicelessness; (5) long and lenis; (6) long with downdrift of pitch. The choice of allo is dependent upon the place of the word within a phonological phrase or phonological sentence (see §4, 5).

Phonological words contain the obligatory syllable, with or without other nonobligatory syllables. Examples: *ki[3]* 'he went', *ca [3]ka[2]te[4]**hna[3]** 'I stayed', *čho[4]ta[4]mi[2]y o[4]le[4]* 'his friend.'

Within a stream of speech, change of speed (fast on words of many syllables, slow on words of one syllable) makes the length of time taken for the pronunciation of the various words more nearly the same. Thus when the words *ni[3]nta[3]* 'bone' and *khoa[4]vi[3]-hna[3]čọ[3]* 'life' are in analogous places in the phonological sentence, the pronunciation of the word 'life' is speeded up to the extent that the obliagory syllable in the word for 'life' is definitely shorter than the nonobligatory syllable in the word 'bone'.

Syllables which precede the obligatory syllable are often faster and more fortis than syllables following the obligatory syllable. Therefore a border between words occurs at any such point of increasing speed and intensity. This has been indicated by word space. Example: *ma[3]čo[4]**ya[3]**na[3]hị[4] **nt[ʔ]ai[4]**vi[4]*. 'It is understood by us now'.

This observation was made from a tape on which a man with deliberate speech was talking. On a tape in which a fourteen-year-old girl was speaking rapidly, I could not identify such a point. In these instances the presence of two phonological words is made certain by the presence of two phonological word centers with an indeterminate border between them—just as a sequence of phonemes may be identified by their centers even though there are slurred indeterminate borders between. The optional audible border phenomenon is an optional contrastive feature of the larger phonological unit—the phonological word.

4. PHONOLOGICAL PHRASE. Each phonological phrase ends with a phonological word whose obligatory syllable is lengthened, unless it coincides with the ballistic syllable of the phonological sentence (see §5). Such a syllable is indicated, in section 4–6, by ° immediately preceding it.

A phonological phrase may contain one or more phonological words. It may optionally

313

be followed by the contrastive feature pause. Example: *vha³²ai³ nti⁴⁰cị⁴*, 'They arrive at the market'.

The lengthened syllable which is obligatory to the phonological phrase occurs near the end of it. Optionally there may also be an even longer and louder nonfading syllable near the beginning. It emphasizes the word in which it occurs. I have indicated such a syllable by an exclamation point immediately following it.

Within a phonological phrase, all syllables following the one with obligatory length are lenis. Therefore an increase in speed and intensity indicates a different phonological phrase.

Thus far I have noted four types of phonological phrases.

(1) In the nonfinal phonological phrase, the most common type, the lengthened syllable fades in intensity while staying more or less the same pitch. This type of phonological phrase has been indicated by a comma. Example: *nkhị²! khoa⁴šị³ ki³⁰s²ị̄a³, koa²⁰ce³.* 'There were many things that I did long ago'.

The nonfinal phonological phrase is often used in utterance-response situations. Example: *ho¹ thị¹ ᵒčhi¹le⁴*, 'How much does it cost'?

(2) In the series phonological phrase, the lengthened syllables fades less in intensity, but glides down in pitch—unless the lengthened syllable already has tone ⁴. This series type of phonological phrase most frequently occurs when it is one of a sequence of coordinate grammatical units. It has been indicated by a hyphen preceding a comma.

Example: *k²oa⁴⁰ti⁴ ki³kha³⁰²a³, ²a:³ na⁴⁰-hme¹-, k²oa⁴ti⁴ ki³kha³⁰²a³, nta⁴⁰hai³-, k²oa⁴-ti⁴ ki³ka³te³ ka³⁰vhe²-.* 'Also, I went to get (hesitation) corn, also I went to get, sugarcane, also I went to cut coffee'.

(3) In the hesitation phonological phrase, the obligatory syllable is loud, very long, with sustained intensity. It has been indicated by colon. Example: *ka²vhị²hto:³ ᵒya⁴ve⁴*. 'She went behind—over there'.

314

(4) In the deliberation phonological phrase, the obligatory syllable is soft, and medium length. Its most frequent occurrence is on introducers. In the text in which the mayor's speech was mimicked, 15 out of 20 subordinate clauses started with soft length on the introducer. It has been indicated by a raised dot after the vowel. Example: *he² nčo² ᵒkhoạ³na⁴, šị³k²oa⁴s²ị̄² ki³⁰kao⁴na³, nka·³ he² šị³k²oa⁴ki³⁰co²na³*, 'It was my aunt, who thus went with me, because (hesitation) she thus told me. . . .'

5. PHONOLOGICAL SENTENCE. Each phonological sentence must have a ballistic syllable. A ballistic syllable starts loud—but not as loud as a syllable signaling emphasis—and has a quick fade to soft, sometimes even to voicelessness. It fades so abruptly that in a two syllable word, the length of the ballistic obligatory syllable may be as short or shorter than the nonobligatory syllable of that word. If the ballistic syllable is not the last one in the phonological sentence, the fade on that syllable may be less, since it is continued over on to the following syllable.

I have noted four types of phonological sentences.

(1) The terminal phonological sentence has a ballistic syllable with the characteristics described above. It is the one used most frequently and signals finality. It is also used when trying to get someone's attention. It has been indicated by a period. Example: *ma³⁰ria²· n²ion¹! ma³⁰čhẹ²¹, nka³ ni²⁰ša¹.* 'Mary, it is very needful that we work'.

(2) The series phonological sentence has a sharp downglide on the ballistic syllable. It differs from that of a series phonological phrase in that the downglide is faster. It has been indicated by a hyphen preceding a period.

(3) The breathy phonological sentence ends with a ballistic syllable but has breathiness added to the final vowel. It signals a request for immediate attention. This is frequently used when trying to get someone's attention without shouting. I have indicated

it with an *h* preceding period. Example: *ma³ºriah²*. 'Mary!'

(4) The intensified phonological sentence ends with a ballistic syllable which fades, but then picks up intensity again. If the ballistic syllable of the intensified phonological sentence is other than last, the last syllable is long and intense. It signals irritation and has been indicated by a raised dot preceding a period. Example: *tʔai² ºnai¹³ ntʔai·⁴*. 'Give it to me now!'

A short text follows in which the various phonological units have been indicated. *ºhe³², nʔiǫ¹! kǫa³ nkhį² ºno¹-, kʔia⁴ nka·³ ya⁴ te⁴ºhao⁴, ca³ka²te⁴ºhna³· kʔia⁴nka³ to⁴ho³· te·³ no¹ ºthį¹na³· nka³nchai² ni⁴ºchį³, ki³kha³ºa³ či³ºkį¹· ya⁴ nki³čao³ši³ ºthį¹na³hį⁴*. 'Very many years ago, when (hesitation) there Huautla, I stayed. When only (hesitation) ten (hesitation) years were had by me. Every day, I went to get firewood. There in the ranch which was had by us'.

6. RELATIONSHIP BETWEEN PHONOLOGY AND GRAMMAR. A grammatical word and a phonological word usually but do not always coincide (see §10 and 11 for skewing).

A grammatical phrase may coincide with a grammatical word if the grammatical word is the complete filler of a slot in a grammatical clause. (For special definition of phrase, see §10.) The number of grammatical phrases included within one phonological phrase is variable. In slow precise speech, if the sentence has only independent grammatical words, there may be a one for one correspondence. Example: *ºkʔia⁴, vhi²ºkao⁴, ºkʔęˀle⁴, ºnčˀoa¹*. 'Then they go with their dead to the cemetery.' If the same sentence is repeated at a faster speed, the phonological phrase becomes more inclusive, extending over several grammatical phrases. The reverse is not true. Even in slow speech, phonological phrases do not normally end in the middle of a grammatical phrase. (For discussion of when they do, see §6.2.)

An independent clause is a filler of the obligatory slot of a grammatical sentence. A dependent clause is a filler of one of the optional slots of a grammatical sentence. There is nothing in the phonological hierarchy that corresponds with the grammatical clause. The grammatical clause may consist of one or of several phonological phrases.

A phonological sentence is a phrase or sequence of phrases, the last of which has a ballistic syllable. A grammatical sentence is a filler of a slot in a narrative monologue. In one ten-page sample of narrative text, the end of each grammatical sentence coincided with the end of a phonological sentence. However, the end of a phonological sentence did not always coincide with the end of a grammatical sentence. Many of the grammatical sentences were long, with several dependent clauses in each, and occasionally a phonological sentence ended between dependent clauses. Also, three times in that text the phonological sentence ended in the middle of a grammatical clause. Each of the three times, however it gave the impression that the part which followed the phonological sentence was added as an "afterthought." Example: *to⁴hnko³ ºtho², ha³ʔ-ai³ºkao⁴ni³· hnko³ na⁴ºšį¹*. 'They came with (it) quickly. A horse'.

6.1. MINIMAL PAIRS occur not only between words composed of different phonemes, but also between units on higher levels.

When a sequence of two phonological words is replaced by an otherwise homophonous sequence of three phonological words, the meaning of the total may be changed. A third phonological contour has been added to the linear phonemic sequence, forming a minimal pair on the higher level of the phonological hierarchy. (Grammatical changes accompany the phonological change but are not as such under attention here.) Examples: *ki³ski³ʔnta¹hao² ša⁴ºnta⁴*. 'The rooster crowed the second time'. *ki³ski³ʔnta¹ hao² ša⁴ºnta⁴*. 'Two roosters crowed'. *ca³ka³ce³ yao³ºnti¹*. 'He bought tenderloin'. *ca³ka³ce³ yao³ ºnti¹*. 'The baby bought meat'.

Similarly, when a phonological phrase is

replaced by an otherwise homophonous sequence of two phonological phrases, the added phonological high-level contour may (in conjunction with changes in grammatical structure) change the meaning of the whole. Examples: *vi³tho³hę³ ni³ʔya³le⁴ ᵒti³*. 'They came down from the boy's house'. *vi³tho³hę³ ni³ᵒʔya³le⁴, ᵒti³*. 'The boy came down from somebody's house'. *vhi²kǫ³le⁴ nka³cʔi³ mi²ᵒyo⁴le⁴*. 'They went to see all their friends'. *vhi²kǫ³le⁴ nka³ᵒcʔi³, mi²ᵒyo⁴le⁴*. 'Their friends went to see them all'.

In fast speech each sentence might be composed of just one phonological phrase, in which case the pairs of utterances would be homophonous and ambiguous. Such variations within the phonological hierarchy emphasize the partial independence of the phonological hierarchy from the grammatical one.

When a phonological sentence is added to a phonological sentence, or to a sequence of sentences (even though the phonological phrases remain the same), the meaning of the total may be changed. Example: *khai¹nka³ ᵒsi³na³, koi⁴so¹ᵒthę⁴*. 'It's a nuisance to me to get up. (I don't like to get up.)' *khai¹nka³ ᵒsi³na³· koi⁴so¹ᵒthę⁴*. 'It's a nuisance to me. I'll get up.' (Meaning that he'd rather get up than endure.)

6.2. PHONOLOGICAL PHRASES WHICH END IN THE MIDDLE OF A GRAMMATICAL SENTENCE. In the introduction to §6 it was stated that even in slow speech, phonological phrases do not, in most instances, end in the middle of a grammatical phrase. There are two specific circumstances when they do.

When a sequence of co-ordinate words is the filler of one subject or object slot, it is, by definition, just one grammatical phrase. It is, however, a sequence of phonological phrases. Example: *ca³ki³ᵒntai¹⁴hi⁴ bo¹ᵒrro¹-, na⁴ᵒši¹-, čo⁴ta²ᵒha³*. 'We bought donkeys, horses, mules'.

When the filler of a subject or of an object slot is composed of a noun with two co-ordinate modifying parts, the entire thing is, by definition, one grammatical phrase. It is, however, two phonological phrases. Example: *he² ši³ki³choa³le⁴ na⁴ši¹, ši³sʔa⁴ha³ᵒʔai³, thi¹le⁴ ᵒtǫo⁴*. 'He who gave him the horse, and who just came, has money'. In that example, the modifying parts were co-ordinate. If, however, the two modifying parts are included within one phonological phrase, then the second is subordinate to the first. The meaning would be, 'He who gave him the horse that just came, has money'.

The meaning would be the same if, instead of just one phonological phrase, the speaker had paused after the second connector *ši³*. To have done so would have broken up the modifying unit, but by pausing there he would have signaled that the expression was subordinate to the preceding predicate rather than co-ordinate with it. In such instances there is a skewing of the borders of the phonological and grammatical units.

There is a similar situation in relation to clauses. Each dependent clause has an introducer which distinguishes it from other dependent clauses and from an independent clause. A clause which is a modifying part within a phrase may have a similar introducer. If a sentence is to be unambiguous, if it is specific that the clause is subordinate to another clause and not co-ordinate with it, there must be no pause preceding the introducer; that is, the introducer must be included in the same phonological phrase as the clause to which it is subordinate. Example: (indep. clause) *kʔoa⁴co² čho⁴ta⁴ᵒša¹*, (*nka*-clause) *nka³kʔoa⁴sʔi̧²² va³te¹šo³ᵒma³na³nka³*, (subordinate *nka*-clause) *si⁴tho³šǫ̧² nka³yi³hę³ ᵒkhoa⁴*. 'That's what the officials say, because they thus order us to obey all things'.

7. MONOLOGUE. There are several contrastive types of monologue in Mazatec speech. Among them are: official speech, Christian prayer, prayer to native deities, narrative.

7.1. OFFICIAL SPEECH is formal and has long complicated sentences. They may have one independent clause and then many dependent clauses in sequence. Such sequences of dependent clauses are used when the occasion calls for elegance. Salesmen may use them.

Example:[4] (indep.)[5] $t^?e^2ški^4$-nai^{13} $taǫ^4$. (indep.) $k^?oe^3nta^3$-le^{23} $šǫ^4$-le^4, (purpose) hme^1-ni^3 nka^3 $hča^4$-si^1ni^3 (nka-clause subordinate to purpose) nka^3 $ña^3ki^3$ $c^?ą^4$ bo^1rro^1-ve^4, (limiting subordinate to nka-clause) sa^3?nta^3 $a^3li^2koi^3$ $koa^3te^3na^{13}$ ca^3kai^3-ni^3, (nka-clause subordinate to limiting) to^4nka^3 $taǫ^4$ $khai^7nka^3$ $n^?iǫ^1$ $ma^3čhę^1$-na^3, (result subordinate to limiting) koi^{32} nka^3 $ti^1va^3te^1na^3$-si^1nia^3 bo^1rro^1-na^4. 'Count out the money for me. I'll make you a bill of sale, so that you can know that the donkey is really mine—so much so I wouldn't even be selling it, but I very much need money, that's why I'm selling my donkey'.

This type of monologue is especially noticeable when the mayor is giving the people the news, telling them about the work of the town.[6] I recorded a text of someone mimicking the mayor. It consisted of a greeting: ?nta^{34}-no^3 $čho^4ta^4na^4ši^4na^3nta^1$. 'Hello to you citizens'. Then there was an independent clause followed by seven dependent clauses each subordinate to the preceding one; then another independent clause and fourteen more dependent clauses; then the closure, $nkhi̧^2$ $k^?a^3$ $ni^3na^1ši^3ka^2t^?e^2čhi^{14}$-$no^3$. 'Many times thank you'.

7.2. CHRISTIAN PRAYER is characterized by equational and imperative sentence types. A section of one prayer: hi^3 ni^{13} $ši^3$ $ti^3ni^2thao^2$-$ča^3$-$nai^1hi̧^4$. hi^3 ni^{13} $ši^3$ $ti^3v^?ai^2$-$nai^1hi̧^4$ $ši^3$?yo^3, $ši^3$ $či^3ne^3$. hi^3 ni^{13} $ši^3$ $khi^3ma^3ma^4ča^3$-$nai^1hi̧^4$.

---

[4] In the examples written in §7–11, the obligatory syllable of the phonological word is followed by a hyphen unless it is the last syllable in the word, in which case it is followed by space. Arbitrarily introducers have been followed by word space. Phonological phrase is indicated by comma, and a phonological sentence by period.

[5] In the parentheses preceding each clause, its function has been indicated.

[6] For a discussion of the content of such speeches, see F. H. Cowan, 1952.

'You are the one who loves us. You are the one who gives us what we drink, what we eat. You are the one who takes pity on us'.

7.3. PAGAN PRAYER. Some prayers to native deities are characterized by vocatives. Each hilltop has a god and he is called upon for help.

Example: $k^?oa^4$ $hǫ^{23}$-vi^4, $či^3kǫ^3$ $to^3ko^2šo^4$, $či^3kǫ^3$ $ni^3nto^3nto^3va^3$, $či^3kǫ^3$ $na^4ši^4nka^3nai^{23}$, $či^3kǫ^3$ $nta^1čo^4$, si^4he^{14}-no^3 nka^3 $k^?oa^4$-$s^?i̧^2$ $ti^4sę^4$-kao^4-nao^{13}. 'And you plural there, Holy Tokoso, Holy Nintontova, Holy Nasinkanai, Holy Ntacho, I ask of you plural that you thus help me?' (I know of no way of translating the names of the various hilltops.)

7.4. NARRATIVE MONOLOGUE frequently begins with a topic sentence which is a dependent clause but which has the characteristics of a phonological sentence. Example: $k^?ia^4$ nka^3 $m^?ę^3$ $hnko^3$ $čho^4ta^4$?i^4 $na^4ši^4na^3nta^1$-vi^4. 'When a person dies here in this city'. The monologue usually ends with a summary sentence that begins with $k^?oa^4$-$s^?i̧^2$ 'thus'. The body of the narrative monologue is made up of a series of independent sentences.

7.5. NON-MONOLOGUE SPEECH, especially in question-response situations, has many sentence fragments which do not contain an independent clause. Such sentences are not treated in this paper. For the most part the grammatical constructions described here are restricted to those which appear in the body of a narrative monologue.

8. GRAMMATICAL SENTENCE. There are five different classes of sentence types which constitute the body of a narrative monologue. They are: declarative, imperative, equational, demonstrative, interrogative.

Any of the sentence types may begin with $k^?oa^4$ the co-ordinator. Example: $k^?ia^4$ va^1ya^3 $ka^2ša^4$. $k^?oa^4$ $k^?ia^4$ $si^1k^?ę^3$ $nkhi̧^2$ $ša^4$?nta^4. 'Then they put (him) in a box. And then they kill many chickens'.

Each sentence has an obligatory part which is an independent clause. Optionally a sentence may contain two independent clauses. If both independent clauses are contained within one phonological sentence, then they are one grammatical sentence. Example: *li²koi³ me³-na³, ʔą³ coa³*. 'It is not wanted by me, I pick up'. ('I don't want to pick it up').

In addition to the obligatory part, there are optional parts—various dependent clauses. These dependent clauses are: time, if-clause, purpose, manner, result, limiting, but-clause, although-clause, and *nka*-clause.

8.1. DECLARATIVE SENTENCES may be considerably longer than other types, first because of more parts in their grammatical phrases, and second, because they have more dependent clauses.

When there are several clauses in a sentence, the most frequent order is: time, if-clause, independent clause, *nka*-clause. The sequence of the other clauses has not been determined. If the independent clause is negative, it may, but does not necessarily, precede the time or if-clause.

Example of a declarative sentence with an independent transitive clause: (time) *kʔia⁴ nka³ ci² ma³-le⁴ šǫ⁴*, (indep.) *to⁴ho³ khaʔai¹ čho⁴ta⁴ vhi²kʔeˡšaˡ-le⁴ ši³ vʔeˡnta³-le⁴ šǫ⁴ ši³ si⁴²ka³sęˡ-nkaˡniˡle⁴ ʔntiˡ-le⁴*, (result) *koi³² nka³ ma³čhę¹-siˡni³ ntʔai⁴-vi⁴* (*nka*-clause subordinate to result) *nka³ nka³cʔi³ šti³ kao⁴ čho⁴ta⁴-hčiˡnka³ ka²ta³koˑtʔ a³ya³ šǫ⁴*, (purpose subordinate to *nka*-clause) *hmeˡ-ni³ nka³ kǫq³čo⁴ya³-siˡniˑle⁴ nka³cʔi³ na⁴šiˡna³nta¹*. 'When paper is not known by him, he takes it to a different person who[7] will make a paper that[7] he will send to his son, that's why it is now necessary that all children and old people study paper, in order that all the towns can understand'.

(if-clause) *ca² ma³čo⁴ya³-le⁴*, (indep.) *skoeˡla⁴ ska⁴ni² nka³cʔi³ šti³-le⁴*, (purpose) *hmeˡ-ni³ nka³ skoe⁴-siˡni³ ha⁴šti³-le⁴ hme³ khoa⁴-ma³ ši³ sʔį⁴² kʔia⁴ nka³ kǫq⁴hčiˡnka³*. 'If they understood, they would send all their children to school, in order that all their children

[7] These have not been marked as sentence parts since they are part of the recipient phrase; the first is modifying "person" in that phrase and the second "paper."

might know what[8] business they would do when[8] they become old'.

Example of a declarative sentence with an independent impersonal clause: (if-clause) *ca² hnko³ čho⁴ta⁴ ši³ čʔį³ tiˡmʔę³-ni³*, (indep.) *ma³²(nka*-clause) *nka³ vʔai²⁴-le² koi²nta⁴ čho⁴-ta⁴šaˡ*, (purpose) *hmeˡ-ni³ nka³ vhi²kho³mi³thę⁴-siˡni³*. 'If a person who has sickness is dying, it is acceptable that we give the officials an account (tell them), in order that they go pick (him) up'.

Declarative sentences which have independent intransitive clauses in my data have only two types of dependent clause, namely the time and *nka*-clause. Example: (time) *kʔia⁴ nka³ he³kǫq³ ntʔai⁴*, (indep.) *ki³ ʔnta³ sia²*. 'When it was over, they went as far as the outskirts'.

(indep.) *kʔia⁴ he² čho⁴ta⁴-ve⁴ khai¹ nka³ siˡkhao³hį³*, (*nka*-clause) *nka³ ci² ca² ki³ skoe²-la⁴*. 'Then this person grieves because he did not go to school'.

8.2. IMPERATIVE SENTENCES may have any of the various dependent clauses in addition to the independent clause; there is, however, seldom more than one in a sentence.

Examples: (if-clause) *ca² ma³sǫ²-ni³li² tąǫ⁴*, (indep.) *čʔai⁴-ni¹³*, (if-clause) *ca² ci² ma³sǫ²-ni³li² tąǫ⁴*, (indep.) *ka²ta³vʔe²*. 'If money is left over, buy; if money is not left over, let it go'.

(indep.) *nki²hnko³ šǫ⁴ ka²ta³si³ca³sęˡ-na³ te³re²sa⁴*, (if-clause) *ca² nka³ ma³chę¹-le⁴ nka³ skoˡya³-nai¹³*. 'Another letter let Teresa send me, if she needs to wait for me'.

8.3. EQUATIONAL SENTENCES which have dependent clauses are rare. There are, however, a few examples in my data.

Numerative equational sentence: (indep.) *to⁴hnko³ ma³-ni³* (*nka*-clause) *nka³² he³kʔ ę³ ši³ kʔa³*. 'There is just one because the rest are dead'.

Adjectival equational sentence: (indep.) *khai¹ nka³ škǫ¹* (*nka*-clause) *nka³ sʔe³nta³*. 'It

[8] These have not been marked as sentence parts since together they make up a relative phrase (see §10.2.8) filling the object slot of the purpose clause.

318

is very dangerous to make'. (indep.) ci^{42} $khoa^4$, (if-clause) $ca^2\ ca^3h\underline{i}^3\text{-}li^2$. 'It's your affair (trouble), if you forget'.

In my data the appearance equational sentence and the copulative equational sentence consist of the independent clause only. The description of them will come in §9.1.3 and 10.1.5–7.

8.4. DEMONSTRATIVE SENTENCES may have a dependent clause. Example: (indep.) $he^2\ \check{s}i^3\ k\underline{o}\underline{a}^3nka^3\text{-}le^4$, (nka³-clause) $nka^3\ koi^{32}$ $^{?}vi^3\ nka^3nchai^{23}$. 'That's what he's accustomed to, because that's what he always drinks'.

8.5. INTERROGATIVE SENTENCES which have dependent clauses are rare. I have examples with a time clause, an if-clause, and an nka-clause. In all examples, the independent clause is initial.

Example: (indep.) $hme^1\ \check{s}a^1\ \check{s}i^3\ s^{?}\underline{i}a^3$ (time) $k^{?}ia^4\ nka^3\ ca^2\ khoia^{13}$. 'What work would I do, when-if I go?' (indep.) $^{?}a^3\ nta^3\ th\underline{i}^{14?}ni^3$ (nka-clause) $nka^3\ k^{?}\underline{e}^3\ ki^3ni^2k^{?}\underline{q}\underline{i}^3$. 'Is it good that you killed a dead one (murdered)?'

9. CLAUSE. All clauses which fill the obligatory slot of a sentence are independent. All which fill one of the optional slots of a sentence are dependent.

9.1. TYPES OF CLAUSE. There are six types of independent clauses, and the predicate is obligatory to all. Included within the predicate is a fused subject and sometimes a fused recipient. One clause type differs from another by the lists of verbs used in the predicate, and by the relationship of the predicate to the other grammatical phrases, which are optional, obligatorily absent, or also obligatory.

The grammatical phrases other than the predicate are: independent subject, object, instrumental, independent recipient, location, time, quantifier, manner, specifier, interrogative.

Although there are eleven of these which may be used in a clause, I have never found all of them in the same clause. One bit of narrative monologue contained 145 inde-

pendent clauses. Of those, 11 had the predicate phrase only, 75 had the predicate and one other phrase, 41 had the predicate and 2 other phrases, 17 had the predicate and 3 other phrases. Only one of the clauses had 5 phrases.

There is considerable flexibility in the order of the phrases. One of the predominant factors influencing this order is that the position for emphasis is clause initial. The sequence changes as the emphasized phrase is put first. Example:[9] (pred.) $th\underline{i}^1\text{-}le^4$ (obj.) $\check{c}^{?}\underline{i}^3$. 'Is had by him sickness'. (obj.) $\check{c}^{?}\underline{i}^3\check{s}k^{?}\underline{e}^1$ (pred.) $th\underline{i}^1\text{-}le^4$. 'Old age is had by him'.

Another factor which influences the order is $-\check{s}o^1$ 'it is indicated (by words or actions)'. Any part which contains this particle is put clause initial. Examples: (subj.) $co^2ti^3\text{-}\check{s}o^1$ (pred.) $ca^3ka^3ce^3$ (obj.) $nio^4\check{s}ti^2la^4$. 'The girl, they say, bought bread'. (obj.) $nio^4\check{s}ti^2la^4\text{-}\check{s}o^1$ (pred.) $ca^3ka^3ce^3$ (subj.) co^2ti^3. 'Bread, they say, the girl bought'. (pred.) $ca^3ka^3ce^3\text{-}\check{s}o^1$ (obj.) $nio^4\check{s}ti^2la^4$ (subj.) co^2ti^3. 'The girl bought, they say, bread'.

9.1.1. DECLARATIVE CLAUSES are the most common of the clause types. The types differ from one another by the verbs which are used and by the obligatory absence of an object in intransitive clauses, and the obligatory absence of a subject in impersonal clauses. The interrogative phrase is obligatorily absent from all three types.

9.1.1.1. DECLARATIVE TRANSITIVE CLAUSES must have a transitive verb. It may have any of the optional phrases but the interrogative one. Examples: (obj.) $na^3h\tilde{n}o^3$ (pred.) $ti^2va^3ne^3\text{-}le^4$ (recipient) $na^4\text{-}na^4$. 'I wash clothes for my mother'. (obj.) $hnko^3$ nka^4hao^4 (pred.) $ca^{3?}nki^3$ (subj.) $\check{c}ho^4ta^4$. 'The people dug a hole'. (pred.) $li^2koi^3\ nta^3\ si^1koi^2\text{-}nta^4$. 'He doesn't take care of (it) well'.

9.1.1.2. DECLARATIVE INTRANSITIVE CLAUSES must have an intransitive verb. The object is obligatorily absent. Examples: (instr.) nco^4ko^4 (pred.) $ka^2vha^{3?}ai^3\text{-}ni^3$ (loc.)

---

[9] In the examples in this section, the function of each phrase has been indicated in parentheses.

te^4hao^4. 'On foot he arrived in Huautla'. (time) k^2ia^4 (pred.) ki^3 (loc.) $nti^4c\underset{.}{i}^4$ (subj.) na^4-le^4. 'Then his mother went to market'. (pred.) $n\check{c}ha^1 vhi^{24}$-no^3 (recipient) $h\underset{.}{o}^2$ (subj.) $ntia^{42}$. 'The road goes hard for you'. ('Walking is hard for you'.)

9.1.1.3 DECLARATIVE IMPERSONAL CLAUSES must have an impersonal verb. It differs from the transitive and intransitive clauses in that the subject is obligatorily absent. (These clauses are most easily translated into English as a passive verb with subject, but in Mazatec the noun phrase patterns as an object. For example, it may have a relative phrase as filler of the object slot, see §10.2.8.) Another difference is the frequency of the recipient phrase. An intransitive clause only occasionally has a recipient phrase, whereas it is one of the most frequent parts of an impersonal clause. Examples: (pred. with dep. rec.) $s^2e^3h\underset{.}{i}^3$-le^4 (obj.) $nta^1na^{4?}yo^4$ (recipient) $nka^3c^2i^3$. 'Corn-drink is served to all'. (pred. with dep. rec.) me^3-na^3 (obj.) na^3nta^1 (specifier) $\check{s}i^3 t^2a^3c^2e^4 ti^3$-$na^4$. 'Water is wanted by me for my boy'. (pred. with dep. rec.) $li^2koi^3 \check{s}o^1$-na^3 (obj.) ka^3vhe^2. 'Coffee will not boil for me'.

9.1.2. IMPERATIVE CLAUSES differ from declarative clauses in the composition of the verb and in the low frequency of an independent subject. Imperative clause types differ from one another in the same way that declarative clause types differ.

Examples of imperative transitive clause: (pred.) ti^4ntai^{13} (time) nt^2ai^4-vi^4. 'Buy now'. (pred. with dep. rec.) ti^4he^1-lai^4 (obj.) $khoa^4$-nta^3 (rec.) ni^3na^1. 'Ask for grace from God'. (subj.) $a^3li^2 hi^3 h\underset{.}{i}^{23}$ (pred.) no^2khoai^4. 'Don't you talk'. (pred. with dep. rec.) $t^2e^2\check{s}ki^4$-nai^{13} (obj.) $ta\underset{.}{o}^4$ (specifier) $\check{s}i^3 t^2a^3c^2e^4 ^2nti^1$-$na^4$. 'Count out money for me for my son'.

Examples of imperative intransitive clause: (pred.) $th\underset{.}{i}\underset{.}{a}^1$ (loc.) $c^2e^4 \check{s}ka^2le^4$. 'Let's go to the judge's'. (loc.) $a^3li^2 ti^{4?}i^4 h\underset{.}{i}^2$ (pred.) $n\check{c}oa^1$-ni^3. 'Don't come here again'.

Examples of imperative impersonal clause: (pred.) $ka^2ta^3ma^3\check{c}o^4ya^3$-$le^4$ (obj.) ni^4ma^4-le^4

(spec.) $\check{s}i^3 t^2a^3c^2e^4 n^2ai^3$-$na^1$. 'Let their hearts understand concerning our inclusive father'. (pred.) $ka^2ta^3ma^3nta^3ya^3$ (obj.) $^2nti^1$-na^4 (time) nt^2ai^4-vi^4. 'Let my son get better now'. (pred.) $ka^2ta^3n\check{c}a^3$ (loc.) ya^4-ve^4. 'Let them stay there'.

9.1.3. EQUATIONAL CLAUSES all have as an obligatory part the equational-predicate phrase, and in this respect they differ from the declarative, imperative and demonstrative clauses. They differ from one another according to the filler of that obligatory part. Any equational clause may have an independent subject and perhaps one other part, but seldom do they have more than that. (For a discussion of equational verbs see §11.1.1.)

The appearance equational clause may have a recipient, but that part is obligatorily absent from other equational clauses. Examples: (equa.-pred.) $nta^3 \check{c}\underset{.}{o}^3$-$le^4$ (subj.) te^4hao^4 (recipient) ma^3ria^2. 'Huautla appears good to Mary'. ('Mary likes Huautla'.)

Examples of the adjectival equational clause: (equa.-pred.) ce^3 (subj.) $ta\underset{.}{o}^4 \check{s}i^3 k\underset{.}{o}a^4$-$\check{c}h\underset{.}{e}^{21}$. 'Much is the money that's needed'. (equa.-pred.) $khai^1 kh\underset{.}{i}^3$. 'It is very far'.

Examples of the numerative equational clause: (equa.-pred.) $hao^2 ma^3$-ni^3 (subj.) $\check{c}ho^4ta^4$. 'There are two people'. (equa.-pred.) $li^2koi^3 nkh\underset{.}{i}^2 ma^3$-$ni^3$. 'There are not many'.

Examples of the copulative equational clause: (equa.-pred.) $\check{c}h\underset{.}{o}^{42} nia^{13}$. 'I'm a woman'. (equa.-pred.) $he^2 ni^1$ (subj.) $\check{s}i^3 \check{c}i^4$-$nka^4 ^2mi^2$. 'That's the one called "pig".'

9.1.4. DEMONSTRATIVE CLAUSES differ from the declarative, imperative, and equational in that they have two obligatory parts —the predicate phrase and another which is the part under attention. It is this demonstrative part which is first in the clause, and if it is a noun it must be accompanied by he^2 'this, that'. Subject, object, instrumental and other parts can be specified in this way.

The demonstrative clause also differs from the others in that $\check{s}i^3$ is an obligatory part of the predicate, but the *ši³* must follow the demonstrative item, and therefore in a clause with optional parts it may be noncontiguous to the verb.

Examples: (subj.) *he² čho⁴ta⁴* (pred.) *ši³ ki³*. 'That's the person who went'. (obj.) *he² šo⁴* (pred.) *ši³ ti¹v²e¹škia⁴* (subj.) *čho⁴ta⁴*. 'That's the paper the man is reading'. (subj.) *ʔa³li²* *ca² he² čho⁴ta⁴* (pred.) *ši³ khȩ²*. 'It's not that man who eats'.

9.1.5. INTERROGATIVE CLAUSES differ from the others in that they must have an interrogative phrase as well as a predicate phrase. The clause may have transitive, intransitive, impersonal, or equational verbs. When, however, *hme¹* 'what', *ʔya¹* 'who', or *hña¹-le⁴* 'which' is the interrogative used, the clause must be a demonstrative one.

The interrogative phrase occurs initial in the clause and the thing about which the question is asked immediately follows. Therefore the order of the various phrases varies in accordance with the question asked.

Examples: (inter.) *ʔya¹* (subj.) *čho̧⁴²* (pred.) *ši³ ti¹va³ne¹* (obj.) *na³hño³*. 'What woman is washing clothes?' (inter.) *hme¹* (obj.) *na³hño³* (pred.) *ši³ ti¹va³ne¹* (subj.) *čho̧⁴²*. 'What clothes is the woman washing?' (inter.) *hña¹-le⁴* (equa.-pred.) *ši³ c²q̧⁴*. 'Which is mine?' (inter.) *hme¹* (pred.) *ši³ s²i̧q⁴-ni³* (instr.) *ši³ thi̧¹-li²ve⁴*. 'What do you do with what you have'?

When *hña¹* 'where', *ho¹* 'how', *k²ia⁷* 'when', *ʔa¹-ni³* 'why' are filling the interrogative slot, the clause is other than demonstrative. Examples: (inter.) *k²ia⁷* (pred.) *khoa²²ai⁴-ni³*. 'When will you come back'? (inter.) *ho¹* (equa.-pred.) *kho̧q̧³* (loc.) *ya⁴ nta¹he⁴²*. 'How is it there in Río Santiago'?

When *ʔa¹-ni³* 'why' is used, it is, in general, in cross reference to *-si¹ni³* which is part of the verb. Examples: (inter.) *ʔa¹-ni³* (pred.) *k²oa⁴to⁴ko³cȩ³-si¹ni³na¹* (subj.) *čho̧⁴²*. 'Why the woman looking at us like that'?

The most common filler of the interrogative slot is *ʔa³* 'indicator of a yes-no question'. It differs from the other interrogatives

in that it is dependent—it does not occur alone, even in an utterance-response situation. When the *ʔa³* is preceding anything but the predicate phrase, it occurs in a demonstrative clause. When preceding the predicate, it may occur in anything but a demonstrative or imperative clause.

Examples: (inter.) *ʔa³* (subj.) *he² čho⁴ta⁴* (pred.) *ši³ ki³*. 'Is this the person who went'? (inter.) *ʔa³* (recipient) *ʔq̧³²* (pred.) *ši³ si⁴ki³-nčha⁴-nai¹³*. 'Am I the one you are making talk'? (inter.) *ʔa³* (equa.-pred.) *hao² ma³-ni³*. 'Are there two'? (inter.) *ʔa³* (equa.-pred.) *ci²* *ca² nta³*. 'Isn't it good'?

When a yes-no question is asked, the thing about which the information is desired is contiguous to the interrogative. Examples: (inter.) *ʔa³* (obj.) *he² šo̧⁴* (pred.) *ši³ ka²v²ai²-lai⁴*. 'Is this the paper you gave him'? (inter.) *ʔa³* (subj.) *hi³²* (pred.) *ši³ ka²v²ai²-lai⁴*. 'Are you the one who gave to him'? (inter.) *ʔa³* (pred.) *ka²v²ai²-lai⁴* (obj.) *šo̧⁴*. 'Did you give him paper'?

9.2. DEPENDENT CLAUSES are fillers of the optional slots of a sentence. They are: if-clause, but-clause, purpose, manner, result, time, limiting, although-clause, and *nka*-clause. Each has an introducer plus one of the clause types as described in §9.1. The declarative types are the most frequent, but a few demonstrative, equational, and third person imperative are also used. There are none in my data with second person imperative, and none are interrogative. When the demonstrative construction is a part of a dependent clause, the *he²* 'this, that' is not obligatory.

9.2.1. THE *nka*-CLAUSE follows the clause to which it is subordinate. The meaning of *nka³* is 'subordination'. Any other meaning is derived from the context. Examples: (indep. impersonal) *li²koi³ ko̧q³hti³-le⁴ či³ko̧³šo⁴nka¹-ve⁴* (nka-clause) *nka³ he³ki³c²ai²-le⁴ khoa⁴thao²*. 'The river gods did not get angry because/ when gifts were given to them'. (indep. transitive) *koi³ ha³²q̧i̧¹-ve⁴ si¹čhȩ²¹ na⁴⁹mi³*, (nka-clause) *nka³ va³te¹nta¹ he² ʔnti¹-ve⁴*. 'The priest uses that name because/when he baptizes that baby'.

There is another situation in which nka^3 may be used. If two like dependent clauses are co-ordinate and in sequence, nka^3 may substitute for the second introducer. (See §9.2.5 where nka^3 substitutes for the purpose introducer; see §9.2.6 where it substitutes for the limiting introducer; see §9.2.7 where it substitutes for the manner introducer.)

9.2.2. THE TIME CLAUSE has k^9ia^4 nka^3 'when' as introducer. Example: (time) k^9ia^4 nka^3 he^3ma^3 $he^2\text{-}vi^4$, (indep. intransitive) $nčoa^{21}\text{-}ni^3$ $nka^3c^9i^3$ $čho^4ta^4$. 'When this is over, all the people come'.

9.2.3. THE RESULT CLAUSE has koi^3 nka^3 'therefore' as introducer. Example: (indep. impersonal) $k^9oa^4\text{-}s^9i̧^2$ $me^3\text{-}le^4$ $čho^4ta^4ša^1$, (result) koi^3 nka^3 $thio^1v^9e^1\text{-}ni^3$ $skoe^2la^4$. 'Thus it is wanted by the officials, therefore they are opening schools'.

9.2.4. THE 'BUT'-CLAUSE has to^4nka^3 'but' as introducer. Example: (indep.) $ko̧ą^3$ $choa^3\text{-}le^{23}$, (but-clause) to^4nka^3 $k^9oe^1nta^3\text{-}nai^1$ $šo̧^4\text{-}le^4$. 'I can give it to you, but you will make a paper for me'.

9.2.5. THE PURPOSE CLAUSE has $hme^1\text{-}ni^3$ nka^3 'in order to' as introducer. It differs from the other dependent clauses in that -si^1ni^3 is added to the stem of the verb. Examples: (indep. transitive) $v^9e^1hca^3ne^2$ $ni^3\text{-}$ $^9nte^3ka^2ša^4\text{-}le^4$ $k^9ȩ^3\text{-}ve^4$, (purpose) $hme^1\text{-}ni^3$ nka^3 nta^3 $s^9e^3hna^3ñai^3\text{-}si^1ni^3$ $k^9ȩ^3\text{-}ve^4$. 'They throw dirt on the coffin in order that the dead be buried well'. (indep. impersonal) $ka^2ta^3sȩ^1\text{-}le^4$ se^2yo^4 he^2 $šo̧^4\text{-}le^4$ $bo^1rro^1\text{-}ve^4$, (purpose) $hme^1\text{-}ni^3$ nka^3 nta^3 $s^9e^4\text{-}si^1ni^3$, (co-ordinate purpose) k^9oa^4 nka^3 ci^2 ca^2 $^9ya^3$ $ši^3$ ho^3 $koi^4co^4\text{-}na^3$. 'Let the donkey's paper be sealed, in order that all will be well, and that no one will say anything to me'.

9.2.6. THE LIMITING CLAUSE has $sa^{3?}nta^3$ 'until' as introducer. Examples: (indep.) ce^{32} $koa^3sȩ^3$, (limiting) $sa^{3?}nta^3$ $^9a^3li^2koi^3$ $ti^4koa^3te^3\text{-}na^3\text{-}nia^3$ (nka-clause) nka^3 he^2 $čo^4$ $ši^3$ nta^3 $khai^1$ nka^3 nta^3 $si^1ša^1$. 'I will keep it a long time, until I would not sell again, because the animal that goes well works well'. (indep.

impersonal) k^9ia^4 $s^9e^3t^9a^3čoa^4\text{-}le^4$ $ki^4ča^4\text{-}le^4$, (limiting) ho^3 $sa^{3?}nta^3$ nka^3 nta^3 $s^9e^4\text{-}le^4$, (co-ordinate limiting) nka^3 ci^2 $ti^4v^9i^1š^9a^1nki^3\text{-}ni^3$ $yo^4nčo^4\text{-}le^4$. 'Then the horseshoe is measured, until it fits well, until his hoof is no longer open underneath'.

9.2.7. THE MANNER CLAUSE has $ho^3\text{-}s^9i̧^2$ 'about how' as introducer. Example: (indep. demonstrative) he^2 ti^3 $ši^3$ he^3nta^1 ti^1hna^3, $ši^3$ $khi^3\text{-}le^4$ $n^9ai^3\text{-}le^4$ (nka-clause) nka^3 $si^1ka^3sȩ^1$ $khoa^4\text{-}le^4$, (manner) $ho^3\text{-}s^9i̧^2$ $ti^1hna^3\text{-}ni^3$, (co-ordinate manner) k^9oa^4 nka^3 $ta̧o̧^4$ $ma^3čhȩ^{21}\text{-}le^4$. 'The boy who is in Tehuacán and who writes his father to send a message about how he is, and about how he needs money'.

9.2.8. THE 'IF'-CLAUSE has ca^2 'if' as introducer. Examples: ('if'-clause) ca^2 $thi̧^1$ $ši^1nkhi̧^1$, (indep. demonstrative) he^2 $ši^3$ $si^1koi^2nta^4$. 'If there are relatives, they are the ones who take care of him.' (indep. impersonal) $a^3li^2koi^3$ $ko̧ą^4nta^3\text{-}le^4$ $čho^4ta^4$, (if-clause) ca^2 to^4he^2 $čho^4ta^4$ $ši^3$ $ma^3\text{-}le^4$ $v^9e^1nta^3$, $si^1si̧^3\text{-}le^4$. 'The person will not get better, if just the people who know native cures take care of him. ('if'-clause) ca^2 $k^9ȩ^3$ koi^4ya^1, (co-ordinate 'if'-clause) k^9oa^4 ca^2 $ta̧o̧^4\text{-}le^4$ $čho^4ta^4$ $ki^3thȩ^4$, (indep. transitive) ya^4 $ko^3so̧^2\text{-}ni^3le^4$. 'If a dead one dies (if there is a murder), and if money is owed, it is judged there'.

9.2.9 THE 'ALTHOUGH'-CLAUSE has nta^3 ca^2 'although' as introducer. Example: (although-clause) nta^3 ca^2 to^4ho^3 $thi̧^1\text{-}na^3$ $č^9i̧^3$, (indep. intransitive) $si^3ša^1\text{-}nia^{13}$ 'Even though I am still sick, I work'.

9.2.10. SECONDARILY DEPENDENT CLAUSES may modify preceding dependent clauses. Examples with secondarily dependent clauses have been given in §7.1 and 8.1. (An alternate solution would treat the secondarily dependent clause as modifying the predicate of the preceding clause.)

10. GRAMMATICAL PHRASE. By special definition here, a grammatical phrase is filler of a slot in a clause. Any filler of a slot in a clause is considered to be a grammatical phrase regardless of its internal structure. Sometimes, therefore, it is simultaneously a single word, or a word sequence, or even a clause.

10.1. A PREDICATE PHRASE is the filler used in the predicate slot of a clause. Predicate phrase types contrast with one another by the lists of verbs in their obligatory parts. They also differ in the way these list differences correlate with permitted-nonpermitted occurrence of the optional parts.

10.1.1. TRANSITIVE VERB PHRASES differ from the others by the list of verbs used. The other parts of the phrase are as follows: intensifiers $khai^1 nka^3$ 'very,' $n^?i̱o̱^1$ 'forcefully'; negativizer li^2koi^3 (but the intensifier and the negativizer do not occur in the same phrase); $-šo^1$ 'it is indicated'; one of several modifiers, nta^3 'well,' $ša^1ti^1$ 'soon', etc.; to^4- 'only'; aspectual auxiliary verb he^3 'done,' ma^3 'it is acceptable', etc.; go-come auxiliary verb vhi^2 'goes', $vha^3{}^?ai^3$ 'arrives', etc.; the obligatory main verb; locational, $-vi^4$ 'here', etc.; emphasis $-^{4?}ni^3$ 'of course', etc.

Examples of transitive verb phrases: (neg.) li^2koi^3 (indicator) $-šo^1$ (verb) ki^3choa^3. 'They say he didn't give (it)'. (aux. verb) $koai^4$ (main verb) ka^3ko^1. 'He will go to show (it)'.

10.1.2. INTRANSITIVE VERB PHRASES have a different list of verbs from the transitive phrase, but they have similar optional parts. In the intransitive verb phrase, however, the intensifiers and the auxiliary verb ma^3 'it is acceptable' are used with greater frequency. (Note that the transitive and intransitive verbs differ also in respect to the correlation of optional presence or obligatory absence of an independent object. This occurs outside the predicate phrase, but within the transitive and intransitive clauses.)

Examples of intransitive verb phrases: (intensifier) $khai^1 nka^3$ (modifier) nta^3 (verb) $si^1ša^1$. 'He works very well'. (neg.) li^2koi^3 (aux. verb) ma^3 (main verb) $si^1ša^1$. 'He is not able to work'. (verb) $ka^2nc̣oai^{23}$ (emph.) $-^{4?}ni^3$. 'You came of course'.

10.1.3. IMPERSONAL VERB PHRASES differ from other verb phrases in that there is obligatory absence of both dependent and independent subject. It also differs from the intransitive verb phrase in that the in-

transitive only occasionally has a dependent recipient (see §11.1.1), whereas it is a frequent part of the impersonal verb phrase.

Examples: (intensifier) $khai^1 nka^3$ (verb) $ma^2c̣he̱^{21}$ (dep. rec.) $-le^4$. 'It is very much needed by him.' (aux. verb) he^3 (main verb) $ki^3so^3ko^3$ (dep. rec.) $-na^3$. 'It has been found by me.' ('I found it.') (intensifier) $khai^1 nka^3$ (modifier) nta^3 (verb) ka^3 (dep. rec.) $-le^4$ (obj. phrase) $c̣^?a^1$. 'A load can be carried by him very well.'

10.1.4. ADJECTIVAL PHRASES (those occurring in the equational-predicate slot of the adjectival equational clause) have an adjective or possessive pronoun as an obligatory part. In addition it may have an intensifier, or a negative. The dependent recipient is obligatorily absent.

Examples: (intensifier) $khai^1 nka^3$ (adj.) $c̣^?a̱i̱^4$ (subj. phrase) hi^3-vi^4. 'You are very bad'. (neg.) li^2koi^3 (poss. pronoun) $c̣^?a̱^4$ (subj. phrase) $c̣i^2to^3-ve^4$. 'That cat is not mine.' (intensifier) $khai^1 nka^3$ (adj.) nta^3. 'It is very good.'

10.1.5. APPEARANCE VERB PHRASE (those occurring in the equational-predicate slot of the appearance equational clause) have two obligatory parts. The first is an adjective, or—infrequently—a noun. The second obligatory part is one of the three verbs, khi^3 'appearance, in respect to singular things', $kho̱a̱^3$ 'appearance, in respect to plural things', $c̣o̱^3$ 'appearance, in respect to climate', etc. There is obligatory absence of auxiliary verbs and modifiers, but there is optional occurrence of the dependent recipient.

Examples: (adj.) nta^3-la^4 (verb) $c̣o̱^3$ (loc. phrase) ya^4. 'It's probably pretty there.' (adj.) $c̣^?ao^3$ (verb) $khi^3²ya^4$ 'I'm ugly'. (inter. phrase) $^?a^3$ (adj.) nta^3 (verb) khi^3 (dep. rec.) $-li^2$. 'Does it look good to you?' ('Do you like it'?) (noun) $c̣ho^4ta^4$ (verb) khi^3. 'It looks like a man'.

10.1.6. NUMERATIVE VERB PHRASES (those occurring in the equational-predicate slot of the numerative equational clause) have two obligatory parts. The first is a numeral or some kind of measure. The second is the verb *ma³* 'is, in relation to quantity'. There is obligatory absence of auxiliary verbs and modifiers. (This verb should not be confused with the impersonal verb *ma³* 'it is acceptable', or 'possible', which may occur as a complete utterance.)

Examples: (numeral) *hao²* (verb) *ma³-ni³* (subj. phrase) *čho⁴ta⁴*. 'There are two people'. *nkhį̃² ma³-ni³*. 'There are many'.

10.1.7. COPULATIVE VERB PHRASES (those occurring in the equational-predicate slot of the copulative equational clause) have two obligatory parts. The first is a noun, a pronoun, a possessive pronoun, or—occasionally—an adjective. The second is the verb *ni¹* 'is, in relation to quality'. There is obligatory absence of the dependent recipient.

Examples: (noun) *či⁴ne⁴ya¹* (verb) *ni¹* (subj. phrase) *he² čho⁴ta⁴*. 'That person is a carpenter'. (noun) *co²ti³-na⁴* (verb) *ni¹*. 'She is my daughter'. (pronoun) *ʔą³* (verb) *nia¹³*. 'I'm the one'.

10.1.8. DEMONSTRATIVE VERB PHRASES differ from the other types in that an introducer, *ši³* 'the one which', is obligatory.

Example: (subj. phrase) *he² čhǫ⁴²* (introducer) *ši³* (verb) *ti¹va³ne¹* (obj. phrase) *na³-hño³*. 'That's the woman who's washing clothes.'

10.2. TYPES OF SUBJECT AND OR OBJECT FILLERS. Six types of fillers are used in the subject and/or object slots of a clause. They contrast one from another by the list of items which fill their obligatory part, and also by the relationship of their constituent parts. The various types follow.

10.2.1. NOUN PHRASES are the most common filler and may be made up of the following parts: *ca²* 'perhaps' (this is translated 'if' when used as the introducer of a see §9.2.8); *to⁴*- 'only'; *he²* 'this, that', or *koi³* 'that previously identified' (this is translated 'therefore' when the introducer of a clause, see §9.2.3); *hnko³* 'one, a'; *nka³cʔi³* 'all, in relation to people', *nka³yi³he³* 'all, in relation to things', *hao²* 'two', etc., 'some

kind of measure'; *ʔnti¹* 'dear little'; the obligatory part—a noun—*ni³ʔya³* 'house', *na⁴hča¹* 'grandmother', etc. (see §11.1.2); *-vi⁴* 'here', *-ve⁴* 'there'.

Examples: (subj.) *he² ʔnti¹ ša⁴ʔnta⁴ʔnti¹-ve⁴* (pred.) *khę²nki³* (obj.) *škoa⁴-le⁴*. 'Those dear little chicks eat the fallen pieces'. (subj.) *nka³cʔi³ čho⁴ta⁴-ve⁴* (pred.) *ki³*. 'All the people there went'. (pred.) *choa¹-le⁴* (obj.) *ca² hnko³ ca² hao² ko¹lo¹*. 'He gives them perhaps one perhaps two turkeys'.

If the noun has a third person possessive pronoun (see §11.1.2), it may be followed by another noun. Examples: (subj.) *čho⁴ta²-ha³-le⁴ ti³* (pred.) *ki³to²ka³*. 'The boy's mule ran'. (manner) *kʔoa⁴-sʔį̃²* (pred.) *si¹khe³tʔa³-ni³* (subj.) *khoa⁴vi³šą³-le⁴ čho⁴ta⁴na⁴ši⁴na³nta¹-te⁴hao⁴*. 'Thus is finished off the wedding of the Huautla people'.

There may be co-ordinate noun phrases in either the object or the subject slot. The co-ordinator is *kao⁴* 'and'. Example: (pred.) *va³ne¹hǫ³* (obj.) *ncha³ mpa²-le⁴ kao⁴ ko²rre⁴-le⁴*. 'They wash the hands of their compadre and comadre.'

The noun phrase may be discontinuous. In the following example part of the object precedes the predicate, and part follows. Example: (obj.) *he² ko¹lo¹-ve⁴* (pred.) *vhi²-ka²ni¹-le⁴* (recipient) *mpa²-le⁴* (obj.) *kao⁴ hao² ni⁴sį̃⁴ nio⁴ti⁴²-, yao³ki³čhą¹-, na⁴hme¹-, skǫą⁴-ka³vhe²*. 'That turkey there they take to their compadre and two baskets of tamales, and cooked meat, and corn, and ground coffee.'

10.2.2. PRONOUN PHRASES may be used as filler of a subject or object slot. Since, however, there is always a dependent pronoun fused to the verb (third person is zero), when the independent pronoun occurs it adds emphasis. They are: *ʔą³* 'I', *hi³* 'you', *he²* 'he, she, it, they', *ña¹* 'we inclusive', *hį̃⁴/hąį̃⁴/hį̃⁴-hį̃⁴/hąį̃⁴-hį̃⁴* (free variation) 'we exclusive', *hǫ²* 'you plural'. Optional additions preceding the pronoun are: *nka³* (the combination is more emphatic than the pronoun alone), and *nta³ ca²* 'even', as in *nta³*

$ca^2 \, {}^?\underline{a}^3$ 'even I'. Optional additions following the pronoun are: $-šo^1$ 'it is indicated'; $-la^2$ 'maybe'; $-vi^4$ 'here', $-ve^4$ 'there'.

Example: (pro.) ${}^?\underline{a}^3$ (pred. phrase) $ka^2va^3ne^3ya^{23}$, (pro.) hi^3 (pred. phrase) $ka^2vi^3šoi^3$ (obj. phrase) $nch\underline{e}^1\text{-}ve^4$. 'I washed, you boiled the sweet.' (pred.) $khoia^{13}$ (pro. phrase) nka^3 ${}^?\underline{a}^3$. 'I'm going'.

10.2.3. POSSESSIVE PRONOUN PHRASES have a possessive pronoun in the obligatory part. They are: $c^?e^4$ 'his', $c^?\underline{a}^4$ 'mine', ci^4 'yours', $c\underline{a}^{42}$ 'ours inclusive', $c\underline{a}\underline{i}^4\text{-}h\underline{i}^4$ 'ours exclusive', $c\underline{a}\underline{o}^{43}$ 'yours plural'. Optional addition, $-la^2$ 'maybe'. Example: (pred. phrase) $ca^3ka^3ce^3$ (poss. pro.) $c^?\underline{a}^4$. 'He bought mine'.

10.2.4. DEMONSTRATIVE CLAUSES may be used as a filler of the subject or object slot. It differs from that used as a filler of the obligatory sentence slot (see §9.1.4) in that here the demonstrative he^2 'this' is optional.

Examples: (obj.-dem. clause) he^2 $š\underline{o}^4$ $ši^3$ $choa^1\text{-}le^4$ $čho^4ta^4ša^1$, (pred.) $choa^1\text{-}le^4$ (recipient) $na^{4?}mi^3$. 'The paper that the officials gave to them, they gave to the priest.' (pred.) $khai^1$ nka^3 nta^3 vhi^2 (subj.-dem. clause) bo^1rro^1 $ši^3$ $ca^3k^?e^2hna^3s\underline{o}^2$ to^3ma^2. 'Goes very well, the donkey that Thomas rode.' (manner) $k^?oa^4\text{-}s^?\underline{i}^2$ (pred.) $si^1khe^3t^?a^3\text{-}ni^3$ (subj.-dem. clause with included time clause) $s^?oi^1$ $ši^3$ $se^3hna^3\text{-}le^4$ $k^?ia^4$ nka^3 $hnko^3$ $khoa^4vi^3s\underline{a}^3$ $s^?e^3\text{-}le^4$ $šti^3\text{-}le^4$. 'Thus is finished off the party which is had by them when their children have a wedding.' (subj.-dem. clause) he^2 $čho^4ta^4$ $ši^3$ $s^?a^4ha^3{}^?ai^3$ (pred.) ti^1co^2. 'The person who just came is saying (it).'

10.2.5. DEMONSTRATIVE NOUN PHRASES are composed of a noun, or a pronoun, plus $ši^3$ 'the one which', plus another noun, possessive pronoun, or possessed noun.

Examples: (pred.) te^2 (subj.-dem. noun phrase) $mi^2yo^4\text{-}le^4$ $ši^3$ $š^?\underline{i}^4$. 'The friends of the man (the groom's friends) dance.' (subj.-dem. noun phrase) he^2 $ši^3$ $n^?ai^3\text{-}le^4$ kao^4 $ši^3$ $na^4\text{-}le^4$ ${}^?nti^1$, (pred.) vha^2kao^4 (obj.) $mpa^2\text{-}le^4$. 'He who is the father, and (she) who is mother of the baby, talk with their compadre.'

10.2.6. $ši^3$ PLUS DECLARATIVE PHRASE. One type of $ši$-phrase has the introducer, $ši^3$ 'the one which', plus a declarative clause. It occurs more frequently as filler of the object slot than it does as filler of the subject slot.

Examples: (time) $k^?ia^4$ (pred.) koa^3hnkia^3 (obj.-$ši$-phrase) $ši^3$ koa^4te^3 ${}^?nti^1$ $ka^3vhe^2\text{-}ve^4$. 'Then I will look for one who will cut that dear little coffee.' (manner) $ti^1th\underline{o}^2$ (pred.) vi^3nta^{32} (obj.-$ši$-phrase) $ši^3$ $he^3me^3v^?e^1$ $čhao^{42}$. 'First we buy one that is almost now laying eggs.'

10.2.7. $ši^3$ PLUS POSSESSIVE PRONOUN OR POSSESSED NOUN. A second type of $ši$-phrase has the introducer, $ši^3$ 'the one which', plus a possessive pronoun or possessed noun. Example: (time) $k^?ia^4$ (pred.) $nčha^4$ (subj.-$ši$-phrase) $ši^3$ $nai^3\text{-}le^4$ $čo^4ta^2ha^3$. 'Then the owner of the mule speaks.'

10.2.8. RELATIVE PHRASES may fill the object, but not the subject, slot of a clause. They are introduced by a relative pronoun, hme^3 'what', ${}^?ya^3$ 'who', or ho^3 'how', and is followed by a noun, a noun phrase, or a $ši$-phrase.

Examples: (obj.-relative phrase) ho^3 ye^4 (pred.) $ma^3\text{-}na^3$. 'To me it seems a snake.' ('I thought it was a snake'.) (pred.) $ka^2ta^3\text{-}co^2\text{-}li^2$ (obj.-relative phrase) hme^3 he^1 $ši^3$ $ka^2\text{-}s^?\underline{i}^1\text{-}na^3$. 'Let him tell you what harm he did to me'.

10.3. INSTRUMENTAL FILLERS may be a noun or a specifier phrase (see §10.2, 10.5). In general it is in cross reference to the morpheme-ni^3 which is part of the verb which follows it.

Examples: (instr. -noun phrase) $hnko^3$ ya^1 (pred. with included ni^3) $ca^3k^?e^1\text{-}ni^3le^4$. 'He hit him with a stick'. (instr.-noun phrase) $t\underline{a}\underline{o}^4škoa^4$ (pred. with included ni^3) $t^?e^2čhi^1\text{-}ni^3nai^{13}$. 'Pay me with change.' (instr.-specifier phrase) $to^4t^?a^3ci^4$ (pred. with included ni³) $ki^3\text{-}ni^3$ (loc.) $nki^3čao^3$. 'Because of you, he went to the ranch.'

10.4 INDEPENDENT RECIPIENT FILLERS may be a pronoun or noun phrase. These occur in cross reference to one of the dependent recipients which are fused with the dependent subject (see §11.1.1).

Examples: (pred. with intrans. verb and dep. rec.) ska^4-li^2 (indep. rec.) hi^3. 'It will fall in reference to you.' ('You will drop it.') (pred. with trans. verb and dep. rec.) ki^3-$si^3\check{c}h\d{a}^1$-le^4 (obj.) $nhi\d{o}^2yao^3$ (indep. rec.) ti^3. 'She cooked meat tamales for the boy'. (pred. with impersonal verb and dep. rec.) li^2koi^3 me^3-na^3 (indep. rec.) $?\d{a}^3$. 'It is not wanted by me'.

10.5 SPECIFIER PHRASES are the filler of the specifier slot. It has two obligatory parts $\check{s}i^3t^?a^3$ or $t^?a^3$ plus a possessive pronoun.

Example: (pred. with dep. rec.) si^4he^1-le^{23} (obj.) $khoa^4nta^3$ (spec.) $\check{s}i^3$ $t^?a^3c^?e^4$ co^2ti^3. 'I ask a favor of you for the girl'. (obj.) he^2-ve^4 $khoa^4nta^3$ (pred.) $\check{s}i^3$ si^3he^{13} (spec.) $t^?a^3c^?e^4$ $\check{c}ho^4ta^4\check{s}a^1$. 'That is the favor that I ask of the officials.'

10.6. MANNER FILLERS are of two types. (1) The manner phrase has an obligatory manner word. Some of them are: to^4hnko^3 $k^?a^2$ 'once', $ti^1th\d{o}^2$ 'first' $k^?oa^4$-$s^?\d{\imath}^2$ 'thus'. Examples: (manner) $k^?oa^4$-$s^?\d{\imath}^2$ (pred.) si^1ki^3-$tho^3s\d{o}^2$ (obj.) to^4hme^3-ni^3 $\check{s}i^3$ $?mi^2$-le^4. 'Thus he obeys anything he is told.' (manner) nki^2hnko^3 $k^?a^2$ (pred.) $ma^3\tilde{n}a^3$ (obj.) mi^2yo^4-le^4. 'Once more their friends gather.'

(2) The equality phrase has the introducer ho^3-ni^3 'as' plus a noun phrase. Example: (pred.) $ve^3\check{s}k\d{o}^1$ (manner) ho^3-ni^3 ca^2 $\check{s}i^3h\check{c}a^1$-$le^4$. 'He respects them as (he would) his parents.'

10.7. LOCATION SLOT FILLERS are of four types. (1) The location phrase has an obligatory location word. This word may optionally be followed by a noun. Some of the location words are: ya^4 'there'; $?i^4$ 'here'; $ha^4h\d{\imath}^3$, 'inside'; $ha^4h\check{c}o^3$ 'at the opening of'; $nki^3\check{s}k\d{o}^4$ 'in front of', etc. Examples: ha^4ya^3 $ka^2\check{s}a^4$ 'inside the box'; $ha^4s\d{o}^2$ $nt^?ia^3$ 'on top of the house'.

(2) Noun or possessive pronoun phrases may also be fillers of the location slot. Example: (pred.) va^1ya^3 (loc.) $ka^2\check{s}a^4$ (obj.)

$?nti^1k^?\d{e}^3$. 'They put the dear-little-dead in a box.'

(3) The limiting phrase has the introducer $sa^3{}^?nta^3$/$?nta^3$ 'as far as'. It is followed by a noun. Example: (time) $k^?ia^4$ (pred.) $si^{42}ka^3$-$s\d{e}^1$ (loc.) $?nta^3$ $hn\check{c}i^4$ (obj.) $\check{c}ho^4ta^4$-$ve^4{}^?ni^3$. 'Then they send the person to Teotitlán'.

(4) The where-phrase is introduced by $h\tilde{n}a^3$ 'where' or ya^4 $h\tilde{n}a^3$ 'there where'. It is followed by a declarative intransitive or impersonal clause. Examples: (pred.) $th\d{a}\d{\imath}^1ka^3$-$shao^3$ (loc.) $h\tilde{n}a^3$ $th\d{\imath}^1$ na^3nta^1. 'Go look where there is water'. (pred.) ki^3kao^4 (loc.) ya^4 $h\tilde{n}a^3$ ti^1hna^3 $n^?ai^3$-le^4. 'They went with (it) to where his father is'.

10.8 INTERROGATIVE SLOT FILLERS were discussed in §9.1.5.

10.9. TIME SLOT FILLERS are of five types. (1) A time phrase has an obligatory time word, which optionally may be preceded by $sa^3{}^?nta^3$/$?nta^3$ 'since, until'. Some of the time words are: $nt^?ai^4$-vi^4 'today', $nko^3h\tilde{n}a^4$ 'yesterday', $k^?ia^4$ 'then'. Examples: (time) $nko^3h\tilde{n}a^4$ (pred.) ki^3, 'He went yesterday'. $?a^3$ $c\d{\imath}^2$-ni^1 $?nta^3$ $nko^3h\tilde{n}a^4$. 'Has it been missing since yesterday?'

(2) A noun phrase. Example: (pred.) va^3-$tio^2ko^2kao^4$ (time) $hnko^3$ $ni^4th\d{e}^4$. 'They stay awake with (him) one night.'

(3) A demonstrative clause. Example: (time) he^2 $ni^4\check{c}h\d{\imath}^3$ $\check{s}i^3$ $v^?i^1hna^3\check{c}oa^4$-le^4 mi^2yo^4-le^4, (pred.) $ma^3\tilde{n}a^3$ (subj.) $nka^3c^?i^3$. 'The day that he tells his friends, everybody gathers.'

(4) When a $\check{s}i$-phrase is used as a filler of the time slot, there is usually an auxiliary verb with a completed aspect. The main verb is frequently followed by $k^?ia^4$ 'then'. Example: (time) $\check{s}i^3$ he^3 $ki^3s^?e^3nta^3$, $k^?ia^4$ (pred.) $ca^3kha^3{}^?a^1\check{s}\d{\imath}^2$. 'After it was made, then they took (it) away'.

11. GRAMMATICAL WORD. A grammatical word is a filler of a slot in one of the various types of grammatical phrases.

Independent grammatical words are, in general, found only in the obligatory slot of a phrase. When, however, words which occur in these obligatory slots also occur in optional slots of other phrases, they are still treated as independent words even when occurring in those optional slots. Any independent grammatical word may on occasion constitute a complete utterance under conditions of normal discourse.

Dependent grammatical words are, in general, found only in optional slots of a phrase. Dependent grammatical words have not been found constituting a complete utterance. Words which fill obligatory slots but which never constitute a complete utterance are also considered to be dependent (see §11.2.2).

Both independent and dependent grammatical words are simultaneously phonological words. There are, however, a few elements whose distributional characteristics suggest their treatment as dependent grammatical words but since they are phonologically dependent they are treated here as semiwords.

These semiwords are as follows: (1) The introducers nka^3 and $ši^3$ and the interrogative $^{?}a^3$ (see §11.2.2, 9.1.5).

(2) Certain phrase parts are also semiwords: to^4- 'only' is phonologically dependent on the following item. The parts -$šo^1$ 'it is indicated', -vi^4 'here', -$^{4?}ni^3$ 'of course' are phonologically dependent on the preceding item. (see §10.1.1).

(3) Certain parts of words (see §11.1.1) are semiwords: the dependent recipient, 'augmentation' -$^3sa^3$, 'doubt' -la^2, 'relationship'-ni^3.

11.1. INDEPENDENT GRAMMATICAL WORDS can be grouped into eight parts of speech in accordance with their distribution in the obligatory slots.

11.1.1. A VERB is the filler of the obligatory slot of a verb phrase. The verb has fused forms consisting of person with stem and at times with an overlapping fusion of aspect. These lead to a very large number of regular and irregular forms. Since these were described in K. L. Pike, 1948, pp. 106–64, only the nonfused forms of the dependent subject suffixes and the aspect prefixes are listed here.

The dependent subject suffixes are obligatorily present in transitive and intransitive verbs. They are: -a^3 'first person', -i^3 'second person', $zero$ 'third person', -a^2 'first person inclusive', -i^4 'first person exclusive', -o^3 'second person plural'.

Examples: si^1cho^2 'he toasts (it)', si^3choa^{23} 'I toast (it)', ni^2choi^{23} 'you toast (it)', ni^2-cho^{23} 'you plural toast (it)', ni^2choi^{24} 'we exclusive toast (it)', ni^2choa^2 'we inclusive toast (it)'.

The nonfused forms of the aspect prefixes are: ki^3- 'completed', koi^4- 'incomplete', ti^1- 'continuing', ka^2- 'recently completed', ka^2ta^3- 'to order to do it', $čǫ^3$- 'eventually', $s^?a^4$- 'soon'.

Examples: $ki^3si^3cho^2$ 'he toasted (it)', koi^4-ti^4 'it will burn', ti^1ti^2 'it is burning', ka^2ti^2 'it burned', $ka^2ta^3ti^2$ 'let it burn', $čǫ^3kǫǫ^4$-le^4 'eventually it will be known by him', ('He will learn some day.')

There is an optional dependent recipient which fuses with the dependent subject as indicated in the chart. The action of the verb is directed to, from, or concerning, the person or thing indicated by the dependent recipient.

Examples: koa^3ce^3-le^{23} 'I will buy (it) for you'. (Ambiguous with, 'I will buy (it) from you'.) $t^?ai^2$-nai^{13} 'Give (it) to me'. ki^3choa^3-na^3 'He gave (it) to me'.

Fusion of Dep. Recipient with Dep. Subject

RECIPIENT	SUBJECT	
3rd sing. and plur.	and 3rd sing. and plur.	-le^4
1st sing.	and 3rd sing. and plur.	-na^3
2nd sing.	and 3rd sing. and plur.	-li^2
2nd* plur.	and 3rd sing. and plur.	-$^4no^3$
1st plur. exc.	and 3rd sing. and plur.	-na^3hi^4
1st plur. inc.	and 3rd sing. and plur.	-na^1
3rd sing. and plur.	and 1st sing.	-le^4
2nd sing.	and 1st sing.	-le^{23}
2nd* plur.	and 1st sing.	-$^4no^3$

* These fused forms are preceded by a tone ^{4} which results in a down-glide on the preceding syllable unless that syllable already has tone ^{4}.

3rd sing. and plur.	and 2nd sing.	-*lai*⁴
1st sing.	and 2nd sing.	-*nai*¹³
1st plur. exc.	and 2nd sing.	-*nai*¹*hi*⁴
3rd* sing. and plur.	and 2nd plur.	-⁴*lao*³
1st sing.	and 2nd plur.	-*nao*¹³
1st plur. exc.	and 2nd plur.	-*nai*³*hi*⁴
3rd sing. and plur.	and 1st plur. exc.	-*lai*⁴*hi*⁴
2nd sing.	and 1st plur. exc.	-*lai*¹*hi*⁴
2nd plur.	and 1st plur. exc.	-*lai*³*hi*⁴
3rd* sing. and plur.	and 1st plur. incl.	-⁴*le*²

There are optional indicators of 'augmentation' -³*sa*³ (This is preceded by tone ³ which results in a down-glide if the preceding syllable has tone ¹ or tone ².), 'doubt' -*la*², 'relationship' -*ni*³ or -*si*¹*ni*³ which fuse with the dependent subject when they immediately precede it.

The stem of a transitive, intransitive, or impersonal verb is frequently a compound one. The first part must be predicating, and and is one of a list of about 150 verbs, most of which may be the entire filler of the obligatory slot. A few have not been found apart from the compound form.

This verbal part combines with a noun, an adjective, another verb, or a directional to form a compound stem of two parts. The third part of a compound stem is usually a directional: -*sǫ*² 'on top of', -ʔ*nčo*² 'between', -*nki*³ 'below', etc. (See Cowan and Cowan, 1947 for a discussion of directionals.)

Examples: *si*¹*tǫą*²¹*nthai*² 'he defends' (*tǫą*²¹ 'fierce', -*nthai*² 'in behalf of'); *ve*³*čho*⁴*ta*⁴ 'he respects' (*ve*³ 'he knows', *čho*⁴*ta*⁴ 'person'); *v*ʔ*e*¹*se*³ 'he whistles' (*se*³ 'he sings', *v*ʔ*e*¹ (he hits').

Equational verbs differ from other verbs in that even though they are phonologically independent, they are grammatically dependent; they cannot be used as a complete utterance even in answer to a question. The adjective equational predicate, the appearance equational verbs *khi*³, *čǫ*³, *khǫą*³, and the copulative equational *ni*¹ indicate person, but do not indicate aspect. The numerative equational verb *ma*³ indicates aspect but not person.

328

11.1.2. A NOUN is a filler in the obligatory slot of a noun phrase. There are three types: personal, nonpersonal, and relational.

The personal nouns have fused possessive pronouns which are the same as the dependent subjects fused to a verb (see §11.1.1). Example: *škǫ*⁴ 'his eye', *škǫą*³ 'my eye', *škǫį*³ 'your eye'.

Nonpersonal nouns have nonfused possessive pronouns. Example: *na*⁴-*na*⁴ 'my mother', *na*⁴-*li*⁴ 'your mother', *na*⁴-*le*⁴ 'his mother', *na*⁴-*na*¹ 'our incl. mothers', *na*⁴-*na*⁴*hi*⁴ 'our exc. mothers', *na*⁴-*no*³ 'your plur. mothers' (K. L. Pike, 1948, pp. 95–106).

The relational nouns are like the nonpersonals except that they never have the down-glide in pitch which is characteristic of the series phonological phrase (see §4).

The stem of a noun can be simple, or it can be a compound. Example: *n*ʔ*ai*³*či*¹*ko*³-*va*³*te*¹*nta*¹ 'baptismal godfather' (*n*ʔ*ai*³ 'father', *či*³*kǫ*³ 'holy', *n*ʔ*ai*³*či*³*kǫ*³ 'godfather', *va*³*te*¹ 'he covers', *na*³*nta*¹ 'water', *va*³*te*¹*nta*⁷ 'he baptizes'); *he*² *ni*¹ *n*ʔ*ai*³*či*³*kǫ*³*va*³*te*¹*nta*¹-*na*⁴. 'He is my baptismal godfather.'

11.1.3. A PRONOUN fills the obligatory slot of type two of a subject phrase (see §10.2.2). Example: (subj.-pro.) *hǫ*² (pred.) *k*ʔ*oa*⁴*ki*³*n*ʔ-*įǫ*²³. 'You plur. did it'.

11.1.4. A POSSESSIVE PRONOUN fills the obligatory slot of type three of a subject or object phrase (see §10.2.3). Example: (pred.) *t*ʔ*ai*²-*nai*¹³ (obj.-poss. pro.) *ci*⁴. 'Give me yours'.

11.1.5. AN ADJECTIVE is a filler in the obligatory slot of a predicate phrase in an adjectival-equational clause (see §10.1.4). Example: (equa.-pred.) *nta*³ (subj.) *čho*⁴*ta*⁴. 'He is a good person'.

11.1.6. A TIME WORD fills the obligatory slot of type one of a time phrase (see §10.9). Example: (time) *nčąǫ*³ (pred.) *khoia*¹³. 'Tomorrow I will go'.

11.1.7. A MANNER WORD fills the obligatory slot of type one of a manner phrase (see §10.6). Example: (manner) *ta*⁴*nhįǫ*² (pred.) *ti*²*so*⁴*thąį*⁴ (time) *nčąǫ*³. 'Get up early tomorrow.'

11.1.8. A SPECIFIER WORD fills the obligatory slot of a specifier phrase (see §10.5). Example: (pred.) *ka²ta³se³* (spec.) *ši³ t²a³ci⁴* (time) *ni⁴či̧³ nka³ nča̧³*. 'Let them sing for you every day.'

11.1.9. CLAUSE FILLERS FOR GRAMMATICAL PHRASES. If the filler of a grammatical phrase is a clause, it in turn contains a sequence of phrases with independent words in their obligatory slots, and dependent ones in their optional slots. Thus, one grammatical phrase may contain a sequence of words of various parts of speech. Example: (pred. phrase) *ha³²ai³* (subject phrase with introducer, verb, noun) *ši³ ca³ka³ce³ čhao⁴²*. 'The one who bought eggs came'.

11.2. DEPENDENT GRAMMATICAL WORDS are divided between those which occur in optional slots and those which occur in obligatory slots.

11.2.1. OPTIONAL SLOT FILLERS. The most common dependent grammatical words which fill optional slots are: the demonstratives *he²* 'this', *koi³* 'that'; the locationals *-vi⁴* 'here', *-ve⁴* 'there', *ha̧¹* 'over there'; *-šo¹* 'it is indicated'; intensifiers *khai¹ nka³* 'very', *n²ǫi̧¹* 'forcefully': auxiliary verbs (see K. L. Pike, 1948, pp. 136–37); the negative *²a³li²-koi³*; the co-ordinators *kao⁴, k²oa⁴* 'and'.

There are a number of allomorphs of the negative morpheme. There is free variation in that the initial *²a³* may be absent. The other allomorphs occur in accordance with their distribution as follows:

(1) *²a³li²koi³* occurs when part of a predicate phrase of the independent declarative clauses and the independent adjectival or appearance-equational clauses. Example: *he² čho⁴ta⁴ li²koi³ choa¹²nte³*. 'The man doesn't allow (it)'.

(2) *ci² ca²* (optionally the *ca²* is omitted) is used in an interrogative clause, and in any dependent clause but the limiting dependent clause. It also occurs when part of a *ši*-phrase.

Examples: *²a³ ci² ca² he² čho⁴ta⁴ ši³ choa¹²nte³*. 'Isn't it this person who allows (it)?' *kǫa̧³hti³-le⁴ nka³ he² čho⁴ta⁴ ci² ca³ choa¹²nte³*.

'He is angry because the person doesn't allow (it)'. *he² čho⁴ta⁴ ši³ ci² ca² choa¹²nte³, ki³*. 'The person who doesn't allow (it) left.'

(3) *²a³li² ~ ²a³li² ca²* (free variation) occurs when part of a nonpredicate phrase in a declarative or demonstrative clause. It also occurs when part of an equational-predicate phrase in the copulative and numerative equational clauses.

Examples: *²a³li² ²ya³ thi̧¹*. 'Nobody is present'. *²a³li² he² čho⁴ta⁴ ši³ choa¹²nte³*. 'It isn't that man who allows (it)'. *²a³li² he² hi̧² čho⁴ta⁴ ši³ choa¹²nte³*. 'That's not the man who allows (it)'.

(4) *²a³li²...hi̧²* occurs with imperative clauses. Examples: *²a³li² v²ai²²nte³-hi̧²lai⁴*. 'Don't give him permission'. *²a³li² k²oa⁴-hi̧² ma³-li²*. 'Don't be concerned'.

The co-ordinator *kao⁴* occurs between nouns, or between demonstrative noun phrases; *k²oa⁴* occurs between other co-ordinates. The two may occur in sequence at the beginning of a phonological sentence if the preceding phonological sentence ended in the middle of a grammatical phrase. This unusual distribution is due to the fact that *k²oa⁴* but not *kao⁴* may be initial in a phonological sentence.

Examples: *ca³ki³ntai¹⁴-hi̧⁴ bo¹rro¹, kao⁴ na⁴-ši̧¹*. 'We bought donkeys and horses'. *ha³²-ai³ka³ce³ na⁴hme¹, k²oa⁴ ha³²ai³ka³ce³ yao³*. 'He came to buy corn; and he came to buy meat.'

11.2.2. OBLIGATORY SLOT FILLERS. Dependent grammatical words which fill obligatory slots in a grammatical phrase, but which never occur as complete utterances, are also considered dependent. They are: the indicator of a yes-no question, *²a³*; the predicating part of the equational-predicate phrases, specifically, *khi³/khǫa̧³/čǫ³* 'it appears', *ni¹* 'is, in quality', *ma³* 'is, in quantity'; the introducers.

The introducers are divided into those which introduce phrases, those which introduce clauses, and those which may introduce both.

Those which introduce phrases, but never

329

clauses, are obligatory to the phrase they are introducing. Introducers to a relative phrase (see §10.2.8) are ho^3 'how', hme^3 'what', $^{\prime}ya^3$ 'who'; introducer to a where-phrase $h\tilde{n}a^3$ 'where'; introducer to a specifier phrase $\check{s}i^3$ $t^{\prime}a^3$ or $t^{\prime}a^3$ 'concerning'; the introducer $\check{s}i^3$ is used in several phrases: the demonstrative verb phrase, the demonstrative noun phrase, the $\check{s}i$-phrase (see §10.1.8, 10.2.5–7, 10.9).

Those which introduce clauses are obligatory to the clause. They are: nka^3 'sub-ordination', $k^{\prime}ia^4$ nka^3 'when', koi^3 nka^3 'therefore', to^4nka^3 'but', hme^1-ni^3 nka^3 'in order to', $sa^{3\prime}nta^3$ 'until', ho^3-$s^{\prime}\underset{\sim}{i}^2$ 'about how', ca^2 'if', nta^3 ca^2 'although' (see §9.2).

Four of the clause introducers (nka^3 'sub-ordination', $sa^{3\prime}nta^3$ 'until', ca^2 'if', nta^3 ca^2 'although') may also be used to introduce a phrase. At such times they are followed by pronouns, time words, or location words—not verbs. Their meanings differ slightly in the two environments (see §10.2.2, 10.7, 10.9).

REFERENCES

Cowan, F. H., 1947, 1952
—— and Cowan, 1947
Cowan, G. M., 1948
Gudschinsky, 1955, 1958a, 1958b, 1959a, 1959b, 1959c

Pike, E. V., 1954, 1956
Pike, K. L., 1948, 1954, 1955, 1960
—— and Pike, 1947
Villa Rojas, 1955

7G. Jiliapan Pame

LEONARDO MANRIQUE C.

0.   Introduction
1.   Phonology
1.1.   Inventory of phonemes
1.2.   Description of segmental phonemes
1.3.   Syllable
1.4.   Sentence melody
2.   Formative processes and morphophonemics
3.   Classes of elements
3.1.   Interrogatives
3.2.   Locatives
3.3.   Temporals
3.4.   Negative
3.5.   Pronouns
3.6.   Verb auxiliaries
3.7.   Adjectives
3.8.   Quantitatives
3.9.   Numerals
3.10. Demonstratives
3.11. Conjunctions
3.12. Nouns
3.13. Possessives
3.14. Verbs
3.15. Prefixes of number of nouns
3.16. Prefixes of tense-aspect and person
3.17. Nominalizers
3.18. Suffix markers of plural of nouns
3.19. Suffix markers of plural of verbs
3.20. Markers of verb object
4.   Construction
4.1.   Verb syntax
4.2.   Noun syntax
4.3.   Complex subjects and objects
4.4.   Syntactic clause
4.5.   Paratactic constructions

0. INTRODUCTION. Pame is spoken in the the Sierra Gorda, a branch of the Sierra Madre Oriental running from the southern part of San Luis Potosi to the north of Hidalgo, approximately between 99° and 100° W. and from 20°45′ to 22°30′ N. The Pame area covers almost all the length of the Sierra Gorda, but not its width. It forms a band more than 150 km. long and less than 50 km. wide; it is not continuous, but consists of a series of small nuclei more or less isolated, with some new extensions. Pame nuclei, north to south, are: Ciudad del Maiz, Alaquines, La Palma and Gamotes, Santa Maria Acapulco, Tilaco, Pacula, Jiliapan.

Today, the situation of Pame is weak. It has been replaced by Spanish in most places, and in others it is being lost, except in Santa Maria Acapulco. Pame is known by only one speaker in Pacula, for instance; five or six persons in Jiliapan are able to speak it, but they use Spanish customarily.

Since the writings of Manuel Orozco y Berra (1864, p. 48) and Francisco Pimentel (1904, p. 412) Pame has been considered a single language, and so it was recorded by Jacques Soustelle (1937), but more recent researches (Manrique, 1958; Swadesh, 1959b, 1960a) postulate the existence of two distinct languages: North Pame and South Pame. The former comprises the dialects of Ciudad del Maiz, also spoken in some new settlements; Alaquines, especially in the Colonia Indigena (it has disappeared from the neigh-

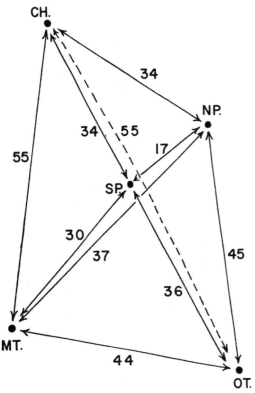

CH.

34

NP.

34   55

55   17

SP.

30

37   45

36

MT.

44

OT.

FIG. 1—INTERNAL RELATIONSHIPS OF
OTOPAMEAN FAMILY. CH, Chichimec; NP,
North Pame; SP, South Pame; MT, Matlatzinca
(and Ocuiltec); OT, Otomí (and Mazahua).

Luis de la Paz, shows a somewhat remote
genetic relationship with Pame, in spite of
what we supposed on the basis of certain
historical data and some striking phonetic
and lexical resemblances.

To give a brief idea of the genetic relationships of South Pame we can say that it is a
member of the Otopamean family, together
with Otomí, Mazahua, Ocuiltec, Matlatzinca, North Pame, and Chichimec. The
internal relationships of this family as lexicostatistically established are shown in Table
1 and in figure 1, which is a graphic expression of the table; both are taken from Manrique, 1958, slightly modified according to
the latest revised cognate count.

In contrast to former classifications, the
table and diagram clearly show that there
are two absolutely different Pame languages
(which for easy reference and identification
in other works we still call Pame, but label
North and South in order to distinguish
them); both languages are also completely
different from Chichimec. Today Otopamean
can be classified as follows:

borhood where Soustelle still found it); La
Palma, in some hamlets around the Mestizo
town of that name; Gamotes, and Santa
Maria Acapulco, the last one very divergent.

South Pame is now a dead language. It is
known to only a few people in Jiliapan and
Pacula. The more divergent dialect of Tilaco
is completely lost.

It is worth noting that Chichimec, a
language spoken only in La Mision, near San

Otopamean family

I. Otomí-Mazahua group
    a. Otomí (it may comprise only three
       main dialect subdivisions)
    b. Mazahua
II. South Pame, with three closely related
    dialects
III. North Pame
    a. Ciudad del Maíz and La Palma dia-
       lects, closely related
    b. Santa María Acapulco dialect, more
       differentiated in some respects

TABLE 1—INTERNAL DIVERGENCES OF THE OTOPAMEAN FAMILY (in minimum centuries)

	Otomí-Mazahua	S. Pame	N. Pame	Matlatzinca-Ocuiltec	Chichimec
Otomí- Mazahua	...	36	45	44	55
South Pame	36	...	17	30	34
North Pame	45	17	...	37	34
Matlatzinca-Ocuiltec	44	30	37	...	55
Chichimec	55	34	34	55	...

IV. Matlatzinca-Ocuiltec group
    a. Matlatzinca
    b. Ocuiltec
V. Chichimec

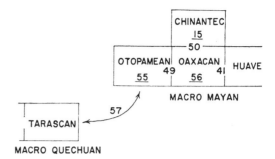

FIG. 2—RELATIONSHIPS OF OTOPAMEAN WITH THE MOST CLOSELY RELATED FAMILIES OF THE MACRO-MAYAN AND MACRO-QUECHUAN PHYLA. Underlined figures represent greatest internal divergences; other figures indicate divergences between families and phyla. (After Swadesh, 1960b.)

Figure 2, taken from Swadesh (1960b), shows the relations of Otopamean with the most closely related families of the Macro-Mayan phylum, in which it is included, and with the Macro-Quechuan phylum, because Otopamean is the link between these two phyla. In this diagram the underlined figures represent the greatest internal divergences; other figures indicate divergences between families and phyla. Some figures have been modified following recent researches; all are subject to slight changes when a better knowledge of the phonology of the group will permit more accurate cognate counts.

Descriptive works on South Pame are listed below in chronological order:

(a) The *Arte*, by Fray Juan Guadalupe Soriano (1776). Lost manuscript of which only a later copy survives. The copy, perhaps incomplete, includes a *Prólogo Historial* of great ethnohistorical value; a Spanish-Pame - Otomí - Nahuatl - Chichimec vocabulary fairly complete for the first three languages, not so complete for Nahuatl, and very brief for Chichimec. It also includes a list of verbs of each of the two "conjugations," and a few unsystematic grammatical remarks. As Pimentel (1904) says, "it looks like a rough draft which has not received the final revision."

(b) The work of Fray Francisco Valle, manuscript of the 18th century, now in the Archivo Histórico de Madrid. It was published almost entire by the Count of Viñaza (Viñaza, 1892), and a small part of this publication was later re-edited by Rudolf Schuller (1925b). For his investigations, the late Dr. Antonio de la Maza obtained a complete copy of the Madrid manuscript, including a short vocabulary and texts used in Confession, not published by Viñaza. The most interesting fact of Valle's work is his astonishing analysis of the verb; it is a pity that Valle did not make the same kind of analysis of other parts of the grammar.

(c) The very short descriptions of Orozco y Berra (1864) and of Pimentel (1904) are not based on fieldwork, but on Soriano's *Arte*. The main purpose of these descriptions was to provide a basis for their comparative work and for the classifications of the languages of Mexico which they made.

(d) In his *La Famille Otomi-Pame . . .*, Jacques Soustelle (1937) published a sketch of North Pame based on fieldwork with the Alaquines dialect, and short notes on Jiliapan Pame. The notes on South Pame are based on fieldwork, on Soriano's manuscript, and on Schuller's edition of Valle.

(e) Robert J. Weitlaner and Carlo Antonio Castro gathered vocabularies and texts in La Misión, near Jacala, and in Pacula. None of their material has been published, except an article on plural formation (Castro, 1955).

(f) For the 58th annual meeting of the American Anthropological Association I prepared a few descriptive remarks on the works of Soriano and Valle, published by the Instituto Nacional de Antropología e Historia of Mexico (Manrique, 1960). This analysis is the basis for the present description, checked and supplemented with new materials gathered in Jiliapan from the informants

Abundia Santana Bartolejo and María Andablo.[1]

1.1. INVENTORY OF PHONEMES. The table below charts the phonemes of Jiliapan Pame.

Consonants:

voiceless stops	*p*	*t*	*¢*	*č*	*k*	*ʔ*
voiced stops	*b*	*d*	*z*	*ž*	*g*	
voiceless fricatives			*s*	*š*		*h*
nasals	*m*	*n*				
oral sonorants	*w*	*r*		*y*		

Vowels:

high orals	*u*	*i*	*ɨ*
low orals	*o*	*e*	*a*
high nasals	*ų*	*į*	*ɨ̨*
low nasals	*ǫ*	*ę*	*ą*

Besides these segmental phonemes, there are three tone-stress phonemes: high (´), low (`) and falling glide (^). One of these and only one is found in each word. There are, of course, secondary tones on the unstressed syllables of a word; their production seems mechanical, but they have not been sufficiently analyzed. The tone-stresses are considered phonemes because they differentiate minimal pairs, but as far as I know they have no grammatical function. Some examples follow:

kudû 'devil'   *kudù* 'stone'
tikî 'arrow'   *tikî* 'rubber'

1.2. DESCRIPTION OF SEGMENTAL PHONEMES. The placing of each of the phonemes in the table shows its point of articulation. This section, therefore, deals only with some further characteristics, and with allophones. Brackets are used to indicate phonetic characteristics; forms not in brackets are written phonemically.

The stops *p, t, k*, are voiceless and usually unaspirated but they may be slightly as-

pirated, especially when not in clusters; when a strong aspiration is heard, it is to be interpreted as cluster of stop plus *h*:

[*p*] *pi¢ʔ* 'mushroom'   [*pʰ*] *mphą¢ʔ* 'sandal'
[*t*] *tanáyn* 'tail'   [*tʰ*) *šuthųnt* 'five'
[*k*] *ketʔę* 'atole'   [*kʰ*] *khɨ̀* 'blood'

¢, č are voiceless affricates; sometimes, when not in cluster, they are slightly aspirated:

[*¢*] *masú¢* 'knot'   [*č*] *gyų̌či* 'firewood'

The glottal stop *ʔ* varies in strength: between two different vowels it is clearly and easily distinguishable, but between identical vowels it is weakened and sometimes disappears, especially in rapid speech. When it follows a voiceless stop or an affricate it is heard as a glottalization of them:

[*ʔ*] *krų́ ʔa* 'skunk'
['] *ntʔu* 'louse'; *pi¢ʔ* 'mushroom';
      rčʔi 'vein'; *hukʔ* 'you' (sing.)

Voiced stops *b, d, g* are slightly fricative, fluctuating to completely fricative between vowels; *b* and *d* lose all or almost all their fricative quality when they follow the corresponding homorganic nasals (in the materials at hand there is no example of *ng*):

[*ƀ*] *sibi¢ʔɨ* 'lime'   [*b*] *numbú ʔu* 'wooden
[*đ*] *tide* 'forty'   hammer'
[*g*] *negû* 'pine'   [*d*] *nde¢ʔ* 'stair'

Sibilant fricatives *s, š* are respectively apico-alveolar and lamino-palatal; both are voiceless:

[*s*] *-su¢ʔ* 'tie'   [*š*] *šinyu* 'nose'

Fricative *h* has positional allophones when occurring intervocalically between vowels of front, central, or back articulation. Front and back allophones also occur when preceding semiconsonants *y* and *w* in the clusters *hy* and *hw*. Between nasal vowels *h* is also nasalized. After a voiceless stop it is heard as aspiration of the stop.

[*h*]	*ntihin*	'corn dough'
[*h*]	*mųhų*	'pumpkin'
[*h*]	*kahan*	'star'
[*h*N]	*bąhą*	'far'
[*Cʰ*]	*štha*	'rabbit'

Voiced fricatives *z, ž* have a very restricted occurrence; the first one appears only in

---

[1] Although it is a description of North Pame, not of South Pame, Gibson's "Pame (Otomí) Phonemics and Morphophonemics" (1956) is worth mention because it provides a good basis for comparing the two languages.

seven words of a 600-word vocabulary and the second one in no more than six. They are homorganic too, but contrast with, the voiceless fricatives *s, š*:

z   *kizín*   'hole'   *s*   *kisáyn* 'eagle'
ž   *ži?*   'teeth'   *š*   *šiši?* 'breast'

Nasals *m, n* are bilabial and alveolar. *n* has a velar allophone [ŋ] before *k*; *m* and *n* are palatalized before *y*, but not before *i*:

[*m*]   *miši*   'cat'
[*mʸ*]   *msa-mye?e* 'the other side of the sea'
[*n*]   *nidí?i*   'straight'
[*nʸ*]   *šinyú*   'nose'
[*ŋ*]   *nk?u*   'snail'

The *r* has special allophones: it is a flap [ř] before a vowel, it is trilled [r̃] more or less long before a consonant other than *?* (the only example of *r?* is in final position), and it is lateral [*l*] in final position, followed or not by glottal stop. Besides this, it develops a brief supporting vocalic sound when in initial cluster of three or more consonants:

[ř]   *-?ęrų* 'alive', *krų́?a* 'skunk'
[r̃]   *byarma?a* 'coyote', *rsi* 'leaf'
[r̃̆]   *rč?i* 'vein', *rk?wę* 'mezquite tree'
[*l*]   *-níur?* 'want', *mpáhar* 'horse'

The semivowel *w* always has a timbre like [*u*]; it is distinguished from the homophonous vowel because it never takes a tone-stress phoneme nor is it nasalized, and because of its relative shortness. The *y* frequently sounds like [*i*], and in that case it is distinguished from the corresponding vowel for reasons parallel to those distinguishing *w* and *u*. When in initial position or intervocalic the *y* is slightly fricative, nevertheless contrasting with the fricative *ž*. The *w* gives a slight labial quality to certain preceding consonants; *y* palatalizes any consonant immediately preceding it:

[*u*]   *idiwe*   'capulín'
[*hʷ*]   *škuhwá* 'palm'
[*i*]   (with palatalization) *ihyaw* 'earth'
[*y*]   *yurthi* 'root'

The norms of the vocalic phonemes are

sufficiently described in the table; here I need only to describe their outstanding allophones:

Besides the norm [*i*], the phoneme *i* has a lower and somewhat backed allophone [ɨ]:

[*i*]   *tłi* 'two'   [ɨ]   *siné?ę?* 'small'

When in cluster with *y* or in final position, *e* is pronounced somewhat *open* [ɛ]; when these two conditions occur together the vowel is still more open [ɛˇ]:

[*e*]   *merî*   'fast'
[ɛ]   *tikyent* 'six'
[ɛ]   *bi?e*   'few'
[ɛˇ]   *nimbye* 'nest'

o has, similar to *e*, more open allophones [ɔ] in final position and in other situations not yet well defined:

[*o*]   *komú* 'butterfly'
[ɔ]   *m?mǫ* 'moon'

The central vowel *i* has been postulated because of the impossibility of transcribing certain words using only *i, e, a, o, u* (and the corresponding nasals); it has three frequent allophones [ə], [ɨ], [ʉ], and other not so common variants [ɐ], [ø]. Undoubtedly, there is sometimes a vocalic development within certain consonant clusters, with the characteristics of *i*; sometimes a fronted allophone [ʉ] of *u* is found, and occasionally *i* is pronounced further back than [ɨ]; the result of this is that under certain circumstances the oppositions of these three phonemes are neutralized:

[ə]   *-mikinɖáw* 'burn'
[ʉ]   *bi?í*   'chili pepper'
[ɨ]   *kisáyn*   'eagle'

Besides the more common vocalic allophones just described, all unstressed vowels tend to be more or less obscure, increasing the difficulties of phonemic interpretation.

The nasal vowels have more or less the same phonetic timbres as the oral ones, including the obscure pronunciation in unstressed syllables. They have not been interpreted as *oral vowel plus nasalization*, because nasalization would be a suprasegmental phoneme not easy to match with tone-stress, and if counted as a consonantic phoneme, a much more difficult description and analysis of distribution would be required:

i̧	ȼi̧ 'above'	ę	-tęhę 'laugh'
ą	mpą 'sun'	i̧	škị̂nî 'skin'
ų	nkų 'tree'	ǫ	mpǫˀ 'snake'

The system of vowels in terms of their contrasts is shown in the following scheme:

All vowels, whether oral or nasal, have certain traits in common which are not merely phonetic, but phonemic and are related to the syllable and word structure. The vowels, and only they, constitute the syllable peak; only vowels can support the suprasegmental phoneme of tone-stress, and when they are not stressed they bear secondary tones contrasting with that of the stressed syllable (in fact, in certain clusters also m or n have secondary tones which make of them peaks of phonetic, but not phonemic, syllables). All vowels are longer still when these two conditions coincide. These characteristics serve as differential criteria in distinguishing between w-u, y-i.

1.3. SYLLABLE. Jiliapan Pame has junctures (for "juncture" see Hockett, 1955, p. 52) that make the syllabic analysis easier, but not all junctures are equally clear; e.g. between two vowels junctures are almost inaudible, but between a vowel and a following voiceless stop they are strongly marked. Phonetically junctures are marked by the lengthening of the vowel in an open syllable, or by sustaining the final occlusion in a syllable closed by a voiceless stop, or by the lengthening of the syllable final nasal, and by lowering the word melody in the final syllable; the last characteristic gives a stronger mark for junctures between words than for junctures between syllables of the same word.

Syllables conform to the patterns (CCCC)V, (CCCC)VC and (CCC)VCC; in other words, they can be constituted by a single vowel or vowel preceded and/or followed by consonants. Consonants following the vowel may be one or two; those preceding it may be one to four (if only one consonant follows), or one to three (if two

336

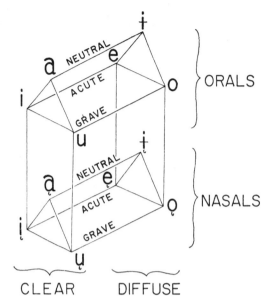

Fig. 3—JILIAPAN PAME VOWELS

consonants follow). There are no more than five consonants in a single syllable, and the largest consonant cluster has no more than four phonemes.

Open syllables occur in all positions within the word. (In the examples given below, syllable division is marked by a lowered point [.]):

V: i.hyầw 'earth', na.ų.hwę 'nine', šma.só.a 'skin'

CV: mi.ȼú.hu 'sat', ȼi̧ 'above'

CCV: ȼˀi.nkî 'jar', ke.nta.mpaˀ 'sky'

CCCV: mphú.stˀi 'table', i.šnkî.hin 'bush'

CCCCV: nkhwé.hen 'mirror', nsa.žmphú 'muddy place'

Syllables closed by a consonant occur mainly in word final position:

VC: -ndó.ak 'walk'

CVC: šku.muˀ 'hip', ba.ˀa.ȼán 'poor'

CCVC: di.pyęt 'rich', ti.nyìn 'lightning'

CCCVC: bi.khioˀ 'knife', štˀíw 'nit'

CCCCVC: štˀweˀ 'sheep', nkˀyáˀ 'wet'

Such syllables occur in other positions only under certain limited conditions: (a) when the syllable final consonant is followed by an identical consonant which is part of a syllable of pattern CV(CC): kon.nó.a 'guava'; (b) when the syllable final consonant is a voiceless stop followed by another voiceless stop which is part of a syllable of pattern $CV(CC)$: *tik.ti* 'seven'; and (c) when the syllable final consonant is a glottal stop followed by a syllable of pattern $mV(CC)$: *bu⁷.ma.⁷a* 'amate tree'.

Syllables closed by two consonants occur only in word final position:

VCC: *-nỉ.ur⁷* 'want'

$CVCC$: *pị¢⁷* 'mushroom', *ta.nayn* 'tail'

$CCVCC$: *šu.thunt* 'five', *mbu⁷t* 'grinding stone'

$CCCVCC$: *ntyawš* 'round', *mphạ¢⁷* 'sandal'

The distribution of consonants is so complex that it is preferable to give only a few general remarks:

(1) All of them occur as single consonants preceding a vowel.

(2) As single consonants in syllable final position only *t, ¢, k, ⁷, s, š, m, n, r, w, y* occur.

(3) Two identical consonants never occur in a single syllable, excepting *⁷, m, n*. Two glottal stops in the same syllable have at least a vowel between them. Two nasals in the same syllable occur in the clusters *nhn, mhm, m⁷m, n⁷n*.

(4) The only consonant which may occur in all positions within clusters is *n*.

(5) The consonants with a broader distribution are *n, t, k, ⁷, š, h*.

(6) *w, y* never occur as first member of an initial cluster.

(7) All consonants, excepting *č, b, z, w, y*, are found as first member of an initial cluster of two consonants.

(8) In final clusters only *t, ¢ k, ⁷, š, r, w, y* occur.

(9) Voiced fricatives have the most limited distribution.

Vowels occur only singly, that is, one in each syllable, constituting its peak; they may be preceded and/or followed by consonants in the way already described. The frequency of occurrence of vowels is not equal for all; in the materials at hand vowels are found in all environments, except the syllables $(CCC)wu$, $(CCC)wụ, o, ọ, ỉ, ị$.

1.4. SENTENCE MELODY. The melody of the sentence rises gradually towards the end, and then it falls sharply; different melodies for different types of sentences are not to be found. As explained, each syllable has its own melody: when it is stressed it has high, low, or glide tone, and when unstressed it has secondary tones contrasting with that of the stressed syllable; in this way a peculiar melody for each word is formed. The ascending melody of the sentence refers then to a slight progressive rising of the tones of each syllable when compared with the same tones occurring at the beginning of the sentence; the same applies to the final falling of the melody. These intonational features delimit the sentences.

2. FORMATIVE PROCESSES AND MORPHOPHONEMICS. The formative processes of Jiliapan dialect are prefixation, suffixation, and juxtaposition. Suffixation is scarce, but juxtaposition and especially prefixation are abundant. In another section I shall deal in some detail with classes of affixes; for the present it may be observed that they serve mainly in conjugation. In what we call juxtaposition the elements do not cause or suffer regular morphophonemic changes; nevertheless, they are in certain ways fused, as shown by certain melodic and stress features.

A root never bears more than one prefix, never more than two suffixes. The structure of suffixes is very simple: they are formed by a single consonant. Most prefixes are of pattern CV-, but there are also prefixes formed by a single vowel or by a single consonant, and there is one of pattern CCV- (*mdu*-). Though some roots have the same limited patterns of affixes, most of them have more complex ones.

The combinatory processes are accompanied by many morphophonemic changes. To explain them it is convenient to recognize a set of morphophonemes related to the segmental phonemes, but at times otherwise represented. We use capital letters for these morphophonemes so indicating the part of an affix which is lost under certain circumstances which will be described later.

Prefixes containing the morphophoneme *I* palatalize the root or stem to which they are jointed but the vowel does not appear as such. It is worth noting that probably in the 18th century, when Soriano and Valle wrote their *Artes*, this (and the other morphophonemes here transcribed with capitals) had a simple segmental form, but they must already have acquired their modern form when Soustelle gathered his materials in Jiliapan. That would be the explanation of Soustelle's difficulties which led him to postulate an almost unpredictable series of "functional variations."

Prefixes containing the morphophoneme *I* are: *I-, nI-, mI-, gI-, kI-, KI-, tI-*, markers of tense-aspect and person. The palatalization they produce has several particular forms:

(a) When the root initial is *t, k, m, n, nd* followed by a vowel, the palatal semiconsonant is infixed between the consonant and the vowel:

> *I+tao⁷ > tyao⁷* 'I am cutting'
> *I+kų¢ > kyų¢* 'I am following'
> *I+mą > myą* 'I am sowing'

(b) When the root begins with *¢* or *s* followed by vowel, the initial consonant is palatalized respectively to *č* or *š*, and *y* is infixed:

> *nI+¢u > nčyu* 'you chided'
> *mI+su¢⁷ > mšyu¢⁷* 'if you had tied'
> *nI+sáhot > nšyahot* 'you dug'

(c) When there is a *w*, whether alone or in cluster, palatalization consists in changing *w* to *y*:

> *kI+hwa > kihya* 'you loosened',
> *nI+k⁷wa⁷+n > nk⁷ya⁷n* 'you (pl.) wet'

(d) When the root begins with *p* followed by a vowel, the vowel is changed to *i*:

> *I+pá⁷at > pí⁷at* 'I am helping'
> *I+puhin > pihin* 'I am covering'

(e) When for the processes just described *i* and *y* are brought together, *y* is lost:

> *nI+hwi¢⁷ > *nhyi¢⁷ > nhi¢⁷*
> 'you lifted up'
> *gI+¢in > *gičyin > gičin* 'you are piercing'
> *I+ndíis > *ndyíis > ndíis* 'I am fighting'

(f) When roots have forms different from those described they are not palatalized or are palatalized irregularly.

Prefixes *nU-, nI-, r-, nA-, mU-, mdu-*, also markers of tense aspect and person, change initial *p* followed by a vowel into *w*. When *nI-* is employed, this *w* suffers the palatalization produced by the morphophoneme *I*, as explained above. In the examples given below we find also two phenomena described in the section devoted to phonology: loss of intervocalic *⁷*, and vowel reduction. These are not morphophonemic changes, but free phonetic variations, although it is probable that this kind of variation had been fixed in certain roots and became now a regular alternation not explainable by formative processes:

> *nU+pa⁷at > nuwaat* 'I helped'
> *nI+pa⁷at > niyat* 'you helped'

As already pointed out, some prefixes and parts of others are written with capital letters to indicate the changes they produce, and to register its complete form which occurs only under certain circumstances. These circumstances are:

(a) Prefixes *I-, A-* are never found in segmental form. The changes *I-* produces are enough for postulating it. *A-* is kept to complete the prefix series, and also for purposes of comparison with other languages. The vowel morphophoneme of prefix *nA-* is kept for similar reasons.

(b) Prefix *KI-* occurs only with certain verbs, perhaps only to avoid confusing them with other verbs of simpler pattern:

> *KI+ku¢ > kikyu¢* 'you are following'

$KI+hwa > kihya$ 'you are loosening'

(c) nU-, nI-, mU-, mI-, gA-, gI-, kI occur most frequently in the shortened forms n-, n-, m-, m-, g-, g-, k-. They appear in their complete form when the root begins with a bilabial, whether or not preceded by h (probably also when preceded by $ʔ$, but there are no examples of this in the materials at hand):

$nU+sáhot > nsáhot$ 'I dug'
$nI+tut > ntyut$ 'you broke'
$mU+¢u > m¢u$ 'if I had chided'
$mI+kʔwaʔn > mkʔyaʔn$ 'if you had wet'
$gA+ku¢ > gku¢ʔ$ 'I will follow'
$nU+pihin > nuwihin$ 'I covered'
$nI+ma > nimya$ 'you rolled'
$mU+hwi̧¢ʔ > muhwi̧¢ʔ$ 'If I had lifted up'

(d) Commonly mdu- occurs in its complete form. The only case I have of the occurrence of the shortened form may be due to the haplology of $mdu+nd$:

$mdu+paʔat > mdumbaat$ 'if he had helped'
$mdu+sáhot > mdusáhot$ 'if he had dug'
$mdu+ndíis > mdíit$ 'if he had fought'

Besides the conjugational prefixes there are three prefixes of number of the nouns. Two of them (na-, re-) do not produce changes; the third, Y- apparently, behaves exactly like I-; we use a different symbol as a convenient way to distinguish the two morphemes:

$Y+(nu)dúe > dyúe$ 'capulines'
$Y+mpahan > yahan$ 'horses'
$Y+ntao > dyao$ 'eyes'
$Y+(k)ne > nye$ 'mouths'

The suffixes so far found in this language are $-m$, $-n$, $-\#$ (zero), $-k$, $-t$, $-s$. The last three do not produce or suffer changes; the first three (plural markers in conjugation) display a series of changes almost as rich as that of prefixes:

(a) Verbs ending in a vowel take $-m$, $-n$ without change of the root or the suffix:

$ntaʔo+m > ntaʔom$ 'to look for' (1st pers. pl.)
$nI+ču+n > nčyun$ 'to chide' (2nd pers. pl.)

(b) Usually $-m$, $-n$ are lost when the verb ends with voiceless stop, especially in progressive tense-aspect:

$I+paʔat+m > piʔat$ 'we are helping'
$KI+taoʔ+n > tyaoʔ$ 'you (pl.) are cutting'

(c) When the verbal root ends with n, this is fused with $-m$ or $-n$:

$I+puhin+m > pihim$ 'we are covering'
$t+pwi̧n+n > tpwi̧n$ 'you are punishing'

(d) When the root ends in s, $¢$, $¢ʔ$, the ending is palatalized to $š$, and the suffixes are not modified:

$nU+ku̧¢+m > nuku̧šm$ 'we followed'
$nI+ndíis+n > ndíišn$ 'you (pl.) fought'
$nU+hwi̧¢ʔ+m > nuhwi̧šm$ 'we lifted up'

(e) If the root has $¢$ not in cluster, it becomes glottalized when $-\#$ is added; but after the n of the infinitive $¢ > z$:

$r+ku¢+\# > rku¢ʔ$ 'they followed'
$A+¢u+\# > ¢ʔu$ 'they are chiding'
$nA+¢u+\# > nzu$ 'to chide' (3rd pers. pl.)

(f) When $-\#$ is suffixed, final s becomes d or t:

$t+ndíis+\# > tndíit$ 'they are fighting'
$nA+mdíis+\# > ndíid$ 'they fought'

In still other situations the suffix $-\#$ does not affect the endings, but the initial consonants:

(a) Initial *s* becomes affricate:

$A + sáhot + \# > \not{c}ahot$ 'they are digging'

(b) When the verbal root begins with *t* or *m*, the suffix -\# produces its aspiration:

$A + tut + \# > thut$ 'they are breaking'

$A + mą + \# > mhą$ 'they are sowing'

(c) The cluster *hw* is changed into *th* when -\# is added:

$r + hwa + \# > rtha$ 'they loosened'

$nA + hwį\not{c}^{\textrm{?}} + \# > nthį\not{c}^{\textrm{?}}$ 'if they had lifted up'

(d) Initial *p* followed by vowel becomes *mb* when -\# is suffixed, but *p* in cluster has no change:

$r + pa^{\textrm{?}}at + \# > rmba^{\textrm{?}}at$ 'they helped'

$A + pwįhi + \# > pwįhi$ 'they are entreating'

It must be explained that the morphophonemic changes just described are not absolutely regular, that certain verbs with apparently the same patterns show changes different from those here explained; e.g., the verb *tu^{?}u*, 'to sow', does not take the infix *y* we would expect, but changes the vowel, as do verbs beginning with *pV*: *nI+tu^{?}u > nti^{?}u*. Moreover, still other verbs have no changes or have particular changes so special that they can not be systematized. These variant treatments are selective, i.e., they are always the same for certain roots.

Many other words, mostly nouns, show another kind of non-systematizable variations. Although these sometimes seem to respond to the phonetic environment, or depend on the grammatical function, they in part involve free alternation unrelated to special conditions. These changes make the phonemic analysis very difficult, because they sometimes entail the neutralization of phonemic oppositions. This phenomenon was

340

already present in the 18th century, as is clearly noted by Valle. Some examples are given below:

mǫhǫ / bǫhǫ / mbǫhǫ 'good'
byarma^{?}a / mbyarma^{?}a 'coyote'
bisa / bsa / msa / sa 'water'
kęzę / gęzę 'pig'
kumpu / kmpu / gmpu 'black'
kudù / kdù / gdù 'stone'
ksi / si 'ice'
gyų / yių 'firewood'
n¢^{?}i / ¢^{?}i 'pot'
n¢i^{?} / ¢i^{?} 'tooth'
čye / šye 2nd person possessive
či^{?} / ši^{?} / ži^{?} 'teeth'
škandoa / škindoa 'white'

Juxtaposition in Pame consists in the union of two words, forming a new unit with a new sense. This union does not always agree with normal syntax; occasionally there may be phonetic changes similar to those found in syntactic constructions, but they are not obligatory, i.e., they may or may not occur in the same expression uttered at different times. Nevertheless, juxtaposed compounds tend to fix one of the free variants and to reduce the pause between the juxtaposed words, along with frequent loss of the stress of one of them; for these reasons juxtaposed compounds are transcribed in a single word:

(a) noun + verb
kuduksì 'hail' < *kudù* 'stone' and *ksi* 'ice'
mahašk^{?}íš 'cigarette' < *máha* 'tobacco', and *šk^{?}íš* 'paper'

(b) noun + verb
šk^{?}išnú^{?}u 'read' < *šk^{?}íš* 'paper', and *nú^{?}u* 'hear'

(c) noun + adjective
bikhyomądą 'a kind of machete' < *bikhyo* 'knife', and *mądą* 'big'
msamądą 'river' < *msa* 'water', and *mądą* 'big'

(d) adjective + adjective
n¢^{?}ę^{?}ši^{?}i 'narrow' < *n¢^{?}ę^{?}* 'small', and *niši^{?}i* 'broad'

3. CLASSES OF ELEMENTS. Although the division of classes is primarily based on structural traits, I have preferred to call them "classes of elements" instead of "structural classes" because semantic and functional criteria are also taken into account. These criteria have the advantage of avoiding the need for a different classification based on syntactic categories, when we speak of constructions:

Classes of Elements

I. Roots
  A. Independent non-inflective
    1. Interrogatives
    2. Locatives
    3. Temporals
    4. Negative
  B. Satellite non-inflective
    a. Adverbials
      5. Pronouns
      6. Verb auxiliaries
    b. Adnominals
      7. Adjectives
      8. Quantitatives
      9. Numerals
      10. Demonstratives
    c. Endoclitics
      11. Conjunctions
  C. Inflective
    a. Pluralizable
      12. Nouns
      13. Possessives
    b. Temporalizable
      14. Verbs
II. Affixes
  A. Prefixes
    a. Of nouns
      15. Markers of number
    b. Of verbs
      16. Markers of tense-aspect and person
      17. Nominalizers
  B. Suffixes
    a. Of nouns
      18. Markers of number
    b. Of verbs
      19. Markers of plural
      20. Markers of object

Independent non-inflective roots may form sentences by themselves or serve as one of the segments of a paratactic construction (see §4.5). The four classes of these roots are interrogatives, locatives, temporals, and negative.

3.1. INTERROGATIVES (class 1). It is necessary to join in a single class all interrogatives (including those which express location or time), because they are always initial in the clause.

či	'what?'	*nʔni*	'what?'
čibi	'where?'	*nȼa*	'who?'
čiru	'how?'	*nȼaʔnu*	'who?'
čiti	'when?'	*kįʔę*	'when?'
šunkwa	'how many?'		

3.2. LOCATIVES (class 2). We include here expressions of location other than interrogative locatives:

kúwa	'here'		
kubú	'there'		
wiʔi/wiʔ/wi	'there (away)'		
šnu	'near'	*kumpuʔ*	'below'
bąhą	'far'	*nihiʔ*	'under'
ȼį	'above'	*kaʔa*	'upon'

3.3. TEMPORALS (class 3). This class includes expressions of time other than the verb auxiliaries and the interrogatives:

mwę	'already'
štaʔ	'yesterday'
čegmpa	'the day before yesterday'
mpįʔa	'tomorrow'
če	'today'
turumpa	'the day after tomorrow'
bahansą	'last night'
wahanidyet	'at noon'

3.4. NEGATIVE (class 4). This class consists of only one particle, used alone to express negation, or in a clause to negate it:

mwį 'no, not'

Satellite non-inflective roots are so called because they always enter into syntactic constructions as verb satellites (adverbials) or as noun satellites (adnominals). They differ from inflective roots in not having inflexion:

3.5. PRONOUNS (class 5). Usually they are employed as the subject of a sentence when the corresponding noun is not used in the expression; less frequently they are used as verb objects. There are only three (differentiating person but not number):

kak / ka 'I, we'
hukʔ / huk / hu 'you' (singular or plural)
kunu / kuru 'he, she, it, they'

341

The forms ending in nasal (for first, second and third persons plural), and the form for third person singular feminine (*kunea*), mentioned by Soriano and Valle, do not occur now. It seems to me that *kunea* never existed, and that the plural forms, if they existed, have now disappeared; it is possible that these authors were attempting to provide equivalents for the Spanish pronouns.

3.6. VERB AUXILIARIES (class 6). These are only two invariable particles used to form the future tense-aspect of verbal inflexion:

ma	marker of simple future
ma nuwa	marker of immediate future

3.7. ADJECTIVES (class 7). These are noun modifiers, and for this they are always syntactically related to nouns, although they may be morphologically unrelated:

mǫhǫ	'good'	*nȼʔę̌ʔ*	'small'
niši ʔi	'broad'	*štinkąw*	'new'
kų ʔúa	'red'	*mądą̌*	'big'

3.8. QUANTITATIVES (class 8). Quantitatives are noun or adjective modifiers, and as such they are always bound to the elements they modify. I have so far found no more than two quantitatives:

bidí	'much, many, very'
bíʔe	'few, a few'

3.9. NUMERALS (class 9). In normal constructions they are always related to nouns, forming plurals of determinate number. They occur isolated only in the process of counting. Some numerals are:

ʔna/nada	'one'
tíi	'two'
hníų̌ʔ	'three'
pyę̌	'four'
šuthų̌nt	'five'
tíkyent	'six'
tíktí	'seven'
tignyíu	'eight'
nau̯hwę̌	'nine'
sthú̌	'ten'
sthutná̌	'eleven'
sthuti	'twelve'

sthutešthų̌nt	'fifteen'
ʔnade	'twenty'
tide	'forty'
ʔnante ʔe	'one hundred'

3.10. DEMONSTRATIVES (class 10). These always precede a noun. I have found only three:

kení 'this'

kunú 'that' (homophonous with the third person pronoun)

če 'this, present' used only in temporal constructions like 'this year', 'this month' (homophonous with the temporal 'today')

3.11. CONJUNCTIONS (class 11). They have a very restricted use. Their function is to co-ordinate two expressions or two nouns in an expression; the first use is very infrequent, because paratactic constructions are preferred; co-ordination of nouns is more frequent. Conjunctions are considered endoclitics because, lacking semantic value, they are imbedded in endocentric constructions. There are only two conjunctions, and both have the same function:

ti / te 'and'   *ra* 'and'

Inflective roots have the distinctive mark of inflexion. Pluralizable ones (nouns and possessives) have a much more limited inflexion than temporalizables (verbs).

3.12. NOUNS (class 12). Nouns have the obligatory category of number. Number is singular, plural, or dual, and is not always overtly marked. The affixes of nouns pertain to classes 13 and 18 (prefix and suffix markers of number); their syntax will be described in §4.2.

Besides single-root and juxtaposed nouns (as those at the end of §2), there are also nouns formed of a verbal base plus a nominalizing prefix of class 17:

bisa	'water'	*ihyaw*	'earth'
škidi	'cicada'	*nčúą̌ȼ*	'bat'
kumuy	'squirrel'	*kudù̌*	'stone'

mink ʔya ʔ 'a wet thing' < *m*-nominalizer, *nk ʔya ʔ* variant form of the verb *nk ʔwa ʔ*

3.13. POSSESSIVES (class 13). Possessives are always placed immediately before a noun which is the thing possessed. In free translation possessives could be translated as 'my' (and 'our'), 'your' (sing. and pl.). and 'his/her' (and 'their'), but they are better translated, in singular, as 'it is mine' (and 'it is ours') 'it is yours' (sing. and pl.), and 'it is his/it is hers' (and 'it is theirs'). When the things possessed are plural, whether marked or not, the possessive is pluralized by means of the prefix *Y-*, also used as noun pluralizer. Class 11 is formed only by the following elements:

mpą? 'it is mine, it is ours'
čą? 'it is yours' (sing. and pl.)
mą 'it is his, it is hers, it is theirs'
yią(?) 'they are mine, they are ours'
čyą? 'they are yours' (sg. and pl.)
myą 'they are his, they are hers, they are theirs'

3.14. VERBS (class 14). Verbs have the richest inflexion of this language, with categories of tense-aspect and person (marked by prefixes of class 16), and number (marked by suffixes of class 19). Verbs are also bases for nouns formed by prefixing an element of class 17. They can take suffixes of class 20 (object markers), but these are not obligatory.

Verbal roots fall into two subclasses, according to their inherent voice; the voice determines which prefixes of class 16 should be employed. The two subclasses are: transitives—those roots which admit an object, and intransitives—those roots which exclude the object.

Several transitives can get the intransitive voice by taking the prefixes of intransitive. A secondary voice, that of reflexive, is formed by using a special set of prefixes with inherently transitive roots. Some verb roots are:

-ndoa	'to walk'	*-tų?ų*	'to sow'
-paha	'to hit'	*-suȼ*	'to tie'
-ȼe?et	'to split'	*-igin*	'to weep'
-aw	'to eat'	*-sáhot*	'to dig'
	-tišin	'to take a bath'	

3.15. PREFIXES OF NUMBER OF NOUNS (class 15). I have referred, when speaking of class 12, to the number inflexion of nouns. Prefixes of class 15 are markers (along with suffixes of class 18) of this category. Class 15 is constituted by three elements:

na- marker of singular.
Y- marker of plural used most frequently.
re- marker of plural used with a few roots, it may be a recent loan from Otomi.

3.16. PREFIXES OF TENSE-ASPECT AND PERSON (class 16). I shall explain the inflective categories of verbs in §4.1; here I give an almost complete list of tense-aspect and person prefix markers, excluding those of future because they are nearly out of use. The list contains forms I gathered in the field, as well as forms reconstructed according to data provided by Valle; reconstructed forms are marked by an asterisk, as is customary, and it is not possible to guarantee that they actually exist in the language as it is remembered by the few present-day speakers. I have not included Valle's *third conjugation* prefixes because, according to data he himself provides, it seems to have been an optative set of stylistic prefixes used instead of the usual sets:

(a) prefixes of transitive voice verbs:

	progressive	perfective	infinitive	hypothetic	imperative
1st	*I-/ t-*	*nU-*	*nU-*	*mU-*	
2nd	*KI-/ t-*	*nI-*	*nA-*	*mI-*	*k-...-t/I-...-t/s-...-t*
3rd	*A-/ t-*	*r-*	*nA-*	*mdu-*	

(b) prefixes of intransitive voice verbs:

	progressive	perfective	infinitive	hypothetic	imperative
1st	*I-*	**tA-*	**tA-*	**tA-*	
2nd	*gI-*	**kI-*	**kI-*	**kI-*	*k-...-t/I-...-t/s-...-t*
3rd	*U-*	**gU-*	**nA-*	**mI-*	

(c) prefixes of reflexive voice:

	progressive	perfective	infinitive	imperative
1st	**tI-*	**nI-*	**mI-*	**I-...-t*
2nd	**tI-*	**nI-*	**mI-*	
3rd	**tI-*	**nI-*	**mI-*	

343

The alternate sets of markers for the progressive of transitives and for the three forms of imperative, not differentiated for voice, are used selectively, i.e., one series inflects certain roots, and the other inflects other roots.

3.17. Nominalizers (class 17). There are nouns formed by adding prefixes of class 17 to the transitive voice roots. These prefixes are: *k-* agentive, *s-* instrumental, *m*(I)- resultative:

> *k-sáhot* 'digger, a person who digs'.
> *k-dao*ʔ 'cutter, a person who cuts'.
> *s-kíbi* 'the instrument that serves for unloading'
> *s-tao*ʔ 'the instrument that serves for cutting'
> *m-¢oa* 'something split'
> *m-tao*ʔ 'something cut'

3.18. Suffix markers of plural of nouns (class 18). Besides prefixes of class 15 (markers of number) there is a suffix of plural used selectively with words of class 12 formed on a verb-root base: it is the suffix *-t*. Almost unused, and entirely optional is suffix *-s*, marker of dual:

kuhú 'sorcerer'   *kuhút* 'sorcerers'
m¢oa 'something split'   *m¢oat* 'some things that have been split'

3.19. Suffix markers of plural of verbs (class 19). Number inflexion of verbs has three suffix markers of plural (singular being unmarked) *-m* is used with first person, *-n* is used with second person, and *-#* (zero) is used with third person. In §2 I referred to the morphophonemic changes produced by these suffixes:

> *ndíwa+m > ndíwam* 'we walk'
> *ndíwa+n > ndiwan* 'you walk'
> *¢u+# > ¢*ʔ*u* 'they are chiding'
> *píhin+m > píhim* 'we are covering'
> *čyu+n > čyun* 'you (pl.) are chiding'
> *hwa+# > tha* 'they are loosening'

3.20. Markers of verb object (class 20). The two elements of this class indicate the grammatical person which is the object of the verb to which they are suffixed: *-k* is used for first and second person; *-p* is used for third person, but seldom, and, perhaps, optionally:

> *rwáha-k*   'he hit me',
> *nuwáha-k*   'I hit you',
> *rwáha-p*   'he hit him'

4. Construction. In Jiliapan Pame there are syntactic and paratactic constructions. Syntactic constructions are those in which there is grammatical subordination or dependence among the component elements; paratactic constructions are those in which two or more independent expressions are set side by side without formal indication of their connection. Entities taking part in paratactic constructions may be one-element clauses or syntactic clauses, so we have three types of clauses: (a) one-element clauses, depending on the total situational context in which they are uttered, being mainly answers to questions; (b) syntactic clauses, the normal basic expressions (discussed in §4.4); and (c) paratactic clauses, the product of combining two or more clauses of types (a) and (b).

One-element sentences consist of a single word of the group of independent roots, i.e., an interrogative, locative, temporal, or negative.

It is not normal to make a sentence with a noun or verb alone, even in answer to a question. Instead these forms are combined with at least one other even if it involves repeating the verb of the question.

Syntactic clauses basically consist of a verb (with its bound person and tense-aspect marker) and an independent subject, and sometimes also an independent object. The subject and object may in turn be complex, as will be explained later.

Paratactic sentences unite simple elements and syntactic formations by placing them one behind the other, without establishing a subordination relationship, and seldom a co-ordination relationship.

In the following descriptions I shall not make special reference to simple expressions because, as they consist of a single word of classes 1, 2, 3, or 4, they present no difficulties.

4.1. VERB SYNTAX. The verb has inflection for tense-aspect, for person, and for number. Persons are first, second and third; numbers are singular and plural (and, occasionally, dual); tense-aspects are progressive, perfective, future, hypothetic and imperative, with the following values:

Progressive. This tense indicates continuing action, which is assumed to refer to present time if there is no contrary indication. However, used with an appropriate temporal, it refers to past time:

    ka tyao^ʔ 'I am cutting, I cut'
    šta^ʔ ka tyao^ʔ 'I was cutting yesterday, I cut yesterday'

Perfective. This tense indicates concluded action. In the absence of specific indication past tense is implied, but with the appropriate temporal it can also refer to the future:

    ka ntut 'I broke [it]'
    turumpa ka ntut 'I will have broken [it] the day after tomorrow'

Hypothetic. It can be translated by 'if I had...', 'if you had...', 'if he had...', in sentences like 'if you had seen'.

Future and Imperative. These have approximately the same values as the English future and imperative.

Tense-aspects (excepting future) and persons are marked by prefixes of class 16 which I have already listed. The prefix markers of future mentioned by Valle have disappeared, and now this tense is expressed by auxiliaries (class 6) placed before a verb bearing the infinitive prefix. Possible confusions between verbal forms are avoided by the regular employment of pronouns:

    ka šyáhot 'I am digging, I dig'
    huk šyáhot 'you are digging'
    kunu sáhot 'he is digging'
    ka nsáhot 'I dug'

    huk nišyáhot 'you dug'
    kunu rsáhot 'he dug'
    ka msáhot 'if I had dug'
    hu mšyáhot 'if you had dug'
    kunu mdusáhot 'if he had dug'
    ka ma nsáhot 'I am going to dig, I will dig'
    hu ma nsáhot 'you are going to dig'
    kunu ma nsáhot 'he is going to dig'

    ksáhot 'dig!' (imperative)

The singular forms of verbs have no special markers. Forms in the plural have suffixes of class 19; although very infrequent, when the subject is dual, the forms may optionally have the suffix of dual (-*s*) instead of the corresponding suffix of plural. In other words, verbs in the singular bear only a prefix of class 16, and in plural bear one prefix and one suffix. When an object suffix (class 20) is employed with verbs in plural, it is placed between the root and the suffix of number:

    t-ta^ʔo 'I am seeking'
    n-tya^ʔo-n 'you (pl.) sought'
    nu-waha-k 'I hit (past tense) you'
    nu-waha-k-m 'we hit (past tense) you'

4.2. NOUN SYNTAX. The noun has inflexion for number as an obligatory but not always overt category. Usually singular is unmarked (the old prefix *n*-, marker of singular, has fused with the root and is no longer a living prefix), but when it is necessary to emphasize the singular character of a noun, this is done by placing the numeral *nada* 'one' before the noun, or by means of the bound proclitic *na*-. Dual is almost unused, but, when found, it is marked by the suffix -*s*. Plural may be expressed by special affixes (classes 15 and 18) or by using numerals (class 9), or quantitatives (class 8):

Singular	Marked Singular	Plural
	use of affixes:	
šthe 'nopal'	*na-šthe*	*re-šthe*
n-ȼi^ʔ 'tooth'	*na-nȼi^ʔ*	*či^ʔ* (Y+ȼi^ʔ)
n-t^ʔu 'louse'	*na-nt^ʔu*	*tyu^ʔ*
kuhú 'sorcerer'	*nada kuhú*	*kuhut*

345

use of numerals:

n-tao 'eye'	*nada ntao*	*tii dyao*
m-páhan 'horse'	*nada mpáhan*	*hniu yáhan*

use of quantitatives

n-ku̧ 'stick'	*nada nku̧*	*bidi gyu̧*
kudù 'stone'	*nada kudù*	*kuru kudù*

4.3. COMPLEX SUBJECTS AND OBJECTS. In general, it may be said that subjects and objects have the same structure, but with certain limitations in use. Both are formed by a noun, a pronoun, or by several nouns:

ka čyú 'I chide'

šuwa sáhot 'John digs'

šuwa ra mle ma t-tehes 'John and Mary will marry'

Each noun can serve as a base for more elaborate constructions. When there is more than one noun, they are co-ordinated by conjunctions. The elaboration of noun bases consists in using their own modifiers: adjectives, numerals, quantitatives and demonstratives. In their turn, adjectives can be elaborated by the use of quantitatives.

Numerals, quantitatives, and demonstratives are placed before the noun; numerals and quantitatives are mutually exclusive. Demonstratives are placed before other modifiers when they appear together in a complex subject. The adjective (and its modifier, when it has one) usually follows the noun, especially in more complex constructions, but it may also be placed before the noun. The modifier of an adjective precedes it. Some examples follow:

kudù 'stone'

pyȩ kudù 'four stones'

kudù škandóa 'white stone' (also: *škandóa kudù*)

bidi kudù 'many stones'

bidi kudù škandóa 'many white stones'

kudù bidi škandóa 'very white stone'

pyȩ kudù škandóa 'four white stones'

kunu kudù 'that stone'

Although basically the object may have

the same elaborations, objects of complex formation are not frequent.

4.4. SYNTACTIC CLAUSE. The syntactic clause has always two parts, each of which may consist of one or two entities (shown in the formula by $\sum_2^1 + \sum_2^1$).

The first part may contain an introductive (I), a verb auxiliary (X), or both. In constructions with only one entity in the first part the introductive is found more frequently than the auxiliary; in constructions with two entities the obligatory order is *introductive* first, *auxiliary* second (in the formula this is represented by [I.X]).

The second part may contain a verb (V), a complement (C), or both. In constructions with only one entity in the second part, the verb is found more frequently than the complement. In constructions with two entities there is no fixed order, but usually the verb precedes the complement (shown in the formula by [V, C]).

Then, the basic formula for syntactic clause in Jiliapan Pame is:

$$\sum_2^1 [I.X] + \sum_2^1 [V, C]$$

The introductive may be an interrogative (i) of class 1, or a simple or complex subject (s) of the forms already described. Clauses with an interrogative word as introductive are, of course, questions. The verb auxiliary is a member of class 6.

The verb is of class 14. The complement may have the same components as the subject, but as already indicated, it is usually simpler. In constructions with a complement and a verb (which must be transitive) the complement functions as object (o) of the verb. In constructions with complement only it is a predicate (p) modifier of the subject, or, in other words an equational expression is formed:

$I_s + V + C_o$ *ka gtao? mugu* 'I am cutting the meat'

$I_i + V + C_o$ *čton du̧hȩ?t mpu̧hi̧* 'how do you weave the hat?'

$X + V + C_o$ *ma nuwa nsuȼ gyu̧* 'I am going to cut firewood'

$I_i + X + V$ *kị?ę́ ma kikye* 'when will you come back?'

$I_s + C_p$ *mbyarma?a ti nk?a?oȼ bidi mothi* 'coyote and fox are very bad'

$I_s + C_o + V$ *ka nȼ?i kyo?a* 'I make pots'

4.5. PARATACTIC CONSTRUCTIONS. In an effort to interpret accurately the syntactic structure of Pame, we note which components are complete in themselves and do not acquire additional meaning by inclusion in a larger complex, as against those which cannot be used alone or which take on some implicit additional notion in context. A construction entirely made up of the first kind of form is paratactic; other types are syntactic.

Since in a few details Pame parallels Spanish, we may illustrate with a Spanish example like *yo trabajo*, freely translated as 'I work' but more strictly as 'I, I-work'. That is, *trabajo* includes the subject (marked by the suffix *-o*) and is complete in itself. Hence, the addition of *yo*, also self-sufficient, is paratactic. In contrast, 'I work' in English is syntactic because one of the parts of the construction, 'work', is incomplete by itself. Incidentally it may be observed that, generally speaking, paratactic formations more readily admit variations in order than do syntactic ones; for example, *trabajo yo* is perfectly correct in Spanish. There are, of course, paratactic formations in English, as 'I work now' in which the segments 'I work' and 'now' are related only paratactically. Syntactic character may also be given by the use of relational particles, such as the prepositions in English.

Paratactic sentences in Jiliapan Pame result from combining in parataxis two or more expressions, at least one of which is a syntactic clause. The paratactic nature of these constructions is seen in the lack of specific relational elements and in the fact that each component is complete in itself. Members of classes 1, 2, 3, and 4 (interrogatives, locatives, temporals, and the nega-tive), entering into a paratactic construction may be placed either before or after the syntactic clause, and have no fixed order among themselves:

šta thyų ntu?u 'I sowed corn yesterday' (literally: 'yesterday I-sowed corn'

ka thyų ntu?u šta 'I sowed corn yesterday (I I-sowed corn yesterday)'

Note that the independent subject may disappear in paratactic constructions; the rule is that, if some other element precedes the verb, it is normal to omit the independent subject. Perhaps as an extension of this principle, when an English sentence with several co-ordinate verbs is translated into Pame, the subject is kept in the first expression, but lost in the others:

šuwa rwahak te ginti rnaha 'John hit me and went away running (John he-hit-me and he-left he-ran)'

If an English sentence with several co-ordinate subjects is translated, the Pame language favors the use of a paratactic sentence with the verb repeated in each clause, rather than use a co-ordinate subject:

wi kenèn mphagyų šthe naw, stit?iȼ rešthe naw 'there in the town the ox and the donkey are eating the nopals (there (in)-town ox nopal he-is-eating, donkey nopals he-is-eating)'

In the following small text (given as an example of longer utterances) slant lines separate the major divisions. A single stroke marks the division between clauses, a pair of strokes mark the division between sentences:

ma nuwa unahao nuwehe / ma nuwa nk?uš nuwehe // šndabi nuwehe // ma ntuhin nk?uš // mwę / unahao nk?wa?n // ma nȼ?i nkú?a // ma nuwa unahao nk?wa?n // ma nme mọhọ una-hao // ma nȼ?i nkú?a.

Literal translation:

'[I] will go-now earth seek / will go-now

347

"guija" seek / finished seek / will grind "guija" /now // earth [I will] wet // will pot make // will go-now earth wet // will now earth good // will pot make'.

Free translation:

I am going to seek earth and "guija" (a mineral pottery temper). I have brought the things I went to gather. I will grind the "guija," and in this moment I am going to wet the earth. The earth is ready now, and I will make my pot.

REFERENCES

Castro, 1955
Gibson, L. F., 1956
Hockett, 1955
Manrique, 1958, 1960
Orozco y Berra, 1864
Pimentel, 1904

Schuller, 1925b
Soriano, 1776
Soustelle, 1937
Swadesh, 1959b, 1960a, 1960b
Valle, n.d.
Viñaza, 1892

7H. Huamelultec Chontal

VIOLA WATERHOUSE

0. Introduction
1. Phonemes
1.0. Inventory of phonemes
1.1. Phoneme-set descriptions
1.2.1. Distribution in syllables
1.2.2. CV sequences
1.2.3. Consonant clusters
2. Morphophonemics
3. Morphology
3.0. Word-classes
3.1. Verbs
3.1.1. Verb bases
3.1.2. Verb margins
3.2. Nouns
3.2.1. Noun stems
3.2.2. Noun margins
3.3. Pronouns
3.4. Particles
4. Syntax
4.0. Types of syntactic units
4.1. Phrase types
4.2. Clause types
4.2.1. Predicative clauses
4.2.2. Exclamatory clauses
4.2.3. Negative clauses
4.2.4. Interrogative clauses
4.2.5. Subordinate clauses
4.3. Sentence types
4.3.1. Independent sentences
    Affirmative (with *statement intonation*)
    Interrogative (with *non-affirmative intonation*)
    Negative
      General (with *statement intonation*)
      Intensive (with *non-affirmative intonation*)
      Question (with *interrogative intonation*)
    Command (with *statement intonation*)
4.3.2. Dependent sentences
4.4. Discourse types

0. INTRODUCTION. Chontal de Oaxaca is a Hokan language spoken by 9000 Indians in southern Oaxaca, Mexico. The name Tequistlatec (given to avoid confusion with the Mayan Chontal de Tabasco) properly applies to the dialect formerly spoken in the town of Tequisistlan and still surviving in the central core of mountain villages two days' trail from Tequisistlan. The other major dialect (here called Huamelultec) is spoken in the villages of Astata and Huamelula in the coastal plain south of the Tequistlatec area, a day and a half by trail from the Pacific seaport of Salina Cruz.

Tequistlatec (T) has been described by Belmar (1900) and by de Angulo and Freeland (1925), and is now being investigated further by Paul and Shirley Turner of the Summer Institute of Linguistics; Huamelultec (H) has been described only by Waterhouse (Waterhouse, 1949a,b, 1961, 1962), and a colleague (Waterhouse and Morrison, 1950). The present description is only of Huamelultec, with a brief mention of major dialect differences.

Huamelultec shows a high degree of acculturation and bilingualism with, however, the Indian language as the language of choice and prestige in the adult community (Waterhouse, 1949a), and the structure of the Spanish spoken showing a high degree of Chontal influence (see Waterhouse, 1961). In contrast, Tequistlatec-speakers retain a high degree of monolingualism except in the villages closest to the Oaxaca-Isthmus highway.

Major dialect differences are in the phonemics and the grammar; there are many cognate vocabulary items. Some common expressions are completely different, however, making communication between speakers of the two dialects difficult. Common cognates are illustrated in the sentences for 'the child went to sleep': H, *šmánapa law'á*; T, *tišmáynaba law'á*;[1] major differences in the expressions for 'where are you going?': H, *xáape má ʔáypa*; T, *pégof céeya*.

Differences in phonemics and grammar may be summed up by saying that Huamelultec has more phonemic contrasts than Tequistlatec; Tequistlatec has more grammatical contrasts than Huamelultec.

Phonemic differences are voiced-voiceless stop contrast in H, free variation between them in T; alveopalatals *tʸ*, *lʸ*, *ɬʸ* in H, not in T (though both have *š*, *č*, and *ñ*); preglottalized voiced continuants in contrast with *ʔC* in H, not in T; phonemic *ŋ* in T, not in H.

Morphological differences are seen in both noun and verb classification. Both dialects distinguish between consonant-initial (*C*) and vowel-initial (*V*) nouns; in H, however, *C* nouns occur with definitive *el-*; *V* nouns with *l-*; whereas in T, *C* nouns are divided into those which occur with definitive *kal-* and those with *al-*, *V* nouns into those with *l-* and those with *ɬ-*. In H, verbs have no prefixes except first person marker *el-*; in T, verbs are divided into four classes, each of which has distinct person prefix sets for affirmative and negative, completive and incompletive. The H prefix has no cognates in T; the T Class I affirmative completive set is cognate with the H relational set of noun prefixes.[2]

The plan of this article is in the traditional order of phonemics, morphophonemics, morphology, and syntax. For a different order, see the full grammar (Waterhouse, 1962). The analysis of both the morphology and the syntax is based on Pike's tagmemic theory (K. L. Pike, 1954, 1955, 1958, 1960); the term tagmeme, however, and tagmemic formulas have been omitted. Rather, reference has been made to slot and function, which are tagmemic slot and function. For a full tagmemic presentation the reader is again referred to the complete grammar.

1.0. INVENTORY OF PHONEMES. Huamelultec segmental phonemes include 35 consonants and 5 vowels; suprasegmental phonemes are length and stress.

Consonant phonemes are shown on Table 1, arranged to show maximum contrasts within the consonant system. Major contrasts are between voiceless and voiced articulation on the vertical axis, and between central and lateral on the horizontal axis. Both voiceless and voiced central consonants show three-way vertical contrast between glottalic, continuant and obstruent types of articulation, and four-way horizontal contrast between labial, alveolar, alveopalatal, and velar points of articulation. Glottal stop contrasts with all the consonants but fits distributionally with voiceless glottalic rather than with voiceless obstruent.[3] Lateral consonants show two-way contrast between glottalic and continuant type of articulation in both voiceless and voiced categories, and be-

---

[1] Data for Tequistlatec examples are phonetic, taken from my field notes. For the structural information I am indebted to Shirley Turner.

[2] T has a similar noun set as well, thus showing more overlap between the noun and verb classes than there is in H.

[3] Obstruent is defined for this language as any consonant which has stop, affricate or flap allophones in at least some environments. This definition is set up explicitly to allow us to handle voiceless spirants as a separate set from voiceless stops, since they form separate distributional sets.

TABLE 1

Voiceless							Central			Lateral	
1. Glottalic	f'			c'			č'	k'	ʔ	l'	
2. Continuant	f			s			š	x		l	lʸ
3. Obstruent	p	t		c	tʸ		č	k			
Voiced											
4. Glottalic	m'	n'			ñ'			w'		l'	
5. Continuant	m	n	ř		ñ	y		w		l	lʸ
6. Obstruent	b	d	r					g			

tween alveolar and alveopalatal points of articulation. Distributionally, central and lateral consonants combine into horizontal sets numbered 1–6 on Table 1.

Articulation is fortis for Set 4 (voiced glottalic), lenis for other sets. Alveopalatals *tʸ, lʸ, ñ', ñ, lʸ* are made with tongue blade, have no appreciable offglide. They contrast both with alveolars and with clusters with *y*, although in clusters the quality of the consonant before the *y* is alveopalatal: *tépa yáʔ* 'I bit it', *tʸépa* 'he bit it', *tʸyépa* 'fell'; *lóʔpa yá* 'I moved it', *lʸóʔpa* 'he moved it', *miilʸá* 'tell him', *pilʸyá* 'might kill'; *n'ápa yá* 'I bought it', *ñ'ápa* 'he bought it', *peñ'úupa* 'brought', *ʔoyñ'yópa* 'put'; *nápa yá* 'I hit', *ñápa* 'he hit', *fañú* 'seed corn', *lansañyú* 'the people'; *lóopa yá* 'I played', *lʸóopa* 'he played', *lʸyóopa* 'took'.

1.1. PHONEME-SET DESCRIPTIONS. Set 1, voiceless glottalic, includes four glottalized affricates: *f', c', č', lʸ'*, one glottalized stop *k'*, and glottal stop *ʔ*. *f'ónlexmáʔ* 'ladder', *c'óos* 'cold', *č'óospa* 'it got cold', *lʸ'íguy* 'he cleans', *k'éduy* 'he carries water,' *ʔawá* 'squash'.

Set 2, voiceless continuant, consists of spirants *f, s, š*, which have no marked allophones, *x* which varies freely from velar [x] to [h], [axáʔ] or [aháʔ] 'water,' and laterals *l* and *lʸ* which are almost frictionless between vowels (*koláʔ* 'say it', *miilʸá* 'tell him'), lightly fricative elsewhere (*imól* 'sheep', *askúlʸ* 'tortilla'). *fápa* 'he sowed', *símpa yá* 'I saw', *šimpa* 'he saw', *xápa* 'it melted,' *lóʔpa yá* 'I moved it', *lʸóʔpa*

'he moved it'. Voiceless laterals contrast with clusters of *x* plus lateral in *waláʔ* 'take it', *paxláʔ* 'wash it'; *kulʸáʔ* 'give it', *kuxlʸáʔ* 'sell it'.

Set 3, voiceless obstruent, includes stops *p, t, tʸ, k*, and affricates *c, č*. *pánáʔ* 'river', *tánduy yáʔ* 'I'm pounding', *tʸánduy* 'he's pounding', *kánaʔ* 'when', *céepa yáʔ* 'I went', *čéepa* 'he went'.

Set 4, voiced glottalic includes preglottalized nasals *m', n', ñ'*, velar vocoid *w'*, and lateral *l'*. These contrast with phonemic clusters of glottal stop plus *m, n, ñ, w*, and *l*: *pém'a* 'carry', *péʔma* 'believe'; *kán'eláʔ* 'leave it', *máʔneláʔ* 'fish it'; *sáñ'í* 'just so,' *xáʔñí* 'no'; *lʸiw'á* 'his child', *xučíʔwá* 'he is lying to you'; *xáal'e* 'that which', *náʔléʔ* 'tell it (pl.)'.

Set 5, voiced continuant, includes nasals *m, n, ñ*, trill *ř*, vocoids *y, w*, laterals *l, lʸ*. *n* has a velar allophone in word final and before velars, is alveolar elsewhere (*čin* 'quiet', *panxáa* 'slowly', *náana* 'mother'). *w* is velar rather than labial, has no appreciable lip rounding. *mápa* 'died,' *náfpa yáʔ* 'I shook it', *ñáfpa* 'he shook it', *řénka* 'lame', *yáguy* 'he is making noise', *wáduy* 'he is carrying it', *láxlá* 'rinse it off', *lʸáxpa* 'he rinsed it off'.

Set 6, voiced obstruent, includes flap *r*, and *b, d, g*, which have stop allophones after nasals, fricative elsewhere. *náanará* 'wasp'; *mbamáʔ* 'ten', *bíida* 'grandmother'; *kánduy* 'he is leaving it', *odóy* 'straight'; *pánguy* 'he is sitting', *páguy* 'she is washing it'.

Vowels are of the common 2+2+1 pattern: *i, e, a, o, u. e* is mid front open; *a* has a raised allophone before *k'*; other vowels have no marked allophones and the symbols are used with their traditional phonetic values. *ípa* 'flower', *épa* 'sugar cane', *awáʔ* 'wind', *ñáylᵛoxmák'* 'daily', *odóy* 'straight', *uw'é* 'salt'.

Prosodic phonemes are length and stress. Each may occur independently on any vowel and in any position; they may also occur together.

Length does not alter the quality of the vowel with which it occurs; long vowels are only slightly longer than short vowels. The phonemic status of length is well-attested: *eltaxí* 'the crab', *awixtí* 'sleepiness'; *lᵛégopa* 'he was hungry', *lᵛéegopa* 'he took him'; *páguy* 'she is washing it', *páaguy* 'it is dying down'; *tok'ém'a* 'raise', *took'ém'a* 'give a bite'; *tᵛúpa* 'he nursed', *tᵛúupa* 'soft-fibered basket'.

Stress may occur on adjacent syllables: *pánáʔ* 'river', on alternate syllables: *pácedúy* 'he is doing it', or on only one syllable: *pulᵛáypa* 'carried in arms'. Since the multiple stress pattern was discovered at a late stage of field work, not all possible patterns have been checked as yet.

Changes in stress and length occur as suprafixes marking certain plurals. In addition, certain sentence types appear to have a type of overriding stress, and intonational lengthening, much longer than normal lengthening, occurs for emphasis in excited speech.

1.2.1. DISTRIBUTION IN SYLLABLES. All consonants occur as syllable onsets; *d* and *r*, however, are found only in non-initial syllables. Examples are given above.

Only sets 1, 2, and 5 occur as codas. All members of sets 1 and 2 so occur; of Set 5 all but *w* so occur, but *ñ* is found only in non-final codas: Set 1, *wáf'* 'tousled', *amác'* 'land', *ampúč'* 'wild squash', *ʔéek'* 'firewood', *axúl'* 'house', *akáʔ* 'bird'; Set 2, *xóf* 'open', *monl'és* 'mamey fruit', *kúš* 'curly', *fúx* 'white', *fol* 'wet', *askúlᵛ* 'tor-

tilla'; Set 5, *tóm* 'stingy', *c'iñín* 'early morning', *xóřxóř* 'snore', *píñyuy* 'he is pounding', *paafúy* 'straight', *čičakwál* 'booth', *múlᵛmúlᵛ* 'muddy'.

All vowels occur as syllable peaks without either onsets or codas, as seen above. They all also occur as peaks of syllables with onsets, with codas, or with both. With onset: *pípa* 'it got burned', *pépa* 'he sent him', *šápa* 'it itched', *kópa* 'he said', *kúpa* 'he gave it'. With coda: *ínxa* 'wild pig', *énteda* 'liver', *ámpa* 'wide spaced', *onsáale* 'wildcat', *uñtᵛášpo* 'scorpion'. With both onset and coda: *tᵛíšmú* 'shrimp', *péspa* 'weighed', *pánguy* 'he is sitting', *kónta* 'heavy', *kúxpa* 'he sold it'.

1.2.2. CV SEQUENCES. The distribution of consonants next to vowels shows certain systematic gaps, as well as certain sporadic gaps due to low frequency of occurrence. The following consonants are found next to all vowels: *f', k', ʔ, l'; f, š, x; p, tᵛ, č, k; m'; m, ñ, lᵛ; b, d, r, g*. It will be noted that most alveopalatal consonants show unlimited distribution next to vowels; those which have some limitation are *č'*, which does not occur before *e* nor next to *o*, *lᵛ* which does not follow *e*, and *ñ'* which does not precede *o*. Alveolar consonants are almost all restricted in distribution with regard to high vowels: *c'* and *s* do not follow *u*; *l, t, n'*, and *l* do not occur next to *i* or *u*; *c* does not occur before *i* nor next to *u*; *n* does not precede *i* or *u*. Vocoid *y* does not precede *i*; *w* and *w'* do not precede *o* or *u*. Sporadic gaps due to low frequency of occurrence of either consonant or vowel are the non-occurrence of *w'* and *l'* after *e*, of *l'* before *o* and *u*, and of *ř* next to *i* or after *a*.

1.2.3. CONSONANT CLUSTERS of two or three occur as complex onsets, and clusters of two as complex codas. Clusters may be viewed as basic, that is, part of the stem; or derived, that is, resulting from the prefixation or suffixation of some morpheme consisting of a single consonant. Derived clusters forming complex onsets result from prefixing the first person allomorph *l-* to person-marking verbs. Derived clusters forming complex codas result from suffixing plural allomorph -ʔ to certain nouns ending in *n*, or *l*, or suffixing plural allomorph -*yʔ* to certain nouns ending in vowel *a*.

Basic clusters of two occurring as complex onsets consist of any set but 4 as initial member, and any set as second member, with restrictions as to specific combinations. Thus, Set 1 only precedes 5, and the only combination found is *k'w*. Of Set 2, only *s* and *š* occur in complex onsets, and precede any set but 2 and 6, with *k'* and *ʔ* the sole representatives of Set 1, giving clusters *sk'*, *šk'*, *sʔ*, *šʔ*. 2 + 3 combinations have only stops as second members, with specific combinations *sp*, *st*, *sk*, *šp*, *štᵛ*, *šk*. In 2 + 4 combinations *m'*, *n'*, *ñ'*, and *w'* occur, with specific clusters *sm'*, *sn'*, *sw'*, *šm'*, *šñ'*, *šw'*. In 2 + 5 combinations *m*, *n*, *ñ*, *y*, and *w* occur, with specific clusters *sm*, *sn*, *sy*, *sw*, *šm*, *šñ*, *šw*. Only the stop members of Set 3 occur as first member of clusters, with only Set 5, *w*, *y*, and Set 6, *r*, as second member. Specific combinations of 3 + 5 are *pw*, *tᵛy*, *kw*; of 3 + 6, *tr*. Only *m*, *n*, *w*, *lᵛ* of Set 5 occur as first member, and only Set 2, *x*, Set 5, *y*, and Set 6, *b*, *d*, with specific combinations 5 + 2 *wx*, 5 + 5 *lᵛy*, 5 + 6 *mb*, *nd*. The only combination with Set 6 as first member also has 6 as second member and is a loan:[4] 6 + 6 *br* (*brúxu* 'witch-doctor'). Examples of many of these may be seen in later sections.

In basic clusters of three as complex onsets, the first member is Set 2 *s* or *š*, the second, Set 1 *k'* or Set 3 *k*, the third, Set 5, *w*: *sk'w*, *šk'w*, *skw*, *škw*.

Basic clusters forming complex codas have Set 5 *m* or *n* as first member, and Set 1 *f'* or *k'* or Set 2 *s* as second member, with specific combinations 5 + 1 *mf'*, *nk'*, 5 + 2 *ns*.

Complex interludes consist of two or three consonants. Combinations are more numerous and varied than those found in onsets or codas: 86 basic cluster types as interludes, over against 36 onsets and 3

---

codas. Many more would be added if derived clusters were considered.

Basic clusters of two occurring as interludes, like onsets, consist of any set but 4 as first member and any set as second member, with restrictions as to specific combinations. With a few exceptions, all clusters found as onsets and codas are also found as interludes. In addition, the following types occur: Set 1 precedes 2, 3, and 5, with the only 2 + 1 combination *ʔš*, and the only 2 + 3 *lʔp*. Combinations of 1 + 5 are *f'n*, *č'w*, *k'n*, *k'l*, *ʔn*, *ʔñ*. Set 2 precedes all sets but 6. The 2 + 1 combinations are the same as those found as onsets; the only 2 + 2 is *xs*. Combinations of 2 + 3 are *ft*, *ftᵛ*, *xč*, *lt*, *lᵛk*; 2 + 4 combinations are the same as onsets. Combinations of 2 + 5 are *fm*, *fñ*, *xm*, *xn*, *lm*, *lw*, *lᵛñ*. The only combination with Set 3 is 3 + 5 *cy*. Set 5 precedes all sets. Combinations of 5 + 1 are *nc'*, *nč'*, *nl'*, *lʔ*; of 5 + 2 are *nx*, *nl*, *ñs*, *lf*; 5 + 3, *mp*, *nt*, *nc*, *nk*, *ñtᵛ*, *ñč*, *ytᵛ*, *lp*; 5 + 4, *mm'*, *yw'*, *nl'*; 5 + 5, *mm*, *nn*, *nw*, *nl*, *ñy*, *ym*, *yñ*, *yw*, *ylᵛ*; 5 + 6, *ng*, *yg*. The only combination with Set 6 is 6 + 6 *dr*, found only in a loan.

Basic clusters of three as interludes, in addition to all complex onsets except *šk'w* include the following types: 5 + 1 + 5 *yʔlᵛ*, 5 + 2 + 3 *nxtᵛ*, 5 + 2 + 5 *mxm*, *yxm*, *yxñ*, 5 + 3 + 5 *nkw*, *ykw*.

Vowel clusters are extremely rare, and occur only in free alternation with combinations of *yV*: *paceáxkuy/pacyáxkuy* 'he does stupidly'; *miónawa/myónawa* 'he goes on repeating'.

2. MORPHOPHONEMICS. The following morphophonemic processes are operative in Huamelultec: (1) assimilation, (2) unvoicing, (3) palatalization, (4) glottalization, (5) dissimilation, (6) intercalation, and (7) elision.

(1) Assimilation. Nasals assimilate to the point of articulation of the following consonant. *siñyuy* 'see', *simpa* 'saw', *tánduy* 'pound', *támpa* 'pounded', *lánsañyú* 'the people', *lambamúukwéʔ* 'the twelve'. Only *n* occurs before velars, but it is the velar al-

---

lophone which occurs: *pángúk'* 'seated', *sinwáypa* 'came to see', *lánk'epa* 'chose'.

(2) Unvoicing of *g* occurs before consonants: *páguy* 'washes', *páxpa* 'washed', *paxwáypa* 'came to wash', *pánguy* 'sit', *pánxpa* 'sat', *poygi* 'cry', *póyxpa* 'cried'.

(3) Palatalization occurs after high vowels and *y*: *lotáata* 'your father', *lʸitʸáata* 'his father', *laytʸáata* 'my father', *kónapa* 'finally said', *kúñapa* 'finally gave', *falá?* 'sow it', *pulʸá?* 'dig it', *miilʸá?* 'tell him', *paylʸá?* 'give it to him'. Palatalization occurs across glottal stop: *wi?lʸá?* 'look'. While it occurs with stops, nasals and laterals universally, it does not occur with affricates: *lʸicál* 'his roughness', and occurs with sibilants in some cases but not in others: *lʸiš?ápi* 'his older female relative', but *lʸisáñyú?* 'his folks'.

(4) Glottalization occurs when certain morphemes beginning with or consisting of glottal stop follow morphemes ending in a voiceless continuant. The resulting glottalized consonant is the corresponding glottalized affricate or stop: *xoloxóf* 'trousers', *xoloxóf'* 'pl.'; *mónl'és* 'mamey fruit', *mónl'éc* 'pl.'; *piš-* 'get wet', *pič'e-* 'make wet'; *páaxpa* 'got calm', *páak'epa* 'made calm', *imól* 'sheep', *imól'* 'pl.'

(5) Dissimilation (in combination with palatalization) occurs in the general imperative suffix *-La?*. Following stems with high vowels, the lateral is alveopalatal; after low vowels it is alveolar; after voiced sounds it is voiceless; after voiceless sounds it is voiced: *pulʸá?* 'dig it!', *falá?* 'sow it!', *kanlá?* 'leave it!', *piñlʸa?* 'pound it!', *panxlá?* 'sit down!', *fušlʸá?* 'blow it!'

(6) Intercalation of velars occurs mainly between words, but is sometimes also found within words, especially the intercalation of *g* between vowels: *Romego* for 'Romeo, proper name'. The choice of velar is on the following pattern: between voiceless consonant and vowel, *k* occurs: *kúškawxáx* 'curlytop' (*kúš* 'curly', *awxáx* 'head'), *ñáylʸoxmák'* *kitʸiñe* 'every day'. Between

vowel or *y* and vowel, *g* occurs: *elc'ée gamác'* 'the first of the year', *kúgay gápi?e* 'they-sell eggs'. Between vowel and consonant, *x* occurs: *ltépax mílʸa* 'a dog bit me', *lakwéx bořáču* 'the drunkard', *ñ'áč'ipax tónto* 'too stupid'. This tendency is reflected, but not completely operative, in certain sets of allomorphs of suffixes: *kogómpa* 'said again', *pa?kómpa* 'came again', *piñyómpa* 'received again'.

(7) Elision occurs between words according to the following pattern: If the second word begins with a prefix *el-* or *el-* the prefix vowel is lost following another vowel: *pánxa ltangím'a* 'can take-me-out', *ñúlʸi l?asyénto* 'one seat'. In other cases, when two vowels come together, the final vowel of the first word is lost: *ltép-úñči* 'an ant bit me', *táw-itʸtiñe* 'first day', *lákw-išñáxa* 'the drunkard'.

3.0. WORD-CLASSES. Huamelultec has four classes of words: verbs, nouns, pronouns, and particles. Divisive formal criteria for each class are: verb stems co-occur with aspect suffix class 410;[5] noun stems co-occur with definitive prefix 41; pronoun stems have unique pluralizers; particle stems do not co-occur with affixes. Divisive functional criteria are: verbs function only as predicates in certain types of classes; nouns occur as predicates of other types of clauses, also as subject, goal, recipient, means and referent; pronouns occur only as subject, goal or recipient; particles are divided into a number of function classes according to the slots they fill.

3.1. VERBS are divided into four major form classes: intransitive, transitive, recipient, and process. Intransitives are not marked for person, transitives are marked for goal, recipients for indirect object (recipient), process verbs for subject. These classes differ as to base.

Verbs are further divided into six function

[5] For the decade system of classifying affixes I am indebted to C. F. Voegelin. The particular modification of the system used here is similar to that of Shell (1957).

classes: active, reflexive, stative, imperative, hortatory, and subordinate. These classes differ formally as to margin, and functionally as to type of predicate slot they fill.

Verbs are composed of obligatory base plus obligatory margin.

3.1.1. VERB BASES consist of stem plus optional modal suffix class 300. Verb margin consists of aspect-mode-person suffix classes 400 and 500.

Verb stem includes root, adjunct suffix class 100, derivational suffix class 200.

Six classes of roots occur in verb stem: intransitive, transitive, recipient, process, neutral, and noun. Neutral roots are of three subclasses: (1) those with which class 200 is obligatory, (2) those which function unaffixed in Description predicate, but must have class 200 to function in Action predicate, (3) those which occur with 200 as verb stem and with prefix class 10 or 20 as noun stem.

Adjunct suffixes occur with any class of root, do not usually change the class of verb root. They add some specialized meaning to the basic notion of the verb. Class 110 occurs with transitive classifier roots (TCR) as well as with other roots; class 120 does not occur with TCR.[6] Class 110: -*ay* 'give', -*f* 'raise', -*f'i* 'put down', -*g* 'lower', -*ki* 'remove', -*goy* 'remain', -*m'i* 'put in', -*ñi* 'receive'. Class 120: -*ču* 'above', -*ing* 'edge', -*loo* 'motion', -*may* 'settled', -*ñug* 'take hold', -*ol* 'wide-spaced', -*čo* 'together', -*way* 'stooping'.

Suffix class 200 occurs obligatorily to form stems of different class from the root. It includes three subclasses: 210, intransitivizers -*ko*, -*ay*; 220, transitivizers -*ʔe*, -*m'e*, -*ʔi*, -*o*; 230, recipientizers -*ʔin*, -*n'e*.

Intransitive stem denotes simple action and consists of intransitive root, root plus

100, or neutral root, process root, or noun root plus 210. *či*- 'grind', *may*- 'go'; *xulaf*- 'dry up', *w'ang*- 'walk along edge'; *tilay*- 'shine', *mesko*- 'go bad', *fuxko*- 'get white'.

Transitive stem denotes action toward goal and consists of transitive root, alone or with suffix class 220 or 230; root plus 100; intransitive, process or neutral root plus 220. *kan*- 'leave', *xas*- 'break'; *xac'e*- 'crush', *peʔne*- 'believe someone'; *ñilay*- 'sketch', *xasñi*- 'split in two'; *xulʔe*- 'cause to dry up'; *mesm'e*- 'ruin', *xučiʔ*- 'deceive'.

Recipient stem denotes action toward recipient (indirect object) and comprises two subclasses: those which occur in context with goal as well as recipient and those which do not occur with goal. It consists of recipient root, TCR plus 100, verb root or neutral root plus 230, transitive root plus 220. *n'ax*- 'buy', *poy*- 'come out'; *pay*- 'give'; *xoyʔne*- 'call for', *mayʔiñ*- 'take to', *čiñ'i*- 'grind for', *tenk'iñ*- 'ring for'; *kuk'i*- 'sell to'.

Process stem denotes action performed by subject and consists of process root, or intransitive or neutral root plus 100. *xul*- 'get dry', *mu*- 'go down'; *xoygi*- 'fade', *mulʸaf*- 'sweat'.

Modal suffix class 300 is optionally added to verb stem to form verb base. There are eight classes of these; 310, -*k'oy* 'augmentative'; 320, -*ale* 'indefinite object, reciprocal'; 330, -*gax* 'derogatory'; 340, -*gon* 'iterative', 350, -*na* 'finalitive'; 360, -*go*, 'definite'; 370, 'passives', -*nay*, -*goy*, -*yuu*; 380, 'movational', -*way* 'motion toward', -*s* 'motion away'. Not more than four of these can occur together, usually not more than two or three. When they occur together, it is in the relative order given. Classes 350, 360 and 370 are mutually incompatible; others are mutually compatible. 310, 320, 350 and 380 may occur verb final: the base so occurring fills a description predicate slot rather than an action one, since verb margin is obligatory to action predicative verb. Examples: *w'ak'óy* 'he is walking all over', *čufk'óypa* 'he entered inside'; *kégalé* 'he barbers'.

---

[6] TCR includes the following roots which in their simple form indicate fetching an object of the stipulated shape: *č'u*- 'grains', *k'e*- 'water', *lee*- 'animate' or 'long thin object', *pe*- 'small object', *wa*- 'food or something carried in a round container'.

xáak'alepá? 'they answered each other'; *maygáxpa* 'he went off stupidly'; *maygómpa* 'he went again'; *páyñapa* 'he finally gave it to him', *máyña* 'he had gone', *mágopa* 'he died'; *xasnáypa* 'it got ripped', *čogóypa* 'it got spilled', *puyúupa* 'it was dug'; *wi?wáypa* 'he came to look at it', *wi?kišpa* 'he went to look at it', *tʸéxmáš* 'it fits well'. Examples of combinations: *siñalyómm'é?* 'we shall see each other again' (*siñ-* 'see'), *pánxkaxkónspa* 'he stupidly went off and stayed again'.

3.1.2. VERB MARGINS consist of suffix classes 400 and 500. Class 500 suffixes are mutually exclusive and final; class 400 may be followed by 550, 560 or 570.

Class 410 indicates aspect: *-pa* 'punctiliar', *-m'a* 'incompletive', *-ta* 'incompletive movational', *-uy* 'durative', *-wa* 'continuative', *-xmaa* 'customary'. *kópa* 'said', *wi?ma* 'will see', *wi?tʸa* 'will go see', *kódúy* 'says', *šmánawá* 'sleeps', *pálmaa* 'it is clear'.

Class 420 indicates 'imperative': *-la?* 'general imperative', *-ski* 'movational imperative', *-wata* 'requestive'. *pánxlá?* 'sit down', *kánski* 'go leave it', *lnáy?watá* 'please let me know'.

Class 430 indicates 'subjunctive': *-da*. *pánxda* 'might sit'. A prefix *en-* (*em-* or nasal alone) may optionally co-occur with this suffix with no discernible addition or change of meaning. Classes 510, 520 and 530 are plurals of 410, 420 and 430: 510, *-pa?*, *-m'e?*, *-ta?*, *-ay?*, *-way?*, *-xmay?*;[7] 520, *-le?*, *-ca?*, *-wata?*; 530, *-gu?*. Classes 510 and 520 replace 410 and 420; 530 follows 430. *šmápá?* 'they slept', *fám'é?* 'they will sow', *páxtá?* 'she will go wash it', *kodáy?* 'they say', *póyxñawáy?* 'they are shouting', *šyóxmáy?* 'they laugh'; *sáawáylʸé?* 'come and eat!',

kancá? 'go leave it!', *náy?watá?* 'please advise'; *pánxdagú?* 'they might sit'.

Class 540 indicates 'stative': *-a* 'singular', *-olenna?* 'plural'. *kása* 'stands'. *xulíngolénná?* 'they lean'.

Class 550 indicates 'resultant': *-k'* 'singular', *-eeda?* 'plural'. *simpík'* 'seen', *pángeedá?* 'seated'.

Class 560 indicates 'person': 'first', *l-* 'singular', *-nga?* 'plural'; 'second', *-o?* 'singular', *-lwa?* 'plural'; 'third', singular unmarked, *-la?* 'plural'. With transitive verbs, 560 marks 'goal', with recipient verbs 'recipient', with process verbs 'subject'; *napónga?* 'he hit us', *páypó?* 'he gave it to you', *lsóxta* 'I got tired'.

Class 570 indicates 'reflexive': *-si* 'singular', *-lči* 'plural'. *w'áposi* 'he walked by himself', *?éedelčí?* 'they do it to themselves'.

Suffixes 512 *-m'e* and 513 *-ta?* indicate 'hortatory' when used without subject: *?áym'é?* 'let's go', *sánsetá?* 'let's go see the fun'.

3.2. NOUNS are divided into two major form classes: free and bound. These are further subdivided into those which begin with consonant and those which begin with vowel. Bound nouns must occur with prefix *a-* or with a relational prefix. Prefix *a-* precedes initial consonant, replaces initial vowel. Vowel-initial free nouns occur with combiner *p-* in the relational form, vowel-initial bound nouns with combiner *n-*. Consonant-initial nouns do not occur with combiner.

Nouns are further divided into five function classes: quality, location, person, time, and item. Quality nouns are those which function as Quality predicate. Location nouns are those which co-occur with locative prefix to function in Location slot. Person nouns are those which co-occur with vocative prefix to function in Vocative slot. Time nouns are those which occur in Time slot. Item nouns are those which co-occur with definitive prefix to function in Subject or Goal slot, or without prefix in Means slot,

---

[7] An alternate analysis for some of these plural forms would be to consider that they are made up of the singular plus a pluralizer, e.g., *-pa?* = *-pa* + *-?*. Such a solution makes for fewer plurals but does not allow for a neat statement of distribution of the class, and one is still left with the handling of the suffixes which are genuinely suppletive, hence the solution given in the body of this article has been considered preferable.

but which do not belong to any of the other classes.

Nouns are composed of obligatory stem plus optional margin.

3.2.1. NOUN STEMS consist of noun root, root plus nominalizer, verb form plus nominalizer, noun-noun compound, or verb-noun compound with prefix *a-*.

There are five nominalizing affixes: *ap-* 'likeness', and *an-* 'item', which occur only with noun or neutral roots; prefix *in-* 'doer', suffixes *-da* 'agent', and *-f* 'division', which occur only with verb forms; prefixes *a-* and *i-* 'quality', and suffix *-xma²* 'implement', which occur with noun or neutral roots and verbs. Examples: *apekál* 'skinny' (*ekál* 'bone'), *ánkrús* 'cross', *ánskwilᵛé* 'adobe'; *inšó²edá* 'singer', *páñif* 'half', *a²ú* 'eye', *apí²* 'ashes', *ipa* 'flower', *ifú²* 'boil'; *awéxmá²* 'mirror', *táfúxma²* 'broom'.

Examples of noun roots: *méxul* 'hammock', *píime* 'plate', *íkušíš* 'smoke', *úunkwa* 'fire', *álewá²* 'gourd cup'; of compounds: *té²asáns* 'elder person', *tíñingaxá²* 'cool drink'; *apóykó²* 'cry-baby', *amífáy²ú* 'blinker'.

3.2.2. NOUN MARGINS consist of prefixes indicating definitive, locative, vocative, and relational; and infixes, suffixes and suprafixes indicating plural.

The definitive prefix has allomorphs *l-* before vowels, *el-* (singular) and *lan-* (plural) before consonants: *laxúl²* 'the house', *elméxul* 'the hammock', *lánsañyú²* 'the people'.

The locative prefix has allomorphs *m-* before vowel (with lengthening of the vowel), and *max-* before consonant: *máaxúl²* 'in the house', *máxméxul* 'in the hammock'.

The vocative prefix has allomorphs *m-* before vowel, *ma²-* before consonant: *mákán'o²* 'woman!', *má²múlᵛi* 'boy!'

The relational prefixes consist of three elements: 'person possessors', *ay-* 'first person', *o-* 'second', *i-* 'third'; 'pluralizer' of person *l-* (with *a-* allomorph of *ay-*), 'combiners' *p-* for free vowel-initial nouns, and *n-*

for bound vowel-initial nouns. Noun plus relational prefix functions as Relation predicate: *áyméxul* 'I have a hammock', *ópiĺimm'a* 'you have sense', *iñeskúlᵛ* 'he has a tortilla', *álnes²é* 'we have corn gruel'. When the relational is preceded by the other prefixes, the resultant noun functions in the slot appropriate to simple noun marked by the other prefixes: with definitive, as subject or object: *líñeskúl* 'his tortilla'; with locative in Location slot: *máyméxul* 'in my hammock'; with vocative in Vocative slot: *máyw'á* 'my child!'

Pluralizing infixes are *-l-* (*akáln'ó²* 'women'), *-n-* (*mínlᵛé²* 'dogs'), *-we-* (*fáwexmá²* 'nets'). Pluralizing suffixes are *-²* (*mulᵛí²* 'boys'), *-y²* (*aw'áy²* 'children'), *-e²* (*áywalé²* 'horses'), (*aywalá* 'horse'), *-la²* (*apóykolá²* 'cry-babies'), *-da²* (*w'áatedá²* 'brides'), *-yu²* (*lánsañyú²* 'the people'), *-či²* (*asmačí²* 'ears'). Pluralizing suprafixes are shift of stress (*añčupí²* 'baskets', *añčúpi²* 'basket'), and addition of length (*amáac* 'years', *amác* 'year'). Pluralizers may be combined; the most common combination is suffix *-²* plus shift of stress and loss of length: *apalᵛú²* 'messengers' (*apáalᵛu* 'messenger'), the most complex, infix plus suffix plus shift of stress and loss of length: *awalté²* 'girls' (*awáata* 'girl').

3.3. PRONOUNS are divided into two major form classes: personal and demonstrative. Personal and demonstrative pronouns belong to the same function class, filling subject, goal, recipient, and referent slots, but not predicate.

Personal pronouns are *iyá²* 'I', *imá²* 'you'. They co-occur with the unique pluralizer *-nk'*: *iyánk'* 'we' (exclusive), *imánk'* 'you (pl.)'. The inclusion of the first person plural pronoun indicates exclusive, the absence of the pronoun marks inclusive. There is no third person pronoun; its function is filled by a demonstrative or by a third person relational noun *itᵛuwá²* 'himself alone' (literally, 'his otherness'), *iltᵛuwá²* 'themselves alone'.

357

Demonstrative pronouns are composed of first elements and second elements. Members of either set may occur alone, or certain first and second elements may occur together, or with certain particles or personal pronouns between the two elements.

First elements are: *ga-* 'this', *na-* 'these', *xaa-* 'which', *tʸii-* 'that', *tya-* 'that one'. Second elements are: *-ʔa* 'here', *-ge* 'person', *-xne* 'persons', *-l'e* 'thing'. Particles which occur between them are: *ñ'i* 'just', *ča* 'now', *la* 'perhaps', *sa* 'so', *leʔ* 'only', *imáane* 'the very'. Examples of separate elements: *gá lkóofiʔ* 'this pot', *tyá lakán'óʔ* 'that woman'; *máypa gé* 'he went', *lakán'ó l'é* 'it belongs to the woman'.

Combinations: *gáʔa* 'this one', *tʸiige* 'that one', *xáaxne* 'which ones', *tʸiil'e* 'that thing'.

Examples with particles: *tʸiiñ'ixne* 'the same ones', *tʸiičage* 'that one there', *ságe* 'that one', *sáxne* 'those'.

3.4. Particles are divided into eleven function classes, differing according to the slots they fill in the clause.

Modal particles fill mode slot: *k'á* 'just', *lék'* 'only', *máxči* 'apparently'.

Locative particles fill location slot: *l'á* 'over there', *xifa* 'on top', *kulʸiʔ* 'far', *fáʔa* 'here', *sáxpe* 'there'.[8]

Temporal particles fill time slot: *čiča* 'now', *wxéwilʸi* 'a while ago', *kánna* 'sometimes'.

Negative particles fill negative slot: *máa* 'not', *ñi* 'not even', *xáʔñi* 'no'.

Interrogative particles fill introductory interrogative slot: *née* 'who', *tés* 'what', *tʸiñči* 'why', *kánaʔ* 'when', *táxna* 'how much'.

Exclamatory particles fill exclamatory and response slots: *xée* 'yes', *inkóʔ* 'who knows', *xáanaʔ* 'fine', *čúwáʔ* 'like so much'.

Imperative particles fill imperative slot: *kálʸi* 'bring it here', *náʔké* 'leave it alone', *lixéero* 'hurry up'.

---

[8] The last two locatives are comparable in form to the demonstrative pronouns; they are classed as particles rather than pronouns because they do not participate in pronoun pluralization, the criterion for the pronoun class.

The quotative particle fills quotative slot: *náaʔ* 'it is said'.

The conditional particle fills introductory conditional slot: *xóola* 'if'.

The hortatory particle fills hortatory slot: *xinsa* 'let's go'.

The connective particle fills connective slot: *ʔáytʸa* 'and'.

4.0. Types of syntactic units. Huamelultec has five kinds of syntactic units: words, phrases, clauses, sentences, and discourse.

Words are constituent parts of phrases and clauses, can constitute sentences only of an exclamatory or dependent type.

Phrases are composed of two or more words, enter into clauses, can constitute sentences only of a dependent type and in conversation.

Clauses are of two types: principal and subordinate. Principal clauses can constitute independent sentences; subordinate clauses can constitute only dependent sentences and that only in conversation.

Sentences are of two major types: independent and dependent. Independent sentences can constitute a complete narrative; dependent sentences occur only as response within conversation, or in sequence within narrative.

Discourse is of two types: conversation and narrative. Conversation involves the alternation of two or more speakers; narrative is the speech of a single individual at a given time.

4.1. Phrase types. There are two major classes of phrases: noun phrases and verb phrases.

Noun phrases are divided into five subclasses: qualitative, possessive, relative, locative, and temporal.

Qualitative noun phrase consists of quality noun plus definitive noun: *pilki linʔóyk'-óykómon* 'all the town-officials'; *ñúlʸi lakán'óʔ* 'one woman', or of definitive noun plus noun: *lyákwexbólsa mélʸu* 'the big bag of money'.

Possessive noun phrase consists of definitive relational noun plus definitive noun or proper name. The first noun denotes the possessed item, the second the possessor: *lⱽikwáana lakwé?* 'the sickness of the man', *lⱽitⱽáata Dábɨd* 'the father of David'.

Relative noun phrase consists of relative pronoun plus noun: *xáal'e lmélⱽu* 'that which was money', *xáal'e ñɨk'ata* 'that which is pretty', *xáaxne láypɨxedá?* 'those from my town'.

Locative noun phrase consists of locative particle *xáape* 'where' plus noun, or qualitative noun plus locational noun: *xáape itⱽuwá?* 'where he (to, at, by him)', *xáape lⱽiwá* 'where the hole (in the hole)'; *ac'éex ládo* 'new side (another place)', *ñulⱽɨk' elcáye* 'all over the street'.

Temporal noun phrase consists of temporal noun preceded by qualitative noun or by particle: *kánč'úš múul'a* 'six months', *ñúlⱽɨ lⱽipúgi* 'one night'; *?ásta číča* 'till now'.

The only type of verb phrase is that made by the combination of forms of the verbs *?ee-* or *pase-* 'both meaning 'do') with Spanish infinitive: *pásedúy mándár* 'order', *?eem'a ařépentír* 'repent'.

4.2. CLAUSE TYPES. There are two major classes of clauses: principal and subordinate. Principal clauses can constitute independent sentences, subordinate clauses cannot. Subordinate clauses are marked by the presence of a subordinating particle or by a subordinate predicate or both, or by *nonfinal intonation*; a clause not so marked is a principal clause.

Principal clauses are divided into two major types: predicative and exclamatory. Predicative clauses have a bipartite structure, consisting of a predicate plus another unit called a concomitant which includes such items as subject, modal, locative, time, and the like. The most common concomitant is the subject but it is not obligatory. More than one concomitant may occur, but at least one must occur. Exclamatory clauses have a unitary structure, consisting of a predicate only, of a different sort than the predicative predicate.

Both predicative and exclamatory principal clauses are subdivided according to the word class of the predicate. Predicative clauses with verb predicates are: Intransitive Action, Action toward Goal, Action toward Recipient, Subjective Action, Reflexive Action, State, Description, and Quotation; with noun predicates: Quality, Identity and Relation; Location clause may have either locative particle or locative noun as predicate. Exclamatory clauses with verb predicates are Imperative and Hortatory; with noun predicates, Vocative and Comment.

Predicative clauses have both negative and interrogative counterparts; some exclamatory clauses also have a negative counterpart.

4.2.1. PREDICATIVE CLAUSES. Intransitive Action clause has intransitive verb as predicate. Concomitant may be subject noun or pronoun or noun phrase; modal particle; locative particle or noun; temporal particle, noun, or verbal; quotative particle; or noun indicating means. Predicate normally precedes concomitant, although occasionally time word may precede predicate. Predicate plus subject: *šmánapa law'á* 'the-child went-to-sleep';[9] mode: *máypa sá* 'so he-went'; locative: *poyčodúy máxpáná?* 'she-is-washing at-the-river'; time: *máyñapá wxéwilⱽɨ* 'he-went a-while-ago'; quotative: *šñáxuy náa?* 'he-is-drinking so-they-say', means: *máypa abyón* 'he-went by-plane'; with subject and time: *máyñapa lakwé wxéwilⱽɨ* 'the-man went a-while-ago'; with subject and location, *šmánapa yá? máxméxuł* 'I went-to-sleep in-the-hammock'; with time, quotative, and location: *číča náa póyčodúy lⱽɨñexúł* 'now it-is-said she-washes at-her-house'.

Action toward Goal clause has transitive verb as predicate. In addition to the set of concomitants found in Intransitive clause, this clause can have a goal concomitant, but

[9] An attempt has been made to combine a free translation of clauses and sentences with a hyphenation of items which are multiple in English but single words in Chontal. Since English order is followed rather than Chontal order in most cases, the words do not always coincide.

LINGUISTICS

like the rest it is not obligatory. Action toward Goal clause differs from Intransitive Action clause both in the verb class which functions as predicate and in the possibility of goal versus its impossibility of occurrence. Non-third person singular goal is marked in the verb by suffix class 560 of person markers; third person singular is not marked. Transitive predicate with subject concomitant: *łépa mílʸa* 'a-dog bit me'; with goal: *pulʸáygilʸa law'áyʔ* 'he-embraces-them the-children'; with goal and subject: *tʸéxuy mángo láyw'á* 'my-child is-eating mangoes'; with location and time: *pílʸpa múuxa pwíʔa* 'they-butchered down-yonder this-morning'; with means: *napóngax ʔéex* 'they-hit-us with-a-stick'.

Action toward Recipient clause has recipient verb as predicate. In addition to the concomitants found in Action toward Goal clause, this clause can have a recipient concomitant, although it, too, is not obligatory. There are two types of recipient verbs, those which can occur with both goal and recipient and those which occur only with recipient. Non-third singular recipient is marked in the verb by suffix class 560. Examples of the first type with subject: *páypola lakwéʔ* 'the-man gave-it-to-them'; with goal: *łmúk'ipa lʸiw'á* 'they-showed-me their-child'; with recipient and time: *číča páypola pílki lánsañyúʔ* 'now they-gave-it-to-them all the-people'; with location: *wáypa míiñexúłʔ* 'they-gave-food-to-him at-his-house', with subject, means, recipient and goal: *páyʔímpá imáʔ plómo láyw'a lʸiwxáx* 'you broke-for-him with-lead my-child his-head'. Examples of the second type with subject: *kúškínga lałpič'áleʔ* 'our-clothes got-sour-on-us'; with time: *xóypa č'íñčuxpólaʔ* 'now it-got-dark-on-them'.

Subjective Action clause has process verb as predicate. This clause type has the same set of concomitants as Intransitive, but differs from Intransitive in the class of verb which functions as predicate. Process verb has non-third singular subject marked in the verb by suffix class 560. Process predi-

cate with subject: *xúłpa lʸič'aléʔ* 'the-clothes got-dry'; *pánxtola kwési* 'two were-born'; with time: *pwíʔa pánxtoláʔ* 'this-morning they-were-born'; with means: *łsóxta añílya* 'I-got-tired writing'.

Reflexive Action clause has reflexive verb as predicate. The verb base is usually transitive, but may be intransitive. Reflexive predicate with subject: *píč'édesi imáʔ* 'you-are - getting - yourself - wet'; *fóol'epólči lánsañyúʔ* 'the-people gathered-themselves'; with mode: *kúuč'epósí ákoló* 'it-curled-itself into-a-ball'; with subject, time, and means: *íya ráto ráto ʔéedesi axáʔ* 'I every minute douse-myself with-water'; with intransitive reflexive and subject: *w'áposi ilʸuwáʔ* 'he walks-by-himself'.

Stative clause has stative verb as predicate. The underlying verb base may be of any class. Simple stative verbs end in suffix -*a* or -*olennaʔ*, resultant statives in -*k'* or -*eedaʔ*. Stative predicate with subject: *ʔék'ñúuyák' laxúl* 'the-house is-open'; with location and subject: *kasínxa l'á láypépo* 'my-little-brother is-standing-leaning over-there'; with time: *xólgolénna číčá* 'they-live-there now'; with location: *fáʔa pángedáʔ* 'here they-live'.

Description clause has verb base or neutral root as predicate. Verb base predicate with subject: *páylʸo lapálʸu* 'the-messenger is-wandering-around'; *pílkale yáʔ* 'I'm butchering'; with locative: *k'ónxmay l'á* 'it-is-setting (hen) there'. Neutral root is usually reduplicated when it occurs as descriptive predicate. Neutral root predicate with mode and subject: *xás xás sáñ'i láypíč'aléʔ* 'my-clothes are just all ripped'; with time: *gólof síʔmáane* 'it-swelled-up right-away'.

A special type of clause with verb predicate is the Quotative clause: the predicate is either the intransitive verb *ko-* 'say', or the recipient verb *mii-* 'say to'. This clause combines with the Quotation clause, or with a non-clause response to form a Quotational sentence. The Quotation clause can be any clause type. Examples are found under Quotational sentences.

360

Quality clause has quality noun as predicate. Quality predicate with subject: *áwixti yáʔ* 'I'm sleepy'; *epálma lᵛiwʼá* 'her-child has-a-fever'; with mode and location: *iwa sáamʼa lʼá* 'there's-a-hole maybe there'; with mode, location, and subject: *iwxalá sá fá lané* 'so here the-road is-hilly'; with location and time: *iñú lʼá láypíxedá číčá* 'it's-hot there in-my-town now'.

Relation clause has relational noun as predicate. It is the normal way of stating possession. Relation predicate with subject: *ilᵛpóyxña lᵛiñánxmáyʔ* 'the-lakes have-an-owner'; with time: *alpipúfki číča* 'we-have-health now'; with subject and quotative: *itayér gá náaʔ* 'this-one he-has-a-shop it-is-said'; with subject and mode: *opilᵛimmʼa sá imáʔ* 'you really you-have-sense'.

Identity clause has definitive noun as predicate and subject is obligatory: *gáʔa láywʼá* 'this-is my-child'; *láywʼá gé* 'it-is my-child'; with referent: *lakánʼo lʼé lᵛixútᵛi* 'the-woman, it is her-waterjar'; *lakúlwé lʼá lᵛinʔóykʼóykómon* 'the-men there are the-town-officials'.

Location clause has either locative noun or locative particle as predicate: *máyñegá lakúlwéʔ* 'the-men are-in-the-cornfields', *wxáyñíf lᵛiwxalá, tᵛiixpe lᵛipánka láywʼá* 'the-other-side of-the-hill, there-is my-son's ranch', *lʼá láyñexúlʼ* 'there-is my-house'.

4.2.2. EXCLAMATORY CLAUSES. Imperative exclamatory clause has imperative verb as predicate. The verb base may be of any class. *koláʔ* 'say it!'; *miilᵛáʔ* 'tell him!'; *smáski* 'go sleep!'; *sáawáylᵛéʔ* 'come eat!'; *lnáyʔwatá* 'please let me know'; *kúnáski lamúlᵛáʔ* 'go-give-out tamales'.

Hortatory clause has incompletive plural verb as predicate: *ʔáymʼéʔ* 'let's go'; *píltᵛáʔ* 'let's kill it'; *kʼéta axá* 'let's-go-get water'.

Vocative clause has vocative noun as predicate: *máʔmúlᵛi* 'boy!'; *máywʼá!* 'my child!'

Comment clause has quality noun as predicate. It differs from Quality clause in that it does not have obligatory concomitant, though a simple noun of address may ac-

company it: *iñúʔ* 'it's hot!'; *ñíʔi náana, ñíʔi* 'delicious, ma'am, delicious!'

4.2.3. NEGATIVE CLAUSES. Any predicative clause may be made negative by adding *máa* 'general negative', or *ñí* 'intensive negative'; *máa čéeduy elʔeskwéla* 'she doesn't go to school'; *ñí wxéduy* 'she doesn't even want to'; *ñí ya ʔáymʼa* 'I didn't even go; *máa lpépa* 'he didn't send me'; *ñí tyépólaʔ* 'they didn't even fall'; *máa iwxala lané* 'the road isn't hilly'; *máa gáʔa láywʼá* 'this isn't my-child'.

Only the imperative of the exclamatory clauses is negativized. The negative used is *xáʔñi*, and the imperative verb is replaced by the incompletive: *xáʔñi kómʼa* 'don't say-it!' *xáʔñi smáta* 'don't go-and-sleep!', *xáʔñi miimʼoláʔ* 'don't tell-them!'

4.2.4. INTERROGATIVE CLAUSES are of two types: those obligatorily introduced by an interrogative particle, and those optionally introduced by interrogative particle *tés* 'what'.

Those introduced by *née* 'who' are interrogative counterparts of any predicative clause type: *née ʔáymʼa* 'who's going?', *née pasépa* 'who made-it?' *née páypoʔ* 'who gave-it-to-you?' *née išíñakʼ* 'who knows?' *née tᵛiixpe* 'who's there?' Those introduced by *tés* 'what' are the interrogative forms of Transitive or Recipient clauses: *tés pasépa* 'what did-he-make?' *tés páypoʔ* 'what did-he-give-you?' Those introduced by *xáape* 'where' are either the interrogative counterpart of Location clause, or of any clause with location concomitant: *xáape láywʼá* 'where-is my-child?' *xáape má xoláyʔuy* 'where do-you-live?' Those introduced by *kána* 'when' correspond to any clause with time concomitant; those with *táxna* 'how much' to various clauses; those with *tᵛíñči* 'why' have no exact counterpart: *kána ima símpa* 'when did-you see-him?' *kána mayyaguʔ* 'when are-they-going?'; *táxna ipilᵛáalᵛi* 'how-much is-its-price?' *táxna lonáskeʔ* 'how-many children-do-you-have?' *táxna šímpa* 'how-many did-he-see?'; *tᵛíñči má wxéduy* 'why do-you-want-it?'

Those optionally introduced by *tés* are any predicative clause type: *tés* is obligatory if no other concomitant occurs, is optional otherwise: *tés, mayñápa* 'what, did-he-go?' *tés, máyñápa lákwé?* 'what, did the-man go?'; *pácepa lonáana* 'did your-mother make-it?'; *máypa sá elpáná?* 'so did-he-go to-the-river?' Only this type of interrogative clause occurs in negative form; the negative particle that occurs is *xá?ñi: tés, xá?ñi máyñápa lákwé?* 'what, didn't the-man go?' *xá?ñi máypa elpáná?* 'didn't he-go to-the-river?'

4.2.5. SUBORDINATE CLAUSES are subdivided according to the subordinating particle that introduces them. Relative and temporal and locative clauses fill slots in complex sentences comparable to those filled by corresponding words and phrases in simple sentences; conditional, purpose, and causal clauses have no counterparts in simple sentences.

Relative clauses are introduced by relative pronouns: *xáage té?a empánxda* 'the-one-who first should-be-born'; *xáaxne mál-napá?* 'those-who went'; *xáal'e ?ípa lakwé?* 'that-which happened to the-man'. They fill subject, goal and recipient slots, or expand simple fillers of these slots.

Temporal clauses are introduced by *lék'* 'when', *?ásta* 'until', *káda* 'each time', and fill time slots: *lék' sa kwáyñáta* 'so when he arrived'; *lék' yá pácyóna* 'when I make-it-again'; *lék' yán aw'áy?* 'when we were-children'; *?ásta yá kána enkóda* 'until I say when'; *kádá imá nañyóoda* 'each-time you pass'.

Locative clauses are introduced by *xáape* 'where', and fill location slots: *xáape ñóygolénna?* 'where they - were - lying - down'; *xáape yá mpánxda ñúl^vi el?asyénto* 'where I might-sit-down on a chair'.

Conditional clauses are introduced by *xóola* 'if': *xóola ?aygúpa ñúl^vi lapóyxña* 'if there-came a mountain-man'; *xóola ?óyn'-edágu?* 'if they-should-carry-it-out'.

Purpose clauses are introduced by *pára* 'in order to': *pára wím'a elréy* 'in-order-to

see the-king': *pára yá pá?nam'a ñ'í?* 'in-order-that I just come'.

Causal clauses are introduced by *pórke* 'because', or *tánto* 'so much': *pórke íya lakwé?* 'because I'm the-man'; *pórke ñú?eduy* 'because he-asked-for-it'; *tánto páyčúxpa* 'because she was so scared'.

Any subordinate clause can be negativized by the inclusion of the negative particle *xá?ñi*: negative relative clause, *xáage xá?ñi wxéduy* 'whoever doesn't want-to'; negative temporal clause, *lék' xá?ñi ?óyya* 'when there isn't any'; negative locative clause, *xáape xa?ñi asáns* 'where there wasn't a soul'; negative conditional clause, *xóola xá?ñi lmiiya* 'if he doesn't tell-me'; *xóola xá?ñi* 'if not'; negative purpose clause, *pára xá?ñi šmpolá?* 'so-that he didn't see-them; negative causal clause, *pórke xá?ñi ñík'ata tónxl'e* 'because it-isn't good that-way'.

4.3. SENTENCE TYPES. There are two major types of sentences: independent and dependent. Independent sentences are divided into four major classes: Affirmative, Interrogative, Exclamatory, and Negative. Sentences of any of these classes may be simple: composed of a single principal clause; or complex: composed of more than one clause, of which at least one must be a principal clause. Dependent sentences are divided into two major classes: Completive, which consists of less than a full clause; and Sequentially Marked, which consists of a principal clause plus a sequence introducer, which is different from the subordinating particles which introduce subordinate clauses.

4.3.1. INDEPENDENT SENTENCES. Affirmative sentences have a predicative clause as basic and are spoken with *statement intonation*: a final contour with low pitch and heavy stress on the penult and high or rising pitch on the final syllable. Affirmative sentences include: Intransitive Action, Transitive Action, Recipient Action, Subjective Action, Reflexive Action, Stative, Description, Quotation, Quality, Relation, Identity, and Location. Simple examples of each of these have been given under the corresponding clause types except for Quotation; Quotational sentences are always complex. Complex examples of each affirmative type will now be given, but not every possible combination of clause types will be included under each sentence type. The variety given will be illustrative of the range of possibility, with more scope given to subordinate types than to combinations with other principal clauses, since the former are more common.

Intransitive sentence with temporal clause: *lék' yá sǐmpa, máyñápa* 'When I saw-him, he-was-leaving'; with locative clause: *xáape č'íňčuxpóla⁷, t⁴iixpe šmúngopá⁷* 'Where night-overtook-them, there they-slept'.

Transitive sentence with temporal clause: *láyčóoponga lék' yán aw'áy⁷* 'She-had-us when we were-children'; with relative clause functioning as goal: *wxéduy yá xáal'e ñík'ata* 'I want what is-pretty'; with two principal clauses: *pánxpa max⁷asyénto, píñipa lanyáwi⁷* 'He-sat-down on-the-chair; he-picked-up the-keys'.

Recipient Action sentence with locative clause: *kán'espóla xáape ñóygolénna il⁴kwáana* 'He-went-and-left-it-for-them where they-lay sick'; with relative clause expanding goal: *lláym'á imá low'á xáage té⁷a empánxda* 'You will-give-me your-child which is first born'.

Subjective Action sentence with temporal clause: *t⁴óxpa lakán'o, t⁴éconawá* 'When a-woman gets-old, she-gets-sick'; with conditional clause: *xóola xá⁷ñi ⁷óyn'edágu⁷, mám'olá⁷* 'If they don't follow-the-custom, they-will-die'.

Reflexive Action sentence with conditional clause used in a purpose sense: *wí⁷kesi xóola ñík'ata awáata* 'She-is-looking at-herself (to see) if she-is-a-pretty girl'; with causal clause: *tánto ⁷ípa sǐt⁴a, mélofpósi yá ukwéeda* 'It was so cold I-wrapped-myself with-a-blanket'.

Stative sentence with locative clause:

xáape ⁷óyya ⁷awé elmángu, t⁴iixpe xólgolénna⁷ 'Where there-are many mangoes, there they-live'; with temporal clause: *lék' yá náñyóopa špémf'úuyak' pélta lék'* 'When I passed-by, it-was-open only a little-bit'.

Description sentence with conditional clause: *xóola xá⁷ñi ipiñík' layw'á, púro w'ák'oy ínko xáape* 'If my-child doesn't have-work-to-do, he just wanders-around who-knows where'; with temporal clause: *lék' nda t⁴áy⁷pa, mas ñúl⁴e nda sagé lakwé⁷* 'When it-is-said he-heard-it, this man ran all-the-more it-is-said'; with causal clause: *tánto št⁴úuyuy lakwé⁷, kác' sáñ'i li⁷á* 'The-man gets-angry so-much, his-face is-just chewy'.

Quotational sentence with Response quotation: *xáana⁷, kópa lampóbré⁷* 'Fine, said the-poor-folks'; with intransitive quotation: *púro nda kwá, imánk' xúčolayyáy⁷* 'He always said it-is-said, You-all are-lying'; with interrogative quotation: *míipa nda⁷, tés má mpáceda fá⁷a* 'He-said-to-him it-is-said, What might you be-doing here?'.

Quality sentence with temporal clause: *lék' xpé kwáyt⁴a xáape ñúl⁴i el⁷áwe⁷éex, t⁴iixpe fáane láneedáy⁷* 'When there they-arrived where there-was-one big-tree, there there-were-three roads'; with causal clause: *ákwe ákwe layw'á, tánto pánxa pacém'a* 'My-son is very manly, he's-able to-do so-much'.

Relational sentence with causal clause: *pórke púro šáagoduy ñík'ata, poréso ipúfki gé lawáata* 'Because she always eats well, therefore that girl is-healthy'; with coordinate relational clause: *imáyña ge lakán'o, iñekwé ac'ée ládo* 'That woman had-a-vice, she-had-a lover in-another-place'.

Identity sentence with relative clause: *ná⁷a sá lanwagáč' xáaxne ⁷óyya fá⁷a* 'These-are then the-cattle which there-are here'; with conditional clause: *xóola elpáná', elpáná⁷ sal'é* 'If it's-to-be-the-river, then let-it-be-the-river'.

Location sentence with relative clause: *t⁴iixpe laxúl' xáal'e pácepa layw'á* 'There-is the-house that my-son built'; with temporal clause: *lék'yán aw'áyˀ, míiši iñánxmaˀ lalpánka* 'When we-were children, our-ranch was-on-the-bank-of the-river'.

Interrogative sentences are of two types: Information questions, and Yes-or-no questions. Information questions are introduced by an obligatory interrogative particle, and are spoken with *nonaffirmative intonation*, consisting of high pitch on the penult and low pitch on the final syllable. Interrogative particles include: *tés* 'what', *née* "who,' *kána* 'when', *xáape* 'where', *táxna* 'how much', *tᵘíñči* (or *ténsa*) 'why'. Yes-or-no questions are optionally introduced by *tés* 'what', and are spoken with *interrogative intonation*, consisting of high pitch on both the last two syllables.

Information question with temporal clause: *ténsa náˀa lawáltéˀ tᵘóxom'edáyˀ káda náñyoodáguˀ* 'Why are those girls chattering every-time we go-by?'; with conditional clause: *xóolá imá xáˀñi pánk'éda, tés yá ˀéedágoˀ* 'If you don't have-a-baby, what shall I do-to-you?'; with coordinate stative clause: *tés kipúftᵘíiñe lakán'o kása l'á* 'What is-the-name-of the-woman, she-is-standing over-there?'; with information asked about subject and temporal clause included: *née wálwaˀ lék' xáˀñi fáˀa lonáana* 'Who takes-care-of-you when your-mother is'nt here?'; with relative clause expanding goal: *tᵘíñči ma mpáyˀoda layxutᵘí xáal'e yá inkóxma n'áspa* 'Why should-you-break my-water-jar that I just went-and-bought?'

Yes-or-no questions are the same as affirmative sentences in basic form, but are made interrogative by the interrogative intonation, and by the optional inclusion of *tés*, which seems to be used in the sense of a mild 'well,' or 'is it true that', although it may be used in an excited sentence of this type with more exaggerated height of pitch to add a meaning of 'you don't really mean that . . .'' Examples: with basic subjective action clause and causal subordinate clause: *tés šóxtóˀ tánto páylᵘo* 'Well, did-you-get-tired from-so-much running-around?'; with

basic recipient clause and relative clause expanding goal: *tés ˀayñáspóˀ elmáge péšu xáal'e ˀéeñugúk'* 'Well, did-they-give-you the-five pesos that they-owed?'; with basic hortatory clause and response-modal particle: *ˀáym'e čúwáˀ* 'Shouldn't we maybe go?'; with basic relational clause and locative subordinate clause: *tés onéxúl' xáape lopíxedá xoláˀúy* 'What, do-you-have-a-house where you-live in-your-town?'; with basic location clause: *tés tᵘíixpe lotáata máyñegá* 'Say, is your-father there in-the-cornfield?'; with basic transitive clause: *xóypá imá xoláf'ípa* 'Did you get-it-written-down?'; with basic intransitive clause: *kwáyñam'a lᵘítᵘáata c'íitᵘéˀ* 'Did his-father really come?'

Negative sentences are of four types: General Negative, Intensive Negative, Negative Question, and Negative Command. The first two types are negative forms of any affirmative sentence. General Negative is introduced by *máa* 'not' and is spoken with statement intonation. Intensive Negative is introduced by *ñi* 'not even', and is spoken with nonaffirmative intonation. Negative Question is introduced by *xáˀñi* 'not, no' and is spoken with interrogative intonation; it is the negative of yes-or-no questions. Negative Command is also introduced by *xáˀñi* but has statement intonation; it is the negative form of Imperative but differs by having the incompletive form of the verb rather than the imperative. Because of this difference of form, plus the variety of negatives and of intonation, it has been deemed more feasible to treat negative sentences and clauses as separate types rather than subtypes of the respective affirmative, interrogative and imperative types.

General Negative sentence with intransitive principal clause and conditional subordinate clause: *máa yá ˀaym'a xóola tánto iñúˀ* 'I'm not going if it's-so hot'; with recipient principal clause and relative subordinate clause functioning as goal: *máa lpáypa layñáana xáal'e má lmíipa*

'My-mother didn't give-me what you told-me'; with subjective action principal clause and causal subordinate clause: *máa yánk' šúškoxmónga lalpíxedá? tánto alpiñík' fán ládo* 'We don't stay-long in-our-town we have so-much work-to-do here in-this-place'; with quality principal clause and relative subordinate clause expanding the subject: *máa l'é c'iit*v*é xáal'e imán kodáy?* 'It isn't true what you-all say'.

Intensive Negative sentence with transitive principal clause and causal subordinate clauser *tánto šúšpa l'á, ñí faskúupa liñáana* 'She stayed so-long there, she didn't-even remember her-mother'; with recipient clause: *ñí el'éen'eduy aywxíx* 'He doesn't even give-me a-party'; with subjective action clause: *ñí xóygipa laypíč'alé?* 'My-clothes didn't even fade'; with relational clause, and intransitive clause: *ñí ipilímm'a lawáata, púro l*v*óoduy* 'The-girl doesn't-even have-any-sense, all-she-does is-play'; with location clause and intransitive clause: *ñí t*v*íixpe lakulwé?, xóypa máyñápa* 'The-men weren't-even there, they-had-already left'.

Negative Question with recipient clause: *xá?ñi má, táata, l'áyyagónga alposáda* 'Won't you, sir, give-us a-place to-stay?'; with intransitive recipient principal clause and temporal subordinate clause: *xá?ñi póyyagólwa láxá? lék' mánda* 'Doesn't the-water leak-out-on-you when it-is-filled?'; with coordinate intransitive clauses, one affirmative and the other negative: *xúñči sáagom'a sáñ'i imá?, t*v*íige xá?ñi šáagódá* 'And-so you will just eat, and this-one isn't to-eat?'

Negative Command with coordinate imperatives: *lixéero, mayl*v*á?, xá?ñi pánxta ñ'í?* 'Get-a move on (lit. quickly go), don't just sit-there'; *xá?ñi sagím'a, pánxla al*v*íč'* 'Don't breathe, hold your breath!'; with coordinate subjective action clause: *xá?ñi wasm'ím'a, ñ'ač'ím'a* 'Don't put-it-in, it-will be-too-much'. In occasional conversation, a negative command may omit the predicate if the sense is clear from context in terms of the life situation: *xá?ñi max-*

mésa, máa ñík'ata 'Not on-the-table (i.e. don't put the baby on the table), it's not good'.

Negative subordinate clauses occur in any type of complex sentence; they are introduced by *xá?ñi* or contain *xá?ñi* as the negating particle. Example with negative conditional clause: *xóola xá?ñi wxéduy, wxéduy más astoráke, xúu, šó?em'a lúunkwa* 'If it doesn't like-it, it-wants more incense, oooh, the-fire will-sing'; with negative purpose clause: *f'íñčiguy yá? laytwáya ñík'ata pára xá?ñi pém'a lawá?* 'I hold my-towel tight so-that the-wind won't take-it-off'; with negative clause in indirect discourse: *kópá imá xá?ñi póygowá péro póygowá sal'é* 'You said it wasn't going-to-come-out but it's-coming-out all-right'.

4.3.2. DEPENDENT SENTENCES are of two classes. Completive, and Sequentially Marked.

Completive sentences are of two formal types: those which consist of a single predicative predicate by itself, and those which consist of a concomitant. Both types may function as Response dependent sentences in conversational discourse; only the first type may function as a Sequence dependent sentence in narrative discourse.

Sequentially Marked sentences consist of any simple or complex sentence type plus a sequence introducer such as *?áyt*v*a* 'and', *xóyya* 'thereupon', *xóypa* 'then,' *entónse* 'so', *péro* 'but', *poréso* 'therefore'.

Obviously, when sentences are looked at within a matrix of discourse rather than as the top-level units of a language, many of them are contextually conditioned. Much more work needs to be done on a variety of languages to find out more about the nature of contextually conditioned, and therefore dependent, sentences. Those which at this stage are treated as dependent are the types listed above which clearly show by their structure that they are different from the sentences previously described.

In illustrating Completive sentences, the sentence on which they are dependent is given in parentheses, followed by the Completive sentence outside the parentheses.

Completive predicate-type sentences as Responses: (*tés ʔípa low'á* 'What happened-to your-child?') *máfpa* 'Had a fit'. (*kwáym'a c'iitʷé losʔápi* 'Did your-older-sister really come?') *kwáym'a* 'Came'. (*tʷíñči xáʔñi má mʔáygóda* 'Why shouldn't you go?') *kúlʷíʔ* 'Far'. (i.e. 'it's too far').

Completive concomitant sentences as Responses: (*née pacépa* 'Who made-it?') *iyáʔ* I. (*xápe xólgolénna* 'Where do-they-live?') *l'á xápe Tína Síkyo* 'There in-the home-of Tina Sikyo'. (*tés xigáfʔpó* 'How did-you-wake-up?') *ñík'ata ñ'í ʔása* 'Just fine'. (*wxéduy má tónx táʔa* 'Do you want-it like this?') *xée čičá, máskesá* 'Sure thing, no-matter-what'.

Response dependent sentences may also consist of response particles, such as *xée* 'yes', *xénáʔ* 'really?', *xáʔñi* 'no,' *čúwá* 'you-don't-mean-it!'; or of subordinate clauses: *pórsa, xáy, elʔéepa epálmá* 'Because, friend, I-had a-fever'.

Completive predicate-type sentences are found in narrative discourse as an after-thought or amplification or explanation of a previous independent sentence. They occur rather infrequently but are clearly set off by final intonation contours as being separate sentences. Examples: (*máloolóopa náa, fúxfúx náa ʔípa liʔá, ñí pélta íwxac* 'She-was-terrified they-say, perfectly-white her-face got, not-even a-drop of-blood') *páyčúxpa* 'Was-scared'. (*lʷikwéeniitʷíiñe náʔa xóypa lísto xápe ságe kwáyñeñóxmaa* 'The-next-day that-one was ready where this-one usually-came') *w'éexposi* 'Hid-himself'. (*apénas šagímpa tánto páyčúxpa* 'He scarcely revived he was so scared') *máyñápa* 'Went'.

Sequentially Marked sentences are found both in conversational and narrative discourse, but generally in sequence with other sentences. Occasionally one may occur as the comment or question of one speaker after the speech of another: *ʔáytʷa tés má*

pacém'a čiča* 'And-so, what are you going-to-do now?'; *péro máa yá táyʔpá l'é* 'But I didn't hear that'.

Other examples of Sequentially Marked sentences: *ʔáytʷa wxérsa lʷikwáana* 'And his-fever is-very-high'; *xóyya, šwéday lastoráke* 'Next, they-count the-incense-sticks'; *xóypa, xóyʔpolá liñáske* 'Then, he-called-them, his-children'; *entónse šmáf'ipa lakwé* 'And-so the-man woke-up'; *péro móygi móygi tónxl'e pácedúy* 'But every day thus she-was-doing'; *poréso ʔéeday guftʷíiñe lʷilʷmélʷu* 'Therefore they baptize their-money'.

4.4. DISCOURSE TYPES. There are two major types of discourse: Conversation and Narrative. Conversation is the alternating discourse of two or more speakers. Conversational sentences tend to be shorter than narrative sentences, with speaker units frequently beginning with a completive sentence.

A sample conversation: A. *w'áytʷa lá mánapa layw'á.* 'My child was just about to die'. B. *tés ʔípa* 'What happened?' *máfpa.* 'Had a fit'. *ínxkó ténsal'e ʔípa layw'a.* 'Who knows what happened to my child.'

Another: A. *xósa, xáy, tés má pacépa wxéwilʷí pwíʔa* 'Hello, friend, what did you do a while ago this morning?' B. *ñítés, čípa yá* 'Nothing, I ground corn'. A. *xáʔñi má céepa meemáyñe* 'Didn't you go to the funeral?' B. *máa yá céepa.* 'I didn't go'. A. *tʷíñči sal'é* 'How come?' B. *sañ'i.* 'Just because.'

Narrative discourse is the unitary discourse of a single individual. Formal narrative is now restricted to the speech of the marriage go-between in asking for the hand of the bride, and the exhortation of the godfather of the newlyweds at the wedding. Informal discourse includes a variety of instructive, cultural and folklore material.

An example of earlier formal exhortation is the speech formerly delivered by the town president in the streets upon taking office. It was directed to the youth of the town, and my informant remembered it from her younger days. Since the youth are not addressed much in Chontal these days until their marriage, such a speech is no longer given.

*máyw'á, pén'elé lolnáana, lolté⁹asáns. lek'-síñyágu l*in⁹óyk'oykómon, púlᵛaylᵛé lolmáne⁹ pára imánk' wespík'ilᵛem'é andyós. xá⁹ñi wxáyñóota lantuwálč'á⁹, xá⁹ñi wágim'e lambará⁹, k'iñčotá líwxalá, xá⁹ñi nánseta frúta,* xá⁹ñi nánseta mángu. xóola xá⁹ñi, sáxkom'é imánk' elpéna, máyw'á.

'My child, obey your mothers, obey your elder brothers. When you see the town-officials, cross your arms on your chest so that you may give them the greeting of God. Don't jump into the cornfields, don't take away the poles, hunt for wood in the hills, don't steal fruit, don't steal mangoes. If not, you will find punishment, my child'.

REFERENCES

Angulo and Freeland, 1925
Belmar, 1900
Elson, 1961b
Pike, K. L., 1954, 1955, 1958, 1960

Shell, 1957
Waterhouse, 1949a, 1949b, 1961, 1962
——and Morrison, 1950

8. Language-in-Culture Studies

MIGUEL LEÓN-PORTILLA

0. Introduction
1. Cultural implications in language
1.1. Sapir's approach
1.2. Whorf's hypothesis
1.3. Pike's unified theory
1.4. Swadesh's glottochronology
2. Evaluation
3. Language in ethnographic studies
4. Language and prehistory
5. Language and archaeology
6. Conclusion

0. INTRODUCTION. To outline the role of language-in-culture studies in Middle America presupposes an answer to an old and difficult problem. The following question summarizes it: What are the relations between language and the other aspects of culture?

From a merely factual point of view, it is clear that for the ethnologist, the ethnohistorian, or the social anthropologist the mastering of the language of a group, ancient or contemporary, whose culture is to be studied, is a great aid—in fact, a must. It is also true, among other things, that often language and linguistic similarities have furnished the ethnologist with a reliable medium for the classification of different human groups. Obviously, language and culture are related when we consider these and similar factual points of view. But in a purely scientific frame the question remains open. To state what are the possible cultural contents or implications of the words, structure, and semantics of a given language —this is the old and difficult problem.

Some of the earliest philosophers were concerned with this question. In such an ancient book as the *Tao Tê Ching* we read, "there are names but not nature in words," meaning perhaps that no word can disclose the deepest secrets of nature and man (Blakney, 1955, p. 53). In the Western philosophical tradition Plato's speculations in his *Cratylus* on the origin and implications of language are often quoted. Among the modern thinkers Wilhelm von Humboldt and more recently Ernst Cassirer have discussed the problem. From their point of view language not only reflects the degree of evolution of a human group but the inner structure of their world view (Cassirer, 1933, 1944). Others, like Rudolf Carnap, had a somewhat different critical approach. According to them, language has determined the trends of thinking in classical philosophy, leading it into false problems, particularly in the field of metaphysics (Carnap, 1942).

In the contemporary anthropological sciences, as Robert Redfield (1954, p. v) has put it, "interest in these problems was suddenly mobilized by the publication of that series of papers by Benjamin L. Whorf. . . ." He refers to Whorf's *Collected Papers on Metalinguistics* (1952). Redfield himself was

369

aware of the importance of the subject. One year after the publication of Whorf's Papers, he conceived the idea of a symposium in which a group of social scientists—anthropologists, psychologists, philosophers and, of course, linguists—could discuss the old problem of the possible interrelations of language and other aspects of culture.

The conference took place at the University of Chicago March 23–27, 1953. Among the participants who presented papers were J. H. Greenberg, N. A. McQuown, C. F. Voegelin, F. Fearing, S. Newman, and H. Hoijer. Some were linguists or anthropologists in various ways concerned with the pre-Columbian or contemporary Indian cultures and languages of Middle America. This is relevant here, since in some instances mention was made of possible relations between Middle American languages and other cultural elements in this area.

The present article is conceived as an evaluation of the attempts made to study the possible implications of language-in-culture studies. I shall first discuss some theories dealing with the general problem of language in culture, then concentrate on a few specific examples—possible applications in the instance of language-in-culture studies in Middle America.

1. CULTURAL IMPLICATIONS IN LANGUAGE. Some years before Benjamin Whorf formulated his theory, which is the most elaborated one on the subject, Franz Boas, Edward Sapir, and Leonard Bloomfield, among others, were also aware of this problem. Boas, for instance, had noted the variety of linguistic expression among the Eskimos and among the Kwakiutl Indians of British Columbia. He had remarked (1911, pp. 40–41) on their demonstrative terms, which supposed in the various groups of speakers divergent ways of pointing at an object.

1.1. SAPIR'S APPROACH. Sapir, in his classic work *Language* (1921, p. 22) characterized language as, "The specific association of speech elements with concepts and the delicate provision for the formal expression of all manner of relations. . . ."

Considering language not only in itself but as the formal expression of all sort of possible relations, its functional character in any specific cultural context becomes apparent. For Sapir, any existing unit of any given language corresponds to a unit of experience. This applies not only to the isolated person but to the social group which speaks, preserves, and enriches the language. With this in mind, Sapir wrote (1929c, p. 207) that, "language is a guide to social reality." This statement, which first appeared in an article written with another purpose in mind, is, as Hoijer has observed (1954, p. 92), the initial formulation of what later would be called the Sapir-Whorf hypothesis. Quoting further from the same paragraph, written by Sapir in 1929, Hoijer makes the formulation of the hypothesis clearer:

Though language is not ordinarily thought of as of essential interest to the students of social science, it powerfully conditions all our thinking about social problems and processes. Human beings do not live in the objective world alone, nor alone in the world of social activity as ordinarily understood, but are very much at the mercy of the particular language which has become the medium of expression for their society. It is quite an illusion to imagine that one adjusts to reality essentially without the use of language and that language is merely an incidental means of solving specific problems of communication or reflection. The fact of the matter is that "the real world" is to a large extent unconsciously built up on the language habits of the group. . . .

Words, structure, and connotation are not, therefore, neutral devices or pure instruments in communication. They are factors in defining experience, dynamic elements through which the members of a group who possess the same language adjust to reality. Close to this is Leonard Bloomfield's concept of the "speech-community," i.e., "a group of people who interact by means of speech." The importance of "speech communities" should be realized, according to Bloomfield, through analyzing how "all the so-called higher activities of man, our specifically human activities, spring from the close adjustment among individuals we call society, and this adjustment, in turn, is based upon language . . ." (Bloomfield quoted by Herskovits, 1948, p. 442).

1.2. WHORF'S HYPOTHESIS. Statements like those quoted can be found here and there in the works of Sapir, Bloomfield, and other linguists. No doubt they anticipated the direct formulation of the Whorfian hypothesis. Whorf, "a businessman who became a specialist in language study," as F. M. Keesing has put it, delving into the subject, opened new perspectives, pushing his hypotheses probably too far, but presenting interpretations which nontheless deserve to be carefully analyzed. We will proceed to do this, taking advantage of the remarks made in reference to it in the conference organized by Redfield.

In presenting his hypothesis, Whorf takes examples specially from the language of the Hopi Indians he had studied. Comparing the grammars of Hopi and of what he designates as Standard Average European languages, he arrives at what he terms "a new principle of relativity." He states (1952, p. 5), "We are thus introduced to a new principle of relativity, which holds that all observers are not led by the same physical evidence to the same picture of the universe, unless their linguistic backgrounds are similar. . . ." Precisely because in the Standard Average European languages there is a time-specific structural background, experience and thought appear always to be time-colored: "The three-tense system of Standard Average European verbs colors all our thinking about time. This system is amalgamated with that larger scheme of objectification of the subjective experience of duration . . . (ibid., p. 33).

This does not happen among the Hopi, who possess an entirely different linguistic structural background (ibid., p. 44):

Our own "time" differs markedly from Hopi "duration." It is conceived as a space of strictly limited dimensions, or sometimes as a motion upon such a space, and employed as an intellectual tool accordingly. Hopi "duration" seems to be inconceivable in terms of space or motion, being the mode in which life differs from form and consciousness in toto from the spatial elements of consciousness. Certain ideas born of our own time-concept, such as that of absolute simultaneity, would be either very difficult to express or impossible and devoid of meaning under the Hopi conception, and would be replaced by operational concepts.

Standard Average European languages transform the idea of time into an object of strictly limited dimensions. Time—or rather duration—in Hopi "seems inconceivable in terms of space" because the linguistic patterns of Hopi are different. In Whorf's terms, they are "essentially ahistorical." For Whorf, to accept the linguistic principle of relativity means the recognition of such differences as correlated with "the kingly role of language, as shaper of ideas." "Users of markedly different grammars," he says (p. 11), "are pointed by their grammars toward different types of observations and different evaluations of externally similar acts of observation, and hence are not equivalent observers, but must arrive at somewhat different views of the world."

Emphasizing the effect that linguistic structures exert on human thinking, the linguistic principle of relativity presupposes, as Franklin Fearing has noted (1954, p. 47), "that the commonly held notion that the cognitive processes of all human beings possess a common logical structure . . . which operates prior to and independently of communication through language, is erroneous." Whorf himself arrived at this explicit conclusion, which is at the core of his hypothesis (1952, p. 4):

The phenomena of language are to its own speakers largely of a background character and so are outside the critical consciousness and control of the speaker who is expounding natural logic. Hence, when anyone, as a natural logician, is talking about reason, logic and the laws of correct thinking, he is apt to be simply marching in step with purely grammatical facts that have somewhat of a background character in his own language or family of languages but are by no means universal in all languages and in no sense common substratum of reason.

The affirmation of this background character of language, prior to natural logic, implied in Whorf's hypothesis the consequence that "language represents the mass mind," determines the different approaches to the world of experience, is a "shaper of ideas," and is responsible in its "kingly role" for the appearance of different world views. If all this is so, the possible cultural inferences to be drawn from language materials are almost without limit. First of all, ethnologists and ethnohistorians would have, in the analysis of the various grammars and their linguist patterns, the key to the origin and meaning of the most different world views. The archaeologist would have the possibility of establishing parallels between the evolution of language, "that shaper of ideas," and development of artistic forms in ceramics, painting, sculpture, and architecture. The social anthropologist, studying and analyzing the languages, would be able to grasp the intricacies of the "mass mind" of the group he studies. And it is possible that even the physical anthropologist could also discover parallels between linguistic structures and semantics on the one hand, and human evolution on the other.

Obviously Whorf's ideas, even when presented in a schematic and perhaps oversimplified form, bring forth numerous questions of interest in the fields of anthropology and the social sciences in general.

Before attempting an evaluation of the relevance of Whorf's hypothesis in the analysis of the cultural contents of language materials, I shall refer briefly to two other scientific hypotheses. Both are connected with the interrelations of language and culture. One is K. L. Pike's hypothesis on language in relation to a unified theory of the structure of human behavior, and the other is M. Swadesh's often discussed glottochronology.

1.3. PIKE'S UNIFIED THEORY OF THE STRUCTURE OF HUMAN BEHAVIOR. The study of Indian languages, particularly Mixtec, and the analysis of linguistic structures led Kenneth L. Pike to formulate a new behaviorist hypothesis. Far from Whorf's conceptions about language as "the shaper of ideas and world views," Pike considered the structured dynamics of language, especially syntax and morphology, as the key to study of any kind of structured human activity. After developing an explanatory theory and an operational technique for dealing with syntactic and morphological materials, he began the formulation of what he called "Language in Relation to a Unified Theory of the Structure of Human Behavior" (Pike, 1954, 1955). Pike describes the origin and purpose of his hypothesis (1956, p. 659):

The thesis which for the past seven years I have been exploring is the following: that every purposeful activity of man is structured, and that certain basic characteristics are common to every such activity, so that it would be possible to develop a theory and a technique which would pass without jar from the study of the structure of one kind of activity of man to that of any other kind. Ideally this would result in one basic theory of structure, one basic set of terms, and one basic methodology, which could be applied to the analysis of language, the analysis of ritual behavior, the analysis of sports, the analysis of occupational activity, or even to the processes of thought itself.

Pike's technique for analyzing the various patterns of human activity closely follows his basic methodology for working with linguistic structures, especially in the specific areas of phonemics, morphology, and syntax. As an example of this, in analyzing human behavior, Pike describes it as made up of "waves and particles," that is, as a physical continuum in which there are waves with ups and downs, with nuclei or particles at the peaks and ebbs of activity. He calls these nuclei *emes* or *emic units*, "deriving the terms from the latter part of the word *phoneme*, or the phrase *phonemic unit*" (*ibid.*, p. 661).

Since I can here not present all the principles underlying Pike's hypothesis, I mention only one interesting possible application of it, in what Pike designates as "the predictability of difficulties in acculturation." Applying his concept of "emic units," Pike (p. 662) considers "every person emically structured." He means by this that persons have grown up in an environment in which their elicited answers are divided, in certain discrete ways, into emic units, which are part of a total system of possible elicited responses. If we consider this an essential aspect of the structure of human behavior, it may be stated that the members of a community have developed specific forms of responding within the limits of their own language and culture. For instance, if the words "mate" and "met" occur in a particular context, an English-speaking person would easily detect and answer in accordance with the different emic units represented by the different sounds of the vowels in the two words. A Spanish-speaking individual would probably have difficulty in differentiating the emic units and his reaction and possible answer would be entirely different. This simple example shows, according to Pike, how the unified theory of the structure of human behavior can permit certain predictions of emic clash, "not only in respect to language learning but also in respect to acculturation, in the field of etiquette, or of ritual, or of law, of commerce, and so on" (*ibid.*, p. 664). Obviously, from this and other

points of view, Pike's hypothesis, if demonstrated and tested, could be of great significance in the correlation of language and other cultural institutions.

1.4. SWADESH'S GLOTTOCHRONOLOGY. Before attempting an evaluation of Pike's hypothesis, I shall briefly outline Swadesh's glottochronology. Lexicostatistical glottochronology starts from the idea that linguistic changes are not merely occasional phenomena, but represent constant and continuous movements that can be discovered and precisely described. By finding an index which will manifest the rhythm of change in the lexicon of a language, one may establish its degree of relationship with other languages. Further, the number of centuries or even of millennia in which various languages or dialects suddenly or gradually became separate may be determined.

The techniques used in glottochronology imply several fundamental principles. The first is that the existence in all languages of a noncultural basic vocabulary, described by Swadesh, as the one whose terms express "things, qualities and activities universal and simple, which depend in the least possible degree on the particular environment and the cultural status of the group" (Swadesh, 1960e, p. 134). In order to find this basic vocabulary, consisting of 100 words which will allow one to determine the rhythm of change in the various languages (*ibid.*, p. 134):

"a diagnostic" list of words was prepared formed mainly by pronouns, some quantitative concepts, parts and simple activities of the body, movements, and some general qualities of size, color, etc. Aside from the cultural material, we avoided the inclusion of words which in many languages imitate sounds (onomatopoetic words), as this characteristic may give them a persistence, such as terms with a very specific meaning might have, and this might hinder the identification of equivalent words in different languages. The first experiences in the use of the diagnostic list gave rise to reforms, in which elements were eliminated or substituted, until the actual diagnostic list of 100 elements was reached.

The second principle of the method of glottochronology consists in determining the maximum and minimum changes in the basic vocabulary of any language. For this, examples were looked for in languages with texts from two different periods, both historically known and separated by at least several centuries. Among others, Latin and certain Romance languages were chosen, as well as 1000-year-old classic Chinese, which was compared with present-day Chinese. In order to appreciate the changes in the lexicon of these languages through these periods of time, the diagnostic list of 100 words of noncultural basic vocabulary was applied. It turned out that in a thousand years a maximum of 90 per cent of the basic vocabulary and no less than 81 per cent was retained. The average of retention consequently was 86 per cent of the vocabulary in a millennium of evolution of a particular language.

Swadesh acknowledges that there may be

Percentage:		70	69	68	67	66	65	64	63	62	61	60
Minimum centuries of divergence:		11.8	12.3	12.8	13.3	13.8	14.3	14.9	15.3	15.8	16.4	16.9

fluctuations in the percentage of retention of the basic vocabulary. But at the same time he points out the very limited amount of such variation of that vocabulary over a 1000-year period. From this, Swadesh deduces the following principle (1960e, pp. 134–35):

The existence of a limited continuum of variation provides a basis on which to measure time, at least in an approximate way. In order to profit from this knowledge in glottochronology, we must consider the relation between the lineal change and the parallel differentiation between dialects that become separate. In these cases the actual difference is the product of the changes undergone by each one after its separation. The modifications experienced by one have not reached the others, as they have

had a separate divergent development. The whole of the lexical changes in both lines is the same as twice as much time would produce in one of them. The common residue may be calculated by multiplying the two individual residues. For instance, if each language has 80 per cent of the original vocabulary, and if they have continued to develop entirely without mutual contact, then they will have 80 per cent of 80 per cent of cognates, that is, 64 per cent. If they have had partial contacts, this may have caused some additional agreements, including cases where the same original element has been mantained and cases where the same new word has been introduced. In this way partial contact may produce in the case of 80 per cent retention in each line, more than 64 per cent of correspondences—with a possibility that it may be almost 100 per cent if the separation has been very slight.

This criterion may be applied to languages known to have a common origin. The percentage of shared cognate words, according to the diagnostic list, must be determined. The separation of these languages will be translated into minimum centuries of divergence, according to the following conversion table (*ibid.*, p. 135):

The method of lexicostatistical glottochronology has been applied by Swadesh to various languages of Middle America and of this continent in general. One of the applications of this method could be to establish with greater precision different degrees of linguistic relationship. There could be other applications (Swadesh, 1955, pp. 121–22):

This development is of great interest for the reconstruction of prehistory because it offers a time dimension for ethnic contacts shown by linguistic relationship. In the light of historically known locations of peoples, it gives evidence regarding their prehistoric location and movements at given periods of the past. These data can be correlated with the indications of archeology, comparative ethnography, geography of loan-words, geographic distribution of phonetic and morphologic features, and many other kinds of evidence. It frequently gives important clues for connecting prehistoric archeologic sites with historically known peoples.

These are, in a few words, the possibilities and the basic principles of glottochronology. As one may easily see, this hypothesis enters fully into the field of the possible relations between language and culture. Before referring to concrete applications of it to cultural studies in Middle America, we must briefly evaluate the various hypotheses that have been considered: Benjamin Whorf's on language as a shaper of ideas, Pike's on language in relation to a unified theory of the structure of human behavior, and Swadesh's lexicostatistical method.

2. EVALUATION. Norman A. McQuown (1960a, p. 79) notes that those who have analyzed the various theories on the relationship between language and culture "fall into two general groups, those which emphasize the difficulties, and those which point out that it is somehow being done every day."

Referring specifically to the theory of Benjamin Whorf, in the symposium organized by Redfield in 1953, a whole series of questions was prepared, upon the answer to which the applicability of this theory fundamentally depends. The cultural inferences that can be drawn from specific aspects of a language may stem from the phonology, vocabulary, structure, or semantics.

Obviously, the first step would be to determine the phonological, structural, and semantic patterns of a given language. Without doubt, from the point of view of the theories of perception and cognition, it can be stated that "the special character of Whorf's conceptions consists in the central role of linguistic patterns" (Fearing, 1954, p. 49). In the giving of first place to the linguistic factor as the determining one in the way of thinking, in world views and in

communicational behavior, numerous objections and problems arise.

But, it is worthwhile emphasizing that, if the point of departure is an analysis of these linguistic patterns in a certain language, it would be possible to attempt, in a critical sense, applications of Whorf's theory in concrete cases. Rather than doing it in the abstract, it would be worthwhile evaluating that theory in its applications to specific studies of correlation between a language and specific cultural elements. The results of each study, without forcing the elements analyzed, could demonstrate to what degree language has an influence on, or is related to, other aspects of a specific culture.

If Pike's unified theory of the structure of human behavior, taking as the fundamental case linguistic behavior, is applicable, this would demonstrate that in many cases, more than of a relationship of dependency, we could speak of relationships of parallelism between language and other aspects of culture. Undoubtedly, above all a priori considerations, the validity of these theories would depend on their applications. For this to be possible, it would always be necessary to start with a careful analysis of the cultural and linguistic elements to be compared. In the field of linguistics, works like those of Velma Pickett on the analysis of grammatical structures (Pickett, 1956) and of Benjamin Elson on morphology and syntax (Elson, 1958) could become excellent tools for this purpose. Later, it would be necessary to examine critically the possible inferences, parallelisms, and conclusions. This could be done only on the basis of a thorough acquaintance with the languages and the cultural institutions and patterns being studied for such relationships.

Whorf's theory on the one hand, and Pike's on the other, from very different angles, attempt principally to relate the linguistic patterns to other types of patterns, either in the field of thought, art, world view, or in that of human communicational behavior.

375

The case of glottochronology is different. Here, inferences are sought starting basically with vocabulary. The lexicostatistical method, with its diagnostic list of 100 non-cultural words, is aimed at discovering another sort of conclusion. These are also of a cultural character. But they refer to the relationships and kinship between the different languages and, therefore, also to the relationships and kinship between different peoples, their mutual cultural influences, determinable by the study of loan-words, their degree of persistence, etc.

Among the basic questions on which the applicability of Swadesh's method depends are: How is it possible to determine beyond all doubt the correctness of the selection of the diagnostic list of the 100 noncultural words? Is it possible to state that throughout the whole of linguistic evolution the changes in the noncultural vocabulary always follow the same rhythm? Would not application of that diagnostic list to various languages suppose in reality a profound knowledge of them, in order not to err with respect to the identification of the basic vocabulary in languages which are thought to be closely related?

The possible answers to these and other questions in each concrete case will probably determine the applicability of glottochronology to specific situations. Once more, it must be repeated that, as in the case of the theories of Whorf and Pike, a careful analysis of the linguistic elements in play must first be made. In the application of the theory, the greatest critical judgment must be exercised. It would be risky in the case of glottochronology to apply the diagnostic list to languages which are known only superficially.

We now consider briefly some concrete studies related to the area of Middle America in which, in one form or another, relationships have been established between language and culture.

3. LANGUAGE IN ETHNOGRAPHIC STUDIES.

The same idea—that it is necessary to start with an adequate knowledge of the Indian languages to be able to establish relationships between them and other cultural elements—is expressed by McQuown (1960b, pp. 14–15), referring especially to the problem of cultural genesis, migrations, and contacts among various groups:

For fruitful pursuit of hints as to common genesis or culture contact such as those we have listed above, tantalizing and inconclusive as they almost without exception are, and for the profitable study of culture history via the linguistic record, it might be well to specify certain requirements:
(1) more full-fledged grammars and dictionaries;
(2) more comparative and historical work of two kinds:
    (a) preliminary mapping out of areas worthy of work in depth, such preliminary mapping being carried out by: inspection, lexicostatistical dating, probabilistic reasoning, and
    (b) definitive establishment of genetic relationship and full working out of contactual history by: correspondence matrices, etymological dictionaries, historical grammars;
(3) language and culture studies, both descriptive and historical;
(4) dialect geographical work (in the Nahuatl-speaking area, for example, or in the lake region of the highland of Guatemala);
(5) full decipherment of the available glyphic material, with collaboration between archaeologists, linguists and cryptanalysts;
(6) full utilization of the documentary material in Nahuatl and in such other languages as it may turn up, such utilization involving:
    (a) revival and continuation of *Tlalocan* and
    (b) expansion of philological training in Nahuatl and in such other languages as may prove useful towards this end.

It should be recognized that all these requirements now exist only in very limited form, and that in reality only a very few studies to determine cultural contacts have been made on a firm basis. Following principally the evaluation prepared by McQuown on the linguistic studies carried out in Middle America during the last decades, the following can be mentioned:

Both Walter Lehmann (1920) and Oliver LaFarge (1927), note loan words of Nahuatl origin existing in the various Mayan languages and others of Middle America, showing that at various times there were probably cultural contacts between Nahuatl-speakers and the persons speaking those languages.

Other signs of cultural contacts among peoples of Mayan languages and others of Middle America are visible in the presence of terms like the one for 'alligator' *?ain* used by the Huichol and which is very similar to the Maya word (*?áxʸin*) and the Huastec *?áhin*. Another probable loan from Mam or Tzetzal is to be found among the Xincas. That is the word *činaq̇* (Mam) or *čenek'* (Tzetzal) which means 'bean', and which among the Xincas appears slightly modified as *šinak* (Whorf, 1949; McQuown, 1960b, p. 326).

McQuown's studies, aimed at classifying the various languages of the Mayan family as well as at finding the lines of their internal differentiation, have also thrown considerable light on the study of the ancient history and ethnography of these peoples. According to McQuown (1956, pp. 191–95), by drawing a triangle it can be stated that there is a core in the highlands of Guatemala, with Huastec and Yucatec at the two extremes, with the Chontal-Chol-Chortí axis and the peripheral highland languages of Chiapas in a sort of intermediate position. In addition, there are various studies, broader in character, which attempt to relate these languages with others within a Macro-Mayan stock. According to McQuown (1942, pp. 37–38), Totonac and Mixe-Zoque could be included within this stock. Swadesh

(1954b, pp. 306–32) has tried to relate the Huave language with the Macro-Mayan stock, although this cannot be considered as something definitive.

Many other studies by Swadesh, applying the lexicostatistical method, have led him to establish five first-line linguistic groups in Mexico: Tarasco, Macro-Mixtec, Macro-Mayan, Macro-Nahua, and Macro-Yuman. According to his conclusions, the first and the last are to be found at the same linguistic distance, whereas the other three offer points of contact within a 51–80 minimum-century range. Swadesh considers that Macro-Mixtec includes four subgroups: Otopamean; Oaxacan (Chocho-Popoloca-Ixcatec - Mazatecan - Mixtec - Cuicatec-Amuzgan), Trique, and Zapotecan; Chinantecan; and Huave (Swadesh, 1959b, pp. 9–10). Swadesh' theory of Macro-Mixtec particularly has been the object of study and criticism (Longacre, 1957, 1961a).

Finally, as another outcome of his glottochronological studies, Swadesh has suggested a remote kinship between Tarasco and Quechua and between Uto-Aztecan and Chibcha (Swadesh, 1954b, pp. 324–25; 1956, pp. 32–33). It is evident that if this theory can be demonstrated, many and important conclusions can be deduced concerning the migrations that occurred on this continent millennia ago.

Important contributions for future ethnolinguistic studies are also to be found in periodicals offering modern texts in the Indian languages of Middle America: *Tlalocan, The International Journal of American Linguistics, América Indígena* (published by the Instituto Indigenista Interamericano), *Anthropological Linguistics, American Anthropologist*, and the various linguistic series published by the Summer Institute of Linguistics.

4. LANGUAGE AND PREHISTORY. Although several of the studies we have already mentioned could imply conclusions of importance for prehistory, we should like to refer here

377

in particular to another work in which Swadesh concerns himself directly with possible inferences deriving from application of the lexicostatistical method to Nahua prehistory. To give only one example, the Pipil group of Salvador appear to have separated from the Nahua of the Mexico region only approximately ten centuries ago (Swadesh, 1954c, p. 178). In the same study (p. 180) he shows the results of the application of this method to the calculation of the varying amounts of separation between the Nahua language and others of the Uto-Aztecan family. Thus for example, Cora has at least 38 mc. of separation with respect to Nahuatl, whereas Huichol has only 15.

These are a few examples of the applications, carried out by Swadesh, of the lexicostatistical method. From the separation of the languages the separation of the ethnic groups in prehistoric times may be inferred. Obviously, these conclusions are subject to modification as more adequate account is taken of factors which we analyzed on presenting Swadesh's theory and evaluating it.

5. LANGUAGE AND ARCHAEOLOGY. As McQuown has already noted, to be able to establish relationship between language and culture in specific cases, it is necesary to begin with what might be considered obvious: an adequate acquaintance with the language in question. It should be recognized that there are few languages in Middle America on which there is adequate grammatical and lexical material available for which critical analysis of texts and documents, contemporary as well as of pre-Hispanic origin, has been carried out. The latter is true to a certain degree only of some few languages of the Mayan and Nahua families.

With reference to Nahuatl language and culture, it can be said that, especially since the last third of the last century, there have been scholars who have occupied themselves with the analysis and translation of texts, as well as with the publication of some grammars and dictionaries, outstanding among them being the *Dictionaire de la Langue Nahuatl*, published by Rémi Siméon (1885). Francisco del Paso y Troncoso also made possible the study of the Nahuatl manuscripts gathered by Fray Bernardino de Sahagún, thanks to the facsimile publication he made of them in 1906–07. Paso y Troncoso also published a version of some of the texts, such as *La Leyenda de los Soles* (1903) as well as other texts in the series *Papeles de la Nueva España* (1905–06).

Eduard Seler was probably the first investigator who tried to relate various of the texts and documents in Nahuatl language to archaeology. Many of these studies, published in magazines, were included in his *Gesammelte Abhandlungen* (1902–23). After his death, the sections from the Nahuatl texts of the Indian informants of Sahagún that he translated into German were also published in a separate volume (1927).

Continuing in the tradition of Seler, two other German investigators, Walter Lehmann and Leonhard Schultze-Jena, also prepared versions of other sections of the aforementioned texts compiled by Sahagún. as well as the *Anales de Cuauhtitlan*, part of the work of the Indian historian Chimalpahin (Lehmann, 1938, 1949; Lehmann and Kutscher, 1958; Schultze-Jena, 1950, 1952, 1957).

Konrad Theodor Preuss in Germany and Ernst Mengin in Denmark have published bilingual editions of Nahuatl documents (Preuss and Mengin, 1937–38; Mengin, 1950) as well as a series of six volumes containing facsimile reproductions of Nahuatl and Mayan texts under the title *Corpus Codicum Americanorum Medii Aevi* (Mengin, 1942–50).

In Mexico, Angel M. Garibay K. has begun the publication and analysis of Indian texts. His *Llave del Náhuatl* (1940a, 1961) offers, in outline form, an analysis of the structure of Classical Nahuatl. Later studies of Garibay (1940b, 1943a, 1943b, 1945, 1946, 1948, 1953–54) have demonstrated the enormous abundance of this

Indian literature. It can be said that this illustrious tradition of Nahuatl studies from Siméon to Garibay has now opened the way for possible studies of correlation between Indian texts and archaeology.

In the three published volumes of the magazine *Tlalocan* (1943–57) various texts in Nahuatl have also been made available, classical as well as of various contemporary modern dialects, by investigators such as Robert H. Barlow, Fernando Horcasitas, Byron McAfee, Miguel Barrios, and Garibay. Others, like Adrián León (1949) and Primo F. Velázquez (1945), have also contributed with publications of several important Nahuatl documents.

Finally, the Seminar of Nahuatl Culture, organized by Angel M. Garibay and Miguel León-Portilla, has been functioning within the Institute of History of the National University of Mexico since 1956. The Seminar, in addition to preparing students for the investigation of Nahuatl language and culture, has begun to edit three series of publications. In the first, entitled *Fuentes Indígenas de la Cultura Nahuatl*, three volumes of the texts compiled by the informants of Sahagún, with paleography and translation of the Nahuatl text (León-Portilla, 1958; Garibay, 1958, 1961), have been published. The second series (monographs) contain León-Portilla's *La Filosofía Náhuatl, estudiada en sus Fuentes* (1956), which tries to discover via the Nahuatl texts what could have been the world view of the pre-Columbian Aztecs and other Nahua-speaking peoples; and a study on pre-Hispanic law, based on Nahua Indian texts, by Alfredo López Austin (1961). The third series constitutes the yearbook entitled *Estudios de Cultura Náhuatl*, of which five volumes have appeared (1959, 1960, 1962–1965). This publication contains studies on language, archaeology, ethnography, and other aspects of the Nahuatl-speaking peoples.

It remains to be added that in the United States investigators have also undertaken studies of the Nahuatl language. Among them are McQuown and, above all, Arthur J. O. Anderson and Charles E. Dibble, who in 1950 began the publication of the *Códice Florentino* (1950–60) in a bilingual (Nahuatl-English) edition, of which ten volumes have been published to date (1966).

Undoubtedly, this resurgence of studies of the Nahuatl language and culture will make it possible to establish language-in-culture relationships on a firm basis, beginning, as is desirable, with at least an adequate knowledge of the language. It would be interesting, for example, to apply Whorf's theory to the specific case of the philosophy or world view of the Nahuatl-speaking peoples, utilizing the texts included in the work of León-Portilla, already mentioned.

With respect to the Mayan world, there are also studies of literary texts in the Maya of Yucatan, in Quiché, and in Cakchiquel. As it is not possible to list here all the studies made during the 19th century, we mention only the names of the principal investigators: Brasseur de Bourbourg, Daniel G. Brinton, Molina y Solís, Juan Pío Pérez, Bishop Carrillo y Ancona, Leon de Rosny, Karl Hermann Berendt; at the beginning of this century, Eduard Seler, Walter Lehmann, and Juan Martínez Hernández. More recent are the studies of G. B. Gordon (1913) and of A. M. Tozzer who, beginning in 1901, published several modern Maya texts, as well as many other studies, among them his *Maya Grammar* (1921), intended to seek out the categories and structure peculiar to this language.

In the United States, Ralph L. Roys (1920, 1929, 1933, 1940, 1943) has studied texts of the Maya culture of Yucatan. Thanks to the William Gates Collection, it has been possible to continue these studies on a broad scale in the United States.

In Mexico, Alfredo Barrera Vásquez has given special attention to the texts of the Maya world (Barrera Vásquez, 1935, 1939; Barrera Vásquez and Morley, 1948; Barrera Vásquez and Rendón, 1949). Especially

379

valuable are his studies on the books of Chilam Balam and of the Maya Chronicles. Concerning texts in Quiché and Cakchiquel of Guatemala are studies of the Popol Vuh made by investigators at the end of the last century. In this century, Adrían Recinos has published several studies of this same book (1947, 1950a, 1953), of the Annals of Totonicapan (1950b, 1953), and of other Indian chronicles of lesser importance (1957). The translation of the Popol Vuh into German was prepared and published by Leonhard Schultze-Jena (1944). In addition to these studies of Indian texts in various Mayan languages are the major works on decipherment of the glyphs of the Maya pre-Hispanic writing. There are the studies of Hermann Beyer, who tried to identify series of two or more glyphs occurring together, forming what J. E. S. Thompson has called clauses. This approach allowed Beyer to give more attention to the affixes of the principal elements, their functions, the laws which govern their use and their interchangeability (Beyer, 1937). Gates published a dictionary (1931) of the Maya glyphs appearing in the codices. Thompson continued the work of Beyer, trying to discover the rules to be found in the Maya hieroglyphic writing. He also offered a good number of decipherments, some certain and others tentative (Thompson, 1950). Thomas Barthel has attempted a series of decipherments (1952, 1953, 1954, 1955b). He has published an analysis of the glyphs (1955a) in the buildings at Chichen Itza, proposing some impressive equivalents in the inscriptions that he has tentatively interpreted and that seem to recall the contents of the books of Chilam Balam.

Günther Zimmermann introduced a methodical and practical system for classifying the glyphs. As can be seen in Thompson's recent publications (1954, 1961, 1962) there is continuing interest in the attempts at deciphering the Maya glyphs, which in the future will undoubtedly result in important contributions toward knowledge of the language and culture of the peoples of this zone of Middle America.

In the field of Mixtec archaeology and linguistics the study and partial decipherment of some of the pre-Columbian Mixtec codices has been helpful in understanding the life and institutions of the Indian cultures of Oaxaca (Caso, 1928, 1949, 1951, 1960; Dark, 1958).

A modern grammar of the Mitla Zapotec has been worked out by Elinor Briggs (1961). Studies on the Otomí-Pame linguistic family have been made by Jacques Soustelle (1937, 1951).

As for Nahuatl culture, a Seminar on Maya Culture was established in 1960 at the National University of Mexico. This Seminar, directed by Alberto Ruz, has started an annual publication, *Estudios de Cultura Maya*, with the same character and function as its equivalent devoted to Nahuatl culture.

6. CONCLUSION. Although there are many studies on language and culture—Nahuatl, Mayan, and others—much still remains to be investigated. As these studies advance, it will be possible to establish relationships and come much closer to integral knowledge of these cultures and of their respective languages. Only by relating the content of the ancient texts, as well as the cultural implications inherent in the linguistic forms themselves, with other data supplied by archaeology can we some day arrive at an over-all view of these great cultures of Middle America. The general conclusion of this article we have already anticipated: there is continuing need for more profound studies of the languages, for grammars and dictionaries in the modern sense, for the philological study of the texts which have been preserved, and for a wide variety of derivative language-in-culture studies. Only in this way can account be taken, on a firm basis, of the relationships undoubtedly existing between language and culture.

REFERENCES

Anderson and Dibble, 1950–66
Barrera Vásquez, 1935, 1939
——and Morley, 1949
——and Rendón, 1948
Barthel, 1952, 1953, 1954, 1955a, 1955b
Beyer, 1937
Blakney, 1955
Boas, 1911
Briggs, 1961
Carnap, 1942
Carroll, 1956
Caso, n.d., 1928, 1949, 1951, 1960
Cassirer, 1933, 1944
Dark, 1958
Elson, 1958
Estudios de Cultura Náhuatl, 1959, 1960, 1962–65
Fearing, 1954
Garibay K., 1940a, 1940b, 1943a, 1943b, 1945, 1946, 1948, 1953–54, 1958, 1961
Gates, 1931
Gordon, 1913
Greenberg, 1948, 1957a
Herskovits, 1948
Hoijer, 1954
Kroeber, 1940
LaFarge, 1927
Lehmann, 1920, 1938, 1949
——and Kutscher, 1958
León, A., 1949

León-Portilla, 1956, 1958
Longacre, 1957, 1961a
López Austin, 1961
McQuown, 1942, 1954, 1955a, 1956, 1957, 1960a, 1960b
Mengin, 1942–50, 1950
Olmsted, 1950
Paso y Troncoso, 1903, 1905–06, 1906–07
Pickett, 1956
Pike, K. L., 1944, 1954, 1955, 1956, 1959, 1960
Preuss and Mengin, 1937–38
Recinos, 1947, 1950a, 1950b, 1953, 1957
Redfield, 1954
Roys, 1920, 1929, 1933, 1940, 1943
Sapir, 1921, 1927, 1929c, 1949
Schultze-Jena, 1944, 1950, 1952, 1957
Seler, 1902–23, 1927
Siméon, 1885
Soustelle, 1937, 1951
Swadesh, 1954b, 1954c, 1955, 1956, 1959b, 1959c, 1960e, 1960f, 1962, 1964a, 1964b, 1966
Thompson, J. E. S., 1950, 1954, 1961, 1962
Tlalocan, 1943–57
Tozzer, 1921
Velázquez, 1945
Voegelin, 1950, 1953
——and Harris, 1945
Whorf, 1943, 1950, 1952

REFERENCES

REFERENCES

ADAMS, R. M., AND N. A. McQUOWN
1959 Pre-history, proto-history, and post-conquest developments. *In* McQuown, 1959a.

ALBORNOZ, J. DE
1691 Arte de la lengua chiapaneca. MS in Bibliothèque Nationale.

ALDAMA Y GUEVARA, J. A. DE
1754 Arte de la lengua mexicana. (Mexico, 1892.)

ALEJANDRE, M.
1890 Cartilla huasteca con su gramática, diccionario.... Mexico.

ALEMÁN, L.
1884 Grammaire élémentaire de la langue Quiché. Suppl. to Compte-rendu, Int. Cong. Amer., 1883. Copenhagen.

ALVARADO, F. DE
1593 Vocabulario en lengua misteca.... Photograph in Newberry Library. 419 pp.

ANDERSON, A. J. O., AND C. E. DIBBLE
1950–66 Florentine codex. *See* Sahagún, 1575–77.

ANDRADE, M. J.
1940 A grammar of modern Yucatec. *Micro. Coll. MS Middle Amer. Cult. Anthr.*, no. 41 (1957), Univ. Chicago Library. 476 pp.
1946 Materials on the Quiche, Cakchiquel, and Tzutuhil languages. *Ibid.*, no. 11. 942 pp.

ANGEL, FR.
18thC [a] Arte de lengua cakchiquel.... MS in Bibliothèque Nationale.
18thC [b] Vocabulario de la lengua cakchiquel. *Ibid.* 452 pp.
18thC [c] Vocabulario de la lengua cakchiquel. Photograph in Newberry Library. 718 pp.

ANGULO, J. DE
1925 The linguistic tangle of Oaxaca. *Language*, 1: 96–102.
1926a Tone patterns and verb forms in a dialect of Zapotek. *Ibid.*, 2: 238–50.
1926b The development of affixes in a group of monosyllabic languages of Oaxaca. *Ibid.*, 2–46–61.
1933 The Chichimeco language (central Mexico). *IJAL*, 7: 152–94.
—— AND L. S. FREELAND
1925 The Chontal language (dialect of Tequisistlan). *Anthropos*, 20: 1032–52.
1935 The Zapotekan linguistic group. *IJAL*, 8: 111–30.

ANLEO, B.
1744 Arte de lengua quiché.
1865 Arte de lengua Giche. *In* Squier, 1865.

ANONYMOUS
1590 Dictionarium ex bismensi.... MS in Newberry Library. 314 pp.
1598 Vocabulario mexicano. Photograph in Newberry Library. 236 pp.
17thC? [a] Bocabulario en lengua cakchiquel y quiche. Photograph in Newberry Library. 706 pp.
17thC? [b] Bocabulario de lengua quiché. Photograph in Newberry Library. 78 pp.
17thC? [c] Bocabulario en lengua quiché y castellana. Photograph in Newberry Library. 372 pp.
17thC? [d] Calepino grande, castellano y quiché. Photograph in Newberry Library. 480 pp.
17thC [e] Diccionario de San Francisco: maya-español, español-maya. Photograph in Newberry Library. 402 pp.
17thC [f] Noticia breve de los vocablos más usuales de la lengua cakchiquel. MS in Bibliothèque Nationale. 182 pp.
17thC [g] Vocabulario en lengua castellana y ... cakchiquelchi. Photograph in Newberry Library. 500 pp.
18thC? [a] Vocabulario de la lengua castellana y quiché. MS in Bibliothèque Nationale. 200 pp.
18thC [b] Vocabulario hispano-hyaqui. MS in Newberry Library. 999 pp.
1733 Vocabulario de la lengua çoque. MS in John Carter Brown Library. 354 pp.
1750 Vocabulario otomí [Spanish-Otomi]. MS in Newberry Library. 571 pp.
1800 Arte zaapoteco.... MS in Newberry Library. 309 pp.
1838 Requête de plusieurs chefs indiens d'Atitlan à Philippe II. *In* H. Ternaux-Compans, Voyages, relations et mémoires originaux ...: Receuil de pièces relatives à la conquête du Mexique. Paris.
1862 Grammar of the Pima or Névome.... Buckingham Smith, ed. *J. G. Shea's Library of American Linguistics*, no. 5.
1884 A grammar of the Cakchiquel language. ... *Proc. Amer. Phil. Soc.*, 21: 345–412.
1887 Gramática de la lengua zapoteca.... Antonio Peñafiel, ed. Mexico.

1890 Arte de la lengua cahita.

1893a Vocabulario castellano - zapoteco. . . . Mexico.

1893b Luces del otomí. Mexico.

1902 Are va vuhil tioxilah evangelio rech ka nima ahaval Jesucristo kereka San Marcos. Belize. (San Jose, 1899.)

1950 Alfabeto para los cuatro idiomas mayoritarios de Guatemala. *Pub. Especiales Inst. Ind. Nac.*, no. 10. Guatemala.

Ara, D. de

16thC [Copanaguastla Tzeltal grammar.] MS in Newberry Library, subtitled Egregium opus. . . . 40 pp.

1571 Bocabulario en lengua tzeldal. Photograph in Newberry Library. 328 pp.

Arana O., E.

1953 Reconstrucción del Protototonaco. *In* Huastecos, Totonacos y sus vecinos, pp. 123–30.

1957 Relaciones internas del tronco Mixteco. Master's thesis. [Published in 1960 in *An. Inst. Nac. Antr. Hist.*, pp. 22–73.]

1959a Relaciones internas del Mixteco-Trique. *An. Inst. Nac. Antr. Hist.*, 12: 219–73.

1959b Afinidades lingüísticas del Cuitlateco. *Acts 33d Int. Cong. Amer.*, 2: 560–72.

1964 La posición lingüística del huave. *Acts 35th Int. Cong. Amer.*, 2: 471–75.

1966 Posibles relaciones externas del grupo lingüístico maya. MS.

Arenas, P. de

n.d. Vocabulario manual de las lenguas castellana y mexicana. . . . Calderón ed. 151 pp. (Other eds.: n.d., 1611, 1728; Puebla, 1793, 1887.)

Arndt, W. W.

1959 The performance of glottochronology in Germanic. *Language*, 35: 180–92.

Aschmann, P.

1956 Vocabulario totonaco: coordinación alfabética del totonaco de la Sierra de Veracruz y de Puebla. *Inst. Ling. Verano.* Mexico.

Atwood, E. B.

1953 A survey of verb forms in the eastern United States. *Studies Amer. English*, no. 2. Ann Arbor.

Barberena, S. J.

n.d. Quicheísmos. San Salvador.

Barrera, F.

1745 Vocabulario castellano - quiché. Photograph in Newberry Library. 201 pp.

Barrera Vásquez, A.

1935 Baltasar Mutul, autor de un libro de la pasión de Jesucristo y de un discurso sobre la Misa, en la langua maya. *Maya Research*, 2: 299–301.

1939 El Códice Pérez. *Rev. Mex. Estud. Antr.*, vol. 3, no. 1.

1940 Idioma Quiché. *An. Inst. Nac. Antr. Hist.*, 1: 179–80.

—— and S. G. Morley

1949 The Maya chronicles. *Carnegie Inst. Washington*, Pub. 585, Contrib. 48.

—— and S. Rendón

1948 El libro de los libros de Chilam Balam. *Bib. Amer.*, Serie de Lit. Ind. Mexico.

Barrett, W.

1956 The phonemic interpretation of "accent" in Father Rincón's "Arte mexicana." *General Ling.*, 2: 22–28. Lexington.

Barthel, T. S.

1952 Der Morgensternkult in den Darstellungen der Dresdener Mayahandschrift. *Ethnos*, 17: 73–112.

1953 Religion des Regengottes: zur Deutung der unteren Teile der Seiten 65–69 in der Dresdener Mayahandschrift. *Ibid.*, 18: 86–105.

1954 Maya epigraphy: some remarks on the affix 'al.' *Proc. 30th Int. Cong. Amer.* (1952), pp. 45–49.

1955a Versuch über die Inschriften von Chichen Itza viejo. *Baessler Archiv*, n.s., 3: 5–33.

1955b Maya-Paleographik: die Hieroglyphe Strafe. *Ethnos*, 20: 146–51.

Bartholomew, D.

1959 Proto-Otomi-Pame. Master's thesis. [Expanded in her 1965.]

1960 Some revisions of Proto-Otomi consonants. *IJAL*, 26: 317–29.

1965 The reconstruction of Otopamean (Mexico). Doctoral dissertation, Univ. Chicago.

Basalenque, D.

1640 Arte de la lengua matlaltzinga. Photograph in Newberry Library.

1642a Vocabulario . . . castellano . . . matlaltzinga. Photograph in Newberry Library. 411 pp.

1642b Vocabulario . . . matlaltzinga . . . castellano. Photograph in Newberry Library. 286 pp.

1886 Arte de la lengua tarasca. . . . Mexico.

Basseta, D. de

1698? Vocabulario de la lengua quiché. MS in Bibliothèque Nationale. 172 pp.

Becerra, M. E.

1937 Vocabulario de la lengua chol. *An.*

Mus. Nac. Arqueol., Hist., Etnol., s. 5, 2: 249–78.

BELMAR, F.
1892 Ligero estudio sobre la lengua mazateca. Oaxaca.
1897 Ensayo sobre la lengua trique. Oaxaca.
1899 Idiomas indígenas del estado de Oaxaca: el Chocho. Oaxaca.
1900 Estudio de el chontal. Oaxaca.
1901a Investigación sobre el idioma amuzgo. ... Oaxaca.
1901b Lenguas del estado de Oaxaca: estudio del huave. Oaxaca.
1902a Estudio del idioma ayook. ... Oaxaca.
1902b Idiomas del estado de Oaxaca: el cuicateco. Oaxaca.

BELTRÁN DE SANTA ROSA, P.
1746 Arte del idioma maya.
1859 *Idem*, 2d ed. Merida.

BERLIN, O. B.
1962a The Tenejapa dialect of Tzeltal: an outline of morphology. *In* McQuown, 1962.
1962b Some further notes on Tenejapa syntax. *Ibid*.

BERNAL, I., AND E. DÁVALOS HURTADO, eds.
1953 *See* Huastecos, Totonacos y sus Vecinos.

BEYER, H.
1937 Studies on the inscriptions at Chichen Itza. *Carnegie Inst. Washington*, Pub. 483, Contrib. 21.

BLAKNEY, R. B.
1955 The way of life, Lao Tzu. New York.

BLOOMFIELD, L.
1933 Language. New York.

BOAS, F.
1911 [ed.] Introduction. *In* Handbook of American Indian Languages, pt. 1. Washington.
1913 Notes on the Chatino language of Mexico. *Amer. Anthr.*, 15: 78–86.

BRASSEUR DE BOURBOURG, C. E.
1861 Popol Vuh: le livre sacré et les mythes de l'antiquité américaine, avec les livres héroiques et historiques des Quichés. Paris.
1862 Grammaire de la langue Quiché. Paris.
1869–70 Manuscript troano. Paris.
1872 Dictionnaire, grammaire et chrestomathie de la langue maya. ... Paris.

BRIGGS, E.
1961 Mitla Zapotec grammar. *Inst. Ling. Verano* and *Centro Invest. Antr. Mex.*

BRIGHT, W.
1956 Glottochronologic counts of Hokaltecan material. *Language*, 32: 42–48.
1960 Accent in classical Aztec. *IJAL*, 26: 66–68.

BURGESS, D. M.
1946 Quiche translation of the New Testament. *Amer. Bible Soc.*

—— AND P. XEC
1955 Popol Wuj. Quezaltenango.

BURGESS, P. (pseud. Bopal Resgubs)
n.d., *a* Quech'aw ri Awaj. Quezaltenango.
n.d., *b* Quincojon che ri Dios Tataxel. Quezaltenango.
n.d., *c* Ri u Pix K'ak'. [Weekly.] Quezaltenango.
n.d., *d* Himnario en Quiché. Quezaltenango.
1924 Ch'abal Bixobal che ri kajawal Dios. Tip. "El Noticiero." Quezaltenango.
1925 Ri utzilaj tzijobal jas ri xubij ri Xuan. Quezaltenango.

CABALLERO, D. J.
1880 Gramática del idioma mexicano. ... Mexico.

CACALCHEN, LIBRO DE
1647–1826 Manuscript. Photograph in Newberry Library. 167 pp.

CADENA, C.
1892 Vocabulario Quiché. *In* León Fernández, ed., Lenguas indígenas de Centro-America en el siglo XVIII. San Jose.

CALKINI, CHILAM BALAM DE
n.d. Manuscript. Photograph in Newberry Library. 30 pp.

CALVO, T.
1726 Bocabulario español-quiché. Photograph in Newberry Library. 144 pp.

CÁRDENAS, T. DE
17thC? Arte de la lengua cacchi de Coban. MS in Bibliothèque Nationale.

CARNAP, R.
1942 Introduction to semantics. New York.

CAROCHI, H.
1645 Arte de la lengua mexicana. *In* Col. de gramáticas, pp. 395–538. (Mexico, 1759, 1892.)

CARROLL, J. B., ed.
1956 Language, thought and reality. Selected writings of Benjamin Whorf.

CASAGRANDE, J. B.
1948 Comanche baby language. *IJAL*, 14: 11–14.
1954–55 Comanche linguistic acculturation. *Ibid.*, 20: 140–51, 217–37; 21: 8–25.

CASO, A.
1928 Las estelas zapotecas. *Monogr. Mus. Nac. Arqueol., Hist., Etnog.* Mexico.
1949 El mapa de Teozacoalco. *Cuad. Amer.,* 8: 145–81.
1950 Explicación del reverso del Codex Vindobonensis. *Mem. Colegio Nac.,* vol. 5, no. 5. Mexico.
1951 Base para una sincronología mixteca y cristiana. *Ibid.,* vol. 6, no. 6. Mexico.
1960 Interpretación del Códice Bodley 2858. *Soc. Mex. Antr.*

CASSIRER, E.
1933 La langue et la construction du monde des objets. *Jour. Psychologie Normale et Pathologie,* 30: 18–44.
1944 An essay on man: an introduction to a philosophy of human culture. New Haven.

CASTRO, C. A.
1955 La pluralización en pame meridional. *Rev. Mex. Estud. Antr.,* 14: 213–18.

CHARENCEY, H. DE
1883 Des suffixes en lengua Quiché. Louvain.

CHICXULUB, CRÓNICA DE
1542–62 Manuscript. Photograph in Newberry Library. 26 pp.

CHIMALPOPOCA GALICIA, F.
1869 Epítome ó modo fácil de aprender el idioma nahuatl. . . . Mexico.

CHRÉTIEN, C. D.
1956 Word distributions in southeastern Papua. *Language,* 32: 88–108.

CIUDAD REAL, A. DE
1600? Vocabulario en la lengua maya. MS in John Carter Brown Library. Maya-Español, 465 f.; Español-Maya, 236 f. Photograph in Newberry Library. Constitutes Diccionario de Motul.
1929 *Idem,* first printing. Merida.

COLECCIÓN DE GRAMÁTICAS
1904 Colección de gramáticas de la lengua mexicana. Vol. 1, 1457–1673. Mexico.

CONKLIN, H. C.
1956 Tagalog speech disguise. *Language,* 32: 136–39.
1959 Linguistic play in its cultural context. *Ibid.,* 35: 631–36.

CÓRDOVA, J. DE
1578a Vocabulario castellano - zapoteco. Ed. with introduction and notes by W. Jiménez Moreno. (Mexico, 1942.)
1578b Arte del idioma zapoteca. Ed. Nicolás León. (Morelia, 1886.)

CORONEL, J. DE
1620 Arte en lengua maya. . . . Mexico.

CORTÉS Y ZEDEÑO, J. T.
1765 Arte, vocabulario, y confessionario en el idioma mexicano. . . . Guadalajara, Puebla de los Angeles.

COTO, T.
17thC Vocabulario de la lengua cakchiquel. MS in American Philosophical Society. 955 pp.

COWAN, F. H.
1947 Linguistic and ethnological aspects of Mazateco kinship. *SW. Jour. Anthr.,* 3: 247–56.
1952 A Mazateco president speaks. *Amer. Indígena,* 12: 323–41.

—— AND G. M. COWAN
1947 Mazateco: locational and directional morphemes. *Aboriginal Ling.,* 1: 1–9.

COWAN, G. M.
1948 Mazateco whistle speech. *Language,* 24: 280–86.

CROFT, K.
1951 Practical orthography for Matlapa Nahuatl. *IJAL,* 17: 32–36.
1953a Matlapa Nahuatl II: affix list and morphophonemics. *Ibid.,* 19: 274–80.
1953b Six decades of Nahuatl: a bibliographical contribution. *Ibid.,* 19: 57–73.
1954 Matlapa Nahuatl III: morpheme arrangements. *Ibid.,* 20: 37–43.

DAHL, O. C.
1953 Malgache et maanjan: une comparaison linguistique. *Word,* 29: 577–97.

DARK, P.
1958 Mixtec ethnohistory, a method of analysis of the codical art. Oxford Univ. Press.

DÁVILA GARIBI, J. I.
1938 Epítome de raíces nahuas. Mexico.
1948 La escritura del idioma náhuatl a través de los siglos. 2d ed. Mexico.

DAVIS, A. L., AND R. I. MCDAVID, JR.
1950 Northwestern Ohio: a transition area. *Language,* 26: 264–73.

DIBBLE, C. E.
See A. J. O. Anderson.

DIEBOLD, A. R., JR.
1960 Determining the centers of dispersal of language groups. *IJAL,* 26: 1–10.

DIGUET, L.
1911 Idiome huichol. *Jour. Soc. Amer. Paris,* 8: 23–54.

DIXON, R. B., AND A. L. KROEBER
1919 Indian linguistic families of California. *Univ. California Pub. Archaeol. Ethnol.,* 16: 47–118.

REFERENCES

DOLORES, J.
1911–14 Papago verb stems. *Ibid.*, 10: 241–63.
1923 Papago nominal stems. *Ibid.*, 20: 19–31.

DOZIER, E. P.
1956 Two examples of linguistic acculturation: the Yaqui of Sonora and Arizona and the Tewa of New Mexico. *Language*, 32: 146–57.

DYEN, I.
1953 *Review of* O. C. Dahl, Malgache et Maanjan: une comparaison linguistique. *Ibid.*, 29: 577–90.
1956a The Ngaju-Dayak 'old speech stratum.' *Ibid.*, 32: 83–87.
1956b Language distribution and migration theory. *Ibid.*, 32: 611–26.

EBNETER, T.
1960 Report on classical Quiché. Mimeo. Austin.

ECKER, L.
1939 Relationship of Mixtec to the Otomian languages. *El Mex. Antiguo*, 4: 209–40.

EDMONSON, M. S.
1965 Quiche-English dictionary. *Tulane Univ., Middle Amer. Research Inst.*, Pub. 30.

ELLEGÅRD, A.
1959 Statistical measurement of linguistic relationship. *Language*, 35: 131–56.

ELSON, B. F.
1947a Sierra Popoluca syllable structure. *IJAL*, 13: 13–17.
1947b The Homshuk: a Sierra Popoluca text. *Tlalocan*, 2: 193–214.
1948 Sierra Popoluca personal names. *IJAL*, 14: 191–93.
1951 *Review of* Foster and Foster, Sierra Popoluca Speech. *IJAL*, 17: 57–61.
1954 Sierra Popoluca intonation. Master's thesis, Cornell Univ.
1958 Beginning morphology-syntax. *Summer Inst. Ling.* Glendale.
1960a Sierra Popoluca morphology. *IJAL*, 26: 206–23.
1960b Gramática del Popoluca de la Sierra. *Bib. Facultad Filosofía y Letras*, no. 6. Univ. Veracruzana. Jalapa.
1961a Person markers and related morphemes in Sierra Popoluca. In his 1961b.
1961b [ed.] A William Cameron Townsend en el vigésimoquinto aniversario del Instituto Lingüístico de Verano. Mexico.

EMENEAU, M. B.
1956 India as a linguistic area. *Language*, 32: 3–16.

ESCALANTE, R., AND L. FAIER
1959 Relaciones del Linca y Xinca. Paper presented to annual meeting, Amer. Anthr. Assoc.

ESTUDIOS DE CULTURA NÁHUATL
1959, 1960, 1962, 1964, 1965 Yearbook of the Seminario de Cultura Náhuatl I–V. Univ. Nacional. Mexico.

FEARING, F.
1954 An examination of the conceptions of Benjamin Whorf in the light of the theories of perception and cognition. *In* Language in culture, Amer. Anthr. Assoc., Memoir 79.

FERGUSON, C. A.
1956 Arabic baby talk. *In* Halle, Lunt, McLean, and Van Schooneveld, 1956, pp. 121–28.
1959 Diglossia. *Word*, 15: 325–40.
—— AND J. J. GUMPERZ, eds.
1960 Linguistic diversity in south Asia: studies in regional, social and functional variation. *Indiana Univ. Research Center Anthr., Folklore, Ling.*, Pub. 13.

FERNÁNDEZ, J.
1937 Diccionario poconchí. *An. Soc. Geog. Hist.*, 14: 47–70, 184–200.

FERNÁNDEZ DE MIRANDA, M. T.
1951 Reconstrucción del Protopopoloca. *Rev. Mex. Estud. Antr.*, 12: 61–93.
1956 Glotocronología de la familia Popoloca. *Mus. Nac. Antr., Ser. Cien.*, no. 4. Mexico.
1960 Reflejos consonánticos de Proto-Zapoteco. MS.
—— AND R. J. WEITLANER
1961 Sobre algunas relaciones de la familia mangue. *Anthr. Ling.*, 3 (7): 1–99.

FERNÁNDEZ FERRAZ, J.
1902 Síntesis de constructiva gramatical de la lengua Quiché: ensayo lingüístico. San Jose.

FISCHER, J. L.
1958 Social influences on the choice of a linguistic variant. *Word*, 14: 47–56.

FLORES, I. J.
1753 Arte de la lengua metropolitana del reyno cakchiquel. . . . Antigua.

FÖRSTEMANN, E. W.
1880 Die Maya-Handschrift der Königlichen öffentlichen Bibliothek zu Dresden. Leipzig.
1892 *Idem*, 2d ed. Dresden.

FOSTER, G. M.
1943 The geographical, linguistic, and cultural position of the Popoluca of Veracruz. *Amer. Anthr.*, 45: 531–46.

1949 Sierra Popoluca kinship terminology and its wider relationships. *SW. Jour. Anthr.*, 5: 330–44.

FOSTER, M. L., AND G. M. FOSTER
1948 Sierra Popoluca speech. *Smithsonian Inst., Inst. Social Anthr.*, Pub. 8.

FRENCH, D.
1958 Cultural matrices of Chinookan noncasual language. *IJAL*, 24: 258–63.

FRIEDRICH, J.
1955 Kurze Grammatik der alten Quiché-Sprache im Popol Vuh. *Akad. der Wissenschaften und der Literatur in Mainz, Abhand. der Geistes-u. Soz.-Wissenschaftlichen Klasse*, Jahr. 1955, no. 4. Wiesbaden.

FRIES, C. C., AND K. L. PIKE
1949 Coexistent phonemic systems. *Language*, 25: 29–50.

GALDO GUZMÁN, D. DE
1642 Arte mexicano. *In* Col. de gramáticas, pp. 281–394.

GAMBOA, R. P., ed.
1942 *See* Mayas y Olmecas.

GARIBAY K., A. M.
1940a Llave del Náhuatl. (2d ed., 1961.) Otumba, Mexico.
1940b La poesía indígena de la altiplanicie. *Bib. Estudiante Universitario*, no. 11. Mexico.
1943a Huehuetlatolli, documento A. *Tlalocan*, 1: 31–53, 81–107.
1943b Paralipómenos de Sahagún. *Ibid.*, 1: 307–13.
1945 Épica Náhuatl. *Bib. Estudiante Universitario*, no. 57. Mexico.
1946 Paralipómenos de Sahagún. *Tlalocan*, 2: 167–74, 249–54.
1948 Relación breve de las fiestas de los dioses, fray Bernardino de Sahagún. *Ibid.*, 2: 289–320.
1953–54 Historia de la literatura Náhuatl. 2 vols. Mexico.
1958 [ed.] Veinte himnos sacros de los Nahuas. Textos de los informantes indígenas de Sahagún. *Univ. Nac., Seminario de Cultura Náhuatl.* Mexico.
1961 [ed.] Vida económica de Tenochtitlan y Pochtecáyotl. *Ibid.*

GARVIN, P. L.
1947 Distinctive features in Zoque phonemic acculturation. *Studies in Ling.*, 5: 13–20.

GATES, W. E.
1920 Distribution of the several branches of the Mayance linguistic stock. *Carnegie Inst. Wash.*, Pub. 219, pp. 605–15.
1924 The William Gates Collection. *American Art Assoc.* New York.
1931 An outline dictionary of Maya glyphs. *Maya Soc.*, Pub. 1.
1938 A grammar of Maya. *Maya Soc.* Baltimore.

GIBSON, G. D.
1960 Bibliography of anthropological bibliographies: the Americas. *Current Anthr.*, 1: 61–73.

GIBSON, L. F.
1956 Pame (Otomi) phonemics and morphophonemics. *IJAL*, 22: 242–65.

GILBERTI, M.
1558 Arte de la lengua tarasca ó de Michoacán. (Mexico, 1898.)
1559 Diccionario de la lengua tarasca ó de Michoacán. (Mexico, 1901.)

GLEASON, H. A., JR.
1959 Counting and calculating for historical reconstruction. *Anthr. Ling.*, 2: 22–32.

GÓMEZ, A. M.
1935 Estudios gramaticales de la lengua cora. *Invest. Ling.*, 3: 79–142.

GONZÁLEZ, L.
1672 Arte breve y vocabulario de la lengua tzoque . . . de Tecpatlan. MS in Bibliothèque Nationale.

GORDON, G. B.
1913 *Introduction to* The Book of Chilam Balam of Chumayel. *Univ. Mus. Anthr. Pub.*, vol. 5. Philadelphia.

GOUBAUD CARRERA, A.
1946a Distribución de las lenguas indígenas actuales en Guatemala. *Bol. Inst. Ind. Nac.*, 1 (2, 3): 63–76. Guatemala.
1946b La población de habla indígena en Guatemala. *Ibid.*, 1 (4): 17–21.

GRACE, G. W.
1959 The position of the Polynesian languages within the Austronesian (Malayo-Polynesian) language family. *Indiana Univ. Pub. Anthr. Ling.*, Memoir 16.

GREENBERG, J. H.
1948 Linguistics and ethnology. *SW. Jour. Anthr.*, 4: 140–47.
1954 A quantitative approach to the morphological typology of language. *In* R. F. Spencer, ed., Method and perspective in anthropology: papers in honor of Wilson D. Wallis. Reprinted in *IJAL*, 26: 178–94.
1957a Essays in linguistics. *Viking Fund Pub. Anthr.*, no. 24.

REFERENCES

1957b The nature and uses of linguistic typologies. *IJAL*, 23: 68–77.

1960 A quantitative approach to the morphological typology of language. *IJAL*, 26: 178–94.

—— AND M. SWADESH

1953 Jicaque as a Hokan language. *IJAL*, 19: 216–22.

GRIMES, J. E.

1955 Style in Huichol structure. *Language*, 31: 31–35.

1960 Spanish - Nahuatl - Huichol monetary terms. *IJAL*, 26: 162–65.

GUDSCHINSKY, S. C.

1955 Lexico-statistical skewing from dialect borrowing. IJAL, 21: 138–49.

1958a Mazatec dialect history: a study in miniature. *Language*, 34: 469–81.

1958b Native reactions to tones and words in Mazatec. *Word*, 14: 338–45.

1959a Discourse analysis of a Mazatec text. *IJAL*, 25: 139–46.

1959b Mazatec kernel constructions and transformations. *Ibid.*, 25: 81–89.

1959c Proto-Popotecan: a comparative study of Popolocan and Mixtecan. *Indiana Univ. Pub. Anthr. Ling.*, Memoir 15.

GUERRA, J.

1692 Arte de la lengua mexicana . . . de Guadalaxara. Mexico. (2d ed., Guadalajara, 1900.)

GUZMÁN, A. DE

16thC Bocabulario de lengua tzeldal. . . . Photograph in Newberry Library. 294 pp.

HAAS, M. R.

1959 Tonkawa and Algonkian. *Anthr. Ling.*, 1: 1–6.

HAJDA, Y.

1959a Dialect areas as determined by isogloss bundles (transect map). *In* McQuown, 1959a, fig. 17.

1959b Linguistic cross-influences: phonemic isoglosses on lexicostatistical clustering diagram. *Ibid.*, fig. 18.

1959c Linguistic cross-influences: grammatical isogloss on lexicostatistical clustering diagram. *Ibid.*, fig. 19.

1959d Linguistic cross-influences: phonetic isoglosses on lexicostatistical clustering diagram. *Ibid.*, fig. 20.

1959e Linguistic cross-influences: lexical isoglosses on lexicostatistical clustering diagram. *Ibid.*, fig. 21.

1959f Loan word charts. *Ibid.*, fig. 22.

—— AND M. E. VERBITSKY

1959a Percentages of retention of native

Mayan lexicon on pre-Hispanic traits map. *Ibid.*, fig. 40.

1959b Percentages of early Spanish loans on colonial Spanish introductions map. *Ibid.*, fig. 41.

1959c Percentages of recent Spanish loans on recent Mexican introductions map. *Ibid.*, fig. 42.

HALE, K.

1958 Internal diversity in Uto-Aztecan: I. *IJAL*, 24: 101–07.

1959 Internal diversity in Uto-Aztecan: II. *Ibid.*, 25: 114–21.

HALL, R. A., JR.

1958 Creolized language and "genetic relationships." *Word*, 14: 367–73.

HALLE, M., H. G. LUNT, H. MCLEAN, AND C. H. VAN SCHOONEVELD, comps.

1956 For Roman Jakobson. The Hague.

HALPERN, A. M.

1942 A theory of Maya tš-sounds. *Carnegie Inst. Wash., Notes on Middle Amer. Archaeol. Ethnol.*, no. 13.

HAMP, E. P.

1958 Protopopoloca internal relationships. *IJAL*, 24: 150–53.

1960 Chocho-Popoloca innovations. *Ibid.*, 26: 62.

HASLER, J. A.

1954–55a Los cuatro dialectos de la lengua Nahua. *Rev. Mex. Estud. Antr.*, 14: 145–46.

1954–55b Cinco elementos clasificatorios del Nahua del oeste. *Ibid.*, 14: 147.

1954–55c Método de clasificación dialectal por correspondencia. *Ibid.*, 14: 148.

HATTORI, S.

1960 *Discussion of* D. H. Hymes, Lexicostatistics so far. *Current Anthr.*, 1: 40–42.

HAUGEN, E.

1949 Problems of bilingualism. *Lingua*, 2: 271–90.

1950 The analysis of linguistic borrowing. *Language*, 26: 210–31.

1953 The Norwegian language in America: a study in bilingual behavior. 2 vols. Univ. Pennsylvania Press.

1954 Some pleasures and problems of bilingual research. *IJAL*, 20: 116–22.

1956 Bilingualism in the Americas: a bibliography and research guide. *Amer. Dialect Soc.*, Pub. 26.

HAY, C. L., and others

1940 *See* The Maya and their Neighbors.

HENESTROSA, A.
1933 Estudios sobre la lengua zapoteca. *Invest. Ling.*, 1: 27–30.

HERNÁNDEZ SPINA, V.
1932 Calendario Quiché. *Maya Soc. Quar.*, March.

HERSKOVITS, M. J.
1948 Man and his works. New York.

HERVÁS Y PANDURO, L.
1800 Catálogo de las lenguas de las naciones conocidas. 6 vols. Madrid. (Lenguas y naciones americanas in vol. 1.)

HERZOG, G.
1941 Culture change and language: shifts in the Pima vocabulary. *In* Spier, Hallowell, and Newman, 1941.

HOCKETT, C. F.
1947 Componential analysis of Sierra Popoluca. *IJAL*, 13: 258–67.
1955 A manual of phonology. *Indiana Univ. Pub. Anthr. Ling.*, Memoir 11.

HOENIGSWALD, H. M.
1960 Language change and linguistic reconstruction. Chicago.

HOIJER, H.
1948 Linguistic and cultural change. *Language*, 24: 335–45.
1954 The Sapir-Whorf hypothesis. *In* Language in culture, *Amer. Anthr. Assoc.*, Memoir 79.

—— and others
1946 Linguistic structures of native America. *Viking Fund Pub. Anthr.*, no. 6.

HOLLAND, W. R.
1959 Dialect variations of the Mixtec and Cuicatec areas of Oaxaca, Mexico. *Anthr. Ling.*, 1 (8): 25–31.

HOPKINS, N. A.
1962a A phonology of Zinacantan Tzotzil. Master's thesis, Univ. Texas. *Also in* McQuown, 1962.
1962b A short sketch of Chalchihuitan Tzotzil *In* McQuown, 1962.

HOUSEHOLDER, F. W., JR.
1960 First thoughts on syntactic indices. *IJAL*, 26: 195–97.

HUASTECOS, TOTONACOS Y SUS VECINOS
1953 Huastecos, Totonacos y sus vecinos. Ed. by Bernal and Dávalos Hurtado. *Rev. Mex. Estud. Antr.*, vol. 13, nos. 2 and 3.

HYMES, D. H.
1958 Linguistic features peculiar to Chinookan myths. *IJAL*, 24: 253–57.

1959 Genetic classification: retrospect and prospect. *Anthr. Ling.*, 1 (2): 50–66.
1960 Lexicostatistics so far. *Current Anthr.*, 1: 3–44.

IBARRA GRASSO, D. E.
1958 Lenguas indígenas americanas. Buenos Aires.

IZIL, CHILAM BALAM DE
n.d. Manuscript. Photograph in Newberry Library. 85 pp.

JOHNSON, F.
1940 The linguistic map of Mexico and Central America. *In* The Maya and their neighbors, pp. 88–113.

JOHNSON, J. B.
1943 A clear case of linguistic acculturation. *Amer. Anthr.*, 45: 427–34.

KAUFMAN, T. S.
1961 Tzeltal grammar code. Mimeographed. Stanford Univ., Anthr. Research Center. *Also in* McQuown, 1962.
1962 A sketch of Tenejapa Tzeltal syntax. *In* McQuown, 1962.

KEY, H.
1952–53 Algunas observaciones preliminares de la distribución dialectal del náhuatl en el área Hidalgo-Veracruz-Puebla. *Rev. Mex. Estud. Antr.*, 13: 131–43.
1960 Stem construction and affixation of Sierra Nahuat verbs. *IJAL*, 26: 130–45.

—— AND M. KEY
1953 The phonemes of Sierra Nahuat. *Ibid.*, 19: 53–56.

KIRCHHOFF, P.
1943 Mesoamérica, sus límites geográficos, composición étnica y caracteres culturales. *Acta Amer.*, 1: 92–107.

KLAUSNER, S. Z.
1955 Phonetics, personality and status in Israel. *Word*, 11: 209–15.

KROEBER, A. L.
1940 Language history and culture history. *In* The Maya and their Neighbors, pp. 463–70.
1960a Statistics, Indo-European, and taxonomy. *Language*, 36: 1–21.
1960b On typological indices I: ranking of languages. *IJAL*, 26: 171–77.

—— AND C. D. CHRÉTIEN
1937 Quantitative classification of Indo-European languages. *Language*, 13: 83–103.

LaFARGE, O.
1927 Comparative wordlists: Yocotan, Chontal, Tzeltal, Chaneabal, Jacalteca. *In* Blom and LaFarge, Tribes and tem-

ples, 2: 487–98. *Tulane Univ., Middle Amer. Research Ser.*, Pub. 1.

—— AND D. BYERS

1931 The jacalteca language. *In* their The year bearer's people, pp. 244–366. *Ibid.*, Pub. 3.

LA GRASSERIE, R. DE

1898 Langue Zoque et Mixe.... Paris.

—— AND N. LEÓN

1896 Langue Tarasque.... Paris.

LAGUNAS, J. P. DE

1574 Arte y diccionario tarascos. Mexico. (Morelia, 1890.)

LAMB, S. M.

1958 Linguistic prehistory in the Great Basin. *IJAL*, 24: 95–100.

1959 Some proposals for linguistic taxonomy. *Anthr. Ling.*, 1: 33–49.

LARSON, K.

1949 Huasteco baby talk. *El Mex. Antiguo*, 7: 295–98.

LAW, H. W.

1948 Greeting forms of the gulf Aztecs. *SW. Jour. Anthr.*, 4: 43–48.

1958 Morphological structure of Isthmus Nahuat. *IJAL*, 24: 108–29.

LEAL, M.

1950 Patterns of tone substitution in Zapotec morphology. *Ibid.*, 16: 132–36.

1954 Noun possession in Villa Alta Zapotec. *Ibid.*, 20: 215–16.

LEES, R. B.

1953 The basis of glottochronology. *Language*, 29: 113–27.

LEHMANN, W.

1920 Zentral-Amerika: Erster Teil: die Sprachen Zentral-Amerikas. 2 vols. Berlin.

1938 [ed.] Die Geschichte der Königreiche von Culhuacan und Mexiko. *Quellenwerke zur alten Geschichte Amerikas*, vol. 1. Stuttgart.

1949 [ed.] Sterbende Götter und christliche Heilsbotschaft: Wechselreden indianischer Vornehmer und spanischer Glaubensapostel in Mexiko, 1524. *Ibid.*, vol. 3.

—— AND G. KUTSCHER, eds.

1948 Das 'Memorial breve acerca de la fundación de la ciudad de Culhuacán' von Domingo de S. Anton Muñon Chimalpahin. *Ibid.*, vol. 3.

LEÓN, A., ed.

1949 Crónica mexicáyotl, by F. Alvarado Tezozómoc. Mexico.

LEÓN, N.

1901 Familias lingüísticas de México. *Mem.*

Soc. Cien. "Antonio Alzate," 15: 275–87. Mexico.

1902 Familias lingüísticas de México. *Mus. Nac.* Mexico.

1912 Vocabulario de la lengua popoloca chocha ó chuchona.... *An. Mus. Nac.*, 3d ser., 3: 1–48.

1922 Familias lingüísticas de México. 5th rev. ed., abridged.

LEÓN-PORTILLA, M.

1956 La filosofía Náhuatl, estudiada en sus fuentes. *Inst. Ind. Interamer.* Mexico.

1958 [ed.] Ritos, sacerdotes y atavíos de los dioses. Textos de los informantes indígenas de Sahagún. *Univ. Nac., Seminario de Cultura Náhuatl.* Mexico.

1959 La filosofía Náhuatl.... 2d ed.

LEWY, E.

1937 Die Sprache der Quiche (Kičé) von Guatemala. *Anthropos*, 32: 929–58. Mödling.

LOMBARDO, N.

1702 Arte de la lengua teguima llamada vulgarmente ópata. Mexico.

LONGACRE, R. E.

1957 Proto-Mixtecan. *Indiana Univ. Research Center Anthr., Folklore, Ling.*, Pub. 5.

1960 String constituent analysis. *Language*, 36: 63–88.

1961a Swadesh's Macro-Mixtecan hypothesis. *IJAL*, 27: 9–29.

1961b *Review of* M. Swadesh, Mapas de clasificación lingüística de México y las Américas. *Language*, 36: 397–410.

1964 Grammar discovery procedures. The Hague.

1966 On linguistic affinities of Amuzgo. *IJAL*, 32: 46–49.

LÓPEZ, J. J.

1892 Cachiquel, Quiché y Sutugil. *In* León Fernández, ed., Lenguas indígenas de Centroamérica en el siglo XVIII. San Jose.

LÓPEZ AUSTIN, A.

1961 El abogado náhuatl. *Debate*, 2: 22–24. Ciudad Juarez.

LÓPEZ OTERO, D.

1914 Gramática maya. Merida.

McDAVID, R. I., JR.

1946 Dialect geography and social science problems. *Social Forces*, 25: 168–72.

1951 Dialect differences and inter-group tensions. *Studies in Ling.*, 9–27–33.

—— AND V. G. McDavid
1952 *h* before semivowels in the eastern United States. *Language*, 28: 41–62.

McIntosh, J. B.
1945 Huichol phonemes. *IJAL*, 11: 31–35.

McQuown, N. A.
n.d. Quiché phonemes and vocabulary. Univ. Chicago, Dept. Anthr.
1942 Una posible síntesis lingüística Macro-Mayance. *In* Mayas y Olmecas, 2: 37–38.
1954 Content analysis of language in culture. *In* Language in culture, *Amer. Anthr. Assoc.*, Memoir 79.
1955a The indigenous languages of Latin America. *Amer. Anthr.*, 57: 501–70.
1955b *Review of* Chrétien, Beeler, Emeneau, and Haas, eds., Papers from the symposium on American Indian linguistics. *IJAL*, 21: 73–77.
1956 The classification of the Mayan languages. *IJAL*, 22: 191–95.
1957 Linguistic transcription and specification of psychiatric interview materials. *Psychiatry*, 20: 79–86.
1959a [ed.] Report on the 'Man-in-Nature' project of the Department of Anthropology of the University of Chicago in the Tzeltal-Tzotzil-speaking region of the state of Chiapas, Mexico. MS.
1959b Overview and preview. *In* his 1959a, ch. 4.
1959c Measures of dialect distance in Tzeltal-Tzotzil. *Ibid.*, ch. 21.
1960a Discussion of the symposium on translation between language and culture. *Anthr. Ling.*, 2(2): 79–80.
1960b Middle American linguistics: 1955. *Pan Amer. Union, Middle Amer. Anthr.*, 2: 12–36.
1962 [ed.] Report on the 'Natural History' of the Tzeltal-Tzotzil speaking region of the state of Chiapas, Mexico. MS.
—— and others
1959 Internal linguistic groupings in the transect communities. *In* his 1959a, fig. 23.

Mak, C., and R. E. Longacre
1960 Proto-Mixtec phonology. *IJAL*, 26: 23–40.

Maldonado, F.
16thC Arte, pronunciación y ortografía de ... cakchiquel. Photograph in Newberry Library.

Mandelbaum, D. G., ed.
1949 Selected writings of Edward Sapir, in language, culture, and personality. Berkeley.

Manrique Castañeda, L.
1958 Sobre la clasificación del otomí-pame. *Acts 33d Int. Cong. Amer.*, 2: 551–59.
1960 Dos gramáticas pames del siglo XVIII. *An. Inst. Nac. Antr. Hist.*, vol. 11, no. 40.

Marino Flores, A.
1957 Bibliografía lingüística de la República Mexicana. *Inst. Ind. Interamer.* Mexico.

Martinet, A.
1954 Dialect. *Romance Philology*, 8: 1–11.

Martínez Hernández, J., ed.
1926 Crónica de Yaxkukul. Merida.
1929 Diccionario de Motul: Prólogo; Arte de lengua maya [por Fray Juan Coronel, 1620]; Carta de los diez caciques [1567]; Diccionario Maya-Español [Fray Antonio de Ciudad Real, 1600?]. Merida.

Mason, J. A.
1917 Tepecano.... *Ann. New York Acad. Sci.*, 25: 309–416.
1923 A preliminary sketch of the Yaqui language. *Univ. California Pub. Amer. Archaeol. Ethnol.*, 20: 193–212.
1939 Los quatro grandes filones lingüísticos de México y Centro América. *27th Int. Cong. Amer.*, 2: 282–88.
1940 The native languages of Middle America. *In* The Maya and their neighbors, pp. 52–87.
1952 Some initial phones and combinations in Utaztecan stems. *IJAL*, 18: 9–11.

Maya and their Neighbors, The
1940 The Maya and their neighbors. Ed. by C. L. Hay and others. New York.

Maya Society
1937 The Maya society and its work. Baltimore.

Mayas y Olmecas
1942 Mayas y Olmecas. Segunda reunión de mesa redonda sobre problemas antropológicos de México y Centro América, Tuxtla Gutiérrez. *Soc. Mex. Antr.*

Mayers, M. K.
1959 Maya area linguistics. *In* McQuown, 1959a, fig. 14.
1960 The linguistic unity of Pocomam-Pocomchi. *IJAL*, 26: 317–29.
——, Y. Hajda, and N. A. McQuown
1959 Tzeltal-Tzotzil linguistics description, distributions, relations. *In* McQuown, 1959a, ch. 8.
—— and N. A. McQuown
1959a Lexicostatistics of transect informant short list. *Ibid.*, fig. 15.

1959b Dialect areas as determined by lexicostatistical distance counts (transect map). *Ibid.*, fig. 16.

MEDIZ BOLIO, A.
1943 Introducción al estudio de la lengua maya. Mexico.

MEILLET, A., AND M. COHEN
1924 Les langues du monde. Paris. (Rev. ed., 1952.)

MENA, C.
n.d. [Medicina maya.] MS. Photograph in Newberry Library. 159 pp.

MENDIZÁBAL, M. O. DE, AND W. JIMÉNEZ MORENO
1936 Mapa lingüístico de Norte- y Centro-América. *Inst. Panamer. Geog. Hist.* Mexico.
1937 Distribución prehispánica de las lenguas indígenas de México. Mapa. *Ibid.*
1939 Lenguas indígenas de México. Mapa de su distribución prehispánica. *Ibid.*

MENGIN, E., ed.
1942-50 Corpus codicum Americanorum medii aevi. 6 vols. Copenhagen.
1950 Diferentes historias originales de los reynos de Culhuacan y de México y de otras provincias. 5a Relación de Chimalpahin. *Mitteilungen aus dem Mus. für Völkerkunde in Hamburg*, 22.

MILLON, R., AND R. E. LONGACRE
1961 Proto-Mixtecan and Proto-Amuzgo-Mixtecan vocabularies: a preliminary cultural analysis. *Anthr. Ling.*, 3 (4): 1–44.

MOLINA, A. DE
1555 Aquí comiença un vocabulario en lengua castellana y mexicana.... Mexico.
1571a Arte de la lengua mexicana y castellana. *In* Col. de gramáticas, pp. 127–224. (2d ed., 1576.)
1571b Vocabulario de la lengua mexicana. Mexico. (Leipzig, 1880.)

MORÁN, F.
1685-95 Arte en lengua cholti. MS.

MORÁN, P.
n.d. Bocabulario de solo los nombres de la lengua pokoman.... Photograph in Newberry Library. 242 pp.
1720 Arte breve y compendiosa de la lengua pocomchi.... MS in Bibliothèque Nationale.

MORLEY, S. G., AND G. W. BRAINERD
1956 The ancient Maya. 3d ed. Stanford.

MÜLLER, M.
1888 Grundriss der Sprachwissenschaft. Vienna.

MUÑOZ Y MANZANO, C.
1892 Bibliografía española de lenguas indígenas de América. Madrid.

NAH, CHILAM BALAM DE
n.d. Manuscript. Photograph in Newberry Library. 56 pp.

NÁJERA, M. DE SAN JUAN CRISÓSTOMO
1870 Gramática del tarasco. Morelia.

NASH, M., M. E. VERBITSKY, J. C. HOTCHKISS, AND N. A. McQUOWN
1959 Present-day socio-cultural-linguistic-ethnohistorical correlations. *In* McQuown, 1959a, ch. 3.

NEBRIJA, E. A. DE
1492 Gramática castellana. 2 vols. (Madrid, 1946.)

NELLIS, J. G.
1947 Sierra Zapotec forms of address. *IJAL*, 13: 231–32.

NEVE Y MOLINA, L. DE
1767 Reglas de ortografía, diccionario, y arte del idioma othomi.... Mexico. (Mexico, 1863.)

NEWMAN, S.
1955 Vocabulary levels: Zuñi sacred and slang usage. *SW. Jour. Anthr.*, 11: 345–54.
1964 Comparison of Zuñi and Californian Penutian. *IJAL*, 30: 1–13.

—— AND R. J. WEITLANER
1950a Central Otomian I: Proto-Otomi reconstructions. *IJAL*, 16: 1–19.
1950b Central Otomian II: primitive central Otomian reconstructions. *Ibid.*, 16: 73–81.

NIDA, E. A., AND M. ROMERO C.
1950 The pronominal series in Maya (Yucatec). *Ibid.*, 16: 193–97.

OLMOS, A. DE
1547 Arte para aprender la lengua mexicana. *In* Col. de gramáticas, pp. 1–126.

OLMSTED, D. L.
1950 Ethnolinguistics so far. *Studies in Ling.*, Occasional Papers, no. 2

OLSON, R. D.
1964 Mayan affinities with Chipaya of Bolivia I: correspondences. *IJAL*, 30: 313–24.
1965 Mayan affinities with Chipaya of Bolivia II: cognates. *Ibid.*, 31: 29–38.

OPLER, M. E., AND H. HOIJER
1940 The raid and war-path language of the Chiricahua Apache. *Amer. Anthr.*, 42: 617–34.

OROZCO Y BERRA, M.
1864 Geografía de las lenguas y carta etnográfica de México. Mexico.

ORTEGA, J. DE
1732 Vocabulario en lengua castellana y cora.... Mexico. (Tepic, 1888.)

PACHECO CRUZ, S.
1920 Compendio del idioma maya. Merida.
1938 *Idem*, another ed. Merida.
1939 Léxico de la fauna yucateca. Merida.
1948 Compendio del idioma maya. 4th ed. Mexico.

PALMA, M. T.
1886 Gramática de la lengua azteca.... Puebla.

PARRA, M. G., AND W. JIMÉNEZ MORENO
1954 Bibliografía indigenista de México y Centroamérica (1850–1950). *Inst. Nac. Ind.* Mexico.

PASO Y TRONCOSO, F., ed.
1903 Leyenda de los soles. Florence.
1905–06 Papeles de la Nueva España. 2d ser. 7 vols. Madrid.
1906–07 Códices Matritenses del Palacio Nacional y de la Real Academia de la Historia. Vols. 6–8. Madrid.

PATIÑO, C.
1907 Vocabulario totonaco. Jalapa.

PEÑAFIEL, A.
1887 *See* Anonymous, 1887.

PÉREZ, J. P.
n.d. [Recetarios de indios; indices de plantas medicinales y de enfermedades coordinadas.] MS. Photograph in Newberry Library. 58 pp.
1866–67 Diccionario de la lengua maya. Merida.
1898 Coordinación alfabética de las voces del idioma maya. Merida.

PICKETT, V. B.
1951 Nonphonemic stress: a problem in stress placement in Isthmus Zapotec. *Word*, 7: 60–65.
1953 Isthmus Zapotec verb analysis I. *IJAL*, 19: 292–96.
1955 Isthmus Zapotec verb analysis II. *Ibid.*, 21: 217–32.
1960 The grammatical hierarchy of Isthmus Zapotec. Baltimore.

—— AND B. F. ELSON
1962 An introduction to morphology and syntax. *Summer Inst. Ling.* Santa Ana.

PIKE, E. V.
1948 Problems in Zapotec tone analysis. *IJAL*, 14: 161–70.
1954 Phonetic rank and subordination in consonant patterning and historical change. *Misc. Phonetica*, 2: 25–41.

1956 Tonally differentiated allomorphs in Soyaltepec Mazatec. *IJAL*, 22: 57–71.

PIKE, K. L.
1944 Analysis of a Mixteco text. *Ibid.*, 10: 113–38.
1945a Tone puns in Mixteco. *Ibid.*, 11: 129–39.
1945b Mock Spanish of a Mixteco Indian. *Ibid.*, 11: 219–24.
1946a Phonemic pitch in Maya. *Ibid.*, 12: 82–88.
1946b Another Mixteco tone pun. *Ibid.*, 12: 22–24.
1947 A text involving inadequate Spanish of Mixteco Indians. *Ibid.*, 13: 251–57.
1948 Tone languages. Univ. Michigan Press
1954 Language in relation to a unified theory of the structure of human behavior, part I. *Summer Inst. Ling.* Glendale.
1955 *Idem*, part II.
1956 Towards a theory of the structure of human behavior. *In* Estudios antropológicos publicados en homenaje al doctor Manuel Gamio. *Soc. Mex. Antr.* Mexico.
1958 On tagmemes, née gramemes. *IJAL*, 24: 273–78.
1959 Language as particle, wave and field. *Texas Quar.*, 2 (2): 37–54.
1960 Language in relation to a unified theory of the structure of human behavior, part III. *See* his 1954, 1955.

—— AND E. V. PIKE
1947 Immediate constituents of Mazateco syllables. *IJAL*, 13: 78–91.

PIMENTEL, F.
1874–75 Cuadro descriptivo y comparativo de las lenguas indígenas de México. 3 vols. 2d ed. Mexico.
1904 *Idem*, another ed.

PINEDA, V.
1888 Gramática de la lengua tzeltal y diccionario.... Chiapas.

PITTMAN, R. S.
1948 Nahuatl honorifics. *IJAL*, 14: 236–39.
1954 A grammar of Tetelcingo (Morelos) Nahuatl. *Ling. Soc. Amer.*, Language Dissertation 50.

PREUSS, K. T.
1932 Grammatik der Cora-Sprache. *IJAL*, 7: 1–84.
1935 Wörterbuch Deutsch-Cora. *Ibid.*, 8: 79–102.

—— AND E. MENGIN
1937–38 Die Mexikanische Bilderhandschrift

Historia Tolteca-Chichimeca. Parts I and II. *Baessler Archiv.* Berlin.

PULGRAM, E.
1956 On prehistoric linguistic expansion. *In* Halle, Lunt, McLean, and Van Schooneveld, 1956, pp. 411–17.

QUINTANA, A. DE
1729 Arte de la lengua mixe. Puebla. (Reprinted 1891.)

RADA Y DELGADO, J. DE LA, AND J. LÓPEZ DE AYALA Y DEL HIERRO
1892 Códice maya denominado cortesiano. Madrid.

RADHAKRISHNAN, R.
1962 An outline of Pinolteca [Tzeltal] morphology. Master's thesis, Univ. Chicago. *Also in* McQuown, 1962.

RADIN, P.
1916 On the relationship of Huave and Mixe. *Amer. Anthr.*, 18: 411–21.
1919 The genetic relationship of the North American Indian languages. *Univ. California Pub. Amer. Archaeol. Ethnol.*, 14: 489–502.
1930 A preliminary sketch of the Zapotec language. *Language*, 6: 64–85.
1933 Notes on the Tlappanecan language of Guerrero. *IJAL*, 8: 45–72.
1935 An historical legend of the Zapotecs. Berkeley.
1944 The classification of the languages of Mexico. *Tlalocan*, 2: 259–65.
1946 Zapotec texts: dialect of Juchitán-Tehuano. *IJAL*, 12: 152–72.

RAVICZ, R., AND A. K. ROMNEY
n.d. Sixteen centuries of structural continuity in Mixtec kinship. MS.

RECINOS, A.
1916 Estudios de antropología y etnografía: razas y lenguas indígenas de Guatemala. *Centroamérica*, 8: 607–18. Guatemala.
1917 Lenguas indígenas de Guatemala. *Proc. 2d Pan Amer. Sci. Cong. Anthr.*, 1: 209–19.
1947 Popol Vuh: las antiguas historias del Quiché. Mexico.
1950a The Popol Vuh. Univ. Oklahoma Press.
1950b [ed.] Memorial de Sololá: anales de los Cakchiqueles seguido del título de los señores de Totonicapán. Mexico.
1953 [ed.] The Annals of the Cakchiquels. Univ. Oklahoma Press.
1957 Crónicas indígenas de Guatemala. Guatemala.

REDFIELD, R.
1954 *Foreword to* Language in culture. *Amer. Anthr. Assoc.*, Memoir 79.

REED, D. W., AND J. L. SPICER
1952 Correlation methods of comparing idiolects in a transition area. *Language*, 28: 348–59.

REYES, A. DE LOS
1593 Arte en lengua mixteca.... Mexico. (Alençon, 1889.)

REYES, G. DE LOS
1891 Gramática de las lenguas zapoteca-serrana y zapoteca del valle. Oaxaca.

REYNOSO, D. DE
1644 Arte y vocabulario en lengua mame. ... Mexico.

RINALDINI, B.
1743 Arte de la lengua tépeguana.... Mexico.

RINCÓN, A. DEL
1595 Arte mexicana. *In* Col. de gramáticas, pp. 225–80.

ROBLES URIBE, C.
1962 Manual del Tzeltal (gramática Tzeltal de Bachajón). *Univ. Iberoamericana* (Antropología: Lingüística I).

RODAS, F.
n.d. Vocabulario en idioma kiché. Guatemala.

ROMERO FUENTES, L. C.
1910 La lengua maya al alcance de todos. Merida.

ROSNY, L. DE
1887 Codex Peresianus manuscrit hiératique des anciens Indiens de l'Amérique Centrale. Paris.

ROYS, R. L.
1920 A Maya account of creation. *Amer. Anthr.*, 22: 360–66.
1929 Annotated transcription of the Chilam Balam of Kaua. MS. *Tulane Univ., Middle Amer. Research Inst.*
1933 The book of Chilam Balam of Chumayel. *Carnegie Inst. Wash.*, Pub. 438.
1939 The titles of Ebtun. *Ibid.*, Pub. 505.
1940 Personal names of the Maya of Yucatan. *Ibid.*, Pub. 523, Contrib. 31.
1943 The Indian background of colonial Yucatan. *Ibid.*, Pub. 548.
1944 The Vienna dictionary. *Ibid., Notes on Middle Amer. Archaeol. Ethnol.*, no. 41.

SAHAGÚN, B. DE
1575–77 Florentine codex: general history of the things of New Spain. Original Nahuatl text and English tr. by A. J. O. Anderson and C. E. Dibble. Books 1–5, 7–12. Univ. Utah and School Amer. Research, Santa Fe.

SALZMANN, Z.
1954 The problem of lexical acculturation. *IJAL*, 20: 137–39.

SAN BUENAVENTURA, G. DE
1684 Arte de la lengua maya. Mexico.
1888 *Idem*, 2d ed. Mexico.

SÁNCHEZ, J. M.
1877 Gramática de la lengua zoque.

SÁNCHEZ DE LA BAQUERA, J.
1747 Modo breve de aprender a ler, escrevir, pronunciar, y ablar el idioma othomi. MS in Newberry Library.

SANDOVAL, R. T.
1810 Arte de la lengua mexicana. Mexico.

SAN FRANCISCO, DICCIONARIO DE
n.d. Manuscript, maya-español, español-maya. Photograph in Newberry Library. 402 pp.

SANTO DOMINGO, T. DE
1693 Vocabulario en la lengua cakchiquel. MS in Bibliothèque Nationale. 286 pp.

SAPIR, E.
1915 Abnormal types of speech in Nootka. *Canada, Dept. Mines, Geol. Surv.*, Memoir 62, Anthr. Ser. 5. (Reprinted *in* Mandelbaum, 1949, pp. 179–96.)
1916 Time perspective in aboriginal American culture. *Ibid.*, Memoir 90, Anthr. Ser. 13. (Reprinted *in* Mandelbaum, 1949, pp. 389–462.)
1917 The position of Yana in the Hokan stock. *Univ. California Pub. Amer. Archaeol. Ethnol.*, 13: 1–34.
1920 The Hokan and Coahuiltecan languages. *IJAL*, 1: 280–90.
1921 Language. New York. (Reprinted 1949.)
1925 The Hokan affinity of Subtiaba in Nicaragua. *Amer. Anthr.*, 27: 402–35.
1927 The unconscious patterning of behavior in society. *In* Mandelbaum, 1949.
1929a Central and North American languages. *Encyclopaedia Britannica*, 14th ed., 5: 138–41.
1929b Male and female forms of speech in Yana. *In* St. W. J. Teeuwen, ed., Donum Natalicium Schrijnen. (Reprinted *in* Mandelbaum, 1949, pp. 206–12.)
1929c A study in phonetic symbolism. *In* Mandelbaum, 1949.
1949 The status of linguistics as a science. *Ibid.*, pp. 160–66.

SAPON, S. M.
1953 A methodology for the study of socio-economic differentials in linguistic phenomena. *Studies in Ling.*, 11: 57–68.

SAPPER, C.
1927 La lengua tapachulteca. *El Mex. Antiguo*, 2: 259–68.

SARLES, H. B.
1962 A grammar of San Bartoleño Tzotzil. MS. *In* McQuown, 1962.

SCHERZER, K.
1855 Sprache der Indianer von Ixtalavacan (Quiché), von Quezaltenango, Guatemala. *Sitzungsberichte der Philos. Histor. Klasse der Kaiserl. Akad. der Wissenschaften*, 18: 227–41. Vienna.

SCHMIDT, J.
1872 Die Verwandschaftsverhältnisse der indo-germanischen Sprachen. Weimar.

SCHMIDT, P. W.
1926 Die Sprachfamilien und Sprachenkreise der Erde. Heidelberg.

SCHOEMBS, J.
1949 Aztekische Schriftsprache. Heidelberg.

SCHUCHARDT, H.
1900 Über die Klassifikation der romanischen Mundarten. Graz. (Presented orally 1870.)

SCHULLER, R.
1920 Zur sprachlichen Verwandtschaft der Maya-Qu'itše mit den Carib-Aruac. *Anthropos*, 14–15: 465–91.
1925a La lengua ts'ots'il *IJAL*, 3: 193–218.
1925b La única gramática conocida de la lengua pame. *Talleres gráficos del Depto. Antr.* Mexico.

SCHULTZE-JENA, L. S.
1933 Leben, Glaube und Sprache der Quiche von Guatemala. Indiana I. Jena.
1944 Popol Vuh: das heilige Buch der Quiche-Indianer von Guatemala. *Quellenwerke zur alten Geschichte Amerikas*, Vol. 2. Stuttgart.
1950 [ed.] Wahrsagerei, Himmelskunde und Kalender der alten Azteken. Aus dem aztekischen Urtext des B. de Sahagún. *Ibid.*, Vol. 4.
1952 [ed.] Gliederung des alt-aztekischen Volks in Familie, Stand und Beruf. Aus dem aztekischen Urtext des B. de Sahagún. *Ibid.*, Vol. 5.
1957 [ed.] Alt-aztekische Gesänge. *Ibid.*, Vol. 6.

SELER, E.
1887 Das Konjugationssystem der Maya-sprachen. Berlin.
1902 *Idem*, in his 1902–23, 1: 65–126.

1902–23 Gesammelte Abhandlungen zur Amerikanischen Sprach- und Alterthumskunde. 5 vols. Berlin.

1927 Einige Kapitel aus dem Geschichtswerk des B. de Sahagún. Herausgegeben von C. Seler-Sachs in Gemeinschaft mit W. Lehmann. Stuttgart.

SHELL, O.
1957 Cashibo II: grammemic analysis of transitive and intransitive verb patterns. *IJAL*, 23: 179–218.

SIMÉON, R.
1885 Dictionaire de la langue Nahuatl. Paris.

SMITH, B., ed.
1862 *See* Anonymous, 1862.

SMITH, P., AND R. J. WEITLANER
1957 Detalles de la fonología del idioma Proto-Chinanteco. MS.

SOLÍS ALCALÁ, E.
1949 Diccionario español-maya. Merida.

SORIANO, J. G.
1776 Difícil tratado del arte y unión de los idiomas othomii y pamee. MS.

SOTUTA, LIBRO DE
n.d. [Medicina maya.] MS. Photograph in Newberry Library. 108 pp.

SOUSTELLE, J.
1937 La famille Otomi-Pame du Mexique central. *Inst. Ethnol.* Paris.
1951 Documents sur les langues Pame et Jonaz du Mexique central. *Jour. Soc. Amer. Paris*, 60: 1–20.

SPICER, E. H.
1943 Linguistic aspects of Yaqui acculturation. *Amer. Anthr.*, 45: 410–26.

SPIER, L., A. I. HALLOWELL, AND S. S. NEWMAN
1941 Language, culture, and personality: essay in memory of Edward Sapir. Menasha.

SQUIER, E. G.
1861 Monograph of authors who have written on the languages of Central America. London.
1865 [ed.] The Quiches. London.

STEWART, D.
1957 Reconstrucción de tono para Otomí-Mazahua. MS.

STOLL, O.
1884 Zur Ethnographie der Republik Guatemala. Zurich.
1887 Die Sprache der Ixil-Indianer. Leipzig.
1888 Die Sprache der Pokonchi-Indianer. Vienna.
1913 Zur Psychologie der indianischen Hochlandssprachen von Guatemala. *Ann. Geog. Ethnog. Geschichte*, 1912/13: 34–36.

SUMMER INSTITUTE OF LINGUISTICS
1960 Twenty-fifth anniversary bibliography. Glendale.
1964 Bibliography, February, 1964. Santa Ana, Calif.

SWADESH, M.
1947 The phonemic structure of Proto-Zapotec. *IJAL*, 13: 220–30.
1951 Lexicostatistic dating of prehistoric contacts. *Proc. Amer. Phil. Soc.*, vol. 96
1952 Salish phonologic geography. *Language*, 28: 232–48.
1953 The language of the archaeologic Huastecs. *Carnegie Inst. Wash., Notes Middle Amer. Archaeol. Ethnol.*, no. 114.
1954a On the Penutian vocabulary survey. *IJAL*, 20: 123–33.
1954b Perspectives and problems of Amerindian comparative linguistics. *Word*, 10: 306–32.
1954c Algunas fechas glotocronológicas importantes para la prehistoria nahua. *Rev. Mex. Estud. Antr.*, 14: 173–92.
1955 Towards greater accuracy in lexicostatistic dating. *IJAL*, 21: 121–37.
1956 Problems of long-range comparison in Penutian. *Language*, 32: 17–41.
1959a La lingüística de las regiones entre las civilizaciones mesoamericanas y andinas. *Acts 33d Int. Cong. Amer.*, 2: 551–59.
1959b Mapas de clasificación lingüística de México y las Américas. *Univ. Nac. Autónoma Mex., Inst. Hist.*, Pub. 51, Antr. Ser. no. 8.
1959c Indian linguistic groups of Mexico. *Escuela Nac. Antr. Hist.* Mexico.
1959d Linguistics as an instrument of prehistory. *SW. Jour. Anthr.*, 15: 20–35.
1959e The mesh principle in comparative linguistics. *Anthr. Ling.*, 1 (2): 7–14.
1960a The Oto-Manguean hypothesis and Macro-Mixtecan. *IJAL*, 26: 79–111.
1960b Tras la huella lingüística de la prehistoria. *Univ. Nac. Autónoma Mex., Cuad. Seminario de Problemas Cien. y Filo.*, no. 26.
1960c Algunos reflejos lingüísticos de la prehistoria de Chiapas. *Rev. Mex. Estud. Antr.*, 17: 145–59 [1961].
1960d Interrelaciones de las lenguas mayas. *An. Inst. Antr.*, 11: 231–67.
1960e Estudios sobre lengua y cultura. *Acta Antr.*, época 2, II–2.
1960f Afinidades de las lenguas amerindias. *Acts 34th Int. Cong. Amer.*, pp. 729–38.

399

1962   Nuevo ensayo de glotocronología Yuto-nahua. *An. Inst. Antr.*, 15: 263–302.

1964a Interim notes on Oaxacan phonology. *SW. Jour. Anthr.*, 20: 168–89.

1964b Algunos problemas de la lingüística otomangue. *An. Sección Antr.*, 1: 91–123.

1966   Porhé y maya. *Ibid.*, 3: 173–204.

TAPIA ZENTENO, C. DE

1753   Arte novissima de lengua mexicana. Mexico. (Mexico, 1885.)

1767   Noticia de la lengua huasteca. . . . Mexico.

TAX, S.

1960   Aboriginal languages of Latin America. *Current Anthr.*, 1: 430–38.

TELETOR, C. N.

n.d.   Compendio de la doctrina cristiana en lengua quiché y castellano. Guatemala.

1942   Breve manual de conversación quiché. Guatemala.

1943   Toponimia guatemalteca. *An. Soc. Geog. Hist. Guatemala*, 19 (2): 116–24.

1949   Algunos apuntes sobre Rabinal, Baja Verapaz, y algo sobre fonética del dialecto Quiché. *Ibid.*, 24 (3–4): 208–19.

1959   Diccionario castellano-quiché y voces castellano-pokoman. Guatemala.

TELLECHEA, M.

1826   Compendio gramatical para la inteligencia del idioma tarahumar. . . . Mexico.

THIEME, P.

1958   The Indo-European language. *Sci. Amer.* (October), pp. 63–74.

THOMAS, C.

1902   Provisional list of linguistic families, languages and dialects of Mexico and Central America. *Amer. Anthr.*, 4: 207–16.

——AND J. R. SWANTON

1911   Indian languages of Mexico and Central America and their geographical distribution. *Smithsonian Inst., Bur. Amer. Ethnol.*, Bull. 44.

THOMPSON, J. E. S.

1950   Maya hieroglyphic writing: introduction. *Carnegie Inst. Wash.*, Pub. 589.

1954   Memoranda on some dates at Palenque, Chiapas. *Ibid., Notes Middle Amer. Archaeol. Ethnol.*, no. 120.

1961   Investigaciones en la escritura jeroglífica maya. *Bol. Centro Invest. Antr. Mex.*, 11: 3–12.

1962   A catalog of Maya hieroglyphs. Univ. Oklahoma Press.

TICUL, DOCUMENTOS DE

1642–1761 Manuscript. Photograph in Newberry Library. 62 pp.

TIZIMIN, CHILAM BALAM DE

1870   Manuscript. Photograph in Newberry Library. 55 pp.

TLALOCAN

1943–57 A journal of source materials on the native cultures of Mexico. 3 vols. Sacramento, Calif., and Azcapotzalco, Mexico.

TORRESANO, E.

1754   Arte de la lengua kakchiquel. . . . MS in Bibliothèque Nationale.

TOVAR, A.

1954   Linguistics and prehistory. *Word*, 10: 333–50.

TOZZER, A. M.

1921   A Maya grammar. *Papers Peabody Mus., Harvard Univ.*, vol. 9.

TREND, J. B.

1953   The language and history of Spain. London.

ULLMANN, S.

1953   Descriptive semantics and linguistic typology. *Word*, 9: 225–40.

VALLE, F.

n.d.   Quaderno de algunas reglas y apuntes sobre el idioma pame. MS.

1925   La única gramática conocida de la lengua pame. . . . Mexico.

VARELA, F. DE

17thC? Calepino en lengua cakchiquel. MS in American Philosophical Society. 477 pp.

VÁZQUEZ GAZTELU, D.

1726   Arte de lengua mexicana. . . . Puebla.

VELÁZQUEZ, P. F., ed.

1945   Anales de Cuauhtitlán, Códice Chimalpopoca. Mexico.

VETANCURT, A. DE

1673   Arte de la lengua mexicana. . . . Mexico.

VICO, D. DE

17thC? Vocabulario quiché-cakchiquel. MS in Bibliothèque Nationale. 572 pp.

1675? Arte de la lengua quiché. . . . MS in Bibliothèque Nationale.

VIENNA, DICCIONARIO DE

n.d.   Bocabulario de Mayathan por su abecedario. MS in National Library, Vienna. 199 pp.

VILLA ROJAS, A.

1955   Los Mazatecos y el problema indígena de la cuenca del Papaloapan. *Mem. Inst. Nac. Indig.*, vol. 7. Mexico.

VILLACORTA C., J. A.

1934   Estudios sobre lingüística guatemalteca.

An. Soc. Geog. Hist. Guatemala, 10: 41–81, 170–205, 331–73, 431–77.

VIÑAZA, CONDE DE LA [C. Muñoz y Manzano]
1892 Bibliografía española de lenguas indígenas de América. Madrid.

VIVÓ, J. A.
1941 Razas y lenguas indígenas de México, su distribución geográfica. *Inst. Panamer. Geog. Hist.*, Pub. 52. Mexico.

VOEGELIN, C. F.
1945 Influence of area in American Indian linguistics. *Word*, 1: 54–58.
1950 A testing frame for language and culture. *Amer. Anthr.*, 52: 432–34.
1953 [ed.] Results of the conference of anthropologists and linguists. Supplement to *IJAL*, 19: 2.
1956 Subsystems within systems in cultural and linguistic typologies. *In* Halle, Lunt, McLean, and Van Schooneveld, 1956, pp. 592–99.

——AND Z. S. HARRIS
1945 Linguistics in ethnology. *SW. Jour. Anthr.*, 1: 455–65.
1950 Methods of determining intelligibility among dialects and natural languages. *Proc. Amer. Phil. Soc.*, 95: 322–29.

——AND F. M. ROBINETT
1954 'Mother language' in Hidatsa. *IJAL*, 20: 65–70.

VOGT, H.
1954 Language contacts. *Word*, 10: 365–74.

WALLIS, E.
1956 Simulfixation in aspect markers of Mesquital Otomi. *Language*, 32: 453–59.

WATERHOUSE, V.
1949a Learning a second language first. *IJAL*, 15: 106–09.
1949b Oaxaca Chontal: sentence types and text analysis. *El Mex. Antiguo*, 7: 299–314.
1961 The psychological reality of linguistic structure. *In* Elson, 1961b, pp. 687–92.
1962 The grammatical structure of Oaxaca Chontal. *IJAL*, vol. 28, pt. 2, 121 pp.

——AND M. MORRISON
1950 Chontal phonemes. *IJAL*, 16: 35–39.

WEINREICH, U.
1953 Languages in contact: findings and problems. *Ling. Circle New York*, Pub. 1.
1954 Is a structural dialectology possible? *Word*, 10: 388–400.
1957a On the description of phonic interference. *Ibid.*, 13: 1–11.

1957b Functional aspects of Indian bilingualism. *Ibid.*, 13: 203–33.
1958 On the compatibility of genetic relationship and convergent development. *Ibid.*, 14: 374–79.

WEITLANER, R. J.
1942 La rama olmeca del grupo Macro-Otomangue. *In* Mayas y Olmecas, pp. 33–35.

——, M. T. FERNÁNDEZ DE MIRANDA, AND M. SWADESH
1959 Some findings on Oaxaca language classification and culture terms. *IJAL*, 25: 54–58. Abbreviated version of their 1960.
1960 El panorama etno-lingüístico de Oaxaca y el istmo. *Rev. Mex. Estud. Antr.*, 16: 137–57.

WELLS, R.
1954 Archiving and language typology. *IJAL*, 20: 101–07.

WHITE, L. A.
1944 A ceremonial vocabulary among the Pueblos. *Ibid.*, 10: 161–67.

WHORF, B. L.
1935 The comparative linguistics of Uto-Aztecan. *Amer. Anthr.*, 37: 600–08.
1943 Loan words in ancient Mexico. *Tulane Univ., Middle Amer. Research Inst.*, Pub. 11, no. 1.
1946 The Milpa Alta dialect of Aztec, with notes on the classical and Tepostlan dialects. *In* Hoijer and others, 1946, pp. 367–97.
1950 An American Indian model of the universe. *IJAL*, 16: 2.
1952 Collected papers on metalinguistics. U.S. Dept. State, Foreign Service Inst.

WICK, S. A.
1951 Phonemics of the Quiché language. Master's thesis, Univ. Chicago.

WOLFF, H.
1959a Intelligibility and inter-ethnic attitudes. *Anthr. Ling.*, 1 (3): 34–41.
1959b Subsystem typologies and area linguistics. *Ibid.*, 1 (7): 1–88.

WONDERLY, W. L.
1946 Phonemic acculturation in Zoque. *IJAL*, 12: 92–95.
1949 Some Zoquean phonemic and morphophonemic correspondences. *Ibid.*, 15: 1–11.
1953 Sobre la propuesta filiación lingüística de la familia totonaca con las familias zoqueana y mayense. *In* Huastecos, Totonacos y sus vecinos, pp. 105–13.

XEC, P., AND G. MAYNARD
  1954 Diccionario quiché preliminar: quiché-español, español-quiché. Mimeographed. Quezaltenango.
XIMÉNEZ, F.
  1722? Arte de las tres lenguas cacchiquel, quiche y tzutuhil. . . . MS in Newberry Library.
XIU CHRONICLES
  1608–1817 [Constitutes Ticul MS and Crónica de Oxhutzcab.] Photograph in Newberry Library of original in Peabody Museum, Harvard Univ. 164 pp.

ZAMBRANO BONILLA, J.
  1752 Arte de lengua totonaca, conforme a el arte de Antonio Nebrija. Puebla.
ZAVALA, M.
  1898 Gramática maya. Merida.
——AND A. MEDINA
  1898 Vocabulario español-maya. Merida.
ZUÑIGA, D.
  1720 Arte de la lengua pocomchi . . . y traducido en la lengua pocoman de Amatitlán. MS in Bibliothèque Nationale.